FOUNDATIONS OF OPERATIONS MANAGEMENT

FOUNDATIONS OF OPERATIONS MANAGEMENT

third canadian edition

LARRY P. RITZMAN

PROFESSOR EMERITUS AT THE OHIO STATE UNIVERSITY AND BOSTON COLLEGE

LEE J. KRAJEWSKI

UNIVERSITY OF NOTRE DAME

MANOJ K. MALHOTRA

UNIVERSITY OF SOUTH CALIFORNIA

ROBERT D. KLASSEN

UNIVERSITY OF WESTERN ONTARIO

PEARSON

Toronto

Vice-President, Editorial Director: Gary Bennett
Editor-in-Chief: Nicole Lukach
Acquisitions Editor: Megan Farrell
Marketing Manager: Claire Varley
Supervising Developmental Editor: Paul Donelley
Lead Project Manager: Avinash Chandra
Manufacturing Manager: Susan Johnson
Production Editor: Nidhi Chopra, Cenveo Publisher Services
Copy Editor: Rodney Rawlings
Proofreader: Heather Sangster
Compositor: Cenveo Publisher Services
Permissions Researcher: Karen Hunter
Art Director: Julia Hall
Cover and Interior Designer: Opus House Inc./Sonya Thursby
Cover Image: Getty Images/Ryan McVay

Credits and acknowledgments for material borrowed from other sources and reproduced, with permission, in this textbook appear on page 455.

If you purchased this book outside the United States or Canada, you should be aware that it has been imported without the approval of the publisher or the author.

10 9 8 7 6 5 4 3 2 1 [CKV]

Library and Archives Canada Cataloguing in Publication

Foundations of operations management / Larry P. Ritzman ... [et al.]. — 3rd Canadian ed.

Canadian ed. written by Robert D. Klassen.
Includes index.
ISBN 978-0-13-231753-5

1. Production management--Textbooks. I. Ritzman, Larry P. II. Klassen, Robert D. (Robert David), 1963-

TS155.F69 2012   658.5   C2011-905518-X

ISBN 978-0-13-231753-5

PEARSON

Dedicated with love to our families.

Barbara Ritzman
Karen and Matt; Kristin and Alayna
Lisa and Todd; Cody, Cole, Taylor, and Clayton
Kathryn and Paul
Mildred and Ray

Judie Krajewski
Gary
Lori and Dan; Aubrey, Madeline, and Amelia
Carrie and Jon; Jordanne and Alaina
Selena and Jeff
Virginia and Jerry
Virginia and Larry

Maya Malhotra
Vivek, Pooja, and Neha
Santosh and Ramesh Malhotra
Indra and Prem Malhotra; Neeti and Deeksha
Sadhana Malhotra
Leela and Mukund Dabholkar
Aruna and Harsha Dabholkar; Aditee
Mangala and Pradeep Gandhi; Priya and Medha

Lorraine Klassen
Nicholas
Benjamin

About the Authors

LARRY P. RITZMAN is Professor Emeritus at the Ohio State University and Professor Emeritus at Boston College. While at the Ohio State University, he served as department chairman and received several awards for both teaching and research, including the Pace Setters' Club Award for Outstanding Research. While at Boston College, he held the Thomas J. Galligan, Jr. chair and received the Distinguished Service Award from the School of Management. He received his doctorate at Michigan State University, having had prior industrial experience at the Babcock and Wilcox Company. Over the years, he has been privileged to teach and learn more about operations management with numerous students at all levels—undergraduate, MBA, executive MBA, and doctorate.

Particularly active in the Decision Sciences Institute, Larry has served as council coordinator, publications committee chair, track chair, vice-president, board member, executive committee member, doctoral consortium coordinator, and president. He was elected a Fellow of the Institute in 1987 and earned the Distinguished Service Award in 1996. He has been a frequent reviewer, discussant, and session chair for several other professional organizations.

Larry's areas of particular expertise are service processes, operations strategy, production and inventory systems, forecasting, multistage manufacturing, and layout. An active researcher, Larry's publications have appeared in such journals as *Decision Sciences*, *Journal of Operations Management*, *Production and Operations Management*, *Harvard Business Review*, and *Management Science*. He has served in various editorial capacities for several journals.

LEE J. KRAJEWSKI is Professor Emeritus at the Ohio State University and Professor Emeritus at the University of Notre Dame. While at the Ohio State University, he received the University Alumni Distinguished Teaching Award and the College of Business Outstanding Faculty Research Award. He initiated the Center for Excellence in Manufacturing Management and served as its director for four years. In addition, he received the National President's Award and the National Award of Merit of the American Production and Inventory Control Society. He served as president of the Decision Sciences Institute and was elected a Fellow of the Institute in 1988. He received the Distinguished Service Award in 2003.

Lee received his Ph.D. from the University of Wisconsin. Over the years, he has designed and taught courses at both graduate and undergraduate levels on topics such as operations strategy, introduction to operations management, operations design, project management, and manufacturing planning and control systems.

Lee served as the editor of *Decision Sciences*, was the founding editor of the *Journal of Operations Management*, and has served on several editorial boards. Widely published himself, Lee has contributed numerous articles to such journals as *Decision Sciences*, *Journal of Operations Management*, *Management Science*, *Production and Operations Management*, *International Journal of Production Research*, *Harvard Business Review*, and *Interfaces*, to name just a few. Lee's areas of specialization include operations strategy, manufacturing planning and control systems, supply chain management, and master production scheduling.

MANOJ K. MALHOTRA is the Jeff B. Bates Professor and Chairman of the Management Science Department at the Moore School of Business, University of South Carolina (USC), Columbia. He holds an engineering undergraduate degree from the Indian Institute of Technology (IIT) Kanpur, India, and a Ph.D. in operations management from the Ohio State University. He is certified as a Fellow of the American Production and Inventory Management Society (CFPIM), and has conducted seminars and consulted with John Deere, Metso Corporation, Phelps Dodge, Sonoco, UCB Chemicals, Milliken, and Verizon, among others. Manoj has won several teaching awards, including the Michael J. Mungo Outstanding Graduate Teaching Award in 2006 from the University of South Carolina and the Alfred G. Smith Jr. Excellence in Teaching Award in 1995 from the Moore School of Business.

Manoj's research has thematically focused on the deployment of flexible resources in manufacturing and service firms, and on the interface between operations and supply chain management and other functional areas of business. His work on these and related issues has been published in refereed journals, such as *Decision Sciences, European Journal of Operational Research, IIE Transactions, International Journal of Production Research, Journal of Operations Management, OMEGA,* and *Production and Operations Management*. Manoj is currently an associate editor of *Decision Sciences* and *Journal of Operations Management*. He is a recipient of the Decision Sciences Institute's Outstanding Achievement Award for the Best Application Paper in 1990 and the Stan Hardy Award in 2002 for the best paper published in the field of operations management.

ROBERT D. KLASSEN is Professor of Operations Management and holds the Magna International Inc. Chair in Business Administration at the Richard Ivey School of Business, University of Western Ontario. He earned his doctorate from the University of North Carolina at Chapel Hill. He has also worked as an environmental engineer in the steel industry, following earlier experience in the consumer products and petroleum sectors.

Since joining Ivey in 1995, Robert has enjoyed teaching students at all levels, including undergraduate, MBA, executive MBA, and doctoral students. He has developed and delivered courses in operations management, operations strategy, service management, management of technology, and most recently, sustainable development.

Robert has also written more than two dozen teaching cases to help students bridge from research to teaching, concept to application, and theory to practice. His research interests focus on exploring the challenges for and linkages between supply chain management and the natural environment, encompassing both better process design and management practices. His research has been published in *Management Science, Journal of Operations Management, Academy of Management Journal, Production and Operations Management, Manufacturing & Services Operations Management,* and *Decision Sciences*, among others. He has also served as the chair of the operations management division of the Academy of Management, and currently serves as an associate editor for the *Journal of Operations Management* and *Production and Operations Management*, as well as on the editorial boards of several other journals.

Brief Contents

MyOMLab assets

SUPPLEMENTAL TOPICS

Contents

MyOMLab assets

Preface

As this third Canadian edition was developed, my primary emphasis was to expand and further refine three critical themes for operations management: effective process management, the role that operations managers play in the design and execution of effective supply chains, and, ultimately, the pivotal importance of operations in the creation of customer value. Moreover, this edition better captures and reinforces the importance of effective processes for service firms. Highlights of new sections and changes to the third Canadian edition are as follows:

- Chapter 1, "Creating Customer Value Through Operations," opens with an innovative Canadian service firm, AutoShare, that offers both customer-friendly processes and improved sustainability in operations. Four core processes that integrate across supply chains also are overviewed: supplier relationship process, order fulfillment process, customer relationship process, and new service or product development process. Finally, a new conceptual model is offered to provide structure for the following chapters.

- Chapter 2, "Supply Chain Management," previously a later chapter, has been moved to the front of the book to reflect the central and critical role of supply chains for many firms. The four core processes from the first chapter are further detailed, as well as performance measurement. A new section on sustainability defines and highlights the growing importance of reverse supply chains.

- Chapter 3, "Process Configuration," opens with a new vignette exploring the improvement of processes in a healthcare setting. More broadly, configuration of processes in services is given expanded treatment, and process improvement is introduced (and expanded later in Chapter 5).

- Chapter 4, "Capacity," now considers the differences and similarities in service processes between Starbucks and Tim Hortons. Both offer customer value but manage capacity quite differently. Challenges related to managing capacity are also illustrated in the growing ethanol industry.

- Chapter 6, "Quality and Process Improvement," explores the role of quality in mobile phone network firms. The discussion of Six Sigma has been moved much earlier, and expanded to cover the DMAIC steps. In response to reviewer feedback, the chapter has refined its presentation of process control and process capability. Last, the discussion of ISO 9001 has been brought up to date, and other related standards, such as ISO 14001, SA8000, and ISO 26000, are briefly noted.

- Chapter 7, "Lean Systems," is now positioned as integrating the preceding five chapters. After explaining the overarching philosophy, forms of waste and strategic implications of lean, a more detailed discussion of key process levers is presented. A new section covers the design of layouts for lean systems.

- Chapter 8, "Managing Projects," is now viewed as offering managers a means to bridge from strategy to implementation of new systems, processes, and products.

- Chapter 9, "Location and Layout," previously the longest chapter, has been streamlined to focus on fewer key concepts.

- Chapter 10, "Managing Demand and Forecasting," now highlights the importance of jointly managing demand, of developing collaborative forecasts with inputs from across the supply chain, and of systematically seeking to improve forecasting methods.

- Chapter 11, "Operations Planning and Scheduling," has been rewritten to emphasize planning for both services and goods (rather than "aggregate planning," as in previous editions.) In addition, a new section has been introduced to cover three common scheduling rules and two related performance measures.

- Chapter 12, "Resource Planning," includes new opening and managerial practice vignettes that highlight the challenges of managing resources on the front lines. We also have added a new section that summarizes the planning and coordinating functions performed by an Enterprise Resource Planning (ERP) system.

- New student problems. The total number of end-of-chapter assignment problems has been expanded by 10%, of which over 40% are new to this edition. Supplemental problems are included in MyOMLab for instructors seeking further variety, or students looking for extra practise.

- MyOMLab. A key capability of this online resource is the streamlined presentation of chapter-specific materials, such as video cases, assignment problems, full-colour supplements, and commercial software. These are designed to help students improve their understanding of course concepts.

MOTIVATION AND OBJECTIVES

As with previous Canadian editions, this book continues to focus on meeting the need in many educational settings for a brief book that has strong coverage of critical concepts *and* retains a rich set of pedagogical features. Most students who take an operations management course are pursuing a business degree in functional areas other than operations, or seek to develop a general management perspective.

Business students—who will develop into our future managerial leaders—need to understand the interrelated processes of a firm, which connect operations with all other functional areas of an organization. Just as importantly, it is also critical that they understand the many processes that serve to connect firms forming a supply chain, which in turn influence service and product design, quality, and staffing issues, to name a few. For courses that prefer a strong pedagogical structure, a number of instructional features clarify and reinforce student learning (clear, short definitions; step-by-step examples of quantitative techniques; numerous solved problems; and homework problems).

This relatively concise textbook conveys the essential ideas and techniques without the encyclopedic volume of information found in many others. Yet the book is written to simultaneously fit the perspectives, strengths, and pedagogical approaches of individual faculty. Consequently, many advanced concepts, tools, and topics that faculty may wish to explore in greater detail are included as full-length, full-colour supplements in MyOMLab, along with experiential exercises, discussion questions, and cases.

As a starting point, this edition of *Foundations of Operations Management* draws much from the newly updated U.S. ninth edition. However, several shifts in emphasis and development are notable. First, the linkages between customer value and operations management are more strongly stressed and developed, beginning with Chapter 1, and then carried throughout. Operations management creates value through the effective and efficient management of processes, including services, products, and process design. I also present here a remarkable array of interesting Canadian companies that leverage their operations as an important competitive weapon as they battle in the global arena.

Second, the central emphasis on process management now focuses on services. This is a clear message behind the introduction of new service vignettes in many chapters, as well as more detailed aspects such as service productivity, customer involvement, or process improvement. To support this broader emphasis, supply chain management and four core processes are emphasized in the first two chapters. Also, the process management framework in Chapter 4 conceptually links the three critical factors of capacity, variability, and customer queues/inventory. The configuration of service and manufacturing processes—whether a project, batch, line, or continuous process—implicitly combines these factors to deliver customer value. As we explore these topics, I also frequently reinforce the notion that operations management involves coordination across the firm and the supply chain, and quantitative tools can be used to help managers make better operating decisions.

Finally, the facilitating role of operations in creating a more environmentally and socially sustainable organization is a recurring theme throughout the book. Environmental and social concerns are not unique to one region, one industry, or one type of firm; instead, these issues cut across the entire supply chain. For example, concerns about hazardous materials in products, large volumes of used products and waste in both developing and developed countries, supplier working conditions, and sizable carbon footprints are but a few of the issues that have attracted media scrutiny, and, more recently, managerial attention. And, in an Internet-connected world, businesses may be located geographically far from their customers, yet be scrutinized closely for sustainability practices. Framed around the triple bottom line, operations management concepts, insights, and tools are linked to sustainability in virtually all chapters.

CHAPTER OVERVIEW

The text is organized so that several basic strategic issues are covered before delving deeper into a range of tactical decisions.

Chapter 1, "**Creating Customer Value through Operations**," sets the tone for the text. Organizations comprise many processes, and operations principles and techniques are particularly well suited for their management and analysis. The central message—the contribution of operations management and effective processes to value—is emphasized. This perspective, which is carried forward throughout the text, appeals to students regardless of their academic major. This chapter also establishes the basic principles of operations strategy and four core processes that tie together all functions (and the broader supply chain), their primary purpose being the creation of customer value.

Chapter 2, "**Supply Chain Management**," extends the consideration of operations beyond a single site or firm to operational linkages between firms. This chapter delves further into operationalizing the four core processes introduced in first chapter, namely those that manage supplier relationships, order fulfillment, customer relationships, and new service or product development. Measures for supply chain performance also are summarized. Both efficient and responsive supply chains are covered.

Chapter 3, "**Process Configuration**," provides more insight into the management and fundamental structure of processes. Using as a starting point four key decision areas, specifically customer involvement, process structure, capital intensity, and flexibility, process configuration is dissected. Decisions about customer interaction are particularly critical for service processes. And just as importantly, the linkages between these four areas are stressed. The chapter closes with a systematic approach to improving processes and linkages to greener processes.

Chapter 4, "**Capacity**," begins our integrative development of critical process levers that every manager must understand. The process management triangle serves as the conceptual framework that links capacity, variability, and queues/inventory, which are covered in this chapter and the two that follow. Process bottlenecks, economies and diseconomies of scale, capacity strategies, theory of constraints, and a systematic approach to capacity planning are also highlighted. At the end of this chapter, Supplement 4S bolsters the discussion on variability by specifically considering waiting lines. If desired by individual faculty, several related supplements are available online in MyOMLab to deepen student understanding of related topics such as decision making, financial analysis, work measurement, and learning curves.

Chapter 5, "**Inventory Management,**" identifies the functions, costs, and managerial actions that can be taken to effectively use or reduce inventory. Basic inventory models and control systems are covered, and a number of quantitative examples walk students through the application of these concepts. More advanced inventory models are treated on the supplements available online in MyOMLab.

Chapter 6, "**Quality and Process Improvement,**" begins with a quick overview of quality management through the lenses of three quality gurus and underscores the multifaceted definition of quality as an aspect of customer value. Quality includes both high performance design and conformance, which, when coupled with tight tolerances, yields services and products with low variability. Under the conceptual umbrella of total quality management, statistical process control techniques and a number of quality improvement tools are detailed. More advanced students can study acceptance sampling using the supplement available online in MyOMLab.

Chapter 7, "**Lean Systems,**" draws together and reinforces concepts discussed in preceding chapters, and re-emphasizes the central importance of the process management triangle from the fourth chapter. Quality at the source, elimination of waste, small lot sizes, pull flow of materials, process visibility, and continuous improvement are linked and illustrated in both manufacturing and service settings. The overarching message is one of integrating mutually supportive elements to implement highly efficient methods for processes, firms, and supply chains.

Chapter 8, "**Managing Projects,**" has substantial managerial material regarding project management. The material follows the introduction to projects as one type of process in the chapter about process configuration. However, as is noted in Chapter 1, projects are important for both developing and implementing operations strategy. Here, the basic aspects of project management are considered, both qualitative and quantitative. As noted above, an understanding of these issues by students is important regardless of their functional major, and project management tools will undoubtedly be used by many throughout their careers.

Chapter 9, "**Location and Layout,**" continues the book's study of decisions that require long-term commitments about the process. Students can use both qualitative approaches and quantitative tools to make important decisions about the location of new facilities, as well as how to organize processes within a facility. Faculty also can encourage their students to explore the managerial insights from global positioning systems for making location decisions (using MapPoint software available online in MyOMLab). In addition, related quantitative topics such as linear programming and simulation are addressed in supplements in MyOMLab.

Chapter 10, "**Managing Demand and Forecasting,**" begins with an overview of multiple options available to managers to adjust or shift customer demand. From there, the remainder of the chapter considers a wide variety of forecasting approaches. While this forecasting can be used for strategic planning and tactical decisions, the primary emphasis here is on the latter. This chapter also includes information on combination forecasts and focus forecasting.

Chapter 11, "**Operations Planning and Scheduling,**" brings together planning for workforce levels across multiple service and product processes, and, where possible, inventory holdings. The planning process is explored using straightforward spreadsheet tools. Scheduling in small batch processes, flow shops, and service operations are each treated in turn. This approach allows students to understand the whole continuum of planning levels of output and workforce levels over time, as illustrated in the Air New Zealand vignette. The chapter closes with a brief discussion of priority rules for scheduling and performance measurement.

Chapter 12, **"Resource Planning,"** begins with presenting dependent demand as a basis for materials requirements planning in manufacturing. Moreover, these concepts can be extended and combined with a bill of resources for service firms and virtual organizations. Given its importance to practice, an overview of enterprise resource planning systems is provided. These final sections also address also resources such as financial assets, human resources, equipment, and inventories. If desired, the topic of master production scheduling can be covered using an online supplement in MyOMLab.

SPECIAL FEATURES OF THE BOOK

Many features are included to stress foundational concepts and to support the overall philosophy of any operations management course.

- **Central Role of Processes.** The book focuses on processes—the fundamental unit of work in all organizations. It is all about processes! This unifying theme for service and manufacturing organizations builds bridges between chapters and opens up the topics in operations to all students, regardless of their majors or planned career paths. Simultaneously, the focus on processes can create better "buy-in" for a course in operations management because students understand that processes underlie activities throughout the organization, not just in one functional area.

- **Streamlined.** The textbook is designed to have just 12 chapters that can be effectively covered in a 12-week course. Supplemental materials such as short cases and experiential exercises, as well as commercial software, are available online in MyOMLab.

- **A Balanced Perspective.** An effective operations management textbook should address both the "big picture" strategic issues and also the analytic tools that facilitate decision making. It is not just about "concepts" or just about "numbers"—it's about both dimensions. This edition also offers greater emphasis of services, while maintaining a balanced view of resource- and manufacturing-based processes.

- **Integration of Sustainability,** including both environmental and social issues, into the strategy underlying operations, as well as the management of processes. This rapidly emerging linkage resonates with our students, and can be a critical contributor to creating customer value.

- **Chapter-Opening Vignettes and Managerial Practices.** To help stimulate student interest, each chapter opens by profiling how real, world-class companies apply specific process issues. A second example illustrates how companies deal—either successfully or unsuccessfully—with the operations issues as they run their operations. Collectively, these highlight strong examples of best practices from notable Canadian and international firms.

- **Pedagogical Structure.** Colourful and instructive formatting is used throughout the book and online in MyOMLab. Full-colour figures, clear explanations, step-by-step examples of quantitative techniques, solved problems, and numerous homework exercises assist students with identifying key concepts, understanding the linkages between concepts, solving problems, and using powerful decision-making tools.

- **Examples.** Numerous examples throughout each chapter are a popular feature and are designed to help students understand the quantitative material presented. Each concludes with a "Decision Point," which focuses on the decision implications for managers.

- **Across the Organization.** Each chapter begins with a short listing of how the topics that follow are important to professionals throughout the organization, including linkages to accounting, finance, human resources, and marketing.

- **Margin Items.** Margin items have been simplified to focus on key definitions for quick student reference.

- **Solved Problems.** At the end of each chapter, detailed solutions demonstrate how to solve problems with the techniques presented in the chapter. The solved problems reinforce basic concepts and serve as models for students to refer to when doing the other problems that follow.

TEACHING AND LEARNING SUPPORT

MyOMLab

A key capability of MyOMLab is as an online homework and assessment tool designed to help students practise operations management problems and improve their understanding of course concepts, and to give their instructors feedback on their performance. This online product lets professors assign homework that is automatically graded but also serves as a tutorial experience for students.

MyOMLab can be used by itself or linked to any learning management system. To learn more about how MyOMLab combines proven learning applications with powerful assessment, visit **www.myomlab.com.**

MyOMLab lets you teach your course your way. Use it as an out-of-the-box resource for students who need extra help, or take full advantage of its advanced customization options.

- *Commercial software tools.* Microsoft MapPoint, Extend, Microsoft Project, and OM Explorer collectively illustrate the use of software tools to complex management problems. For example, see Chapter 8 for Microsoft Project, Chapter 4 for Extend, Chapter 9 for Microsoft MapPoint, and Chapter 11 for OM Explorer. The use of these tools is optional for students, based on the course time available to the faculty member.

- *Video cases.* Cases and video footage show how operations management can be used to solve real-world problems. For example, one case demonstrates how Southwest Airlines copes with gate turnaround operations and the passenger boarding process. Other examples include Autoliv for lean systems, and Clif Bar & Company for supply chain design and sustainability.

- *Cases.* A wide range of cases can either serve as a basis for classroom instruction or provide an important capstone problem to each chapter. These challenge students to grapple with the issues presented in a chapter in a less structured and more comprehensive way. A number of these cases can be used as in-class exercises without prior student preparation.

- *Experiential learning exercises.* Exercises are offered for most chapters, including Supply Chain Management (Sonic Distributors), Capacity

(Min-Yo Garment Company), Inventory Management (Swift Electronic Supply), and Quality and Process Improvement (SPC with a Coin Catapult). Each of these actively involves students, has been thoroughly tested in class, and has proven to be a valuable learning tool.

- *Supplemental chapters.* Full-colour supplements cover 11 topics such as decision making and master production scheduling.

FOR INSTRUCTORS

INSTRUCTOR'S SOLUTIONS MANUAL

The Instructor's Solutions Manual, created by the authors so as to ensure its currency and accuracy, provides complete solutions to all problems and notes for every case and experiential exercise. Each case includes a brief synopsis, a description of the purposes for using the case, recommendations for analysis and goals for student learning from the case, and detailed teaching suggestions for assigning and discussing the case with students. The Instructor's Solutions Manual is available for download from Pearson Canada's online catalogue and on the Instructor's Resource CD-ROM.

INSTRUCTOR'S RESOURCE MANUAL

The Instructor's Resource Manual features detailed instructor notes and teaching tips for all the textbook and supplemental chapters. It is available for download from Pearson Canada's online catalogue and on the Instructor's Resource CD-ROM.

TEST ITEM FILE

This resource offers an array of questions and problems ranging from easy to difficult. It includes true/false, multiple-choice, short-answer, and essay questions. The Test Item File is available for download from Pearson Canada's online catalogue and on the Instructor's Resource CD-ROM.

TESTGEN

A computerized test bank containing true/false, multiple-choice, short-answer, and problem questions for each textbook and supplemental chapter is available in the latest version of TestGen software. This software package allows instructors to custom-design classroom tests. Instructors can edit, add, or delete questions from the test banks; edit existing graphics and create new graphics; analyze test results; and organize a database of tests and student results. The TestGen is available for download from Pearson Canada's online catalogue and on the Instructor's Resource CD-ROM.

POWERPOINT PRESENTATIONS

This comprehensive set of PowerPoint slides illustrates and builds upon key concepts in the text. The slides are available for download from Pearson Canada's online catalogue and on the Instructor's Resource CD-ROM.

INSTRUCTOR'S RESOURCE CD-ROM

This valuable, time-saving resource provides instructors with electronic files for the complete Instructor's Solutions Manual, Test Item File, TestGen, PowerPoint Presentations, and Instructor's Resource Manual. Offering these materials as MS Word, PowerPoint, and PDF files (where appropriate) allows instructors to customize portions of the material to enhance their students' classroom learning experience.

TECHNOLOGY SPECIALISTS

Pearson's Technology Specialists work with faculty and campus course designers to ensure that Pearson technology products, assessment tools, and online course materials are tailored to meet your specific needs. This highly qualified team is dedicated to helping schools take full advantage of a wide range of educational resources, by assisting in the integration of a variety of instructional materials and media formats. Your local Pearson Education sales representative can provide you with more details on this service program.

PEARSON CUSTOM LIBRARY

For enrollments of at least 25 students, you can create your own textbook by choosing the chapters that best suit your own course needs. To begin building your custom text, visit www.pearsoncustomlibrary.com. You may also work with a dedicated Pearson Custom editor to create your ideal text—publishing your own original content or mixing and matching Pearson content. Contact your local Pearson Education sales representative to get started.

COURSESMART FOR INSTRUCTORS

CourseSmart goes beyond traditional expectations—providing instant, online access to the textbooks and course materials you need at a lower cost for students. And even as students save money, you can save time and hassle with a digital eTextbook that allows you to search for the most relevant content at the very moment you need it. Whether it's evaluating textbooks or creating lecture notes to help students with difficult concepts, CourseSmart can make life a little easier. See how when you visit www.coursesmart.com/instructors.

FOR STUDENTS

Besides having access to study plans in MyOMLab, students can find a wealth of other resources within MyOMLab, including the following:

- eText
- **Assignment questions**
- **Glossary Flashcards**
- **PowerPoints**
- **Equation Summaries**
- **Discussion Questions**
- **Cases**
- **Tours**
- **Videos**
- **Experiential Exercises**
- **Extend LT Simulations**

COURSESMART FOR STUDENTS

CourseSmart goes beyond traditional expectations—providing instant, online access to the textbooks and course materials you need at an average savings of 60 percent. With instant access from any computer and the ability to search your text, you'll find the content you need quickly, no matter where you are. And with online tools like highlighting and note-taking, you can save time and study efficiently. See all the benefits at www.coursesmart.com/students.

ACKNOWLEDGMENTS

I wish to thank the many people at Pearson Canada who inspired this project and made up the publishing team. My deeply felt thanks to Megan Farrell, who supervised the overall project, and Paul Donnelly, who kept me moving forward on the manuscript revisions with many helpful suggestions and feedback. Thanks also to Avinash Chandra for his work in coordinating the production of this text.

I also wish to thank my Canadian colleagues who provided very useful feedback and guidance for this edition. They include the following:

Neil Bishop, Fanshawe College

Paul Callaghan, Acadia University

Lloyd Clive, Fleming College

Mohamed Dia, Laurentian University

Laurel Donaldson, Douglas College

Mary Drane, Seneca College

Brian Graystone, University of British Columbia

Kalinga Jagoda, Mount Royal University

Shailendra Jha, Wilfrid Laurier University

Sam Lampropoulos, George Brown College

Rob Shepherd, Niagara College

I am much indebted to my colleagues at the University of Western Ontario, who have greatly influenced and developed my thinking on the teaching of operations management to business students. In particular, John Haywood-Farmer, Fraser Johnson, and Larry Menor provided much-needed discussion and feedback for this edition.

Finally, I thank my family for their patience during the many long hours preparing this book. My wife, Lorraine, provided the love and encouragement that I needed to complete this edition.

Robert D. Klassen
Ivey Business School
University of Western Ontario

Creating Customer Value Through Operations

Learning Goals

After reading this chapter, you will be able to:

1. describe operations and supply chains in terms of inputs, processes, outputs, information flows, suppliers, and customers.

2. define how operations can contribute to customer value.

3. explain how operations strategy is a pattern of decisions about processes and supply chains that achieves specific competitive priorities.

4. explain how to link marketing strategy to operations strategy through the use of competitive priorities.

5. give examples of how operations can be used as a competitive weapon.

Across the Organization

Competitive operations is important to:

- **marketing**, which helps create the demand that operations must satisfy, links customer demand with staffing and production plans, and keeps the operations function focused on satisfying customers' needs.

- **human resources**, which hires and trains employees to match process needs, location decisions, and planned production levels.

- **accounting**, which prepares financial and cost accounting information that aids operations managers in designing and operating production systems.

- **finance**, which manages the cash flows and capital investment requirements that are created by the operations function.

- **operations**, which designs and operates processes to give the firm a sustainable competitive advantage.

AutoShare is a car-sharing service that leverages an integrated network of locations, people, and Web-enabled technology to provide greater mobility to customers. Customer value is based on the simple premise that many people living in large cities don't drive enough to justify the expense and hassles of owning a car, but still need to occasionally drive a car for appointments, shopping, or other short excursions. The chairman of Ford once remarked, "If you live in a city, you don't need to own a car."

In principle, car-sharing is straightforward: have a car parked nearby that can be shared among several people using a simple reservation system. But in practice, processes have to be worked out to manage access to keys and cars, negotiate convenient parking locations, organize reservations, collect fees from users, respond to customer accidents, and provide routine vehicle maintenance, among other tasks. Operations are based on a self-serve model: Walk to one of the parking locations scattered around the city, unlock your car with a smart card or a key from a lockbox, and off you go. And don't forget to clean up the car before you return it, if you make a mess. Cars can be rented for as briefly as 30 minutes, adding to the complexity of delivering reliable service.

Adapting a European car-sharing model that originated in the 1990s, AutoShare started its operations in 1998. The president, Kevin McLaughlin, launched his business with a mission to reduce car pollution, promote environmental consciousness, and provide low-cost mobility to the masses. However, he found that having a green, socially responsible message was not enough. He reflected, "It took us years to figure out that the green part

AutoShare members get convenient, self-serve access to vehicles at over 100 locations in Toronto.

is not the reason people were joining. People were joining because car-sharing was convenient and saved them money."

The company has been profitable since 2006, while continuing to underpin operations with a green dimension. At this point, 10 percent of AutoShare's fleet is hybrid vehicles, and car-sharing firms are expected to be at the forefront of adopting plug-in electric cars. Industry research indicates that car-sharing operations reduce greenhouse gas emissions and congestion in large cities, with each fuel-efficient, shared car replacing multiple private cars. Over 40 percent of members end up selling at least one of their cars within a year of joining.

More than 10 000 customers of AutoShare now enjoy convenient, 24/7 access to about 220 vehicles at over 100 locations across Toronto. Pressure for growth continues, as operating costs can be spread across more customers and more locations can be developed. Management's goal is to have a vehicle within a five-minute walk of anywhere in the city, and at every subway station.

Auto manufacturers also have shown an interest in a similar service as a way to interest future buyers, test new technologies, and generate some green marketing. To that end, Daimler launched Car2Go service with its Smart car in several European and U.S. cities last year. Technology further enhances service; customers need not return cars to the original location, as they are tracked in real time using GPS technology. Using smart cards also simplifies operations to unlock vehicles, refuel cars, and access dedicated parking at busy city locations. Initial operations in Ulm, Germany, already have 20 000 members, representing 15 percent of all people with driver's licences there. Other manufacturers are considering a similar expansion into such services, which potentially could build long-term relationships with customers.

The demand for car-sharing services will continue to expand in variety and location. Growth is very strong because, according to McLaughlin, people's relationships with cars are changing.[1]

Managing operations is about creating customer value through the effective and efficient management of processes that provide goods and services that people use every day. In essence, **operations management** refers to the systematic design, direction, and control of processes that transform inputs into services and products for internal, as well as external, customers. Processes are the fundamental activities that organizations use to do work and achieve their goals. Every organization, whether public or private, manufacturer or service provider, must manage processes and the operations where these processes are performed.

Processes of multiple firms can be linked together to form a **supply chain**, which is the interconnected network of processes across different firms that produce a service or good to the satisfaction of customers. A firm can have multiple supply chains, which vary by the particular service or good being delivered to customers. **Supply chain management** is the synchronization of a firm's processes with those of its suppliers and customers to match the flow of materials, services, and information with customer demand.

The growing business developed by AutoShare provides one example of designing processes that generate customer value. Processes must be created for each step of the customer experience at an affordable price. In some areas, managers automated processes, for example, reservations and invoicing. In other areas, such as expanding the number of locations and identifying the mix of cars offered, managers focused on specific attributes. However, all of these processes involved coordination across all functional areas of the firm.

Throughout this book, we explore with you the role of managing processes within the total organization. We explain what managers of processes do, the decisions they make, and some of the tools and concepts that they can use. By developing a sound operations strategy and using appropriate techniques, managers can design and operate processes to give companies a competitive edge. Helping you understand how operations creates customer value and can be a competitive weapon begins with this chapter and continues throughout the book.

PROCESS VIEW

An organization is only as effective as its processes. A **process** is any activity or group of activities that takes one or more inputs, transforms and adds value, and generates one or more outputs for its customers. The types of processes can vary significantly. For example, a primary process in a factory could be a physical or chemical change of raw materials, like wood and leather, into physical products, such as furniture. But there also are many service and support processes at a factory, such as order fulfillment, making due-date promises to customers, and inventory control. In contrast, the primary process for an airline would be the movement of passengers and their luggage from one location to another. Here, too, processes are needed for making reservations, checking in passengers, serving meals, and scheduling crews.

As Figure 1.1 illustrates, processes have inputs and customer outputs. Inputs include human resources (workers and managers), capital (equipment and facilities),

operations management The systematic design, direction, and control of processes that transform inputs into services and products for internal, as well as external, customers.

supply chain An interrelated series of processes within and across firms that produces a service or good to the satisfaction of customers.

supply chain management The synchronization of a firm's processes with those of its suppliers and customers to match the flow of materials, services, and information with customer demand.

process Any activity or group of activities that takes one or more inputs, transforms and adds value to them, and provides one or more outputs for its customers.

FIGURE 1.1   *Processes and Operations*

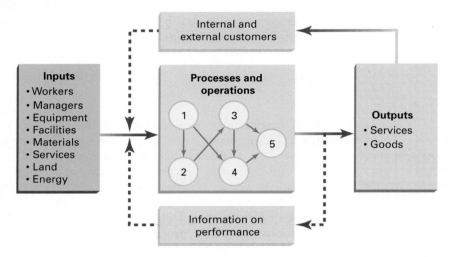

energy, and purchased materials and services, including information. The numbered circles represent operations through which services, products, and customers pass and where activities are performed. The arrows represent flows and can cross because one customer can have different requirements (and thus, a different flow pattern) from another customer. Processes provide outputs—often services, which can take the form of information—to their "customers."

Both manufacturing and service organizations now realize that every process and every person in an organization has customers. Some are **external customers,** who may be either end users or intermediaries (such as manufacturers, wholesalers, or retailers) buying the firm's finished products and services. Others are **internal customers,** who may be one or more other employees who rely on inputs from earlier processes in order to perform processes in the next office, shop, or department. Either way, processes must be managed with the right customer in mind.

Figure 1.1 can represent a whole firm, a department or small group, or even a single individual. Each one has inputs and uses processes at various operations to provide outputs. The dashed lines represent two special types of input: participation by customers and information on performance from both internal and external sources. Participation by customers occurs not only when they receive outputs, but also when they take an active part in the processes, such as when students participate in a class discussion. Information on performance includes internal reports on customer service or inventory levels and external information from market research, government reports, or telephone calls from suppliers. Managers need all types of information to manage processes most effectively.

HOW PROCESSES WORK

Let's take a look at what happens at an ad agency. Suppose a client contacts her account executive (AE) about her need for a memorable ad campaign for the upcoming National Hockey League (NHL) Stanley Cup series. The AE gathers the pertinent information and passes it along to a creative design team and a media planning team that prepare an ad layout and a media exposure plan acceptable to the client. The AE also gives the information to the accounting department, which prepares an account for billing purposes. The creative design team passes the layout design to a production

external customers End users or intermediaries, such as manufacturers, wholesalers, or retailers, who buy a firm's products and services.

internal customers One or more employees who use outputs from earlier, upstream processes to perform processes in the next office, shop, or department.

just example
no need to memorize.

FIGURE 1.2 *Process View of an Ad Agency*

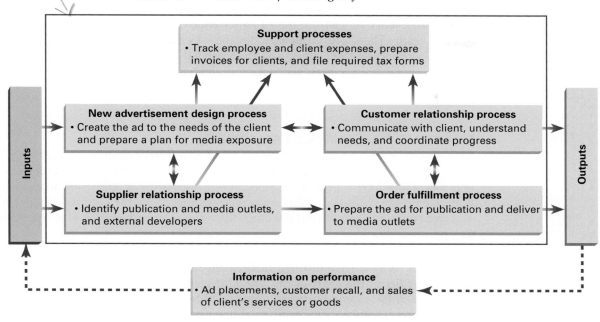

team, which prepares the final layout for publication and delivers it to the selected media outlets according to the schedule developed by the media team and approved by the client. The design team, media team, and production team send their billable hours and expense items to the accounting department, which prepares an invoice that is approved by the AE and then sent to the client for payment.

Figure 1.2 shows a process view of the ad agency at two levels. The red-outlined box represents the ad agency as an aggregate process. Viewed at this level, the ad agency requires inputs from external sources and produces outputs, which are advertisements for external clients. The inputs from external sources are resources used by the ad agency's processes and include employees, managers, money, equipment, facilities, materials, services, land, and energy. The output is the NHL ad campaign for the client. However, inside the red box we see a more detailed process view: the client interface process includes the AE and her interactions with the client. The advertisement design and planning process creates the ad and plans its exposure during the Stanley Cup series. The production process acquires the actors, prepares the production set and props, coordinates the schedules of all involved in the production of the ad, films the content, prepares a video, and delivers the ad to the media outlets on time. The arrows in the diagram indicate information and work flows between the processes, along with feedback on performance.

NESTED PROCESSES

Processes can be broken down into subprocesses, which can in turn be broken down into still more subprocesses. We refer to this concept of a process within a process as a **nested process**. One part of a process can be separated from another for several reasons. One person or one department may be unable to do all parts of the process, or different segments in the process may require different skills. Some segments of the process may be standardized for all customers, making high-volume operations possible. Other segments may be customized, requiring processes best suited to flexible, low-volume operations.

nested process A process within a process.

If we peel away a few more layers of our process view of the ad agency, we can focus on the advertisement design and planning process. The creative design process starts with a work order from the AE, after which the creative design director assembles the team. The work order includes the ad's objective, the overall message, the evidence supporting the claims, and the intended audience. The design team comes up with several designs, gets feedback from the AE, prepares a final design, gets feedback from the client through the client interface process, and revises the design as needed.

SERVICE AND MANUFACTURING PROCESSES

At a simple level, processes are often classified as services or manufacturing (i.e., goods) based on the primary output of the process. Service processes pervade the business world and have a prominent place in our discussion of operations management. Manufacturing processes are also important; without them, the products we that enjoy as part of our daily lives would not exist. In addition, manufacturing gives rise to service opportunities.

DIFFERENCES. Why do we distinguish between service and manufacturing processes? The answer lies at the heart of the design of competitive processes. While Figure 1.3 shows several distinctions between service and manufacturing processes along a continuum, three characteristics tend to differentiate goods-producing processes from service-producing processes. First, customers tend to be highly involved in the operations process for services, particularly those that are experience-based, such as an amusement park. Although tangible facilities might be part of that experience, the output of the process is the enjoyment and memories of the customer.

Second, manufacturing outputs are physical goods that often can be produced in advance, and then held in inventory until needed by the customer. In contrast, because service processes usually require the customer to be directly involved, they cannot be produced in advance to insulate the process from erratic customer demands. For example, the output from the auto loan process of a bank would be a car loan, and an output of the order fulfillment process of Purolator Courier is the delivery of your package.

Third, the quality of goods can often be monitored using physical measures of specific characteristics, with little ambiguity. However, the outputs of many service operations tend to have perceptual characteristics, such as whether a movie was "exciting." Distinctions between manufacturing and service outputs must be reflected in the operations strategies chosen by an organization.

FIGURE 1.3 *Continuum of Service and Manufacturing Process Outputs*

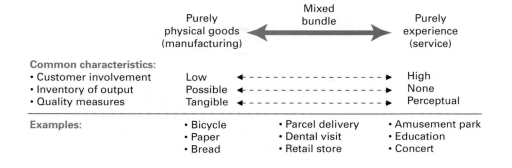

SIMILARITIES. Today, few firms put themselves at either end of the continuum, with manufacturing firms moving into service offerings, and services selling physical goods. For example, some manufacturing firms such as Lexus are strongly committed to outstanding after-sales service support through its dealer network. Moving in the opposite direction, Disney produces and licenses an increasing number of goods related to its cast of characters. As a result, firms must explicitly design and manage a set of processes that bundle both goods and services with strong, convincing customer value.

Further, even though service processes do not keep finished goods inventories, they do inventory their inputs. For example, hospitals keep inventories of medical supplies and materials needed for day-to-day operations. Some manufacturing processes, on the other hand, do not inventory their outputs because they are too costly. Such would be the case with low-volume customized products (e.g., tailored suits) or products with short shelf lives (e.g., daily newspapers).

When you look at what is being done at the process level, it is much easier to see whether the process is providing a service or manufacturing a product. However, this clarity is lost when the whole company is classified as either a manufacturer or a service provider, because it often performs both types of processes. For example, the process of baking a doughnut at Tim Hortons is a manufacturing process, because it changes the food's physical properties. However, most of the other processes visible or invisible to customers are service processes.

SUPPLY CHAIN VIEW

As noted earlier, most services or goods are produced through a series of interrelated business activities. Each activity in a process should add value to the preceding activities; waste and unnecessary cost should be eliminated. Our process view of a firm is helpful for understanding how services or products are produced and why cross-functional coordination is important, but it does not shed any light on the strategic benefits of the processes. The critical strategic insight is that processes must add value for every customer along the supply chain. The concept of supply chains reinforces the link between processes and performance, which includes a firm's internal processes as well as those of its external customers and suppliers. It also focuses attention on the two main types of processes in the supply chain, namely core processes and support processes.

CORE PROCESSES

core process A set of activities that delivers value to external customers.

A **core process** is a set of activities that delivers value to external customers. Managers of these processes and their employees interact with external customers and build relationships with them, develop new services and products, interact with external suppliers, and produce the service or product for the external customer. Examples include a hotel's reservation handling, new car design for an auto manufacturer, or Web-based purchasing for an online retailer like Chapters.Indigo.ca. Of course, each of the core processes has subprocesses nested within it. In this text, we focus on four core processes:

1. *Supplier relationship process.* Employees select the suppliers of services, materials, and information, and facilitate the timely and efficient flow of these items into the firm. Working effectively with suppliers can add significant customer value. For example, negotiating fair prices, scheduling on-time deliveries, and gaining ideas and insights from critical suppliers are just a few of the ways to create value.

2. *Order fulfillment process.* The order fulfillment process includes the activities required to produce and deliver the service or product to the external customer.

3. *Customer relationship process.* Sometimes referred to as *customer relationship management.* Employees involved in the customer relationship process identify, attract, and build relationships with external customers, and facilitate the placement of orders by customers.

4. *New service or product development process.* Employees use a process to design, develop, and launch new services or goods. The services or goods may be developed to external customer specifications or conceived from inputs received from the market in general.

SUPPORT PROCESSES

support process
A process that provides vital resources and inputs to the core processes and therefore is essential to the management of the business.

A **support process** provides vital resources and inputs to the core processes and is essential to the management of the business. Firms have many support processes. Examples include accounting, budgeting, recruiting, and scheduling (see Figure 1.2). Support processes provide key resources, capabilities, or other inputs that allow the core processes to function.

OPERATIONS STRATEGY

operations strategy The pattern of decisions and investments in products, services, and processes used to implement an organization's corporate strategy and to create customer value.

Operations strategy specifies the means by which operations implements corporate strategy and helps to direct processes toward creating customer value. It links long-term and short-term operations decisions to corporate strategy, and develops the capabilities the firm needs to be competitive. It is at the heart of managing processes and supply chains. A firm's internal processes are only building blocks: they need to be organized to ultimately be effective in a competitive setting. Operations strategy is the linchpin that brings these processes together to form supply chains that extend beyond the walls of the firm, encompassing suppliers as well as customers. Because customer segments evolve and new opportunities arise, the firm's operations strategy must be strongly linked to the needs of its customers. We will return to these important ideas at the end of the chapter.

Developing an operations strategy that delivers customer value begins with a corporate strategy, as shown in Figure 1.4, that establishes the firm's overall goals with its core processes. It determines the markets that are served and how the firm responds to changes in the business setting. The corporate strategy also provides the resources to develop the firm's core processes, and identifies how the firm will be positioned in international markets. Based on corporate strategy, a market analysis categorizes the firm's customers, identifies opportunities, and assesses competitors' strengths. This information is used to target customer value and specify competitive priorities. Competitive priorities encompass six key dimensions, and are a central driver for the firm's operations strategy. However, an operations strategy is not static; improvement opportunities and gaps in performance must be addressed through iterative development.

CORPORATE STRATEGY

Corporate strategy provides an overall direction that serves as the framework for carrying out all the organization's functions. It specifies the business or businesses the company will pursue, isolates new opportunities and threats in the environment, and identifies growth objectives.

From an operations perspective, a corporate strategy involves three considerations: (1) monitoring and adjusting to changes in the business setting, (2) targeting resources

FIGURE 1.4 *Customer value is the critical link between corporate strategy, competitive priorities, and operations strategy*

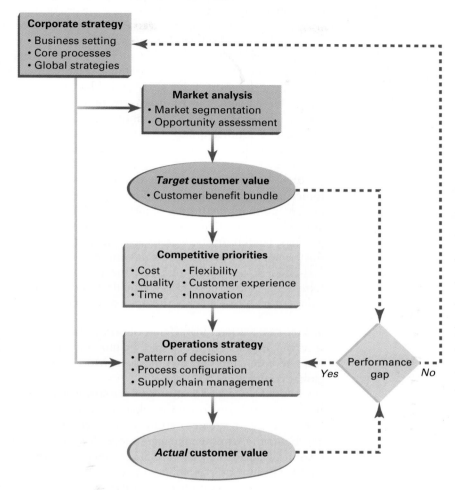

to develop a firm's core processes, and (3) developing the firm's operations with a global perspective.

BUSINESS SETTING. The competitive and regulatory situation in which a firm finds itself frequently changes, and it needs to adapt accordingly. Adaptation begins with scanning of the business setting, whereby managers monitor trends in the industry, marketplace, and society in general. A crucial reason for monitoring is to stay ahead of the competition. Competitors may be gaining an edge by broadening service or product lines, improving quality, or lowering costs. New entrants into the market or competitors that offer substitutes for a firm's service or product may threaten continued profitability. For example, car manufacturers recognize that dwindling oil reserves will eventually require alternative fuels for their cars. Consequently, several are beginning to introduce new cars based on hybrid or electric power systems. Other important environmental concerns are economic trends, technological changes, political conditions, social changes (such as attitudes toward work), the availability of vital resources, and the collective power of customers or suppliers.

DEVELOPING CORE PROCESSES. Firms tend to have a limited quantity of resources—such as workforce, financial, managerial, process, and technological capabilities—to allocate toward developing new core processes or improving existing processes. As a result, while some companies have all four core processes described earlier, many others focus on a subset of them to improve their competitiveness. For instance, in the credit card business within the banking industry, some companies primarily specialize in finding customers and maintaining relationships with them. American Airlines's credit card program reaches out and achieves a special affinity to customers through its marketing database. Alternatively, other specialized credit card companies, such as CapitalOne, focus on service innovation by creating new features and pricing programs. The important point is that every firm must evaluate how to best use its limited resources to develop core processes that differentiate the firm and yield significant customer value.

It is important to recognize that core processes can also be extended into new customer benefit bundles and markets. For example, Honda has strong core processes to design and manufacture small internal combustion engines. These processes have been applied with great success to a wide range of products and markets, including automobiles, lawn mowers, watercraft, and motorcycles. Most recently, Honda has turned this competency toward the small aircraft sector, where it is introducing a new, very fuel-efficient jet engine that has the potential to dramatically reshape this market. Extending core processes is particularly crucial as global competition increases and competitors move quickly to copy basic product and service features.

GLOBAL PERSPECTIVE. Identifying opportunities and threats today requires a global perspective. A global strategy may include buying foreign services or parts, or planning ways to enter international markets. Moreover, defending against threats from other global competitors is a necessity.

Two effective global strategies are strategic alliances and locating abroad. One way for a firm to open foreign markets or leverage resources abroad, such as a low-cost workforce, is to create a strategic alliance. A strategic alliance is an agreement with another firm that may take one of three forms. One form of strategic alliance is the *collaborative* effort, which often arises when one firm has resources and capabilities that another needs but is unwilling (or unable) to duplicate. Such arrangements commonly arise out of buyer–supplier relationships.

Another form of strategic alliance is the *joint venture*, in which two firms agree to produce a service or good jointly. Firms often use this approach to gain access to foreign markets. For example, Bombardier Transportation is a global railway leader with three joint ventures in China, employing more than 4000 people. A recent agreement established the China Railway Signal and Communication Corp. to jointly develop signalling products to meet the requirements in China and abroad.[3] Finally, *technology licensing* is a form of strategic alliance in which one company licenses its service or production methods to another.

Another way to enter global markets is to locate operations in a foreign country. However, managers must recognize that what works well in their home country might not work well elsewhere. For example, McDonald's is known for the consistency of its products—a Big Mac tastes the same anywhere in the world. However, the family-owned chain Jollibee Foods Corporation has become the dominant fast-food chain in the Philippines by catering to a local preference for sweet and spicy flavours, which it incorporates into its fried chicken, spaghetti, and burgers. Employing over 26 000 people at over 1000 locations in seven countries, Jollibee's strengths are its creative marketing programs, an understanding of local tastes, and claims that its burger is similar to the one a Filipino would cook at home. In order to be successful, firms with a global perspective must recognize customs, preferences, and economic conditions in other countries.

MARKET ANALYSIS

One key to successfully formulating a customer-driven operations strategy for both service and manufacturing firms is to understand what the customer wants and how to provide it. A market analysis first divides the firm's customers into market segments, and then identifies the needs and opportunities of each segment.

For operations, each segment might require a different process configuration and supply chain. Not only must the product bundle be clearly defined, but how that service or good will reach the intended customer must also be defined. Core and supporting processes allow a firm to focus on particular segments based on customer requirements for availability, convenience, courtesy, safety, accuracy, reliability, and delivery speed. Other critical attributes related to operations that can differ between segments include the level and predictability of customer demand. Once it makes this assessment, the firm can incorporate the needs of customers into its emphasis on particular competitive priorities.

CUSTOMER VALUE AND COMPETITIVE PRIORITIES

customer value The combination of quality, time, flexibility, customer experience, and innovation relative to price for a particular customer benefit bundle of goods and services. Price translates into cost for operations management.

customer benefit bundle A package of core goods and services along with a set of peripheral goods or services.

For operations management, we focus on aspects of **customer value** that are driven by processes that relate to the product or service itself, to its delivery system, and to related volume factors. Customer value includes both the tangible and the intangible product attributes and features that a customer desires (Collier, 1994). These attributes and features, which can be termed a **customer benefit bundle**, consist of a core good and/or service and a set of peripheral goods and services. For example, when you purchase an automobile, the core product is the car itself—its features and qualities. However, the peripheral services offered by the dealer play a key role in whether you will buy the car. They include the manner in which you are treated by the salesperson, the availability of financing, and the quality of after-sales service at the dealership. Thus, the customer benefit bundle is the automobile plus the services provided by the dealership. Customers won't be completely satisfied unless they receive a well-integrated benefit bundle that addresses all of their needs.

In general, there are six broad dimensions of customer value that collectively create the customer benefit bundle: quality, time, flexibility, customer experience, innovation, and price. Conceptually, customer value is defined as a ratio:

$$\text{Customer value} = \frac{(\text{Quality, time, flexibility, customer experience, innovation})}{\text{Price}}$$

Because price is usually determined by the market and other competitive forces, operations must work to improve *cost* (rather than price), relative to quality, time, and flexibility. An operations strategy is only sustainable if price exceeds cost, as many bankrupt firms have tragically discovered.

For operations management to effectively and efficiently create customer value, a clear understanding of the organization's long-term goals is needed, as embodied in its corporate strategy. Thus, customer value vividly underscores that operations management cannot succeed in isolation, but must be strongly linked both strategically and tactically to other functional areas, such as marketing. The relative emphasis or

competitive priorities
The relative weighting of the dimensions of customer value that operations management must outperform its competitors.

weighting of the dimensions of customer value that operations management must possess to outperform its competitors is called **competitive priorities**.

More specifically, we can dissect the six basic dimensions of customer value into 12 possible competitive priorities for processes. Table 1.1 provides definitions and examples of these competitive priorities, as well as how firms achieve them at the process level.

TABLE 1.1	*Definitions, Process Considerations, and Examples of Competitive Priorities*		
	DEFINITION	**PROCESSES CONSIDERATIONS**	**EXAMPLE**
1. COST			
a. Low-cost operations	Delivering a service or a product at the lowest possible cost to the satisfaction of external or internal customers of the process or supply chain	To reduce costs, processes must be designed and operated to make them efficient using rigorous process analysis that addresses workforce, methods, scrap or rework, overhead, and other factors, such as investments in new automated facilities or technologies to lower the cost per unit of the service or product.	**Costco** achieves low costs by designing all processes for efficiency, stacking products on pallets in warehouse-type stores, and negotiating aggressively with their suppliers. Costco can provide low prices because it has designed operations for low cost.
2. QUALITY			
a. High-performance design	Delivering an outstanding service or good	To deliver top quality, a service process may require a high level of customer contact, and high levels of helpfulness, courtesy, and availability of servers. It may require superior product features, close tolerances, and greater durability from a manufacturing process.	**Ferrari**'s processes deal with providing superior product features and more demanding performance requirements.
b. Consistent quality	Producing services or products that meet design specifications on a consistent basis	Processes must be designed and monitored to reduce errors, prevent defects, and achieve similar outcomes over time, regardless of the "level" of quality.	**Tim Hortons** standardizes work methods, staff training processes, and procurement of raw materials to achieve the same consistent product and process quality from one store to the next.
3. TIME			
a. Delivery speed	Quickly filling a customer's order	Design processes to reduce lead time (elapsed time between the receipt of a customer order and filling it) through keeping backup capacity cushions, storing inventory, and using premium transportation options.	**Dell** engineered its customer relationship, order fulfillment, and supplier relationship processes to create an integrated and agile supply chain that delivers reliable and inexpensive computers to its customers with short lead times.
b. On-time delivery	Meeting delivery-time promises	Along with processes that reduce lead time, planning processes (forecasting, appointments, order promising, scheduling, and capacity planning) are used to increase percent of customer orders shipped when promised (95% is often a typical goal).	**United Parcel Services (UPS)** uses its expertise in logistics and warehousing processes to deliver a very large volume of shipments on time across the globe.

TABLE 1.1 *(cont'd)*

	DEFINITION	PROCESSES CONSIDERATIONS	EXAMPLE
4. FLEXIBILITY			
a. Customization/ variety	Satisfying the unique needs of each customer by changing service or product designs or handling a wide assortment of services or products efficiently	Processes can require low-volume, close customer contact, and an ability to reconfigure processes to meet diverse types of customer needs. Alternatively, higher volume processes can adapt to particular needs using flexible technologies.	**Chapters.Indigo.ca** uses information technology and streamlined customer relationship and order fulfillment processes to reliably deliver a vast variety of items to its customers.
b. Volume flexibility	Accelerating or decelerating the rate of production of services or goods quickly to handle large fluctuations in demand	Processes must be designed for excess capacity and/or excess inventory to handle demand fluctuations that can vary in cycles from days to months. This priority also could be met with a strategy that adjusts capacity without accumulation of inventory or excess capacity.	**Purolator Courier** can have severe demand peak fluctuations at large sorting facilities where processes are flexibly designed for receiving, sorting, and dispatching packages to numerous distribution locations.
5. CUSTOMER EXPERIENCE			
a. Customer participation	Ranges from passive, in which customers are observers, to active, in which customers play key roles in creating the service	Processes can be designed to solicit and capture customer preferences, and engage them with either workers or other customers. Process cues and structured interaction are needed to create a consistent experience.	Theme parks at **Disney** include both passive shows and interactive rides.
b. Customer connection	The extent to which a customer is immersed or absorbed in a service or good	Processes can employ multiple senses (e.g., sight, touch) to provide a deeper, more enriching connection.	3D movies at **Cineplex** and **Apple**'s use of touch screen gestures on the iPhone expand the customer's connection.
6. INNOVATION			
a. Product innovation	Develop a novel service or good	Processes for developing new services and goods requires internal R&D capabilities, access to new technologies, and discerning latent customer needs. Other firms in the supply chain often are critical.	**Monsanto** continues to develop biotech products that insert new plant genes into such crops as potatoes and corn.
b. Process innovation	Develop a novel process or supply chain	Processes aim to develop novel ways of meeting customer needs. Resources must be reconfigured, people trained, and technology developed to create a new process.	**Progressive Insurance** dramatically reinvented the way claims were processed using online systems for both customers and agents, and quick dispatch of adjusters to inspect the damaged vehicle.
c. Development speed	Quickly introducing a new service or good	Processes aim to achieve cross-functional integration and involvement of critical external suppliers in the service or product development process.	**Li & Fung** can get new product idea for clothing from its customer, design the sweater, transmit the design to Southeast Asia where it is produced, ship the sweater back to Canada, and put the sweater on the store shelves of the customer within a few weeks.

MANAGERIAL PRACTICE
Using Operations for Profit at Costco

Looking for bargains on items ranging from watermelons to symphonic baby grand pianos? One company addressing those needs is Costco (www.costco.com), a wholesale club with 77 warehouse stores in Canada. With 566 warehouses worldwide, the firm had revenues of $70 billion and profits of $1 billion in 2009. Capital investment of $1.3 billion was directed at opening 20 new warehouses. Individual and business customers pay Costco a relatively small annual fee for membership and the privilege of buying staple items in bulk quantities and other select items at big discounts.

What makes Costco so successful? It has linked the needs of its customers to its operations by developing a customer-driven operations strategy that supports its retailing concept. Costco's competitive priorities are low-cost operations, customer experience, and quality flexibility. A visit to one of Costco's stores shows how these competitive priorities manifest themselves.

Shoppers checking out the bargains that they found at one of Costco's wholesale clubs. Costco operates member-centred discount warehouse outlets in North America, Europe, Australia, and Asia.

Low-Cost Operations

Customers come to Costco because of low prices, which are possible because processes are designed for efficiency. The store is actually a warehouse where products are stacked on pallets with little signage. Only a limited selection is carried in each product category, reducing inventory and handling. Only 3800 carefully selected items are carried in a typical store, while superstores of competitors might carry over 100 000 items.

Costco managers also focus on an efficient supply chain, in which buying in large volumes reduces prices. Suppliers are expected to change factory runs to produce specially built packages that are bigger but cheaper per unit. In addition, new products are identified to replace old products efficiently.

Customer Experience

Customers are looking, not for high levels of customer service, but for high value. In addition to having low prices, Costco backs everything it sells with generous return policies. Customers trust Costco, which has generated an 87 percent membership renewal rate—among the highest in the industry—helping to make the firm the ninth largest retailer in the world.

Quality

To support the need for high value, operations must ensure that products are of high quality and undamaged when placed in the store. Identifying key partners for their supply chain has been critical to expand Costco's range of private label products based on enhanced quality and special product sizes.[2]

time-based competition
Defining the steps and time needed to deliver a product or service, and then critically analyzing each step to determine whether time can be reduced without hurting quality.

At times, management emphasizes a cluster of competitive priorities together for either internal or external customers. For example, many companies focus on the competitive priorities of delivery speed and innovation speed for their processes, a strategy called **time-based competition**. To implement the strategy, managers carefully define the steps and time needed to deliver a service or produce a product and then critically analyze each step to determine whether they can save time without hurting quality.

Using process innovation, Progressive Insurance has been able to achieve amazing growth in the United States. Under the company's Immediate Response Claims Handling program, for example, claims adjusters are quickly dispatched to the scene of an accident to examine the vehicle and process claims.

order winner A criterion customers use to differentiate the services or goods of one firm from those of another.

order qualifier A demonstrated level of performance of an order winner that is required for a firm to do business in a particular market segment.

More generally, competitive priorities need to be thought of as evolutionary in nature. What do we need to emphasize now, and how will that change over time? For example, consider a high-volume standardized product, such as colour ink-jet desktop printers. In the early stages of the ramp-up period when the printers had just entered the mass market, the manufacturing processes required consistent quality, delivery speed, and volume flexibility. In the later stages of the ramp-up when demand was high, the competitive priorities became low-cost operations, consistent quality, and on-time delivery.

SELECTING COMPETITIVE PRIORITIES

You might wonder why firms have to choose among competitive priorities. Why not compete in all areas at once and dramatically improve your competitive position? In certain situations, firms *can* improve on all competitive priorities simultaneously. For example, in a manufacturing firm, scrap materials from mistakes in operations and the need to rework defective parts sometimes account for a quarter of a product's cost. By reducing defects and improving quality, the firm can reduce costs, improve productivity, and cut delivery time—all at the same time.

At some point, though, further improvements in one area may require a trade-off with one or more of the others. Therefore, firms must select a subset of competitive priorities to emphasize with operations processes and systems. In any given market, one particular dimension of customer value often transcends others to influence purchase behaviour between competing products. This dimension is called an **order winner** (Hill, 2000). For example, consistent quality is an order winner for many of Toyota's automobiles.

Sometimes the minimum level of a particular dimension of customer value has become a requirement for doing business in a specific market segment. Such a requirement is called an **order qualifier**. In such situations, customers will not place orders for products or services unless a certain level of performance can be demonstrated. Fulfilling the order qualifier will not ensure competitive success in a market; it will only position the firm to compete. For example, for television sets, one measure of quality is product reliability. Customers expect to purchase a set that will not require repairs for many years. Products that do not live up to that level of quality do not last long in the market. In the electronics industry in general, product reliability is rapidly becoming an order qualifier.

Figure 1.5 shows how order winners and qualifiers are related to achieving the competitive priorities of a firm. Order winners and qualifiers are often used in competitive bidding. For example, before a buyer considers a bid, suppliers might be required to document their ability to provide consistent quality as measured by adherence to the design specifications for the service or component they are supplying (order qualifier). Once qualified, the supplier might eventually be selected by the buyer on the basis of low prices (order winner) and the reputation of the supplier (order winner).

USING COMPETITIVE PRIORITIES: TARGETING VALUE AT AN AIRLINE

To get a better understanding of how companies use competitive priorities, let us look at a major airline. We will consider two market segments: business-class passengers and economy-class passengers. Core services for both market segments are ticketing and seat selection, baggage handling, and transportation to the customer's destination.

FIGURE 1.5   *Relationship of Order Winners and Order Qualifiers to Competitive Priorities*

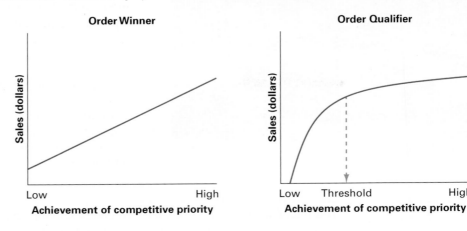

The peripheral services are quite different across the two market segments. Business-class passengers demand separate airport lounges; preferred treatment during check-in, boarding, and deplaning; more comfortable seats; better meals and beverages; more personal attention (cabin attendants who refer to customers by name); more frequent service from attendants; high levels of courtesy; and low volumes of passengers (adding to the feeling of being special). For a lower price, economy-class passengers are satisfied with standardized services (no surprises), courteous flight attendants, and low prices. Both market segments expect the airline to hold to its schedule. Consequently, we can say that the competitive priorities for the business-class segment are top quality and on-time delivery, whereas the competitive priorities for the economy-class segment are low-cost operations, consistent quality, and on-time delivery.

How are these market segments translated into each of its core processes, namely customer relationship, new service/product development, order fulfillment, and supplier relationship? Competitive priorities are assigned to each core process to measure and identify gaps required to provide complete customer satisfaction.

One of the competitive priorities of airline companies is on-time delivery of their services. Being able to repair and maintain planes rapidly to avoid delays are crucial processes.

CUSTOMER RELATIONSHIP. This process involves high levels of customer contact through ticketing (both electronic and telephone), elite lounge service, and boarding. It also has marketing and sales functions. Possible competitive priorities include the following:

- *High-performance design.* High levels of customer contact and lounge service for the business-class passengers.

- *Consistent quality.* The information and service must be error-free.

- *Delivery speed.* Customers want immediate information regarding flight schedules and other ticketing information.

- *Variety.* The process must be capable of handling the service needs of all market segments and promotional programs, such as frequent-flier services.

ORDER FULFILLMENT. This process is responsible for delivering the service to the customer's satisfaction. It is a huge process in an airline, involving scheduling, gate operations, maintenance, cabin service, pilot operations, and baggage handling. It has many nested processes, and many competitive priorities, which might include the following:

- *Low-cost operations.* Airlines compete on price and must keep costs in check.

- *High-performance design.* The service provided to business-class passengers must be top-notch. To a large extent, this service aspect involves well-trained and experienced cabin attendants and a high-quality meal and beverage service.

- *Consistent quality.* Once the quality level is set, it is important to achieve it every time.

- *On-time delivery.* The airline strives to arrive at destinations on schedule; otherwise, the passengers might miss connections to other flights.

- *Variety.* Maintenance operations are required for a variety of aircraft models.

SUPPLIER RELATIONSHIP. This process is responsible for acquiring all of the inputs the airline requires to do business, which range from human resources to capital goods. Competitive priorities might include the following:

- *Low-cost operations.* The cost of acquiring inputs must be kept to a minimum to allow for competitive pricing.

- *Consistent quality.* The quality of the inputs must adhere to the required specifications. In addition, the information provided to the suppliers must be accurate.

- *On-time delivery.* Inputs must be delivered to tight schedules, particularly meal services.

- *Variety.* Many different inputs must be acquired, including maintenance items, meals and beverages, and even aircraft.

- *Volume flexibility.* The process must be able to handle variations in supply quantities efficiently.

NEW SERVICE DEVELOPMENT. New services must continually be developed to stay ahead of the competition. Such services include tours to the world's vacation paradises, new routes, or new dinner service. Competitive priorities might include the following:

- *Development speed.* It is important to get to market fast to pre-empt the competition.

- *Customization.* The process must be able to create unique services.
- *High-performance design.* New services must be carefully designed, because the future of the airline depends on them.

TRENDS IN OPERATIONS MANAGEMENT

Several trends are currently having a great impact on operations management: productivity improvement; global competition; and sustainability. In this section, we briefly look at these trends and their challenges for operations managers.

PRODUCTIVITY IMPROVEMENT

productivity The value of outputs (goods and services) produced divided by the values of input resources.

Productivity is a basic measure of performance for economies, industries, firms, and processes. Improving productivity of processes and supply chains is of critical importance to both enhance customer value and further develop a firm's competitive positioning. Productivity is the value of outputs (goods and services) produced divided by the values of input resources (wages, cost of equipment, and the like) used:

$$\text{Productivity} = \frac{\text{Output}}{\text{Input}}$$

* Examples in slides

* Standard cost is COGS. *

Many measures of productivity are possible, and all are rough approximations. For example, the value of output can be measured by what the customer pays or simply by the number of units produced or customers served. The value of inputs can be judged by their cost or simply by the number of hours worked.

Managers usually pick several reasonable measures and monitor trends to spot areas needing improvement. For example, a manager at an insurance firm might measure office productivity as the number of insurance policies processed per employee each week. A manager at a carpet company might measure the productivity of installers as the number of square metres of carpet installed per hour. Both of these measures reflect *labour productivity*, which is an index of the output per person or hour worked. Similar measures may be used for *machine productivity*, where the denominator is the number of machines. Accounting for several inputs simultaneously is also possible. *Multifactor productivity* is an index of the output provided by more than one of the resources used in production. For example, it may be the value of the output divided by the sum of labour, materials, and overhead costs. When developing such a measure, you must convert the quantities to a common unit of measure, typically dollars.

The way processes are managed plays a key role in productivity improvement. Labour and multifactor productivity measures can provide a means to monitor improvement over time; however, they can be deceptive. For example, a firm can decide to transfer some of its work to outside suppliers and lay off some of its own workforce. Labour productivity will increase considerably, because the value of the firm's total sales (the numerator) remains unchanged while the number of employees (the denominator) drops. Also, because many processes only have internal customers, it is often difficult to assign a dollar value to the value of process outputs. Thus, productivity measures are often a good starting point, but insufficient in isolation. Just as importantly, managers must monitor performance measures on quality, inventory levels, capacity utilization, on-time delivery, employee satisfaction, customer satisfaction, and the like. The smart manager monitors *multiple* measures of performance, setting goals for the future and seeking better ways to design and operate processes.

FIGURE 1.6   *Growth in Service Sector Employment in Canada*[4]

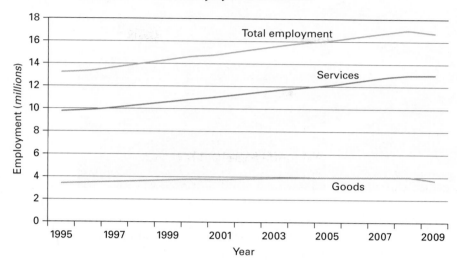

Labour productivity in Canadian business has improved by an average of 2.1 percent annually over the past four decades, although this has slowed recently. Investment in new equipment and technology that substituted for workers, rather than gains in worker skills, was the most important factor contributing to this improvement. It is interesting to further break down productivity improvements between the manufacturing and services sectors. As shown in Figure 1.6, employment growth in Canada has been in the service sector, not manufacturing, over the past 15 years. But historically, productivity gains have been much lower in services than in manufacturing. Fortunately, there are recent signs of improvement,[5] as an increasing number of service firms are using technology to raise productivity and deliver services directly to customers, often using the Internet. Greater international competition, in areas such as financial services, is also motivating service firms to accelerate improvements in the efficiency of their processes.

GLOBAL COMPETITION

Most businesses realize that, to prosper, they must view customers, suppliers, facility locations, and competitors in global terms. Most products today are composites of materials and services from all over the world. Sitting in a Cineplex theatre (Canadian), you munch on a Nestle's Crunch bar (Swiss) while watching a Columbia Pictures movie (Japanese). Five developments spurred the need for sound global strategies: (1) improved transportation and communications technologies, (2) loosened regulations on financial institutions, (3) increased demand for imported services and goods, (4) comparative cost advantages, and (5) reduced international trade barriers due to regional trading blocs, such as the European Union (EU) and the North American Free Trade Agreement (NAFTA). Here, we will just focus on the last two developments.

usually main one

COMPARATIVE COST ADVANTAGES. China and India have recently become the sources for low-cost, skilled labour. Historically, companies have manufactured products in China to gain a foothold in a huge market, or to get cheap labour to produce low-tech products despite concerns about the skills of the workforce and poor infrastructure such as electricity and transportation. Today, however, China's new factories, such as those in

Foreign companies have opened thousands of new factories in China in recent years. Labour costs are low in China, and its workforce is educated and disciplined.

the Pudong industrial zone in Shanghai, produce a wide variety of high-quality products that are sold around the world. But, even in China, companies are seeing new competition from other emerging economies with lower wage costs, such as Vietnam.

What China is to manufacturing, India is to service. As with the manufacturing companies, the cost of labour is a key factor. A programmer in India receives a fraction of the wages of a programmer in Canada with comparable skills and experience. And Indian software companies have grown very sophisticated in their applications. For example, to remain competitive, Electronic Data Systems increased its staff in India almost tenfold over a three-year period. Back-office support operations are also affected for the same reason. Many firms are using Indian companies for customer-support call centres, accounting and bookkeeping, preparing tax returns, and processing insurance claims.

Operations in these countries can extend into research and development (R&D), with a number of Canadian high-tech companies opening, acquiring, or expanding significant development capabilities in India. For example, ATI Technologies, now owned by AMD, acquired a subsidiary located in Hyderabad to both gain access to a strong talent pool and cut development costs. The Indian subsidiary creates software to compress and decompress audio and video data for hand-held game and mobile phone developers (Holloway, 2005).

TRADING BLOCS. Regional trading blocs such as NAFTA and the EU further change the competitive landscape in both services and manufacturing. As a result, Canadian manufacturers have been under increasing competitive pressure in domestic and international markets in areas such as financial services, steel, appliances and household durable goods, machinery, and chemicals. The recent rise in the Canadian dollar relative to U.S. and European currencies has added another challenge for exporters. Yet managers must continue to build operational capabilities through investment in human resources, quality, and product and process technologies.

DISADVANTAGES OF GLOBALIZATION. Of course, operations in other countries can have disadvantages. A firm may have to relinquish proprietary technology if it turns over some of its component manufacturing to offshore suppliers or if suppliers need the firm's technology to achieve desired quality and cost goals. Political risks may also be involved. The extreme case is nationalization, in which a government may take over a firm's assets without paying compensation. Exxon and other large multinational oil firms are scaling back operations in Venezuela due to nationalization concerns. Further, a firm may actually alienate customers in its home market if jobs are lost to offshore operations.

Employee skills may be lower in foreign countries, requiring additional training time. South Korean firms moved much of their sports shoe production to low-wage Indonesia and China, but they still manufacture hiking shoes and in-line roller blades in South Korea because of the greater skills required. In addition, when a firm's operations are scattered globally, customer response times can be longer. We discuss these supply chain issues in more depth in later chapters. Coordinating components from

Shortage of components from suppliers and capacity shortfalls prevented Nintendo from meeting the customer demand for its popular Wii game system.

sustainability Designing and managing process to ensure that we meet humanity's needs today without hurting the ability of future generations to meet their own needs. Performance is assessed using a triple bottom line.

a wide array of suppliers can be challenging, as Nintendo found out in the production and worldwide distribution of its Wii game systems.[6] Despite twice increasing capacity over an eight-month period before the 2007 holiday season, up to 1.8 million Wiis a month, Nintendo could ship only limited quantities to major retailers, both forgoing profits and hurting customer satisfaction.

SUSTAINABILITY AND OPERATIONS

Environmental and social concerns are not unique to one region, one industry, or one type of firm. Instead, these issues cut across the entire supply chain. For example, concerns about hazardous materials in products, large volumes of used products and waste in both developing and developed countries, and sizable carbon footprints are but a few of the issues that have attracted media scrutiny, and more recently, managerial attention. Also, new regulations seek to simultaneously protect both the environment and human health. For example, the Registration, Evaluation, Authorisation and Restriction of Chemicals (REACH) regulation in the European Union forces companies to evaluate the human health and environmental impact of a broad range of chemicals, and then to track them throughout their supply chain.

Businesses also face more difficult social issues than ever before, intensified by an increasing global presence and rapid technological change. Companies are locating new operations, and have more suppliers and customers, in other countries. Potential ethical dilemmas arise when business can be conducted by different rules. Some countries are more sensitive than others about employee working conditions, conflicts of interest, bribery, poverty and minimum-wage levels, unsafe workplaces, and workers' rights. Managers must decide in such cases whether to design and operate processes that do more than just meet local standards that are lower than those back home. In an electronic world, businesses are geographically far from their customers, and a reputation for trust may become even more important.

Reflecting this reality, **sustainability** captures both the environmental and the social implications of operations. Processes are designed and managed to ensure that we meet humanity's needs today without hurting the ability of future generations to meet their own needs. In a general sense, a firm's sustainability can be viewed as having a triple bottom line, with financial, environmental, and social performance (Elkington, 1998). Conceptually, this view can be represented by the three sides of a triangle, each side representing performance against peer firms and its area providing an indication of value (see Figure 1.7). For instance, improved environmental performance can result from fewer hazardous materials and lower toxic emissions, which in turn can reduce or eliminate the need for employee protective equipment—a social aspect of sustainable development.[7] In Figure 1.7, both firms generate the same financial performance, but the competitor generates much lower environmental and social performance. As a result, the total customer value offered by the competitor is lower. Naturally, managing and improving the triple bottom line is much more difficult than just focusing on a single bottom line.

In a promising change of direction, managers are increasingly shifting their attention away from just controlling pollution, to designing greener services, processes, and products (Vachon and Klassen, 2008). Greener processes actually work to prevent the generation of pollution. For example, in manufacturing, finishes for furniture replace

FIGURE 1.7 *Sustainability Translates into the Triple Bottom Line for Operations*

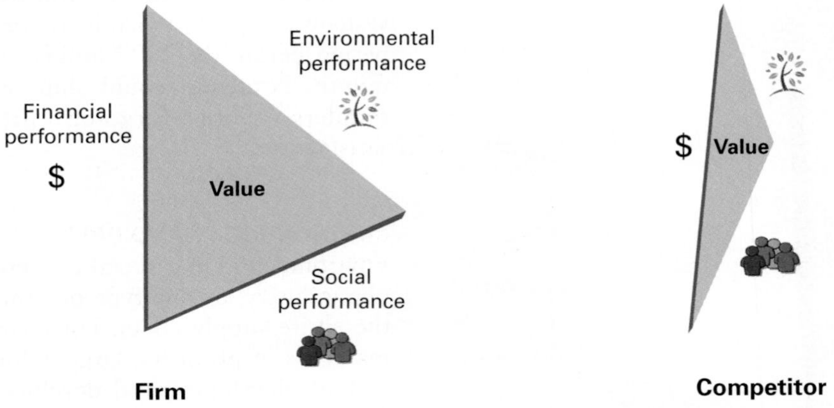

organic solvents with water-based finishes that are cured by UV light, preventing the release of harmful vapours. Paper can increase recycled fibre content, and be whitened with alternatives to elemental chlorine.

Service firms also are actively working with customers to reduce the environmental impact of their processes. For example, hotels have reduced laundry needs by asking customers to reuse towels, and financial institutions have shifted the flow of some information from paper-based mail to electronic delivery. Delivery firms can use biodiesel to fuel their vehicles. Finally, large computer firms, such as Google, can use solar energy to power their server operations, while simultaneously designing their facilities to use natural cooling methods.

Greener products are also being developed. To illustrate, Apple has recently begun to report environmental burden for at least one dimension of its popular products. The 13-inch (33-centimetre) MacBook Pro has a carbon footprint of 440 kilograms of carbon dioxide equivalent, of which two-thirds comes from the supply chain, including production (59%), transport (8%), and recycling (1%). Improvements since introducing the original MacBook model include lowering energy consumption by 32 percent and reducing packaging volume by 41 percent.[8] However, in other products, trade-offs may occur. For example, fluorescent lamps consume much less energy during use than incandescent bulbs, but also require small amounts of mercury as a key material. As a result, additional supply chain activities might facilitate recycling or reduce hazards from disposing of fluorescent lamps.

The message is clear: Consideration of environmental and social issues is becoming part of every manager's job. When designing and managing processes, managers must consider the triple bottom line that extends beyond traditional measures such as productivity, quality, cost, and profit. This triple-bottom-line theme will be developed further in each chapter.

OPERATIONS STRATEGY AS A PATTERN OF DECISIONS

Competitive priorities provide a basis for the design of processes and the formulation of an effective and sustainable operations strategy. An operations strategy is not a single initiative, such as a quality improvement program, more automated machinery, or even a new facility located abroad, but rather a pattern of decisions and investments over time that develop a competitive advantage. An operations strategy translates plans for goods and services, and competitive priorities for each market segment, into decisions affecting the supply chains that support those market segments. Even if not formally stated by senior managers, the current operations strategy for any firm reflects the collective past decisions made for its processes and supply chains. As noted previously in Figure 1.4, developing capabilities and closing performance gaps is the thrust of operations strategy.

In this text, we cover the major decisions that collectively form an operations strategy (Figure 1.8). Driven by customer value at the apex, operations managers are involved in the design of supply chains and process configuration. These strategic decisions are covered in the next two chapters. These systems rely on implementing many different capabilities (and developing new ones) that collectively provide value for the firm's customers (process implementation). It is very important to emphasize that plans, policies, and actions of operations should be aligned and linked to those of other functional areas to support the firm's overall goals and objectives. Taking a process view of a firm helps us to understand these linkages. Finally, project management is widely used whenever change is planned, whether at the strategic level or within particular processes.

Regardless of whether you aspire to be an operations manager, or you just want to use the principles of operations management to become a more effective manager, remember that effective management of people, capital, information, and materials is critical to the success of any process and any supply chain.

As you study operations management, keep two principles in mind:

1. Each part of an organization, not just the operations function, must design and operate processes that are part of a supply chain and deal with quality, technology, and staffing issues.

2. Each function of an organization has its own identity and yet is connected with operations through shared processes.

FIGURE 1.8   *Operations Strategy as a Coordinated Pattern of Decisions*

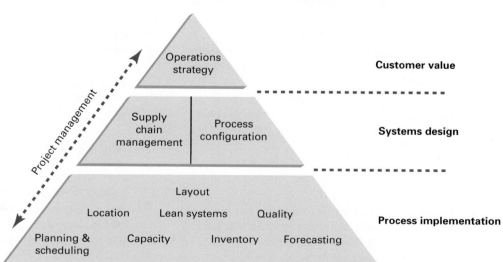

Overall, the ideal outcome is a strong alignment between corporate and operations strategies. And most organizations commit the bulk of their human and financial assets to operations. Unfortunately, great strategic decisions lead nowhere if the tactical process implementation that supports them is wrong. Too often, tactical decisions covering capacity, inventory levels, and scheduling reflect incorrect assumptions about customer value and corporate strategy—ultimately working at cross-purposes to a firm's strategic goals. This lack of understanding can waste a firm's resources for years. The rest of this book explores these issues in greater detail.

Due to an increasing array of competitors and an explosion of new technologies, recognition is growing that a firm competes not only by offering new products and services, creative marketing, and skillful finance but also by having unique skills and capabilities in operations. The organization that can offer superior products and services produced at lower cost is a formidable competitor.

EQUATION SUMMARY

1. Productivity is the ratio of output to input, or:

$$\text{Productivity} = \frac{\text{Output}}{\text{Input}}$$

CHAPTER HIGHLIGHTS

- Every organization must manage processes and the operations by which these processes are performed. Processes are the fundamental means by which organizations perform work and achieve their goals. Processes transform inputs into outputs, and are ideally designed to create customer value. Inputs include human resources (workers and managers), capital resources (equipment and facilities), purchased materials and services, land, and energy. Outputs are goods and services that firms combine into a customer benefit bundle.

- Conceptually, for operations management, customer value is defined as the ratio of quality, time, flexibility, customer experience, and innovation to cost.

- The concept of processes applies not just to an entire organization but also to the work of each department and individual. Each has work processes and customers (whether internal or external).

- A process can be broken down into subprocesses, which in turn can be broken down still further. A process within a process is known as a nested process.

- The outputs from manufacturing and service processes range from pure goods to pure experience. Three primary characteristics tend to differentiate goods-producing

processes from service-producing processes: customer involvement, potential inventory of outputs, and measurement of quality. These differences must be reflected in the operations strategy used by an organization.

- Decisions within operations should be linked. For example, quality, process, capacity, and inventory decisions affect one another and should not be made independently. Strategy (long-range plans) and tactical implementation (for short-range decision making) should complement each other.

- Smart managers use multiple performance measures, including productivity, to monitor and improve performance.

- Several trends are at work in operations management: productivity is a major concern, particularly in the service sector; a global perspective must be encouraged; and sustainability must be integrated into operations. The importance of the natural environment, ethics, and workforce diversity is increasing.

- Firms expanding and competing internationally may form strategic alliances through collaborative efforts, joint ventures, or licensing of technology.

- Market analysis is key to formulating a customer-driven operations strategy. Market segmentation and needs assessment are methods of pinpointing elements of a good or service that satisfy customers.

- Customer-driven operations strategy requires translating market needs into specific operating advantages, called competitive priorities. There are six basic dimensions that cover 12 priorities: low-cost operations; quality, including high-performance design and consistent quality; time, including fast delivery time and on-time delivery; flexibility, including customization and volume flexibility; customer experience, including participation and connection; and innovation, including product, process, and development speed. Management must decide on which dimensions the firm's processes should excel, sometimes requiring difficult trade-offs.

- With time-based competition, managers seek to significantly reduce time in the various steps required to deliver a product or service.

- Operations strategy is a pattern of decisions and investments in products, services, and processes used to implement an organization's corporate strategy and to create customer value.

- Sustainability has become an important issue for operations management. Managers must increasingly design and manage their firm's processes and supply chains to ensure that we meet humanity's needs today without harming future generations. Firm performance is viewed as a triple bottom line, including financial, environmental, and social performance.

- Operations strategy integrates supply chain management and lean systems. Implementing effective processes encompasses decisions about process configuration, capacity, quality, inventory, location, forecasting, and planning and scheduling. Finally, project management enables change, whether at the strategic or the process level.

SOLVED PROBLEM

Student tuition at Boehring University is $150 per semester credit hour. The province supplements school revenue by $100 per semester credit hour. Average class size for a typical 3-credit course is 50 students. Labour costs are $4000 per class, materials costs are $20 per student per class, and overhead costs are $25 000 per class.

a. What is the *multifactor* productivity ratio for this course process?

b. If instructors work an average of 14 hours per week for 16 weeks for each 3-credit class of 50 students, what is the *labour* productivity ratio?

SOLUTION

a. Multifactor productivity is the ratio of the value of output to the value of input resources.

$$\text{Value of output} = \left(\frac{50 \text{ students}}{\text{Class}}\right)\left(\frac{3 \text{ credit hours}}{\text{Student}}\right)\left(\frac{\$150 \text{ tuition} + \$100 \text{ provincial support}}{\text{Credit hour}}\right)$$

$$= \$37\,500/\text{class}$$

$$\text{Value of inputs} = \text{Labour} + \text{Materials} + \text{Overhead}$$

$$= \$4000 + (\$20/\text{student} \times 50 \text{ students/class}) + \$25\,000$$

$$= \$30\,000/\text{class}$$

$$\text{Multifactor productivity} = \frac{\text{Output}}{\text{Input}} = \frac{\$37\,500/\text{class}}{\$30\,000/\text{class}} = 1.25$$

b. Labour productivity is the ratio of the value of output to labour hours. The value of output is the same as in part (a), or $37 500/class, so

$$\text{Labour hours of input} = \left(\frac{14 \text{ hours}}{\text{Week}}\right)\left(\frac{16 \text{ weeks}}{\text{Class}}\right) = 224 \text{ hours/class}$$

$$\text{Labour productivity} = \frac{\text{Output}}{\text{Input}} = \frac{\$37\,500/\text{class}}{224 \text{ hours/class}}$$

$$= \$167.41/\text{hour}$$

PROBLEMS

Software is available in MyOMLab. Check with your instructor on how best to use it. In many cases, the instructor wants you to understand and practise how to do the calculations by hand. Alternatively, if the calculations are particularly complex and the goal is to learn how to interpret the results to make a decision, the software could replace the manual calculations.

1. (Refer to Solved Problem 1.) Coach Bjourn Toulouse led the Big Red Herrings to several disappointing football seasons. Only better recruiting will return the Big Red Herrings to winning form. Because of the current state of the program, Boehring University fans are unlikely to support increases in the $192 season ticket price. Improved recruitment will increase overhead costs to $30 000 per class section from the current $25 000 per class section. The university's budget plan is to cover recruitment costs by increasing the average class size to 75 students. Labour costs will increase to $6 500 per 3-credit course. Material costs will be about $25 per student for each 3-credit course. Tuition will be $200 per semester credit, which is supplemented by provincial support of $100 per semester credit.

   a. What is the multifactor productivity ratio? Compared to the result obtained in Solved Problem 1, did productivity increase or decrease for the course process?
   b. If instructors work an average of 20 hours per week for 16 weeks for each 3-credit class of 75 students, what is the *labour* productivity ratio?

2. CD players are produced on an automated assembly line process. The standard cost of CD players is $150 per unit (labour, $30; materials, $70; and overhead, $50). The sales price is $300 per unit.

   a. To achieve a 10 percent multifactor productivity improvement by reducing materials costs only, by what percentage must these costs be reduced?
   b. To achieve a 10 percent multifactor productivity improvement by reducing labour costs only, by what percentage must these costs be reduced?
   c. To achieve a 10 percent multifactor productivity improvement by reducing overhead costs only, by what percentage must these costs be reduced?

3. Alyssa's Custom Cakes currently sells 5 birthday, 2 wedding, and 3 specialty cakes each month for $50, $150, and $100 each, respectively. The cost of labour is $50 per hour including benefits. It takes 90 minutes to produce a birthday cake, 240 minutes to produce a wedding cake, and 60 minutes to produce a specialty cake. Alyssa's multifactor productivity ratio is 1.25, and each type of cake has the same cost for ingredients.

   a. What is the average cost to produce a cake?
   b. Calculate Alyssa's labour productivity ratio in dollars per hour for each type of cake.
   c. Based solely on the labour productivity ratio, which cake should Alyssa try to sell the most?
   d. Based on your answer in part (a), is there a type of cake Alyssa should stop selling?

4. Mack's guitar fabrication shop produces low-cost, highly durable guitars for beginners. Typically, out of the 100 guitars that begin production each month, only 80 percent are considered good enough to sell. The other 20 percent are scrapped due to quality problems that are identified after they have completed the production process. Each guitar sells for $250. Because some of the production process is automated, each guitar requires only 10 labour hours. Each employee works an average 160 hours per month. Labour is paid at $10/hour, materials cost is $40/guitar, and overhead is $4000.

   a. Calculate the labour and multifactor productivity ratios.
   b. After some study, the operations manager, Darren Funk, recommends three options to improve the company's multifactor productivity: (1) increase the sales price by 10 percent, (2) improve quality so that only 10 percent are defective, or (3) reduce labour, material, and overhead costs by 10 percent. Which option has the greatest impact on the multifactor productivity measure?

NOTES FOR CHAPTER

1. J. Pachner, "The AutoShare Saga: A Long, Strange Trip," *The Globe and Mail*, September 9, 2010; J. Motavalli, "Daimler's Car2go Sharing Program Continues to Expand," *New York Times Blogs*, October 18, 2010; T. Luntz, "Smaller Towns Fuel Rise of Nonprofit Car-Sharing Programs," *Greenwire*, December 24, 2008; J. Brown, "Cars by the Hour: Sharing Saves," *The Toronto Star*, August 2, 2008; and www.autoshare.com, accessed December 7, 2010.

2. "Inside the Cult of Costco," *Fortune*, September 6, 1999, pp. 184–190; Costco annual report, 2009.

3. R. Marowits, "Bombardier Signs Deal That Could Lead to Export of Chinese Made Trains," *The Canadian Press*, December 7, 2010.

4. Statistics Canada, *Canada Year Book* (Ottawa: Statistics Canada, 2010); CANSIM, Table 282-0008.

5. Statistics Canada, *The Canadian Productivity Accounts: Data, 1961 to 2006*, Catalogue No. 15-003-X (2007).

6. P. Svensson, "GameStop to Sell Rain Checks for Wii," *The State*, December 18, 2007.

7. For a more complete discussion of sustainability and what major corporations are doing, see Marc J. Epstein, *Making Sustainability Work* (Sheffield, UK: Greenleaf Publishing, 2008); Pete Engardio, "Beyond the Green Corporation," *Business Week*, January 29, 2007, pp. 50–64.

8. Apple, "13-Inch MacBook Pro Environmental Report," accessed May 10, 2010, from www.apple.com/environment/reports.

FURTHER READING

Berry, W. L., C. Bozarth, T. Hill, and J. E. Klompmaker. "Factory Focus: Segmenting Markets from an Operations Perspective." *Journal of Operations Management*, vol. 10, no. 3 (1991), pp. 363–387.

Blackburn, Joseph. *Time-Based Competition: The Next Battle-Ground in American Manufacturing*. Homewood, IL: Business One-Irwin, 1991.

Chase, R. B., and U. M. Apte. "A History of Research in Service Operations: What's the Big Idea?" *Journal of Operations Management*, vol. 25, no. 2 (2007), pp. 375–386.

Chatterjee, S. "Delivering Desired Outcomes Efficiently: The Creative Key to Competitive Strategy." *California Management Review*, vol. 40, no. 2 (1998), pp. 78–95.

Collier, David A. *The Service Quality Solution*. Milwaukee: ASQC Quality Press, and Burr Ridge, IL: Irwin Professional Publishing, 1994.

Elkington, J., *Cannibals with Forks: The Triple Bottom Line of 21st Century Business*. Gabriola Island (British Columbia): New Society Publishers, 1998.

Fitzsimmons, James A., and Mona Fitzsimmons. *Service Management*. New York: McGraw-Hill, 2005.

Gilmore, James H., and B. Joseph Pine II. "The Four Faces of Mass Customization." *Harvard Business Review*, vol. 75, no. 1 (1997), pp. 91–101.

Goldstein, Susan Meyer, Robert Johnson, JoAnn Duffy, and Jay Rao. "The Service Concept: The Missing Link in Service Design Research?" *Journal of Operations Management*, vol. 20 (2002), pp. 121–134.

Hammer, Michael. "Deep Change: How Operational Innovation Can Transform Your Company." *Harvard Business Review* (April 2004), pp. 85–93.

Hayes, Robert H., and Gary P. Pisano. "Beyond World-Class: The New Manufacturing Strategy." *Harvard Business Review* (January–February 1994), pp. 77–86.

Heineke, Janelle, and Mark Davis. "The Emergence of Service Operations as an Academic Discipline." *Journal of Operations Management*, vol. 25, no. 2 (2007), pp. 364–374.

Heskett, James L., and Leonard A. Schlesenger. "The Service-Driven Service Company." *Harvard Business Review* (September–October 1991), pp. 71–81.

Hill, Terry. *Manufacturing Strategy: Text and Cases*, 3rd ed. Homewood, IL: Irwin/McGraw-Hill, 2000.

Holloway, A. "Hand-Helds across the Water," *Canadian Business*, vol. 78, no. 13 (2005), pp. 63–65.

Jack, Eric P., and Thomas L. Powers. "Volume Flexible Strategies in Health Services: A Research Framework." *Production and Operations Management*, vol. 13, no. 3 (2004), pp. 230–244.

Kaplan, Robert S., and David P. Norton. *Balanced Scoreboard*. Boston, MA: Harvard Business School Press, 1997.

Menor, Larry J., Mohan V. Tatikonda, and Scott E. Sampson. "New Service Development: Areas for Exploitation and Exploration." *Journal of Operations Management*, vol. 20 (2002), pp. 135–157.

Porter, Michael E., and Mark R. Kramer. "Strategy and Society: The Link Between Competitive Advantage and Corporate Social Responsibility." *Harvard Business Review*, vol. 84, no. 12 (2006), pp. 78–92.

Prahalad, C. K., and Venkatram Ramaswamy. "Co-Opting Customer Competence." *Harvard Business Review* (January–February 2000), pp. 79–87.

Rayport, Jeffrey F., and Bernard J. Jaworski. "Best Face Forward." *Harvard Business Review*, vol. 82, no. 12 (2003), pp. 47–58.

Rudberg, Martin, and Jan Olhager. "Manufacturing Networks and Supply Chains: An Operations Strategy Perspective." *Omega*, vol. 31, no. 1 (2003), pp. 29–39.

Skinner, Wickham. "Manufacturing—Missing Link in Corporate Strategy." *Harvard Business Review* (May–June 1969), pp. 136–145.

Skinner, Wickham. "Manufacturing Strategy on the 'S' Curve." *Production and Operations Management*, vol. 5, no. 1 (1996), pp. 3–14.

Vachon, Stephan, and Robert Klassen, "Environmental Management and Manufacturing Performance: The Role of Collaboration in the Supply Chain," *International Journal of Production Economics*, vol. 111, no. 2 (2008), pp. 299–315.

van Biema, Michael, and Bruce Greenwald. "Managing Our Way to Higher Service-Sector Productivity." *Harvard Business Review* (July–August 1997), pp. 87–95.

Ward, Peter T., and Rebecca Duray. "Manufacturing Strategy in Context: Environment, Competitive Strategy and Manufacturing Strategy." *Journal of Operations Management*, vol. 18 (2000), pp. 123–138.

Wheelwright, Steven C., and H. Kent Bowen. "The Challenge of Manufacturing Advantage." *Production and Operations Management*, vol. 5, no. 1 (1996), pp. 59–77.

Womack, James P., Daniel T. Jones, and Daniel Roos. *The Machine That Changed the World*. New York: HarperPerennial, 1991.

MyOMLab ASSETS

MyOMLab offers the following resources, which allow you to further practise and apply concepts presented in this chapter.

- **Key Equations:** All the equations for this chapter can be found in one convenient location.

- **Discussion Questions:** These questions challenge your understanding of the role of operations management and operations strategy.

- **Case and Video:**
  - *Operations as a Competitive Weapon at Starwood.* What are the key inputs and outputs associated with Starwood's new meeting planning process? How does this process interact with other core processes in their hotels?

- **Case:**
  - *Chad's Creative Concepts.* How should Chad Thomas, traditionally a custom manufacturer, cope with the new move into standard products sold by retail outlets?

- **OM Explorer Tutor:** OM Explorer contains one tutor program that will help you explore productivity measures.

- **Supplement A: Decision Making.** This supplement provides the background to use break-even analysis, preference matrices, decision theory, and decision trees.

Supply Chain Management

Learning Goals

After reading this chapter, you will be able to:

1. define the nature and strategic importance of supply chains, and their linkage to core processes.
2. define the key design issues associated with supply chain processes.
3. discuss how critical operating measures of supply chain performance are linked to key financial measures.
4. distinguish between efficient and responsive supply chains and understand how each offers particular competitive benefits in different business settings.
5. describe the major causes of supply chain dynamics, their effects, and how integrated supply chains can mitigate supply chain dynamics.
6. explain how integrated supply chains can help firms achieve goals related to sustainability.

Across the Organization

Supply chain management is important to:

- **distribution,** which determines the best placement of finished goods inventories and selects the appropriate modes of transportation for serving the external supply chain.
- **marketing,** which involves contact with the firm's customers and needs a supply chain that ensures responsive customer service.
- **operations,** which is responsible for managing effective supply chains.
- **purchasing,** which selects the suppliers for the supply chain.
- **finance and accounting,** which must understand how the performance of the supply chain affects key financial measures and how information flows into the billing process.

Customer service after the sale, which requires having the right repair part in the right location in the service parts supply chain, is a key competitive dimension of business today for service providers as well as manufacturers. Overstocking the parts throughout the supply chain is not an option because of the expense. Eastman Kodak, a $13.3 billion manufacturer of digital imaging products, found this out for its digital aftermarket parts. These parts, which become obsolete quickly and are very expensive, included circuit boards, print head controllers, CPUs, optical drives, and monitors. Kodak faced a typical conflict: the product group managers wanted low inventories, and the field engineers, who did the repair in the field and had to face the customer, wanted high inventories. Facing a need to reduce the cost of inventories while maintaining or improving service, Kodak needed to redesign its supply chain and integrate the entities for smooth operations.

Rather than allowing the expensive parts to reside with the field engineers, Kodak managers realized that centralizing expensive parts at strategic field

Kodak makes a diverse range of digital products, from user-friendly Picture Maker photo kiosks found in retail stores to sophisticated computer radiology equipment for trauma centres and hospitals. Here Tina Burke, author of children's books, uses the touchpad to demonstrate the Kodak digital photo printing kiosk.

locations and delivering them on demand to field engineers was an option worth pursuing. Kodak made three major decisions to implement the new supply chain design. First, the number of forward stock locations (FSLs) to stock the expensive parts and the inventory levels at each stock location had to be determined using software from Baxter Planning Systems. Second, UPS Supply Chain Solutions was chosen as the logistics provider to operate the more than 100 FSLs and deliver the parts as needed to the field engineers. Finally, and perhaps most importantly, Kodak fully incorporated the field engineers and service parts supply chain personnel employees in the design process and executed a four-month pilot program to help employees accept the new design.

Kodak showed that fully integrating the key elements of the new supply chain, including the software provider, logistics provider, and internal employees, can lead to significant results. During the first year of operation, the new program reduced FSL inventory items by 66 percent, central inventory by 32 percent, and priority shipments by 22 percent, and has had no negative impact on call duration.[1]

supply chain management
The synchronization of a firm's processes with those of its suppliers and customers to match the flow of materials, services, and information with customer demand.

Supply chain management seeks to synchronize a firm's processes and those of its suppliers and customers to match the flow of materials, services, and information with customer demand. Supply chain management has strategic implications, because the supply system can be used to achieve important competitive priorities, as with Eastman Kodak. It also involves the coordination of key processes in the firm, such as order placement, order fulfillment, and purchasing, which are supported by marketing, finance, engineering, information systems, operations, and logistics. To achieve competitive advantage, the firm's operations strategy and competitive priorities must guide management decisions for its supply chain.

To get a better understanding of the importance of supply chain management, consider Figure 2.1, which conceptually shows the challenges facing operations managers. The blue line is the performance curve (sometimes called the efficiency frontier) that shows the trade-off between costs and supply chain responsiveness, such as delivery speed, for the current supply chain design if the supply chain is operated as efficiently as possible. This curve illustrates the best possible performance when we consider all of the leading firms in the same industry. (Of course, other competitive priorities, such as quality or flexibility, could be substituted for the horizontal axis.)

Now, suppose that your firm plots its actual costs and responsiveness, as indicated by the red dot. It is far off of the performance frontier, which is not an uncommon occurrence. The challenge is to move operations into the tinted area, as close to the frontier as possible. This change in position can be accomplished using a better supply chain design, superior quality processes, more accurate planning, and leaner operations systems. We discuss these topics in the chapters that follow. In addition, if new competitive innovations are developed, the firm might be able to push the entire performance frontier outward, as shown by the dashed red line. Dell is such an example: using innovative supply chain processes, it created an extremely responsive supply chain, which in turn pushed the rest of the industry to perform better. In essence, the goal is to reduce costs as well as increase other dimensions of customer value.

We begin by taking a bird's-eye view of supply chain management, focusing on its implications for service providers and manufacturers. We then describe how companies manage their customer and supplier interfaces. Next, we discuss the important operating and financial measures of supply chain performance, followed by a discussion of the dynamics of supply chains. We conclude with a comparison of basic supply chain designs, their competitive implications, and options for structuring supply chains.

FIGURE 2.1 *Supply Chain Efficiency Curve*

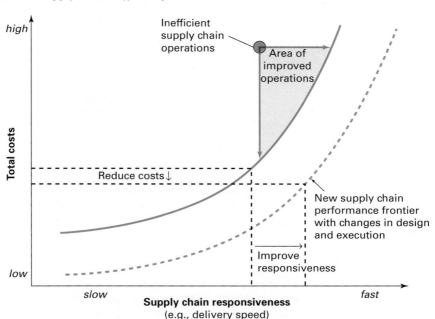

OVERVIEW OF SUPPLY CHAIN MANAGEMENT

LINKING FIRMS TO DELIVER VALUE

Supply chain design for a service provider is driven by the need to provide support for the essential elements of the various service packages it delivers. Recall that a customer benefit bundle consists of a core service along with a set of peripheral products and services. Management must design and leverage the firm's supply chain both to acquire supporting goods and services and to reach the customer.

To see the connection between supply chains and customer benefit bundle, consider the example of atWork Office Furniture (www.atwork.ca), a service provider that offers customized office design and a wide variety of business furnishings, from a single workstation to an entire office. Customers can view new and used furniture online, consult with staff using a 1-800 number, or visit one of six retail locations across Ontario. The new furnishings are sourced globally, and used products are acquired from many local businesses (essentially suppliers, who, in turn, are likely to be customers).

A simplified supply chain for this firm is illustrated in Figure 2.2, which shows how the suppliers support various elements of the service. Each of the suppliers, of course, has its own supply chain (not shown). For example, the supplier of desks may get steel tubes from one supplier and wood panels from another. All of the suppliers in this firm's supply chain play an integral role in its ability to meet its competitive priorities for the customer benefit bundle, such as top quality, delivery speed, and customization.

FIGURE 2.2 *Supply Chain for an Office Furniture Retailer*

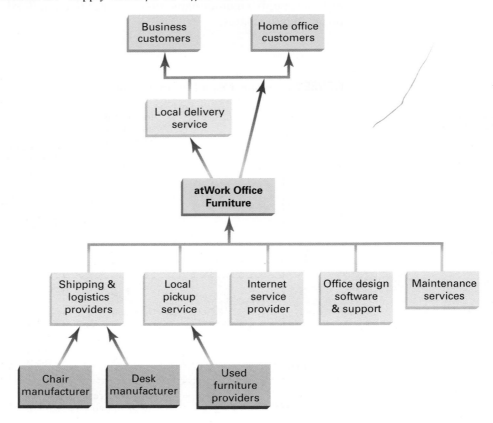

As the degree of customer interaction increases in the service process, the complexity and challenges also tend to increase. For example, an airline's supply chain provides soft drinks, peanuts, in-flight meals, and airsickness bags, as well as maintenance and repair items such as engine parts and motor lubricants. Timing and coordination in this supply chain are often very visible to customers, and any miscues are immediately evident and often interpreted as poor service.

The supply chain for manufacturing firms, such as the chair manufacturer shown at the bottom of Figure 2.2, can also be very complicated because many companies have hundreds, if not thousands, of suppliers (Figure 2.3 is a generalization). Suppliers are often identified by their position in the supply chain. Here, tier 1 suppliers provide materials or services that are used directly by the firm, tier 2 suppliers supply tier 1 suppliers, and so on. In this diagram, the firm owns its own distribution and transportation services. However, companies that engineer products to customer specifications normally do not have distribution centres as part of their supply chains. Such companies often ship products directly to their customers.

The value of careful design and consistent execution for supply chain management becomes apparent when the complexity of the supply chain is recognized. However, the challenges don't stop here. As we later show in Chapter 4, "Capacity," inventory levels combine with variability and capacity utilization to affect the flow of materials.

FIGURE 2.3 *Illustrative Supply Chain for a Chair Manufacturer*

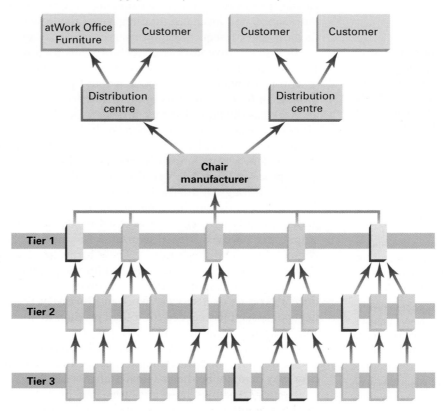

FIGURE 2.4 *Inventory at Successive Stocking Points*

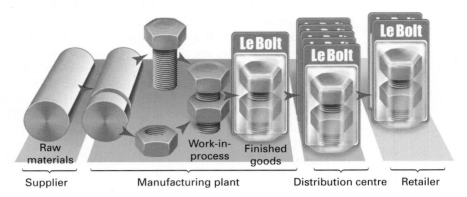

Raw materials | Work-in-process | Finished goods

Supplier | Manufacturing plant | Distribution centre | Retailer

FORMS OF INVENTORY

The value of supply chain management becomes apparent when the complexity of the supply chain is recognized. The performance of numerous suppliers upstream determines the flow of materials and services to a firm. The performance of the firm determines the flow of services or products downstream to the next stage of the supply chain. Moreover, the flow of materials determines inventory levels. Too much inventory can happen to the best of companies. For example, one year Amazon.com overestimated the amount of demand for Kermit the Frog telephones and ended up with a 50-week supply, which contributed to a strain on warehouse operations and service to customers. Improved forecasting processes, selective outsourcing of warehouse operations, and state-of-the-art automation and mechanization improved the flow of materials through Amazon.com's facilities and consequently improved the efficiency and performance of the supply chain.[2]

> **inventory** A stock of items, including materials, orders, information, and people, that flow through or are used in a process to satisfy customer demand.

In essence, **inventory** is a stock of items used to satisfy customer demand or support the production of goods or services. A traditional accounting definition limits inventory to materials, components, and products. The typical manufacturer spends more than 60 percent of its total income from sales on purchased services and materials, whereas the typical service provider spends only 30 to 40 percent. Because materials comprise such a large component of the sales dollar, manufacturers can reap large profits with a small reduction in the cost of materials, which makes supply chain management a key competitive weapon. However, a more general definition for managing processes must be expanded to include materials, orders, information, and people that flow through or are used in a process.

Inventory exists in three aggregate forms: raw materials, work-in-process, or finished goods. Identifying each form is based partly on the process (Where does it start and stop?) and partly on the organization (Where do hand-offs occur and what is the degree of vertical integration?). These forms are also useful for accounting purposes.

> **raw materials** Materials and items used as inputs for the production of goods and services.

> **work-in-process (WIP)** Items partway through a process that are needed for a final product or service.

> **finished goods** Items that have completed the manufacturing or service process.

Raw materials are inventories needed for the production of goods or services. They are considered to be inputs to the transformation processes of the firm, whether they produce a product or a service. **Work-in-process (WIP)** consists of items such as components or assemblies needed for a final product in manufacturing. WIP is also present in some service operations, such as repair shops, restaurants, cheque-processing centres, and package delivery services. **Finished goods** in manufacturing plants, warehouses, and retail outlets are the items sold to the firm's customers. The finished goods of one firm may actually be the raw materials for another.

Figure 2.4 shows how inventory can be held in different forms and at various stocking points for a typical manufacturing firm. In this example, raw materials—the finished goods of the supplier—are held by both the supplier and the manufacturer.

Raw materials at the plant pass through one or more processes, which transform them into various levels of WIP inventory. Final processing of this inventory yields finished goods inventory. Finished goods inventory can be held at the plant, the distribution centre (which may be a warehouse owned by the manufacturer or the retailer), and retail locations.

Imagine the chaos if a firm's suppliers and customers all acted independently and never communicated changes in demand or adjusted to changes in others' schedules. Reducing inventory and speeding the flow of goods and services in the supply chain is covered in greater detail in Chapter 10, "Lean Systems."

INVENTORY PLACEMENT

inventory pooling A reduction in inventory and safety stock because of the merging of variable demands from customers.

A fundamental supply chain decision is where to locate inventories of raw materials, work-in-process, or finished goods. At one extreme, the firm could keep the entire finished goods inventory at the manufacturing plant and ship directly to each of its customers. The advantage would come from what is referred to as **inventory pooling**, which is a reduction in inventory and safety stock because of the merging of variable demands from many customers. A higher-than-expected demand from one customer can be offset by a lower-than-expected demand from another. However, a disadvantage of placing the entire inventory in one location is the added cost of shipping smaller, uneconomical quantities directly to the customers, typically over long distances.

forward placement Locating stock closer to customers at a warehouse, distribution centre (DC), wholesaler, or retailer.

Another approach is to use **forward placement**, which means locating stock closer to customers at a warehouse, distribution centre (DC), wholesaler, or retailer. Forward placement can have two advantages for the order-fulfillment process—faster delivery times and reduced transportation costs—that can stimulate sales. As inventory is placed closer to the customer, such as at a DC, the pooling effect of the inventories is reduced because safety stocks for the item must increase to take care of uncertain demands at each DC, rather than just a single location. However, the time to get the product to the customer is reduced. Consequently, service to the customer is quicker, and the firm can take advantage of larger, less costly shipments to the DCs from the manufacturing plant, at the expense of larger overall inventories.

MEASURES OF SUPPLY CHAIN PERFORMANCE

As we have shown, supply chain management involves managing the flow of materials that create inventories in the supply chain. For this reason, managers closely monitor inventories to keep them at acceptable levels. Inventory levels also have implications for the responsiveness of the supply chain and, ultimately, the level of customer service. In this section, we first define the typical inventory measures used to monitor supply chain performance and then discuss some process measures. Finally, we relate some commonly used supply chain performance measures to several important financial measures.

INVENTORY MEASURES

All methods of measuring inventory begin with a physical count of units, volume, or weight. However, measures of inventories are reported in three basic ways: average aggregate inventory value, weeks of supply, and inventory turnover.

average aggregate inventory value The total value of all items held in inventory by a firm.

First, the **average aggregate inventory value** is the total value of all items held in inventory for a firm. Consistent with accounting conventions, valuation is at cost, summing the value of individual items in raw materials, work-in-process, and finished goods. Because this measure is taken at a particular point in time, it is usually more meaningful to estimate the average inventory investment over some period of time.

The raw materials typically cost much less than a finished product, which includes the costs of labour, technology, and other value-added operations performed in manufacturing the product. For example, the value of raw materials, such as iron ore, must be added to that of finished products, such as steel coils, for a steel manufacturer. To estimate the approximate average aggregate inventory value, sum the values of individual inventory items:

$$\text{Average aggregate inventory value} = (N_a c_a) + (N_b c_b) + \ldots + (N_n c_n)$$

where:

N_a = Average quantity of materials, part, component, or product a

c_a = Average cost per unit of materials, part, component, or product a

n = Total number of materials, parts, components, and products

Summed over all items in an inventory, this total value tells managers how much of a firm's assets are tied up in inventory. Manufacturing firms typically have about 25 percent of their total assets in inventory, whereas wholesalers and retailers average about 75 percent.

weeks of supply An inventory measure obtained by dividing the average aggregate inventory value by sales per week at cost.

Second, to some extent, managers can decide whether the aggregate inventory value is too low or too high by historical or industry comparison or by managerial judgment. However, a better performance measure would take demand into account. **Weeks of supply** is an inventory measure obtained by dividing the average aggregate inventory value by sales per week, again at cost. (In some low-inventory operations, days or even hours of supply are a better unit of time for measuring inventory.) The formula expressed using weeks is:

$$\text{Weeks of supply} = \frac{\text{Average aggregate inventory value}}{\text{Weekly sales (at cost)}}$$

Although the numerator includes the value of all items (raw materials, WIP, and finished goods), the denominator represents only the finished goods sold—at cost rather than the sale price after markups or discounts. This cost is referred to as the *cost of goods sold*. (Within the supply chain, the weeks of supply can be calculated for specific items in a similar way, using the average inventory value for that item and the demand for that item.)

inventory turnover A measure of the rate at which inventory is consumed, obtained by dividing annual sales at cost by the average aggregate inventory value maintained during the year.

Third, **inventory turnover** (or *turns*) is an inventory measure obtained by dividing annual sales at cost by the average aggregate inventory value maintained during the year, or:

$$\text{Inventory turnover} = \frac{\text{Annual sales (at cost)}}{\text{Average aggregate inventory value}}$$

The "best" inventory level, even when expressed as turnover, cannot be determined easily. Although six or seven turns per year is typical, the average high-tech firm settles for only about three turns. At the other extreme, some automobile firms report 40 turns per year for selected products. See the Solved Problem at the end of this chapter for a detailed example of the three inventory measures.

PROCESS MEASURES

We have discussed four core processes in Chapter 1, "Creating Customer Value Through Operations," namely, supplier relationship, order fulfillment, customer relationship, and new product design. These processes must be translated by supply chain managers into specific operating measures, as illustrated in Table 2.1. Collecting data on these measures allows managers to track changes in level or direction. In addition, statistical process control charts can be used to determine whether the changes are statistically significant, thereby prompting management's attention (see Chapter 6, "Quality and Process Improvement").

TABLE 2.1	*Supply Chain Process Measures*		
Supplier Relationship	**Order Fulfillment**	**Customer Relationship**	**New Service/ Product Development**
● Percentage of suppliers' deliveries on time ● Suppliers' lead times ● Percentage of defects in purchased materials and services ● Cost of purchased materials and services	● Percentage of incomplete orders shipped ● Percentage of orders shipped on time ● Time to fulfill the orders ● Percentage of returned items or botched services ● Cost to produce the item or service ● Customer satisfaction with the order-fulfillment process	● Percentage of orders taken accurately ● Time to complete the order-placement process ● Customer satisfaction with the order-placement process ● Availability of services ● Customer's evaluation of firm's sustainability	● Time to develop a new service or product ● Cost to develop, including supplier-led efforts ● Time to launch and ramp up, including new process implementation, employee training, and process debugging

LINKS TO FINANCIAL MEASURES

The design and management of the supply chain has a huge financial impact on the firm. Inventory should be considered an investment, because it is created for future use. However, inventory is also a liability, in that it ties up funds that might be used more profitably elsewhere or can hide operational problems. Figure 2.5 shows how supply chain decisions can affect financial measures.

TOTAL REVENUE. Supply chain performance measures related to time, which is a critical dimension of supply chain operations, have financial implications. As noted earlier in Table 2.1, timely availability of services and speedy delivery of goods to customers, for example, will increase total revenue because satisfied customers will buy more services and products from the firm.

COST OF GOODS SOLD. Being able to buy materials or services at a better price and transform them more efficiently into services or products improve a firm's cost of goods sold, and ultimately, its net income. These improvements also have an effect on contribution margin, which is the difference between price and the variable costs to produce a service or good. Reducing the cost of order fulfillment, including purchased materials, production, logistics, and poor-quality costs, increases the contribution margin. Managers often use contribution margin as one factor to decide which services or products to offer in the firm's portfolio.

OPERATING EXPENSES. Changes to the supply chain infrastructure can have an effect on overhead, which is considered a fixed expense. Also, designing a supply chain with minimal capital investment can reduce depreciation charges.

cash flow The difference between the flows of funds into and out of an organization over a period of time, including revenues, costs, and changes in assets and liabilities.

CASH FLOW. The supply chain design can improve positive net cash flows by focusing on reducing lead times and backlogs of orders. **Cash flow** is the difference between the flows of funds into and out of an organization over a period of time, including revenues, costs, and changes in assets and liabilities. The Internet brings another financial measure related to cash flows to the forefront: cash-to-cash is the time lag between paying for the services and materials needed to produce a service or product and receiving payment for it. The shorter the time lag, the better the cash flow

FIGURE 2.5 *How Supply Chain Decisions Can Affect Financial Performance*

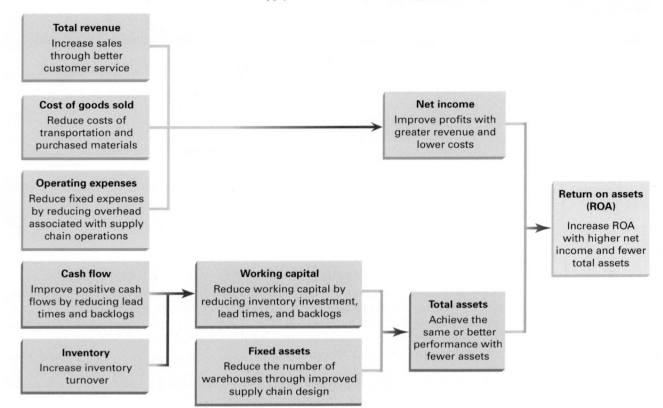

position of the firm, because it needs less working capital. Ideally, a firm can build a *negative* cash-to-cash situation, which is possible when the customer pays the firm before it pays for the resources and materials needed to produce a service or product. Redesigning the customer relationship process can allow for payment by customers immediately when their orders are placed. The firm also must have supplier inventories on consignment, which allows it to pay for materials as it uses them.

WORKING CAPITAL. Inventory turns are reflected in another financial measure, working capital, which is money used to finance ongoing operations. Increasing inventory turns reduces the working capital needed to finance inventories. Reductions in working capital can be accomplished by improving the customer relationship, order fulfillment, or supplier relationship processes. For example, reducing supplier lead times has the effect of reducing weeks of supply and increasing inventory turns. Matching the input and output flows of materials is easier because shorter-range, more reliable forecasts of demand can be used.

RETURN ON ASSETS. The design and management of the supply chain affects fixed investments, such as warehouses, and aggregate inventory investment, both of which are listed as assets on a firm's balance sheet. A related, important financial measure is return on assets (ROA), defined as net income divided by total assets. Consequently, reducing these investments or increasing net income through better cost management increases ROA. Techniques for reducing inventory, transportation, and operating costs related to resource usage and scheduling are discussed in the chapters to follow.

We now turn to a brief discussion of how four core processes are critically linked to supply chain decisions.

SUPPLIER RELATIONSHIP PROCESS

The supplier relationship process focuses on the interaction of the firm and upstream suppliers. In this section we focus on several important decision areas that affect the design of the supplier relationship process. We focus our discussion on five nested processes: sourcing, design collaboration, negotiation, buying, and information exchange.

SOURCING

The purchasing function is the eyes and ears of the organization in the supplier marketplace, continuously seeking better value from suppliers. Consequently, purchasing is in a good position to select suppliers for the supply chain and to conduct certification programs.

SELECTION. Three criteria most often considered by firms selecting new suppliers are price, quality, and time. (The other three dimensions of customer value often have lower priority.) Because firms spend a large percentage of their total income on purchased items, finding suppliers that charge *low prices* is a key objective. However, as noted by Deming (see Chapter 6, "Quality"), lowest price should not be the only purchasing criterion. The *quality* of a supplier's materials can dramatically affect the *total* cost of using that supplier. The hidden costs of poor quality can be high, particularly if defects are not detected until after considerable value has been added by subsequent operations. For a retailer, poor merchandise quality can mean loss of customer goodwill and future sales. Finally, shorter lead times and on-time *delivery* help the buying firm maintain acceptable customer service with less inventory.

Another criterion is becoming increasingly important in the selection of suppliers—environmental performance. Many firms are engaging in **green purchasing**, which involves buying from firms with strong environmental management systems. This typically includes identifying, assessing, and managing the flow of environmental waste and finding ways to reduce it and minimize its impact on the environment. Suppliers are being asked to be environmentally conscious when designing and manufacturing their products, and claims such as *green*, *biodegradable*, *natural*, and *recycled* must be substantiated when bidding on a contract. This criterion has become increasingly important in the selection of suppliers over the past few years, particularly for consumer-oriented markets.

green purchasing Using environmental criteria in purchasing decisions to favour suppliers (and inputs) with strong environmental management systems, performance, or certification.

SUPPLIER CERTIFICATION. Supplier certification programs verify that potential suppliers have the capability to provide the materials or services the buying firm requires. Certification typically involves site visits by a cross-functional team from the buying firm who do an in-depth evaluation of the supplier's capability to meet cost, quality, delivery, and flexibility targets from process and information system perspectives. Every aspect of producing the materials or services is explored through observation of the processes in action and review of documentation for completeness and accuracy. Once certified, the supplier can be used by purchasing without having to make background checks. Performance is regularly monitored, and the supplier may need recertification if performance declines.

An alternative approach is supplier certification audited by a third party, which is somewhat similar to a financial audit. Certifications such as ISO 14001 assess the environmental management systems of suppliers, and others such as SA8000 or Fair Trade evaluate working conditions or wages paid by suppliers, for example with coffee plantations. These certifications are increasingly being used in such industries as electronics, food, and clothing to assure retail buyers about the nature of supplier processes and practices.

DESIGN COLLABORATION

This process focuses on jointly designing new services or products with key suppliers; it facilitates concurrent engineering, discussed later in this chapter, by drawing key suppliers into the new service or product development process. This process seeks to eliminate costly delays and mistakes incurred when many suppliers design service packages or manufactured components in parallel.

An approach that many firms are using is called **early supplier involvement,** which leverages the expertise of suppliers during the design phase of a new service or product. Suppliers provide suggestions for design changes and materials choices that will result in more efficient operations and higher quality. Taken one step further, **presourcing** involves suppliers during a product's concept development stage, and they are given significant, if not total, responsibility for the design of certain components or systems of the product. This approach is described in the Managerial Practice about Boeing.

Firms can also improve performance by engaging in **value analysis,** which is a systematic effort to reduce the cost or improve the performance of services or products, either purchased or produced. It is an intensive examination of the services, materials, processes, information systems, and flows of material involved in the production of a service or an item. Benefits include reduced production, materials, and distribution costs; improved profit margins; and increased customer satisfaction. Because teams involving purchasing, production, and engineering personnel from both the firm and its major suppliers play a key role in value analysis, another potential benefit is increased employee morale. Value analysis should be part of continual efforts to improve the performance of the supply chain.

NEGOTIATION

The negotiation process focuses on obtaining an effective contract that meets the price, quality, and other requirements from suppliers. The orientation of a firm toward its suppliers will affect the negotiation and design collaboration processes.

COMPETITIVE ORIENTATION. The **competitive orientation** toward suppliers views negotiations between buyer and seller as a zero-sum game: whatever one side loses, the other side gains. Short-term advantages are prized over long-term commitments. The buyer may try to beat the supplier's price down to the lowest survival level or to push demand to high levels during boom times and order almost nothing during recessions. In contrast, the supplier presses for higher prices for specific levels of quality, customer service, and volume flexibility. Which party wins depends largely on who has the most clout.

Purchasing power determines the clout that a firm has. A firm has purchasing power when its purchasing volume represents a significant share of the supplier's sales or the purchased item or service is standardized and many substitutes are available. For example, Staples is the world's largest office products firm, with outlets in 27 countries and more than 300 stores in Canada. The buying power of this growing company has become enormous. Home Hardware, a lumber and home improvement cooperative with almost 1000 stores across Canada, aggregates the purchases of independent dealers to reduce the costs for materials and services for its members. Suppliers are willing to give Home Hardware lower prices because of the large-scale purchasing power.

early supplier involvement A program that includes suppliers in the design phase of a service or product.

presourcing A level of supplier involvement in which suppliers are selected early in a product's concept development stage and are given significant, if not total, responsibility for the design of certain components or systems of the product.

value analysis A systematic effort to reduce the cost or improve the performance of services or products, either purchased or produced.

competitive orientation A supplier relation that views negotiations between buyer and seller as a zero-sum game: whatever one side loses, the other side gains; short-term advantages are prized over long-term commitments.

cooperative orientation
A supplier relation in which the buyer and seller are partners, each helping the other to achieve mutually beneficial objectives.

COOPERATIVE ORIENTATION. With the **cooperative orientation** to supplier relations, the buyer and seller are partners, each helping the other as much as possible. A cooperative orientation translates into a longer-term commitment, joint work on quality improvement, and support by the buyer of the supplier's managerial, technological, and capacity development. A cooperative orientation favours few suppliers of a particular item or service, with just one or two suppliers being the ideal number. As order volumes increase, the supplier gains repeatability, which helps movement toward high-volume operations at a low cost. When contracts are large and a long-term relationship is ensured, the supplier might even build a new facility and hire a new workforce, perhaps relocating close to the buyer's plant.

A cooperative orientation means that the buyer shares more information with the supplier on its future buying intentions. This forward visibility allows suppliers to make better, more reliable forecasts of future demand. The buyer visits suppliers' plants and cultivates cooperative attitudes. The buyer may even suggest ways to improve the suppliers' operations. Similarly, the supplier may offer suggestions to the buyer to improve quality and reliability, or reduce costs. This close cooperation with suppliers could even mean that the buyer does not need to inspect incoming materials. It also could mean giving the supplier more latitude in specifications, involving the supplier more in designing parts, implementing cost-reduction ideas, and sharing in savings.

A cooperative orientation has opened the door for innovative arrangements with suppliers. One extreme example of such an arrangement is the Sharp plant, detailed at the beginning of Chapter 7, "Lean Systems," where suppliers are located on-site. This arrangement has several advantages. First, Sharp's capital investment is lower. Second, parts will arrive just before they are needed, so everyone's inventory costs will be low. Finally, improvements by suppliers in the assembly process will benefit all parties.

One advantage of reducing the number of suppliers in the supply chain is a reduction in the complexity of the procedures needed to support and manage them. However, reducing the number of suppliers for an item or service may have the disadvantage of increased risk of an interruption in supply, and less leverage to drive a good bargain in prices. The extreme situation, **sole sourcing**, is the awarding of a contract for an item or service to only one supplier. Doing so is particularly attractive if development and market risks are shared, as with key suppliers for Boeing's new 787 Dreamliner; however, such an arrangement can amplify any supply problems that may arise over the life of the product. Managers can use a mixed strategy, such as a competitive approach for commodity-like supplies and a cooperative approach for complex, high-valued services and materials.

sole sourcing The awarding of a contract for an item or service to only one supplier.

BUYING

The buying process relates to the actual procurement of the service or material from the supplier. This process includes the creation, management, and approval of purchase orders and determines the locus of control for purchasing decisions. Although not all purchasing opportunities involve the Internet, the emergence of the virtual marketplace has provided firms with many opportunities to improve their buying and information exchange processes. Here we discuss four approaches to e-purchasing, and close with the implications of choosing centralized versus decentralized buying.

electronic data interchange (EDI) A technology that enables the transmission of routine business documents having a standard format from computer to computer over telephone or direct leased lines.

ELECTRONIC DATA INTERCHANGE. The most used form of e-purchasing is **electronic data interchange (EDI)**, a technology that enables the transmission of routine business documents having a standard format from computer to computer. Invoices, purchase orders, and payments are some of the routine documents that EDI can handle—it

MANAGERIAL PRACTICE
Building a Supply Chain for the Dreamliner

Suppose that you had the freedom to totally design the supply chain for one of the most highly anticipated airliners of modern times. The airliner, the Boeing 787 Dreamliner, is a super-efficient commercial airplane that can carry up to 290 passengers on routes as long as 15 750 kilometres, at cruising speeds of over 1000 kilometres per hour. It is to be constructed with carbon-fibre composite materials, which are lightweight and not susceptible to corrosion or fatigue like aluminum. This plane will be manufactured using 50 percent composite materials; Boeing used only 10 to 12 percent in the 777. Boeing's goal is to bring the most complex machine in mass production to market in just over four years, one-third less time than other projects. And when delivered to customers, the plane must meet demanding performance specifications, such as using 20% less fuel to reduce its carbon footprint and the environmental impact.

Boeing had two options for the design of the supply chain: (1) Produce about 50 percent of the plane in-house, including the wing and fuselage as in existing Boeing planes, and run the risk that production lead times will suffer because of capacity constraints; or (2) outsource about 85 percent of the plane, essentially only constructing the vertical fin in-house, and manage the global suppliers responsible for design as well as production of major components. Boeing's senior managers chose the second option.

There are some good reasons for this choice. First, a number of big customers for the 787, such as India and Japan, require that significant portions of the aircraft must be manufactured in their countries. Using major contractors within those countries satisfies the requirement. Second, a shortage of high-quality engineering talent encourages further outsourcing. Third, the sheer complexity of the airplane makes it necessary to share the load. Boeing, even with all of its resources, could not build all of the components and pieces in one facility or region. Finally, work on the plane can proceed concurrently, rather than sequentially, thereby saving time and money. For example, the modular design of the plane allows Boeing to utilize flexible tooling to move planes through the factory much more quickly. Also, suppliers design and deliver the subsystems on a just-in-time basis where they are "snapped" together by a smaller number of factory workers in a matter of days rather than a month, the typical time for a plane of that complexity.

The first Boeing 787 Dreamliner takes shape in the final assembly plant in Everett, Washington. The new commercial airplane is assembled with major components produced worldwide.

Boeing chose to design its supply chain with 43 top-tier suppliers on three continents. Outsourcing so much responsibility requires a lot of managerial attention; you have to know what is going on in each factory at all times. As expected with something so complex, major glitches developed unexpectedly. The first Dreamliner to show up at Boeing's factory was missing tens of thousands of parts. Supplier problems ranged from language barriers to problems caused by some contractors who outsourced major portions of their assigned work and then experienced problems with their suppliers.

Cutting edge design choices that simplify the supply chain and final assembly also presented difficult challenges. For example, the fuselage section—the big multi-part cylindrical barrel that encompasses the passenger seating area—was constructed as a single piece to eliminate 1,500 aluminum sheets and over 40 000 fasteners. However, the first fuselage failed in company testing, causing Boeing to make more sections than planned and to reexamine quality and safety concerns. Software programs designed by a variety of manufacturers had trouble talking to one another and the overall weight of the airplane was too high, especially the carbon-fiber wing. These and many other glitches caused a three-year delay in the deliveries of the first 787s. Finally, in September 2011, the first plane was delivered to a customer with great fanfare, and production capacity is being ramped up to 2.5 planes per month.

Will the advantages of collaboration on such a large scale outweigh the loss of logistical and design control? Moreover, will the $32 billion spent on developing the 787 provide Boeing a competitive advantage? Managers bet that these actions will payoff; by 2011, the firm had received more than 820 orders for the Dreamliner from 56 customers.[3]

replaces the phone call or mailed document. An electronic purchasing system with EDI might work as follows. Buyers browse an electronic catalogue and click on items to purchase from a supplier. A computer sends the order directly to the supplier. The supplier's computer checks the buyer's credit and determines whether the items are available. The supplier's warehouse and shipping departments are notified electronically, and the items are readied for shipment. Finally, the supplier's accounting department bills the buyer electronically. EDI saves the cost of opening mail, directing it to the right department, checking the document for accuracy, and re-entering the information in a computer system. It also improves accuracy, shortens response times, and can even reduce inventory. Savings (ranging from $5 to $125 per document) are considerable in the light of the hundreds to thousands of documents many firms typically handle daily.

catalogue hubs
Centralized electronic online catalogues that enable employees to place orders for preapproved items.

CATALOGUE HUBS. The costs of placing orders to suppliers, as well as the goods and services themselves, can be reduced through the use of **catalogue hubs**. Suppliers post their catalogue of items on the hub, and buyers select what they need and purchase them electronically. Moreover, a buying firm can negotiate prices with specific suppliers for items such as office supplies, technical equipment, specialized items, services, or furniture. The catalogue that the buying firm's employees see consists only of the approved items and their negotiated prices. The hub connects the firm to potentially hundreds of suppliers through the Internet, saving the costs of EDI, which requires one-to-one connections to individual suppliers.

exchange An electronic marketplace where buying firms and selling firms come together to do business.

EXCHANGES. An **exchange** is an electronic marketplace where buying and selling firms come together to do business. The exchange maintains relationships with buyers and sellers, making it easy to do business without the aspect of contract negotiations or other sorts of long-term conditions. Exchanges are often used for "spot" purchases, which are needed to satisfy an immediate need at the lowest possible cost. Commodity items such as oil, steel, or energy fit this category. However, exchanges can also be used for almost any item. For example, Marriott International, Hyatt Hotels, Fairmont

Hotels, and others formed an exchange for hotels (www.avendra.com). This exchange allowed hotels to do one-stop shopping for such items as soap, food, and equipment, rather than having to individually approach thousands of suppliers using faxes, telephones, and forms.

auction An extension of the exchange in which firms place competitive bids to buy something.

AUCTIONS. An extension of the exchange is the **auction**, where firms place competitive bids to buy something. For example, a site may be formed for a particular industry at which firms with excess capacity or materials can offer them for sale to the highest bidder. Bids can be either closed or open to the competition. Industries where auctions have value include steel, chemicals, and the home mortgage industry, where financial institutions can bid for mortgages.

An approach that has received considerable attention is the so-called *reverse auction*, in which suppliers bid for contracts with buyers. Each bid is posted, so suppliers can see how much lower their next bid must be to remain in the running for the contract. Each contract has an electronic prospectus that provides all the specifications, conditions, and other requirements that are non-negotiable. The only thing left to determine is the cost to the buyer, and savings can be dramatic.

Our discussion of these electronic approaches in purchasing should not leave the impression that cost is the only consideration in selecting a supplier. Exchanges and auctions are more useful for commodities, near-commodities, or infrequently needed items that require only short-term relationships with suppliers. The past two decades have taught us the lesson that suppliers should be thought of as partners when the needed supply is significant and steady over extended periods of time.

CENTRALIZED VERSUS LOCALIZED BUYING. When an organization has several facilities (e.g., stores, hospitals, or plants), management must decide whether to buy locally or centrally. This decision has implications for the control of supply chain flows.

Centralized buying has the advantage of increasing purchasing clout. Savings can be significant, often on the order of 10 percent or more. Increased buying power can mean getting better service, ensuring long-term supply availability, or developing new supplier capability. Companies with overseas suppliers favour centralization because of the specialized skills (e.g., understanding of foreign languages and cultures) needed to buy from foreign sources. Buyers also need to understand international commercial and contract law regarding the transfer of goods and services. Another trend that favours centralization is the growth of computer-based information systems and the Internet, which give specialists at headquarters access to data previously available only at the local level.

Probably the biggest disadvantage of centralized buying is loss of control at the local level. When facilities or divisions are evaluated as profit or cost centres, centralized buying is undesirable for items unique to a particular facility. These items should be purchased locally whenever possible. The same holds for purchases that must be closely meshed with process schedules. Further, localized buying is an advantage when the firm has major facilities in foreign countries, because the managers there, often foreign nationals, have a much better understanding of the culture than staff would at the home office. Also, centralized purchasing often contributes to longer lead times and another hierarchical level in the organization, which can slow decision making and hurt responsiveness.

Often, management must develop a mixed approach and leverage both centralized buying and local autonomy. For example, the corporate purchasing group at IBM negotiates contracts on a centralized basis only at the request of local plants. Then management at one of the facilities monitors the contract for all the participating plants. Alternatively, commodity-based purchases might be made by a centralized group, while specialized parts and services are bought at the local level in a decentralized fashion.

INFORMATION EXCHANGE

The information exchange process facilitates the exchange of pertinent operating information, such as forecasts, schedules, and inventory levels, between the firm and its suppliers. New technology in the form of radio frequency identification facilitates the flow of inventory information. Beyond inventory information, the exchange of forecasts and other demand-related data facilitates integrating activities such as vendor-managed inventories.

radio frequency identification (RFID)
A method for identifying items through the use of radio signals from a tag attached to an item.

vendor-managed inventories (VMI) An extreme application of the forward placement tactic that involves locating the inventories at the customer.

RFID tags can be attached to containers or pallets of product to aid in managing the flow of inventories in a supply chain. This RFID tag card has a transponder with antenna and embedded integrated electronic circuit on a chip for receiving and transmitting Electronic Product Code signals.

RADIO FREQUENCY IDENTIFICATION. An important requirement for the execution of order-fulfillment processes is accurate information regarding the quantity and location of inventories. A new application of an old technology presents some tantalizing benefits. **Radio frequency identification (RFID)** is a method for identifying items through the use of radio signals from a tag attached to an item. The tag has information about the item and sends signals to a device that can read the information and even write new information on the tag. Data from the tags can be transmitted wirelessly from one place to another through electronic product code (EPC) networks and the Internet, making it theoretically possible to uniquely identify every item a company produces and track it until the tag is destroyed.

Walmart and Gillette, among a number of large retailers, manufacturers, government agencies, and suppliers, are in the process of implementing RFID in their supply chains. In Walmart's case, RFID tags on cases and pallets will be read when inventory enters a stockroom and when those cases and pallets go to the retail floor. Walmart will use the data to draw conclusions about when to bring additional stock to the floor and to figure out if too much of a product has been ordered by a store and is sitting in the stockroom or in the distribution centre. The data could also help some 30 000 suppliers check inventory levels and sales. The use of RFID data can increase a supplier's service level to Walmart. Pilferage reduction is another major advantage of the RFID technology. Gillette hopes to use RFID to reduce the amount of razor-blade theft, which amounts to as much as 30 percent.

Whether RFID will be universally accepted is still unknown. Global data synchronization using industry standards is critical to ensure that accurate and consistent product information is exchanged between trading partners. Much work is still to be done. According to Walmart managers, the best way to make RFID happen is if retail stores work collaboratively on the project.

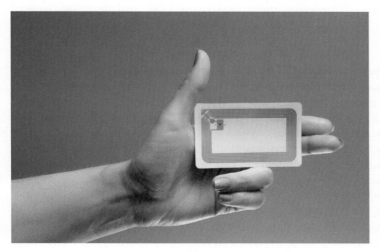

VENDOR-MANAGED INVENTORIES. A tactic that employs an extreme case of forward placement is **vendor-managed inventories (VMI)**, a system in which the supplier has access to the customer's inventory data and is responsible for maintaining the inventory level required by the customer. Service providers and manufacturers use VMI, including such firms as AT&T, Roadway Express, Walmart, Dell, Westinghouse, and Bose. In some cases, although the inventory is on the customer's site, the supplier retains possession of the inventory until it is used.

Vendor-managed inventories have several key elements.

- *Collaborative effort.* For VMI to succeed, the customers must be willing to allow the supplier access to their inventory. The implication is that the supplier assumes an important administrative role in the management of the inventory. Thus, an atmosphere of trust and accountability is required.
- *Cost savings.* Suppliers and customers eliminate the need for excess inventory through better operational planning. VMI reduces costs by removing administrative and inventory costs. Order placement costs are also reduced.
- *Customer service.* The supplier is frequently on site and better understands the operations of the customer, improving response times and reducing stockouts.
- *Written agreement.* It is important that both parties fully understand the responsibilities of each partner. Areas such as billing procedures, forecast methods, and replenishment schedules should be clearly specified. Further, the responsibility for obsolete inventory resulting from forecast revisions and changes in contract lengths should be included.

continuous replenishment
A VMI method in which the supplier monitors inventory levels at the customer and replenishes the stock as needed to avoid shortages.

If stock is replenished only as needed to avoid shortages, called **continuous replenishment**, inventories can be reduced while achieving greater efficiencies in warehousing and transportation.

ORDER FULFILLMENT PROCESS

The order fulfillment process produces and delivers the service or product to the firm's customers. There are four key nested processes: customer demand planning, supply planning, internal service/production activities, and logistics.

CUSTOMER DEMAND PLANNING

Customer demand planning (CDP) facilitates the collaboration of a supplier and its customers to more accurately forecast customer requirements for a service or product. CDP is a business-planning process that enables sales teams (and customers) to develop demand forecasts as input to service-planning processes, production and inventory planning, and revenue planning. Forecasts must generally precede plans: it is not possible to make decisions on staffing levels, purchasing commitments, and inventory levels until forecasts are developed that give reasonably accurate views of demand over the forecasting time horizon. Chapter 10, "Managing Demand and Forecasting," provides more details on CDP and describes several practical tools.

SUPPLY PLANNING

The supply planning process takes the demand forecasts produced by CDP and the capacity available to generate a plan to meet the demand. This process is both critical for effective execution in the supply chain and very complex. For this reason we devote four later chapters to its important elements: capacity, inventory management, operations planning, and resource scheduling.

In a nutshell, the capacity of individual operations, facilities, and the broader supply chain must be assessed to determine if demand can be filled, as discussed in Chapter 4, "Capacity." For retailers or manufacturers, inventory offers one option to have the product available ahead of a new product launch or in anticipation of future customer demand (see Chapter 5, "Inventory Management"). For example, a Nokia repair service facility must have enough components and materials on hand to fulfill its requirements for the repair of the various Nokia products under warranty. Alternatively, other services might use reservation systems, such as dental offices, or call in additional staff on overtime, such as UPS before the Christmas delivery rush. In Chapters 11 and 12, we show how firms plan, and then schedule productive resources to provide an appropriate level of supply for services or products.

INTERNAL SERVICE/PRODUCTION ACTIVITIES

The internal service or production activities encompass all of the tasks required to deliver a product or service to a customer. These activities might be focused on addressing any of the competitive priorities, and might be done by either employees or customers. For example, a customer at a Loblaw grocery store in Canada has in effect ordered groceries, performed the work to actually find it in the inventory, and taken delivery when the groceries were paid for at the checkout cashier. However, Grocery Gateway in Toronto (www.grocerygateway.com) uses a Web page, which separates order placement (discussed in the next section under "Customer Relationship Process") from order fulfillment. Customers doing business on its Web page must accept a delay in receiving their groceries, a delay that Grocery Gateway seeks to minimize through effective management of its supply chain. Offering a new order-fulfillment process can have significant competitive implications, particularly in terms of changing the value offered to customers.

LOGISTICS

A key aspect of order fulfillment is the logistics process, which delivers the product or service to the customer. Five important decisions determine the design and implementation of logistics processes: degree of ownership, facility location, shipment mode, level of capacity, and amount of cross docking.

OWNERSHIP. The firm has the most control over the logistics process if it operates as a private carrier. Although this approach may help to better achieve some competitive priorities, the cost of equipment, labour, facilities, and maintenance could be high. The firm could instead leave the distribution to a contract carrier, negotiating with the carrier for specific services. Those services could involve taking over a major portion of the order fulfillment process. For example, UPS's Supply Chain Solutions unit controls more than 92 900 square metres of warehouse space to help manage inventories for clients near Shanghai and Guangzhou in China. The clients use UPS to ship items to the warehouse, and then UPS manages the deliveries to the specific sites in China.

FACILITY LOCATION. A critical decision affecting the effectiveness of supply chains is the location of facilities that serve as points of service, storage, or manufacture. Key decisions focus on whether facilities might be located in close proximity to suppliers or customers. Because of the importance of this decision, we have devoted a major portion of Chapter 9, "Location and Layout," to a more complete discussion.

SHIPMENT MODE. The five basic modes of transportation are truck, train, ship, pipeline, and airplane. The drivers for the selection should be the firm's competitive priorities. Trucks provide the greatest flexibility, because they can go wherever roads go. Transit times are good, and rates are usually better than trains for small quantities and short distances. Rail transportation can move large quantities cheaply; however, the transit times are long and often variable. Water transportation provides high capacity and low costs, and is necessary for overseas shipments of bulky items; however, the transit times are slow, and then long-haul highway or rail transportation is often needed to get the product to its ultimate destination. Pipeline transportation is highly specialized and is used for liquids, gases, or solids in slurry form. Although it has limited geographical flexibility, transporting via pipeline requires no packaging, and the operating costs per kilometre are low. Finally, air transportation is the fastest and most costly mode per kilometre. Nonetheless, getting a product to the customer fast using truck or air transportation may actually reduce total costs when the costs of inventory and warehouse handling are considered.

CAPACITY. The performance of a logistics process is directly linked to its capacity and variability of demand. Moreover, the ownership and shipment mode decisions are often intertwined, because the question of how much capacity is needed must be resolved. If ownership of the equipment and facilities is under consideration, capital costs as well as variable operating costs must be weighed against the costs of obtaining the logistics services from a supplier.

CROSS-DOCKING. Low-cost operations and delivery speed can be enhanced with a technique called **cross-docking**, which is the packing of products on incoming shipments so that they can be easily sorted at intermediate warehouses for outgoing shipments based on their final destinations; the items are carried from the incoming-vehicle docking point to the outgoing-vehicle docking point without being stored in inventory at the warehouse. For example, a truck from Montreal carrying shipments to customers in Ontario might arrive at a warehouse in Mississauga, where warehouse personnel unload its contents and reload them on trucks headed for destinations in neighbouring cities, such as Toronto, Hamilton, and London. Inbound shipments must be tightly coordinated with outbound shipments for cross-docking to work. The warehouse becomes a short-term staging area for organizing efficient shipments to customers. The benefits of cross-docking include reductions in inventory investment, storage space requirements, handling costs, and lead times, as well as increased inventory turnover and accelerated cash flow.

CUSTOMER RELATIONSHIP PROCESS

The customer relationship process addresses the interface between the firm and its customers downstream in the supply chain. We use the term customer to refer to an entity the firm is trying to serve, which might be a consumer or a business. The purpose of the customer relationship process is to identify, attract, and build relationships with customers and to facilitate the transmission and tracking of orders.

ORDER-PLACEMENT PROCESS

The **order-placement process** involves the activities required to register the need for a product or service and to confirm the acceptance of the order. These activities are initiated by the customer but consummated by the firm producing the product or service. Because it is the order-placement process that generates demand backward through the supply chain, it is to the firm's advantage to make it simple and fast. The Internet has enabled firms to re-engineer their order-placement process to benefit both the customer and the firm. Some companies, however, have been able to use the Internet to eliminate certain elements of their supply chains by substituting information for inventories. Other firms have used it to reduce the transaction costs in their supply chains. Still others have used it to expand the reach and responsiveness of the supply chain. The Internet provides the following advantages for a firm's order-placement process.

- *Cost reduction.* Using the Internet can reduce the costs of processing orders because it allows for greater participation by the customer. Customers can select the products or services they want and place an order with the firm without actually talking to anyone.

cross-docking The packing of products on incoming shipments so that they can be easily sorted at intermediate warehouses and immediately transferred for outgoing shipment based on their final destinations.

order-placement process The activities required to register the need for a product or service and to confirm the acceptance of the order.

- *Revenue flow increase.* A firm's Web page can allow customers to enter billing information during the order-placement process, and suggest related goods or services. This approach also reduces the time lags for payment collection.

- *Global access.* The Internet also allows firms to accept orders 24 hours a day from virtually any location, potentially reducing the time it takes to satisfy a customer.

- *Pricing flexibility.* Firms with their products and services posted on the Web can easily change prices as the need arises. For example, online bookstores can suggest items to customers that are overstocked, or provide time-limited discounts.

CUSTOMER SERVICE

The customer service process helps customers with answers to questions regarding the service or product, resolves problems, and, in general, provides information to assist customers. It is an important point of contact between the firm and its customers, who may judge the firm on the basis of their experiences with this process. The age-old trade-off between cost and quality, however, enters the picture, especially for call centres. In an effort to reduce the cost of their customer service process, many firms have opted to replace human service agents with automated systems, which often require customers to wade through an exhausting sequence of options that sometimes only lead to frustration. Other firms are using Verbots®, or "verbal robots," which are supported by sophisticated artificial intelligence. They have personalities, ask and respond to questions, and in some cases are almost indistinguishable from humans over the phone. Nonetheless, most customers and others seeking information about a service or product prefer interaction with a real person.

Consequently, in consideration for the cost involved, many companies have expanded their supply chain by outsourcing the customer service process to an offshore site where labour costs are low. In this regard, India has responded in a big way to the international need for low-cost call centers. For example, you might have a problem with your Hewlett-Packard ink-jet printer and solve that problem by talking to a technician in Bangalore, India. Of course, the big risk in outsourcing the customer service process, or a part of it, is that the firm loses some control over a process that has direct interface with its customers. This consideration should be carefully weighed in the final analysis.

NEW SERVICE OR PRODUCT DEVELOPMENT PROCESS

New services or products are essential to the startup of many entrepreneurial firms and the long-term survival of established firms. As a result, the new service or product development process is a core process that fundamentally shapes the supply chain. Times change, people change, technologies change, and so services and products change. "New" refers to novel, new-to-the-world products and services, as well as significant changes to existing ones. For the customer, technology can increase service customization, expand product variety, add new features, dramatically reduce cost, or improve consistency of the benefit bundle. For the firm, this means better profitability for existing offerings, new customers, stronger loyalty from existing customers, and opening new markets. As we discuss the nature and importance of the new service and product development process, we will frequently refer to a firm's services or products as its "offerings."

Firms must also define the pace of their technology development and adoption relative to competitors. A firm can emphasize being a *market leader* (also known as *first mover*, who is first to introduce an innovative service or product), a *fast-follower*

FIGURE 2.6 *New Service and Product Development Process*

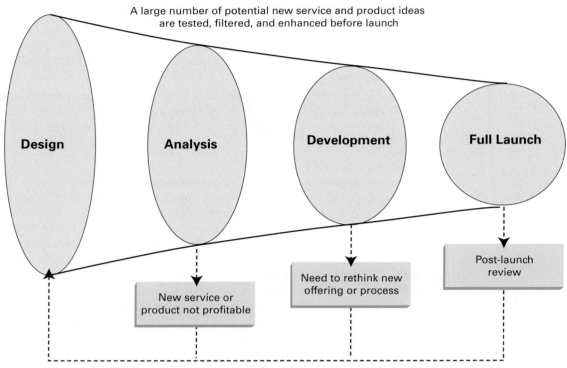

(who allows a leader to incur innovation costs and then introduces a very similar offering after the market has started to develop), or a *laggard* (who waits to see whether the service or product idea catches on in the market). This overall pace of development determines when the firm will initiate the new service or product development process.

The new service/product development process begins with design and ends with the launch of the new offering. Figure 2.6 shows the four stages of the development process. For the market leader, many ideas might be put forward, relative to the few new offerings that are finally launched into the market. A quote attributed to Linus Pauling, winner of two Nobel Prizes, sums up product and service development in these firms: "The best way to have a good idea is to have lots of ideas . . . then throw away the bad ones!" At the other end of the spectrum, the laggard may also be very successful by learning from the trials, miscues, and mistakes that frequently come with being the first to market with a new product or service.

DESIGN. The *design* stage is critical, because it links the creation of new services or products to the corporate strategy of the firm. Ideas for new offerings are generated and screened for feasibility and market-worthiness. Particular attention must be paid to customer needs that are largely unmet or novel attributes that might offer significant differentiation relative to those of competitors. As the basic concept starts to take specific shape, these ideas specify which technologies are being considered, what role they play, how the customer connects with the product or service, how the product or service is delivered, and the benefits and value for the customer. The most promising new ideas are selected for more detailed attention, which includes diagramming processes, providing specifications for performance dimensions, and investigating costs. In this stage, firms need to engage a variety of individuals, including engineering, operations, and marketing personnel, to ensure that any new offering can be reasonably delivered to the market. Even though the detailed specifications of the service or product have not yet been developed, this interaction of designers and manufacturing engineers can avoid costly mistakes.

ANALYSIS. The second stage, *analysis*, involves a critical review of the new offering and how it will be produced to make sure that it fits the corporate strategy, is compatible with regulatory standards, presents an acceptable market risk, and satisfies the needs of the intended customers. The resource requirements for the new offering must be examined from the perspective of the capabilities of the firm and the need to acquire additional resources or form strategic partnerships with other firms. If the analysis reveals that the new offering has good market potential and that the firm has the capability (or can acquire it), development proceeds.

DEVELOPMENT. The third stage, *development*, brings more specificity to the new offering. The required competitive priorities are used as inputs to the design (or redesign) of the processes that will be involved in delivering the new offering. Pilot testing in limited markets might occur in this stage as product or service mock-ups are developed. Such testing allows for further refinement of the design. Once the new offering is specified and the processes have been designed, the market program can be developed. Finally, personnel are trained and some test runs can be conducted to iron out the kinks in production.

To avoid costly mismatches between the design of a new offering and the capability of the processes required to produce it, many firms engage in a concept called **concurrent engineering**, which brings product engineers, process engineers, marketers, buyers, information specialists, quality specialists, and suppliers together to design a product and the processes that will meet customer expectations. Changes are much simpler and less costly at this stage. However, if major problems with the product design or the capability to deliver the product are uncovered, the product proposal may have to be completely rethought.

FULL LAUNCH. The final stage, *full launch*, involves the coordination of many processes. Promotions for the new offering must be initiated, sales personnel briefed, distribution processes activated, and old services or products that the new offering is to replace withdrawn. A particular strain is placed on the processes needed to produce the offering during a period referred to as *ramp-up*, when the facilities and suppliers must increase volume to meet customer demand while coping with quality problems and last-minute design changes. Finally, post-launch review will compare the competitive priorities of the processes with their competitive capabilities and may signal a need to rethink the original product idea.

Competitive priorities may change over time. For example, consider what we now see as a high-volume standardized product, such as

concurrent engineering
A concept that brings product engineers, process engineers, marketers, buyers, information specialists, quality specialists, and suppliers together to work jointly to design a service or product and the required processes that will meet customer expectations.

Former Apple CEO Steve Jobs emphasizes Apple Computer's innovation during the launch of each generation of the iPhone.

3.5 inch display

960 x 640 pixels (4X more)

326 pixels per inch

800:1 contrast ratio (4X better)

IPS technology for superb color and wide viewing angle

Incredibly sharp text & image

colour ink-jet desktop printers. Initially after market launch, when the printers were just beginning to appeal to the mass market, manufacturing processes required flexibility to adapt to changing volumes, features, and engineering specifications. Later, after the product was widely adopted and demand was high, the competitive priorities became low-cost operations, consistent quality, and on-time delivery.

SUPPLY CHAIN DYNAMICS

Supply chains often involve linkages among many firms, and supply chain dynamics can wreak havoc on performance. Each firm in a supply chain depends on other firms for services, materials, or the information needed to supply its immediate external customer in the chain. Yet, the actions of downstream supply chain members (positioned nearer the ultimate consumer of the service or product) can indirectly affect the operations of upstream members, even several tiers away.

As you examine the order patterns of firms in a supply chain, you will frequently see the variability in order quantities increase as you proceed upstream. This increase in variability is referred to as the **bullwhip effect**, which gets its name from the action of a bullwhip—the handle of the whip initiates the action; however, the tip of the whip experiences the wildest action. The slightest change in customer demands can ripple through the entire chain, with each member receiving more variability in demands from the member immediately downstream.

bullwhip effect The phenomenon in supply chains whereby ordering patterns show increasing variance as you move upstream in the chain.

The bullwhip effect in a supply chain for facial tissue is depicted in Figure 2.7. The retailer's orders to the manufacturer exhibit more variability than the actual demands from the consumers of the facial tissue because shipments to a retailer occur much less frequently than a customer buying individual packages. The manufacturer's orders to the package supplier have more variability than the retailer's orders. Finally, the package supplier's orders to the cardboard supplier have the most variability. Because supply patterns do not match demand patterns, inventories accumulate in some firms and shortages occur in others. The firms with too much inventory stop ordering, and those that have shortages place expedited orders. The culprits are unexpected changes in demands or supplies that are based on a number of causes.

EXTERNAL CAUSES

A firm has the least amount of control over its external customers and suppliers, who can periodically cause disruptions. Typical disruptions include:

- *Volume changes.* Customers may change the quantity of the service or product they had ordered for a specific date or unexpectedly demand more of a standard service or product. If the market demands short lead times, the firm needs a quick reaction from its suppliers.

The bullwhip effect can cause costly disruptions to upstream facilities of a supply chain, such as a paperboard manufacturing process at this Weyerhaeuser Co. plant.

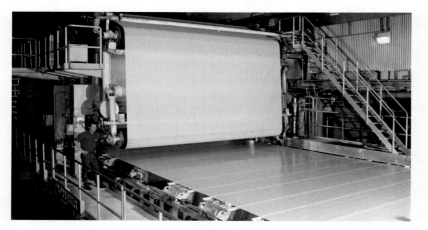

- *Service and product mix changes.* Customers may change the mix of items in an order and cause a ripple effect throughout the supply chain. For example, a major-appliance store chain may change the mix of washing machines in its orders from 60 percent Whirlpool brand and 40 percent Kitchen Aid brand to 30 percent Whirlpool and 70 percent Kitchen Aid. This decision

FIGURE 2.7   *Supply Chain Dynamics for Facial Tissue*

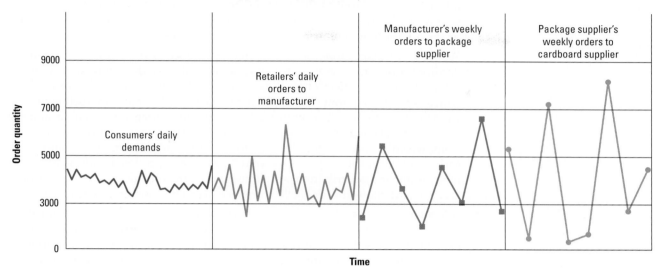

changes the production schedule of the Whirlpool plant that makes both brands, causing imbalances in its inventories. In addition, companies that make faceplates for the washing machines must change their schedules, thereby affecting their suppliers.

- *Late deliveries.* Late deliveries of materials or delays in essential services can force a firm to switch its schedule from production of one product model to another. Suppliers that provide model-specific parts then may have their schedules disrupted. For example, the Whirlpool plant may find that a component supplier for its Model A washing machine could not supply a component on time. To avoid shutting down the assembly line, which is an expensive action, Whirlpool may decide to switch to Model B production. Suddenly, the demand on the suppliers of Model B–specific components increases.

- *Underfilled shipments.* Suppliers that send partial shipments do so because of disruptions at their own plants. The effects of underfilled shipments are similar to those of late shipments unless they contain enough to allow the firm to operate until the next shipment.

INTERNAL CAUSES

A famous line from a Pogo cartoon is "We have seen the enemy, and he is us!" Unfortunately, this statement is true for many firms when it comes to disruptions in the supply chain. Typical internal disruptions that cause increased variability include the following:

- *Internally generated shortages.* There may be a shortage of parts manufactured by a firm because of machine breakdowns or inexperienced workers—all sources of variation discussed in Chapter 4, "Capacity." A labour shortage, possibly caused by absenteeism, has a similar effect.

- *Technology changes.* Changes to the design of services or products can have a direct impact on suppliers. For example, changing cable TV feed lines to fibre-optic technology increases the benefits to the cable company's customers but affects the demand for cable.

- *New service or product introductions.* A firm decides on the number of introductions, as well as their timing, and hence introduces variability in the supply chain. New services or products may even require a new supply chain or the addition of new members to an existing supply chain.

- *Service or product promotions.* A common practice of firms producing standardized products or services is to use occasional price discounts to promote sales. This has the effect of creating a spike in demand followed by a trough, which is felt throughout the supply chain. That is what the Campbell Soup Company found out when its annual deep-discount pricing program in January caused retailers and customers to stock up with large quantities of chicken soup, which in turn created the need for overtime production at its plants as early as October. Moving to "everyday" low pricing, coupled with daily replenishment to distribution warehouses, smoothed the demand pattern from grocers, and allowed Campbell's to reduce overtime costs and expand sales.

- *Information errors.* Demand forecast errors could cause a firm to order too many, or too few, services and materials. Also, forecast errors can result in expedited orders that force suppliers to react more quickly to avoid shortages in the supply chain. In addition, errors in the physical count of items in stock can cause shortages (leading to panic purchases) or too much inventory (leading to a slowdown in purchases).

Many disruptions are simply caused by ineffective coordination in the supply chain because so many firms and separate operations are involved. It is therefore unrealistic to think that all disruptions can be eliminated. As firms move toward more integrated supply chains, described earlier in this chapter, it is possible to reduce the number of disruptions and minimize the impact of those that cannot be eliminated.

SUPPLY CHAIN STRATEGIES

A supply chain is a network of firms, each with its own core processes. Yet each firm in the chain must build its own supply chain with a consistent understanding and support for the competitive priorities of the overall supply chain. This challenge helps to explain why the performance of many supply chains has been dismal, with high costs and slow response times, despite great investment in advanced technologies such as the Internet, flexible manufacturing, and automated warehousing. For example, the design of supply chain for a firm with innovative, customized high-margin products should be quite different from that of another firm providing basic functional, low-margin products. Overall, the design of the supply chain must be aligned with a firm's strategy and the characteristics of the service or product. In this section, we highlight two distinct supply chain designs and demonstrate how they can support the operations strategies of firms. We also discuss how a firm can trade off greater vertical integration with outsourcing, and we close the chapter by listing some levers to improve performance.

EFFICIENT VERSUS RESPONSIVE SUPPLY CHAINS

Depending on the characteristics of the product or service, two distinct supply chain designs can be used for competitive advantage: *efficient* or *responsive* supply chains (Fisher, 1997). The purpose of efficient supply chains is to coordinate the flow of materials and services so as to minimize inventories and maximize the efficiency of the chain. Responsive supply chains are designed to react quickly to market demands by positioning inventories and capacities in order to hedge against variation and uncertainties in demand. Table 2.2 shows the business settings that best suit each design.

TABLE 2.2	Business Settings Best Suited for Efficient and Responsive Supply Chains	
Factor	**Efficient Supply Chains**	**Responsive Supply Chains**
Demand	Predictable; low forecast errors	Unpredictable; high forecast errors
Competitive priorities	Low cost; consistent quality; on-time delivery	High innovation; fast delivery times; customization; volume flexibility; high-performance design quality
New-product introduction	Infrequent	Frequent
Contribution margins	Low	High
Product variety	Low	High

EFFICIENT SUPPLY CHAINS. The pattern of demand for the firm's products or services is a key factor in the best choice of supply chain design. Efficient supply chains work best in settings where demand is highly predictable, such as demand for staple items purchased at grocery stores or demand for a package delivery service. The focus of the supply chain is on the efficient flows of materials and services, that is, keeping inventories to a minimum. Product or service designs last a long time, new introductions are infrequent, and variety is small. Such firms typically produce for markets in which price is crucial to winning an order; therefore, contribution margins are low and efficiency is important. Consequently, the firm's competitive priorities are low-cost operations, consistent quality, and on-time delivery.

RESPONSIVE SUPPLY CHAINS. Responsive supply chains work best when firms offer a great variety of products or services and demand predictability is low. Demand may also be short-lived, as in the case of fashion goods. The focus of responsive supply chains is reaction time to meet rapidly changing demand, with judiciously placed inventories along the supply chain to meet peak demand. In other markets, firms may not know what products or services they need to provide until customers place orders. To be competitive, such firms must frequently develop new products or services to generate high contribution margins. Typical competitive priorities are development speed, fast delivery times, customization, volume flexibility, and high-performance design quality.

IMPLEMENTING THE RIGHT DESIGN

The alignment with operations strategy and implementation for efficient and responsive supply chains are summarized in Table 2.3. The further upstream in an efficient supply chain that a firm is positioned, the more likely it is to have a process that supports high volumes of standardized products or services. Consequently, suppliers in efficient supply chains tend to have little excess capacity because high utilization helps to keep the cost per unit low. Higher inventory turnover is desired to keep inventory investment low, and thus reduce costs. Firms should work with their suppliers to shorten lead times, but care must be taken to use tactics that do not appreciably increase costs. For example, lead times for a supplier could be shortened by switching from rail to air transportation; however, the added cost may offset the savings obtained from the shorter lead times. Suppliers should be selected with emphasis on low prices, consistent quality, and on-time delivery. Because of low capacity cushions, disruptions in an efficient supply chain can be costly and must be avoided.

TABLE 2.3	*Design Features for Efficient and Responsive Supply Chains*	
Factor	**Efficient Supply Chains**	**Responsive Supply Chains**
Operations strategy	Emphasize high-volume, standardized products or services, such as make-to-stock	Emphasize product or service variety, including assemble-to-order, make-to-order, or customization
Inventory investment	Low; focus on high inventory turnover	Higher at critical points in supply chain to enable fast delivery time; use modular components
Lead time	Shorten, if possible without driving up cost	Shorten aggressively
Supplier selection	Emphasize low prices, consistent quality, on-time delivery	Emphasize fast delivery time, customization, volume flexibility, high-performance design quality

Because of the need for quick reactions and the high levels of product or service variety, firms in a responsive supply chain must have a more flexible process. Consequently, suppliers also tend to have very flexible operations. Inventories should be positioned in the chain to support delivery speed, but inventories of expensive finished goods should be avoided. Firms should aggressively work with their suppliers to shorten lead times because that allows managers to wait longer before committing to customer orders. Firms should select suppliers to support the competitive priorities of the products or services provided, which in this case would include the ability to provide quick deliveries, customize parts or components, adjust volumes quickly to match demand cycles in the market, and provide high performance quality.

Poor supply chain performance is often the result of using the wrong supply chain design for the products or services provided. A common mistake is to use an efficient supply chain in a business setting that calls for a responsive supply chain, or, alternatively, a single design across all market segments. Instead, a firm may need to utilize more than one supply chain design when its operations compete in multiple market segments. For example, the supply chain for a standard product such as an oil tanker has different requirements than that for a customized product such as a luxury liner, even though both are ocean vessels and both may be manufactured by the same company.

Finally, the design of supply chains becomes more complex as markets evolve and firms move to reposition products over time. Over time, a firm may add options to its basic product, or introduce variations of that product, so that the variety of products and options increases dramatically. Yet, all too often, the design of the supply chain changes little, and the firm continues to measure the supply chain's performance as it always has, emphasizing efficiency, even when characteristics of the product and market require a more responsive supply chain design.

For some firms, an intermediate design step is to identify modular subassemblies or service elements that can be combined using postponement. For example, Gillette uses an efficient supply chain to manufacture some products so that it can more fully utilize a capital-intensive manufacturing process. However, in response to increasingly uncertain and fragmented retail markets, managers have developed a supply chain that postpones the packaging of the products until the very last moment. The packaging operation involves customization in the form of printing different graphics and languages. Clearly, effective alignment of operations and its competitive priorities with supply chain design has strategic implications for a firm.

OUTSOURCING PROCESSES

All businesses buy at least some inputs to their processes, such as professional services, raw materials, or manufactured parts, from other producers. Vertical integration is the degree to which a firm's own production system or service facility handles the entire supply chain. The more processes that are performed in-house rather than by suppliers or customers, the greater the degree of vertical integration. Management decides the level of vertical integration by looking at all the processes performed between the acquisition of raw materials or outside services and the delivery of finished goods or services.

If a company doesn't perform some processes itself, it must rely on **outsourcing**, or paying suppliers and distributors to perform those processes and provide needed services and materials. When managers opt for more vertical integration, there is by definition less outsourcing. These decisions are sometimes called **make-or-buy decisions**, with a make decision meaning more integration and a buy decision meaning more outsourcing. After deciding what to outsource and what to do in-house, management must find ways to coordinate and integrate the various processes and suppliers involved.

VERTICAL INTEGRATION. Vertical integration can be in two directions. **Backward integration** represents movement upstream toward the sources of raw materials and parts, such as a major grocery chain having its own plants to produce house brands of ice cream, frozen pizza dough, and peanut butter. Alternatively, **forward integration** represents movement downstream, such as acquiring new channels of distribution, warehouses, and retail stores. It can also mean that a firm begins to acquire or compete

outsourcing Allotting payment to suppliers and distributors to provide needed services and materials and to perform those processes that the organization does not perform itself.

make-or-buy decisions Decisions that involve either more integration (a *make* decision) or more outsourcing (a *buy* decision).

backward integration A firm's movement upstream toward the sources of raw materials and parts.

forward integration A firm's movement downstream by acquiring channels of distribution, finished goods manufacturing, or supplemental service.

A key consideration in designing global supply chains is to focus on the total cost of manufacturing and delivering the product to customers. Often increased logistics costs are offset by lower manufacturing costs, promoting greater movement of goods. Here a vessel loaded with containers berths at Halifax's port, an important port of entry to Canada.

against its customers. Vincor Canada, this country's largest producer of wine, is a model of vertical integration. The firm's dozens of brands run the gamut from basic to premium wines. Upstream, it owns or leases thousands of hectares of vineyards in Ontario, British Columbia, and California. Downstream, it sells its products through its own chain of Wine Rack stores. Finally, winery tours through new state-of-the-art operations and a 500-seat amphitheatre have been developed and built to lure wine lovers and concertgoers to increase cellar-door sales in the Niagara region of Ontario.

ADVANTAGES OF VERTICAL INTEGRATION. A firm tends to choose vertical integration when it has the skills, volume, and resources to perform processes at lower cost and produce higher-quality goods and services than outsiders can. Doing the work in-house may mean better quality and more timely delivery—and taking better advantage of the firm's human resources, equipment, and space. Extensive vertical integration is generally attractive when input volumes are high, because high volumes allow for task specialization and greater efficiency. It is also attractive if the firm has the relevant skills and views the processes that it is integrating as particularly important to its future success. Thus, managers must look upstream toward its suppliers and downstream toward its customers, and bring in-house those processes that give it the right skills and capabilities—those that allow the firm to organize work and deliver value better than its competitors. However, management should also realize that if the firm outsources a critical process, it might lose control over that area of its business—and perhaps foster future competition.

offshoring A supply chain strategy that involves moving processes to another country.

OFFSHORING. The strategy of globalizing a firm adds a new twist to vertical integration. **Offshoring** is a supply chain strategy that involves relocating internal processes to another country, with either a wholly owned subsidiary or a joint venture. Firms are motivated to initiate operations offshore by the market potential and the cost advantages it provides. The firm may be able to create new markets because of its presence in other countries and its ability to offer competitive prices due to its cost efficiencies. Competitive priorities other than low costs, such as delivery speed to distant customers, can drive the decision too.

ADVANTAGES OF OUTSOURCING. Outsourcing, in contrast to vertical integration and offshoring, offers several advantages to firms. It is particularly attractive to those that have low volumes or need specialized expertise. Outsourcing can also provide better quality and cost savings. For example, foreign locations managed by a supplier can offer lower wages and yield higher productivity. Firms are doing more outsourcing than ever before. Two factors contributing to this trend are global competition and information technology. Globalization creates more supplier options, and advances in information technology make coordination with suppliers easier. IKEA, the largest retailer of home furnishings, has 30 buying offices around the world to seek out suppliers. Its Vienna-based business service department runs a computer database that helps suppliers locate raw materials and new business partners. Cash registers at its stores around the world relay sales data to the nearest warehouse and to its operational headquarters in Älmhult, Sweden, where its information systems provide the data needed to control its shipping patterns worldwide.

PITFALLS OF OUTSOURCING. Even though offshoring and outsourcing appear to offer some big advantages, they also have some pitfalls that firms should carefully explore before using these strategic options:

● *Moving too quickly.* A critical mistake is to decide to outsource or move a process offshore before making a major effort to fix the existing one. As we will discuss in the next few chapters, there are many ways to improve processes in the areas of quality, efficiency, and customer responsiveness. These methods should be explored first. It is not always the case that offshoring or outsourcing is the answer, even if local labour wages far exceed those of other countries. Canon, for example, decided to keep its manufacturing in Japan rather than shift it to lower-cost countries in Southeast Asia. The strategy was to compete on technology innovations in its line of high-end cameras. To achieve that strategy, Canon kept its new product development process and its manufacturing process close to each other to support speedy new product introductions and communication between engineers and manufacturing managers. Assembly lines were replaced with manufacturing cells (see Chapter 7, "Lean Systems"), thereby improving teamwork, reducing its inventory and factory costs, and increasing its ability to make innovative products faster. The message: Make sure you really need to outsource or offshore in order to accomplish your operations strategy.

- *Technology transfer.* Often an offshoring strategy involves creating a joint venture with a company in another country. With a joint venture, two firms agree to jointly produce a service or product together. Typically, a transfer of technology takes place to bring one partner up to speed regarding the service or product. The danger is that the firm with the technology advantage will set up the other firm to be a future competitor. For example, Chinese rail companies that were once junior partners with Japanese, European, and Canadian companies, such as Bombardier Inc., have recently been competing against them in the growing global market for super-fast train systems. According to a senior executive at Kawasaki, "How are you supposed to fight rivals when they have your technology, and their cost base is so much lower?"[4]

- *Process integration.* Despite the power of the Internet, it is difficult to fully integrate outsourced or offshore processes with the firm's other core processes. Time, distance, and communication can be formidable hurdles. Managing offshore processes won't be the same as managing processes located next door. Often considerable managerial time must be expended to coordinate offshore processes.

Thus, these strategic options carry opportunities, challenges, and threats. As with any critical decision affecting operations strategy, trade-offs must be carefully assessed and risks actively managed.

LEVERS FOR IMPROVED SUPPLY CHAIN PERFORMANCE

Now that we have discussed strategies for supply chain management, we can return to the problems caused by supply chain dynamics and options to improve performance.[5]

- *Sharing data.* One source of dynamics in supply chains is the lack of visibility of end-user demand by suppliers upstream in the supply chain. To facilitate planning at all levels in the supply chain, point-of-sale (POS) data, which records actual customer purchases of the final service or product, can be shared with all suppliers. RFID can also be used to track quantities of inventory throughout the supply chain.

- *Collaborative activities.* Working closely with customers and suppliers in customer demand planning (CDP) and environmental health and safety programs, as well as the design collaboration process, improves information flows, improves environmental stewardship, and reduces surprises from demand spikes due to promotions or supply hangups because of poorly designed services or products.

- *Reduce replenishment lead times.* Improving internal processes and working with suppliers to reduce lead times allows the firm to wait longer before reacting to a change in demand levels, mitigating the bullwhip effect. In addition, shorter lead times lead to smaller pipeline inventories.

- *Reduce order lot sizes.* Working on ways to reduce the costs associated with ordering, transporting, and receiving inventory throughout the supply chain will reduce order lot sizes and thereby decrease the amount of fluctuation in the size of orders in the supply chain.

- *Ration short supplies.* When a shortage exists, customers sometimes artificially inflate their orders to protect themselves, only to cancel them later when the shortage is relieved. To counteract this behaviour, suppliers can ration short supplies to customers on the basis of their past sales, rather than their current orders.

- *Use everyday low pricing (EDLP).* Promotional or discount pricing encourages spikes in demand. Using a stable pricing program such as EDLP, as is done by Walmart, discourages customers from buying excess stock at discounted prices so they can offer price promotions, a practice called *forward buying*. EDLP levels the demand.

- *Be cooperative and trustworthy (to a point).* Being cooperative in solving supply issues and providing information that can be trusted serves to reduce costs for all members of the supply chain and mitigates environmental problems and the deleterious effects of supply chain dynamics. However, it is critical to protect core processes and technologies.

SUPPLY CHAINS AND SUSTAINABILITY

As is noted in Chapter 1, environmental concerns regarding business are voiced every day in the popular media. Service providers are examining ways to increase efficiency and reduce the impact of their operations on the environment. Manufacturers are feeling pressure to take responsibility for their products "from cradle to grave." In this section we will discuss how integrated supply chains can address some of these issues. We will also discuss the supply chain implications for implementing an approach called "reverse supply chain," which responds to the need to salvage products at the end of their life cycles.

BASIC PROCESS CONCERNS

A growing theme among many firms is that of environmental stewardship and social responsibility. In essence, this means that managers must actively work toward designing and delivering services, products, and processes that take into account both the environment and other people (beyond customers) throughout the supply chain. A first step is better communication across the supply chain to work toward common goals. Second, any materials used or produced (and their wastes) must be tracked from cradle to grave (disposal), or, better yet, to cradle (recycle or reuse).

Being more sustainable is no easy task for any firm. However, managers can move closer to that goal by working to address the following areas with targeted investments and innovation:

- *Environmental protection.* Firms need to monitor their own processes and those of their suppliers to reduce the pollution of the air, streams, and rivers, and to increase efforts at ecological stewardship for the protection of flora and fauna.

- *Productivity improvement.* Firms can examine processes up and down the supply chain to increase material conservation, to increase energy efficiency, and to look for ways to convert waste into useful byproducts.

- *Social responsibilities.* Firms also must evaluate, and possibly encourage improvement of labour conditions at suppliers, particularly in developing economies. Worker safety, protecting human rights, and paying fair wages are but a few issues that customers now require supply chain partners to address.
- *Risk minimization.* As the supply chain grows, particularly on a global basis, managers must take great care to ensure that the materials that go into their services, products, or processes do not pose health or safety hazards to customers.
- *Innovation.* As new services, products, or technologies are developed, firms can identify new, greener ways to deliver better customer value, or improve the quality of life in local communities.

Sustainability is not the easiest strategy to sell to every investor. While seemingly intuitive, investors expect a tangible return on investment to justify up-front costs. However, benefits may take years to materialize, for example, from recycled products or green energy. Similar challenges face any new technology idea or entry into new markets. Likewise, managers must have a long-term view: uncertain, but smart, investment in more sustainable solutions now can improve competitiveness and customer value in the future.

REVERSE SUPPLY CHAIN

reverse supply chain The process of planning for, collecting, and controlling flow of new, used, or end-of-life products from customers to supply chain partners for reuse, repair, remanufacturing, or recycling.

Firms such as Xerox, ABInBev, and Caterpillar are developing reverse supply chains to manage their products throughout their life cycles. A **reverse supply chain** includes all processes that plan for, collect, and control the flow of products, materials, and information from the point of consumption back to reuse, repair, remanufacture, or recycle. Of course, this chain should be both efficient and cost-effective, just like the forward supply chain. Taken one step further, a supply chain that integrates forward flow with reverse flows is called a *closed-loop supply chain*, because it focuses on the complete chain of operations from cradle to cradle (producing a new product).[6]

More generally, Figure 2.8 shows how a product starts its journey at the new service/product development process, makes its way to the customer, and then enters the reverse supply chain that attempts to maximize the value of all materials and components after either an early or end-of-life return. Products can be returned either shortly after initial purchase because the product was unsatisfactory or defective, i.e., *early returns*, or after being used until they wear out, i.e., *end-of-life returns*.

It is clear that the processes for reverse supply chains can be quite different from forward supply chains. A firm must locate convenient collection points to receive the used goods from the final customer and transport used goods to a returns processor, which can involve either vertical integration or outsourcing. Following inspection and sorting, which can use sophisticated tests for electronic or mechanical components, several options are possible. If the item no longer works, it might be *repaired*, and then returned to the customer or sold in another market.

A second option is to partially disassemble, clean, and *recondition* the product, either to be sent to the distribution channel, which is the case with leased products, or to be completely disassembled and completely *remanufactured* by combining new parts with repaired or adjusted used parts. Unlike reconditioning, a remanufactured product loses its original identity (e.g., its serial number changes) as new materials and components are mixed with quality-checked used parts. Finally, used parts or packaging that cannot be salvaged can be *recycled* for their material value (e.g., aluminum). Naturally, waste can be created at each step in the forward or reverse supply chain.

Three aspects should be stressed. First, services often generate large amounts of waste, and the reverse supply chain is frequently overlooked. For example, operating rooms in hospitals often use many disposable supplies that might be recycled (or if

FIGURE 2.8 *Closing the loop in the supply chain*

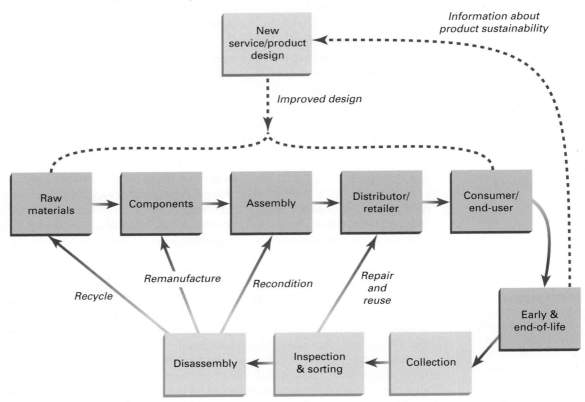

Products flow to and from consumers, potentially offering multiple points to introduce consumed materials. Wastes might also be generated at each tier in the supply chain.

autoclaved, even reused). Medical supply firms are beginning to explore options to safely, yet responsibly, develop closed-loop supply chains, which can also provide new business opportunities.

Second, reverse supply chains can be particularly important in the industries with short-lived products, such as electronics. Have you ever wondered what happens to your old cell phone after you purchase a new one? You may have given it to the store where you purchased your new one, or merely slipped it into the household trash. Old cell phones can contain toxins that leach into the soil if these components are left unprocessed, for example lead and cadmium in circuit boards. Some regions, such as the European Union, have passed laws requiring electronics manufacturers to take back and recycle products that they sell.

Third, information about a product or service's sustainability performance across the supply chain, if measured, can be sent back to the new service/product development process to introduce improvements in future generations and new services (Rothenberg, 2007). For example, environmental performance includes waste created by the product throughout the forward and reverse supply chains (and customer use), leading to redesign with a smaller impact. Xerox has leveraged information from its used products and customers' experience to develop more reliable and durable products that have less waste, which, in turn, also can be remanufactured and leased for multiple cycles.

EQUATION SUMMARY

1. Weeks of supply $= \dfrac{\text{Average aggregate inventory value}}{\text{Weekly sales (at cost)}}$

2. Inventory turnover $= \dfrac{\text{Annual sales (at cost)}}{\text{Average aggregate inventory value}}$

3. Average aggregate inventory value $= (N_a c_a) + (N_b c_b) + \ldots + (N_n c_n)$

CHAPTER HIGHLIGHTS

- A supply chain is a set of linkages among suppliers of materials and services that spans the transformation of raw materials into services and products that are delivered to customers.

- A basic purpose of supply chain management is to control inventory by managing the flows of materials. Three aggregate categories of inventories are raw materials, work-in-process, and finished goods. Both inventory pooling and forward placement of inventories can reduce the total inventory in the supply chain.

- Supply chain performance is tracked with inventory measures such as aggregate inventory level, weeks of supply, and inventory turnover. Supply chain process measures include broader measures that assess performance related to the four core processes, that is, supplier relationship, order fulfillment, customer relationship, and new service or product development. Outcomes from these core processes drive financial measures such as total assets, return on assets, working capital, cost of goods sold, and cash flow.

- When sourcing, firms can select suppliers using multiple criteria related to their competitive priorities for creating customer value. Verification of supplier capabilities rely on either a firm's own staff, or an external audit and certification by a third party. Early supplier involvement in new service or product development and presourcing can yield reduced costs, higher quality, and better employee morale.

- Buyers can take two approaches in dealing with their suppliers. The competitive orientation pits supplier against supplier in an effort to get the buyer's business. Alternatively, the cooperative orientation seeks to make long-term commitments to a small number of suppliers, with advantages accruing to both parties. The orientation chosen should be aligned with the firm's operations strategy to create customer value.

- The Internet is changing how many firms handle purchasing. Internet-based catalogue hubs, exchanges, and auctions are recent innovations.

- The customer relationship process is continuing to change using technology. Order placement can be re-engineered to allow more customer involvement, to lower labour costs, to enable remaining open 24/7, and to enable the use of pricing as a means to influence demand to accommodate product shortages. Customer service also can be automated or moved offshore to call centres in developing economies.

- Because supply chains consist of many independent firms linked to other firms, disruptions with customers (i.e., downstream) can cascade upstream to suppliers, growing ever larger with each upstream tier in the supply chain. Both internal and external sources of variability contribute to this problem through a process termed the *bullwhip effect*.

- Efficient supply chains are designed to coordinate the flows of materials and services so as to minimize inventories and maximize the efficiency of the firms in the supply chain. Responsive supply chains are designed to react quickly to market demand through judicious use of inventories and flexible capacity. Each can be effective, if matched correctly with service or product characteristics.

- Other strategic decisions for supply chain managers include vertical integration, outsourcing, and offshoring. Competitive priorities, combined with the firm's operational strategy, guide managers as they balance benefits and risks, such as the potential loss of technological advantages to former suppliers.

- More sustainable supply chains must consider multiple environmental and social outcomes, and work toward reducing pollutants across the supply chain, improving energy and resource efficiency, enhancing product safety, and monitoring social responsibilities in suppliers. However, products, parts, and components now also flow backward from customers, in a *reverse supply chain*. Competitive benefits are possible through better service and product design and cost savings.

SOLVED PROBLEM

A firm's cost of goods sold last year was $3 410 000, and the firm operates 52 weeks per year. It carries seven items in inventory: three raw materials, two work-in-process items, and two finished goods. The following table contains last year's average inventory level for each item, along with its value.

CATEGORY	PART NUMBER	AVERAGE LEVEL	UNIT VALUE
Raw materials	1	15 000	$ 3
	2	2 500	5
	3	3 000	1
Work-in-process	4	5 000	14
	5	4 000	18
Finished goods	6	2 000	48
	7	1 000	62

a. What is the average aggregate inventory value?

b. How many weeks of supply does the firm maintain?

c. What was the inventory turnover last year?

SOLUTION

a.

PART NUMBER	AVERAGE LEVEL		UNIT VALUE		TOTAL VALUE
1	15 000	×	$ 3	=	$ 45 000
2	2 500	×	$ 5	=	$ 12 500
3	3 000	×	$ 1	=	$ 3 000
4	5 000	×	$14	=	$ 70 000
5	4 000	×	$18	=	$ 72 000
6	2 000	×	$48	=	$ 96 000
7	1 000	×	$62	=	$ 62 000
	Average aggregate inventory value			=	$360 500

b. Average weekly sales at cost = $3 410 000/52 weeks = $65 577/week

$$\text{Weeks of supply} = \frac{\text{Average aggregate inventory value}}{\text{Weekly sales (at cost)}} = \frac{\$360\ 500}{\$65\ 577} = 5.5 \text{ weeks}$$

c. $$\text{Inventory turnover} = \frac{\text{Annual sales (at cost)}}{\text{Average aggregate inventory value}} = \frac{\$3\ 410\ 000}{\$360\ 500} = 9.5 \text{ turns}$$

PROBLEMS

1. Buzzrite ended the current year with annual sales (at cost) of $48 million. During the year, the inventory turnover was six turns. For the next year, Buzzrite plans to increase annual sales (at cost) by 25 percent.

a. What is the increase in the average aggregate inventory value required if Buzzrite maintains the same inventory turnover during the next year?

b. What change in inventory turnover must Buzzrite achieve if, through better supply chain management, it wants to support next year's sales with no increase in the average aggregate inventory value?

2. Jack Jones, the materials manager at Precision Enterprises, is beginning to look for ways to reduce inventories. A recent accounting statement shows the following inventory investment by category: raw materials $3 129 500; work-in-process $6 237 000; and finished goods $2 686 500. This year's cost of goods sold will be about $32.5 million. Assuming 52 business weeks per year, express total inventory as:

a. Weeks of supply

b. Inventory turnover

3. Sterling, Inc. operates 52 weeks per year, and its cost of goods sold last year was $6 500 000. The firm carries eight items in inventory: four raw materials, two work-in-process items, and two finished goods. Table 2.4 shows last year's average inventory levels for these items, along with their unit values.

a. What is the average aggregate inventory value?

b. How many weeks of supply does the firm have?

c. What was the inventory turnover last year?

4. One product line has 10 turns per year and an annual sales volume (at cost) of $985 000. How much inventory is being held, on average?

5. The following data were collected for a retailer:

Cost of goods sold	$3 500 000
Gross profit	$ 700 000
Operating costs	$ 500 000
Operating profit	$ 200 000
Total inventory	$1 200 000
Fixed assets	$ 750 000
Long-term debt	$ 300 000

Assuming 52 business weeks per year, express total inventory as

a. Weeks of supply

b. Inventory turns

TABLE 2.4	*Inventory Items*		
CATEGORY	PART NUMBER	AVERAGE INVENTORY UNITS	VALUE PER UNIT
Raw materials	RM-1	20 000	$ 1
	RM-2	5 000	5
	RM-3	3 000	6
	RM-4	1 000	8
Work-in-process	WIP-1	6 000	10
	WIP-2	8 000	12
Finished goods	FG-1	1 000	65
	FG-2	500	88

NOTES FOR CHAPTER

1. Mark Brienzi and Dr. Sham Kekre, "How Kodak Transformed Its Service Parts Supply Chain," *Supply Chain Management Review*, (October 2005), pp. 25–32; www.kodak.com.
2. Nick Wingsfield, "Amazon Vows to Avoid Mess of 1999 Christmas Rush: Too Many Kermit Phones," *Wall Street Journal*, (September 25, 2000), p. B1.
3. Sources: Elizabeth Rennie, "Beyond Borders," *APICS Magazine* (March 2007), pp. 34–38; Stanley Holmes, "The 787 Encounters Turbulence," *Business Week* (June 19, 2006), pp. 38–40; J. Lynn Lunsford, "Boeing Scrambles to Repair Problems With New Plane," *The Wall Street Journal* (December 7, 2007), p. A1; "Manufacturing,"
The Globe and Mail: Report on Business (September 27, 2011), p. B2; www.boeing.com/commercial/787family/background.html.
4. Norihiko Shirouzu, "Train Makers Rail Against China's High-Speed Designs," *Wall Street Journal*, (November 17, 2010).
5. For more coverage of levers, see Sunil Chopra and Peter Meindl, *Supply Chain Management*, 3rd ed. (Upper Saddle River, NJ: Prentice Hall, 2007), pp. 506–511.
6. See Hau Lee, "Don't Tweak Your Supply Chain—Rethink It End to End," *Harvard Business Review*, vol. 88, no. 10 (2010), pp. 62–69; Cris Prystay, "Recycling E-Waste," *Wall Street Journal*, (September 23, 2004).

FURTHER READING

Aron, Ravi, and Jitendra V. Singh. "Getting Offshoring Right." *Harvard Business Review* (December 2005), pp. 135–143.
Bowersox, D. J., and D. J. Closs. *Logistical Management: The Integrated Supply Chain Process*. New York: McGraw-Hill, 1996.
Brienzi, Mark, and Dr. Sham Kekre. "How Kodak Transformed Its Service Parts Supply Chain." *Supply Chain Management Review* (October 2005), pp. 25–32.

Champion, David. "Mastering the Value Chain." *Harvard Business Review* (June 2001), pp. 109–115.

Chopra, Sunil, and ManMohan S. Sodhi. "Looking for the Bang from the RFID Buck." *Supply Chain Management Review* (May/June 2007), pp. 34–41.

Conner, Martin P. "The Supply Chain's Role in Leveraging Product Life Cycle Management." *Supply Chain Management Review* (March 2004), pp. 36–43.

Cook, Robert L., Brian Gibson, and Douglas MacCurdy. "A Lean Approach to Cross-Docking." *Supply Chain Management Review* (March 2005), pp. 54–59.

de Waart, Dick, and Steve Kemper. "5 Steps to Service Supply Chain Excellence." *Supply Chain Management Review* (January/February 2004), pp. 28–35.

Ellram, Lisa M., and Baohong Liu. "The Financial Impact of Supply Management." *Supply Chain Management Review* (November/December 2002), pp. 30–37.

Farrell, Diana. "Beyond Offshoring: Assess Your Company's Global Potential." *Harvard Business Review* (December 2004), pp. 82–90.

Fiksel, Joseph, Douglas Lambert, Les B. Artman, John A. Harris, and Hugh M. Share. "Environmental Excellence: The New Supply Chain Edge." *Supply Chain Management Review* (July/August 2004), pp. 50–57.

Fisher, Marshall L. "What Is the Right Supply Chain for Your Product?" *Harvard Business Review* (March/April 1997), pp. 105–116.

Fleck, Thomas. "Supplier Collaboration in Action at IBM." *Supply Chain Management Review* (March 2008), pp. 30–37.

Grey, William, Kaan Katircioglu, Dailun Shi, Sugato Bagchi, Guillermo Gallego, Mark Adelhelm, Dave Seybold, and Stavros Stefanis. "Beyond ROI." *Supply Chain Management Review* (March/April 2003), pp. 20–27.

Handfield, Robert B., and Kevin McCormack. "What You Need to Know About Sourcing from China." *Supply Chain Management Review* (September 2005), pp. 28–33.

Hindo, Brian. "Everything Old Is New Again." *BusinessWeek* (September 25, 2006), pp. 64–70.

Kulwiec, Ray. "Reverse Logistics Provides Green Benefits." *Target,* vol. 22, no. 3 (2006), pp. 11–20.

Lee, Hau L., and Corey Billington. "Managing Supply Chain Inventory: Pitfalls and Opportunities." *Sloan Management Review* (Spring 1992), pp. 65–73.

Liker, Jeffrey K., and Thomas Y. Choi. "Building Deep Supplier Relationships." *Harvard Business Review* (December 2004), pp. 104–113.

Metersky, Jeff, and J. Michael Kilgore. "How to Improve Your Inventory Deployment." *Supply Chain Management Review* (October 2004), pp. 26–32.

Miller, Jamey. "Shared Success: Working Together to Find the Value of VMI." *APICS Magazine* (November/December 2007), pp. 37–39.

Mollenkopf, Diane A., and David J. Closs. "The Hidden Value in Reverse Logistics." *Supply Chain Management Review* (July/August 2005), pp. 34–43.

Murphy-Hoye, Mary, Hau L. Lee, and James B. Rice, Jr. "A Real-World Look at RFID." *Supply Chain Management Review* (July/August 2005), pp. 18–26.

Plambeck, Erica L. "The Greening of Wal-Mart's Supply Chain." *Supply Chain Management Review* (July/August 2007), pp. 18–25.

Reeve, James M., and Mandyam M. Srinivasan. "Which Supply Chain Design Is Right for You?" *Supply Chain Management Review* (May/June 2005), p. 57.

Rothenberg, S. "Sustainability through Servicizing," *MIT Sloan Management Review*, vol. 48, no. 2 (2007), pp. 83–91.

Slone, Reuben E., John T. Mentzer, and J. Paul Dittmann. "Are you the Weakest Link in Your Supply Chain?" *Harvard Business Review* (September 2007), pp. 116–127.

Tiede, Tom, and Kay Ree Lee. "What Is an Optimal Distribution Network Strategy?" *Supply Chain Management Review* (November 2005), pp. 32–39.

Trent, Robert J. "What Everyone Needs to Know About SCM." *Supply Chain Management Review* (March 2004), pp. 52–59.

Venkatesan, Ravi. "Strategic Sourcing: To Make or Not to Make." *Harvard Business Review* (November/December 1992), pp. 98–107.

MyOMLab ASSETS

MyOMLab is a unique online set of cases, videos, decision tools, and software to further practise and apply concepts presented in this chapter.

- **Key Equations:** All the equations for this chapter can be found in one convenient location.

- **Discussion Questions:** Several questions will challenge your understanding of supply chain management and how to work with suppliers.

- **Video Cases:**

  - **Clif Bar: Supply Chain:** Explore how this firm has expanded its supply chain to provide customers with tasty energy bars.

  - **Inventory and Textbooks:** By following one product, a typical textbook, from printing through distribution to the final retail sale, different types and forms of inventory and the design of the supply chain are illustrated.

  - **Supply Chain Strategy at Starwood:** Bath towels. Televisions. Fresh produce. Uniforms. How can the supply chain manager at this hotel leverage these purchases to gain a competitive advantage?

- **Cases:**

  - *Wolf Motors.* How should John Wolf restructure the purchasing process at his newly acquired automotive dealership?

  - *Brunswick Distribution Inc.* Use the DuPont Analysis spreadsheet to determine the effects of purchasing additional warehouse facilities or investing in an improved distribution system on key business measures.

- **Virtual Tours:**

  - **Yamaha Corporation,** a manufacturer of musical instruments.

  - **Jagger Yarn,** a producer of worsted yarn.

- **Internet Exercises:** Walmart and Nokia have supply chains with different challenges to create customer value.

- **Experiential Exercise:** Sonic Distributors. You will experience the challenges of managing a distribution chain in this exciting in-class simulation.

- **OM Explorer Tutor:** OM Explorer contains a tutor program that will help you learn how to calculate inventory measures.

- **Extend LT:** Managing the supply chain at Compware Peripherals. Options to improve the cost and timely delivery of components along Compware's supply chain were being assessed.

Process Configuration

Learning Goals

After reading this chapter, you will be able to:

1. describe the four major decisions for process configuration and how they must relate to customer value.

2. describe how each of the basic forms of process structure are best suited to particular levels of customization and volume.

3. discuss how customer involvement influences the processes of service providers.

4. define capital intensity and calculate the break-even volume to compare processes of different capital intensity.

5. discuss the meaning of automation and economies of scope.

6. explain the concept of process focus and how it can contribute to better customer value.

7. analyze a process for key areas of improvement by constructing flow diagrams and process charts.

8. describe the key elements of process re-engineering and improvement.

Across the Organization

Process management is important to:

- **accounting,** which seeks better ways to perform its work processes and provides cost analyses of process improvement proposals.

- **human resources,** which melds process and job design decisions into an effective whole.

- **marketing,** which seeks better processes to perform its work and explores opportunities to expand market share by encouraging ongoing customer dialogue.

- **operations,** which designs and manages production and service processes in order to maximize customer value and enhance a firm's core competencies.

When an emergency arises, sick or injured patients and their families expect fast, high-quality service from a nearby hospital. Guelph General Hospital in Ontario, with 1200 staff providing a wide range of care, is working hard to do just that by examining and improving processes in its Emergency Department (ED). Since the hospital opened with 12 beds in 1875, medical care has changed dramatically. Today, a patient arrives on average every 11 minutes in the ED, with over 46 000 visits annually. But certain basic process steps remain: welcoming patients, assessing their condition, identifying treatment, and administering care.

Long wait times, dissatisfied patients and staff, and new provincial funding prompted the GGH to undertake a Process Improvement Program (PIP). The Chief of Emergency Medicine reflected, "We were a group of really good people trapped in a really bad process." The province established target wait times for ED: 90 percent of patients with less serious conditions should be seen, treated, and discharged or admitted within four hours. For more complex conditions, the target is twice that time.

To begin, physicians, nurses, and staff undertook process-related training. Weekly meetings provided a forum for the PIP team to explore ways to improve patient care, assess opportunities for improvement, and decide what ideas should be tested. Clear process metrics also were developed, which established the basis for both reducing the average time and decreasing variation between patients. "We have to collect the data and show them," noted one senior physician. Staff members were motivated, but graphs illustrated ongoing results, spurring continued efforts.

Both the physical space and patient processes had to be redesigned over an eight-month period. Old equipment was removed, and critical materials were carefully selected. For example, orthopaedic

Team-based efforts to improve patient care processes have cut emergency department wait times dramatically over a two-year period.

supplies, which once occupied an entire storage room, were pared down to a single cart that could be rolled to where it was needed with a patient. And restocking now took place using a standardized checklist to ensure the right materials were always available.

Focused processes were developed for both high-volume and specialized care. A rapid "See and Treat" area was created for patients suffering from relatively minor ailments such as cuts, asthma, back pain, or even some broken bones. It functions much like a walk-in clinic: a triage nurse makes an initial assessment when the patient arrives and directs him or her to a designated area. Treatment by a doctor or nurse practitioner typically occurs within 30 minutes. A nurse-manager remarked, "It's a very rapid cycle, but it's not in any way giving up quality of care. It's getting the patient to the physician a lot faster." This process now handles about one-quarter of patients who come to the ED.

Another new process is used to care for patients who require mental health treatment. The newly opened Emergency Mental Health Unit is staffed with a specialized, highly trained team, and currently cares for about 7 percent of incoming patients.

Over the past two years, patients are spending 31 percent less total time in the ED—while total patient visits rose by 2.4 percent. Nine out of ten patients with less serious conditions are being seen within 4.1 hours. "These results would not be possible without a total team effort from the staff and physicians in our inpatient units, diagnostic departments, and other support services who worked with staff in the ED to develop new ways to improve the flow of our patients," observed the GGH's president and CEO. Or, in the words of an enthusiastic front-line physician, "The change to me has been extraordinary."[1]

Essential issues in the design of processes are deciding how to make products and to provide services, the results of which are often presented to the customer as a customer benefit bundle. Deciding on processes involves many different choices in selecting human resources, equipment, and materials. Processes are involved in how marketing prepares a market analysis, how accounting bills customers, how a retail store provides services on the sales floor, and how a manufacturing plant performs its assembly operations. Process configuration affects an organization's ability to compete over the long run.

Process configuration is strategic in nature. As we saw in Chapter 1, processes should further a company's long-term competitive goals and are linked to a firm's supply chain. In developing or redesigning a firm's process configuration, managers focus on controlling such competitive priorities as quality, flexibility, time, cost, customer experience, and innovation. For example, firms can improve their ability to compete on the basis of time by examining each step of their processes and finding ways to respond more quickly to their customers. Productivity (and, therefore, cost) is affected by choices made when processes are designed. Process management is an ongoing activity, with the same principles applying to both first-time and redesign choices. Thus, the configuration of processes at Canadian hospitals, such as Guelph General Hospital, must change and evolve with new technology and patient demands.

We begin by defining four basic decisions for process configuration: customer involvement, process structure, resource flexibility, and capital-intensity. In addition, important differences between service and manufacturing firms will be highlighted. We then present a systematic approach to designing processes, using flow diagrams, process charts, and simulation. We conclude with two basic philosophies of analyzing and modifying processes—re-engineering and process improvement.

WHAT IS PROCESS MANAGEMENT?

A process involves the use of an organization's resources to provide something of value. No product can be made and no service provided without a process, and no process can exist without a product or service.

process management
The selection of the inputs, operations, work flows, and methods that transform inputs into outputs.

Process management is the design and selection of the inputs, operations, work flows, and methods that transform inputs into outputs. Input selection begins by deciding which processes are to be done in-house and which processes are to be done outside and purchased as materials and services. Process decisions also deal with the proper mix of human skills and equipment and which parts of the processes are to be performed by each. Decisions about processes must be consistent with competitive priorities and the organization's ability to obtain the resources necessary to support them.

Three principles concerning process configuration are particularly important:

1. The key to successful process design is to make choices that both make sense for the competitive situation and cohesively fit together. They should not work at cross-purposes, with one process optimized at the expense of other processes. A more effective process is one that matches major process decisions and has close strategic alignment with customer value (see Figure 3.1).

2. Although this section focuses on individual processes, they are the building blocks that eventually create the firm's whole supply chain. The cumulative effect on customer value and competitive advantage is huge.

FIGURE 3.1 *Major Decisions for Process Configuration*

Customer involvement
• Customer interaction
• Service encounter

Process structure
• Customization-volume positioning
• Customer, material, and information flows

Process Configuration

Resource flexibility
• Specialized or general-purpose technology
• Workforce and equipment

Strategic Alignment

Capital-intensity
• Economies of scale
• Degree of automation

Customer value
• Customer benefit bundle: cost, quality, time, flexibility, customer experience, and innovation

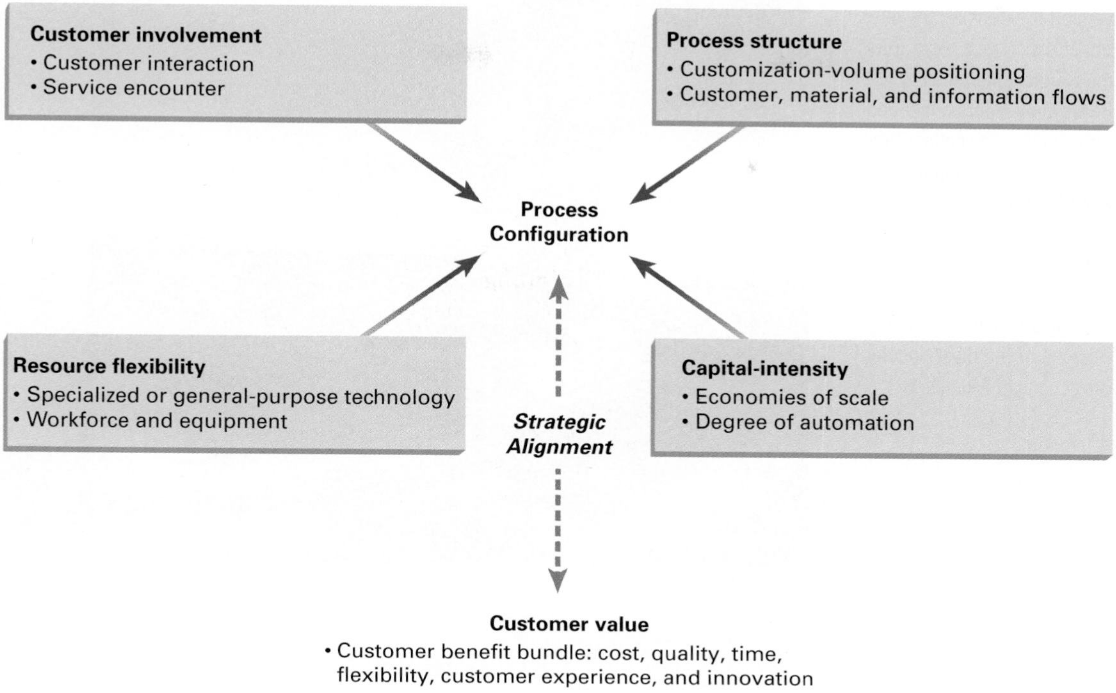

3. Whether processes in the supply chain are performed internally or by outside suppliers, managers must pay particular attention to the interfaces between processes that connect the firm to suppliers and customers (see Chapter 2, "Supply Chain Management"). Having to deal with these interfaces underscores the need for cross-functional coordination.

MAJOR PROCESS DECISIONS

Process decisions directly affect the process configuration and indirectly affect the products and services that it provides. Whether dealing with processes for offices, service providers, or manufacturers, operations managers must consider four common process decisions: *customer involvement*, *process structure*, *resource flexibility*, and *capital-intensity*. Collectively, these four act as building blocks to determine the process configuration, as depicted in Figure 3.1. However, management must work to ensure that this configuration is aligned with the firm's definition of customer value.

CUSTOMER INVOLVEMENT

customer involvement
The ways in which customers become part of the process and the extent of their participation.

A fundamental process decision deals with **customer involvement**, the ways in which customers become part of the process and the extent of their participation. This is particularly important in services, as the customer is frequently being transformed by the process. A good way to begin increasing customer involvement is by making more of the process visible to the customer. Letting customers see what normally is hidden from them is part of the service design at Harvey's, a fast-food restaurant. There you can see

BMW Welt established a venue for extending the customer experience. As a truly multi-functional building, the BMW Welt offers a location for customers to collect their new cars, to participate in a manufacturing plant tour, and to explore a world-class automotive museum, among other activities. With around two million visitors annually, it is one of the most popular attractions in Munich.

service encounter
The time during which a customer is in contact with a service process, starting from when the customer and process first meet, and finishing when the customer completes the process.

customer interaction
The extent to which the customer is present, is actively engaged, and receives personalized, face-to-face attention during the process.

workers in a sanitary and neat workplace grilling your meat, and you can pick the kinds and quantities of toppings desired as they assemble your hamburger.

To be sure, customer involvement also affects manufacturing firms, and is increasingly being used to improve competitiveness. Customers can provide detailed specifications used to customize products ranging from home furnishings to automobiles. One luxury manufacturer has taken customer involvement a significant step further. BMW has developed a service initiative, called BMW Welt ("world" in English), that offers personalized delivery service of new vehicles directly from the manufacturer to their new owners. Up to 250 vehicles every day can be picked up by customers at the manufacturing plant in Munich.

Two dimensions are important to consider for customer involvement, particularly in service processes. First, management can choose to vary the extent of customer interaction or contact during the service process (Chase, 1981). Second, and just as critical, the amount of time that the customer interacts with the process, termed the **service encounter**, can vary significantly even within an industry (Schmenner, 2004). The service encounter begins when the customer and service process first meet, and continues until the customer completes the process. However, it should be stressed that the customer need not actually be transformed in the process, as with auto repair.

There are five factors that gauge the level of **customer interaction**, each of which forms a continuum: physical presence, what is being processed, intensity, personal attention, and mode of delivery (see Figure 3.2). The first factor is the extent to which the customer is *physically present* during the process. This can be approximated as the percentage of the total time the customer is at the process, relative to the total time to complete the service. When physical presence is required, either the customer comes to the facility, or the service providers and equipment travel to meet the customer.

FIGURE 3.2   *Factors for Assessing Customer Interaction*

High interaction	Factor	Low interaction
Present	*Physical presence* ←——————————→	Absent
People	*What is processed* ←——————————→	Possessions
Active, visible	*Contact intensity* ←——————————→	Passive, out of sight
Personal	*Personal attention* ←——————————→	Impersonal
Immediate, face to face	*Method of delivery* ←——————————→	Delayed, textual

The second factor is *what is being processed*, which could include the customer, the customer's possessions, or information. People-processing services involve tangible actions to people, such as transportation on an airline or filling a cavity. Naturally, these services require a customer to be present for at least part of the service. Possession-processing services, such as pet grooming or auto repair, provide a transformation for a person. The object must be present, but the customer may not be until the service is completed. Finally, information processing collects, analyzes, and transmits data, possibly with new insights, either using facts or opinions supplied by the customer or others. Financial planning, education, and legal services are examples of such services.

The *intensity* of contact goes beyond physical presence to examine the degree of interaction between the service provider and the customer. Active contact means that the customer is very much part of the creation of the service and affects the service process itself. The process is also very visible to the customer. Passive contact means that the customer is not interacting with the process, but instead may simply be waiting in line. Passive processes can include public transportation or theatres.

A fourth factor is the extent of *personal attention* offered. Highly attentive processes tend to be more intimate, with a higher degree of trust and richer range of information exchanged. As a result, the customer often experiences the service rather than simply receiving it. Impersonal contact at times can translate into customers feeling as if they are merely numbers in the system, as may be the case when waiting in line for government services.

The final factor of customer contact is the *mode of delivery*. A high-interaction mode would use face-to-face or telephone contact (with a human operator), assuring more clarity in identifying and satisfying customer needs. Low-interaction modes might include postal mail and billboard advertising.

Customer interaction and service encounter time combine to form a wide range of service processes, even within the same industry (see Figure 3.3). At one extreme, we have services that are factory-like, such as a fast-food restaurant or cheque-clearing operation in a bank, where the service encounter is very short and interaction is low. At the other extreme, professional services, such as a gourmet restaurant or design

FIGURE 3.3   *Customer Involvement for Service Processes[2]*

by an architect, require interaction with highly skilled staff over a relatively longer period of time. Two other categories, service shop or mass service, capture either more interaction or a longer service encounter when compared to the service factory. However, both scales really form a continuous spectrum, and service processes should usually be compared relative to each other within the same industry. Overall, productivity improves as a service process shifts toward the lower-right quadrant (Schmenner, 2004).

SERVICE FACTORY. The service factory has low customer interaction and a short service encounter. The work tends to be standardized and routine, with line flows from one operation to another until the service is completed. An example is the monthly production of client fund balance reports for a mutual fund company. The process doesn't vary, is repeated frequently, and requires very little attention. Because these processes usually occur behind the scenes and are not visible to the customer, the term "back office" is sometimes used. The primary emphasis here is often cost efficiency, and, not surprisingly, these processes also tend to be highly automated.

SERVICE SHOP. The service shop tends to have a higher level of customer interaction than the service factory because the service must be at least partially customized to meet the unique needs of individuals or small groups (i.e., small batches). Workstations and equipment tend to be organized by task with various routings between them. The work is reasonably complex, possibly involving skilled professionals for at least part of the process, such as a hospital emergency room or auto repair, but the overall time for the service encounter remains relatively short. Moreover, some steps may be performed ahead of time (e.g., preparation of medical instruments), while other steps, such as the doctor–patient diagnosis, must be tailored to the individual. Thus, some efficiency may be sacrificed to improve overall effectiveness in meeting individual needs.

MASS SERVICE. In contrast to the service shop, mass services tend to have much less interaction to improve efficiency and cost. As a result, the service encounter tends to be longer with little customization. Also, to improve productivity, many mass services, such as education and public transit, handle large groups of customers simultaneously (i.e., large batches). Customers follow the same ordering of steps through the process, although the particular product or service may vary. Web-based retailing is typically a mass service, with relatively little interaction with customers (although new designs and customer tracking capabilities are increasing this process), and additional time required for the service encounter. While different products are purchased by customers, they all follow the same basic steps: visit the retail Web site, search for merchandise, add to shopping cart, make payment, assemble and ship the order, and receive delivery.

PROFESSIONAL SERVICE. Finally, both high customer interaction and long service encounters characterize a professional service, with the service provider working directly with the customer. The service is usually adjusted and tailored to individual customer needs, with a wide variety of options. The process is complex, and steps may be followed in a flexible order to suit individual requirements. Rather than focus on low cost, professional services emphasize effectiveness, including high quality, timely responsiveness, and flexibility. Examples include law offices and tax accountants.

INTERNET-BASED INVOLVEMENT. The Internet, including such technologies as Web browsers, search engines, and e-mail, has added a rich new mode of customer interaction. Collectively, these technologies offer the potential to greatly expand the scope, flexibility, location, and variety in the service or manufacturing process. Internet-based customer involvement offers process managers much more than simply automating the buying and selling of goods electronically. Firms can significantly improve their processes to yield competitive advantages by cutting costs, improving quality, and increasing speed and flexibility.

At first glance, managers might be tempted to think that Web-enabled processes only work to increase customer involvement by reducing the time for the service encounter, by expanding access and variety, and by increasing customization. However, managers can use the Web to either increase *or* decrease the level of customer involvement depending on the service strategy. Processes that traditionally had high-contact modes, such as telephone contact with a staff member or physical presence in a retail branch, can be altered to lower Web-based interaction. Banking is one such service, where customers can now do virtually all of their banking over the Internet rather than in a physical bank branch. However, other services, such as billing and monthly statements, have been moved from a low-contact mode with slow postal mailings to the immediate delivery of e-mail statements.

PROCESS STRUCTURE

process structure
A process decision that determines whether resources are organized around products or processes.

The second significant process decision that a manager makes in designing a well-functioning process is the **process structure**, which determines whether resources are organized around products or processes. The structure is strongly influenced by the competitive priorities (see Chapter 1, "Creating Customer Value Through Operations") given to the process. However, what is emphasized for the overall facility or product line is not necessarily what should be emphasized for each of the processes or subprocesses that contribute to creating the customer benefit bundle. The manager

FIGURE 3.4   *The Influence of Customization and Volume on Process Structure*

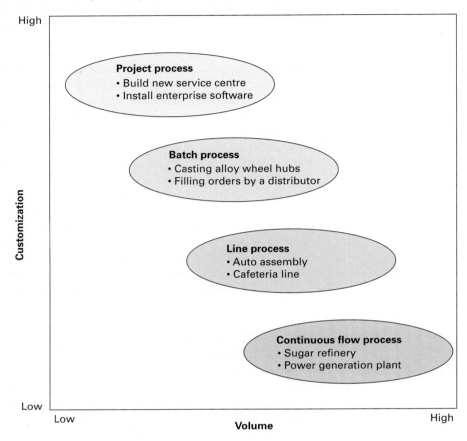

has four basic process structures, which form a continuum, to choose from: project, batch, line, and continuous flow.

Figure 3.4 shows that these types of processes are found in service and manufacturing organizations alike. The fundamental message in Figure 3.4 is that the best choice for a process structure depends on the volume and degree of customization required of the process. One structure might apply to an entire process or just one subprocess within it. For example, one of a service facility's processes might best be characterized as a batch process and another process as a line process. Because our definition of a process in Chapter 1 provides a basic understanding of processes in general, we now concentrate on the differences among the four process structures.

project process
A process characterized by a high degree of job customization, the large scope of each project, and the release of substantial resources once a project is completed.

PROJECT PROCESS. Examples of a project process are building a shopping centre, installing new enterprise resource planning (ERP) software, planning a major event, running a political campaign, putting together a comprehensive training program, doing management consulting work, or developing a new technology or product. A **project process** is characterized by a high degree of job customization, the large scope of each project, and the release of substantial resources once a project is completed (see Chapter 8, "Managing Projects").

A project process lies at the high-customization, low-volume end of the process-choice continuum. The sequence of operations and the process involved in each are unique to the project, creating one-of-a-kind products or services made specifically to customer order. Although some projects may look similar, each is unique. Project processes are valued on the basis of their capabilities to do certain kinds of work rather than on their ability to produce specific products or services. Projects tend to be complex, take a long time, and be large. Many interrelated tasks must be completed, requiring close coordination. Resources needed for a project are assembled and then released for further use after the project is finished. Projects typically make heavy use of certain skills and resources at particular stages and then have little use for them the rest of the time. With a project process, work flows are redefined with each new project. Professional services (Figure 3.3) often use a project process, or alternatively, a batch process, discussed next.

BATCH PROCESS. Next on the continuum of process structure is the **batch process**. Batches can range in size from very small to much larger in size. Smaller batch processes, sometimes termed a *job shop* in manufacturing, include machining a metal casting for a customized order, providing emergency room care, handling special-delivery mail, and making customized cabinets. In contrast, larger batch processes might include scheduling air travel for a tour group, making components that feed an assembly line, processing a group of similar mortgage loans, and manufacturing large earthmoving equipment.

The batch process creates the flexibility needed to produce a variety of products or services in significant quantities. Customization is relatively high and volume for any one product or service is low. However, volumes are not as low as for a project process, which by definition does not produce in quantity. For manufacturing, products in small batches tend to be produced as needed and not ahead of time. The specific needs of the next customer are unknown, and the timing of repeat orders from the same customer is unpredictable.

A batch process tends to have resources grouped or organized by task rather than allocating them to specific products and services. Thus, equipment and workers capable of certain types of work are located together, and these resources are more flexible than the line process (described next) and handle various tasks. Because of customization, parts, orders, and customers will follow different routings between individual process steps, as needed.

As batches become larger, the service and product range created by a batch process will decrease, and dominant routings emerge between process steps. Also, the greater volumes allow some components or products to be processed in advance or held in stock to improve process speed. Variety can be achieved by assembling standard components as customer orders arrive.

LINE PROCESS. Products created by a line process include automobiles, appliances, consumer electronics, and toys. Services based on a line process are fast-food restaurants and cafeterias. A **line process** lies between the batch and continuous processes on the continuum; volumes are high and products or services are standardized, which allows resources to be organized around a product or service. There are line flows, with little inventory held between operations. Each operation performs the same process over and over, with little variability in the products or services provided. Production, assembly, or processing often is not directly linked to a specific customer order, as is the case with project and small batch processes. Services factories (Figure 3.3) also tend to be structured as a line process.

In some processes, flexible automation or modular product designs allow for some degree of customization as the service or good is being produced. For example, firms

batch process A process with the flexibility needed to produce a wide variety of services and products in small to moderate quantities. Resources such as workers and equipment are usually grouped by task.

line process A process with linear movement of materials, information, or customers from one operation to the next according to a fixed sequence. Volumes are relatively high, allowing resources to be organized around standardized services and products.

selling products online often allow for custom engraving (e.g., Apple's iPod) or gift cards to be inserted before shipping, in what is otherwise a high-volume distribution process. Greater variety is possible by careful control of the addition of standard options to the main product or service. Adding this automation allows the line process to shift upward on Figure 3.4.

CONTINUOUS FLOW PROCESS. Examples of companies that use continuous flow processes are petroleum refineries, chemical plants, and plants making beer, steel, and food. Firms with such facilities are also referred to as the *process industry*. An electric generation plant represents one of the few continuous processes found in the service sector. A **continuous flow process** is the extreme end of high-volume, standardized production with rigid line flows. Its name derives from the way materials move through the process. Usually, one primary material, such as a liquid, gas, or powder, moves without stopping through the facility. The processes seem more like separate entities than a series of connected operations. The process is often capital-intensive and operated round the clock to maximize utilization and to avoid expensive shutdowns and startups.

continuous flow process
The extreme end of high-volume, standardized production with rigid line flows.

#slide → beer & steel don't belong under continuous

COMBINING CUSTOMER INVOLVEMENT AND PROCESS STRUCTURE

What is effective customer involvement or process structure in one circumstance may provide little customer value in another. A quick, streamlined process with little customer interaction might work very well for a fast-food restaurant, yet be totally inappropriate for a five-star restaurant, where customers seek a leisurely dining experience with very attentive servers. Further, the right level of customer involvement for servers at a restaurant might be totally inappropriate for a process back in the restaurant's business office. To get insights, we must jointly consider both customer involvement and the process structure, and also recognize key contextual variables associated with the process. Only by doing so can we recognize appropriate patterns and see how decisions should be grouped together.

FRONT OFFICE. A front-office process has high customer involvement, with the process being directly visible to the internal or external customer. Because this involvement usually results in customizing the service or good, the specific sequence and type of activities in the process can vary significantly. Work flows tend to be flexible, and they vary from one customer to the next. The work involves many exceptions to the usual work pattern. The customer has more choice in how each step of the service process is carried out and sometimes even where the service encounter occurs. Given this variety, a project or batch

The Ritz-Carlton Hotel Company targets luxury travellers, and so puts huge emphasis on customer experience, quality, and flexibility. Its sophisticated processes allow it to manage details as few other hotels do, regardless of customer special requests. These associates at the front desk epitomize a front office, because the customers are present, take an active part in creating the service, receive personal attention, and have face-to-face contact.

process structure is usually used, with the batch size possibly being a single customer. Examples include a patient moving through an emergency room process, or a client working with an architectural firm to design and construct a new building.

HYBRID OFFICE. A hybrid office process tends to be used when many of the five factors of customer involvement (Figure 3.2) are at a moderate level, or perhaps high on some, and low on others. Because customer interaction is lower, some of the steps occur without the customer present, or behind the scenes. Also, many customers use a similar process, with some options available from which the customer chooses. Work flow progresses from one station or activity to the next, with some dominant paths. As a result, process structure tends to either batch or line processes. For example, businesses offering a fast oil change, such as Jiffy Lube, allow for some choices from a standard list of options, and the vehicle moves through a line-like process while the customer waits nearby.

BACK OFFICE. A back-office process has low customer involvement, and takes place out of sight of the customer. Minimal amounts of customization are still possible, but the work is standardized and routine, with a line or continuous process structure. Although service firms tend to use either front- or hybrid-office processes, some subprocesses are back-office processes. Preparing the monthly client fund balance reports in the financial services industry is a good example. The process is almost completely standardized and repeated frequently. Not surprisingly, most processes in manufacturing firms are back-office, although the previous example of BMW Welt illustrates the combination of a back-office assembly of automobiles on a line process with a front-office customer service process.

LINKING PROCESS STRUCTURE TO INVENTORY POLICIES

Depending on the process structure, inventory can play a critical role in the delivery of goods and some services. Manufacturing firms, with a relatively low level of customer involvement, use inventory in their processes to adjust their responsiveness to customers. Service firms also create and use inventory to satisfy customer needs, such as different types of prepared foods in cafeterias.

make-to-stock policy
A policy that involves holding items in inventory for immediate delivery, thereby minimizing customer delivery times.

mass production A term sometimes used in the popular press for a line process that uses the make-to-stock strategy.

assemble-to-order
A policy for producing a wide variety of goods or services from relatively few subassemblies and components after customer orders are received.

MAKE-TO-STOCK POLICY. Firms that hold items in inventory for immediate delivery, thereby minimizing customer delivery times, use a **make-to-stock policy.** This approach is feasible for standardized products with high volumes and reasonably accurate forecasts. It is the inventory policy of choice for line- or continuous-flow processes. For example, a company producing a sensor for the transmission of a Toyota Camry would have enough volume to operate a production line specifically for that sensor, and would carry a stock of the finished product for the scheduled shipments to the factory. Other examples of goods and services produced with a make-to-stock policy include garden tools, electronic components, soft drinks, chemicals, and cafeterias.

Combining a line process with the make-to-stock strategy is sometimes called **mass production.** It is what the popular press commonly envisions as the classical manufacturing process, because the environment is stable and predictable, with workers repeating narrowly defined tasks with low divergence.

ASSEMBLE-TO-ORDER POLICY. The **assemble-to-order** policy is an approach to producing a wide variety of goods or services from relatively few parts and components until the customer is present, or after a specific order is received. Typical competitive priorities are variety and fast delivery times. For example, in a pizzeria, uncooked pizza dough is prepared in advance, but the pizza is then assembled and baked after a specific customer order arrives.

In manufacturing firms, standardized parts and subassemblies are fabricated in high volumes, and held in inventory for later assembly. After a customer order is received, the assembly processes create the product from standardized parts. Alternatives, such as stocking finished products, would be economically prohibitive, because numerous possible options make forecasting inaccurate. In contrast, make-to-order from basic materials would force the customer to wait too long. For example, a manufacturer of upscale upholstered furniture can produce hundreds of a particular style of sofa, with no two alike, to meet customers' selections of fabric and colour of wood finish.

mass customization An assemble-to-order policy combined with flexible processes generates customized products or services in high volumes at reasonably low costs.

MASS CUSTOMIZATION. Using an assemble-to-order policy in high volume markets yields **mass customization**, whereby a firm's flexible processes generate customized products or services at reasonably low cost. A key to being a successful mass customizer is using flexible automated assembly technology and a modular product design. Customization that differentiates a product or service for a specific customer for specific orders typically is delayed until the latest possible moment. Doing so allows the greatest application of standard modules of the product or service before specific customization. For example, Lands' End (www.landsend.com) can create a customized dress shirt for men based on the customer completing a brief online profile by answering a few simple questions regarding things such as height, weight, and shoe size. Using that information, along with a database containing millions of detailed sets of body measurements, an individually cut-and-sewn shirt is produced and shipped.

postponement A tactic used by assemble-to-order and mass-customization firms that refers to delaying the customizing of a product or service until the last possible moment.

channel assembly The process of using members of the distribution channel to put together components as if they were assembly stations in the factory.

POSTPONEMENT. Assemble-to-order and mass-customization firms use a tactic called **postponement**, which involves delaying the customization of a product or service as long as possible (either within the firm or across the supply chain). Mass-customized products are assembled from a variety of standard components according to the specifications from a customer. Hewlett-Packard (HP) provides a good example of mass customization. HP postpones assembly of the printer with the country-specific power supply and packaging of the appropriate manuals until the last link in the process—the distributor in the region where the printer is being delivered. If distributors provide final assembly, it is termed **channel assembly**.

make-to-order policy A policy used by firms that produce goods or services to customer specifications in low volumes.

MAKE-TO-ORDER POLICY. Firms that make products or provide services to customer specifications in low volumes tend to use the **make-to-order policy**, using either project or small batch processes. With this policy, you can think of the firm as selling a collection of processes, which in turn can be used in many different ways to satisfy the unique needs of customers. This policy requires a high degree of flexibility, which is a major competitive priority for these firms. Building custom homes and providing dental crowns for tooth replacement are examples of make-to-order firms.

resource flexibility The ease with which employees and equipment can handle a wide variety of products, output levels, duties, and functions.

RESOURCE FLEXIBILITY

The choices that management makes concerning competitive priorities determine the degree of flexibility required of a company's resources—its employees, facilities, and equipment. **Resource flexibility** is the ease with which employees and equipment can handle a wide variety of products, output levels, duties, and functions. For example, when a process handles products and services with short life cycles or high customization, employees need to perform a broad range of tasks, and equipment must be general-purpose. Otherwise, resource utilization will be too low for economical operation.

flexible workforce
A workforce whose members are capable of doing many tasks, either at their own workstations or as they move from one workstation to another.

WORKFORCE. Operations managers must decide whether to have a flexible workforce. Members of a **flexible workforce** are capable of doing many tasks, either at their own workstations or as they move from one workstation to another. However, such flexibility often comes at a cost, requiring greater skills and, thus, more training and education. Nevertheless, benefits can be large: worker flexibility can be one of the best ways to achieve reliable customer service and alleviate capacity bottlenecks. Resource flexibility helps to absorb the feast-or-famine workloads in individual operations that are caused by low-volume production, varied routings, and fluid scheduling.

MANAGERIAL PRACTICE
eBay

Most manufacturers do not have to contend with customers waltzing around their shop floors, showing up intermittently and unannounced. Such customer involvement can introduce considerable variability, disrupting carefully designed processes. Costs and quality can be adversely affected. While some manufacturers have similar challenges (each process does have at least one customer), extensive customer contact and involvement is business as usual for many processes of service providers. Moreover, customers at restaurants or rental car agencies are directly involved in performing the processes.

How much should customers be involved in a process, so as to provide timely delivery and consistent quality, and at reasonable cost? Various ways are available—some accommodate customer-introduced variability and some reduce it. eBay illustrates one way to accommodate variability. An online auction house, eBay has high variability in the number of items displayed by one group of customers—those that supply a seemingly endless number of articles—and also in the bidding behaviour of another group—those that buy. eBay's customers also vary dramatically in their capabilities, some with considerable online experience, and others needing more hand-holding. Fortunately, its automated processes can adapt to these changes, and continue to provide value by linking buyers to sellers.

In total, eBay connects hundreds of millions of people around the world every day. It has a global presence in 39 markets, with gross merchandise volume of $60 billion in more than

At any given time eBay has approximately 113 million listings worldwide, and yet its workforce consists of just 15 000 employees. The explanation? Customers do most of the work in eBay's buying and selling processes. Here a customer prepares items for shipping from sales on his eBay account.

50 000 categories—and with only 16 400 employees. This relatively small workforce is possible in the face of customer-induced variability, because its customers perform virtually all of the selling and buying processes through the eBay Web site. When the customer is responsible for much of the work, the right labour is provided at the right moment.[3]

The type of workforce required also depends on the need for volume flexibility. When conditions allow for a smooth, steady rate of output, the likely choice is a permanent workforce that expects regular full-time employment. If the process is subject to hourly, daily, or seasonal peaks and valleys in demand, the use of part-time or temporary employees to supplement a smaller core of full-time employees may be the best solution. However, this approach may not be practical if knowledge and skill requirements are too high for a temporary worker to grasp quickly. Controversy continues to grow over the practice of replacing full-time workers with temporary or part-time workers.

EQUIPMENT. When products or services have a short life cycle and a high degree of customization, low volumes mean that process managers should select flexible, general-purpose equipment. Figure 3.5 illustrates this relationship by showing the total cost lines for two different types of equipment that can be chosen for a process. Each line represents the total annual cost of the process at different volume levels. It is the sum of fixed costs and variable costs. When volumes are low (because customization is high), process 1 is the better choice. It calls for inexpensive general-purpose equipment, which keeps investment in equipment low and makes fixed costs (F_1) small. Its variable unit cost is high (v_1), which gives its total cost line a relatively steep slope. However, volumes are not high enough for the high variable costs to outweigh the benefit of low fixed costs.

Conversely, process 2 is the better choice when volumes are high and customization is low. Its advantage is low variable unit cost (v_2), as reflected in the flatter total cost line. This efficiency is possible when customization is low because the equipment can be designed for a narrow range of products or tasks. Its disadvantage is high equipment investment and, thus, high fixed costs (F_2). When the annual volume produced is high enough, spreading these fixed costs over more units produced, the advantage of low variable costs more than compensates for the high fixed costs.

CAPITAL-INTENSITY

capital-intensity The mix of equipment and human skill in a process.

For either the design of a new process or the redesign of an existing one, an operations manager must determine the amount of capital-intensity required. **Capital-intensity** is the mix of equipment and human skills in a process; the greater the relative cost of equipment, the greater the capital-intensity. As the capabilities of technology increase

FIGURE 3.5   *Relationship Between Process Costs and Product Volume*

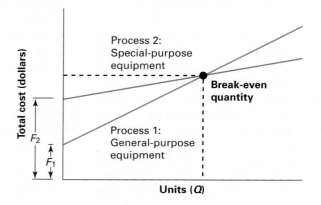

and its costs decrease, managers face an ever-widening range of choices, from operations utilizing very little automation to those requiring task-specific equipment and very little human intervention. **Automation** is a system, process, or piece of equipment that is self-acting and self-regulating. Although automation is often thought to be necessary to gain competitive advantage, it has both advantages and disadvantages. Thus, the automation decision requires careful examination.

automation A system, process, or piece of equipment that is self-acting and self-regulating.

One advantage of automation is that adding capital-intensity can significantly increase productivity and improve quality. One big disadvantage of capital-intensity can be the prohibitive investment cost for low-volume operations. Generally, capital-intensive operations must have high utilization to be justifiable. Also, automation does not always align with an organization's competitive priorities. If a firm offers a unique product or high-quality service, competitive priorities may indicate the need for skilled servers, hand labour, and individual attention rather than new technology.

Look again at Figure 3.5. Financially, this decision about capital-intensity involves a trade-off between fixed and variable costs. By comparing total cost, we can identify the volume at which process 1 is preferred over process 2. Process 1, which uses general-purpose equipment, is not capital-intensive and, therefore, has small fixed costs, F_1. Customer orders can be processed in smaller batches. In contrast, process 2 has greater fixed costs, F_2, and involves more continuous processing. However, process 1 has much higher variable costs, v_1, than process 2 with variable costs, v_2, as indicated by the steeper slope of the total cost line. Thus, the total cost to produce Q (annual quantity) for process 1 is $F_1 + v_1 Q$, and for process 2 is $F_2 + v_2 Q$. To find the annual break-even quantity, we set the two cost functions equal and solve for Q:

$$F_1 + v_1 Q = F_2 + v_2 Q$$

$$Q = \frac{F_1 - F_2}{v_2 - v_1}$$

[handwritten: ×break even will be on exam]

[handwritten: → Break even quantity.]

| EXAMPLE 3.1 | *Break-Even Analysis for Two Process Configurations* |

[handwritten: ① Voting terminal ② vote card.]

A county elections officer is considering installing new voting equipment to replace antiquated equipment. Two options are being considered. The first uses the latest in voting technology with electronic voting terminals. Cast ballots could be processed, checked, and tallied continuously using terminals similar to an ATM. The officer estimates the fixed cost for all the necessary terminals is $131 500 and variable costs total $0.20 per ballot. The second, more traditional process technology uses a centralized optical vote-card reader to process the ballots in a single batch. Ballots would be shipped to the central location from individual polling stations after closing. Estimated costs of this option are $46 800 for new equipment, and $2.40 per vote cast. The officer expects that, on average, a total of 25 000 ballots will be cast in various local, provincial, and federal elections in the county each year.

What is the break-even quantity?

SOLUTION

The formula for the break-even quantity yields:

$$Q = \frac{F_1 - F_2}{v_2 - v_1}$$

$$= \frac{131\ 500 - 46\ 800}{2.40 - 0.20} = 38\ 500$$

[handwritten: $V = \frac{F}{P-C}$
V = break even volume
F = annual FC
P = Rev per unit.
C = cost per unit.]

where:

$$F_1 = \text{Fixed cost for process 1}$$
$$v_1 = \text{Variable cost per unit for process 1}$$
$$F_2 = \text{Fixed cost for process 2}$$
$$v_2 = \text{Variable cost per unit for process 2}$$

The break-even quantity is 38 500 cast ballots. As the 25 000-vote forecast is less than this amount, the centralized optical vote-card reader is preferred. Only if the county expected to have more than 38 500 ballots cast each year would the use of electronic voting terminals be better financially. However, other factors to consider might include monitoring vote quality (including overvoting, in which too many candidates are selected on the ballot), flexibility, and ease of completion.

Decision Point The elections officer chose the traditional process technology with a centralized optical vote-card reader and batch processing. Voter education for proper completion of the ballots was also implemented. A deciding factor was that the annual volume was well below the 38 500-ballot break-even point.

FIXED AUTOMATION. Manufacturers use two types of automation: fixed and flexible (or programmable). Particularly appropriate for line and continuous process choices, **fixed automation** produces one type of part or product in a fixed sequence of simple operations. Until the mid-1980s, many automobile plants were dominated by fixed automation—and some still are. Chemical processing plants and oil refineries also utilize this type of automation.

Operations managers favour fixed automation when demand volumes are high, product designs are stable, and product life cycles are long. These conditions compensate for the process's two primary drawbacks: large initial investment cost and relative inflexibility. However, fixed automation maximizes efficiency and yields the lowest variable cost per unit if volumes are high.

FLEXIBLE AUTOMATION. **Flexible (or programmable) automation** can be changed easily to handle various products. The ability to reprogram machines is useful for both low-customization and high-customization processes. In the case of high customization, a machine that makes a variety of products in small batches can be programmed to alternate between products. When a machine has been dedicated to a particular product or family of products, as in the case of low customization and a line flow, and the product is at the end of its life cycle, the machine can simply be reprogrammed with a new sequence of operations for a new product. However, such flexibility comes at a price, as the operating speed might be slower or the capital cost higher than for fixed automation.

Canada is one of the industrialized-world leaders in applying flexible automation, on the basis of robots per capita. Throughout the 1990s, much of this technology in North America was applied in the automotive sector. However, an increasing number of applications have been developed in the

fixed automation A manufacturing process that produces one type of part or product in a fixed sequence of simple operations.

flexible (or programmable) automation A manufacturing process that can be changed easily to handle various products.

A robotic arm places lenses on a tray for distribution. Robots are ideally suited for routine tasks that require precise movement, and their rate can often be adjusted to match that of other process activities.

food, pharmaceutical, and electronics industries, particularly with materials handling (Guidoni, 2000). For example, ABB Flexible Automation offers systems that can palletize loads to specific customer orders, which reduces the cost of distribution. Another new direction is laser cutting and trimming. Regardless of the application, the president of FANUC Robotics Canada stressed, "The critical element is understanding the process flow."

ECONOMIES OF SCOPE

economies of scope
Economies that reflect the ability to produce multiple products more cheaply in combination than separately.

Note that capital-intensity and resource flexibility tend to vary inversely in Figure 3.6. If capital-intensity is high, resource flexibility is low. In certain types of manufacturing operations, such as machining and assembly, programmable automation breaks this inverse relationship between resource flexibility and capital-intensity. It makes possible both high capital-intensity and high resource flexibility, creating economies of scope. **Economies of scope** reflect the ability to produce multiple products more cheaply in combination than separately. In such situations, two conflicting competitive priorities—customization and low cost—become more compatible. However, taking advantage of economies of scope requires that a family of parts or products have enough collective volume to utilize equipment fully.

Economies of scope also apply to service processes. Consider, for example, Disney's approach to the Internet. When the company's managers entered the volatile Internet world, their businesses were only weakly tied together. They wanted plenty of freedom to evolve in and even shape emerging markets. They wanted flexibility and agility, not control, in these fast-moving markets. Disney's Infoseek business, in fact, was not even fully owned. However, once its Internet markets became more crystallized, managers at Disney moved to reap the benefits of economies of scope. They aggressively linked their Internet processes with one another and with other parts of Disney. A flexible technology that handles many services together can be less expensive than handling each one separately, particularly when the markets are not too volatile.

STRATEGIC ALIGNMENT

The process manager should understand how these four process decisions—process structure, customer involvement, resource flexibility, and capital-intensity—must tie together, so as to spot ways of improving poorly designed processes. Two common elements in these relationships are volume and product/service variety, which in turn are derived from an underlying operations strategy.

Figure 3.6 summarizes the general relationship between volume and process decisions, and applies to all operations. Overall, these relationships illustrate general tendencies rather than rigid prescriptions, and provide a way of understanding how process decisions can be linked coherently. Naturally, for services, customer involvement is particularly critical.

High volumes typically translate into all of the following:

1. *A line or continuous flow process.* Standardized flows are preferred, with customers or products moving through a consistent series of steps. Each customer gets the same basic service, and service specifications are tightly controlled. Standardized products increase volumes and process repeatability. One example is the front-end process of a cafeteria line, where the customer moves from one station to the next, making food selections and then paying at the end of the line. Other examples include processes in public transportation; auto assembly; backroom processes in banking, insurance, and postal service; oil refining; and airport baggage handling.

FIGURE 3.6 *Volume and the Major Process Decisions*

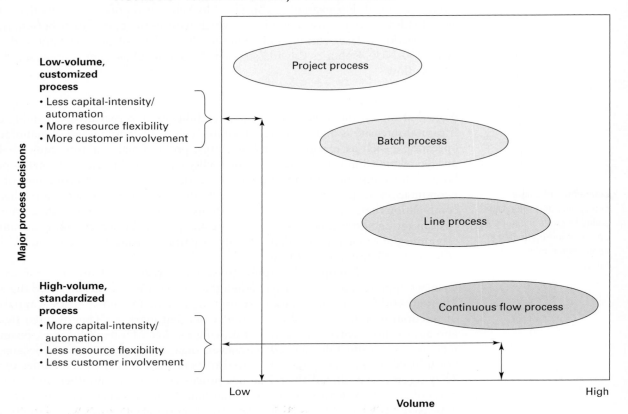

2. *Less customer involvement.* For services, customers may not be present because the process has little variation, as with the backroom operations of financial institutions. Less contact occurs between employees and customers, and customized orders and requests are difficult to accommodate. If the customer is involved in the process, it is in performing self-service activities to get lower prices or in selecting from standard product options rather than getting unique customized treatment.

3. *Less resource flexibility.* High process volumes and repetition create less need for resource flexibility, which is usually more expensive. Instead, specialization and simplification is possible, which reduces capital and labour costs. Resources are dedicated to each standardized product or service, and personnel can focus on a narrower set of tasks repeated more frequently.

4. *More capital-intensity and automation.* High volumes justify large fixed costs and increase repetition, which can improve the efficiency of operations. Capital-intensity is high, with much less labour content needed to deliver the product. Of course, there can be exceptions to always automating processes for standardized high-volume goods and services. Examples are wholesalers and full-service retailers. In such cases, capital-intensity is low because the nature of the work being done makes it difficult to achieve automation for these processes.

Low volumes typically mean all of the following:

1. *A project or small batch process.* Customized treatment means a low-volume process, and each customer requires different changes in the process itself. Examples are processes for management consultants, physicians, gourmet restaurants, and construction. Each customer has individual needs that must be understood and accounted for in the process.

2. *More customer involvement.* Front-line employees interact more frequently with customers, often on a one-to-one basis, to understand and diagnose each customer's individual needs. They must be able to relate well to their customers, not merely possess technical skills. Exercising judgment as they provide new or unique products and services—often termed "solutions"—is commonplace.

3. *More resource flexibility.* Employees and equipment must be trained and able to handle new or unique services as demand occurs and changes. Thus, they must be versatile and flexible and able to handle a wide array of customer requests. Skill levels are high and the scope of activities is enlarged, often with a great deal of operating discretion.

4. *Less capital-intensity and automation.* Because of an almost infinite variability of problems and customer specifications, the process is difficult to automate, although flexible automation might be possible. Generally, capital-intensity is low, which means high labour-intensity. However, exceptions occur if particular equipment is needed regardless of the volume (e.g., medical diagnostics). With specialized processes, such as product design and health care, employee skill levels are very high and expensive.

Because these are general tendencies, exceptions can be found. But these relationships provide a way of understanding how process decisions can be linked coherently.

REGAINING FOCUS

As firms grow, managers often appear willing to endure the additional complexity that comes with size. New products or services are added to a facility in the name of better utilizing fixed costs and keeping everything under the same roof. The result is a jumble of competitive priorities, process choices, and technologies. In the effort to do everything, nothing is done well.

FOCUSED FACTORIES. Canada's Palliser Furniture, Venmar Ventilation, and Magna International, the U.S.'s Hewlett-Packard and SC Johnson, Japan's Ricoh and Mitsubishi, and Britain's Imperial Chemical Industries PLC are some of the firms that have created **focused factories**, splitting large plants that produced all the company's products into several specialized smaller plants. The theory is that narrowing the range of demands on a facility will lead to better performance because management can concentrate on fewer tasks and lead a workforce toward a single goal. In some situations, a plant that used to produce all the components of a product and assemble them may split into one that produces the components and one that assembles them so that each can focus on its own individual process technology.

focused factories The result of a firm's splitting large plants that produced all the company's products into several specialized smaller plants.

FOCUS BY PROCESS SEGMENTS. A facility's process often can neither be characterized nor actually designed for one set of competitive priorities and one process choice. At a services facility, some parts of the process might seem like a job process and other

**plants within plants
(PWPs)** Different opera-
tions within a facility with
individual competitive priorities, processes, and
workforces under the
same roof.

parts like a line process. Such arrangements can be effective, provided that sufficient focus is given to each process. **Plants within plants (PWPs)** are different operations within a facility with individual competitive priorities, processes, and workforces under the same roof. Boundaries for PWPs may be established by physically separating subunits or simply by revising organizational relationships. At each PWP, customization, capital-intensity, volume, and other relationships are crucial and must be complementary. The advantages of PWPs are fewer layers of management, greater ability to rely on team problem solving, and shorter lines of communication among departments.

FOCUSED SERVICE OPERATIONS. Service industries have also implemented the concepts of focus, PWPs, and cells. For example, Toronto's Rogers Centre has executive boxes with unique services and equipment that operate within the same facility and for the same entertainment events as customers purchasing basic tickets. Air Canada also differentiates between first- and economy-class customers with particular service processes. Finally, specialty retailers, such as The Gap, have opened stores that have smaller, more accessible spaces. These focused facilities have generally chipped away at the business of large department stores. Using the same philosophy, some department stores are focusing on specific customers or products, with remodelled interiors creating the effect of many small boutiques under one roof.

PROCESS ANALYSIS

The four main process decisions encompass broad, strategic issues. Process analysis is the documentation and detailed understanding of how work is performed and how it can be redesigned. In essence, we begin with defining our competitive priorities and identifying new opportunities, and end with implementing a revised process. However, it doesn't stop there, as the steps are repeated to create a cycle of continual improvement.

A SYSTEMATIC APPROACH

1. Describe the strategic aspects of the process. How is customer value defined and what is the customer benefit bundle? What are the competitive priorities, operations strategy, and major process decisions that apply?

2. Identify the inputs, outputs, and customers of the process. Make a comprehensive list so that the value-added capability of the process can be evaluated. Consider both internal and external customers.

metrics Measures that
can be used to assess the
performance of a process
and the steps within it.

3. Identify key performance metrics for the process. Performance **metrics**, often termed *measures*, should be specifically tied to dimensions of customer value. Possible performance measures could be multiple measures of quality, customer satisfaction, throughput time, cost, errors, safety, environmental measures, on-time delivery, flexibility, and the like.

4. Document the process. Use "as is" for an ongoing process, and "as proposed" for a process being designed for the first time. A manager or team can use several basic questions to drive this data collection:
   a. What is being done?
   b. When is it being done?
   c. Who is doing it?
   d. Where is it being done?
   e. How is it being done?

Important signals that indicate there are critical problems in particular areas for an ongoing process include one or more of the following characteristics:

- Customers are dissatisfied with the value of the services or goods that they receive from the process.
- The process introduces too many quality problems or errors.
- The process is slow in responding to customers.
- The process is costly.
- The process is often a bottleneck (see Chapter 4, "Capacity"), with work piling up waiting to go through it.
- The process creates pollution or waste, or adds little value.

Collect information on each part of the process and for each of the performance measures selected in step 3. Whenever possible, benchmark against similar processes within or external to the firm to expose areas of substandard performance.

5. Critically question how the process might create better customer value. Metrics provide critical information to identify gaps between actual and desired performance. To help with this open-ended evaluation, managers should push to answer the following questions:

- Why is the process even being done?
- Why is it being done where it is being done?
- Why is it being done when it is being done?

Such questioning often leads to creative answers and breakthroughs in process design. Once again, benchmarking against processes elsewhere, either inside or outside the organization, can pay off with new ideas and substantial improvements.

6. Evaluate the changes and implement those that are expected to yield the best results for the metrics selected in step 3. Later on, after the process has been changed, check to see whether the changes worked. Finally, return to step 1 as needed.

DOCUMENT THE PROCESS

Documenting the process requires a detailed understanding of all of the tasks that happen within a process, including both value-added and non–value-added activities. Doing so allows the manager to "lift the lid" and peer inside how an organization does

McDonald's uses mystery shoppers to evaluate its stores. It also sends operations "emissaries" to its stores to help managers fine-tune their processes, while revising processes and its supply chain to be more environmentally friendly.

its work. They see how a process operates at any level of detail, and how well it is performing. Trying to construct one of these diagrams or charts also may reveal that there is no established process! When breaking down the process into the specific steps performed, the degree of customer involvement and process complexity become much clearer.

Three techniques are effective for documenting and evaluating processes: flow diagrams, process charts, and simulation. Later, we will expand these three techniques to consider additional tools that focus on quality improvement (see Chapter 6, "Quality and Process Improvement"). These techniques involve the systematic observation and recording of process details to allow better assessment. They also lend themselves to brainstorming the process for improvements, which is step 5. Finally, they are useful for performing step 6 because they should be reapplied to the newly proposed process, along with information on how performance measures are affected. Thus, they provide a "before" and "after" look at the process. Important inputs to these three techniques are time estimates of how long it takes to do various tasks.

flow diagram A diagram that traces the flow of information, customers, employees, equipment, or materials through a process.

FLOW DIAGRAMS. A **flow diagram** traces the flow of information, customers, employees, equipment, or materials through a process. Flow diagrams are also known as flowcharts, process maps, or service blueprints. While many variations are possible, a common format is to use a box shape (with a brief description of the step inside) for activities or tasks, and with lines and arrows to show sequencing. Other shapes can differentiate between different types of steps. Thus, a rectangle [■■], inverted triangle [▼], diamond [◆], circle [●], and semicircle [▶] can represent an operation, queue, decision, inspection, and delay, respectively. Steps essential to success and in which failure occurs most often are identified. Also, listing important performance metrics beside each step is helpful, such as total elapsed time, quality losses, error rate, capacity, and cost.

service blueprint A special flowchart of a service process that shows which steps have high customer involvement.

For example, Figure 3.7 is a diagram of an automotive repair process, beginning with the customer's arrival for an appointment and ending with the customer's pickup of the car. In this figure, called a **service blueprint**, the dotted *line of visibility* divides activities that are directly visible (front office) to the customers from those that occur

FIGURE 3.7 *Flow Diagram for Automotive Repair*

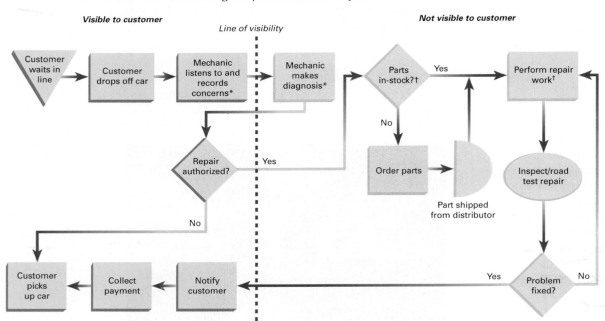

* = Points critical to the success of the service.
† = Points at which failure is most often experienced.

in the back office. Including this information is particularly valuable for service operations involving high customer involvement.

Sometimes flow diagrams are overlaid on a facility's layout. To make this special kind of flow diagram, the analyst first does a rough sketch of the area in which the process is performed. On a grid, the analyst plots the path followed by the person, material, or equipment, using arrows to indicate the direction of movement or flow.

process chart An organized way of documenting all the activities performed on a customer or product by a person, a group of people, equipment, or a workstation.

PROCESS CHARTS. A **process chart** is an organized way of documenting the purpose of all the activities performed on a subject by a person, a group of people, equipment, or a workstation. The subject can be a customer, possession, product, or data. For example, a process chart may track a patient with an ankle injury moving through an emergency room. Data are presented in a tabular form, and can summarize a rich set of information on each step in the process. Often data are used to drill down to the job level for an individual person, a team, or a focused nested process. Here we group the type of activities for a typical process into five categories:

- *Operation.* Changes, creates, or adds something. Drilling a hole and serving a customer are examples of operations.

- *Transportation.* Moves the study's subject from one place to another (sometimes called *materials handling*). A customer walking from one end of a counter to the other, a crane hoisting a steel beam to a location, and a conveyor carrying a partially completed product from one workstation to the next are examples of transportation.

- *Inspection.* Checks or verifies something but does not change it. Checking for blemishes on a surface, weighing a product, and taking a temperature reading are examples of inspections.

- *Delay.* Occurs when the subject is held up awaiting further action. Time spent waiting for materials or equipment, cleanup time, and time that workers, machines, or workstations are idle because there is nothing for them to do are examples of delays.

- *Inventory or queue.* An example of inventory is supplies unloaded and placed in a storeroom. Examples of queues are customers in a waiting line and a backlog of orders waiting to be filled.

To complete a chart for a new process, the analyst must identify each step performed. If the process is an existing one, the analyst can actually observe the steps, categorizing each one according to the subject being studied. The analyst then records the distance travelled and the time taken to perform each step. After recording all the activities and steps, the analyst summarizes the number of steps, the times, and the distances data. Figure 3.8 shows a process chart prepared for a patient with a twisted ankle being treated at a hospital. The process begins at the entrance and ends with the patient exiting after picking up the prescription.

After a process is charted, the analyst sometimes estimates the annual cost of the entire process. It becomes a benchmark against which other methods for performing the process can be evaluated. Annual labour cost can be estimated by finding the product of (1) time in hours to perform the process each time, (2) variable costs per hour, and (3) number of times the process is performed each year:

$$\begin{array}{c} \text{Annual} \\ \text{labour cost} \end{array} = \left(\begin{array}{c} \text{Time to perform} \\ \text{the process} \end{array} \right) \times \left(\begin{array}{c} \text{Variable costs} \\ \text{per hour} \end{array} \right) \times \left(\begin{array}{c} \text{Number of times process} \\ \text{performed per year} \end{array} \right)$$

FIGURE 3.8 *Process Chart for Emergency Room Admission*

Process: Emergency room admission
Subject: Ankle injury patient
Beginning: Enter emergency room
Ending: Leave hospital

Summary

Activity		Number of Steps	Time (min)	Distance (m)
Operation	■	5	23.00	
Transport	➡	9	11.00	255
Inspect	●	2	8.00	
Delay	❭	3	8.00	
Inventory or queue	▼	—	—	

Step No.	Time (min)	Distance (m)	■	➡	●	❭	▼	Step Description
1	0.50	5		X				Enter emergency room, approach patient window
2	10.00		X					Sit down and fill out patient history
3	0.75	15		X				Nurse escorts patient to ER triage room
4	3.00				X			Nurse inspects injury
5	0.75	15		X				Return to waiting room
6	1.00					X		Wait for available bed
7	1.00	20		X				Go to ER bed
8	4.00					X		Wait for doctor
9	5.00				X			Doctor inspects injury and questions patient
10	2.00	60		X				Nurse takes patient to radiology
11	3.00		X					Technician X-rays patient
12	2.00	60		X				Return to bed in ER
13	3.00					X		Wait for doctor to return
14	2.00		X					Doctor provides diagnosis and advice
15	1.00	20		X				Return to emergency entrance area
16	4.00		X					Check out
17	2.00	50		X				Walk to pharmacy
18	4.00		X					Pick up prescription
19	1.00	10		X				Leave the building

In the case of the patient in Figure 3.8, this conversion wouldn't be necessary, with total patient time being sufficient. What is being tracked is the patient's time, not the time and costs of the service providers.

SIMULATION MODELS. A flow diagram is a simple but powerful tool for understanding each of the activities that make up a process and how they tie together. A process chart provides information similar to a table rather than a diagram, but also provides time and cost information for the process. A simulation model goes one step further by showing how the process performs dynamically over time. **Simulation** is an act of reproducing the behaviour of a process using a model that describes each step of the process. Once the current process is modelled, the analyst can make changes in the process to measure the impact on certain performance measures, such as response time, waiting lines, resource utilization, and the like. To learn more about how simulation works, see Supplement G, "Simulation" in MyOMLab.

ROBUST DESIGN. One goal of documenting the process is to assess the robustness of the process. A **robust process design** continues to effectively deliver customer value, despite

simulation The act of reproducing the behaviour of a process using a model that describes each step of the process.

robust process design A process that is less sensitive to or accommodates variation in inputs or operating conditions while maintaining customer value.

uncertainty, changes, and problems. As part of the design process, managers and engineers must specify targets for inputs and operating conditions. However, minor variations from these ideal targets often cause the process to operate poorly, generating waste or creating customer dissatisfaction.

Instead, careful process design and improvement can reduce the sensitivity of the process to small changes from "ideal." For example, a supplier might occasionally ship flour to a cookie bakery with higher or lower moisture content than is ideal. However, a process design that monitors the moisture level of the dough and baked cookies in real time allows the process to adapt to this variation and continue to produce high-quality products with little change in waste and cost.

DEVELOPING A BETTER PROCESS

Process analysis and documentation are really means to an end: a better process with greater customer value (effectiveness) and less waste (efficiency). Generally speaking, waste is a poor use of process resources. Processes can be designed or redesigned using two different approaches: process re-engineering and process improvement (see Figure 3.9). In general, process re-engineering should be viewed as radical, dramatic change; something to be undertaken only occasionally. In contrast, process improvement is an ongoing necessity as customer needs evolve, competitors adapt, and the marketplace develops. We begin with process re-engineering, which is getting considerable attention today in management circles.

re-engineering The fundamental rethinking and radical redesign of processes to improve performance dramatically in terms of cost, quality, service, and speed.

Critical Processes.

PROCESS RE-ENGINEERING

Re-engineering is the fundamental rethinking and radical redesign of processes to improve performance dramatically in terms of cost, quality, customer service, and speed. Process re-engineering is about reinvention rather than incremental improvement. It is

FIGURE 3.9 *Developing a Better Process*

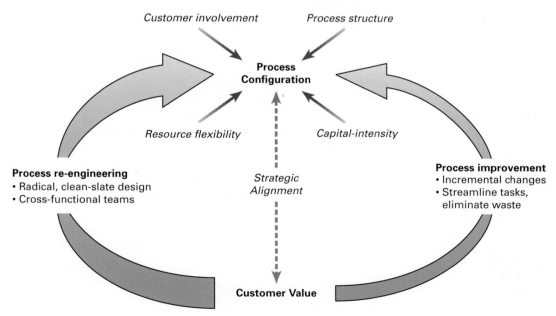

strong medicine and not always needed or successful. Pain, in the form of layoffs and large cash outflows for investments in information technology, almost always accompanies massive change. However, re-engineering processes can have big payoffs. Table 3.1 list the key elements of the overall approach.

Like many new techniques and concepts in operations management, re-engineering has led to many successes, and will continue to do so. For example, Nestlé Canada re-engineered its supply chain, with the objectives of streamlining internal and external information flows and explicitly linking initial consumer demand planning with the final purchase. "The only way that we can compete is if each Nestlé employee takes responsibility to reduce non-value-added costs at every step of our operation," observed Nestlé's chairman and CEO.[4] To create improvement, cross-functional teams applied four core elements: systematic identification of cost drivers, focus on root causes, standardized use of best practices, and ongoing measurement of results. (For a more detailed discussion of these techniques, see Chapter 6, "Quality and Process Improvement.") Over a three-year period, waste was reduced by 35 percent, range of products by 50 percent, and inventory by 40 percent.

Re-engineering is not simple or easily done; nor is it appropriate for all processes or all organizations. Ideally, a core process, such as a firm's order fulfillment, should be the major focus, and simplifying information flows often yields important gains (either with or without new information technology). However, many firms struggle to find the time and resources to implement a radical, clean-slate approach. Moderate gains might give greater cumulative results than the pursuit of huge breakthroughs from re-engineering. Finally, the best understanding of a process, and how to improve it, often lies with the people who perform the work every day, not cross-functional teams or top management.

TABLE 3.1	Key Elements of Re-engineering
Element	**Description**
Critical processes	The emphasis of re-engineering should be on core business processes. Normal process-improvement activities can be continued with the other processes.
Strong leadership	Senior executives must provide strong leadership for re-engineering to be successful. Otherwise, cynicism, resistance ("We tried that before"), and boundaries between departments can block radical changes.
Cross-functional teams	A team, consisting of members from each functional area affected by the process change, is charged with carrying out a re-engineering project. Self-managing teams and employee empowerment are the rule rather than the exception.
Information technology	Information technology is a primary enabler of process engineering. Most re-engineering projects design processes around information flows, such as customer order fulfillment.
Clean-slate philosophy	Re-engineering requires a "clean-slate" philosophy—that is, starting with the way the customer wants to deal with the company. To ensure a customer orientation, teams begin with internal and external customer objectives for the process.
Process analysis	Despite the clean-slate philosophy, a re-engineering team must understand things about the current process: what it does, how well it performs, and what factors affect it. The team must look at every procedure involved in the process throughout the organization.

PROCESS IMPROVEMENT

The systematic study of the activities and flows of each process both precedes and underpins any effective effort at **process improvement**. Only after a process is really understood can it really be improved. Analysis also helps to identify the critical points in the process where the majority of time is wasted, materials are lost, equipment is needlessly idle, and workers are hampered by unavailable resources.

process improvement
The systematic study of the activities and flows of each process to improve its performance.

After a process has been systematically considered, this information becomes the basis for brainstorming about opportunities to achieve better performance. Using flow diagrams, process charts, or other tools, a team must look for ways to streamline tasks, cut expensive materials or services, improve the environment, or make jobs safer. The process analysis also indicates which activities take the most time. The emphasis is on identifying and improving the critical few areas where significant gains can be achieved (sometimes with very little investment).

During this creative part, the team must ask the what, when, who, where, how long, and how questions, challenging each of the steps of the process. To make a process more efficient, the team should question each delay and assess which steps can be combined, rearranged, or eliminated. There is always a better way, but someone must identify a specific problem, and then the team can develop a better way. Improvements in productivity, quality, time, and flexibility can be significant. Unlike process re-engineering, process improvement must be continually and actively pursued—it's an ongoing competitive necessity. Managerial approaches and tools for process improvement are explained in greater detail in Chapter 6, "Quality and Process Improvement."

PROCESS CONFIGURATION AND SUSTAINABILITY

With process configuration comprising four major decisions, several linkages to sustainability are important for managers to consider. To begin, process configuration can influence either environmental or social performance of a firm through the use of resources, efforts to improve efficiency, and working conditions. Increasing customer involvement can serve to better align social aspects of a firm's processes with aspects of customer value. For example, if customers are concerned about the environmental impact or working conditions of facilities located in Canada, Asia, or elsewhere, these concerns can be reflected in management's choice of metrics and auditing of these operations. Moreover, customer involvement in recycling of used products, packaging, or consumables, such as 3D glasses at movie theatres, can serve to enhance the connection between the firm and its customers, to potentially lower costs, and to improve environmental performance.

Processes that use mass customization or flexible technologies also can be an important way to reduce waste as goods are produced exactly when needed in the precise quantities that customer demand. Some of the challenges created by make-to-stock policies, such as product obsolescence, which unnecessarily consumes raw materials, are reduced or even eliminated. Thus, more environmentally friendly processes can be more capital-intensive, yet save money in the long run.

Another example further illustrates this trade-off between fixed and variable costs. Green energy production using wind or solar power requires much more capital investment than a coal-fired power plant, but reduces both pollutants and operating costs over the long run. In a similar way, setting up a process that uses returnable, reusable packing requires managers to invest time and energy in developing a process configuration that accommodates the variability and uncertainty of customer returns. Yet, as noted in Chapter 2, these used products can lower raw materials costs for companies, particularly when the prices of oil-derived commodities, such as plastics, is rising.

EQUATION SUMMARY

1. Break-even analysis:

$$Q = \frac{F_1 - F_2}{v_2 - v_1}$$

2. Annual labour cost estimated from process chart:

$$\begin{array}{c}\text{Annual} \\ \text{labour cost}\end{array} = \left(\begin{array}{c}\text{Time to perform} \\ \text{the process}\end{array}\right) \times \left(\begin{array}{c}\text{Variable costs} \\ \text{per hour}\end{array}\right) \times \left(\begin{array}{c}\text{Number of times process} \\ \text{performed per year}\end{array}\right)$$

CHAPTER HIGHLIGHTS

- Process configuration deals with *how* to make a product or service. Process configuration is of strategic importance and is closely linked to a firm's long-term success. It involves the selection of inputs, operations, work flows, and methods used to produce goods and services.

- Process decisions are made in the following circumstances: a new product is to be offered or an existing product modified, quality improvements are necessary, competitive priorities are changed, demand levels change, current performance is inadequate, competitor capabilities change, new technology is available, or cost or availability of inputs changes.

- The four major process decisions are customer involvement, process structure, resource flexibility, and capital-intensity. Customer involvement is the extent to which customers interact with the process during the service encounter. Basic process structures are project, batch, line, and continuous flow processes. Combined with differing levels of customer involvement, process structure can be in the form of a front-, hybrid-, or back-office process. Resource flexibility is the degree to which equipment is general-purpose and individuals can handle a wide variety of work. Capital-intensity is the mix of capital equipment and human skills in a process.

- Inventory policies provide options for managers to adjust speed and flexibility for customer value. Common policies include make-to-stock, assemble-to-order, mass customization, postponement, and make-to-order. Each has implications for process structure and resource flexibility.

- Fixed automation maximizes efficiency for high-volume products with long life cycles, but flexible (programmable) automation provides economies of scope. Flexibility is gained and setups are minimized because the machines can be reprogrammed to follow new instructions.

- A basic variable underlying the relationships among the four major process decisions is volume, which in turn is shaped by operations strategy. For example, high volume is associated with a line or continuous flow process, little resource flexibility, little customer involvement, and high capital-intensity.

- Customer involvement is central to understanding and categorizing service processes, both between industries and within an industry. Based on the two dimensions of customer interaction and the time for the service encounter, services can be described as professional service, service shop, mass service, and service factory. Process efficiency tends to increase as both the interaction and encounter time decrease. Internet-based involvement offers many options to increase or decrease customer involvement, depending on the need for greater interaction or improved efficiency.

- Focusing operations avoids confusion among competitive priorities, process choices, and technologies. Focused facilities, plants within plants, and cells are ways to achieve focus in both manufacturing and service operations.

- Three basic techniques for analyzing process activities and flows are flow diagrams, process charts, and simulation. Symbols capture operations, decisions, inventory and queues, delays, and inspection.

- Process re-engineering uses cross-functional teams to rethink the fundamental design of critical processes. Process improvement is a systematic analysis of activities and flows that occurs repeatedly to achieve steady incremental improvements in key process metrics.

SOLVED PROBLEM 1

An automobile service is having difficulty providing oil changes in the 29 minutes or less mentioned in its advertising. You are to analyze the process of changing automobile engine oil. The subject of the study is the service mechanic. The process begins when the mechanic directs the customer's arrival and ends when the customer pays for the services.

SOLUTION

Figure 3.10 shows the completed process chart. The process is broken into 21 steps. A summary of the times and distances travelled is shown in the upper right-hand corner of the process chart. The times add up to 28 minutes, which does not allow much room for error if the 29-minute guarantee is to be met and the mechanic travels a total of 131 metres.

FIGURE 3.10 *Process Chart for Changing Engine Oil*

Solver - Process Charts
Enter data in yellow-shaded areas.

Process: *Changing engine oil*
Subject: *Mechanic*
Beginning: *Direct customer arrival*
Ending: *Total charges, receive payment*

Summary

Activity		Number of Steps	Time (min)	Distance (m)
Operation	■	7	16.50	
Transport	➡	8	5.50	131
Inspect	●	4	5.00	
Delay	◗	1	0.70	
Inventory or queue	▼	1	0.30	

Step No.	Time (min)	Distance (m)	■	➡	●	◗	▼	Step Description
1	0.80	15.0		X				Direct customer into service bay
2	1.80		X					Record name and desired service
3	2.30				X			Open hood, verify eng. type, inspect hoses & fluids
4	0.80	10.0		X				Walk to customer in waiting area
5	0.60		X					Recommend additional services
6	0.70					X		Wait for customer decision
7	0.90	22.0		X				Walk to storeroom
8	1.90		X					Look up filter number(s), find filter(s)
9	0.40				X			Check filter number(s)
10	0.60	15.0		X				Carry filter(s) to service pit
11	4.20		X					Perform under-car services
12	0.70	12.0	X	X				Climb from pit, walk to automobile
13	2.70		X		X			Fill engine with oil, start engine
14	1.30				X			Inspect for leaks
15	0.50	12.0		X				Walk to pit
16	1.00				X			Inspect for leaks
17	3.00		X					Clean and organize work area
18	0.70	25.0		X				Return to auto, drive from bay
19	0.30						X	Park the car
20	0.50	20.0		X				Walk to customer waiting area
21	2.30		X					Total changes, receive payment

SOLVED PROBLEM 2

What improvement can you make in the process shown in Figure 3.10?

SOLUTION

Your analysis should verify the following three ideas for improvement. You may also find others.

1. *Move step 17 to step 21.* Customers shouldn't have to wait while the mechanic cleans the work area.

2. *Store small inventories of frequently used filters in the pit.* Step 7 involves travel to the storeroom. If the filters are moved to the pit, a copy of the reference material must also be placed in the pit. The pit will have to be organized and well lighted.

3. *Use two mechanics.* Steps 10, 12, and 15 involve running up and down the steps to the pit. Much of this travel could be eliminated. The service time could be shortened by having one mechanic in the pit working simultaneously with another working under the hood.

PROBLEMS

1. Your class has volunteered to assist with publicizing the campaign of a candidate. The campaign includes assembling 10 000 yard signs (preprinted water-resistant paper signs to be glued and stapled to a wooden stake) on a Saturday. Construct a flow diagram and a process chart for yard sign assembly. What inputs in terms of materials, human effort, and equipment are involved? Estimate the number of volunteers and staples, and the amount of glue, equipment, lawn and garage space, and pizza required.

2. Prepare a flowchart of the field service division process at DEF, as described here. Start from the point at which a call is received and end when a technician finishes the job.

   DEF was a multibillion-dollar company that manufactured and distributed a wide variety of electronic, photographic, and reprographic equipment used in many engineering and medical system applications. The Field Service Division employed 475 field service technicians, who performed maintenance and warranty repairs on the equipment sold by DEF. Customers would call DEF's National Service Centre (NSC), which received about 3000 calls per day. The NSC staffed its call centre with about 40 call takers. A typical incoming service call was received at the NSC and routed to one of the call takers, who entered information about the machine, caller's name, and type of problem into DEF's mainframe computer. In some cases, the call taker attempted to help the customer fix the problem. However, call takers were currently only able to avoid about 10 percent of the incoming emergency maintenance service calls. If the service call could not be avoided, the call taker usually recited the following script: "Depending upon the availability of our technicians, you should expect to see a technician sometime between now and (now + *X*)." ("*X*" was the target response time based on the model number and the zone.) This information was given to the customer because many customers wanted to know when a tech would arrive on-site.

   Call takers entered service call information on DEF's computer system, which then sent the information electronically to the regional dispatch centre assigned to that customer location. (DEF had four regional dispatch centres with a total of about 20 dispatchers.) Service call information was printed on a small card at the dispatch centre. About every hour, cards were ripped off the printer and given to the dispatcher assigned to that customer location. The dispatcher placed each card on a magnetic board under the name of a tech that the dispatcher believed would be the most likely candidate for the service call, given the location of the machine, the current location of the tech, and the tech's training profile. After completing a service call, techs called the dispatcher in the regional dispatch centre, cleared the call, and received a new call assigned by the dispatcher. After getting the service call from a dispatcher, a tech called the customer to give an expected time of arrival, drove to the customer site, diagnosed the problem, repaired the machine if parts were available in the van, and then phoned the dispatcher for the next call. If the tech did not have the right parts for a repair, the tech informed the NSC and the part was express mailed to the customer; the repair was done the next morning.

FIGURE 3.11

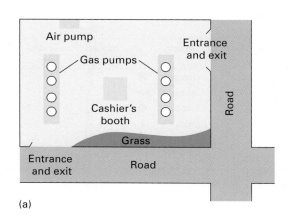

(a)

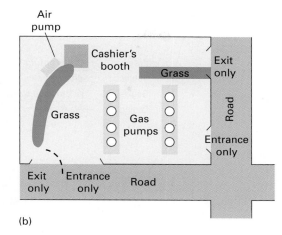

(b)

3. Diagrams of two self-service gasoline stations, both located on corners, are shown in Figure 3.11(a) and (b). Both have two rows of four pumps and a booth at which an attendant receives payment for the gasoline. At neither station is it necessary for the customer to pay in advance. The exits and entrances are marked on the diagrams. Analyze the flows of cars and people through each station.

a. Which station has the more efficient flows from the standpoint of the customer?

b. Which station is likely to lose more potential customers who cannot gain access to the pumps because another car is headed in the other direction?

c. At which station can a customer pay without getting out of the car?

4. The management of the Just Like Home restaurant has asked you to analyze some of its processes. One of these processes is making a single-scoop ice cream cone. Cones can be ordered by a server (for table service) or by a customer (for takeout). Figure 3.12 on the next page illustrates the process chart for this operation.

- The ice cream counter server earns $10 per hour (including variable fringe benefits).

- The process is performed 10 times per hour (on average).

- The restaurant is open 363 days a year, 10 hours a day.

a. Complete the summary (top right) portion of the chart.

b. What is the total labour cost associated with the process?

c. How can this operation be made more efficient? Draw a process chart of the improved process. What are the annual labour savings if this new process is implemented?

5. Refer to the process chart for the automobile oil change in Solved Problem 1. On average, the process is performed twice per hour, and the shop is open 300 days a year, 10 hours per day. A mechanic earns $40 per hour (including benefits).

a. What is the total annual labour cost associated with the process?

b. Assuming steps 7, 10, 12, and 15 were eliminated, estimate the annual labour savings associated with implementing this new process.

6. Dr. Gulakowicz is an orthodontist. She estimates that adding two new chairs will increase fixed costs by $150 000, including the annual equivalent cost of the capital investment and the salary of one more technician. Each new patient is expected to bring in $3000 per year in additional revenue, with variable costs estimated at $1000 per patient. The two new chairs will allow her to expand her practice by as many as 200 patients annually. How many patients would have to be added for the new process to break even?

7. Two different manufacturing processes are being considered for making a new product. The first process is less capital-intensive, with fixed costs of only $50 000 per year and variable costs of $700 per unit. The second process has fixed costs of $400 000 but variable costs of only $200 per unit.

a. What is the break-even quantity, beyond which the second process becomes more attractive than the first?

b. If the expected annual sales for the product is 800 units, which process would you choose?

FIGURE 3.12

Solver - Process Charts
Enter data in yellow-shaded areas.

	Summary			
Activity	Number of Steps	Time (min)	Distance (m)	

Process: *Making one ice cream cone*
Subject: *Server at counter*
Beginning: *Walk to cone storage area*
Ending: *Give it to server or customer*

Activity		Number of Steps	Time (min)	Distance (m)
Operation	■			
Transport	➡			
Inspect	●			
Delay	◗			
Inventory or queue	▼			

Step No.	Time (min)	Distance (m)	■	➡	●	◗	▼	Step Description
1				X				
2			X					
3				X				
4			X					
5				X				
6						X		
7				X				
8			X					
9				X				
10			X					
11			X					
12					X			
13				X				
14			X					

NOTES FOR CHAPTER

1. *WWLHIN Backgrounder,* July 29, 2010; www.gghorg.ca, accessed January 2011; Ministry of Health and Long-Term Care, "Guelph General Hospital ER Seeing More Patients Sooner," news release, November 5, 2010; V. Kirsch, "Emergency Wait Times Shorter Thanks to 'See and Treat' Routine," *Guelph Mercury,* September 16, 2009; V. Kirsch, "Health Minister Offers More Emergency Room Funds," *Guelph Mercury,* November 6, 2010; S. Sheahan and T. Begda-Peyton, "Guelph General Hospital: Physician Leadership in Transformation Work: We Were in a Really Dark Place" (Toronto: Institute of Public Administration of Canada, 2010).

2. Adapted from: Schmenner, R. W. "Service Businesses and Productivity." *Decision Sciences,* vol. 35, no. 3 (2004), pp. 333–347.

3. Frances X. Frei, "Breaking the Trade-Off Between Efficiency and Service," *Harvard Business Review* (November 2006), pp. 93–101; news.ebay.com/about.cfm, accessed April 19, 2008; www.ebayinc.com/who, accessed January 24, 2010; eBay 2009 annual report.

4. S. Gahbauer, "Nestlé Freshens Up Supply Chain Performance," *Modern Purchasing,* vol. 40, no. 5 (1998), p. 26.

FURTHER READING

Anderson, Merrill C. "Transforming Human Resources: Maximizing Value While Increasing Productivity." *National Productivity Review,* vol. 17, no. 3 (Autumn 2000), pp. 75–80.

Anupindi, Ravi, Sunil Chopra, Sudhakar D. Deshmukj, Jan A. Van Mieghem, and Eitan Zemel. *Managing Business Process Flows.* Upper Saddle River, NJ: Prentice Hall, 1999.

Bitner, Mary Jo. "Servicescapes: The Impact of Physical Surroundings on Customers and Employees." *Journal of Marketing,* vol. 56 (April 1992), pp. 57–71.

Bowen, John, and Robert C. Ford. "Managing Service Organizations: Does Having a 'Thing' Make a Difference?" *Journal of Management,* vol. 28, no. 3 (2002), pp. 447–469.

Carey, Susan. "Case of the Vanishing Airport Lines." *Wall Street Journal*, August 9, 2007.

Chase, R. B. "The Customer Contact Approach to Services: Theoretical Bases and Practical Extensions." *Operations Research*, vol. 29 (1981), no. 4, pp. 698–706.

Collier, D. A., and Meyer, S. "An Empirical Comparison of Service Matrices." *International Journal of Operations and Production Management*, vol. 20, nos. 5–6 (2000), pp. 705–729.

Collins, Jim. *Good to Great: Why Some Companies Make the Leap . . . and Others Don't*. New York: HarperCollins, 2001.

Cook, David P., Chon-Huat Goh, and Chen H. Chung. "Service Typologies: A State of the Art Survey." *Production and Operations Management*, vol. 8, no. 3 (1999), pp. 318–338.

Davenport, Thomas H. "The Coming Commoditization of Processes." *Harvard Business Review* (June 2005), pp. 101–108.

Drucker, Peter F. "The Discipline of Innovation." *Harvard Business Review*, vol. 80, no. 8 (August 2002), pp. 95–101.

Fitzsimmons, James A., and Mona J. Fitzsimmons. *Service Management: Operations, Strategy, and Information Technology*. New York: McGraw-Hill, 1998.

Fleming, John H., Curt Coffman, and James K. Harter. "Manage Your Human Sigma." *Harvard Business Review* (July–August 2005), pp. 101–108.

Guidoni, G. "Robotic Renaissance: Auto Sector Still Leading the Way in North American Industry's Unfolding Love Affair with Robotic Technologies." *Canadian Packaging*, vol. 53 (2000), no. 4, pp. 17–18.

Hammer, Michael. "Deep Change: How Operational Innovation Can Transform Your Company." *Harvard Business Review*, vol. 82, no. 4 (April 2004), pp. 85–93.

Karmarkar, Uday. "Will You Survive the Services Revolution?" *Harvard Business Review*, vol. 82, no. 6 (June 2004), pp. 100–107.

Kelliher, Clare, and Michael Riley. "Beyond Efficiency: Some By-products of Functional Flexibility." *Service Industries Journal*, vol. 23, no. 4 (2003), pp. 98–114.

La Ferla, Beverly. "Mapping the Way to Process Improvement." *IEE Engineering Management*, December 2004–January 2005, pp. 16–17.

Lovelock, Christopher H., and George S. Yip. "Developing Global Strategies for Service Businesses." *California Management Review*, vol. 38, no. 2 (1996), pp. 64–86.

Melnyk, Steven A., Douglas M. Stewart, and Morgan Swink. "Metrics and Performance Measurement in Operations Management: Dealing with the Metrics Maze." *Journal of Operations Management*, vol. 22, no. 3 (June 2004), pp. 209–217.

Metters, Richard, Kathryn King-Metters, and Madeleine Pullman. *Successful Service Operations Management*. Mason, OH: South-Western, 2003.

Rampersad, Hubert K. *Total Performance Scorecard*. New York: Butterworth-Heinemann, 2003.

Rayport, Jeffrey F., and Bernard J. Jaworski. "Best Face Forward." *Harvard Business Review*, vol. 82, no. 12 (2003), pp. 47–58.

Safizadeh, M. Hossein, Joy M. Field, and Larry P. Ritzman. "An Empirical Analysis of Financial Services Processes with a Front-Office or Back-Office Orientation." *Journal of Operations Management*, vol. 21, no. 5 (2003), pp. 557–576.

Schmenner, R. W. "Service Businesses and Productivity." *Decision Sciences*, vol. 35 (2004), no. 3, pp. 333–347.

Senge, P. *The Fifth Discipline: The Art and Practice of the Learning Organization*. New York: Doubleday, 1990.

Shapiro, Benson R., V. Kasturi Rangan, and John J. Sviokla. "Staple Yourself to an Order." *Harvard Business Review*, vol. 82, nos. 7–8 (July–August 1992), pp. 113–122.

Wheelwright, Steven C., and Robert H. Hayes. "Competing Through Manufacturing." *Harvard Business Review*, January/February 1985, pp. 99–109.

MYOMLAB

MyOMLab offers the following resources, which allow you to further practise and apply concepts presented in this chapter.

- **Key Equations:** All the equations for this chapter can be found in one convenient location.

- **Discussion Questions:** These questions challenge your understanding of the role of operations management and operations strategy. Several questions also focus specifically on the ethical, environmental, and political dimensions of designing processes.

- **Cases:**

  - *Custom Molds, Inc.* How should the Millers design their processes, given the changing environment?

  - *Car Lube Operations.* How do the competitive priorities of two different firms match their customers' needs?

  - *The Facilities Maintenance Problem at Midwest University.* How would you measure performance of your personnel, and what restructuring is necessary for facilities maintenance?

- **Video Case:**

  - *Process Analysis at Starwood.* How should management improve the process of keeping public areas clean? What benefits would you expect from Starwood's "Power of Innovation" program?

- **Virtual Tours:**

  - *Androsia* manufactures batik fabrics in a labour-intensive, low-volume process at their plant on the island of Andros in the Bahamas.

  - *The Hershey tour* shows how cocoa beans are processed into chocolate using a high-volume, line process.

  - *Three tours—Kokomo Opalescent Glass Factory, Buck Knives, and Marshmallow Peeps Facility Tour—* provide a view of a low-, moderate- and high-volume facility.

- **Experiential Exercise:** King Soopers Bakery. See how three different process structures are used under the same roof, depending on volume and the degree of product customization.

- **Extend LT:** A student version is included to develop and use simulation models. Artistic Glass is considering changes to its process structure, and a simulation exercise and model is included.

- **OM Explorer Tutor:** OM Explorer contains two tutor programs that will help you learn about break-even analysis applied to equipment selection and process charts.

- **Supplement A:** *Decision Making.* This supplement provides the background to use break-even analysis, preference matrices, decision theory, and decision trees.

- **Supplement B:** *Financial Analysis.* Learn about several tools for evaluating revised processes that involve large capital investments.

- **Supplement C:** *Work Measurement.* Learn about several tools for estimating the time it takes for each step in a process.

- **Supplement D:** *Learning Curve Analysis.* Learn about how to account for learning effects when estimating time requirements for new or revised processes.

- **Supplement E:** *Computer-Integrated Manufacturing.* Read about how complex computer systems can give manufacturers more resource flexibility.

- **Supplement G:** *Simulation.* Learn how to simulate a process and understand how it performs dynamically over time.

Capacity

Learning Goals

After reading this chapter, you will be able to:

1. define capacity, and describe different ways to measure capacity, assess process capacity, and calculate capacity utilization.

2. understand the linkages between capacity, inventory, and variability for process management.

3. identify bottlenecks, and discuss short- and long-term strategies to expand bottlenecks (related to the concept of the theory of constraints).

4. identify sources and forms of variability and understand the implications for process capacity.

5. explain the reasons for economies and diseconomies of scale.

6. discuss strategic issues such as capacity cushions, timing and sizing options, and linkages with other decisions.

7. identify a systematic approach to capacity planning.

Across the Organization

Capacity is important to:

- **accounting**, which prepares the cost information needed to evaluate capacity expansion decisions.

- **finance**, which performs the financial analysis of proposed capacity expansion investments and raises funds to support them.

- **human resources**, which must hire and train employees to support capacity plans.

- **marketing**, which provides demand forecasts needed to identify capacity gaps.

- **operations**, which must develop capacity strategies that meet future demand most effectively.

- **purchasing**, which obtains capacity from other firms through outsourcing.

Linking service capacity to customer demand requires management to confront many challenges, whether serving lattés or double-doubles. Starbucks has based its customer value on an "anti-fast-food" concept that continues to this day. Customers enter a café venue, order a customized drink such as a skinny caramel macchiato, and then expect to linger over their hot drink. In contrast, Tim Hortons is designed to minimize the time needed for customers to get their large double-double and a doughnut, and then depart.

A Starbucks barista prepares a beverage.

Given the many permutations of sizes, flavours, and preparation techniques for its beverages, Starbucks doesn't leave customer variability to chance in its process. In order to maximize the efficiency of its staff and ensure that orders are filled accurately, managers train counter clerks to call out orders to beverage makers, called "baristas," in a particular sequence. It is even better when customers do it themselves. First, Starbucks provides a "guide-to-ordering pamphlet" for customers to look over. Second, it trains clerks to repeat the order in the correct sequence for the baristas, which may not be exactly how a customer presented it. This process not only makes it easier for the barista, but also indirectly "trains" the customers for how to correctly place their orders. Increasing capacity of the barista frees up time to interact with customers and improves the Starbucks experience.

But the capacity of the baristas is only one part of the customer experience that must be considered. The recent introduction of free Wi-Fi in 750 stores across Canada was designed to enhance the slow-pace appeal. However, as cus-

Tim Hortons now combines capacity to serve both quick-serve coffee and customized ice cream treats.

tomers stay longer, the seating capacity of the store can become a critical problem during busy times. Historical data shows that the average customer with a laptop uses Wi-Fi for about an hour. Thus, if the average length of the customer stay is expected to increase by 25 percent, seating area should expanded by the same factor to maintain the same customer experience—or risk leaving incoming customers with limited seating.

In contrast, Tim Hortons has designed their store capacity at over 3000 locations in Canada around a high percentage of drive-through and grab-and-go customers. For decades, each was designed with its own in-store kitchen where staff bakers produced fresh batches twice daily. However, in the past few years, Tim Hortons outsourced this baking capacity to Maidstone Bakeries, which now supplies partially cooked and flash-frozen doughnuts to all stores across Canada. The product is then "baked" in the local store in two minutes, as needed, thereby improving product consistency, enabling wider product variety, and ultimately, better matching store-level capacity for fresh product with hour-by-hour customer demand.

Tim Hortons' recent introduction of Cold Stone ice cream in some locations has added its own capacity challenge. Ice cream is mixed as ordered to customer specifications, taking more time to prepare than Tim Hortons' traditional fare. To manage capacity and throughput time, customers are divided into separate queues, with distinct counters, and clear signage. As with Starbucks, expanding product offerings requires changes in both process design and capacity to enhance competitiveness.[1]

A fter deciding what products or services should be offered and how they should be made, management must plan the capacity of its processes. The experiences of Starbucks and Tim Hortons show how important capacity planning and adjustments are to an organization's future. **Capacity** is the maximum rate of output for a process. The operations manager must provide the capacity to meet current and future demand; otherwise, the organization will miss opportunities for growth and profits.

Capacity planning is made at two levels. Long-term capacity plans, which we describe in this chapter, deal with investments in new facilities and equipment. These plans cover at least two years into the future, but construction lead times alone can force much longer time horizons. Canadian firms invest more than $80 billion annually in *new* facilities, plants, and equipment. Service industries account for about three-quarters of this investment. Such sizable investments require top-management participation and approval because they are not easily reversed. Short-term capacity plans focus on workforce size, overtime budgets, inventories, and other types of decisions that we explore in later chapters.

capacity The maximum rate of output for a process.

CAPACITY AND PROCESS CHOICE

Managerial decisions about process configuration have significant implications for planning and managing process capacity (see Chapter 3, "Process Configuration," and Figure 3.1). Process structure—whether a project, batch, line, or continuous flow process (see Figure 3.4)—implicitly combines three process factors: capacity utilization, inventory, and variability. These three factors are related, as a change in any one factor has managerial implications for the other two (Lovejoy, 1998). In a very practical sense, lower capacity utilization, greater inventory, and less variability are substitutes for each other (Figure 4.1). The basic management issues for each factor are first introduced; a more detailed discussion follows in later chapters about the management of variability and inventory.

MEASURING CAPACITY

No single capacity measure is applicable to all types of situations. However, each measure is related to a maximum rate that captures items per unit time, either explicitly or implicitly. For example, an automobile assembly line might be able to produce 62 cars per hour. However, a retailer might measure capacity as annual sales dollars generated per square metre per week, an airline as available seat-miles (ASMs) per month, and a small batch process as number of available machine-hours per week. Even if a theatre states its capacity as number of seats, time must be implicitly included based on the

FIGURE 4.1 *Process Management Triangle*

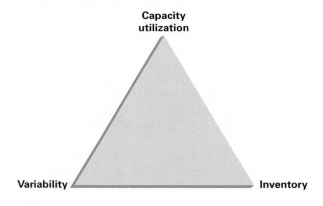

number of shows per day. In general, capacity can be expressed in one of two ways: output measures and input measures.

Output measures are the usual choice for high-volume processes that produce only a limited range of similar products or services, usually expressed in terms of output over a period of time. For example, capacity could be number of customers per day, cars per hour, or litres of water per minute. Naturally, the actual output rate of a process might be much less than the capacity because of inefficiencies or lack of demand.

Measuring output is preferred when the firm provides a relatively small number of standardized products and services, or when applied to individual processes within the overall firm. For example, a restaurant may be able to handle 100 takeout customers *or* 50 sitdown customers per hour. It might also handle 50 takeout *and* 25 sitdown customers or many other combinations of the two types of customers. However, as the range of products and services or degree of customization increases, translating each output into a common metric becomes very challenging. For example, a bank would have one capacity measure for processes that serve customers with the Internet and another measure for customers served with traditional "bricks-and-mortar" facilities.

Input measures are the usual choice for low-volume, flexible processes. For example, in a photocopy centre, capacity can be measured in machine-hours or number of machines. Just as product mix can complicate output capacity measures, so too can demand complicate input measures. Demand, which invariably is expressed as an output rate, must be converted to an input measure. Only after making the conversion can a manager compare demand requirements and capacity on an equivalent basis. For example, the manager of a copy centre must convert its annual demand from different clients for copies to the number of machine-hours required.

As noted in Chapter 1, "Creating Customer Value Through Operations," these measures of output and input can be combined to calculate the ratio of productivity for a process. Comparisons then can be made to industry benchmarks or competitors, and managers can also track internal improvement over time.

capacity utilization The degree to which capacity is currently being used to generate products or services.

UTILIZATION. Capacity planning requires a knowledge of the current capacity of a process, as well as the degree to which a process or resource is actually being used to produce goods and services. **Capacity utilization**, or the degree to which equipment, space, or labour is currently being used, is expressed as a percentage:

$$\text{Capacity utilization} = \frac{\text{Output}}{\text{Effective capacity}} \times 100\%$$

Capacity utilization is an important indicator that helps operations managers decide whether adding extra capacity or eliminating unneeded capacity might improve competitiveness. As technology increases productivity, the mix of products and services changes, or workers develop and learn better methods, capacity utilization of individual operations can shift quite dramatically.

Both output and effective capacity must be measured in the same terms, such as customers per hour, units, minutes, or dollars. Usually, output is based on the *actual* quantity of goods or services produced by the process. However, in some circumstances when the market demand exceeds process capacity, output is better expressed in terms of *required* quantity. The greatest difficulty in calculating capacity utilization lies in defining effective capacity, the denominator in the ratio.

effective capacity The maximum output that a process or firm can reasonably sustain under normal conditions.

EFFECTIVE CAPACITY. The maximum output that a process or firm can reasonably sustain under *normal conditions* is its **effective capacity**. In some organizations, effective capacity implies a one-shift operation; in others, it implies a three-shift operation. The critical issue is identifying the greatest level of output a process can reasonably sustain by using realistic employee work schedules and the equipment currently in place.

PEAK CAPACITY. The maximum output that a process or facility can achieve under *ideal conditions* is called **peak capacity**. When capacity is measured relative to equipment alone, the appropriate measure is "rated" capacity: an engineering assessment of maximum annual output, assuming continuous operation except for an allowance for normal maintenance and repair downtime. Peak capacity can be sustained for only a short time, such as a few hours in a day or a few days in a month. A process reaches it by using marginal methods of production, such as excessive overtime, extra shifts, temporarily reduced maintenance activities, overstaffing, and subcontracting. Although they can help with temporary peaks, these options cannot be sustained for long. Employees do not want to work excessive overtime for extended periods; overtime and night-shift premiums drive up costs and lower the quality.

When operating at close to peak capacity, a firm can make minimal profits or even lose money despite high sales levels. Cummins Engine Company reacted a few years ago to an unexpected demand surge caused by the weakened U.S. dollar by working at peak capacity: the plant operated three shifts, often seven days a week. Overtime soared and exhausted workers dragged down productivity. Productivity suffered when Cummins called back less-skilled workers, laid off during an earlier slump. These factors caused Cummins to report a quarterly loss, even as sales jumped.

CALCULATING PROCESS CAPACITY. Most processes involve multiple operations, and their effective capacities are not usually identical. Within a process, a **bottleneck** is an operation that has the lowest effective capacity of any operation in the process and, thus, limits the system's output. Alternatively, if customer demand exceeds process capacity, a bottleneck is any operation with capacity utilization greater than 100 percent.

For example, let's consider a simplified process for making a wooden drawer that becomes part of a computer desk. Four basic operations are required (Figure 4.2). First, the basic pieces of a drawer (two sides, front, and back) are put together by two people in drawer fabrication. Next, the drawers are moved to an automated operation that nails and glues the sides and bottom of the drawer. Third, another person performs some touchup sanding and places the drawer on a conveyor. Last, the drawer has a clear finish sprayed on as it moves through a spray booth. The effective capacities are noted in Figure 4.2.

peak capacity The maximum output that a process or facility can achieve under ideal conditions.

bottleneck An operation that has the lowest effective capacity of any operation in the process and, thus, limits the output rate of the process. Alternatively, a bottleneck is any operation with capacity utilization greater than 100 percent.

FIGURE 4.2 *Identifying the Capacity Bottleneck*

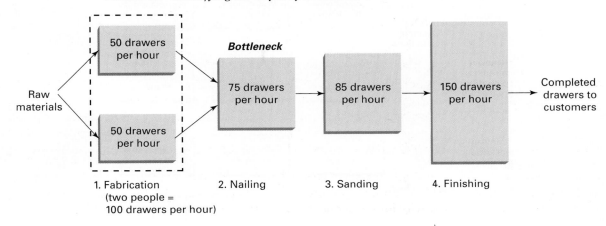

If each operation works without breakdowns or quality problems, the second operation (Nailing) is the bottleneck operation that limits the process output to 75 drawers per hour. In effect, the entire drawer manufacturing *process* can produce only as fast as the slowest operation. So the process capacity is set by this bottleneck, specifically 75 drawers per hour. Expansion of the overall process capacity occurs only when capacity at the bottleneck operation is increased.

CAPACITY CUSHION

capacity cushion The amount of reserve capacity a firm maintains to handle variability in the process or demand. It measures the amount by which the average utilization falls below 100 percent.

Average utilization rates should not get too close to 100 percent. When they do, that is usually a signal to increase capacity or decrease order acceptance so as to avoid declining productivity and maintain customer service. The **capacity cushion** is the amount of reserve capacity a firm maintains to handle sudden increases in demand or temporary losses of production capacity; it measures the amount by which the average capacity utilization falls below 100 percent. Specifically:

$$\text{Capacity cushion} = 100\% - \text{Capacity utilization (\%)}$$

COMPLEX PROCESSES. Many service and manufacturing firms offer multiple products in small volumes, each of which may have a different sequence of operations or workstations. For example, project or small batch processes do not enjoy the simple line flows shown in Figure 4.2. Even if a similar sequence is followed, the operations time may be unique for each customer or product. However, process capacity and bottlenecks can still be identified by computing the average utilization of each operation across a group of projects, customers, or products, as we see in Example 4.1.

EXAMPLE 4.1   *Identifying Capacity in a Service Process*

Speedy Loan, a financial services company, promises fast turnaround on loan applications. It offers three basic types of loans: (A) new mortgage applications; (B) mortgage renewals; and (C) car loans. Loan applications are processed through five different workstations (V, W, X, Y, and Z). Except for workstation X, which has two workers, all workstations are staffed by one worker.

Different types of loan applications require different steps to cross-reference the applicant's financial background, assess the applicant's risk profile, and compile the final loan authorization for signature. The flowcharts in Figure 4.3 note the order of steps and processing

FIGURE 4.3 *Flowcharts for Speedy Loan*

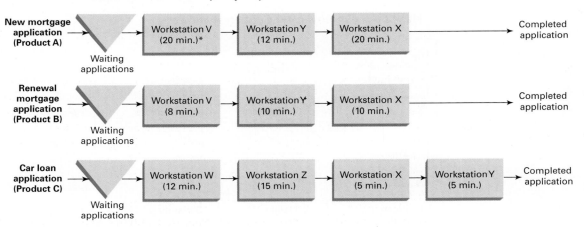

*Note: All processing times are minutes per application.

TABLE 4.1

WORKSTATION	WORKERS (number)	WORKLOAD (minutes)			TOTAL	EFFECTIVE CAPACITY (minutes)	CAPACITY UTILIZATION (percent)
		PRODUCT A	PRODUCT B	PRODUCT C			
V	1	60 × 20 = 1200	80 × 8 = 640	0	1840	2100	88
W	1	0	0	100 × 12 = 1200	1200	2100	57
X	2	60 × 20 = 1200	80 × 10 = 800	100 × 5 = 500	2500	4200	60
Y	1	60 × 12 = 720	80 × 10 = 800	100 × 5 = 500	2020	2100	96
Z	1	0	0	100 × 15 = 1500	1500	2100	71

times per type of application. (Inverted triangles at the beginning of each process represent the inbox or queue of applications waiting for processing.) Workers are currently available for 35 hours per week.

Customer demand currently is 60 new mortgage applications, 80 mortgage renewals, and 100 car loans. Which operation is the bottleneck, limiting the process capacity for Speedy Loan?

SOLUTION

For capacity utilization, the total workload for each workstation is based on the overall mix of applications, and processing time requirements for each application. *Output* is most easily expressed here as total time required to meet all customer demand each week, termed workload. The customer demand for each application, listed as Products A, B, and C, is converted into minutes, and then summed across all three products for each workstation, as noted in the sixth column of Table 4.1. The *effective capacity* is based on the number of workers and the number of available hours for each worker each week. Thus, effective capacity for each workstation is 35 hours, or 2100 minutes, per week, except for workstation X, which has two people, yielding 4200 minutes (see Table 4.1). So now capacity utilization is calculated as the ratio of required output (workload) to effective capacity for each workstation (last column).

Decision Point The process capacity is set by the operation with the highest capacity utilization, workstation Y. This workstation needs the most total time to process all customer demand for the week. If customer demand increases even marginally, Speedy Loan will not be able to meet market requirements.

MARKET DEMAND. More generally, market demand is also an important factor to consider when looking for bottlenecks. If demand exceeds the effective capacity of any individual operation, *each* of these operations is a bottleneck to creating satisfied customers. A clear signal of this unmet demand is to calculate a capacity utilization of greater than 100 percent for any operation.

For example, if the market requires 90 drawers per hour from the drawer manufacturing process, two operations have a capacity utilization of greater than 100 percent. Specifically, Nailing would have utilization of 90 ÷ 75 × 100 = 120 percent; for Sanding, utilization is 90 ÷ 85 × 100 = 106 percent. Both operations are bottlenecks; to fulfill all market demand, the effective capacity of both operations must be increased. So when identifying bottlenecks, it is important to keep two perspectives in mind: internally, the operation(s) that establishes process capacity, and externally, the operation(s) that has insufficient capacity to meet market demand.

ESTIMATING CAPACITY REQUIREMENTS

The demand forecast has to be converted to a number that can be compared directly with the capacity measure being used. Suppose that capacity is expressed as the number of available stations at an operation (e.g., people, equipment, etc.). When just one product (service) is being processed, the number of stations required, M, is:

$$\text{Number of stations required} = \frac{\text{Processing time required to meet demand}}{\substack{\text{Time available from one station,} \\ \text{after deducting desired cushion}}}$$

$$M = \frac{Dp}{N[1 - (C/100)]}$$

where:

D = Forecast demand (e.g., customers per year)

p = Processing time (e.g., hours per customer)

N = Total time during which the station operates (e.g., hours per year)

C = Desired capacity cushion (e.g., $0.18 = 18\%$)

The processing time, p, in the numerator depends on the process and methods selected to do the work. Estimates of p come from established work standards or equipment specifications. The denominator, N, considers the total availability of the station, using the same time interval over which we developed the forecast demand, such as a year. N is then multiplied by a proportion that accounts for the desired capacity cushion, C. The proportion is simply $1 - C$, where C is converted from a percentage to a proportion by dividing by 100.

Other managerial decisions and problems that create variability can reduce the capacity cushion, including scheduled maintenance, breakdowns, and changing from one product to another (i.e., setup time). **Setup time** is the additional time needed to change over from one service or product to the next, and increases the time required (numerator). The setup time needed is found by dividing the forecast demand by the total number of batches produced over a particular time period, which gives the number of setups per year, and then multiplying by the time per setup.

For example, if the monthly demand for a particular wood drawer size is 1200 units, and the average order size is 160, there is an average of $1200/160 = 7.5$ setups per month. If each setup takes 50 minutes, we must account for $(7.5 \times 50) \div 60 = 6.25$ hours lost to setups each month. Accounting for both processing and setup time when there are multiple products and services (remember that time must be expressed consistently in terms of hour, month, year, etc.), we get:

setup time The time required to change or readjust a process or an operation from one service or product to another.

$$\text{Number of stations required} = \frac{\substack{\text{Processing } and \text{ setup time required to} \\ \text{meet demand, summed over all products}}}{\substack{\text{Time available from one station,} \\ \text{after deducting desired cushion}}}$$

$$M = \frac{[Dp + (D/Q)s]_{\text{product 1}} + [Dp + (D/Q)s]_{\text{product 2}} + \cdots + [Dp + (D/Q)s]_{\text{product } n}}{N[1 - (C/100)]}$$

where:

Q = Number of units in each batch

s = Setup time per batch

Always round up the fractional part unless it is cost-efficient to use short-term options such as overtime or stockouts to cover any shortfalls.

| EXAMPLE 4.2 | *Estimating Requirements* |

A copy centre in an office building prepares bound reports for two large clients. The centre makes multiple copies (the batch size) of each report. The processing time to run, collate, and bind each copy depends on, among other factors, the number of pages. The centre operates 250 days per year, with one eight-hour shift. Management believes that a capacity cushion of 15 percent (beyond the allowance built into time standards) is best. It currently has three copy machines. On the basis of the following table of information, determine how many machines are needed at the copy centre.

ITEM	CLIENT X	CLIENT Y
Annual demand forecast (copies)	2000	6000
Standard processing time (hour/copy)	0.5	0.7
Average batch size (copies per report)	20	30
Standard setup time (hours)	0.25	0.40

SOLUTION

$$M = \frac{[Dp + (D/Q)s]_{\text{product 1}} + [Dp + (D/Q)s]_{\text{product 2}}}{N[1 - (C/100)]}$$

$$= \frac{[2000(0.5) + (2000/20)(0.25)]_{\text{client X}} + [6000(0.7) + (6000/30)(0.40)]_{\text{client Y}}}{[(250 \text{ days/year})(1 \text{ shift/day})(8 \text{ hours/shift})](1.0 - 15/100)}$$

$$= \frac{5305}{1700} = 3.12$$

Rounding up to the next integer gives a requirement of four machines for these two clients.

Decision Point   The copy centre's capacity is being stretched and no longer has the desired 15 percent capacity cushion. Not wanting customer service to suffer, management decided to use overtime as a short-term solution to handle past-due orders. If demand continues at the current level or grows, it will acquire a fourth machine.

INVENTORY

Inventory is any stock of items used to support the production of goods and services or satisfy customer demand. Further details are provided in Chapter 5, "Inventory Management," so it is sufficient at this point to recognize that items include any materials, orders, information, and people that flow through a process.

For purposes of process structure, inventory has two critical implications: cost and time. First, increasing the amount of inventory adds to the cost of producing goods and services. For example, if a copy centre holds a stock of raw paper between weekly deliveries from a supplier, the firm must pay for the related direct costs, such as working capital and handling. Even people waiting in line at a restaurant have a cost—for the physical space, customer aggravation, and potentially lost business.

Second, the amount of inventory is related to the time that customers or products take to move through a process. A waiting line at a bank offers a simple example; as the average number of people waiting in line in front of each teller increases, the average overall service time increases. The same principle applies to both manufacturing and services, where items are typically waiting in front of several operations. Thus, the total time that a typical item spends in any process, termed **throughput time**, increases as the average level of inventory in that process increases.

Inventory level and throughput time can be related mathematically using Little's Law (Little, 1992). The *average* throughput time for items in a process is related to

throughput time Total time for an item to move through a process from the first operation to the last, including operations time, movement time between operations, and wait time.

FIGURE 4.4   *Measuring Process Performance[2]*

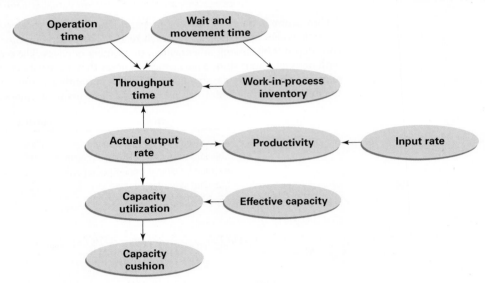

both average work-in-process (WIP) inventory and actual output rate. (The first and last operation for the process must be clearly defined.)

$$\text{Throughput time} = \frac{\text{WIP inventory}}{\text{Output rate}}$$

Note that for this calculation, output rate must always be expressed as "items per time" (unlike capacity utilization, where both output and effective capacity can be expressed in any identical units). Thus, if a copy centre had an average of 80 customer orders waiting for or in various stages of production (e.g., layout, printing, and packaging) and serviced 200 customers each five-day week, an order is expected to take, on average, $80 \div 200 = 0.4$ weeks, or two days, to complete.

The throughput time for a *specific* item as it moves through a process can also be found by summing all the time for individual operations and activities:

$$\text{Throughput time} = \text{Operations time} + \text{Movement time} + \text{Wait time}$$

Wait time captures many sources of delay, including machine setup, waiting for resources (such as people, equipment, and information), and other delays. A summary of the relationships among these process measures is depicted in Figure 4.4. For example, throughput time includes both operation and wait time, and is a function of work-in-process inventory and actual production rate.

If increasing inventory adds to cost and throughput time, why do managers allow inventory to be in a process? This critical question returns us to the process management triangle (see Figure 4.1). Inventory can smooth the flow of customers, parts, or materials through the process, which in turn necessitates less investment in capacity or serves as a buffer to accommodate greater variability.

VARIABILITY

Unfortunately, in practice, designing and evaluating process capacity is rarely as straightforward as illustrated in Figure 4.2. Products, people, and equipment change from minute to minute, day to day, and year to year. Variation is really a measure of how much something changes. Many managers have a general intuition about the average output or demand rates for a process, usually based on observing a process over an extended period of time. Variability is much less intuitive.

For example, Bombardier's sales of a particular model of Sea-Doo watercraft in a particular region might average 27 units per day, based on sales during the previous year. A simple approach might be to install capacity to produce exactly 27 units per day. However, the product manager would quickly point out that the same number of units are not sold each and every day. Instead, sales tend to be much higher before the summer season, and much lower (or nonexistent) during the remainder of the year.

This variability affects Bombardier's entire process. Suppliers, manufacturing, assembly, logistics, and sales support, to name just a few subprocesses, must be designed to take into account this seasonal rise and fall in sales. Managers can choose to build a very large assembly plant to accommodate peak demand (i.e., greater capacity), or, more commonly, manufacture extra units ahead of peak season (i.e., greater inventory). If insufficient capacity or inventory is ready for the peak season, another, much less attractive option is to turn away customers! In essence, this last option reduces variability by lowering the maximum demand filled by operations.

IMPLICATIONS FOR PROCESS CAPACITY. If we return to our simple process in Figure 4.2, how is process capacity related to variability? First, it is important to clearly differentiate between the capacity of individual operations and the overall capacity of the process.

Second, if each individual operation has some variability, then its output rate (i.e., effective capacity) is really an average, with some hour-to-hour variation. So Nailing might produce 77 drawers during one hour and then 71 drawers the next hour because of a significant breakdown or quality problems. If Nailing were working by itself, we know that over the longer term the effective capacity would be 75 drawers per hour.

Third, because processes have operations that are performed in sequence, each operation is linked to, or depends on, those upstream and downstream. These are called *dependent operations*. Variation in one operation, such as breakdowns, can force downstream operations to stop. For example, if Sanding breaks down, Nailing must stop, because the flow of parts is **blocked**, and Finishing must also stop because it is **starved** for drawers. As a result, Nailing (bottleneck) cannot produce the expected 75 drawers during that hour. So we can't simply consider the effective capacity of each *operation*, but instead must consider how they interact to estimate overall process capacity.

Processes with dependent operations are very common. Air Canada offers another example where process delays create variability. After a plane arrives in Halifax with customers, several operations must be performed in sequence. The plane must be cleared to pull up to the terminal gate, passengers must be unloaded, the plane must be cleaned and refuelled, new passengers and baggage must be loaded, and the plane must be cleared to depart. If too many planes arrive simultaneously (possibly because of air traffic congestion or weather), the baggage crew's capacity will be overloaded, resulting in delays in unloading some planes. Processing a full plane also takes longer for some operations than a half-empty plane.

For our furniture manufacturing process to produce 75 drawers per hour, management has two basic options to accommodate the variability in Nailing and Sanding:

1. *Add capacity* to the Nailing bottleneck, so that the *process* is capable of producing the expected 75 parts per hour, even when breakdowns in Sanding occur. The extra capacity needed depends on the variability of Sanding. For example, an effective capacity of 79 drawers per hour at Nailing may be sufficient to accommodate the variability at Sanding (Figure 4.5(a)).

blocked operation An operation that cannot pass work along to the next operation downstream and must stop.

starved operation An operation that runs out of work to process.

FIGURE 4.5 *Maintaining Process Output Rate with Variability*

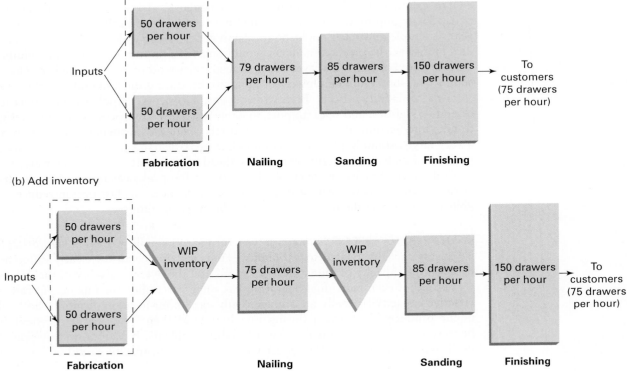

(a) Add capacity

(b) Add inventory

2. *Add inventory* between Nailing and Sanding, so that Nailing can continue to produce when a breakdown occurs in Sanding (Figure 4.5(b)). Because Sanding has a higher capacity, it will eventually catch up. For similar reasons, inventory could also be added ahead of the Nailing operation to accommodate variability in Fabrication and ensure that Nailing is never starved for parts. However, the allowable inventory ahead of Nailing must be limited; otherwise, the faster production of Fabrication will far outpace Nailing.

Naturally, as indicated by the process management triangle, a combination of additional capacity and inventory also would accommodate process variability. As the variability of Sanding increases further, additional capacity and inventory are necessary to maintain an average *process* output rate of 75 parts per hour. Again, the emphasis must be on the overall process capacity, not just on individual operations.

For Air Canada, variability in passenger loads or poor weather creates delays, which adds to work-in-process inventory in the form of stranded passengers (although people undoubtedly dislike being termed "inventory"). To estimate how much additional capacity or inventory is needed, managers must measure variability by gathering data on the frequency and pattern of variability—which then can be translated into the right mix of capacity and inventory. One tool to assist with this analysis is computer simulation (see Supplement G, "Simulation," in MyOMLab).

MEASURING VARIABILITY. For operation processes, variability can occur in the operations time needed by an X-ray technician, the reliability of a laser printer, or the time needed for an airline check-in process. One basic measure for comparing variability between operations or processes is the *coefficient of variation* (cv). This measure is simply a ratio of the standard deviation (a common statistical measure of variation) to the average.

$$\text{Coefficient of variation} = \frac{\text{Standard deviation}}{\text{Average}}$$

The higher that process variability is, the more expensive and difficult the process is to manage. So how high is the cv for a process with high variability? It really depends on both the time horizon and the relative stability of process alternatives. For example, researchers have suggested a high variability process has a cv of greater than 1.33 (Hopp and Spearman, 2001). High process variability is present in situations, for example, where machine breakdowns require long repair times and customer demand fluctuates dramatically.

TWO FORMS OF VARIABILITY. It is important to recognize that variability is not simply uncertainty. When we consider the many ways variability is introduced into a process, it becomes clear that variability takes on two general forms with different implications for managers: random and predictable variation. **Random variation** is introduced by chance and results from small changes or differences in equipment operations, people's behaviour, or environmental conditions. This form corresponds to uncertainty. In contrast, **predictable variation** is determined by specific, usually larger-scale causes, often driven by natural cycles related to time of day, day of week, season of year, or even multiyear economic cycles. Many management decisions also create predictable variation. For example, scheduling preventive maintenance on an aircraft engine reduces the fleet capacity available at that time to serve customers. Examples of each form of variability are illustrated in Table 4.2.

These two forms of variability often combine, making the management of processes quite complicated. For example, a manager at a copy centre might know from past sales data that there is an average of 200 customers per five-day week, but that sales tend to be higher at the end of the week (i.e., Thursday and Friday) with correspondingly lower figures at the beginning of the week (i.e., predictable variation). Yet, even for sales at the end of the week, the process must accommodate the random arrivals of particular customers, each with different copying needs. Customers (and orders) must wait longer for assistance, or more staff and copy machines must be scheduled.

Although both forms of variability can hurt the efficiency of a process, random variability is much more difficult for managers to adjust to—often at significant cost

random variation
Uncertainty that results from chance related to small changes or differences in equipment operations, people's behaviour, or environmental conditions.

predictable variation
Changes determined by specific, usually larger-scale causes, often driven by natural cycles such as time of day. Many management decisions, such as preventive maintenance, also create predictable variation.

TABLE 4.2	*Examples of Variability*	
	FORM OF VARIABILITY	
SOURCE	**RANDOM**	**PREDICTABLE**
Internal (e.g., process)	• Quality defects from a metal stamping press • Equipment breakdowns • Worker absenteeism	• Setup time for a packaging operation • Preventive maintenance • Number of models of an automobile
External (e.g., market or supply chain)	• Arrival of individual customers at a hair salon • Transit time for local delivery of package • Medical treatments needed for emergency patient	• Daily pattern of demand for fast-food restaurant • Seasonal demand for printing of annual reports • More technical support immediately after new product launch

to the firm or the customer. In the short term, random variability must usually be accommodated, possibly by adding extra capacity, coping with longer waiting lines (see Supplement 4S in this book, "Waiting Lines"), or maintaining inventory of extra products (see Chapter 5, "Inventory Management"). Managers can take specific actions over the longer term to reduce random process variability, such as upgrading process technology and reducing poor-quality raw materials (see Chapter 6, "Quality and Process Improvement"), scheduling the arrival of customers (see Chapter 10, "Managing Demand and Forecasting"), or the availability of equipment and parts (see Chapter 12, "Resource Planning").

Because predictable variability is linked to specific cycles or particular management practices, managers can plan and act with greater confidence. Preventive maintenance can be shifted to the weekend, additional staff can be added for service at lunchtime, or larger batches can be produced of a standard, frequently requested item. Predictable customer behaviour can also be modified to some degree, possibly through the use of incentives. Discounts can be offered to customers to shift demand in a relatively predictable manner.

If we return to our earlier discussion of bottlenecks, variability in workload for individual operations along a process can create *floating bottlenecks*. One week the particular mix of work may make Nailing a bottleneck, and the next week it may make Sanding appear to be the bottleneck. This type of variability increases the complexity of day-to-day scheduling. In this situation, management prefers lower utilization rates, which allow greater slack to absorb unexpected surges in demand. For service processes, in addition to lowering capacity utilization, managers can implement a reservation system to adjust the arrival and mix of customers in a predictable way.

Finally, variability should not be viewed as always bad. In fact, customers may desire a broad range of options. If a competitive priority of the firm is to respond to this market need, an operations manager should not be pushing for lower variability! Instead, operations can respond with greater flexibility and customization, which requires the addition of capacity (i.e., lower capacity utilization). Thus, whether good or bad, variability must be actively managed.

STRATEGICALLY MANAGING CAPACITY

Identifying and putting in place the right amount of capacity is central to the long-term success of an organization. In the short term, managers must focus on the levering existing capacity and deciding how large a capacity cushion is needed to handle variable demand. The theory of constraints (TOC) is one approach to ensure that existing resources are used efficiently and effectively by focusing on maximizing the value of the bottleneck. Longer-term, industry-level transformations may push managers to invest in new capacity, driven by changes in product and process technologies. Too little capacity can often be as painful (in terms of lost opportunities) as too much. Managers have to consider if their firm's capacity should expand ahead of demand, or wait until demand arrives. These decisions can be linked to both operations strategy and process configuration to enhance competitiveness for each situation.

WestJet increased capacity by 11 percent from the prior year, and served over 15 million "guests." Yet each time a plane is boarded, bottlenecks must be managed to speed customer service.[3]

THEORY OF CONSTRAINTS

theory of constraints (TOC) An approach to management that focuses on whatever impedes progress toward the goal of maximizing the flow of total value-added funds or sales less discounts and variable costs. Also referred to as the drum-rope-buffer method.

Before expanding the capacity of any process, it is critical to ensure that existing resources are used efficiently and effectively. The fundamental idea underlying the **theory of constraints (TOC)** is to focus on bottleneck resources because increasing their output increases the output of the entire process and financial performance. A bottleneck might appear in any process, such as an activity in order entry, new product development, or manufacturing. The goal is to simultaneously improve net profit, return on investment, and cash flow (Goldratt and Cox, 1992).

In essence, the bottleneck resources must be kept as busy as practical. To do so, managers should minimize the idle time lost at bottlenecks, either due to jobs or customers being delayed at upstream operations in the process, or due to necessary materials and tools being temporarily unavailable. They should also minimize the time spent unproductively for setup time. When a changeover is made at a bottleneck operation, the number of units or customers processed before the next changeover should be large compared to the number processed at less critical operations. Maximizing the number processed per setup means that there will be fewer setups per year, and thus less total time lost to setups.

Using the drum-rope-buffer method, managers must focus on scheduling around bottlenecks. The bottleneck becomes the "drum" for the rest of the process, setting the pace. Inputs are only pulled into the process at that pace (i.e., rope), and extra inventory is placed around the bottleneck so that it is never starved or blocked (i.e., buffer). Minimal inventory is allowed elsewhere in the process to minimize throughput time.

For example, let's return to our drawer manufacturing process (see Figure 4.6). Suppose that the delivery commitments for all styles of computer desk drawers for the next month indicate that Nailing has a capacity utilization of 105 percent. The other three operations will have capacity utilization of less than 100 percent. According to TOC, Nailing is the only bottleneck resource, whereas Fabrication, Sanding, and Finishing are nonbottleneck resources. Any idle time at Nailing is a lost opportunity to generate total value-added funds. To maximize the output rate of the drawer manufacturing system, managers should focus on Nailing's schedule.

APPLYING TOC. The theory of constraints focuses management's attention and action on the bottleneck, and involves the following steps:

1. *Identify the system bottleneck(s).* For the drawer manufacturing example, the bottleneck is Nailing because it is restricting the firm's ability to meet

FIGURE 4.6 *Drum-Rope-Buffer System*

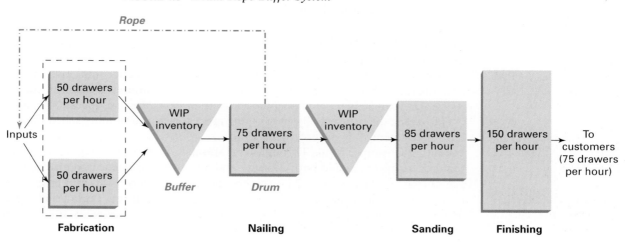

the schedules of subsequent processes. Bottlenecks also can often be identified by looking for the operation with the largest queue of parts being delayed or longest line of customers waiting for service.

2. *Exploit the bottleneck(s).* Create schedules that maximize the throughput of the bottleneck(s). For the drawer manufacturing example, schedule Nailing to maximize its utilization while meeting other commitments to the extent possible. Also make sure that only good-quality parts are passed on to the bottleneck from other operations.

3. *Subordinate all other decisions to step 2.* Nonbottleneck resources should be scheduled to support the schedule of the bottleneck and not produce more than it can handle. That is, Fabrication should not produce more than Nailing can handle, and the activities of Sanding and subsequent operations should be based on the output rate of Nailing.

4. *Elevate the bottleneck(s).* After the scheduling improvements in steps 1–3 have been exhausted and the bottleneck is still a constraint to throughput, management should consider increasing the capacity of the bottleneck. For example, if Nailing is still a constraint after exhausting schedule improvements, consider increasing its capacity by adding another shift or other resources.

5. *Do not let inertia set in.* Actions taken in steps 3 and 4 will improve Nailing's capacity and may alter the loads on other processes. Consequently, the system constraint(s) may have shifted. Then the steps need to be repeated in order to identify and manage the new set of constraints.

Over the longer term, capacity of bottleneck operations can be expanded in various ways. Investments can be made in new equipment or operating additional hours per week. Investing in new information technology can also help highly skilled workers service more customers. More generally, managers might also relieve a bottleneck by redesigning the process, through either process re-engineering or process improvement (see Chapter 3, "Process Configuration").

Because of its potential for improving performance dramatically, many manufacturers have applied the principles of the theory of constraints, including National Semiconductor, Dresser Industries, Allied-Signal, Bethlehem Steel, Johnson Controls, and Rockwell Automotive. All manufacturers implementing TOC principles can also dramatically change the mind-set of employees and managers. Instead of focusing solely on their own functions, they can see the "big picture" and where other improvements in the system might lie.

STRATEGICALLY POSITIONING THE BOTTLENECK. So where would a thoughtful manager ideally want the bottleneck to be located in a process? The natural inclination of many managers is to try to achieve a perfectly balanced process to reduce total investment, where each operation has the same capacity. Alternatively, to simplify the task of coordinating the process, a manager could position the bottleneck as the first operation in a process.

However, the primary objective of any process is not to simplify scheduling or minimize investment, but instead to maximize *customer value* as discussed in Chapter 1, "Creating Customer Value Through Operations." As we saw in Figure 4.5, variability requires managers to add both capacity and inventory (or queues) to produce the average output rate demanded by customers. The logical action is to add both selectively, particularly to those stations where capacity is least expensive. Taking this reasoning a few steps further and continuing to add small amounts of capacity to accommodate variability, we soon see that the most expensive operation is the last place that we want to add capacity—which creates a bottleneck for the process. Then, on the basis of the drum-rope-buffer method, inventory must be added judiciously ahead of the bottleneck, with minimal inventory elsewhere in the process.

Thus, the most expensive operation should be our bottleneck (if it isn't, we have a significant opportunity for improvement!). But the most expensive operation is not necessarily the most expensive piece of equipment. In a software firm such as Corel Corporation, the developer of WordPerfect, the most expensive resource is highly skilled people, such as software engineers. These individuals should never be forced to be idle because they are waiting for other process operations, such as testing for bugs.

RELATING CAPACITY UTILIZATION TO VARIABILITY

Businesses find lower capacity utilization (i.e., larger capacity cushion) appropriate when variability increases. In certain service industries (e.g., groceries), demand on some days of the week is predictably higher than on other days, and there are even hour-to-hour patterns. Long customer waiting times are not acceptable, because customers grow impatient if they have to wait in a supermarket checkout line for more than a few minutes. Prompt customer service requires supermarkets to maintain lower capacity utilization to handle peak demand.

Similar issues arise if long-term future demand is uncertain, particularly if resource flexibility is low. Another type of demand uncertainty occurs with a changing product mix, possibly due to new product introductions or customized orders. Though total demand might remain stable, the load can shift unpredictably from one work centre to another as the mix changes. Supply uncertainty also favours large capacity cushions. Firms need to build in excess capacity to allow for employee absenteeism, vacations, holidays, and any other delays. Penalty costs for overtime and subcontracting can create the need for further increases in capacity cushions.

In general, capacity, inventory, and variability are strongly related to process structure, as depicted in Figure 4.7, with project and batch processes having higher variability, lower capacity utilization (and capital-intensity), and higher work-in-process inventories. At the other end of the spectrum, continuous processes have lower variability, higher capacity utilization, and lower work-in-process inventory.

Over the past ten years, Canadian manufacturers have maintained an average cushion of approximately 20 percent.[4] However, given the linkage between process choice and capacity cushion, it is important to recognize that the average size of the cushion varies by industry. Moreover, for some industries, capacity comes in large, expensive increments, so expanding even by the minimum amount possible may create a large cushion. For example, a new paper plant is sized to capture economies of scale, and adding an airline route often requires flying a minimum number of flights, which can create overcapacity.

The argument in favour of small cushions is simple: unused capacity costs money. For capital-intensive firms, minimizing the capacity cushion is vital, as a low return on investment tends to occur if the utilization is low. As a result, managers in capital-intensive industries such as paper, chemicals, or steel prefer cushions of about 10 percent or lower. Small cushions have other advantages; they reveal inefficiencies that may be masked by excess capacity—problems with absenteeism, for example, or unreliable suppliers. Once managers and workers have identified such problems, they often can find ways to correct them. However, these industries have great difficulty adjusting capacity to match peaks and valleys in market demand.

FIGURE 4.7 *Matching Process Variability and Capacity Cushion*

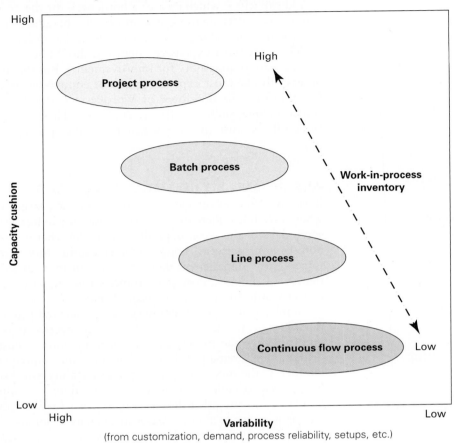

In more labour-intensive industries, where the number of workers can be easily adjusted, a larger capacity cushion is possible, because the lower investment in equipment makes high utilization less critical. For example, the less capital-intensive leather goods industry has a much larger cushion that averages about 30 percent in Canada. This industry can more easily accommodate changes in demand by varying the size of the workforce. Similar challenges arise in service firms. By some estimates, the hotel industry breaks even with 60 percent to 70 percent utilization (40 percent to 30 percent cushion) and begins to suffer customer service problems when the cushion drops to 20 percent.

COMPETITIVE PRIORITIES. Decisions about capacity cushions, inventory, and variability (Figure 4.7) return us to the competitive priorities for operations management introduced in the opening chapter. Consequently, capacity decisions cannot be isolated from major process decisions about customer involvement and resource flexibility, to name a few. For example, a continuous process tends to mean little customer involvement and customization, low capacity cushion (i.e., high utilization), low resource flexibility, and high vertical integration. Collectively, these are consistent with competitive priorities that favour low cost and consistent high quality. In contrast, a project or small batch process tends to mean high customer involvement and customization, high capacity cushion (i.e., low utilization), high resource flexibility, and little vertical integration. These characteristics are consistent with competitive priorities that favour high-performance design, fast delivery, and customization.

A China Southern Airlines (CSA) jetliner taking off at the Guangzhou Baiyun International Airport, China. The Boeing 777-2000, along with the other planes waiting to take off, are part of an expanding CSA fleet. The capacity expansion helped CSA gain economies of scale and garner a greater share of China's domestic market.

economies of scale
A concept that states that the average unit cost of a good or service can be reduced by increasing its output rate.

diseconomies of scale
When the average cost per unit increases as the facility's size increases.

ECONOMIES OF SCALE

A concept known as **economies of scale** states that the average unit cost of a good or service can be reduced by increasing its output rate. There are four principal reasons why economies of scale can drive costs down when output increases: fixed costs are spread over more units, construction costs are reduced, costs of purchased materials are cut, and process advantages are found.

SPREADING FIXED COSTS. In the short term, certain process costs do not vary with changes in the output rate, as noted earlier in Figure 3.4. These fixed costs include equipment, heating costs, debt service, and management salaries. Depreciation of plant and equipment already owned is also a fixed cost in the accounting sense. When the output rate—and, therefore, the facility's utilization rate—increase, the average unit cost drops, because fixed costs are spread over more units.

REDUCING CONSTRUCTION COSTS. Certain activities and expenses are required in building small and large facilities alike: building permits, architects' fees, rental of building equipment, and the like. Doubling the size of the facility usually does not double construction costs.

CUTTING COSTS OF PURCHASED MATERIALS. Higher volumes can reduce the costs of purchased materials and services. They give the purchaser a better bargaining position and the opportunity to take advantage of quantity discounts. Retailers such as Canadian Tire reap significant economies of scale because their national stores sell huge volumes of each item. Producers that rely on a vast network of suppliers (e.g., General Motors) and food processors (e.g., Maple Leaf Foods) can also buy inputs for less because of the potential for competitive bidding and the large quantities that they purchase.

FINDING PROCESS ADVANTAGES. High-volume production provides many opportunities for cost reduction. At a higher output rate, the process shifts toward a line or continuous process, with resources dedicated to individual products. Firms may be able to justify the expense of more efficient technology or more specialized equipment. The benefits of dedicating resources to individual products or services may include speeding up the learning effect, lowering inventory, improving process and job designs, and reducing the number of changeovers. Alternatively, flexible technology and mass customization can allow higher utilization and lower cost.

DISECONOMIES OF SCALE

As a service or manufacturing facility continues to grow, it is possible for it to become so large that **diseconomies of scale** set in; that is, the average cost per unit increases as the facility's size increases. The reason is that excessive size can bring complexity, loss of focus, and inefficiencies that raise the average unit cost of a product or service. There may be too many layers of employees and bureaucracy, and management may lose touch with employees and customers. The organization is less agile and loses the flexibility needed to respond to changing demand. Many large companies become so involved in analysis and planning that they innovate less and avoid risks. The result is that small companies outperform corporate giants in numerous industries.

FIGURE 4.8 *Economies and Diseconomies of Scale*

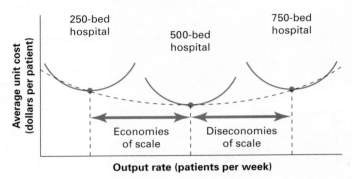

Figure 4.8 illustrates the transition from economies of scale to diseconomies of scale. The 500-bed hospital shows economies of scale because the average unit cost at its *best operating level*, represented by the blue dot, is less than that of the 250-bed hospital. However, further expansion to a 750-bed hospital leads to higher average unit costs and diseconomies of scale. One reason the 500-bed hospital enjoys greater economies of scale than the 250-bed hospital is that the cost of building and equipping it is less than twice the cost for the smaller hospital. The 750-bed facility would enjoy similar savings. Its higher average unit costs can be explained only by diseconomies of scale, which outweigh the savings realized in construction costs.

However, this analysis does not mean that the optimal size for all hospitals is 500 beds. Optimal size depends on the number of patients per week to be served. On the one hand, a hospital serving a small community would have lower costs by choosing a 250-bed capacity rather than the 500-bed capacity. On the other hand, assuming the same cost structure, a large community will be served more efficiently by two 500-bed hospitals than by one 1000-bed facility.

TIMING OF EXPANSION

A basic concern for any long-term planning of capacity is when to expand and by how much. Figure 4.9 illustrates two extreme strategies: the *expansionist strategy*, which involves large, infrequent jumps in capacity, and the *wait-and-see strategy*, which involves smaller, more frequent jumps. The first strategy relies on capacity expansion ahead of demand (i.e., lead), while the second favours trailing demand (i.e., lag).

The timing and sizing of expansion are related; that is, if demand is increasing and the time between increments increases, the size of the increments must also increase. The expansionist strategy, which stays ahead of demand, minimizes the chance of sales

FIGURE 4.9 *Two Capacity Strategies*

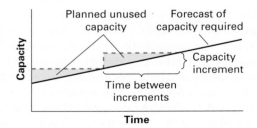

(a) Expansionist strategy

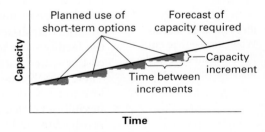

(b) Wait-and-see strategy

lost to insufficient capacity. The wait-and-see strategy lags behind demand, relying on short-term options such as the use of overtime, temporary workers, subcontractors, stockouts, and postponement of preventive maintenance to meet any shortfalls.

Several factors favour the expansionist strategy. Expansion may result in economies of scale and a faster rate of learning, thus helping a firm reduce its costs and compete on price. This strategy might increase the firm's market share or act as a form of pre-emptive marketing. By making a large capacity expansion or announcing that one is imminent, the firm uses capacity to pre-empt expansion by other firms. These other firms must sacrifice some of their market share or risk burdening the industry with overcapacity. To be successful, however, the pre-empting firm must have the credibility

MANAGERIAL PRACTICE
Expansionist Strategy for Capacity in the Ethanol Industry

A search for renewable energy and alternative sources of fuel has made ethanol production a huge growth industry in many parts of the world, including Canada. Ethanol, one form of bio-fuel, is fermented from corn in Canada and the United States; one litre of ethanol requires roughly 3.6 litres of corn. Worldwide capacity has expanded dramatically, by seven times, over the past decade, reaching over 100 billion litres annually in 2010. Some experts predict that biofuels, including ethanol, might represent 20 percent of all transportation fuel within 30 years.

But financial returns from all this capacity expansion remain uncertain. Companies and farm cooperatives have built so many distilleries so quickly that the ethanol market has been plagued by a glut, as demand for ethanol did not increase as much as hoped. Oversupply put downward pressure on price. At the same time, scarcity and price of raw materials needed to feed ethanol plants became an issue. For example, the price of corn rose by 150 percent over a two-year period, further eroding profitability.

Capacity concerns extend down the supply chain, but for very different reasons. Unlike gasoline, traditional pipelines cannot be used to move the fuel because ethanol is corrosive and contains traces of water. Instead, it must be transported by specialized ethanol rail cars, trucks, and barges. Capacity of such a transportation network also has not kept up with the surge in surplus ethanol production. As a result of the global recession, a number of companies moved to modify their plans for new plant construction.

Suncor delayed the planned expansion of its biofuel plant in St. Clair, Ontario, by two years. The plant opened in 2011, at a cost of $120 million, and can now produce a total

An expansion to Suncor's St. Clair ethanol plant, the largest ethanol facility in Canada, was delayed in 2008 due to the global recession.

of 400 million litres of ethanol annually. The plant is located near large farming operations that grow industrial grade corn not fit for human consumption. All the ethanol produced at the St. Clair plant is blended into Suncor's Petro-Canada branded gasoline to provide a cleaner burning fuel option to retail customers and meet Canada's Renewable Fuel Mandate. Going one step further, other firms are exploring next-generation technology that uses switch grass or wheat straw as raw materials, rather than corn, which in turn may fuel another round of industry expansion based on less expensive raw materials.[5]

to convince the competition that it will carry out its plans—and it must signal its plans before the competition can act.

The conservative wait-and-see strategy is to expand in smaller increments, such as by renovating existing facilities rather than building new ones. Because the wait-and-see strategy follows demand, it reduces the risks of overexpansion based on overly optimistic demand forecasts, obsolete technology, or inaccurate assumptions regarding the competition.

However, this strategy has its own risks, such as being pre-empted by a competitor or being unable to respond if demand is unexpectedly high. The wait-and-see strategy has been criticized as a short-term strategy. Managers on the fast track to corporate advancement tend to take fewer risks. They earn promotions by avoiding the big mistake and maximizing short-term profits and return on investment. The wait-and-see strategy fits this short-term outlook, but it can erode market share over the long run.

Management may choose one of these two strategies or one of the many between these extremes. With strategies in the more moderate middle, firms may expand more frequently (on a smaller scale) than with the expansionist strategy but do not always lag behind demand as with the wait-and-see strategy. An intermediate strategy could be to *follow the leader*, expanding when others do. If others are right, so are you, and nobody gains a competitive advantage. If they make a mistake and overexpand, so have you, but everyone shares in the agony of overcapacity.

PLANNING FOR LONG-TERM CAPACITY

Long-term decisions for capacity would typically include whether to add a new plant or warehouse or to reduce the number of existing ones, how many workstations a given department should have, or how many workers are needed to staff a given process. Some of these decisions can take years to become operational. Hence, a systematic approach is needed to plan for long-term-capacity decisions. In describing this procedure, we assume that management already performed the preliminary steps of determining the process's existing capacity and assessing whether its current capacity cushion is appropriate.

1. Estimate future capacity requirements.
2. Identify gaps by comparing requirements with available capacity.
3. Develop alternative plans for filling the gaps.
4. Evaluate each alternative, both qualitatively and quantitatively, and make a final choice.

STEP 1: ESTIMATE CAPACITY REQUIREMENTS

A process's **capacity requirement** is what its capacity should be for some future time period to meet the demand of the firm's customers (external or internal), given the firm's desired capacity cushion. Larger requirements are practical for processes or workstations that could potentially be bottlenecks in the future, and management may even plan for larger cushions than normal.

The foundation for estimating the needed capacity over the long term is forecasts of demand, productivity, competition, and technological change. These forecasts normally need to be made for several time periods in a **planning horizon**, which is the set of consecutive time periods considered for planning purposes. Long-term capacity plans need to consider more of the future (perhaps a whole decade) than do short-term plans. Unfortunately, the farther ahead you look, the more chance you have of making an inaccurate forecast.

capacity requirement The process capacity needed for some future time period to meet the demand of customers, given the firm's desired capacity cushion.

planning horizon The set of consecutive time periods considered for planning purposes.

capacity gap Any
difference (positive or
negative) between
projected demand and
current capacity.

STEP 2: IDENTIFY GAPS

A **capacity gap** is any difference (positive or negative) between projected demand and current capacity. Identifying gaps requires the use of the correct capacity measure. Complications arise when multiple operations and several resource inputs are involved. Expanding the capacity of some operations may increase overall capacity. However, if one operation is a bottleneck, capacity can be expanded only if the capacity of the bottleneck operation is expanded.

STEP 3: DEVELOP ALTERNATIVES

base case The act of
doing nothing and losing
orders from any demand
that exceeds current
capacity.

The next step is to develop alternative plans to cope with projected gaps. One alternative, called the **base case**, is to do nothing and simply lose orders from any demand that exceeds current capacity. Other alternatives are various timing and sizing options for adding new capacity, including the expansionist and wait-and-see strategies illustrated in Figure 4.9. Additional possibilities include expanding at a different location and using short-term options such as overtime, temporary workers, and subcontracting.

STEP 4: EVALUATE THE ALTERNATIVES

In this final step, the manager evaluates each alternative, both quantitatively and qualitatively.

QUALITATIVE CONCERNS. Qualitatively, the manager has to look at how each alternative fits the overall capacity strategy and other aspects of the business not covered by the financial analysis. Of particular concern might be uncertainties about demand, competitive reaction, technological change, and cost estimates. Some of these factors cannot be quantified and have to be assessed on the basis of judgment and experience. Others can be quantified, and the manager can analyze each alternative by using different assumptions about the future. One set of assumptions could represent a worst case, in which demand is less, competition is greater, and construction costs are higher than expected. Another set of assumptions could represent the most optimistic view of the future. This type of "what if" analysis allows the manager to get an idea of each alternative's implications before making a final choice.

QUANTITATIVE CONCERNS. Quantitatively, the manager estimates the change in cash flows for each alternative over the forecast time horizon compared to the base case. The manager is concerned here only with calculating the cash flows attributable to the project.

| EXAMPLE 4.3 | *Evaluating the Alternatives* |

Grandma's Chicken Restaurant is experiencing a boom in business. The owner expects to serve a total of 80 000 meals this year. Although the kitchen is operating at 100 percent capacity, the dining room can handle a total of 105 000 diners per year. Forecast demand for the next five years is 90 000 meals for the next year, followed by a 10 000-meal increase in each of the succeeding years.

One alternative is to expand both the kitchen and the dining room now, bringing their capacities up to 130 000 meals per year. The initial investment would be $200 000, made at the end of this year (year 0). The average meal is priced at $10, and the incremental before-tax profit margin is 20 percent. The 20 percent figure was arrived at by determining that, for each $10 meal, $8 covers variable costs. The remaining $2 goes to pre-tax profit.

What are the pre-tax cash flows from this project for the next five years compared to those of the base case of doing nothing?

SOLUTION

Recall that the base case of doing nothing results in losing all potential sales beyond 80 000 meals. With the new capacity, the cash flow would equal the extra meals served by having a 130 000-meal capacity, multiplied by a profit of $2 per meal. In year 0, the only cash flow is −$200 000 for the initial investment. In year 1, the 90 000-meal demand will be completely satisfied by the expanded capacity, so the incremental cash flow is (90 000 − 80 000)(2) = $20 000. For subsequent years, the figures are as follows:

Year 2:   Demand = 100 000; Cash flow = (100 000 − 80 000)$2 = $40 000
Year 3:   Demand = 110 000; Cash flow = (110 000 − 80 000)$2 = $60 000
Year 4:   Demand = 120 000; Cash flow = (120 000 − 80 000)$2 = $80 000
Year 5:   Demand = 130 000; Cash flow = (130 000 − 80 000)$2 = $100 000

If the new capacity were smaller than the expected demand in any year, we would subtract the base case capacity from the new capacity (rather than the demand).

Decision Point Before deciding on this capacity alternative, the owner should account for the time value of money, applying such techniques as the present value or internal rate of return methods (see Supplement B, "Financial Analysis," in MyOMLab). The owner should also examine the qualitative concerns. For example, the homey atmosphere that the restaurant has projected may be lost with expansion. Furthermore, other alternatives should be considered.

TOOLS FOR CAPACITY PLANNING

Long-term capacity planning requires demand forecasts for an extended period of time. Unfortunately, forecast accuracy declines as the forecasting horizon lengthens. In addition, anticipating what competitors will do increases the uncertainty of demand forecasts. Finally, demand during any period is not evenly distributed; peaks and valleys of demand may (and often do) occur within the period. These realities necessitate the use of capacity cushions. In this section, we introduce three tools that deal more formally with demand uncertainty and variability: waiting-line models, simulation, and decision trees. Waiting-line models and simulation account for the random, independent behaviour of many customers, in terms of both their time of arrival and their processing needs. Decision trees allow anticipation of events such as competitors' actions.

WAITING-LINE MODELS

Waiting-line models often are useful in capacity planning. Waiting lines tend to develop in front of a work centre, such as an airport ticket counter, a machine centre, or a central computer. The reason is that the arrival time between orders or customers varies and the processing time may vary from one customer to the next. Waiting-line models use probability distributions to provide estimates of average customer delay time, average length of waiting lines, and utilization of the work centre. Managers can use this information to choose the most cost-effective capacity, balancing customer service and the cost of adding capacity.

Supplement 4S in this book, "Waiting Lines," which follows this chapter, provides a fuller treatment of these models. It introduces formulas for estimating important characteristics of a waiting line, such as average customer waiting time and average facility utilization, for different facility designs. For example, a facility might be designed to have one or multiple lines at each operation and to route customers through one or multiple operations. Given the estimating capability of these formulas and cost estimates for waiting and idle time, managers can select cost-effective designs and capacity levels that also provide the desired level of customer service.

SIMULATION

More complex waiting-line problems must be analyzed with simulation. This tool helps to identify a process's bottlenecks and appropriate capacity cushions, even for complex processes with random demand patterns and/or with predictable surges in demand during a typical day. Building and working with simulation models is treated in greater detail in Supplement G, "Simulation," in MyOMLab.

DECISION TREES

The decision tree method is a general approach to a wide range of decisions, such as product planning, process management, capacity, and location. A decision tree can be particularly valuable for evaluating different capacity expansion alternatives when demand is uncertain and sequential decisions are involved. For example, the owner of Grandma's Chicken Restaurant (see Example 4.3) may expand the restaurant now only to discover in a few years that demand growth is much higher than forecast. In that case, she needs to decide whether to expand further. In terms of construction costs and down-time, expanding twice is likely to be much more expensive than building a large facility from the outset. However, making a large expansion now when demand growth is low means poor facility utilization. Much depends on the demand.

decision tree A schematic model of alternatives available to the decision maker, along with their possible consequences.

A **decision tree** is a schematic model of alternatives available to the decision maker, along with their possible consequences. The name derives from the tree-like appearance of the model. It consists of a number of square *decision nodes*, representing decision points, that sprout *branches*, which depict multiple alternatives (which should be read from left to right). Branches also come out of circular *event nodes*, which represent chance points where more than one event is possible that influences the decision. The probability of each chance event is shown above each branch. The probabilities for all branches leaving a event node must add up to exactly one. Finally, the payoff at the end of each branch is conditional on a specific alternative-event combination, and is given only at the outset, before the analysis begins. Payoffs are often expressed as the present value of net costs or profits.

After drawing a decision tree, we solve it by working from right to left, calculating the *expected payoff* for each node as follows:

1. For an event node, we multiply the payoff of each event branch by the event's probability. We add these products to get the event node's expected payoff.
2. For a decision node, we pick the alternative that has the best expected payoff. If an alternative leads to an event node, its payoff is equal to that node's expected payoff (already calculated). We "saw off," or "prune," the other branches not chosen by marking two short lines through them. The decision node's expected payoff is the one associated with the single remaining unpruned branch.

We continue this process until the leftmost decision node is reached. The unpruned branch extending from it is the best alternative to pursue. If multistage decisions are involved, we must await subsequent events before deciding what to do next. If new probability or payoff estimates are obtained, we repeat the process.

Figure 4.10 shows a decision tree for this view of the problem with new information provided. Demand growth can be either low or high, with probabilities of 0.4 and 0.6, respectively. The initial expansion in year 1 (square node 1) can either be small or large. The second decision node (square node 2), whether to expand at a later date, is reached only if the initial expansion is small and demand turns out to be high. If demand is high and if the initial expansion was small, a decision must be made about a second expansion in year 4. Payoffs for each branch of the tree are estimated. For

FIGURE 4.10   *Decision Tree for Capacity Expansion (payoffs in thousands of dollars)*

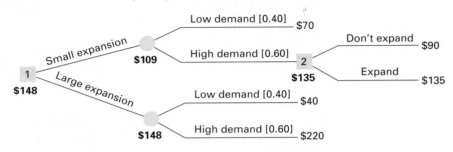

example, if the initial expansion is large, the financial benefit is either $40 000 or $220 000, depending on whether demand is low or high. Weighting these payoffs by the probabilities yields an expected value of $148 000. This expected payoff is higher than the $109 000 payoff for the small initial expansion, so the better choice is to make a large expansion in year 1.

CAPACITY AND SUSTAINABILITY

Capacity management has implications for sustainability beyond direct investments in green production facilities, as described earlier. Smartly exploiting the bottleneck's capacity can reduce the need for new equipment, while improving customer service and value. For example, if a hospital changes patient scheduling to allow for 24-hour use of very expensive test equipment, such as magnetic resonance imaging (MRI), natural resources can be saved and more patients can be served in a timely way. This principle also is very important in capital-intensive processes, such as those found in steelmaking and paper industries. Just as important, reducing variability—whether from internal or external sources—allows managers to reduce their investment in bottleneck capacity.

As shown earlier in Figure 4.9, adding new capacity often is quite "lumpy," with capacity added or subtracted in relatively large jumps. However, this need not always be the case. Managers can work with engineers to develop more flexible capacity that allows for smaller incremental adjustments to be made. Careful planning using design tools, such as simulation, allows for better decision making and less wasted capacity.

For example, while an electronics manufacturer, such as Research In Motion (RIM), might initially erect a large building, it need not immediately fill the entire facility with assembly equipment. Instead, several flexible assembly lines and testing equipment can be installed. As demand increases for its newest BlackBerry models, more lines can be added, and the existing lines rearranged. This approach also relies on programmable equipment that can be repurposed. Taken together, approaches such as these for capacity management can reduce the use of natural resources and better match capacity with market demand.

EQUATION SUMMARY

1. Capacity utilization, expressed as a percent:

$$\text{Capacity utilization} = \frac{\text{Output}}{\text{Effective capacity}} \times 100\%$$

2. Capacity cushion, C, expressed as a percent:

$$C = 100\% - \text{Capacity utilization (\%)}$$

3. Throughput time for a process:

$$\text{Throughput time} = \frac{\text{WIP inventory}}{\text{Output rate}}$$

$$\text{Throughput time} = \text{Operations time} + \text{Movement time} + \text{Wait time}$$

4. Coefficient of variation (cv):

$$\text{cv} = \frac{\text{Standard deviation}}{\text{Average}}$$

5. a. Capacity requirement for one product:

$$M = \frac{Dp}{N[1 - (C/100)]}$$

b. Capacity requirement for multiple products:

$$M = \frac{[Dp + (D/Q)s]_{\text{product 1}} + [Dp + (D/Q)s]_{\text{product 2}} + \cdots + [Dp + (D/Q)s]_{\text{product } n}}{N[1 - (C/100)]}$$

CHAPTER HIGHLIGHTS

- Operations managers plan for timely acquisition, use, and disposition of capacity.

- The process management triangle illustrates the trade-offs between capacity utilization, inventory, and variability, each of which affects process performance.

- Long-term capacity planning is crucial to an organization's success because it often involves large investments in facilities and equipment and because such decisions are not easily reversed.

- Capacity can be stated in terms of either input or output measures. Output measures giving the number of products or services completed in a time period are useful when a firm provides *standardized* products or services. However, a statement of the number of *customized* products or services completed in a time period is meaningless because the work content per unit varies. Demand for customized products and services must be translated into input measures, such as labour hours, machine hours, and material requirements.

- Operating at peak capacity calls for extraordinary effort, using marginal production methods, and is usually not sustainable. Maximum output under normal conditions is called effective capacity. The operation having the lowest effective capacity is called a bottleneck and limits the capacity of the entire system. Variable workloads and changing product mixes complicate measuring capacity and can cause different operations to become bottlenecks under varying circumstances. Such floating bottlenecks make determining a firm's effective capacity difficult.

- Focusing capacity and scheduling decisions on bottleneck resources with an approach called the theory of constraints (TOC) can help maximize the flow of total value-added funds.

- The desirable amount of capacity cushion varies, depending on competitive priorities, cost of unused capacity, resource flexibility, supply uncertainties, shelf life, variability and uncertainty of demand, and other factors.

- Economies of scale derive from spreading fixed costs, reducing construction costs, reducing purchased materials costs, and obtaining process advantages. Diseconomies of scale cause some firms to focus their operations and move to smaller, rather than larger, facilities.

- Three capacity strategies are expansionist, wait and see, and follow the leader. The expansionist strategy is attractive when there are economies of scale, learning effects, and a chance for pre-emptive marketing. The wait-and-see strategy minimizes risk by relying more on short-term options. The follow-the-leader strategy maintains the current balance between competitors.

- The four steps in capacity planning are (1) estimate capacity requirements, (2) identify gaps, (3) develop alternatives, and (4) evaluate the alternatives.

- Waiting-line models help the manager choose the capacity level that best balances customer service and the cost of adding more capacity. As waiting-line problems involve more servers, mathematical models quickly become very complex. Simulation is used to analyze most multiple-server waiting-line situations. Decision trees are schematic models that can be helpful in evaluating different capacity expansion alternatives when demand is uncertain and sequential decisions are involved.

SOLVED PROBLEM 1

You have been asked to put together a capacity plan for a critical bottleneck operation at the Surefoot Sandal Company. Your capacity measure is number of machines. Three products (men's, women's, and children's sandals) are manufactured. On average, about 10 000 sandals are in various stages of production. The time standards (processing and setup), batch sizes, and demand forecasts are given in the following table. The firm operates two eight-hour shifts, five days per week, fifty weeks per year. Experience shows that a capacity cushion of 5 percent is sufficient.

| | TIME STANDARDS | | | |
PRODUCT	PROCESSING (hr./pair)	SETUP (hr./batch)	BATCH SIZE (pairs/batch)	DEMAND FORECAST (pairs/year)
Men's sandals	0.05	0.5	240	80 000
Women's sandals	0.10	2.2	180	60 000
Children's sandals	0.02	3.8	360	120 000

a. How long does a typical pair of sandals take to move through the manufacturing process?

b. How many machines are needed?

c. If the operation currently has two machines, what is the capacity gap?

SOLUTION

a. Using Little's Law:

$$\text{Throughput time} = \frac{\text{WIP inventory}}{\text{Output rate}}$$

$$= \frac{10\,000 \text{ sandals}}{(80\,000 + 60\,000 + 120\,000) \text{ sandals per year}}$$

$$= 0.038 \text{ year}$$

Given that Surefoot Sandal operates 250 days per year, this throughput time translates into 9.6 days, or slightly less than two weeks.

b. The number of hours of operation per year, N, is:

$N = (2 \text{ shifts/day})(8 \text{ hours/shift})(250 \text{ days/machine-year})$

$= 4000 \text{ hours/machine-year}$

The number of machines required, M, is the sum of machine-hour requirements for all three products divided by the number of productive hours available for one machine:

$$M = \frac{[Dp + (D/Q)s]_{men} + [Dp + (D/Q)s]_{women} + [Dp + (D/Q)s]_{children}}{N[1 - (C/100)]}$$

$$= \frac{\begin{array}{c}[80\,000(0.05) + (80\,000/240)0.5] + [60\,000(0.10) + (60\,000/180)2.2] \\ + [120\,000(0.02) + (120\,000/360)3.8]\end{array}}{4000[1 - (5/100)]}$$

$$= \frac{14\,567 \text{ hours/year}}{3800 \text{ hours/machine-year}} = 3.83 \quad \text{or} \quad 4 \text{ machines}$$

c. The capacity gap is 1.83 machines (3.83 − 2). Two more machines should be purchased, unless management decides to use short-term options to fill the gap.

SOLVED PROBLEM 2

Managers at the First Community Bank are attempting to shorten the time it takes customers with approved loan applications to get their paperwork processed. In addition, a busy season ahead is expected, and the capacity of the process must be expanded by 20 percent.

The flowchart for this process, consisting of several different activities, each performed by a different bank employee, is shown in Figure 4.11. Approved loan applications first arrive at step 1, where they are checked for completeness and put in order. At step 2, the loans are categorized into different classes according to the loan amount and whether they are being requested for personal or commercial reasons. While credit checking commences at step 3, loan application data are entered in parallel into the information system for record-keeping purposes at step 4. Finally, all paperwork for setting up the new loan is finished at step 5. The estimated time, in minutes, for each step is given in parentheses in this figure.

Which single step is the bottleneck, assuming that market demand for loan applications exceeds the capacity of the process? If the typical total wait time is two hours as an application moves through the process, what is the expected throughput time? Finally, management is also interested in knowing the number of approved loans that this system can process in an eight-hour workday.

FIGURE 4.11   *Processing Credit Loan Application at First Community Bank*

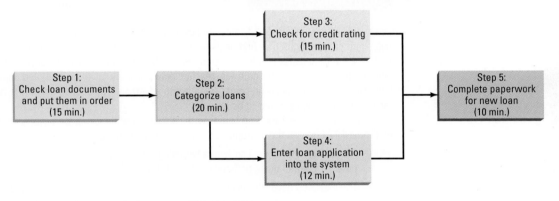

SOLUTION

The capacity for loan completions is derived by translating the "minutes per customer" at each step to "customers per hour." At First Community Bank, process capacity is 3 customers per hour, because the bottleneck step 2 can process only 1 customer every 20 minutes (60/3). This equates to $3 \times 8 = 24$ applications per eight-hour day.

The throughput time to complete an approved loan application is $[15 + 20 + \max(15,12) + 10] + 120 = 180$ minutes, or 3 hours, including waiting time. Naturally, such a smooth process flow is not always the case. So the actual time taken for completing an approved loan might be longer (or shorter) than three hours due to variability in the arrival of applications, actual processing times, and other factors.

Rearranging Little's Law to isolate work-in-process applications (i.e., inventory) yields 3 hours $\times$ 3 customers per hour = 9 customers (on average) somewhere in the loan process.

Decision Point   Wait time currently accounts for half of the total throughput time, so management might be able to shorten the loan application time by ensuring that applications are passed immediately along to the next step. Action also is needed to reduce the variability of the arrival of applications and processing time at each step to reduce queues.

In terms of capacity, step 2 is the bottleneck. The bank can complete a maximum of only 24 per eight-hour day. (All other steps can process at least 32 applications per day.) Managers must focus their efforts to expand capacity at step 2 to reach their 20 percent targeted increase, that is, 27 loans per day. One option might be to redesign that step, for example shifting some elements of the task to step 1 or step 4. Another option might be employing information technology to assist with the categorization.

SOLVED PROBLEM 3

A retailer must decide whether to build a small or a large facility at a new location. Demand at the location can be either low or high, with probabilities estimated to be 0.4 and 0.6, respectively. If a small facility is built and demand proves to be high, the manager may choose not to expand (payoff is $223 000) or to expand (payoff is $270 000). If a small facility is built and demand is low, there is no reason to expand and the payoff is $200 000. If a large facility is built and demand proves to be low, the choice is to do nothing ($40 000) or to stimulate demand through local advertising. The response to advertising may be either modest or sizable, with their probabilities estimated to be 0.3 and 0.7, respectively. If it is modest, the payoff is estimated to be only $20 000; the payoff grows to $220 000 if the response is sizable. Finally, if a large facility is built and demand turns out to be high, the payoff is $800 000.

Draw a decision tree. Then analyze it to determine the expected payoff for each decision and event node. Which alternative—building a small facility or building a large facility—has the higher expected payoff?

SOLUTION

The decision tree in Figure 4.12 shows the event probability and the payoff for each of the seven alternative-event combinations. The first decision is whether to build a small or a large facility. Its node is shown first, to the left, because it is the decision the retailer must make now. The second decision node—whether to expand at a later date—is reached only if a small facility is built and demand turns out to be high. Finally, the third decision point—whether to advertise—is reached only if the retailer builds a large facility and demand turns out to be low.

Analysis of the decision tree begins with calculation of the expected payoffs from right to left, shown on Figure 4.12 beneath the appropriate event and decision nodes.

1. For the event node dealing with advertising, the expected payoff is 160, or the sum of each event's payoff weighted by its probability [0.3(20) + 0.7(220)].

2. The expected payoff for decision node 3 is 160, because *Advertise* (160) is better than *Do nothing* (40). Prune the *Do nothing* alternative.

FIGURE 4.12 *Decision Tree for Retailer*

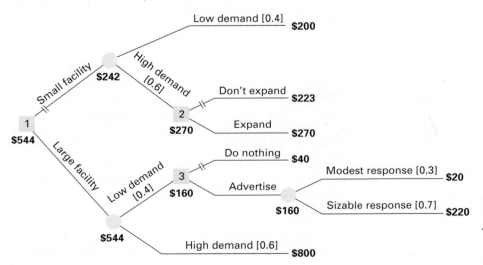

3. The payoff for decision node 2 is 270, because *Expand* (270) is better than *Do not expand* (223). Prune *Do not expand*.

4. The expected payoff for the event node dealing with demand, assuming that a small facility is built, is 242 [or 0.4(200) + 0.6(270)].

5. The expected payoff for the event node dealing with demand, assuming that a large facility is built, is 544 [or 0.4(160) + 0.6(800)].

6. The expected payoff for decision node 1 is 544, because the large facility's expected payoff is largest. Prune *Small facility*.

Decision Point The retailer should build the large facility, given the large expected payoff of $544 000. This initial decision is the only one made now. Subsequent decisions are made after learning whether demand actually is low or high.

PROBLEMS

1. The Dahlia Medical Centre has 30 labour rooms, 15 combination labour and delivery rooms, 3 delivery rooms, and 1 special delivery room reserved for complicated births. All of these facilities operate around the clock. Time spent in labour rooms varies from hours to days, with an average of about 1 day. The average, uncomplicated delivery requires about 1 hour in a delivery room.

   During an exceptionally busy three-day period, 109 healthy babies were born at the Centre. Sixty babies were born in separate labour and delivery rooms, 45 were born in combined labour and delivery rooms, and only 4 required a labour room and the complicated delivery room. Which of the facilities (labour rooms, combination labour and delivery rooms, or delivery rooms) had the greatest utilization rate?

2. A process currently services an average of 50 customers per day. Observations in recent weeks show that its utilization is about 90 percent, allowing for just a 10 percent capacity cushion. If demand is expected to be 75 percent of the current level in five years and management wants to have a capacity cushion of just 5 percent, what capacity requirement should be planned?

3. An airline company must plan its fleet capacity and its long-term schedule of aircraft usage. For one flight segment, the average number of customers per day is 70, which represents a 65 percent utilization rate of the equipment assigned to the flight segment. If demand is expected to increase to 84 customers for this flight segment in three years, what capacity requirement should be planned? Assume that management deems a capacity cushion of 25 percent to be appropriate.

4. Trim Tailor Shop has two general types of customers, labelled A and B, that require custom tailoring and alterations. The process flowcharts for each are shown in Figure 4.13. After step T1, Type A customers proceed to step T2 and then to any of the three workstations at T3, followed by step T4, and then step T7. After step T1, Type B customers proceed to step T5 and then steps T6 and T7.

FIGURE 4.13 *Flowcharts for Trim Tailor Shop*

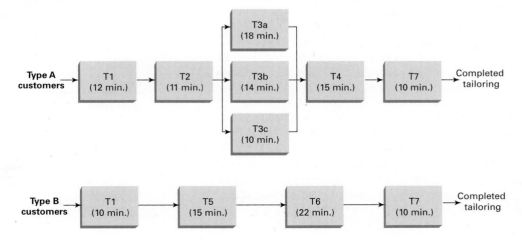

The numbers in parentheses are the minutes it takes to process a customer.

a. What is the effective capacity of Trim Tailor Shop in terms of the numbers of Type A customers who can be served in an hour? Assume no customers are waiting at steps T1 or T7.

b. If 30 percent of the customers are Type A customers and 70 percent are Type B customers, what is the effective capacity of Trim Tailor Shop in customers per hour?

c. Where would you expect Type A customers to experience waiting lines, assuming no Type B customers are in the shop? Where would the Type B customers have to wait, assuming no Type A customers?

5. Sterling Motors is a telephone or mail-order dealer in British auto parts. Sterling has six telephones for receiving orders. Order takers answer the telephones, check inventory availability, and prepare picking tickets for the warehouse stock pickers. One order may consist of several lines, with a different part or multiple of a part ordered on each line. Each order taker can prepare picking tickets at a rate of one line every three minutes. The telephones are normally answered weekdays from 6 a.m. to 4 p.m., Pacific time. Stock pickers can fill and package parts at a rate of one line every five minutes. Sterling employs eight stock pickers, who normally work weekdays from 8 a.m. to 5 p.m. (except for lunch hours).

a. What is the effective capacity of order taking in lines per week? stock picking?

b. For three weeks after the spring catalogue is mailed in May, the eight warehouse employees work 10 hours per day between 7 a.m. and 6 p.m., six days per week. What is the peak capacity of the system in lines per week?

c. During the second week of May, Sterling filled 5000 order lines. What is the capacity utilization?

6. The Clip Joint operates four barber's chairs in the student centre. During the week before semester break and the week before graduation, the Clip Joint experiences peak demands. Military-style haircuts take 5 minutes each, and other styles require 20 minutes each. Operating from 9 a.m. to 6 p.m. on the six days before semester break, the Clip Joint completes 500 military-style haircuts and 400 other haircuts. During a comparable six-day week before graduation, the Clip Joint completes 700 military-style haircuts and 300 other haircuts. In which week is utilization higher? (Assume that each barber is able to work continuously throughout the 9-hour day.)

7. Up, Up, and Away is a producer of kites and wind socks. Relevant data on a bottleneck operation in the shop for the upcoming fiscal year are given in the following table:

ITEM	KITES	WIND SOCKS
Demand forecast	30 000 units/year	12 000 units/year
Batch size	20 units	70 units
Standard processing time	0.3 hr./unit	1.0 hr./unit
Standard setup time	3.0 hr./batch	4.0 hr./batch

The shop works two shifts per day, eight hours per shift, 200 days per year. There currently are four machines, and a 25 percent capacity cushion is desired. How many machines should be purchased to meet the upcoming year's demand without resorting to any short-term capacity solutions?

8. Tuff-Rider, Inc., manufactures touring bikes and mountain bikes in a variety of frame sizes, colours, and component combinations. Identical bicycles are produced in batches of 100. The projected demand, batch size, and time standards are shown in the following table:

ITEM	TOURING	MOUNTAIN
Demand forecast	5000 units/year	10 000 units/year
Batch size	100 units	100 units
Standard processing time	0.25 hr./unit	0.5 hr./unit
Standard setup time	2 hr./batch	3 hr./batch

The shop currently works eight hours a day, five days a week, 50 weeks a year. It has five workstations, each producing one bicycle in the time shown in the table. The shop maintains a 15 percent capacity cushion. How many workstations will be required next year to meet expected demand without using overtime and without decreasing the firm's current capacity cushion?

9. Beta World amusement park has the opportunity to expand its size now (the end of year 0) by purchasing adjacent property for $250 000 and adding attractions at a cost of $550 000. This expansion is expected to increase attendance by 30 percent over projected attendance without expansion. The price of admission is $30, with a $5 increase planned for the beginning of year 3. Additional operating costs are expected to be $100 000 per year. Estimated attendance for the next five years, *without expansion*, follows:

YEAR	1	2	3	4	5
ATTENDANCE	30 000	34 000	36 250	38 500	41 000

a. What are the pre-tax combined cash flows for years 0 through 5 that are attributable to the park's expansion?

b. Ignoring tax, depreciation, and the time value of money, determine how long it will take to recover (pay back) the investment.

10. Roche Brothers is considering a capacity expansion of its supermarket. The landowner will build the addition to suit in return for $200 000 upon completion and a 5-year lease. The increase in rent for the addition is $10 000 per month. The annual sales projected through year 5 are listed. The current effective capacity is equivalent to 500 000 customers per year. Assume a 2 percent pre-tax profit on sales.

    a. If Roche expands its capacity to serve 700 000 customers per year now (end of year 0), what are the projected annual incremental pre-tax cash flows attributable to this expansion?

    b. If Roche expands its capacity to serve 700 000 customers per year at the end of year 2, the landowner will build the same addition for $240 000 and a 3-year lease at $12 000 per month. What are the projected annual incremental pre-tax cash flows attributable to this expansion alternative?

YEAR	1	2	3	4	5
Customers	560 000	600 000	685 000	700 000	715 000
Average sales per customer	$50	$53	$56	$60	$64

11. Yost-Perry Industries (YPI) manufactures a mix of affordable guitars (A, B, C) that are fabricated and assembled at four different processing stations (W, X, Y, Z). The operation is a batch process with small setup times that can be considered negligible. The product information (price, weekly demand, and processing times) and process sequences are shown in Figure 4.14. Raw materials and purchased parts (shown as a per-unit consumption rate) are represented by inverted triangles. YPI is able to make and sell up to the limit of its demand per week with no penalties incurred for not meeting the full demand. Each workstation is staffed by one highly skilled worker who is dedicated to work on that workstation alone and is paid $15 per hour. The plant operates one 8-hour shift per day and operates on a 5-day workweek (i.e., 40 hours of production per person per week). Which of the four workstations, W, X, Y, or Z, has the highest aggregate workload, and thus serves as the bottleneck for YPI?

12. Knott's Industries manufactures standard and super premium backyard swing sets. Currently it has four identical swing-set-making machines, which are operated 250 days per year and 8 hours each day. A capacity cushion of 20 percent is desired. The following information is also known:

	STANDARD MODEL	SUPER PREMIUM MODEL
Annual demand	20 000	10 000
Standard processing time	7 min.	20 min.
Average batch size	50	30
Standard setup time per batch	30 min.	45 min.

FIGURE 4.14   *Flowchart for Yost-Perry Industries (YPI)*

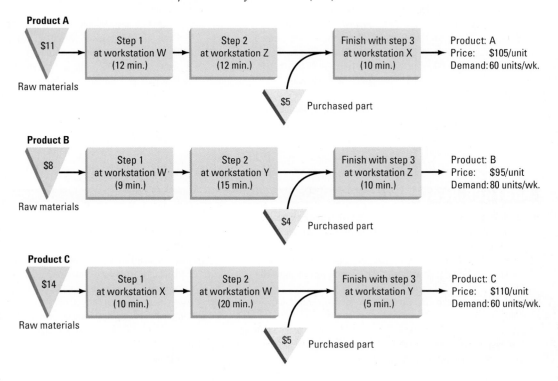

a. Does Knott's have sufficient capacity to meet annual demand?

b. If Knott's could reduce the setup time for the Super Premium Model from 45 minutes to 30 minutes, would there be enough current capacity to produce 20 000 units of each type of swing set?

13. A manager is trying to decide whether to buy one machine or two. If only one machine is purchased and demand proves to be excessive, the second machine can be purchased later. Some sales would be lost, however, because the lead time for delivery of this type of machine is six months. In addition, the cost per machine will be lower if both machines are purchased at the same time. The probability of low demand is estimated to be 0.30 and that of high demand to be 0.70. The after-tax net present value of the benefits (NPV) from purchasing two machines together is $90 000 if demand is low and $170 000 if demand is high.

If one machine is purchased and demand is low, the NPV is $120 000. If demand is high, the manager has three options: doing nothing, which has an NPV of $120 000; subcontracting, with an NPV of $140 000; and buying the second machine, with an NPV of $130 000.

a. Draw a decision tree for this problem.

b. What is the best decision and what is its expected payoff?

14. Acme Steel Fabricators has experienced booming business for the past five years. The company fabricates a wide range of steel products, such as railings, ladders, and light structural steel framing. The current manual method of materials handling is causing excessive inventories and congestion. Acme is considering the purchase of an overhead rail-mounted hoist system or a forklift truck to increase capacity and improve manufacturing efficiency.

The annual pre-tax payoff from the system depends on future demand. If demand stays at the current level, the probability of which is 0.50, annual savings from the overhead hoist will be $10 000. If demand rises, the hoist will save $25 000 annually because of operating efficiencies in addition to new sales. Finally, if demand falls, the hoist will result in an estimated annual loss of $65 000. The probability is estimated to be 0.30 for higher demand and 0.20 for lower demand.

If the forklift is purchased, annual payoffs will be $5000 if demand is unchanged, $10 000 if demand rises, and −$25 000 if demand falls.

a. Draw a decision tree for this problem and compute the expected value of the payoff for each alternative.

b. Which is the best alternative, based on the expected values?

NOTES FOR CHAPTER

1. E. Mathieu, "Starbucks Offers Free Wi-Fi in Canada," www.thestar June 30, 2010; J. Jargon, "Latest Starbucks Buzzword: 'Lean' Japanese Techniques," *Wall Street Journal,* August 4, 2009; D. Calleja, "What Are They Putting in That Coffee?" *The Globe and Mail,* September 24, 2010; "Q4 2009 Tim Hortons Inc. Earnings Conference Call," *CQ Firm D Disclosure,* February 25, 2010; www.timhortons.com/ca/en/about/profile.html, accessed April 12, 2011.

2. Adapted from R. B. Chase, N. J. Aquilano, and F. R. Jacobs, *Operations Management for Competitive Advantage* (New York: McGraw-Hill/Irwin, 2001), p. 100.

3. WestJet Annual Report, 2010.

4. Statistics Canada, CANSIM, Table 028-0002 (Ottawa: Statistics Canada, 2011).

5. "Suncor Energy Doubles Production Capacity at St. Clair Ethanol Plant," *ENP Newswire,* March 28, 2011; "Suncor Energy Delays Plans for Sarnia Ethanol Plant Expansion," *Daily Commercial News,* January 14, 2009; G. Chazan, "Biofuels Industry Battles Past Bumps in the Road," *Wall Street Journal,* April 7, 2011; C. Krauss, "Ethanol's Boom Stalling as Glut Depresses Price," *The New York Times,* September 30, 2007; "Ethanol Plants in Nebraska," Nebraska Ethanol Board site, www.ne-ethanol.org/industry/ethplants.htm, October 16, 2008.

FURTHER READING

Bakke, N. A., and R. Hellberg. "The Challenges of Capacity Planning." *International Journal of Production Economics,* vol. 31–30, no. 1 (1993), pp. 243–264.

Chase, R. B., N. J. Aquilano, and F. R. Jacobs. *Operations Management for Competitive Advantage,* 9th ed. New York: Irwin/McGraw-Hill, 2001.

Goldratt, E. Y., and J. Cox. *The Goal,* 2nd rev. ed. New York: North River, 1992.

Hammesfahr, R., D. Jack, James A. Pope, and Alireza Ardalan. "Strategic Planning for Production Capacity." *International Journal of Operations and Production Management,* vol. 13, no. 5 (1993), pp. 41–53.

Hopp, W. J., and M. L. Spearman. *Factory Physics: Foundations in Manufacturing Management,* 2nd ed. New York: Irwin/McGraw-Hill, 2001.

Klassen, Kenneth J., and Thomas R. Rohleder. "Combining Operations and Marketing to Manage Capacity and Demand in Services." *The Service Industries Journal,* vol. 21, no. 2 (2001), pp. 1–30.

Klassen, Robert D., and Larry J. Menor. "The Process Management Triangle: An Empirical Investigation of Process Tradeoffs." *Journal of Operations Management,* vol. 25 (2007), pp. 1015–1034.

Little, John D. C. "Tautologies, Models, and Theories: Can We Find 'Laws' of Manufacturing?" *IIE Transactions,* vol. 24, no. 3 (1992), pp. 7–13.

Lovejoy, W. S. "Integrated Operations: A Proposal for Operations Management Teaching and Research." *Production and Operations Management,* vol. 7, no. 2 (1998), pp. 106–124.

Ritzman, Larry P., and M. Hossein Safizadeh. "Linking Process Choice with Plant-Level Decisions About Capital and Human Resources." *Production and Operations Management,* vol. 8, no. 4 (1999), pp. 374–392.

Srikanth, M. L., H. E. Cavallaro, and H. E. Cavallaro, Jr. *Regaining Competitiveness; Putting the Goal to Work,* 2nd rev. ed. Guilford, CT: Spectrum Publishing Company, 1995.

Steele, Daniel C., Patrick R. Philipoom, Manoj K. Malhotra, and Timothy D. Fry. "Comparisons Between Drum-Buffer-Rope and Material Requirements Planning: A Case Study." *International Journal of Production Research,* vol. 43, no. 15 (2005), pp. 3181–3208.

MyOMLab ASSETS

MyOMLab offers the following resources, which allow you to further practise and apply concepts presented in this chapter.

- **Key Equations:** All the equations for this chapter can be found in one convenient location.

- **Discussion Questions:** Five questions expand your thinking on economies of scale, safety issues, and capacity cushions.

- **Case:** *Fitness Plus, Part A.* How should Fitness Plus measure its capacity, and what capacity strategy is best?

- **Experiential Exercise:**

  - *Min-Yo Garment Company.* Experience the challenges of matching markets to the capacity of your manufacturing process in this exciting in-class simulation.

- **Video Cases:**

  - *Gate Turnaround at Southwest Airlines.* How can capacity and utilization be measured at an airline such as SWA? What are the important long-term issues relevant for managing capacity, revenue, and customer satisfaction?

  - *Constraint Management at Southwest Airlines.* Analyze Southwest's passenger boarding process using the theory of constraints. Which approach to boarding scenario would you recommend? How should Southwest evaluate the gate boarding and plane turnaround process?

- **Virtual Tours:**

  - *FaucetCraft Manufacturing.* How does firm measure the capacity of their processes and of the entire plant? What levers are does FaucetCraft have to vary capacity in the short term?

  - *Portland Bolt & Manufacturing.* How is capacity measured for each process? Should it measure capacity of the entire plant?

  - *The wastewater treatment plant located in Camarillo* is an example of a high-volume, public project with significant variability in demand.

  - *Los Maestros Cigars* produces its products with a low-volume, labour-intensive process.

- **Internet Exercises:**

  - *Granite Rock* is a supplier of materials to the construction industry with a hundred-year history. Explore the past and present bottlenecks in their process.

  - *Chevron* is a large corporation with many business units, one of which is gas and oil. The amount of petroleum products they can sell is, in part, determined by the amount of their natural resource reserves, and the capacity of refining operations.

- **Extend LT:** A student version is included to develop and use simulation models. Provincial Automobile License Renewals must identify the bottleneck and improve its process for handling customers.

- **OM Explorer Tutor:** OM Explorer contains two tutor programs that will help you learn about capacity (capacity requirements and projecting cash flows).

- **Supplement A:** *Decision Making.* This supplement provides the background to use break-even analysis, preference matrices, decision theory, and decision trees.

- **Supplement C:** *Work Measurement.* Learn about several tools for estimating the time it takes for each step in a process.

- **Supplement G:** *Simulation.* Learn how to simulate a process and understand how it performs dynamically over time.

Waiting Lines

Learning Goals

After reading this supplement, you will be able to:

1. recognize the elements of a waiting-line problem in a real situation.
2. use waiting-line models to estimate the operating characteristics of a system.
3. know when to use single-workstation and multiple-workstation models.
4. describe how waiting-line models can be used to make managerial decisions.

Anyone who has had to wait at a stoplight, a Tim Hortons, or a provincial licence office has experienced the dynamics of queues or waiting lines. Perhaps one of the best examples of effective management of waiting lines is that of Walt Disney World. One day there may be only 25 000 customers, but on another day there may be 90 000. Careful analysis of process flows, technology for people-mover (materials handling) equipment, capacity, and layout keeps the waiting times for attractions at acceptable levels.

The analysis of waiting lines is of concern to managers because it affects design, capacity planning, layout planning, inventory management, and scheduling. However, waiting lines include more than just people. A **waiting line** is one or more customers or items queued for an operation, which can include people waiting for service, materials waiting for further processing, equipment waiting for maintenance, and sales orders waiting for delivery. In a general sense, these items also represent inventory, which is discussed further in Chapter 5, "Inventory Management."

In this supplement we discuss why waiting lines form, the structure of waiting-line models, and the uses of these models in operations management. We also discuss the decisions managers address with the models. In addition, waiting lines can also be analyzed using computer simulation (see Supplement G, "Simulation," in MyOMLab).

WHY HAVE WAITING LINES?

Although people rarely enjoy waiting, waiting lines can serve several managerial purposes to improve the performance of the system and, under

waiting line or **queue**
One or more customers or items waiting for service. Materials, equipment, or products can also form a queue as they wait for further operations.

some circumstances, even improve the customer experience. However, the primary purpose of waiting lines is to balance two types of costs: capacity and waiting. For capacity-related costs, waiting lines allow managers to accommodate short surges in demand with less capacity—provided that, at a minimum, average capacity exceeds average demand. Scheduling fewer workers at a fast-food restaurant, running a limited number of cars on a public transit system, and installing less IT server capacity for a Web service improves the utilization of resources and lowers investment or operating costs. In contrast, as additional capacity is installed, lines will be shorter, but capacity-related investment and operating costs increase.

Although capacity costs decrease with longer average waiting lines, customer-related waiting costs increase as the average number of people, materials, machines, or products in the waiting line increases, as depicted in Figure 4S.1. For example, customer satisfaction can decrease, which in turn reduces the likelihood of future, repeat business. In extreme cases, customers may leave the line before being served or cancel their order (this is called *reneging*). Also, as discussed in greater detail in Chapter 5, "Inventory Management," having more materials or equipment waiting to be processed requires higher levels of investment.

FIGURE 4S.1   *Illustrating the Cost Trade-Off for Waiting Lines*

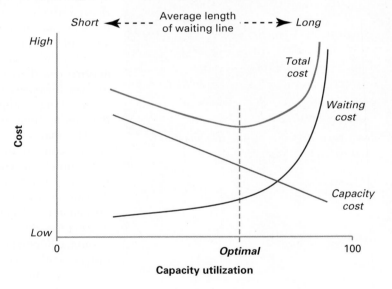

Costs may not be the only management concern. Managers must consider not only the physical arrangement of any waiting line, but in many situations also the customer's perception. Some customer experiences actually benefit from the psychological impact of waiting lines. For example, a short period of waiting in a theme park can contribute to heightening the anticipation and excitement of a thrill ride, such as a roller coaster. Similarly, a queue outside a night club can signal desirability and exclusivity. Through intelligent design, managers can reduce the negative aspects of waiting lines and improve customer service, as described in Table 4S.1.

WHY WAITING LINES FORM
A waiting line forms because of a temporary imbalance between demand and capacity of the system to process customers or items. In most real-life waiting-line problems, the demand rate varies; that is, customers arrive at unpredictable intervals. The rate of service also varies, depending on individual customer needs.

TABLE 4S.1 *Managing Waiting Lines*[1]

1. **Determine the acceptable waiting time for customers.**
   Customer expectations for a reasonable waiting time can be affected by competition, the value of the service provided, and customers' perception of the value of their time.

2. **Segment customers based on value or type of service.**
   Using "express" service lanes can shorten the wait for customers requiring minimal assistance or those customers willing to pay extra for faster service. However, clear, easy-to-monitor criteria for express service must be established, and well-trained people are essential for the express service.

3. **Use distractions to entertain or physically involve the customer.**
   Visual information, possibly presented using TV screens, can distract customers, particularly if light and humorous. In addition, if the customer must provide information as part of the service, install facilities to allow for this while waiting in line. An employee may also assist with pre-processing during peak times.

4. **Move customers out of lines.**
   Reservation systems can smooth demand patterns, and automation, such as Web-based delivery, can encourage self-service.

5. **If customers tend to overestimate waiting times, provide feedback on actual waiting times.**
   Although posting the current wait times for short, relatively predictable wait times (e.g., for fast food) may not be helpful, customers appreciate receiving information for longer, less predictable wait times (e.g., for airline takeoff when there is a delay).

6. **Change customer behaviour.**
   Inform customers about peak times or provide other incentives to shift demand away from peak times.

7. **Resources that are not serving customers should be out of sight.**
   Staff or equipment not directly involved with serving customers should be moved to back rooms. Idle resources signal to customers that they are not the first priority.

8. **Adopt a long-term perspective.**
   For frequently used services, customers expect consistent, predictable waiting times.

9. **Train staff to take the initiative.**
   If a staff member observes an unusual situation developing in line, such as a screaming child, all customers may perceive better service if this situation is dealt with immediately.

10. **Emphasize good service at the front of the line!**
    Managers also must not overlook the primary objective—good service when the front of the line is finally reached. A friendly, attentive employee providing helpful service, along with well-designed equipment and facilities, may overcome any negative impressions of waiting and leave an excellent final impression.

For example, suppose bank customers arrive at an average rate of 15 per hour throughout the day and the bank can process an average of 20 customers per hour. Why would a waiting line ever develop? The answers are that the customer arrival rate varies and the time required to process a customer can vary. During the noon hour, 30 customers may arrive at the bank. Some of them may have complicated transactions, requiring above-average process times. The waiting line may grow to 15 customers for a period of time before it eventually disappears. Even though the bank manager provided for more than enough capacity on average, waiting lines can still develop.

Waiting lines can develop even if the time to process a customer is constant. For example, a subway train is computer-controlled to arrive at stations along its route. Each train is programmed to arrive at a station, say, every 15 minutes. Even with the constant operations time, waiting lines develop while riders wait for the next train or cannot get on a train because of the size of the crowd at a busy time of the day. Consequently, variability in the rate of demand determines the sizes of the waiting lines in this case. In general, if there is no variability in the demand and operations rates and enough capacity has been provided, no waiting lines form.

USES OF WAITING-LINE THEORY

Waiting-line theory applies to both service and manufacturing firms, relating customer or item arrival and process characteristics to output characteristics. It also provides a basis for Little's Law, presented in Chapter 4, "Capacity" (Lovejoy, 1998). Waiting-line models apply to a wide variety of process stuctures, including project, batch, and line processes. In our discussion, we will frequently use the term *customer*, although these principles apply equally well to items waiting ahead of a workstation or operation. The process might be hair cutting at a hair salon, satisfying customer complaints, or processing a production order of parts on a certain machine. Other examples of customers and services include lines of theatregoers waiting to purchase tickets, trucks waiting to be unloaded at a warehouse, machines waiting to be repaired by a maintenance crew, and patients waiting to be examined by a physician. Regardless of the situation, waiting-line problems have several common elements, discussed in the next section.

STRUCTURE OF WAITING LINES

Analyzing waiting-line problems begins with a description of the situation's basic elements. Each specific situation will have different characteristics, but four elements are common to all situations:

customer population
An input that generates potential customer demand.

priority rule A rule that selects the next customer to be served at the service facility.

queuing configuration
The number of lines and the arrangement of the facilities.

1. An input of customers or items, here termed simply **customer population**, that generates potential demand

2. A waiting line of customers or items

3. A workstation or operation, consisting of a person (or crew), a machine (or group of machines), or both, necessary to perform one or more activities

4. A **priority rule**, which selects the next customer to be served or item to be transformed by a workstation or operation

Figure 4S.2 shows these basic elements. The **queuing configuration** describes the number of lines and the arrangement of the workstations or operations. After the service has been performed, the served customers or transformed items leave the system.

FIGURE 4S.2   *Basic Elements of Waiting-Line Models*

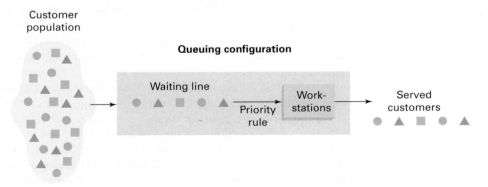

CUSTOMER POPULATION

A customer population is the source of input to the system. An infinite customer population is one in which the number of customers in the system does not affect the rate at which the population generates new customers. For example, consider a mail-order operation for which the customer population consists of shoppers who have received a catalogue of products sold by the company. Because the customer population is so large and only a small fraction of the shoppers place orders at any one time, the number of new orders it generates is not appreciably affected by the number of orders waiting for service or being processed. For this case, the customer population is assumed to be infinite.

In contrast, if the potential number of new customers appreciably affects the number of customers in the system, the input source is said to be finite. For example, suppose that a maintenance crew is assigned to repair five machines. The customer population for the maintenance crew is five machines in good working order. If one of these fails, the available population is clearly affected. In this supplement, we only consider analysis for waiting lines with an infinite customer population.

Customers in waiting lines may be *patient* or *impatient*, which has nothing to do with the colourful language a customer may use while waiting in line for a long time on a hot day. In the context of waiting-line problems, a patient customer is one who enters the system and remains there until being served; an impatient customer is one who either decides not to enter the system (*balks*) or leaves the system before being served (*reneges*). For the methods used in this supplement, we make the simplifying assumption that all customers are patient.

QUEUING CONFIGURATION

The queuing configuration may be described by the number of lines and the arrangement of the workstations.

Sometimes customers are not neatly organized into lines. Here, ships wait to use the port facilities in Vancouver.

NUMBER OF LINES. Waiting lines may be designed to be a *single line* or *multiple lines*. Figure 4S.3 shows an example of each arrangement. Generally, single lines are utilized at airline counters, inside banks, and at some fast-food restaurants, whereas multiple lines are utilized in grocery stores, at drive-in bank operations, and in discount stores.

FIGURE 4S.3 *Waiting-Line Arrangements*

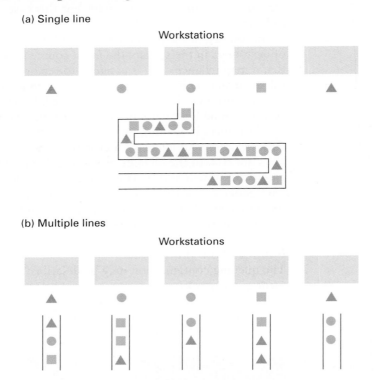

When multiple workstations are available and each can handle general transactions, the single-line arrangement keeps each workstation uniformly busy and gives customers a sense of fairness. Customers believe that they are being served on the basis of when they arrived, not how well they guessed their waiting time when selecting a particular line. The multiple-line design is best when some of the workstations provide a limited set of services. In this arrangement, customers select the services they need and wait in the line where that service is provided, such as at a grocery store where there are special express lanes for customers paying with cash or having fewer than ten items.

Sometimes waiting lines are not organized neatly. Machines that need repair at a customer's site may be left in place, and the maintenance crew comes to them. Nonetheless, we can think of such machines as forming a single line or multiple lines, depending on the number of repair crews and their specialties. Likewise, passengers who telephone for a taxi also form a line even though they may wait at different locations.

ARRANGEMENT OF WORKSTATIONS. Workstations consist of the personnel and equipment necessary to perform an operation for the customer. Figure 4S.4 shows examples of the five basic arrangements. Managers should choose an arrangement based on customer

FIGURE 4S.4 *Examples of Workstation Arrangements*

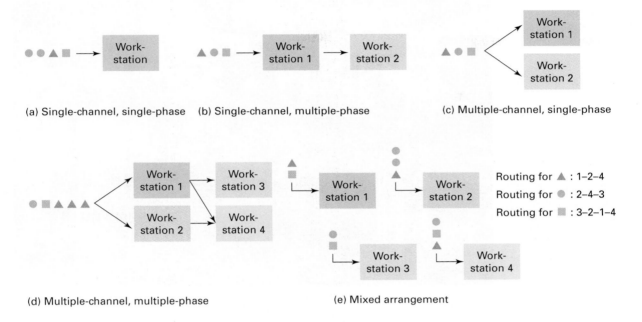

(a) Single-channel, single-phase   (b) Single-channel, multiple-phase   (c) Multiple-channel, single-phase

(d) Multiple-channel, multiple-phase   (e) Mixed arrangement

phase A single step in the process.

volume and the nature of services performed. Some processes require only a single step, also called a **phase**, whereas others require a sequence of steps.

In the *single-channel, single-phase* system, all operations demanded by a customer can be performed by a single workstation, which is also called a single-workstation configuration for service processes. Customers form a single line and go through the process one at a time. Examples are a drive-through car wash and a machine that must process several batches of parts.

The *single-channel, multiple-phase* arrangement is used when several operations are best performed in sequence by more than one workstation, yet customer volume or other constraints limit the design to one channel. Customers form a single line and proceed sequentially from one workstation to the next, with a waiting line between phases. An example of this arrangement is a McDonald's drive-through, where the first workstation takes the order, the second takes the money, and the third provides the food.

The *multiple-channel, single-phase* arrangement is used when demand is large enough to warrant providing the same service at more than one workstation or when the services offered by the workstations are different. Customers form one or more lines, depending on the design. In the single-line design, customers are served by the first available server, as in the lobby of a bank. If each channel has its own waiting line, customers wait until the server for their line can serve them, as at a bank's drive-through facilities.

The *multiple-channel, multiple-phase* arrangement occurs when customers can be served by one of the first-phase workstations but then require another operation from a second-phase workstation, and so on. In some cases, customers cannot switch channels after service has begun; in others they can. An example of this arrangement is a laundromat. Washing machines are the first-phase workstations, and dryers are the

Customers wait in multiple queues to be served at Montréal-Trudeau Airport in Dorval.

second-phase workstations. Some of the washing machines and dryers may be designed for extra-large loads, thereby providing the customer a choice of channels.

The most complex waiting-line problem involves customers who have unique sequences of required services; consequently, service cannot be described neatly in phases. A *mixed* arrangement is used in such a case. In the mixed arrangement, waiting lines can develop in front of each workstation, where each customized order may require the use of various machines and different routings.

PRIORITY RULE

The priority rule determines which customer or item to serve next. Most queuing configurations that you encounter use the first-come, first-served (FCFS) rule. The customer at the head of the waiting line has the highest priority, and the customer who arrived last has the lowest priority. Other priority disciplines might take the customer with the earliest promised due date (EDD) or the customer with the shortest expected processing time (SPT). We focus on FCFS in this supplement and discuss EDD and SPT elsewhere (see Chapter 11, "Operations Planning and Scheduling").

pre-emptive discipline
A rule that allows a customer of higher priority to interrupt the service of another customer.

A **pre-emptive discipline** is a rule that allows a customer of higher priority to interrupt the service of another customer. For example, in a hospital emergency room, patients with the most life-threatening injuries receive treatment first, regardless of their order of arrival. Modelling of systems having complex priority disciplines is usually done using computer simulation (see Supplement G, "Simulation," in MyOMLab).

PROBABILITY DISTRIBUTIONS

The sources of variation in waiting-line problems come from the random arrivals of customers and the variations in times for operations, described earlier as external and internal variability, respectively, in Table 4.2. Each of these sources can be described with a probability distribution.

DISTRIBUTION OF ARRIVALS

Unless scheduled, customers tend to arrive randomly; recall that this is one source of external variability. The variability of customer arrivals often can be described by a Poisson distribution, which specifies the probability that n customers will arrive in T time periods:

$$P(n) = \frac{(\lambda T)^n}{n!} e^{-\lambda T} \quad \text{for } n = 0, 1, 2, \ldots$$

where:

$P(n)$ = Probability of n arrivals in T time periods

λ = Average number of customer arrivals per period   → has to be a rate ex: arrivals per min.

e = 2.7183

The mean of the Poisson distribution is λT, and the variance also is λT. The Poisson distribution is a discrete distribution; that is, the probabilities are for a specific number of arrivals per unit of time.

EXAMPLE 4S.1

Calculating the Probability of Arrivals

Management is redesigning the customer service process in a large department store. Accommodating four customers is important. Customers arrive at the desk at the rate of two customers per hour. What is the probability that four customers will arrive during any hour?

SOLUTION

In this case $\lambda = 2$ customers per hour, $T = 1$ hour, and $n = 4$ customers. The probability that four customers will arrive in any hour is:

$$P(4) = \frac{[2(1)]^4}{4!} e^{-2(1)} = \frac{16}{24} e^{-2} = 0.090$$

Decision Point The manager of the customer service desk can use this information to determine the space requirements for the desk and waiting area. There is a relatively small probability that four customers will arrive in any hour. Consequently, seating capacity for two or three customers should be more than adequate unless the time to service each customer is lengthy. Further analysis on service times is warranted.

---

interarrival times The time between customer arrivals.

service time.

operations time The time required to complete all activities or tasks at a workstation. Also called *service time* or *processing time.*

Another way to specify the arrival distribution is to do it in terms of customer **interarrival times**—that is, the time between customer arrivals. If the customer population generates customers according to a Poisson distribution, the *exponential distribution* describes the probability that the next customer will arrive in the next T time periods. The exponential distribution can also be used to describe the time to complete an operation; we discuss the details of this distribution in the next section.

DISTRIBUTION OF OPERATIONS TIME   → service time

The exponential distribution describes the probability that the **operations time** (sometimes labelled *service time* or *processing time*) at a particular workstation will be no more than a target time (T). The probability can be calculated by using the formula:

$$P(t \leq T) = 1 - e^{-\mu T}$$

where:

> μ = Mean number of customers completing service per period
>
> t = Service time of the customer
>
> T = Target service time

The mean of the operations time distribution is $1/\mu$, and the variance is $(1/\mu)^2$. As T increases, the probability that the operations time will be less than T approaches 1.0. For simplicity, let us look at a single-channel, single-phase arrangement.

EXAMPLE 4S.2   *Calculating the Service Time Probability*

The management of the large department store in Example 4S.1 must determine whether more training is needed for the customer service clerk. The clerk at the customer service desk can serve an average of three customers per hour. What is the probability that a customer will require less than 10 minutes of service?

SOLUTION

We must have all the data in the same time units. Because μ = 3 customers per *hour*, we convert minutes of time to hours, or T = 10 minutes = 10/60 hour = 0.167 hour. Then:

$$P(t \le T) = 1 - e^{-\mu T}$$
$$P(t \le 0.167 \text{ hour}) = 1 - e^{-3(0.167)} = 1 - 0.61 = 0.39$$

Decision Point   The probability that the customer will require only 10 minutes or less is not very high, which leaves the possibility that customers may experience lengthy delays. Management should consider additional training for the clerk so as to reduce the time it takes to process a customer request.

Some characteristics of the exponential distribution do not always conform to an actual situation. The exponential distribution model is based on the assumption that each operations time is independent of those that preceded it. In real life, however, productivity may improve as human workers learn about the work. Another assumption underlying the model is that very small, as well as very large, operations times are possible. However, real-life situations often require a fixed-length startup time, some cutoff on total operations time, or nearly constant operations time, similar to an assembly line.

USING WAITING-LINE MODELS TO ANALYZE OPERATIONS

As noted at the beginning of this supplement, operations managers can use waiting-line models to trade off the costs of waiting against any gains that might be made by minimizing capacity investment in the service system. Managers should therefore be concerned about the following performance characteristics of the system:

1. *Line length.* The number of customers in the waiting line reflects one of two conditions. Short queues could mean either good customer service or too much capacity. Similarly, long queues could indicate either low workstation efficiency or the need to increase capacity.

2. *Number of customers in the system.* The number of customers in the queue and being served also relates to process efficiency and capacity. A large number

of customers in the system causes congestion and may result in customer dissatisfaction, unless more capacity is added.

3. *Waiting time in line.* Long lines do not always mean long waiting times. If the service rate is fast, a long line can be served efficiently. However, when waiting time seems long, customers perceive the quality of service to be poor. Managers may try to change the arrival rate of customers or design the system to make long wait times seem shorter than they really are, as noted in Table 4S.1.

4. *Total time in the system.* The total elapsed time from entry into the system until exit from the system may indicate problems with customers, workstation efficiency, or capacity. If some customers are spending too much time in the service system, there may be a need to change the priority discipline, increase productivity, or adjust capacity in some way.

5. *Capacity utilization.* The utilization of the process or individual operations reflects the percentage of time that they are busy. Management's goal is to maintain high utilization and profitability without adversely affecting the other operating characteristics.

The best method for analyzing a waiting-line problem is to relate the five operating characteristics and their alternatives to dollars. However, placing a dollar figure on certain characteristics (such as the waiting time of a shopper in a grocery store) is difficult. In such cases, an analyst must weigh the cost of implementing the alternative under consideration against a subjective assessment of the cost of *not* making the change.

We now present two models and some examples showing how waiting-line models can help operations managers make decisions. We analyze problems requiring the single-workstation and multiple-workstation models, both of which are single-phase. References to more advanced models are cited at the end of this supplement.

SINGLE-WORKSTATION MODEL

The simplest waiting-line model involves a single workstation and a single line of customers. In service processes, this model is often termed a *single-server* model. To further specify the model, we make the following assumptions:

1. The customer population is infinite, and all customers are patient.

2. The customers arrive according to a Poisson distribution with a mean arrival rate of λ.

3. The operations time distribution is exponential with a mean processing rate of μ.

4. Customers are served on a first-come, first-served basis.

5. The length of the waiting line is unlimited.

With these assumptions we can apply various formulas to describe the operating characteristics of the system:

$$\rho = \text{Average capacity utilization of the system}$$
$$= \frac{\lambda}{\mu}$$

$$P_n = \text{Probability that } n \text{ customers are in the system}$$
$$= (1 - \rho)\rho^n$$

$$L = \text{Average number of customers in the system}$$
$$= \frac{\lambda}{\mu - \lambda}$$

$$L_q = \text{Average number of customers in the waiting line}$$
$$= \rho L$$

$$W = \text{Average time spent in the system, including}$$
$$\text{waiting time and operations time}$$
$$= \frac{1}{\mu - \lambda}$$

$$W_q = \text{Average waiting time in line}$$
$$= \rho W$$

EXAMPLE 4S.3	*Calculating the Operating Characteristics of a Single-Channel, Single-Phase System*

The manager of a grocery store in the retirement community of Sunnyville is interested in providing good service to the senior citizens who shop in his store. Presently, the store has a separate checkout counter for senior citizens. On average, 30 senior citizens per hour arrive at the counter, according to a Poisson distribution, and are served at an average rate of 35 customers per hour, with exponential service times. Find the following operating characteristics:

a. Probability of zero customers in the system
b. Utilization of the checkout clerk
c. Number of customers in the system
d. Number of customers in line
e. Time spent in the system
f. Waiting time in line

SOLUTION

The checkout counter can be modelled as a single-channel, single-phase system.

a. To begin, utilization must be calculated before estimating the probability that no customers are in the waiting line.
   Utilization is:

$$\rho = \frac{\lambda}{\mu} = \frac{30}{35} = 0.857$$

Next, the probability is estimated, where $n = 0$:

$$P_n = (1 - \rho)\rho^n$$
$$= (1 - 0.857)(0.857)^0$$
$$= 0.143$$

b. The utilization is calculated above as 0.857.

c. The average number of customers can be calculated as:

$$L = \frac{\lambda}{\mu - \lambda}$$

$$= \frac{30}{35 - 30} = 6 \text{ customers}$$

d. The average number of customers waiting in line is:

$$L_q = \rho L$$
$$= 0.857 \times 6 = 5.142 \text{ customers}$$

e. Average time spent by customers in the system is:

$$W = \frac{1}{\mu - \lambda}$$

$$= \frac{1}{35 - 30} = 0.2 \text{ hours}$$

f. Finally, the average time spent by customers waiting in line is:

$$W_q = \rho W$$
$$= 0.857 \times 0.2 = 0.171 \text{ hours}$$

Both the average waiting time in the system (W) and the average time spent waiting in line (W_q) are expressed in hours. To convert the results to minutes, simply multiply by 60 minutes/hour. For example, $W = 0.2(60) = 12$ minutes, and $W_q = 0.171(60) = 10.26$ minutes.

EXAMPLE 4S.4   *Analyzing Service Rates with the Single-Workstation Model*

The manager of the Sunnyville grocery in Example 4S.3 wants answers to the following questions:

a. What processing rate would be required to have customers average only eight minutes in the system?

b. For that processing rate, what is the probability of having more than four customers in the system?

c. What processing rate would be required to have only a 10 percent chance of exceeding four customers in the system?

SOLUTION

a. We use the equation for the average time in the system and solve for μ.

$$W = \frac{1}{\mu - \lambda}$$

$$8 \text{ minutes} = 0.133 \text{ hour} = \frac{1}{\mu - 30}$$

$$0.133\mu - 0.133(30) = 1$$
$$\mu = 37.52 \text{ customers/hour}$$

b. The probability that there will be more than four customers in the system equals 1 minus the probability that there are four or fewer customers in the system.

$$P = 1 - \sum_{n=0}^{4} P_n$$

$$= 1 - \sum_{n=0}^{4} (1 - \rho)\rho^n$$

and:

$$\rho = \frac{30}{37.52} = 0.80$$

Then:

$$P = 1 - 0.2(1 + 0.8 + 0.8^2 + 0.8^3 + 0.8^4)$$
$$= 1 - 0.672 = 0.328$$

Therefore, there is a nearly 33 percent chance that more than four customers will be in the system.

c. We use the same logic as in part (b), except that μ is now a decision variable. The easiest way to proceed is to find the correct average utilization first and then solve for the processing rate.

$$P = 1 - (1 - \rho)(1 + \rho + \rho^2 + \rho^3 + \rho^4)$$
$$= 1 - (1 + \rho + \rho^2 + \rho^3 + \rho^4) + \rho(1 + \rho + \rho^2 + \rho^3 + \rho^4)$$
$$= 1 - 1 - \rho - \rho^2 - \rho^3 - \rho^4 + \rho + \rho^2 + \rho^3 + \rho^4 + \rho^5$$
$$= \rho^5$$

or:

$$\rho = P^{1/5}$$

If $P = 0.10$:

$$\rho = (0.10)^{1/5} = 0.63$$

Therefore, for a capacity utilization of 63 percent, the probability of more than four customers in the system is 10 percent. For $\lambda = 30$, the mean processing rate must be:

$$\frac{30}{\mu} = 0.63$$

$$\mu = 47.62 \text{ customers/hour}$$

Decision Point The processing rate would have to increase only modestly to achieve the eight-minute target. However, the probability of having more than four customers in the system is too high. The manager must now find a way to increase the processing rate from 35 per hour to approximately 48 per hour. He can increase this rate in several different ways, ranging from employing a high-school student to help bag the groceries to installing electronic point-of-sale equipment that reads the prices from bar-coded information on each item.

MULTIPLE-WORKSTATION MODEL

With the multiple-workstation model, also labelled the *multiple-server model* for services, customers form a single line and choose one of s workstations when one is available. The system has only one phase. We make the following assumption in addition to those for the single-workstation model: There are s identical workstations, and the distribution of the operations time for each workstation is exponential, with a mean operations time of $1/\mu$.

With these assumptions, we can apply several formulas to describe the operating characteristics of the system:

$$\rho = \text{Average utilization of the system}$$

$$= \frac{\lambda}{s\mu}$$

P_0 = Probability that zero customers are in the system

$$= \left[\sum_{n=0}^{s-1} \frac{(\lambda/\mu)^n}{n!} + \frac{(\lambda/\mu)^s}{s!} \left(\frac{1}{1 - \rho} \right) \right]^{-1}$$

P_n = Probability that n customers are in the system

$$= \begin{cases} \dfrac{(\lambda/\mu)^n}{n!} P_0, & 0 < n < s \\[2ex] \dfrac{(\lambda/\mu)^n}{s! s^{n-s}} P_0, & n \geq s \end{cases}$$

L_q = Average number of customers waiting in line

$$= \frac{P_0 (\lambda/\mu)^s \rho}{s! (1 - \rho)^2}$$

W_q = Average waiting time of customers in line

$$= \frac{L_q}{\lambda}$$

W = Average time spent in the system, including waiting and operations time

$$= W_q + \frac{1}{\mu}$$

L = Average number of customers in the system

$$= \lambda W$$

EXAMPLE 4S.5

Estimating Idle Time and Hourly Operating Costs with the Multiple-Workstation Model

The managers of a Canada Post terminal in New Brunswick are concerned about the amount of time the delivery trucks are idle, waiting to be unloaded. The terminal operates with four unloading bays. Each bay requires a crew of two employees, and each crew costs $30 per hour. The estimated cost of an idle truck is $50 per hour. Trucks arrive at an average rate of three per hour, according to a Poisson distribution. On average, a crew can unload a semi-trailer rig in one hour, with exponential service times. What is the total hourly cost of operating the system?

SOLUTION

The *multiple-workstation model* is appropriate. To find the total cost of labour and idle trucks, we must calculate the average number of trucks in the system.

First, we must calculate capacity utilization, ρ:

$$\rho = \frac{\lambda}{s\mu} = \frac{3 \text{ trucks per hour}}{4 \text{ bays} \times 1 \text{ hour per truck per bay}} = 0.75$$

To estimate the average number of trucks in the system, L, we must calculate (in order) the following, P_0, L_q, W_q, and W:

$$P_0 = \left[\sum_{n=0}^{s-1} \frac{(\lambda/\mu)^n}{n!} + \frac{(\lambda/\mu)^s}{s!} \left(\frac{1}{1-\rho} \right) \right]^{-1}$$

$$= \left[1 + 3 + \frac{3^2}{2} + \frac{3^3}{6} + \frac{3^4}{24} \times \left(\frac{1}{1-0.75} \right) \right]^{-1}$$

$$= \frac{1}{1 + 3 + 4.5 + 4.5 + 13.5} = 0.03774$$

$$L_q = \frac{P_0(\lambda/\mu)^s \rho}{s!(1-\rho)^2}$$

$$= \frac{0.03774 \times (3/1)^4 \times 0.75}{24 \times (1-0.75)^2} = 1.528 \text{ trucks}$$

$$W_q = \frac{L_q}{\lambda}$$

$$= \frac{1.528}{3} = 0.509 \text{ hours}$$

$$W = W_q + \frac{1}{\mu}$$

$$= 0.509 + 1 = 1.509 \text{ hours}$$

We can now estimate the average number of trucks in the system:

$$L = \lambda W$$
$$= 3 \times 1.509 = 4.53 \text{ trucks}$$

Thus, the results show that the four-bay design will be utilized 75 percent of the time and that the average number of trucks either being serviced or waiting in line is 4.53 trucks. We can now calculate the hourly costs of labour and idle trucks:

Labour cost:	$30(s) = \$30(4)$	$= \$120.00$
Idle truck cost:	$50(L) = \$50(4.53)$	$= \underline{226.50}$
	Total hourly cost	$= \$346.50$

Decision Point   Management must now assess whether $346.50 per hour for this operation is acceptable. Attempting to reduce costs by eliminating crews will only increase the waiting time of the trucks, which is more expensive per hour than the crews. However, if the service rate can be increased through better work methods, for example, L can be reduced and daily operating costs will be less.

DECISION AREAS FOR MANAGEMENT

After analyzing a waiting-line problem, management can improve the service system by making changes in one or more of the following areas:

1. *Arrival rates.* Management often can affect the rate of customer arrivals, λ, through advertising, special promotions, or differential pricing. For example, a telephone company uses differential pricing to shift residential long-distance calls from daytime hours to evening hours.

2. *Number of service facilities.* By increasing the number of workstations, such as tool cribs, toll booths, or bank tellers, or by dedicating some workstations in a phase to a unique set of services, management can increase system capacity.

3. *Number of phases.* Managers can decide to allocate tasks to sequential phases if they determine that two sequential workstations may be more efficient than one. For instance, in the assembly-line problem discussed in Chapter 9, "Location and Layout," the decision concerns the number of phases needed along the assembly line. Determining the number of workers needed on the line also involves assigning a certain set of work elements to each one. Changing the arrangement of workstations can increase the processing rate, μ, of each workstation and the capacity of the system.

4. *Number of people per workstation.* Managers can influence the processing rate by assigning more than one person to a workstation.

5. *Worker efficiency.* By adjusting the capital-to-labour ratio, devising improved work methods, or instituting incentive programs, management can increase the efficiency of workers assigned to a workstation. Such changes are reflected in μ.

6. *Priority rule.* Managers set the priority rule to be used, decide whether to have a different priority rule for each workstation, and decide whether to allow pre-emption (and, if so, under what conditions). Such decisions affect the waiting times of the customers and the utilization of workstations.

7. *Line arrangement.* Managers can influence customer waiting times and the utilization of individual workstations by deciding whether to have a single line or multiple lines in a given phase of service.

Obviously, these factors are interrelated. An adjustment in the customer arrival rate, λ, might have to be accompanied by an increase in the processing rate, μ, in some way. Decisions about the number of workstations, the number of phases, and waiting-line arrangements also are related.

For each of the problems we analyzed with the waiting-line models, the arrivals had a Poisson distribution (or exponential interarrival times), the processing times had an exponential distribution, the workstations had a simple arrangement, and the priority discipline was first-come, first-served. Waiting-line theory has been used to develop other models in which these criteria are not met, but these models are very complex. Many times the nature of the customer population, the constraints on the line, the priority rule, the distribution of operations time, and the arrangement of workstations are such that waiting-line theory is no longer useful. In these cases, simulation often is used (see Supplement G, "Simulation").

EQUATION SUMMARY

1. Customer arrival Poisson distribution: $P_n = \dfrac{(\lambda T)^n}{n!} e^{-\lambda T}$

2. Operations-time exponential distribution: $P(t \leq T) = 1 - e^{-\mu T}$

	SINGLE-WORKSTATION MODEL	MULTIPLE-WORKSTATION MODEL
Average capacity utilization of the system	$\rho = \dfrac{\lambda}{\mu}$	$\rho = \dfrac{\lambda}{s\mu}$
Probability that n customers are in the system	$P_n = (1 - \rho)\rho^n$	$P_n = \begin{cases} \dfrac{(\lambda/\mu)^n}{n!}P_0, & 0 < n < s \\[2ex] \dfrac{(\lambda/\mu)^n}{s!\,s^{n-s}}P_0, & n \geq s \end{cases}$
Probability that zero customers are in the system	$P_0 = 1 - \rho$	$P_0 = \left[\displaystyle\sum_{n=0}^{s-1} \dfrac{(\lambda/\mu)^n}{n!} + \dfrac{(\lambda/\mu)^s}{s!}\left(\dfrac{1}{1 - \rho}\right) \right]^{-1}$
Average number of customers in the system	$L = \dfrac{\lambda}{\mu - \lambda}$	$L = \lambda W$
Average number of customers in the waiting line	$L_q = \rho L$	$L_q = \dfrac{P_0(\lambda/\mu)^s \rho}{s!(1 - \rho)^2}$
Average time spent in the system, including waiting and operations time	$W = \dfrac{1}{\mu - \lambda}$	$W = W_q + \dfrac{1}{\mu}$
Average waiting time in line	$W_q = \rho W$	$W_q = \dfrac{L_q}{\lambda}$

SUPPLEMENT HIGHLIGHTS

- Waiting lines form when customers or items arrive at a faster rate than they are being served or processed. Because customer arrival rates vary, long waiting lines may occur even when the system's designed processing rate is substantially higher than the average customer arrival rate.

- Waiting-line models have been developed for use in analyzing service and manufacturing systems. If the assumptions made in creating a waiting-line model are

consistent with an actual situation, the model's formulas can be solved to predict the performance of the system with respect to capacity utilization, average customer waiting time, and the average number of customers in the system.

- Four elements are common to all waiting-line problems: a customer population, a waiting line, a queuing configuration, and a priority rule for determining which customer is to be served next.

SOLVED PROBLEM 1

A photographer at the passport office takes passport pictures at an average rate of 20 pictures per hour. The photographer must wait until the customer blinks or scowls, so the time to take a picture is exponentially distributed. Customers arrive at a Poisson-distributed average rate of 19 customers per hour.

a. What is the capacity utilization of the photographer?

b. How much time will the average customer spend at the photograph step of the passport issuing process?

SOLUTION

a. The assumptions in the problem statement are consistent with a single-workstation model. Utilization is:

$$\rho = \frac{\lambda}{\mu} = \frac{19}{20} = 0.95$$

b. The average customer time spent at the photographer's station is:

$$W = \frac{1}{\mu - \lambda} = \frac{1}{20 - 19} = 1 \text{ hour}$$

SOLVED PROBLEM 2

The Mega Multiplex Movie Theatre has three concession clerks serving customers on a first-come, first-served basis. The processing time per customer is exponentially distributed with an average of 2 minutes per customer. Concession customers wait in a single line in a large lobby, and arrivals are Poisson distributed with an average of 81 customers per hour. Previews run for 10 minutes before the start of each show. If the average time in the concession area exceeds 10 minutes, customers become dissatisfied.

a. What is the average capacity utilization of the concession clerks?

b. What is the average time spent in the concession area?

SOLUTION

a. The problem statement is consistent with the multiple-workstation model, and the average utilization rate is:

$$\rho = \frac{\lambda}{s\mu} = \frac{81 \text{ customers/hour}}{(3 \text{ clerks})\left(\dfrac{60 \text{ minutes/clerk-hour}}{2 \text{ minutes/customer}}\right)} = 0.90$$

The concession clerks are busy 90 percent of the time.

b. The average time spent in the system, W, is

$$W = W_q + \frac{1}{\mu}$$

Here:

$$W_q = \frac{L_q}{\lambda} \qquad L_q = \frac{P_0(\lambda/\mu)^s \rho}{s!(1 - \rho)^2} \qquad \text{and} \qquad P_0 = \left[\sum_{n=0}^{s-1} \frac{(\lambda/\mu)^n}{n!} + \frac{(\lambda/\mu)^s}{s!}\left(\frac{1}{1 - \rho}\right)\right]^{-1}$$

We must solve for P_0, L_q, and W_q, in that order, before we can solve for W:

$$P_0 = \left[\sum_{n=0}^{s-1} \frac{(\lambda/\mu)^n}{n!} + \frac{(\lambda/\mu)^s}{s!}\left(\frac{1}{1 - \rho}\right)\right]^{-1}$$

$$= \frac{1}{1 + \dfrac{(81/30)}{1} + \dfrac{(2.7)^2}{2} + \left[\dfrac{(2.7)^3}{6}\left(\dfrac{1}{1 - 0.9}\right)\right]}$$

$$= \frac{1}{1 + 2.7 + 3.645 + 32.805} = \frac{1}{40.15} = 0.0249$$

$$L_q = \frac{P_0(\lambda/\mu)^s \rho}{s!(1 - \rho)^2} = \frac{0.0249(81/30)^3(0.9)}{3!(1 - 0.9)^2} = \frac{0.4411}{6(0.01)} = 7.352 \text{ customers}$$

$$W_q = \frac{L_q}{\lambda} = \frac{7.352 \text{ customers}}{81 \text{ customers/hour}} = 0.0908 \text{ hour}$$

$$W = W_q + \frac{1}{\mu} = 0.0908 \text{ hour} + \frac{1}{30} \text{ hour} = (0.1241 \text{ hour})\left(\frac{60 \text{ minutes}}{\text{hour}}\right)$$

$$= 7.45 \text{ minutes}$$

With three concession clerks, customers will spend an average of 7.45 minutes in the concession area.

PROBLEMS

1. The Solomon law firm produces many legal documents that must be typed for clients and the firm. Requests average 8 pages of documents per hour, and they arrive according to a Poisson distribution. The secretary can type 10 pages per hour on average according to an exponential distribution.

   a. What is the average capacity utilization of the secretary?

   b. What is the probability that more than 4 pages are waiting or being typed?

   c. What is the average number of pages waiting to be typed?

2. Moore, Aiken, and Leung is a dental clinic serving the needs of the general public on a first-come, first-served basis. The clinic has three dental chairs, each staffed by a dentist. Patients arrive at the rate of five per hour, according to a Poisson distribution, and do not balk or renege. The average time required for a dental checkup is 30 minutes, according to an exponential distribution.

   a. What is the probability that no patients are in the clinic?

   b. What is the probability that six or more patients are in the clinic?

   c. What is the average number of patients waiting?

   d. What is the average total time that a patient spends in the clinic?

3. Fantastic Styling Salon is run by two stylists, Jenny Perez and Bill Sloan, each capable of serving five customers per hour, on average. Eight customers, on average, arrive at the salon each hour.

   a. If all arriving customers wait in a common line for the next available stylist, how long would a customer wait in line, on average, before being served?

   b. Suppose that 50 percent of the arriving customers want to be served only by Perez and that the other 50 percent

want only Sloan. How long would a customer wait in line, on average, before being served by Perez? By Sloan? What is the average customer waiting time in the line?

   c. Do you observe a difference in the answers to parts (a) and (b)? If so, why? Explain.

4. You are the manager of a local bank where three tellers provide services to customers. On average, each teller takes 3 minutes to serve a customer. Customers arrive, on average, at a rate of 50 per hour. Having recently received complaints from some customers that they have had to wait for a long time before being served, your boss asks you to evaluate the service system. Specifically, you must provide answers to the following questions:

   a. What is the average capacity utilization of the three-teller service system?

   b. What is the probability that no customers are being served by a teller or are waiting in line?

   c. What is the average number of customers waiting in line?

   d. On average, how long does a customer wait in line before being served?

   e. On average, how many customers would be at a teller's station and in line?

5. Tram Tweet hosts a psychology talk show on CTPG radio. Tram's advice averages 10 minutes per caller but varies according to an exponential distribution. The average time between calls is 25 minutes, exponentially distributed. Generating calls in this local market is difficult, so Tram doesn't want to lose any calls to busy signals. The radio station has only three telephone lines. What is the probability that a caller receives a busy signal?

6. The supervisor at the Precision Machine Shop wants to determine the staffing policy that minimizes total

operating costs. The average arrival rate at the tool crib, where tools are dispensed to the workers, is 8 machinists per hour. Each machinist's pay is $20 per hour. The supervisor can staff the crib either with a junior attendant who is paid $5 per hour and can process 10 arrivals per hour or with a senior attendant who is paid $12 per hour and can process 16 arrivals per hour. Which attendant should be selected, and what would be the total estimated hourly cost?

7. The daughter of the owner of a local hamburger restaurant is preparing to open a new fast-food restaurant called Hasty Burgers. On the basis of the arrival rates at her father's outlets, she expects customers to arrive at the drive-up window according to a Poisson distribution, with a mean of 20 customers per hour. The service rate is flexible; however, the service times are expected to follow an exponential distribution. The drive-in window is a single-workstation operation.

   a. What service rate is needed to keep the average number of customers in the service system (waiting line and being served) to four?

   b. For the service rate in part (a), what is the probability that more than four customers are in line and being served?

   c. For the service rate in part (a), what is the average waiting time in line for each customer? Does this average seem satisfactory for a fast-food business?

8. You are in charge of a quarry that supplies sand and stone aggregates to your company's construction sites. Empty trucks from construction sites arrive at the quarry's huge piles of sand and stone aggregates and wait in line to enter the station, which can load either sand or aggregate. At the station, they are filled with material, weighed, checked out, and proceed to a construction site. Currently, 9 empty trucks arrive per hour, on average. Once a truck has entered a loading station, it takes 6 minutes for it to be filled, weighed, and checked out.

   Concerned that trucks are spending too much time waiting and being filled, you are evaluating two alternatives to reduce the average time the trucks spend in the system. The first alternative is to add side boards to the trucks (so that more material could be loaded) and to add a helper at the loading station (so that filling time could be reduced), at a total cost of $50 000. The arrival rate of trucks would change to 6 per hour, and the filling time would be reduced to four minutes. The second alternative is to add another loading station at a cost of $80 000. The trucks would wait in a common line and the truck at the front of the line would move to the next available station.

   Which alternative would you recommend if you want to reduce the current average waiting time in the system?

NOTES FOR CHAPTER

1. Adapted from K. L. Katz, B. M. Larson, and R. C. Larson, "Prescription for Waiting-in-Line Blues: Entertain, Enlighten, and Engage," *Sloan Management Review*, vol. 32, no. 2 (1991), pp. 44–53.

FURTHER READING

Cooper, Robert B. *Introduction to Queuing Theory*, 2nd ed. New York: Elsevier-North Holland, 1980.

Hillier, F. S., and G. S. Lieberman. *Introduction to Operations Research*, 2nd ed. San Francisco: Holden-Day, 1975.

Lovejoy, W. S. "Integrated Operations: A Proposal for Operations Management Teaching and Research." *Production and Operations Management*, vol. 7, no. 2 (1998), pp. 106–124.

Moore, P. M. *Queues, Inventories and Maintenance*. New York: John Wiley & Sons, 1958.

Saaty, T. L. *Elements of Queuing Theory with Applications*. New York: McGraw-Hill, 1961.

My OM Lab ASSETS

MyOMLab offers the following resources, which allow you to further practise and apply concepts presented in this chapter.

- **Key Equations:** All the equations for this chapter can be found in one convenient location.

- **Video Case. 1st Bank Villa Italia:** *Waiting Lines*. What are the managerial implications of using different approaches to designing waiting lines? How do different designs change customer value?

- **Virtual Tour:** *New York City Fire Department*. For the fire/paramedic service, what are determinants of response time? Given the average response times for the types of calls, what measures could be taken to reduce the response time? What type of queuing model is best for this situation?

- **Extend LT:** *Security Inspection at the Randville Plant*. The chief of security must explore options to cut delays with employees passing through the security checkpoint.

- **OM Explorer Tutor:** OM Explorer contains two tutor programs that will help you learn about single- and multiple-workstation models.

Inventory Management

Learning Goals

After reading this chapter, you will be able to:

1. describe the cost and service trade-offs involved in inventory decisions.

2. distinguish among the different types of inventory and know how to manage their quantities.

3. compute the economic order quantity and apply it in various situations.

4. develop policies for both continuous review and periodic review inventory control systems.

5. identify ways to maintain accurate inventory records.

Across the Organization

Inventory management is important to:

- **accounting,** which provides the cost estimates used in inventory control, pays suppliers, and bills customers.

- **finance,** which deals with the implications of interest or investment opportunity costs on inventory management.

- **management information systems,** which develop and maintain the technology for tracking and controlling inventories.

- **marketing and sales,** which create the need for inventory systems and rely on inventories to satisfy customers.

- **operations,** which has the responsibility to establish the firm's inventory policies and control inventories.

Although new products are expected to drive future growth at Xerox Canada, it must be supported by strong service of products already in the field. Slow fulfillment of a worn part or needed supplies costs customers time and money. That makes the management of Xerox's inventory of replacement parts absolutely critical. However, managers have also had to make bold cuts in inventory and operating costs to improve financial performance. In the words of Al Gallina, director of logistics, "It has been a delicate balancing act."

First, a forecasting system has proven instrumental in reducing Canadian inventory. Statistical methods are used for a first pass, and then the logistics team meets monthly with sales and marketing to further refine the forecast. Doing so has shifted Xerox away from building and shipping to inventory, with its associated "just-in-case" inefficiencies. Instead, the emphasis is on build-to-order and just-in-time, which require better information flow, as well as greater supply chain speed and flexibility. The net result: with lower inventories, leased warehouse space was reduced by 4500 square metres.

Second, a complete rethinking of how to best deliver critical parts and supplies to Xerox's field technicians was also undertaken. Although technicians travel with much of the inventory in their service vehicles (the target service level is 85 percent for in-the-field repairs), a rapid delivery network is essential for other critical parts. This massive network had grown to two warehouses and 19 depots that shipped more than 1.5 million pieces annually—ranging from fusers and rollers to complete plug-and-play modules—with a targeted service level of 95 percent.

Although service expectations were generally met, Xerox had some glaring inefficiencies in

Timely repair service is critical. Achieving the right balance between inventories stored in centralized versus satellite locations— near field service personnel— can improve customer service while still reducing overall costs.

smaller centres. Some satellite locations needed only half a person to manage the volume, yet two people would be staffed for safety reasons, sick days, and vacation. Maintaining consistency across multiple carriers was also very challenging, with their varying procedures, delivery times, and formal reporting capabilities.

Xerox employed a two-pronged approach. To begin, the parts ordering system was centralized in a St. John, N.B., call centre. Next, Xerox went looking for a strategic partner to manage the depot network. By outsourcing, labour and facility costs for each depot could be spread across several firms to make such a vast network economically feasible. Xerox's partner was Progistix, and the contract included gain sharing—as Progistix added clients to its network, the Xerox share of total costs for the depot network was reduced.

Now, technicians looking for critical parts check in with the central call centre and provide the shipping address. Once Xerox's mainframe identifies the closest depot with the part, it sends the order by EDI link to Progistix, which, in turn, prints out the order at the appropriate depot. Because inventory accuracy is vitally important to maintain service, inventory variances between Xerox and its outsourcing partner are compared and resolved daily. Xerox also tracks the time between when the order came in and delivery.

The results speak for themselves: Canadian inventory was cut in half in just 12 months, and the service level improved to 98 percent. Gallina adds, "But we're not completely satisfied yet and we are going to continue to look for further reductions. That's obviously going to be a challenge, so we need to be thinking how we can do things differently."[1]

inventory A stock of items, including materials, orders, information, and people, that flow through or are used in a process to satisfy customer demand.

Inventory management is an important concern for managers in all types of businesses. **Inventory** is a stock of items used to satisfy customer demand or support the production of goods or services. For companies that operate on relatively low profit margins, poor inventory management can seriously undermine the business. The challenge is not to pare inventories to the bone to reduce costs nor to have plenty around to satisfy all demands, but to have the right amount to achieve the competitive priorities for the business most efficiently. In this chapter, we first introduce the basic concepts of inventory management for all types of businesses and then discuss inventory control systems appropriate for retail and distribution inventories.

INVENTORY CONCEPTS

Inventory is created when items, including materials, parts, or finished goods, are received faster than they are consumed, used, or sold. Considered more generally, items can also include customer orders waiting to be processed, called an *order backlog*, or customers waiting in a service process (see Supplement 4S in MyOMLab, "Waiting Lines"). In this section, the focus is on materials, and we identify the pressures for high and low inventories, define the different types of inventory, discuss tactics that can be used to reduce inventories when appropriate, identify the trade-offs involved in making manufacturing inventory placement decisions, and discuss how to identify the inventory items needing the most attention.

PRESSURES FOR LOW INVENTORIES

An inventory manager's job is to balance the conflicting costs and pressures that argue for both low and high inventories and to determine appropriate inventory levels. There are two primary reasons for keeping inventories low. First, inventory represents a temporary monetary investment in goods on which a firm must pay (rather than receive) interest. Second, as inventory in a process increases, the total time required for items to pass through the process, called *throughput time*, increases (see Chapter 4, "Capacity"). In addition, customer responsiveness for service processes and products slows across the supply chain (see Chapter 2).

inventory holding cost
The variable cost of keeping items on hand, including interest, storage and handling, taxes, insurance, and shrinkage.

Inventory holding cost or carrying cost is the variable cost of keeping items on hand, including such costs as interest, storage and handling, insurance, and shrinkage. When these components change with inventory levels, so does the holding cost. Companies usually state an item's holding cost per period of time as a percent of its value. The annual cost to maintain one unit in inventory typically ranges from 20 percent to 40 percent of its value. Suppose that a firm's holding cost is 30 percent. If the average value of total inventory is 20 percent of sales, the average annual cost to hold inventory is $0.30(0.20) = 6$ percent of total sales. This cost is sizable in terms of gross profit margins, which often are less than 10 percent. Thus, the components of holding cost create pressures for low inventories.

COST OF CAPITAL. The cost of capital is the opportunity cost of investing in an asset relative to the expected return on assets of similar risk. Inventory is an asset; consequently, we should use a cost measure that adequately reflects the firm's approach to financing assets. Most firms use the *weighted average cost of capital (WACC)*, which is the average of the required return on a firm's stock equity and the interest rate on its debt, weighted by the proportion of equity and debt in its portfolio. The cost of capital usually is the largest component of holding cost, and is as high as 15 percent.

STORAGE AND HANDLING COSTS. Inventory takes up space and must be moved into and out of storage. Storage and handling costs may be incurred when a firm rents space on either a long- or a short-term basis. There also is an opportunity cost for storage when a firm could use storage space productively in some other way.

TAXES, INSURANCE, AND SHRINKAGE. Taxes and insurance are often related to total inventory levels. Shrinkage takes three forms. Pilferage, or theft of inventory by customers or employees, is a significant percentage of sales for some businesses. Obsolescence occurs when inventory cannot be used or sold at full value, owing to model changes, engineering modifications, or unexpectedly low demand. Obsolescence is a big expense in electronics and retail clothing, where drastic discounts are often given after new products are introduced. Finally, deterioration through physical spoilage or damage results in lost value. Food and beverages, for example, lose value and might even have to be discarded when their shelf life is reached.

PRESSURES FOR HIGH INVENTORIES

Given the costs of holding inventory, why not eliminate it altogether? Let us look briefly at the pressures related to maintaining inventories.

CUSTOMER SERVICE. Creating finished goods inventory can speed delivery and improve on-time delivery. Inventory reduces the potential for stockouts and backorders, which are key concerns of wholesalers and retailers. A **stockout** occurs when an item that is typically stocked is not available to satisfy a demand the moment it occurs, resulting in loss of the sale. A **backorder** is a customer order that cannot be filled when promised or demanded but is filled later. Customers may be willing to wait for a backorder, but next time they may take their business elsewhere.

ORDERING COST. Each time a firm places a new order, it incurs an **ordering cost,** such as the cost of preparing a purchase order for a supplier. For the same item, the ordering cost is the same, regardless of the order size: the purchasing agent must take the time to decide how much to order and, perhaps, select a supplier and negotiate terms. Time also is spent on paperwork, followup, and receiving. Similar costs occur also for services or products produced within the firm.

SETUP COST. The cost involved in changing over an operation to produce a different component or provide a different type of service is the **setup cost.** It includes labour and time to make the changeover, cleaning, and new tools or fixtures. Scrap or rework costs can be substantially higher at the start of the run. Generally, setup cost also is independent of order size, so there is pressure to order a large supply of the component and hold it in inventory. Setup costs also are present in services, where, for example, an airline must set up each aircraft for each batch of customers taking a new flight.

LABOUR AND EQUIPMENT UTILIZATION. By creating more inventory, management can increase workforce productivity and facility utilization in three ways, all of which are related to reducing variability (see Chapter 4, "Capacity"). First, placing larger, less frequent production orders reduces the number of unproductive setups, which add no value to a product or service. Second, holding inventory reduces the chance of costly rescheduling of production orders, because the components needed to make the product are not in inventory. Third, building inventories improves resource utilization by stabilizing the output rate for industries when demand is cyclical or seasonal. The firm uses inventory built during slack periods to handle extra demand in peak seasons and minimizes the need for extra shifts, hiring, layoffs, overtime, and additional equipment.

stockout An item that is typically stocked is not available to satisfy a demand the moment it occurs, resulting in loss of the sale.

backorder A customer order that cannot be filled when promised or demanded but is filled later.

ordering cost The cost of preparing a purchase order for a supplier or a production order for the shop.

setup cost The cost involved in changing over an operation to produce a different component, item, or service.

TRANSPORTATION COST. Sometimes outbound transportation cost can be reduced by increasing inventory levels. Having inventory on hand allows for more full-load shipments and minimizes the need to expedite shipments by more expensive modes of transportation. Forward placement of inventory can also reduce outbound transportation cost, even though the pooling effect is lessened and more inventory is necessary. Inbound transportation cost also may be reduced by creating more inventory. Sometimes several items are ordered from the same supplier. Combining these orders and placing them at the same time may lead to rate discounts, thereby decreasing the costs of transportation and raw materials.

PURCHASING COST DISCOUNTS. A firm often can reduce total payments to suppliers if it can tolerate higher inventory levels. Suppose that a firm learns that a key supplier is about to increase prices. It might be cheaper for the firm to order a larger quantity than usual—in effect delaying the price increase—even though inventory will increase temporarily. Similarly, a firm can take advantage of quantity discounts. A **quantity discount**, whereby the price per unit drops when the order is sufficiently large, is an incentive to order larger quantities. Quantity discounts are frequently offered by suppliers to reduce their ordering and setup costs.

quantity discount A drop in the price per unit when the order is sufficiently large.

FUNCTIONS OF INVENTORY

Another perspective on inventory is to classify it by how and why it is created. In this context, there are five functions of inventory for an item: safety stock, decoupling, anticipation, cycle, and pipeline. They cannot be identified physically; that is, a manager can't look at a pile of half-assembled computers or waiting customers and see any difference between items that function as cycle inventory or as safety stock inventory. However, conceptually, each of the five types comes into being in an entirely different way. Once you understand these differences, you can prescribe different ways to reduce inventory, which we discuss in the next section.

safety stock inventory Inventory held to protect against uncertainties and random variation in demand, lead time, processing time, quality, and supply.

SAFETY STOCK INVENTORY. To avoid customer service problems and the hidden costs of unavailable components, companies hold safety stock to act as a buffer. **Safety stock inventory** protects against unexpected variation or uncertainty in demand, lead time, processing time, and supply. Safety stocks are desirable when suppliers fail to deliver the desired quantity on the specified date with acceptable quality or when manufactured items have significant amounts of scrap or rework. In addition, safety stock also accommodates random variability that happens with individual operations. For example, a machine may break down or an employee be may be required to handle a particularly difficult customer. Having safety stock as a buffer is critical ahead of a process bottleneck, as discussed in Chapter 4, "Capacity," to maintain process output.

To create safety stock, one option is to place an order for delivery earlier than when the item is typically needed. The replenishment order arrives ahead of time, giving a cushion against uncertainty. For example, suppose that the average lead time from a supplier is three weeks but a firm orders five weeks in advance just to be safe. This policy creates a safety stock equal to a two weeks' supply (5 − 3). Another option is to order or hold extra items based on the degree of variability.

decoupling inventory Inventory held to accommodate different rates or patterns of production between two operations.

DECOUPLING INVENTORY. To accommodate the different processing rates of individual operations in a process, **decoupling inventory** can be used to smooth the flow of customers or items. These different processing rates are reasonably certain and may occur because of the "lumpiness" of investing in capacity at any individual operation. Other factors include the scheduling of preventive maintenance or changes in process choice (e.g., changing from batch process in fabrication to line process for final assembly). Unlike safety stock, decoupling inventory accommodates predictable variation. For example, a plastic moulding machine produces 100 parts per hour, but people assemble the final product at 50 parts per hour. As a result, parts are held between operations to balance production rates and moulding is shut down periodically.

anticipation inventory
Inventory used to absorb uneven, but predictable, rates of demand or supply.

ANTICIPATION INVENTORY. Inventory used to absorb predictable, uneven rates of demand or supply, which businesses often face, is referred to as **anticipation inventory**. Seasonal demand patterns lend themselves to the use of anticipation inventory. Manufacturers of air conditioners, for example, can experience 90 percent of their annual demand during just three months of a year. Such uneven demand may lead a manufacturer to stockpile anticipation inventory during periods of low demand so that output levels do not have to be increased much when demand peaks. Smoothing output rates with inventory can increase productivity because varying output rates and workforce size can be costly. Anticipation inventory also can help when supply, rather than demand, is uneven. A company may stock up on a certain purchased item if its suppliers are threatened with a strike or have severe capacity limitations.

cycle inventory The portion of total inventory that varies directly with lot size.

CYCLE INVENTORY. The portion of total inventory that varies directly with lot size is called **cycle inventory**. Determining how frequently to order, and in what quantity, is called *lot sizing*. The quantity ordered or produced is called a *lot* or *batch*. Two principles apply. First, the lot size, Q, varies directly with the elapsed time (or cycle) between orders. Second, the longer the time between orders, the greater the cycle inventory must be.

Just after a lot has arrived, at the beginning of a cycle, the cycle inventory is at its maximum, or Q. Later, at the end of a cycle, just before a new lot arrives, cycle inventory drops to its minimum, or 0. The average cycle inventory is the average of these two extremes:

$$\text{Average cycle inventory} = \frac{Q + 0}{2} = \frac{Q}{2}$$

This formula is exact only when the demand and processing rates are constant and uniform. However, it does provide a reasonably good estimate even when demand rates are not constant.

pipeline inventory
Inventory moving from point to point in the materials flow system.

PIPELINE INVENTORY. Items moving from point to point in a process are called **pipeline inventory**. Materials move from suppliers to a plant, from one operation to the next in the plant, from the plant to a distribution centre or customer, and from the distribution centre to a retailer. Pipeline inventory consists of orders that have been placed but not yet received. For example, a manufacturer of decorative glass panels in British Columbia uses glass and parts produced in China. Although shipments arrive periodically at the plant, the long transportation time creates a pipeline inventory of parts en route from Asia to Canada. Pipeline inventory is based on the average demand that occurs during an item's lead time, $\overline{D}_L$, that is, demand per period multiplied by the time that the item is being moved or shipped.

$$\text{Pipeline inventory} = \overline{D}_L = dL$$

Note that the lot size does not directly affect the average level of the pipeline inventory. Increasing Q inflates the size of each order, but orders are placed less frequently.

INVENTORY REDUCTION TACTICS

Managers always are eager to find cost-effective ways to reduce inventory. We begin by discussing something fundamental—the basic tactics (which we call *levers*) for reducing inventory. A primary lever is one that must be activated if inventory is to be reduced. A secondary lever reduces the penalty cost of applying the primary lever and the need for having inventory in the first place.

SAFETY STOCK INVENTORY. The primary lever for reducing safety stock inventory is to reduce random variation, including the uncertainty found in demand, supply, delivery, and operations. Four secondary levers can be used:

1. Improve demand forecasts so that fewer surprises come from customers. Customers also can be encouraged to reserve or order items before they need them.

2. Rely more on a capacity cushion of equipment and labour, including more flexible equipment and cross-trained workers. These cushions are particularly critical in services where customers are willing to wait only a very short time.

3. Cut lead times of purchased or produced items to reduce demand uncertainty during lead time. For example, local suppliers with short lead times could be selected whenever possible.

4. Reduce process uncertainties. Suppliers may be more reliable if production plans are shared with them, permitting them to make more realistic forecasts. Analyzing supplier risk may allow reductions where low risks are present. Surprises from unexpected scrap or rework can be reduced by improving manufacturing processes. Preventive maintenance can minimize unexpected downtime caused by equipment failure.

DECOUPLING INVENTORY. The primary lever for reducing decoupling inventory is to reduce predictable variation. Secondary levers emphasize better coordination and adjusting the output rate of individual operations.

1. More closely aligned schedules can be implemented. This usually translates into taking more frequent, but shorter, reductions in output from a higher-capacity operation. For example, rather than simply scheduling an entire shift for preventive maintenance while other operations continue, more frequent but shorter periods of preventive maintenance reduce the quantity amount of decoupling inventory needed.

2. The production rate of individual, higher-output operations might be slowed to more closely match the overall output rate of the system. This may also improve quality at the higher-capacity operations, as people and equipment are not required to work at the maximum output rate.

ANTICIPATION INVENTORY. The primary lever for reducing anticipation inventory is to better match the demand and production rates. Secondary levers are used to level customer demand in one of the following ways:

1. Add new products with different demand cycles so that a peak in the demand for one product compensates for the seasonal low in another.

2. Provide off-season promotional campaigns.

3. Offer seasonal pricing plans.

CYCLE INVENTORY. The primary lever is simply to reduce the lot size. Methods of lean systems (see Chapter 7, "Lean Systems") use small lots relative to traditional lot sizes, which might equal several weeks' (or even months') supply. However, making such reductions in Q without making any other changes can be devastating. For example, setup costs can skyrocket, which leads to use of the two secondary levers.

1. Streamline methods for placing orders and making setups, which reduces ordering and setup costs and allows Q to be reduced.

2. Increase repeatability to eliminate the need for changeovers. **Repeatability** is the degree to which the same work can be done again. It can be increased through promoting product demand; using more flexible automation; devoting resources exclusively to a product; using the same part in many different products; the one-worker, multiple-machines concept; or using group technology (see Chapter 7, "Lean Systems"). Increased repeatability may justify new setup methods, reduce transportation costs, and allow quantity discounts from suppliers.

repeatability The degree to which the same work can be done again.

PIPELINE INVENTORY. An operations manager has direct control over lead time but not demand rate. Because pipeline inventory is a function of demand during lead time, the primary lever is to reduce the lead time. Secondary levers that can help managers cut lead times include finding more responsive suppliers, speeding the ordering and shipment process, or improving materials handling within the plant.

PLACEMENT OF MANUFACTURING INVENTORIES

The positioning of a firm's inventories supports its competitive priorities. Inventories can be held at the raw materials, work-in-process, and finished goods levels. In general, managers make inventory placement decisions on the basis of two basic factors: process configuration and product characteristics. Naturally, these factors are related, and their interaction creates unique challenges and opportunities for individual companies. It must be emphasized that placement refers to the *relative allocation* of inventory across a process, as there are still other pressures that drive managers to increase or decrease overall inventory levels.

Recall that process configuration is related to the degree of product customization. When a company makes many standard items, it tends to place inventory closer to the customer. Inventory held toward the finished goods level means short delivery times—but a higher dollar investment in inventory.

Product characteristics also influence inventory management in a company. If a process has few raw materials and creates many finished goods, such as a petroleum refinery, managers prefer to hold inventory in raw materials as long as possible. In contrast, if many raw materials are used to produce only a few final products, such as automobile assembly, shifting inventory to finished goods improves customer responsiveness. Finally, if a small number of modules (each of which has many raw materials) is needed to create a wide variety of products, the largest allocation of inventory is usually in intermediate modules. For example, computer manufacturing relies on the assembly of a relatively small number of modules. The rationale behind these allocations is based on inventory pooling, where variability from demand is reduced.

Inventory placement can change over time as an operations strategy develops and process choice evolves. For example, McDonald's changed from a make-to-stock process, where finished hamburgers were held in inventory, to an assemble-to-order process, where cooked hamburger patties are held in inventory (explained in greater detail in Chapter 7). This new placement enables greater customization and delivery of fresher final products.

FIGURE 5.1 *Typical Chart from ABC Analysis*

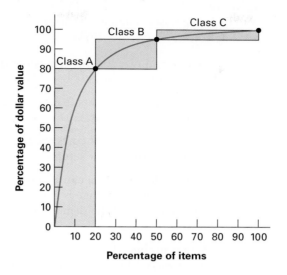

IDENTIFYING CRITICAL INVENTORY ITEMS WITH ABC ANALYSIS

ABC analysis The method of dividing items into three classes according to their dollar usage so that managers can focus on important items.

Thousands of items are held in inventory by a typical organization, but only a small percentage of them deserves management's closest attention and tightest control. **ABC analysis** divides items into three classes according to their dollar usage so that managers can focus on items that have the highest dollar value. This method is the equivalent of creating a *Pareto chart* except that it is applied to inventory rather than process defects. As Figure 5.1 shows, class A items typically represent only about 20 percent of the items but account for 80 percent of the dollar usage. Class B items account for another 30 percent of the items but only 15 percent of the dollar usage. Finally, 50 percent of the items fall in class C, representing a mere 5 percent of the dollar usage. The goal of ABC analysis is to identify the inventory levels of class A items and enable management to control them tightly by using the levers just discussed.

The analysis begins by multiplying the annual demand rate for one item by the dollar value (cost) of one unit to determine its dollar usage. After ranking the items on the basis of dollar usage and creating the Pareto chart, the analyst looks for "natural" changes in slope. The dividing lines in Figure 5.1 between classes are only approximate. Class A items could be somewhat higher or lower than 20 percent of all items, but normally account for the bulk of the dollar usage.

A manager can direct that class A items be reviewed frequently to reduce the average lot size and keep inventory records current. Class B items are candidates for systems where purchase or replenishment decisions can be programmed. Finally, a stockout of a class C item can be as crucial as for a class A or B item, but the inventory holding cost of class C items tends to be low. These features suggest that higher inventory levels can be tolerated and that more safety stock, larger lot sizes, and perhaps even a visual system, which we discuss later, may suffice for class C items. See Solved Problem 2 for a detailed example of ABC analysis.

ECONOMIC ORDER QUANTITY

Recall that managers face conflicting pressures to keep inventories low enough to avoid excess inventory holding costs but high enough to reduce the frequency of orders and setups. A good starting point for balancing these conflicting pressures and

economic order quantity (EOQ) The lot size that minimizes total annual inventory holding and ordering costs.

determining the best cycle-inventory level for an item is finding the **economic order quantity (EOQ)**, which is the lot size that minimizes total annual inventory holding and ordering costs. The approach to determining the EOQ is based on the following assumptions:

1. The demand rate for the item is constant (e.g., always 10 units per day) and known with certainty.

2. There are no constraints (e.g., truck capacity or materials handling limitations) on the size of each lot.

3. The only two relevant costs are the inventory holding cost and the fixed cost per lot for ordering or setup.

4. Decisions for one item can be made independently of decisions for other items (i.e., no advantage is gained in combining several orders going to the same supplier and the demand for one item is not directly linked to another item).

5. There is no uncertainty in lead time or supply. The lead time is constant (e.g., always 14 days) and known with certainty. The amount received is exactly what was ordered and it arrives all at once rather than piecemeal.

The economic order quantity will be optimal when the five assumptions are satisfied. In reality, few situations are so simple and well behaved. In fact, different lot-sizing approaches are needed to reflect quantity discounts, uneven demand rates, or interactions between items (see Supplement H, "Special Inventory Models"). However, the EOQ is often a reasonable first approximation of average lot sizes, even when one or more of the assumptions do not quite apply.

CALCULATING THE EOQ

We begin by formulating the total cost for any lot size, Q. Next, we derive the EOQ, which is the Q that minimizes total cost. Finally, we describe how to convert the EOQ into a companion measure, the elapsed time between orders.

When the EOQ assumptions are satisfied, cycle inventory behaves as shown in Figure 5.2. A cycle begins with Q units held in inventory, which happens when a new

FIGURE 5.2 *Cycle Inventory Levels*

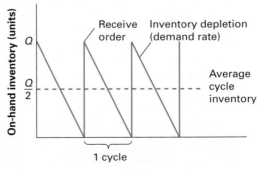

FIGURE 5.3 *Total Inventory Cost*

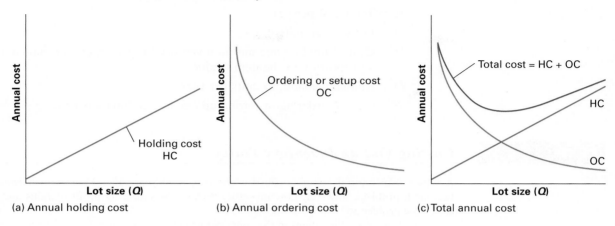

(a) Annual holding cost   (b) Annual ordering cost   (c) Total annual cost

order is received. During the cycle, on-hand inventory is used at a constant rate and, because demand is known with certainty and the lead time is a constant, a new lot can be ordered so that inventory falls to 0 precisely when the new lot is received. Because inventory varies uniformly between Q and 0, the average cycle inventory equals half the lot size, Q.

The annual holding cost for this amount of inventory, which increases linearly with Q, as Figure 5.3(a) shows, is:

Annual holding cost = (Average cycle inventory)(Unit holding cost)

The annual ordering cost is:

Annual ordering or setup cost = (Number of orders/year)(Ordering or setup cost)

The average number of orders per year equals annual demand divided by Q. For example, if 1200 units must be ordered each year and the average lot size is 100 units, then 12 orders will be placed during the year. The annual ordering or setup cost decreases nonlinearly as Q increases, as shown in Figure 5.3(b), because fewer orders are placed.

The total annual cost,* as graphed in Figure 5.3(c), is the sum of the two cost components:†

Total annual cost = Annual holding cost + Annual ordering or setup cost

$$C = \frac{Q}{2}\,(H) + \frac{D}{Q}\,(S)$$

---

*Expressing the total cost on an annual basis usually is convenient (though not necessary). Any time horizon can be selected, as long as D and H cover the same time period. If the total cost is calculated on a monthly basis, D must be monthly demand and H must be the cost of holding a unit for one month.

†The number of orders actually placed in any year is always a whole number, although the formula allows the use of fractional values. However, rounding is not needed, because what is being calculated is an average for multiple years. Such averages need not be integers.

where:

C = Total cost per year

Q = Lot size, in units

H = Cost of holding one unit in inventory for a year, often calculated as a proportion of the item's value

D = Annual demand, in units per year

S = Cost of ordering or setting up one lot, in dollars per lot

---

EXAMPLE 5.1   *Costing Out an Inventory Policy*

A museum of natural history opened a gift shop two years ago. Managing inventories has become a problem, however. Low inventory turnover is squeezing profit margins and causing cash-flow problems.

One of the top-selling items in the container group at the museum's gift shop is a birdfeeder. Sales are 18 units per week, and the supplier charges $60 per unit. The cost of placing an order with the supplier is $45. Annual holding cost is 25 percent of a feeder's value, and the museum operates 52 weeks per year. Managment chose a 390-unit lot size so that new orders could be placed less frequently. What is the annual cost of the current policy of using a 390-unit lot size? Would a lot size of 468 be better?

SOLUTION

We begin by computing the annual demand and holding cost as:

D = (18 units/week)(52 weeks/year) = 936 units

H = 0.25($60/unit) = $15 per unit per year

The total annual cost for the current policy is:

$$C = \frac{Q}{2}(H) + \frac{D}{Q}(S)$$

$$C = \frac{390}{2}(\$15) + \frac{936}{390}(\$45) = \$2925 + \$108 = \$3033$$

The total annual cost for the alternative lot size is:

$$C = \frac{468}{2}(\$15) + \frac{936}{468}(\$45) = \$3510 + \$90 = \$3600$$

Decision Point The lot size of 468 units, which is a half-year supply, would be a more expensive option than the current policy. The savings in order costs are more than offset by the increase in holding costs. Management should use the total annual cost equation to explore other lot-size alternatives.

Taken a few steps further, Figure 5.4 displays the impact of using several Q values for the birdfeeder. Eight different lot sizes were evaluated in addition to the current one. Both holding and ordering costs were plotted, but their sum—the total cost curve—is the important feature. The graph shows that the best lot size, namely the EOQ, is the lowest point on the total cost curve, or between 50 and 100 units. Obviously, reducing the current lot-size policy (Q = 390) can result in significant savings.

A more efficient approach is to use the EOQ formula:

$$EOQ = \sqrt{\frac{2DS}{H}}$$

FIGURE 5.4 *Total Inventory Cost Function for Birdfeeder*

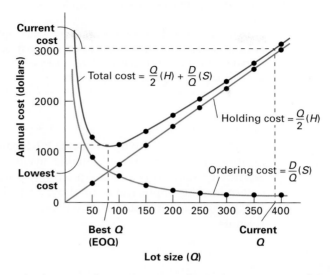

Using basic calculus, we obtain the EOQ from the minimum of the total cost formula. (Take the first derivative of the total cost function with respect to Q, set it equal to 0, and solve for Q.) As Figure 5.4 indicates, the EOQ is the order quantity for which annual holding cost equals annual ordering cost. This is mirrored in Figure 5.4; when the annual holding cost for any Q exceeds the annual ordering cost, as with the 390-unit order, we can immediately conclude that Q is too big. A smaller Q reduces holding cost and increases ordering cost, bringing them into balance. Similarly, if the annual ordering cost exceeds the annual holding cost, Q should be increased.

Sometimes inventory policies are based on the time between replenishment orders, rather than on the number of units in the lot size. The **time between orders (TBO)** is the average elapsed time between receiving (or placing) replenishment orders. For a particular lot size, Q, the TBO_Q is simply Q divided by annual demand. However, the TBO can be stated in any period of time, as demonstrated in Example 5.2, by using demand over that time period.

When we use the EOQ, the TBO is:

$$\text{TBO}_{\text{EOQ}} = \frac{\text{EOQ}}{D}$$

time between orders (TBO) The average elapsed time between receiving (or placing) replenishment orders.

| EXAMPLE 5.2 | *Finding the EOQ, Total Cost, and TBO* |

Using information about the birdfeeder (Example 5.1), calculate the EOQ and its total cost. How frequently will orders be placed if the EOQ is used?

SOLUTION
Using the formulas for EOQ and annual cost, we get:

$$\text{EOQ} = \sqrt{\frac{2DS}{H}} = \sqrt{\frac{2(936)(45)}{15}} = 74.94, \quad \text{or} \quad 75 \text{ units}$$

When the EOQ is used, the time between orders (TBO) can be expressed in various ways for the same time period.

$$\text{TBO}_{\text{EOQ}} = \frac{\text{EOQ}}{D} = \frac{75}{936} = 0.080 \text{ year}$$

This TBO is equivalent to 0.96 months, 4.17 weeks, and 29.25 days.

Decision Point Using the EOQ, about 12 orders per year will be required. In contrast, the current policy of 390 units per order requires an average of 2.4 orders each year (every five months). Thus, the current policy saves on ordering costs but incurs a much larger cost for carrying the cycle inventory. Although it is easy to see which option is best on the basis of total ordering and holding costs, other factors may affect the final decision. For example, if the supplier is willing to reduce the price per unit for large orders, it may be better to order the larger quantity (see Supplement H, "Special Inventory Models").

MANAGERIAL INSIGHTS FROM THE EOQ

Examining the sensitivity of the EOQ formula to small changes, errors, or uncertainties in cost can yield valuable insights into the management of inventories. Sensitivity analysis is a technique for systematically changing crucial parameters to determine the implications of those changes. Table 5.1 shows the effects on the EOQ when we substitute different values into the numerator or denominator of the formula.

TABLE 5.1	*Sensitivity Analysis of the EOQ*			
PARAMETER	**EOQ**	**PARAMETER CHANGE**	**EOQ CHANGE**	**COMMENTS**
Demand	$\sqrt{\dfrac{2DS}{H}}$	↑	↑	Increase in lot size is in proportion to the square root of D.
Order/setup costs	$\sqrt{\dfrac{2DS}{H}}$	↓	↓	Weeks of supply decreases and inventory turnover increases because the lot size decreases.
Holding costs	$\sqrt{\dfrac{2DS}{H}}$	↓	↑	Larger lots are justified when holding costs decrease.

As the table shows, the EOQ provides support for some of the intuition you may have about inventory management. In general, because changes in the crucial values of demand, setup cost, and holding cost fall under the square root, the EOQ changes by a much smaller proportion. For example, a 50 percent increase in demand translates into only a 22 percent increase in the EOQ.

The effect of ordering or setup cost changes on inventories is especially important for lean systems, discussed later in Chapter 7. The EOQ formula explains why managers are so concerned about reducing setup time and costs; small batches are economical with low-cost setups. Moreover, the same process improvements that lead to a lean system also create the basis for a very small EOQ with a very small order or batch size; for example, monthly, daily, or hourly demand rates are known with reasonable certainty in lean systems, and the rate of demand is relatively uniform. In addition, lean systems strive to reduce variability, through either improved quality or reliable delivery lead times from suppliers. Finally, frequent information exchange with and deliveries from suppliers translate into little need to hold inventory. Consequently, the EOQ as a inventory management tool is quite compatible with the principles of lean systems.

INVENTORY CONTROL SYSTEMS

The EOQ and other lot-sizing methods answer the important question: How much should we order? Another important question that needs an answer is: When should we place the order? An inventory control system responds to both questions. In selecting an inventory control system for a particular application, the nature of the demands imposed on the inventory items is crucial. An important distinction between types of inventory is whether an item is subject to dependent or independent demand. Retailers and distributors must manage **independent demand items**—that is, items for which demand is influenced by market conditions and is not related to the inventory decisions for any other item held in stock. Independent demand inventory includes:

1. Wholesale and retail merchandise;

2. Service industry inventory, such as stamps and mailing labels for post offices, office supplies for law firms, and laboratory supplies for research universities;

3. End-item and replacement-part distribution inventories; and

4. Maintenance, repair, and operating (MRO) supplies—that is, items that don't become part of the final product or service, such as employee uniforms, fuel, paint, and machine repair parts.

Managing independent demand inventory can be tricky, because demand is influenced by external factors. For example, the owner of a bookstore may not be sure how many copies of the latest bestseller customers will purchase during the coming month. As a result, she may decide to stock extra copies as a safeguard. Independent demand such as the demand for various book titles must be forecasted. The chapter opener illustrates how Xerox Canada made significant inventory reductions through improved forecasting.

In this chapter, we focus on inventory control systems for independent demand items, which is the type of demand the bookstore owner, other retailers, and distributors face. Even though demand from any one customer is difficult to predict, low demand from some customers is often offset by high demand from others. Thus, total demand for any independent demand item may follow a relatively smooth pattern, with some random fluctuations. *Dependent demand items* are those required as components or inputs to a product or service. Dependent demand exhibits a pattern very different from that of independent demand and must be managed with different techniques (see Chapter 12, "Resource Planning").

In this section, we discuss and compare two inventory control systems: the continuous review system, called a Q system, and the periodic review system, called a P system. We close with a look at hybrid systems, which incorporate features of both the P and the Q systems.

CONTINUOUS REVIEW (Q) SYSTEM

A **continuous review (Q) system**, sometimes called a **reorder point (ROP) system** or *fixed order-quantity system*, tracks the remaining inventory of an item every time a withdrawal is made to determine whether it is time to reorder. In practice, these reviews are done frequently (e.g., daily) or continuously (after every withdrawal). The advent of computers and electronic cash registers linked to inventory records has made continuous reviews easy. At each review a decision is made about an item's inventory position; if it is judged to be too low, the system triggers a new order. The **inventory position (IP)** measures the net quantity of an item available to satisfy future demand.

independent demand items Items for which demand is influenced by market conditions and is not related to the inventory decisions for any other item held in stock.

continuous review (Q) system *or* **reorder point (ROP) system** A system designed to track the remaining inventory of an item every time a withdrawal is made to determine whether it is time to replenish.

inventory position (IP) The net quantity of an item available to satisfy future demand.

scheduled receipts (SR)
or **open orders** Orders
that have been placed but
not yet received.

It includes **scheduled receipts (SR)**, which are orders that have been placed but not yet received, plus on-hand inventory (OH) minus backorders (BO). Sometimes scheduled receipts are called **open orders**. More specifically:

Inventory position = On-hand inventory + Scheduled receipts − Backorders

$$IP = OH + SR - BO$$

reorder point (R) The
predetermined minimum
level that an inventory
position must reach
before a fixed quantity
Q of the item is ordered.

When the inventory position reaches a predetermined minimum level, called the **reorder point (R)**, a fixed quantity Q of the item is ordered. In a continuous review system, although the order quantity Q is fixed, the time between orders can vary. Hence, Q can be based on the EOQ, a price break quantity (the minimum lot size that qualifies for a quantity discount), a container size (such as a truckload), or some other quantity selected by management.

SELECTING THE REORDER POINT WHEN DEMAND IS CERTAIN. To demonstrate the concept of a reorder point, suppose that the demand for feeders at the museum gift shop in Example 5.1 is always 18 per week, the lead time is a constant two weeks, and the supplier always ships on time the exact amount ordered. With both demand and lead time certain, the museum's buyer can wait until the inventory position drops to 36 units, or (18 units/week) × (2 weeks), to place a new order. Thus, in this case, the reorder point, R, equals the *demand during lead time*, with no added allowance for safety stock.

Figure 5.5 shows how the system operates when demand and lead time are constant. The downward-sloping line represents the on-hand inventory, which is being depleted at a constant rate. When it reaches reorder point R (the horizontal line), a new order for Q units is placed. The on-hand inventory continues to drop throughout lead time L until the order is received. At that time, which marks the end of the lead time, on-hand inventory jumps by Q units. A new order arrives just when inventory drops to 0. The time between orders (TBO) is the same for each cycle.

The inventory position, IP, shown in Figure 5.5 corresponds to the on-hand inventory, except during the lead time. Just after a new order is placed, at the start of the lead time, IP increases by Q, as shown by the dashed line. The IP exceeds OH by this same margin throughout the lead time.* At the end of the lead time, when the scheduled

FIGURE 5.5 *Continuous Review System (Q) When Demand and Lead Time Are Constant and Certain*

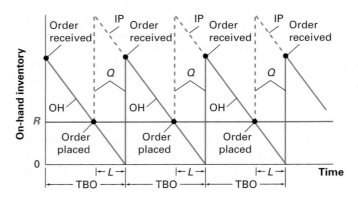

---

*A possible exception is the unlikely situation when more than one scheduled receipt is open at the same time because of long lead times.

receipts convert to on-hand inventory, IP = OH once again. The key point here is to compare IP, not OH, with R in deciding whether to reorder. A common error is to ignore scheduled receipts or backorders.

SELECTING THE REORDER POINT WHEN DEMAND IS UNCERTAIN. In reality, demand and lead times are not always predictable. For instance, the museum's buyer knows that *average* demand is 18 feeders per week and that the *average* lead time is two weeks. That is, a variable number of feeders may be purchased during the lead time, with an average demand during lead time of 36 feeders (assuming that each week's demand is identically distributed). This situation gives rise to the need for safety stocks. Suppose that the buyer sets R at 46 units, thereby placing orders before they typically are needed. This approach will create a safety stock, or stock held in excess of expected demand, of 10 units (46 − 36) to buffer against uncertain demand. In general:

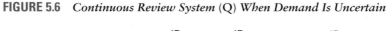

Figure 5.6 shows how the Q system operates when demand is variable and uncertain. We assume that the variability in lead times is negligible and, therefore, can be treated as a constant, as we did in the development of the EOQ model. The wavy downward-sloping line indicates that demand varies from day to day. Its slope is steeper in the second cycle, which means that the demand rate is higher during this time period. The changing demand rate means that the time between orders changes, so $TBO_1 \neq TBO_2 \neq TBO_3$. Because of uncertain demand, sales during lead time are unpredictable, and safety stock is added to hedge against lost sales. This addition is why R is higher in Figure 5.6 than in Figure 5.5. It also explains why the on-hand inventory usually doesn't drop to 0 by the time a replenishment order arrives. The greater the safety stock and, thus, the higher reorder point R, the less likely a stockout.

Because the average demand during lead time is variable and uncertain, the real decision to be made when selecting R concerns the safety stock level. Deciding on a small or large safety stock is a trade-off between customer service and inventory holding costs. Cost minimization models can be used to find the best safety stock, but they require estimates of stockout and backorder costs, which are usually difficult to make with any precision. The usual approach for determining R is for management—based on judgment—to set a reasonable service-level policy for the inventory and then determine the safety stock level that satisfies this policy.

FIGURE 5.6 *Continuous Review System (Q) When Demand Is Uncertain*

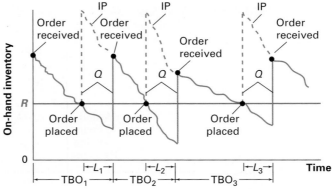

cycle-service level The desired probability of not running out of stock in any one ordering cycle, which begins at the time an order is placed and ends when it arrives in stock.

CHOOSING AN APPROPRIATE SERVICE-LEVEL POLICY. Managers must weigh the benefits of holding safety stock against the cost of holding it when developing a policy for service level. One way to determine the safety stock is to set a **cycle-service level**—the desired probability of not running out of stock in any one *ordering cycle*, which begins at the time an order is placed and ends when it arrives in stock. In a bookstore, the manager may select a 90 percent service level for a book. In other words, the probability is 90 percent that demand will not exceed the supply *during the lead time*. The probability of running short during the lead time, creating a stockout or backorder, is only 10 percent (100 − 90). This stockout risk, which occurs only during the lead time in the Q system, is greater than the overall risk of stockout because the risk is nonexistent outside the ordering cycle.

To translate this policy into a specific safety stock level, we must know how demand during the lead time is distributed. If demand varies little around its average, safety stock can be small. Conversely, if demand during lead time varies greatly from one order cycle to the next, the safety stock must be large. Variability is measured with probability distributions, which are specified by a mean and a variance.

Another measure of customer service is the fraction of total demand met from on-hand inventory. Fill rate can be expressed at several levels, depending on the needs of the customer. If measured for individual items, the **item fill rate** is the quantity of a particular item that is delivered from inventory, relative to the total demand for that item. At a more general level, customers that frequently order multiple items per order might be more interested in *order fill rate*, which captures the number of orders filled completely (no partly filled or backordered items) relative to total orders. This is the most challenging measure and can be appropriate when all items are needed by the customer. For example, a photo finishing shop must have all the right chemicals from a distributor to develop photographs—having most simply won't work.

item fill rate Percentage of demand for an item that is met from on-hand inventory, relative to the total demand for that item.

FINDING THE SAFETY STOCK. When selecting the safety stock, the inventory planner often assumes that demand during lead time is normally distributed, as shown in Figure 5.7. The average demand during the lead time is the centreline of the graph, with 50 percent of the area under the curve to the left and 50 percent to the right. Thus, if a cycle-service level of 50 percent were chosen, reorder point R would be the quantity represented by this centreline. As R equals demand during the lead time plus the safety stock, the safety stock is 0 when R equals this average demand. Demand is less than average 50 percent of the time and, thus, having no safety stock will be sufficient only 50 percent of the time.

FIGURE 5.7   *Finding Safety Stock with a Normal Probability Distribution for an 85 Percent Cycle-Service Level*

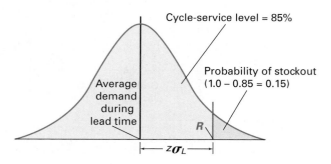

To provide a service level above 50 percent, the reorder point must be greater than average demand during the lead time. In Figure 5.7, that requires moving the reorder point to the right of the centreline so that more than 50 percent of the area under the curve is to the left of R. An 85 percent cycle-service level is achieved in Figure 5.7, with 85 percent of the area under the curve to the left of R and only 15 percent to the right. We compute the safety stock by multiplying the number of standard deviations, z, from the mean needed to implement the cycle-service level, by the standard deviation of demand during lead time probability distribution,[†] σ_L:

$$\text{Safety stock} = z\sigma_L$$

The higher the value of z, the higher the safety stock and the cycle-service level should be. If $z = 0$, there is no safety stock, and stockouts will occur during 50 percent of the order cycles.

| EXAMPLE 5.3 | *Finding the Safety Stock and* R |

Records show that the demand for dishwasher detergent during the lead time is normally distributed, with an average of 250 boxes and $\sigma_L = 22$. What safety stock should be carried for a 99 percent cycle-service level? What is R?

SOLUTION
The first step is to find z, the number of standard deviations to the right of average demand during the lead time that places 99 percent of the area under the curve to the left of that point. One option is to use a "Normal Distribution" table, which we have made available online in MyOMLab, or alternatively, a spreadsheet function in Excel, that is, "NORM.S.INV(0.99)." Thus, the correct z-value is 2.33. With this information, you can calculate the safety stock and reorder point:

$$\text{Safety stock} = z\sigma_L = 2.33(22) = 51.3, \quad \text{or} \quad 51 \text{ boxes}$$

$$\text{Reorder point} = \text{Average demand during lead time} + \text{Safety stock}$$
$$= 250 + 51 = 301 \text{ boxes}$$

We rounded the safety stock to the nearest whole number. In this case, the theoretical cycle-service level will be less than 99 percent. Raising the safety stock to 52 boxes will yield a cycle-service level greater than 99 percent.

Decision Point Management can control the quantity of safety stock by choosing a service level. Another approach to reducing safety stock is to reduce the standard deviation of demand during the lead time, which can be accomplished by closer coordination with major customers through information technology.

Finding the appropriate reorder point and safety stock in practice requires estimating the demand distribution for the lead time. Sometimes average demand during the lead time and the standard deviation of demand during the lead time, σ_L, are not directly available and must be calculated by combining information on the demand

---

[†]Some inventory planners using manual systems prefer to work with the mean absolute deviation (MAD) rather than the standard deviation, because it is easier to calculate. (MAD is discussed in Chapter 10, "Managing Demand and Forecasting.") To approximate the standard deviation you simply multiply the MAD by 1.25. Then proceed to calculate the safety stock.

rate with information on the lead time. There are two reasons for this additional calculation:

1. Developing estimates first for demand and then for the lead time may be easier. Demand information comes from the customer, whereas lead times come from the supplier.

2. Records are not likely to be collected for a time interval that is exactly the same as the lead time. The same inventory control system may be used to manage thousands of different items, each with a different lead time. For example, if demand is reported *weekly*, records can be used directly to compute the average and the standard deviation of demand during the lead time if the lead time is exactly one week. However, the average and standard deviation of demand during the lead time for a lead time of three weeks are more difficult to determine.

We can get at the more difficult case by making some reasonable assumptions (e.g., probability distributions of demand for each time interval are identical and independent of each other). In general, the standard deviation of several periods is equal to the square root of the sum of the variances of those periods. If the time periods are of identical length, t, and total lead time for an order is L:

$$\sigma_L = \sqrt{\sigma_t^2 L} = \sigma_t \sqrt{L}$$

Figure 5.8 shows how the demand distribution for the lead time is developed from the individual distributions of weekly demands ($t = 1$ week), where $d = 75$, $\sigma_t = 15$, and $L = 3$ weeks. In this case, average demand during the lead time is $(75)(3) = 225$ units and $\sigma_L = 15\sqrt{3} = 25.98$, or 26. More complex formulas or simulation must be used when both demand and the lead time are variable or when the supply is uncertain. However, in such cases the safety stock must be larger than otherwise.

FIGURE 5.8   *Development of Demand Distribution for the Lead Time*

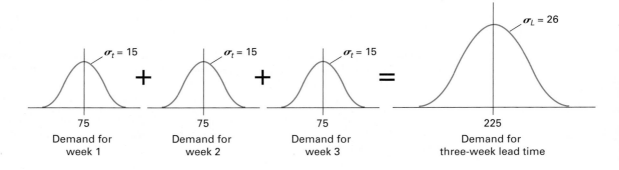

$\sigma_t = 15$	$\sigma_t = 15$	$\sigma_t = 15$	$\sigma_L = 26$
75	75	75	225
Demand for week 1	Demand for week 2	Demand for week 3	Demand for three-week lead time

CALCULATING TOTAL *Q* SYSTEM COSTS. Total costs for the continuous review (Q) system is the sum of three cost components:

Total Q system cost = Annual cycle inventory holding cost + Annual ordering cost + Annual safety stock holding cost

$$C = \frac{Q}{2}(H) + \frac{D}{Q}(S) + Hz\sigma_L$$

The annual cycle inventory holding cost and annual ordering costs are the same equations we used for computing the annual cost for the EOQ. The annual cost of holding the safety stock is computed under the assumption that the safety stock is on hand all the time. Referring to Figure 5.6, in each order cycle, sometimes, we will have experienced a demand greater than the average demand during lead time, and sometimes we will have experienced less. On average over the year, we can assume the safety stock will be on hand.

| EXAMPLE 5.4 | *Finding the Safety Stock and R When the Demand Distribution for the Lead Time Must Be Developed* |

SOLUTION

Let's return to the birdfeeder example. Suppose that the average demand is 18 units per week with a standard deviation of 5 units. The lead time is constant at two weeks. Determine the safety stock and reorder point if management wants a 90 percent cycle-service level. What is the total cost of the Q system?

SOLUTION

In this case, $t = 1$ week, $d = 18$, and $L = 2$, so:

$$\sigma_L = \sigma_t\sqrt{L} = 5\sqrt{2} = 7.1$$

Consult the body of the normal table for 0.9000, which corresponds to a 90 percent cycle-service level. The closest number is 0.8997, which corresponds to a z value of 1.28. (Alternatively, use the spreadsheet function in Excel, that is, "NORM.S.INV(0.90).") With this information, we calculate the safety stock and reorder point as follows:

$$\text{Safety stock} = z\sigma_L = 1.28(7.1) = 9.1, \quad \text{or} \quad 9 \text{ units}$$
$$\text{Reorder point} = dL + \text{Safety stock}$$
$$= 18(2) + 9 = 45 \text{ units}$$

Hence, the Q system for the birdfeeder operates as follows: Whenever the inventory position reaches 45 units, order 75 units. The total Q system cost for the birdfeeder is:

$$C = \frac{75}{2}(\$15) + \frac{936}{75}(\$45) + 9(\$15) = \$562.50 + \$561.60 + \$135 = \$1259.10$$

Decision Point Various order quantities and safety stock levels can be used in the Q system. For example, management could specify a different order quantity (because of shipping constraints) or a different safety stock (because of storage limitations). The total costs of such systems can be calculated, and the trade-off between costs and service levels could be assessed.

visual system A system that allows employees to place orders when inventory visibly reaches a certain marker.

TWO-BIN SYSTEM. The concept of a Q system can be incorporated in a **visual system**, that is, a system that allows employees to place orders when inventory visibly reaches a certain marker. Visual systems are easy to administer, because records are not kept on the current inventory position. The historical usage rate can simply be reconstructed from past purchase orders. Visual systems are intended for use with low-value items that have a steady demand, such as nuts and bolts or office supplies. Overstocking is common, but the extra inventory holding cost is minimal because the items have relatively little value.

two-bin system A visual system version of the Q system, in which an item's inventory is stored at two different locations.

A visual system version of the Q system is the **two-bin system**, in which an item's inventory is stored at two different locations. Inventory is first withdrawn from one bin. If the first bin is empty, the second bin provides backup to cover demand until a replenishment order arrives. An empty first bin signals the need to place a new order. Filled-in order forms placed near the bins let workers send one to purchasing or even directly to the supplier. When the new order arrives, the second bin is restored to its normal level and the rest is put in the first bin. The two-bin system operates like a Q system, with the normal level in the second bin being the reorder point R. The system also may be implemented with just one bin by marking the bin at the reorder point level.

periodic review (P) system A system in which an item's inventory position is reviewed periodically rather than continuously.

PERIODIC REVIEW (P) SYSTEM

An alternative inventory control system is the **periodic review (P) system**, sometimes called a *fixed interval reorder system* or *periodic reorder system*, in which an item's inventory position is reviewed periodically rather than continuously. Such a system can simplify delivery scheduling because it establishes a routine, although the quantity ordered each time varies. A new order is always placed at the end of each review, and the time between orders (TBO) is fixed at P. Demand is a random variable, so total demand between reviews varies. In a P system, the lot size, Q, may change from one order to the next, but the time between orders is fixed. An example of a periodic review system is that of a soft-drink supplier making weekly rounds of grocery stores. Each week the supplier reviews the store's inventory of soft drinks and restocks the store with enough items to meet demand and safety stock requirements until the next week.

Four of the original EOQ assumptions are maintained: (1) no constraints on the size of the lot; (2) only holding and ordering costs are relevant; (3) decisions for one item are independent of decisions for other items; and (4) no uncertainty in lead times or supply quantities. However, demand uncertainty is again allowed for. Figure 5.9 shows the periodic review system under these assumptions. The downward-sloping line again represents on-hand inventory. When the predetermined time, P, has elapsed since the last review, an order is placed to bring the inventory position, represented by the dashed line, up to the target inventory level, T. The lot size for the first review is Q_1, or the difference between inventory position IP_1 and T. As with the continuous review system, IP and OH differ only during the lead time. When the order arrives, at the end of the lead time, OH and IP again are identical. Figure 5.9 shows that lot sizes vary from one order cycle to the next. Because the inventory position is lower at the second review, a greater quantity is needed to achieve an inventory level of T.

FIGURE 5.9 *Periodic Review System* (P) *When Demand Is Uncertain*

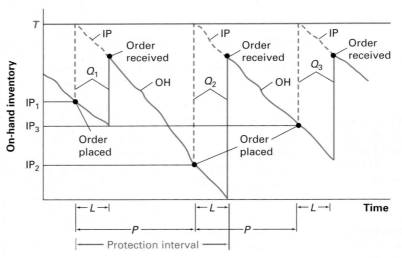

SELECTING THE TIME BETWEEN REVIEWS. To run a P system, managers must make two decisions: the length of time between reviews, P, and the target inventory level, T. Let us first consider the time between reviews, P. It can be any convenient interval, such as each Friday or every other Friday. Another option is to base P on the cost trade-offs of the EOQ. In other words, P can be set equal to the average time between orders for the economic order quantity, or TBO_{EOQ}. Because demand is variable, some orders will be larger than the EOQ and some will be smaller. However, over an extended period of time, the average lot size should equal the

MANAGERIAL PRACTICE
Inventory Systems at Celanese

What do products such as paints, adhesives, coatings, plastics, medicines, cosmetics, detergents, textiles, and fragrances have in common? All these products use acetic acid as a major component. Celanese, a $5.9 billion chemical company with $610 million in total inventories, is a major supplier of acetic acid from nine production plants scattered around the globe. The large investment in inventory forces Celanese to take a hard look at inventory policies for all products, including acetic acid. The key to successful management of these inventories was to acknowledge the interaction between the inventory policies at each stage of the supply chain with the realities of material flows and logistics in the chemical industry.

The supply chain for acetic acid is complex, comprising 90 stages, including vendors supplying a liner to transport the acid, manufacturing sites producing the acid, transportation of acid, warehouses providing storage, and customer demand locations to which the acid is finally shipped. Each plant can supply multiple storage locations worldwide. Transportation can occur using different modes, including rail, barges, trucks, and ocean vessels. Material typically moves in large quantities because of economies of scale and transportation schedules.

The use of periodic review inventory systems at the storage and demand locations in this supply chain makes sense for several reasons. First, each transportation mode has defined schedules of operation. Review periods at storage facilities reflect the schedule of the supplying transportation mode. Second, customer orders are typically batched and timed with weekly, biweekly, or monthly frequencies. Celanese often assigns customers and storage facilities specific days to place orders so that their own production schedules can be coordinated. Finally, the cyclic ordering is often a function of the capital intensity of the industry. Long production runs are scheduled to gain production efficiency; it is costly to set up the equipment for another product.

Specifying the best review period and target inventory levels for the various stages of the supply chain takes sophisticated

Large manufacturers of chemicals often assign schedules to customers and storage facilities for ordering and picking up chemicals. Such a practice facilitates the coordination of the manufacturer's production schedules. Here a tank truck is loaded at its assigned time.

mathematical models. Regardless of the effort required, it is important to recognize the implications of the supply chain when determining inventory policies.[2]

EOQ. If other models are used to determine the lot size (e.g., those described in Supplement H, "Special Inventory Models"), we divide the lot size chosen by the annual demand, D, and use this ratio as P. It will be expressed as the fraction of a year between orders, which can be converted into months, weeks, or days as needed.

SELECTING THE TARGET INVENTORY LEVEL. Now let us consider how to calculate the target inventory level, T. Figure 5.9 reveals that an order must be large enough to make the inventory position, IP, last beyond the next review, which is P time periods away. At that time a new order is placed, but it does not arrive until after the lead time, L. Therefore, as Figure 5.9 shows, a **protection interval** of $P + L$ periods is needed, or the time interval for which inventory must be planned when each new order is placed. A fundamental difference between the Q and P systems is the length of time needed for stockout protection. A Q system needs stockout protection only during the lead time because orders can be placed as soon as they are needed and will be received L periods later. A P system, however, needs stockout protection for the longer $P + L$ protection interval because orders are placed only at fixed intervals and the inventory isn't checked until the next designated review time.

> **protection interval** The time interval for which inventory must be planned when each new order is placed.

As with the Q system, we need to develop the appropriate distribution of demand during the protection interval to specify the system fully. In a P system, we must develop the distribution of demand for $P + L$ time periods. The target inventory level T must equal the expected demand during the protection interval of $P + L$ periods, plus enough safety stock to protect against demand uncertainty over this same protection interval. We use the same statistical assumptions that we made for the Q system. Thus, the average demand during the protection interval is $d(P + L)$, or:

$$T = d(P + L) + \text{Safety stock for protection interval}$$

We compute safety stock for a P system much as we did for the Q system. However, the safety stock must cover demand uncertainty for a longer period of time. When using a normal probability distribution, we multiply the desired standard deviations to implement the cycle-service level, z, by the standard deviation of demand during the protection interval, σ_{P+L}. Thus:

$$\text{Safety stock} = z\sigma_{P+L}$$

Based on our earlier logic for calculating σ_L, we know that the standard deviation of the distribution of demand during the protection interval is:

$$\sigma_{P+L} = \sigma_t \sqrt{P + L}$$

Because a P system requires safety stock to cover demand uncertainty over a longer time period than a Q system, a P system requires more safety stock; that is, σ_{P+L} exceeds σ_L. Hence, to gain the convenience of a P system requires that overall inventory levels be somewhat higher than those for a Q system.

CALCULATING TOTAL P SYSTEM COSTS. The total costs for the P system are the sum of the same three cost elements as for the Q system. The differences are in the calculation of the order quantity and the safety stock. Referring to Figure 5.9, the average order quantity will be the average consumption of inventory during the P periods between orders. Consequently, $Q = dP$. Total costs for the P system are:

$$C = \frac{dP}{2}(H) + \frac{D}{dP}(S) + Hz\sigma_{P+L}$$

| EXAMPLE 5.5 | *Calculating* P *and* T |

Again let us return to the birdfeeder example. Recall that demand for the birdfeeder is normally distributed with a mean of 18 units per week and a standard deviation in weekly demand of 5 units. The lead time is 2 weeks, and the business operates 52 weeks per year. The Q system developed in Example 5.4 called for an EOQ of 75 units and a safety stock of 9 units for a cycle-service level of 90 percent. What is the equivalent P system? What is the total cost? Answers are to be rounded to the nearest integer.

SOLUTION

We first define D and then P. Here P is the time between reviews, expressed as a multiple (or fraction) of time interval t ($t = 1$ week, because the data are expressed as demand *per week*):

$$D = (18 \text{ units/week})(52 \text{ weeks/year}) = 936 \text{ units}$$

$$P = \frac{\text{EOQ}}{D}(52) = \frac{75}{936}(52) = 4.2, \quad \text{or} \quad 4 \text{ weeks}$$

With $d = 18$ units per week, we can also calculate P by dividing the EOQ by d to get $75/18 = 4.2$, or 4 weeks. Hence, we would review the birdfeeder inventory every 4 weeks. We now find the standard deviation of demand over the protection interval ($P + L = 6$):

$$\sigma_{P+L} = \sigma_t\sqrt{P + L} = 5\sqrt{6} = 12 \text{ units}$$

Before calculating T, we also need a z value. For a 90 percent cycle-service level, $z = 1.28$ (see online Appendix, "Normal Distribution," or use the Excel function "NORM.S.INV(0.90)"). We now solve for T:

$$T = \text{Average demand during the protection interval} + \text{Safety stock}$$
$$= d(P + L) + z\sigma_{P+L}$$
$$= (18 \text{ units/week})(6 \text{ weeks}) + 1.28(12 \text{ units}) = 123 \text{ units}$$

Every 4 weeks we would order the number of units needed to bring inventory position IP (counting the new order) up to the target inventory level of 123 units. The safety stock for this P system is $1.28(12) = 15$ units.

The total P system cost for the birdfeeder is:

$$C = \frac{4(18)}{2}(\$15) + \frac{936}{4(18)}(\$45) + 15(\$15) = \$540 + \$585 + \$225 = \$1350$$

Decision Point The P system requires 15 units in safety stock, while the Q system only needs 9 units. If cost were the only criterion, the Q system would be the choice for the birdfeeder. As we discuss in the next section, other factors may sway the decision in favour of the P system.

---

single-bin system
A system of inventory control in which a maximum level is marked on the storage shelf or bin on a measuring rod, and the inventory is brought up to the mark periodically.

SINGLE-BIN SYSTEM. The concept of a P system can be translated into a simple visual system of inventory control. In the **single-bin system**, a maximum level is marked on the storage shelf or bin on a measuring rod, and the inventory is brought up to the mark periodically—say, once a week. The single bin may be, for example, a gasoline storage tank at a service station or a storage bin for small parts at a manufacturing plant.

COMPARATIVE ADVANTAGES OF THE *Q* **AND** *P* **SYSTEMS**

Neither the Q nor the P system is best for all situations. Three P-system advantages must be balanced against three Q-system advantages. The advantages of one system are implicitly disadvantages of the other one. The primary advantages of P systems are the following:

1. Administration of the system is convenient, because replenishments are made at fixed intervals. Employees can regularly set aside a day or part of a day to concentrate on this particular task. Fixed replenishment intervals also allow for standardized pickup and delivery times.

2. Orders for multiple items from the same supplier may be combined into a single purchase order. This approach reduces ordering and transportation costs and may result in a price break from the supplier.

3. The inventory position, IP, needs to be known only when a review is made (not continuously, as in a Q system). However, this advantage is moot for firms using computerized record-keeping systems, in which a transaction is reported upon each receipt or withdrawal. When inventory records are always current, the system is called a **perpetual inventory system**.

The primary advantages of Q systems are the following:

1. The review frequency of each item may be individualized. Tailoring the review frequency to the item can reduce total ordering and holding costs.

2. Fixed lot sizes, if large enough, may result in quantity discounts. Physical limitations such as truckload capacities, materials handling methods, and furnace capacities also may require a fixed lot size.

3. Lower safety stocks result in savings.

In conclusion, the choice between Q and P systems is not clear-cut. Which one is better depends on the relative importance of its advantages in various situations. Management must weigh each alternative carefully in selecting the best system.

HYBRID SYSTEMS

Various hybrid inventory control systems merge some but not all the features of the P and Q systems. We briefly examine two such systems: optional replenishment and base stock.

OPTIONAL REPLENISHMENT SYSTEM. Sometimes called the optional review, min-max, or (s, S) system, the **optional replenishment system** is much like the P system. It is used to review the inventory position at fixed time intervals and, if the position has dropped to (or below) a predetermined level, to place a variable-sized order to cover expected needs. The new order is large enough to bring the inventory position up to a target inventory, similar to T for the P system. However, orders are not placed after a review unless the inventory position has dropped to the predetermined minimum level. The minimum level acts as reorder point R does in a Q system. If the target is 100 and the minimum level is 60, the minimum order size is 40 (or 100 – 60). The optional review system avoids continuous reviews and so is particularly attractive when both review and ordering costs are significant.

BASE-STOCK SYSTEM. In its simplest form, the **base-stock system** issues a replenishment order, Q, every time a withdrawal is made, for the same amount as the withdrawal. This one-for-one replacement policy maintains the inventory position at a base-stock level equal to expected demand during the lead time plus safety stock. The base-stock level, therefore, is equivalent to the reorder point in a Q system. However, order quantities now vary to keep the inventory position at R at all times. Because this position is

perpetual inventory system A system of inventory control in which the inventory records are always current.

optional replenishment system A system used to review the inventory position at fixed time intervals and, if the position has dropped to (or below) a predetermined level, to place a variable-sized order to cover expected needs.

base-stock system An inventory control system that issues a replenishment order, Q, each time a withdrawal is made, for the same amount as the withdrawal.

the lowest IP possible that will maintain a specified service level, the base-stock system may be used to minimize cycle inventory. More orders are placed but each is smaller. This system is appropriate for very expensive items, such as replacement engines for jet airplanes. No more inventory is held than the maximum demand expected until a replacement order can be received. The base-stock system is used in just-in-time systems (see Chapter 7, "Lean Systems").

INVENTORY RECORD ACCURACY

Regardless of the inventory system in use, record accuracy is crucial to its success. One method of achieving and maintaining accuracy is to assign responsibility to specific employees for issuing and receiving materials and accurately reporting each transaction. A second method is to secure inventory behind locked doors or gates to prevent unauthorized or unreported withdrawals. This method also guards against storing new receipts in the wrong locations, where they can be lost for months. **Cycle counting** is a third method, whereby storeroom personnel physically count a small percentage of the total number of items every day, correcting errors that they find. Class A items are counted most frequently. A final method for computerized systems is to make logic error checks on each transaction reported and fully investigate any discrepancies. Discrepancies may include (1) actual receipts when there is no record of scheduled receipts, (2) disbursements that exceed the current on-hand balance, and (3) receipts with an inaccurate (nonexistent) part number.

These methods can keep inventory record accuracy within acceptable bounds. Accuracy pays off mainly through better customer service, although some inventory reductions can be achieved by improving accuracy. A side benefit is that auditors may not require end-of-year counts if records prove to be sufficiently accurate.

cycle counting An inventory control method whereby storeroom personnel physically count a small percentage of the total number of items each day, correcting errors that they find.

CAREFUL INVENTORY MANAGEMENT IMPROVES SUSTAINABILITY

Because inventory management is one component of supply chain management, much of what was described in Chapter 2, "Supply Chain Management," applies to managing inventories in a more sustainable manner. Inventory often inadvertently leads to waste, whether from the energy it takes to light cavernous warehouses, from repeated movement of stored materials, or from shrinkage of stock. Efforts to reduce these types of waste have prompted the development of multi-pronged management efforts to create less wasteful processes, broadly termed *leaner systems,* explored in greater detail in Chapter 7.

For example, let's focus on just two ways that poorly managed inventory creates environmental waste. First, many raw materials and finished goods have "best before" dates, after which the quality performance of the product declines. Pharmaceutical products, paints and finishes, and fresh food are but a few examples. Inventory tracking and rotation is a simple, but effective, means of minimizing waste and improving efficiency. RONA, one of Canada's largest retailers of hardware, gardening, and home renovation products, credits better stock rotation and lower inventory for its improving performance.[3]

Second, obsolescent inventory must often be discounted or scrapped, as when electronic products change or fashions evolve. Clearly, this hurts economic performance, but it also creates additional environmental problems because this waste has to be stored and disposed of. Jones Apparel, including such brands as Nine West footwear, Anne Klein, and Jones New York, is increasingly using its broad store network in combination with large centralized warehouses.[4] New inventory management software has helped managers increase efficiency by using online orders to keep excess inventory from building up in stores. Sales clerks can print out shipping labels and invoices for online orders routed to stores, and then pack the merchandise for same-day pickup. These changes have allowed the firm to directly ship between 30 and 50 percent of orders, depending on the brand, from the company's stores. Energy is potentially saved with shorter shipments, customer service is improved, and less inventory is likely to become obsolete. Smarter inventory management really can improve operational competitiveness.

EQUATION SUMMARY

1. Cycle inventory $= \dfrac{Q}{2}$

2. Pipeline inventory $= dL$

3. Total cost = Holding cost + Ordering or setup cost   (*Note:* All costs calculated for an identical time period, e.g., one year)

   $$C = \frac{Q}{2}(H) + \frac{D}{Q}(S)$$

4. Economic order quantity: $EOQ = \sqrt{\dfrac{2DS}{H}}$

5. Time between orders for EOQ: $TBO_{EOQ} = \dfrac{EOQ}{D}$ (*Note:* Where TBO and D represent the same time period, e.g., weeks)

6. Inventory position = On-hand inventory + Scheduled receipts − Backorders

   $$IP = OH + SR - BO$$

7. Continuous review system:

   Reorder point (R) = Average demand during lead time + Safety stock
   $$= dL + z\sigma_L$$

   Protection interval = Lead time (L)

   Standard deviation of demand during the lead time $= \sigma_L = \sigma_t\sqrt{L}$

   Order quantity = EOQ

   Replenishment rule: Order EOQ units when: $IP \leq R$

   Total Q system cost: $C = \dfrac{Q}{2}(H) + \dfrac{D}{Q}(S) + Hz\sigma_L$

8. Periodic review system:

   Target inventory level (T) = Average demand during the protection interval + Safety stock
   $$= d(P + L) + z\sigma_{P+L}$$

   Protection interval = Time between orders + Lead time $= P + L$

   Review interval = Time between orders $= P$

   Standard deviation of demand during the protection interval $= \sigma_{P+L} = \sigma_t\sqrt{P + L}$

   Order quantity = Target inventory level − Inventory position $= T - IP$

   Replenishment rule: Every P time periods order $T - IP$ units

   Total P system cost: $C = \dfrac{dP}{2}(H) + \dfrac{D}{dP}(S) + Hz\sigma_{P+L}$

CHAPTER HIGHLIGHTS

- Inventory decisions involve trade-offs among the conflicting objectives of low investment, good customer service, and high resource utilization. Benefits of good customer service and high resource utilization may be outweighed by the cost of carrying large inventories, including interest or opportunity costs, storage and handling costs, insurance, shrinkage, and obsolescence. Order quantity decisions are guided by a trade-off between the cost of holding inventories and the combined costs of ordering, setup, transportation, and purchased materials.

- Safety stock, decoupling, anticipation, cycle, and pipeline inventories vary in size with random and predictable variability, production rate flexibility, order quantity, and lead time, respectively.

- Inventory placement at the plant level depends on process configuration and product characteristics. These include the degree to which a process is producing standard or customized items and the trade-off between short customer response time and low inventory costs.

- ABC analysis helps managers focus on the few significant items that account for the bulk of investment in inventory. Class A items deserve the most attention, with less attention justified for class B and class C items.

- Independent demand inventory management methods are appropriate for wholesale and retail merchandise; service industry supplies; finished goods and service parts replenishment; and maintenance, repair, and operating supplies.

- A basic inventory management question is whether to order large quantities infrequently or to order small quantities frequently. The EOQ provides guidance for this choice by indicating the lot size that minimizes (subject to several assumptions) the sum of holding and ordering costs over some period of time, such as a year.

- In the continuous review (Q) system, the buyer places orders of a fixed lot size Q when the inventory position drops to the reorder point. In the periodic review (P) system, every P fixed time interval the buyer places an order to replenish the quantity consumed since the last order. Visual systems, such as single-bin and two-bin systems, are adaptations of the P and Q systems that eliminate the need for records.

- The base-stock system minimizes cycle inventory by maintaining the inventory position at the base-stock level.

SOLVED PROBLEM 1

A distribution centre (DC) experiences an average weekly demand of 50 units for one of its items. The product is valued at $650 per unit. Average inbound shipments from the factory warehouse are 350 units. Average lead time (including ordering delays and transit time) is 2 weeks. The DC operates 52 weeks per year, it carries a 1-week supply of inventory as safety stock, and it has no anticipation inventory. What is the average aggregate inventory being held by the DC?

SOLUTION

TYPE OF INVENTORY	CALCULATION OF AVERAGE INVENTORY QUANTITY	
Cycle	$\frac{Q}{2} = \frac{350}{2} =$	175 units
Safety stock	1-week supply =	50 units
Anticipation	None	
Pipeline	dL = (50 units/week)(2 weeks) =	100 units
	Total average aggregate inventory =	325 units

SOLVED PROBLEM 2

Booker's Book Bindery divides inventory items into three classes according to their dollar usage. Calculate the usage values of the following inventory items and determine which is most likely to be classified as an A item.

PART NUMBER	DESCRIPTION	QUANTITY USED PER YEAR	UNIT VALUE ($)
1	Boxes	500	3.00
2	Cardboard (square metres)	18 000	0.02
3	Cover stock	10 000	0.75
4	Glue (litres)	75	40.00
5	Inside covers	20 000	0.05
6	Reinforcing tape (metres)	3 000	0.15
7	Signatures	150 000	0.45

SOLUTION

PART NUMBER	DESCRIPTION	QUANTITY USED PER YEAR		UNIT VALUE ($)		ANNUAL DOLLAR USAGE ($)
1	Boxes	500	×	3.00	=	1 500
2	Cardboard (square metres)	18 000	×	0.02	=	360
3	Cover stock	10 000	×	0.75	=	7 500
4	Glue (litres)	75	×	40.00	=	3 000
5	Inside covers	20 000	×	0.05	=	1 000
6	Reinforcing tape (metres)	3 000	×	0.15	=	450
7	Signatures	150 000	×	0.45	=	67 500
					Total	81 310

The annual dollar usage for each item is determined by multiplying the annual usage quantity by the value per unit as shown in Figure 5.10. The items are sorted by annual dollar usage, in declining order. Finally,

FIGURE 5.10 *ABC Analysis for Solved Problem 2*

Part#	Description	Qty Used/Year	Value	Dollar Usage	Pct of Total	Cumulative % of Dollar Value	Cumulative % of Items	Class
7	Signatures	150 000	$0.45	$67 500	83.0%	83.0%	14.3%	A
3	Cover stock	10 000	$0.75	$7 500	9.2%	92.2%	28.6%	B
4	Glue	75	$40.00	$3 000	3.7%	95.9%	42.9%	B
1	Boxes	500	$3.00	$1 500	1.8%	97.8%	57.1%	C
5	Inside covers	20 000	$0.05	$1 000	1.2%	99.0%	71.4%	C
6	Reinforcing tape	3 000	$0.15	$450	0.6%	99.6%	85.7%	C
2	Cardboard	18 000	$0.02	$360	0.4%	100.0%	100.0%	C
Total				$81 310				

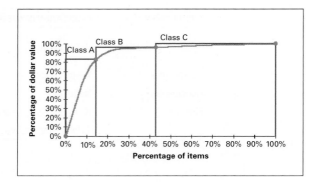

A–B and B–C class lines are drawn roughly according to the guidelines presented in the text. Here, class A includes only one item (signatures), which represents only 1/7, or 14 percent, of the items but accounts for 83 percent of annual dollar usage. Class B includes the next two items, which taken together represent 28 percent of the items and account for 13 percent of annual dollar usage. The final four, class C, items represent more than half the number of items but only 4 percent of total annual dollar usage.

SOLVED PROBLEM 3

In Example 5.2, the economic order quantity, EOQ, is 75 units when annual demand, D, is 936 units/year, setup cost, S, is $45, and holding cost, H, is $15/unit/year. Suppose that we mistakenly estimate inventory holding cost to be $30/unit/year.

   a. What is the new order quantity, Q, if $D = 936$ units/year, $S = \$45$, and $H = \$30$/unit/year?

   b. What is the change in order quantity, expressed as a percentage of the economic order quantity (75 units)?

SOLUTION

   a. The new order quantity is:

$$EOQ = \sqrt{\frac{2DS}{H}} = \sqrt{\frac{2(936)(\$45)}{\$30}} = \sqrt{2808} = 52.99, \quad \text{or} \quad 53 \text{ units}$$

   b. The percentage change is:

$$\left(\frac{53 - 75}{75}\right)(100) = -29.33\%$$

The new order quantity (53) is about 29 percent smaller than the correct order quantity (75).

SOLVED PROBLEM 4

In Example 5.2, the total cost, C, is $1124/year.

   a. What is the annual total cost when $D = 936$ units/year, $S = \$45$, $H = \$15$/unit/year, and Q is the result from Solved Problem 3(a)?

   b. What is the percentage change in total cost?

SOLUTION

   a. With 53 as the order quantity, the annual cost is:

$$C = \frac{Q}{2}(H) + \frac{D}{Q}(S) = \frac{53}{2}(\$15) + \frac{936}{53}(\$45) = \$397.50 + \$794.72$$

$$= \$1192.22$$

   b. The percentage change is:

$$\left(\frac{\$1192 - \$1124}{\$1124}\right)(100) = 6.05\%$$

A 100 percent error in estimating the holding cost caused the order quantity to be 29 percent too small, and that in turn increased annual costs by about 6 percent.

SOLVED PROBLEM 5

A regional warehouse purchases hand tools from various suppliers and then distributes them on demand to retailers in the region. The warehouse operates five days per week, 52 weeks per year. Only when it is open can orders be received. The following data are estimated for 10 millimetre hand drills with double insulation and variable speeds:

Average daily demand = 100 drills
Standard deviation of daily demand (σ_t) = 30 drills
Lead time (L) = 3 days
Holding cost (H) = \$9.40/unit/year
Ordering cost (S) = \$35/order
Cycle-service level = 92%

The warehouse uses a continuous review (Q) system.

a. What order quantity, Q, and reorder point, R, should be used?

b. If on-hand inventory is 40 units, there is one open order for 440 drills, and there are no backorders, should a new order be placed?

SOLUTION

a. Annual demand is:

$$D = (5 \text{ days/week})(52 \text{ weeks/year})(100 \text{ drills/day}) = 26\,000 \text{ drills/year}$$

The order quantity is:

$$\text{EOQ} = \sqrt{\frac{2DS}{H}} = \sqrt{\frac{2(26\,000)(\$35)}{\$9.40}} = \sqrt{193\,167} = 440.02, \quad \text{or} \quad 440 \text{ drills}$$

and the standard deviation is:

$$\sigma_L = \sigma_t\sqrt{L} = (30 \text{ drills}) \sqrt{3} = 51.96, \quad \text{or} \quad 52 \text{ drills}$$

A 92 percent cycle-service level corresponds to $z = 1.41$ (see MyOMLab "Normal Distribution" or use the Excel function "NORM.S.INV(0.92)"). Therefore:

Safety stock = $z\sigma_L$ = 1.41(52 drills) = 73.38,   or   73 drills

Average demand during the lead time = 100(3) = 300 drills

Reorder point = Average demand during the lead time + Safety stock
= 300 drills + 73 drills = 373 drills

With a continuous review system, $Q = 440$ and $R = 373$.

b. Inventory position = On-hand inventory + Scheduled receipts − Backorders:

$$\text{IP} = \text{OH} + \text{SR} - \text{BO} = 40 + 440 - 0 = 480 \text{ drills}$$

IP (480) exceeds R (373); do not place a new order.

SOLVED PROBLEM 6

Suppose that a periodic review (P) system is used at the warehouse, but otherwise the data are the same as in Solved Problem 5.

a. Calculate the P (in workdays, rounded to the nearest day) that gives approximately the same number of orders per year as the EOQ.

b. What is the value of the target inventory level, T? Compare the P system to the Q system in Solved Problem 5.

c. It is time to review the item. On-hand inventory is 40 drills; there is a scheduled receipt of 440 drills and no backorders. How much should be reordered?

SOLUTION

a. The time between orders is:

$$P = \frac{EOQ}{D}(260 \text{ days/years}) = \frac{440}{26\,000}(260) = 4.4, \quad \text{or} \quad 4 \text{ days}$$

b. Before calculating T, we must estimate the standard deviation of demand over the protection interval:

$$\sigma_{P+L} = \sigma_t\sqrt{P + L} = 30\sqrt{4 + 3} = 79.4 \text{ drills}$$

As with Solved Problem 5, for a cycle-service level of 92%, $z = 1.41$.

T = Average demand during the protection interval + Safety stock

$\quad = d(P + L) + z\sigma_{P+L}$

$\quad = 100(4 + 3) + 1.41 \times 79.4$

$\quad = 812 \text{ drills}$

c. Inventory position is the amount on hand plus scheduled receipts minus backorders, or:

$$IP = OH + SR - BO = 40 + 440 - 0 = 480 \text{ drills}$$

The order quantity is the target inventory level minus the inventory position, or:

$$Q = T - IP = 812 \text{ drills} - 480 \text{ drills} = 332 \text{ drills}$$

In a periodic review system, the order quantity for this review period is 332 drills.

PROBLEMS

1. A part is produced in lots of 1000 units. It is assembled from two components worth $50 total. The value added in production (for labour and variable overhead) is $60 per unit, bringing total costs per completed unit to $110. The average lead time for the part is 6 weeks and annual demand is 3800 units. There are 50 business weeks per year.

   a. How many units of the part are held, on average, in cycle inventory? What is the dollar value of this inventory?

   b. How many units of the part are held, on average, in pipeline inventory? What is the dollar value of this inventory? *Hint:* Assume that the typical part in pipeline inventory is 50 percent completed. Thus, half the labour and variable overhead costs have been added, bringing the unit cost to $80, or $50 + $60/2.

2. Stock-Rite, Inc., is considering the use of ABC analysis to focus on the most critical SKUs in its inventory. For a random sample of eight SKUs, the following table shows the SKU's unit value and annual demand. Categorize these SKUs as A, B, and C classes.

SKU CODE	UNIT VALUE	DEMAND (UNITS)
A104	$40.25	80
D205	80.75	120
X104	10.00	150
U404	40.50	150
L205	60.70	50
S104	80.20	20
X205	80.15	20
L104	20.05	100

3. Babble, Inc. buys 400 blank DVDs per month for use in producing foreign language courseware. The ordering cost is $12.50. Holding cost is $0.12 per DVD per year.

   a. How many DVDs should Babble order at a time?

   b. What is the time between orders?

4. Leaky Pipe, a local retailer of plumbing supplies, faces demand for one of its SKUs at a constant rate of 30 000 units per year. It costs Leaky Pipe $10 to process an order to replenish stock and $1 per unit per year to carry the item in stock. Stock is received 4 working days after an order is placed. No backordering is allowed. Assume 300 working days per year.

   a. What is Leaky Pipe's optimal order quantity?

   b. What is the optimal number of orders per year?

   c. What is the optimal interval (in working days) between orders?

   d. What is the demand during the lead time?

   e. What is the reorder point?

   f. What is the inventory position immediately after an order has been placed?

5. Sam's Cat Hotel operates 52 weeks per year, 6 days per week, and uses a continuous review inventory system. It purchases kitty litter for $11.70 per bag. The following information is available about these bags:

   > Demand = 90 bags/week
   > Order cost = $54/order
   > Annual holding cost = 27% of cost
   > Desired cycle-service level = 80%
   > Lead time = 3 weeks (18 working days)
   > Standard deviation of weekly demand = 15 bags

   Current on-hand inventory is 320 bags, with no open orders or backorders.

   a. What is the EOQ? What would be the average time between orders (in weeks)?

   b. What should R be?

   c. An inventory withdrawal of 10 bags was just made. Is it time to reorder?

   d. The store currently uses a lot size of 500 bags (i.e., $Q = 500$). What is the annual holding cost of this policy? Annual ordering cost? Without calculating the EOQ, how can you conclude from these two calculations that the current lot size is too large?

   e. What would be the annual cost saved by shifting from the 500-bag lot size to the EOQ?

6. Consider again the kitty litter ordering policy for Sam's Cat Hotel in Problem 5.

   a. Suppose that the weekly demand forecast of 90 bags is incorrect and actual demand averages only 60 bags per week. How much higher will total costs be, owing to the distorted EOQ caused by this forecast error?

   b. Suppose that actual demand is 60 bags but that ordering costs are cut to only $6 by using the Internet to automate order placing. However, the buyer does not tell anyone, and the EOQ isn't adjusted to reflect this reduction in S. How much higher will total costs be, compared to what they could be if the EOQ were adjusted?

7. Fresh Dessert Inc. is using a continuous review system for its ice cream. The demand rate for strawberry ice cream is normally distributed, with an average of 300 litres per week. The lead time is 9 weeks. The standard deviation of weekly demand is 15 litres.

   a. What is the standard deviation of demand during the 9-week lead time?

   b. What is the average demand during the 9-week lead time?

   c. What reorder point results in a cycle-service level of 99 percent?

8. You are in charge of inventory control of a highly successful product retailed by your firm. Weekly demand for this item varies, with an average of 200 units and a standard deviation of 16 units. It is purchased from a wholesaler at a cost of $12.50 per unit. The supply lead time is 4 weeks. Placing an order costs $50, and the inventory carrying rate per year is 20 percent of the item's cost. Your firm operates 5 days per week, 50 weeks per year.

   a. What is the optimal ordering quantity for this item?

   b. How many units of the item should be maintained as safety stock for 99 percent protection against stockouts during an order cycle?

   c. If supply lead time can be reduced to 2 weeks, what is the percent reduction in the number of units maintained as safety stock for the same 99 percent stockout protection?

   d. If, through appropriate sales promotions, the demand variability is reduced so that the standard deviation of weekly demand is 8 units instead of 16, what is the percent reduction (compared to that in part (b)) in the number of units maintained as safety stock for the same 99 percent stockout protection?

9. Your firm uses a continuous review system and operates 52 weeks per year. One of the items handled has the following characteristics:

   > Demand (D) = 20 000 units/year
   > Ordering cost (S) = $40/order
   > Holding cost (H) = $2/unit/year
   > Lead time (L) = 2 weeks
   > Cycle-service level = 95%

Demand is normally distributed, with a standard deviation of *weekly* demand of 100 units. Current on-hand inventory is 1040 units, with no scheduled receipts and no backorders.

   a. Calculate the item's EOQ. What is the average time, in weeks, between orders?

   b. Find the safety stock and reorder point that provide a 95 percent cycle-service level.

   c. For these policies, what are the annual costs of (i) holding the cycle inventory and (ii) placing orders?

   d. A withdrawal of 15 units just occurred. Is it time to reorder? If so, how much should be ordered?

10. In a continuous review inventory system, the lead time for door knobs is five weeks. The standard deviation of demand during the lead time is 85 units. The desired cycle-service level is 99 percent. The supplier of door knobs streamlined its operations and now quotes a one-week lead time. How much can safety stock be reduced without reducing the 99 percent cycle-service level?

11. Nationwide Auto Parts uses a periodic review inventory control system for one of its stock items. The review interval is six weeks, and the lead time for receiving the materials ordered from its wholesaler is three weeks. Weekly demand is normally distributed, with a mean of 100 units and a standard deviation of 20 units.

   a. What is the average and the standard deviation of demand during the protection interval?

   b. What should be the target inventory level if the firm desires 97.5 percent stockout protection?

   c. If 350 units were in stock at the time of a periodic review, how many units should be ordered?

12. A company begins a review of ordering policies for its continuous review system by checking the current policies for a sample of items. Following are the characteristics of one item (assume 52 weeks per year):

> Demand (D) = 64 units/week
> Ordering and setup cost (S) = $50/order
> Holding cost (H) = $13/unit/year
> Lead time (L) = 2 weeks
> Standard deviation of *weekly* demand = 12 units
> Cycle-service level = 88%

   a. What is the EOQ for this item?

   b. What is the desired safety stock?

   c. What is the reorder point?

   d. What are the cost implications if the current policy for this item is Q = 200 and R = 180?

13. Wood County Hospital consumes 1000 boxes of bandages per week. The price of bandages is $35 per box, and the hospital operates 52 weeks per year. The cost of processing an order is $15, and the cost of holding one box for a year is 15 percent of the value of the material.

   a. The hospital orders bandages in lot sizes of 900 boxes. What *extra cost* does the hospital incur, which it could save by using the EOQ method?

   b. Demand is normally distributed, with a standard deviation of weekly demand of 100 boxes. The lead time is 2 weeks. What safety stock is necessary if the hospital uses a continuous review system and a 97 percent cycle-service level is desired? What should be the reorder point?

   c. If the hospital uses a periodic review system, with P = 2 weeks, what should be the target inventory level, T?

14. Osprey Sports stocks everything that a muskie fisherman could want in the Great North Woods. A particular muskie lure has been very popular with local fishermen as well as those who buy lures on the Internet from Osprey Sports. The cost to place orders with the supplier is $30/order; the demand averages 4 lures per day, with a standard deviation of 1 lure; and the inventory holding cost is $1/lure/year. The lead time from the supplier is 10 days, with a standard deviation of 3 days. It is important to maintain a 97 percent cycle-service level to properly balance service with inventory holding costs. Osprey Sports is open 350 days a year to allow the owners the opportunity to fish for muskie during the prime season. The owners want to use a continuous review inventory system for this item.

   a. What order quantity should be used?

   b. What reorder point should be used?

   c. What is the total annual cost for this inventory system?

15. The Farmer's Wife is a country store specializing in knickknacks suitable for a farmhouse decor. One item experiencing a considerable buying frenzy is a miniature Holstein cow. Average weekly demand is 30 cows, with a standard deviation of 5 cows. The cost to place a replenishment order is $15, and the holding cost is $0.75/cow/year. The supplier, however, is in China. The lead time for new orders is 8 weeks, with a standard deviation of 2 weeks. The Farmer's Wife, which is open only 50 weeks a year, wants to develop a continuous review inventory system for this item with a cycle-service level of 90 percent.

   a. Specify the continuous review system for the cows. Explain how it would work in practice.

   b. What is the total annual cost for the system you developed?

NOTES FOR CHAPTER

1. L. Smyrlis, "Mission Critical," *Canadian Transportation & Logistics,* vol. 105, no. 5 (May 2002), pp. 20–22, 36. Reprinted with permission of Lou Smyrlis, Editorial Director, *Canadian Transportation & Logistics.*

2. J. M. Bossert and S. P. Williams, "A Periodic-Review Modeling Approach for Guaranteed Service Supply Chains," *Interfaces,* vol. 37, no. 5 (September/October 2007), pp. 420–435; finance.yahoo.com; www.celanese.com, 2008.

3. "RONA Ends Year on High Note with Increased Sales and Profits in Fourth Quarter 2009," *Marketwire,* February 25, 2010.

4. G. A. Fowler and R. Dodes, "Retailers Tap Stores to Speed Online Orders," *Wall Street Journal,* May 20, 2010.

FURTHER READING

Bastow, B. J. "Metrics in the Material World." *APICS—The Performance Advantage,* May 2005, pp. 49–52.

Berlin, Bob. "Solving the OEM Puzzle at Valleylab." *APICS—The Performance Advantage,* March 1997, pp. 58–63.

Callioni, Gianpaolo, Xavier de Montgros, Regine Slagmulder, Luk N. Van Wassenhove, and Linda Wright. "Inventory-Driven Costs." *Harvard Business Review,* March 2005, pp. 135–141.

Cannon, Alan R., and Richard E. Crandall. "The Way Things Never Were." *APICS—The Performance Advantage,* January 2004, pp. 32–35.

Greene, James H. *Production and Inventory Control Handbook,* 3rd ed. New York: McGraw-Hill, 1997.

Krupp, James A. G. "Are ABC Codes an Obsolete Technology?" *APICS—The Performance Advantage,* April 1994, pp. 34–35.

Silver, Edward A. "Changing the Givens in Modeling Inventory Problems: The Example of Just-in-Time Systems." *International Journal of Production Economics,* vol. 26 (1996), pp. 347–351.

Silver, Edward A., D. F. Pyke, and Rein Peterson. *Inventory Management, Production Planning and Scheduling,* 3rd ed. New York: John Wiley & Sons, 1998.

Tersine, Richard J. *Principles of Inventory and Materials Management,* 4th ed. Upper Saddle River, NJ: Prentice-Hall, 1994.

Timme, Stephen G., and Christine Williams-Timme. "The Real Cost of Holding." *Supply Chain Management Review,* July–August 2003, pp. 30–37.

MyOMLab ASSETS

MyOMLab offers the following resources, which allow you to further practise and apply concepts presented in this chapter.

- **Key Equations:** All the equations for this chapter can be found in one convenient location.
- **Discussion Questions:** Four questions expand your thinking on approaches to improving the management of inventory.
- **Case:** *Parts Emporium.* Analyze the situation for two parts, develop the appropriate inventory system for each one, and estimate the savings relative to current practice.
- **Video Case:** *Inventory and Textbooks.* Compare and contrast the inventory practices of three organizations, R. R. Donnelley, Pearson, and the University Bookstore, as books are printed and sold.
- **Virtual Tours:**
  - *Stickley Furniture Factory* using a high-volume batch process for furniture, with particular inventory challenges.
  - *United Wood Treating* uses chromated copper arsenate to produce pressure-treated utility poles and marine pilings. Explore the functions that inventory serves and think about the appropriate inventory management approach.
  - *Round House* has manufactured overalls since 1903. Identify the key inventory management issues.
- **Experiential Exercise:** *Swift Electronic Supply Inc.* Design an inventory system and test it under actual conditions in this interactive simulation.
- **OM Explorer Tutors:** Five tutor programs will help you learn how to estimate inventory levels, perform ABC analysis, calculate EOQs and total costs, determine the safety stock and reorder point for Q systems, and calculate the review period and target inventory level for P systems.
- **Extend LT:** *Inventory Management at Ready Hardware.* Inventory replenishment.
- **Supplement A:** *Decision Making.* Use this supplement to get background information on how to do sensitivity analysis.
- **Supplement G:** *Simulation.* Learn how to conduct simulations and keep track of the results.
- **Supplement H:** *Special Inventory Models.* See how to apply additional inventory tools, including the economic production lot size model, the analysis of quantity discounts, and the one-period inventory model.

Quality and Process Improvement

Learning Goals

After reading this chapter, you should be able to:

1. define *quality* from the customer's perspective.

2. discuss the four major cost categories of quality.

3. describe the principles and elements of TQM and six-sigma programs, and how they contribute to improved quality and productivity.

4. distinguish among the various tools for improving quality and explain how each should be used.

5. discuss how control charts are developed and used to determine whether a process is out of statistical control.

6. assess whether a process is capable of producing a product or service to specifications.

Across the Organization

Quality is important to:

- **accounting,** which must measure and estimate the costs of poor quality and provide error-free data to its internal customers.

- **human resources,** which recruits, motivates, and trains employees who value quality work.

- **management information systems,** which design the systems for tracking productivity and quality performance.

- **marketing,** which uses quality and performance data for promotional purposes.

- **operations,** which designs and implements total quality management and six-sigma programs.

Anyone who owns a cell phone knows the agony of poor service quality, whether from established mobile carriers such as Rogers or Bell, or from newer entrants such as Wind Mobile. Dropped calls and sketchy reception have recently become a major battleground for Canada's carriers—prompting media campaigns, counter-campaigns, legal action, and demands for government penalties.

Calls can be dropped for a variety of reasons, such as when customers roam from their home network to an adjacent network, or when they walk into large buildings. But did you know that another cause might be the phone itself? Major network carriers know that if service is lost, it is they—not the manufacturer—who likely will take the blame from the customer. So Canadian carriers can ill afford failure caused by poor design or assembly of their customers' phones. Manufacturers such as Apple, Motorola, Samsung, and LG Electronics are expected to provide defect-free phones; however, experience has indicated that extensive testing by network carriers is needed as well.

For example, Verizon Wireless, a major carrier in the United States, performs a "teardown" analysis that looks for weaknesses in a phone's hardware and components, and tests the device for its ability to withstand temperature extremes, vibration, and stress. Beyond these physical tests, Verizon also uses two approaches to assess a phone's capability to receive cellular signals and clearly communicate to the caller. First, the company hired about a hundred personnel, who drive $300 000 specially equipped vans more than 1.5 million kilometres annually, to measure network performance using prospective new cell phones. They make more than three million voice call attempts and sixteen million data tests annually. The tests check the coverage of the network as well as the capability of the phones to pick up the signals and clearly communicate to the caller. Second, Verizon uses Mr. Head, a robotic mannequin, who has a recorded voice and is electronically equipped with a rubber ear that evaluates how well the phone's mouthpiece transmits certain phonetics. Mr. Head utters what sounds like gibberish; however, it actually covers the range of sounds in normal speech patterns. Other systems monitor the tests and summarize results. Some phones spend so much time in the test phase that ultimately they never make it to the market.

Kristin Desjadon is one of the engineers who inspired Verizon Wireless' long-running "Can You Hear Me Now?" advertising campaign. She is pictured here with her test vehicle and the campaign's popular "Test Man" outside a regional network facility in United States.

Looking forward, customers can anticipate improved service quality in big buildings and rural areas when Canadian mobile carriers begin using new networks that rely on the "premium" 700-megahertz spectrum. The federal government is expected to auction off these airwaves as TV broadcasters discontinue analog channels in 2012. This promises big gains through an improved combination of phone design and network characteristics, yielding much better service quality at lower cost.[1]

The challenge for business today is to produce quality products or services efficiently. This chapter explores the competitive implications of quality, focusing on the philosophy and tools of total quality management, which many firms have embraced. **Total quality management (TQM)** stresses three principles: customer satisfaction, employee involvement, and continuous improvements in quality. As Figure 6.1 indicates, TQM also integrates other areas essential to quality, including benchmarking, product and service design, process design, purchasing, and problem-solving tools. Statistical process control forms a foundational set of techniques to appraise and monitor quality in processes and operating systems.

QUALITY: A MANAGEMENT PHILOSOPHY

We previously identified two competitive priorities that deal with quality: high-performance design and consistent quality (see Chapter 1, "Creating Customer Value Through Operations"). These priorities characterize an organization's competitive thrust. Strategic plans that recognize quality as an essential competitive priority must be based on some operational definition of quality. In this section, we discuss individuals who have shaped the management of quality. We also consider various definitions of quality and emphasize the importance of bridging the gap between consumer expectations of quality and operating capabilities.

GURUS OF QUALITY MANAGEMENT

Many individuals have contributed to the development of quality management over the last 80 years, beginning with Walter Shewhart's development of statistical tools. The distinctive perspectives of three people, Deming, Juran, and Crosby, help us to understand the basis for many of the different approaches and tools in wide use today to monitor and improve quality. That is not to say that others have not been instrumental in shaping the way we conceptualize quality, such as Armand Feigenbaum with his concept of total quality control, and Taguchi with his emphasis on designing in quality through engineering, discussed near the end of this chapter. However, Deming, Juran, and Crosby provide important philosophical starting points for a deeper understanding of how to effectively manage quality.

FIGURE 6.1   *TQM Wheel*

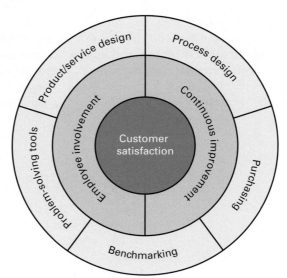

W. EDWARDS DEMING. The foundation to Deming's philosophy to quality management is statistical process control (SPC). SPC, described in much greater detail later in this chapter, uses statistical methods to monitor the quality of output from individual operations along a process. Although Deming initially introduced these techniques to U.S. managers, it was only later, in the 1950s, that his methods proved far more influential with Japanese management. He became a major figure in the Japanese quality movement, where at times he is referred to as the father of quality control. In recognition, the highest industrial award for excellence in Japan has been named the Deming Prize.

In a nutshell, Deming's philosophy advocates continuous improvement of the production process to achieve conformance to specifications and reduce variability. As noted in Chapter 4, "Capacity," higher variability requires additional investment in capacity and inventory. Extensive final inspection and testing comes too late in the process to get rid of poor quality. To reduce variability, Deming's approach to process improvement focuses on two actions: reduce *common* causes of quality problems, such as poor design and inadequate employee training; and reduce *special* causes, such as specific short-term equipment problems or a particular operational practice. Statistical techniques are critical to identifying and reducing both types of causes. Each of these issues is discussed in greater detail later in this chapter.

Deming's 14 points, listed in Table 6.1, go beyond SPC to address management's central role in total quality management. Primary responsibility for quality improvement lies with management, as he argued that 85 percent of quality problems can be attributed to managers or the systems they put in place. His rationale was that management is responsible for designing the system, for leading efforts to improve the system, and for empowering employees. However, employees were not ignored; they must monitor quality throughout the process and systematically analyze and implement improvements using a four-step approach. This approach, termed the Deming wheel, or plan-do-check-act (PDCA) cycle, is discussed in greater detail in the later section titled "Continuous Improvement" (see also Figure 6.2).

JOSEPH M. JURAN. Like Deming, Joseph Juran served as a consultant to Japanese industry. However, Juran defined quality in terms of the customer—as fitness for use.

TABLE 6.1	*Deming's 14 Points for Improving Quality*[2]

1. Create constancy of purpose toward improvement of product and service.
2. Adopt a new philosophy, with management leading change.
3. Cease dependence on inspection to achieve quality—build quality into the product.
4. Stop awarding business on the basis of price; instead minimize total cost.
5. Constantly improve the system of production and service.
6. Institute training on the job.
7. Institute leadership, the aim of which is to help people and equipment do a better job.
8. Drive out fear so that everyone can work effectively.
9. Break down barriers between departments.
10. Eliminate slogans, exhortations, and targets, which only create adversarial relationships.
11. Eliminate quotas, and management by objective and by numbers—substitute leadership.
12. Remove barriers that rob people of their right to pride in their work.
13. Institute a vigorous program of education and self-improvement.
14. Put everybody in the company to work to accomplish the transformation.

He also advocated that the costs of quality can be better understood by explicitly recognizing specific categories: prevention, appraisal, and failure costs. These categories are explained in detail later in this chapter. Only by examining all of these can a complete and accurate picture of the implications of poor quality be understood, which then serves as the basis for delivering optimal levels of quality.

To effectively manage quality, Juran emphasized the critical importance of three interrelated managerial processes: quality planning, control, and improvement. According to Juran, "Quality does not happen by accident; it has to be planned." The planning process, driven by senior managers and experts, ensures that customer needs are well understood, and that systems are designed to attain the particular quality characteristics deemed necessary by the customer. Management sets goals and priorities, assesses the results of previous plans, and coordinates quality objects with other company goals. For this reason, quality training must start at the top of the organization with management.

Quality control is about maintaining a stable, predictable level of quality. To do so, actual performance must be evaluated, comparisons are made to objectives, and, where

TABLE 6.2	*Views of Three Quality Gurus*[3]		
	DEMING	**JURAN**	**CROSBY**
Definition of quality	A predictable degree of uniformity and dependability at low cost and suited to the market	Customer-defined: fitness for use	Conformance to requirements
Senior management responsibility	Responsible for 85% of quality problems; management designs system	Source of more than 80% of quality problems; management plans and reviews improvement projects	Responsible for quality
General philosophy	Reduce variability by continuous improvement; cease mass inspection	Multifaceted management of quality, especially human elements	Prevention, not inspection
Basic structure	14 points for management; PDCA cycle	Quality trilogy: planning, ongoing control, and breakthrough improvement projects	14 steps to quality improvement
Basis for improvement	Continuous to reduce variation; eliminate goals without methods	Project-by-project team approach; set goals	A process, not a program; improvement goals
Costs of quality	No optimum; continuous improvement	Quality is not free; there is an optimum	Quality is free; cost of nonconformance
Performance standard/motivation	Many quality metrics; use statistics to assess performance; critical of zero defects	Avoid campaigns to do perfect work	Zero defects, less emphasis on statistics
Statistical process control (SPC)	Statistical methods of quality control must be used	Recommends SPC but warns that it can lead to tool-driven approach	Rejects statistically acceptable levels of quality
Teamwork	Employee participation in decision making; break down barriers between departments	Quality council and project teams	Quality improvement teams; quality councils
Purchasing and goods received	Statistical evidence and control charts required, as inspection is too late and allows defects to enter system	Problems are complex; carry out formal surveys	State requirements; supplier is extension of business; most faults due to purchasers themselves
Vendor rating	No, critical of most systems	Yes, but help supplier improve using quality trilogy	Rate buyers and suppliers, as both contribute to material faults
Single sourcing of supply	Yes	No, can neglect to sharpen competitive edge	No

discrepancies are found, corrective action is initiated. Finally, quality improvement uses project teams to achieve periodic "breakthroughs" with dramatic gains to address chronic quality problems. Improvement processes must also establish and support the necessary infrastructure, such as employee training and other resources for project teams. Many individual quality improvement projects are under way throughout an organization at any given time. Collectively, these three processes of planning, control, and improvement form what Juran referred to as the *quality trilogy*.

PHILIP CROSBY. A third leader in quality management, Philip Crosby, further explored the costs of poor quality, which he argued are greatly misunderstood and underestimated. The cost of poor quality must include lower productivity, lost sales, equipment downtime, and poor service, to name just a few outcomes. His book *Quality Is Free* stresses that the trade-off between tolerating versus preventing poor quality should always favour prevention and improvement. In Crosby's view, a company's objective must be *zero defects*. Quality excellence is achieved through clear goals and standards (rather than statistical data), strong organizational commitment, redesigned processes to remove error-causing situations, and open communication between management and employees.

To summarize, the views of these three quality gurus are compared in Table 6.2.

CUSTOMER SATISFACTION: DEFINITIONS OF QUALITY

quality The degree of excellence based on meeting or exceeding the expectations of the customer, including both high-performance design and conformance.

Quality is one of the key dimensions of customer value; however, customers define quality in various ways, partly depending on whether the customers are internal or external to the firm. In a general sense, **quality** may be defined as meeting or exceeding the expectations of the customer. For practical purposes, it is necessary to be more precise and identify particular facets or components that apply to the customer benefit bundle of goods and services being produced. Like a diamond, quality looks somewhat different depending on the shape of the bundle, and which facet is presented to the customer. Broadly speaking, the two competitive priorities of high-performance design and conformance relate quality to customer value. Managers can monitor and improve specific quality dimensions, one or more of which may apply at any one time.

HIGH-PERFORMANCE DESIGN

High-performance design includes basic performance, supplemental features, reliability, durability, support, and psychological impressions.

BASIC PERFORMANCE. Customers generally expect products or services to offer key characteristics or technical capabilities. These characteristics are measurable and well understood, allowing customers to make direct comparisons between competitive products. For example, performance characteristics for a computer might include computing power and speed, memory, disk storage, Internet connectivity, and footprint (i.e., the area it takes up on your desk). Unfortunately, such a complex product might require trade-offs in performance, with a larger size being needed to accommodate additional memory and storage. For home delivery of newspapers, performance might include delivering a clean, dry newspaper, even in inclement weather.

SUPPLEMENTAL FEATURES. In addition to key characteristics, customers consider secondary, less important aspects, sometimes termed "bells and whistles," that are merely nice to have. Supplemental features often make the product easier to use or service more pleasant. For example, the layout and backlighting of the keyboard on a laptop computer can make it easier to use in low-light conditions. Setting up water stations for thirsty golfers at several locations around a golf course enhances the experience, particularly during hot weather.

RELIABILITY. The likelihood of a product working properly or service being performed during a specified period is termed reliability. Because any measure of reliability is expected to be very high, firms often report reliability in terms of failure, for example, mean time between failures, failure rate per month, or average percent late. For example, Seagate, a disk drive manufacturer, advertised that a particular disk drive had a "mean time between failures" of 1.2 million hours. Reliability is particularly critical for customers when the costs of failure or downtime are high, such as with the telecommunications industry. Equipment reliability is critical for service providers, where customers can be immediately aware of any downtime.

DURABILITY. In contrast to reliability, durability measures the lifespan of a product before it begins to deteriorate or no longer functions at an acceptable level. For simple products such as fluorescent lights, this might be measured in hours of expected service. However, for other, more expensive capital goods, such as automobiles, durability also captures the costs of repair relative to replacement. Finally, for many high-technology products, durability also can include how long the product is useful before it becomes obsolete. For example, a computer may "work" for ten years, yet still be obsolete for all but the simplest functions in less than five years. Durability reflects the ease with which the computer can be upgraded to maintain compatibility with current standards for software.

SUPPORT. Often the support provided by the company after the initial sale of the product or service is as important to customers as the quality of the basic product or service itself. Customers get upset with a company if financial statements are incorrect, responses to warranty claims are delayed, or advertising is misleading. Serviceability is also very important, as it adds to the overall life-cycle cost of the product. For example, many products need occasional repair, such as the brakes on an automobile. If this can be done quickly and inexpensively, customers perceive higher quality. At times, good product serviceability and support also can reduce the consequences of poor quality. For example, if you had just had brake service done for your car, you would be upset if the brakes began squealing again a week later. If the manager of the brake shop offers to redo the work at no additional charge, the company's intent to satisfy the customer is clear.

PSYCHOLOGICAL IMPRESSIONS. People often evaluate the quality of a product or service on the basis of psychological impressions: atmosphere, image, craftsmanship, or aesthetics. In the provision of services, where the customer is in close contact with the provider, the appearance and actions of the provider are very important. Nicely dressed, courteous, friendly, and sympathetic employees can affect the customer's perception of service quality. For example, rumpled, discourteous, or grumpy waiters can undermine a restaurant's best efforts to provide high-quality service. Also, some patients may judge a dentist's quality of service on the basis of the age of her equipment, because new dental technology greatly reduces the discomfort associated with visits to the dentist. In manufacturing, product quality often is judged on the basis of the knowledge and personality of salespeople, as well as the product image presented in advertisements.

CONFORMANCE

On the basis of customer expectations, a firm must develop specifications for product and service design, as well as any associated operating characteristics. These specifications describe high-performance design in detail, including such aspects as basic performance, supplemental features, and reliability. Conformance captures the consistency with which the firm meets these specifications.

In general, high conformance quality coupled with tight tolerances for specifications yields consistent products with low variability. For example, all the components of the disk drive must conform to particular specifications for size, speed of access, failure rate, and drop distance (i.e., resistance to breakage) to achieve the desired quality of the finished product. In service systems, conformance to specifications is also important, even though tangible outputs may not be created. For example, one specification for a service operation might be response time. Bell Canada measures the performance of its operators in Ontario by the length of time it takes to process a telephone call ("handle time"). In the past, if the group average time exceeded a standard of 23 seconds, managers worked with the operators to reduce it.

QUALITY AS A COMPETITIVE WEAPON

Consumers are much more quality-minded now than in the past, yet attaining quality in all areas of a business is a difficult task. To make things even more difficult, consumers change their perceptions of quality. In general, a business's success depends on the accuracy of its perceptions of consumer expectations and its ability to bridge the gap between those expectations and operating capabilities. Good quality can pay off in higher profits. In many markets, high-quality products and services can be priced higher than comparable lower-quality ones.

Higher quality (i.e., greater consistency and less variability) can also translate into lower costs, which yield a greater return for the same sales dollar. Consistent quality is particularly critical in commodity-based industries, such as mining and forest products, where the price is set by broad market forces. Poor quality erodes the firm's ability to compete in the marketplace and increases the costs of producing its product or service.

For example, poor-quality service has been a frequent complaint about Air Canada to Canada's federal Air Travel Complaints Commissioner. In contrast, relatively few complaints have been received about WestJet's service quality—well below what might be expected given its second-place market share. These reports, which are often published in the media, can contribute to losses in market share for a firm with poor quality, as well as to higher costs associated with resolving those complaints. Historically, Toyota consistently dominated quality surveys of new-car buyers, such as the Initial Quality Survey by J. D. Power, which in turn influenced the purchase decisions of other new customers. However, recent design missteps and supplier problems eroded quality and hurt Toyota's market share. Big Rock Brewery, a regional brewery based in Calgary, Alberta, attributes its continued growth and success against much larger, dominant firms to offering high-quality products. Collectively, high quality means that management is better able to compete on both price and quality, yielding significantly better customer value.

COSTS OF QUALITY

Many companies spend significant time, effort, and expense on systems, training, and organizational changes to improve the performance and quality of their processes. They believe that it is important to be able to gauge current levels of performance so that any process gaps can be determined. Gaps reflect potential dissatisfied customers and additional costs for the firm.

defect Any instance of a process failing to satisfy its customer.

When a process fails to satisfy its customers, the failure is considered a **defect**. Experts have estimated that the losses from the costs of poor quality range from 20 percent to 30 percent of gross sales for defective or unsatisfactory products. Four major categories of costs are associated with quality management: prevention, appraisal, internal failure, and external failure.

PREVENTION COSTS

prevention costs Costs associated with preventing defects before they happen.

Prevention costs are associated with avoiding defects before they happen. They include the costs of redesigning the process to remove the causes of poor quality, redesigning the product to make it simpler to manufacture, training employees in the methods of continuous improvement, and working with suppliers to increase the quality of purchased items or contracted services. In order to improve quality, firms have to invest additional time, effort, and money.

APPRAISAL COSTS

appraisal costs Costs incurred in assessing the level of quality attained by the operating system.

Appraisal costs are incurred to assess and inspect the level of quality attained by the operating system. Appraisal helps managers identify quality problems. As preventive measures improve quality, appraisal costs decrease, because fewer resources are needed for quality inspections and the subsequent search for causes of any problems that are detected.

INTERNAL FAILURE COSTS

internal failure costs Costs resulting from defects that are discovered during the production of a product or service.

Internal failure costs result from defects that are discovered during the production of a service or product. Defects fall into two main categories: *rework*, which is incurred if some aspect of a service must be performed again or if a defective item must be rerouted to some previous operation(s) to correct the defect, and *scrap*, which is incurred if a defective item is unfit for further processing. For example, if the final inspector at an automobile paint shop discovers that the paint on a car has a poor finish, the car may have to be reworked by sanding and repainting. The additional time spent correcting such a mistake results in lower productivity for the sanding and painting departments. In addition, the car may not be finished by the date on which the customer is expecting it.

EXTERNAL FAILURE COSTS

external failure costs Costs that arise when a defect is discovered after the customer has received the product or service.

External failure costs arise when a defect is discovered *after* the customer has received the product or service. For instance, suppose that you have the oil changed in your car and that the oil filter is improperly installed, causing the oil to drain onto your garage floor. You might insist that the company pay for the car to be towed and restore the oil and filter immediately. External failure costs to the company include the towing and additional oil and filter costs, as well as the loss of future revenue because you decide never to take your car back there for service. Dissatisfied customers talk about bad service or products to their friends, who in turn tell others. If the problem is bad enough, consumer protection groups alert the media. The potential impact on future profits is difficult to assess, but without doubt external failure costs erode market share and profits. Encountering defects and correcting them after the product is in the customer's hands is costly.

warranty A written guarantee that the producer will replace or repair defective parts or perform the service to the customer's satisfaction.

External failure costs also include warranty service and litigation costs. A **warranty** is a written guarantee that the producer will replace or repair defective parts or perform the service to the customer's satisfaction. Usually, a warranty is given for some specified period. For example, television repairs might be guaranteed for 90 days and new automobiles for five years or 100 000 kilometres, whichever comes first. Warranty costs must be considered in the design of new products or services, particularly as they relate to reliability.

EMPLOYEE INVOLVEMENT

One of the important elements of TQM is employee involvement, as shown in Figure 6.1. A program in employee involvement includes changing organizational culture and encouraging teamwork.

CULTURAL CHANGE

One of the main challenges in developing the proper culture for TQM is to define *customer* for each employee. As noted earlier, customers can be either internal or external. Some employees, especially those having little contact with external customers, may have difficulty seeing how their jobs contribute to the whole effort. However, each employee also has one or more internal customers—other employees in the firm who rely on that individual's output. For example, a machinist who drills holes in a component and passes it on to a welder has the welder as her customer. Even though the welder is not an external customer, he will have many of the same definitions of quality as an external customer, except that they will relate to the component instead of a complete product.

All employees must do a good job of serving their internal customers if external customers ultimately are to be satisfied. The concept of internal customers works if each *internal* customer demands only value-added activities of their internal suppliers—that is, activities that the external customer will recognize and pay for. The notion of internal customers applies to all parts of a firm and enhances cross-functional coordination. For example, accounting must prepare accurate and timely reports for management, and purchasing must provide high-quality materials on time for operations.

In TQM, everyone in the organization must share the view that high quality is an end in itself. Errors or defects should be caught and corrected at the source, not passed along to an internal or external customer. For example, a consulting team should make sure its billable hours are correct before submitting them to the accounting department. This philosophy is called *quality at the source*. In addition, firms should avoid trying to "inspect quality into the product" by using inspectors to weed out defective products or unsatisfactory services after all operations have been performed. By contrast, in some manufacturing firms, workers have the authority to stop a production line if they spot quality problems.

TEAMS

Employee involvement is a key tactic for improving quality and competitiveness. One way to achieve employee involvement is by the use of **teams**, which are small groups of people who have a common purpose, set their own performance goals and approaches, and hold themselves accountable for success. The three approaches to teamwork most often used are problem-solving teams, special-purpose teams, and self-managing teams. All three use some amount of **employee empowerment**, which shifts responsibility for decisions farther down the organizational chart—to the level of the employee actually doing the job.

PROBLEM-SOLVING TEAMS. First introduced in the 1920s, problem-solving teams, also called **quality circles**, only became popular in the late 1970s after the Japanese used them successfully. These teams are small groups of supervisors and employees who meet to identify, analyze, and solve production and quality problems. The philosophy behind this approach is that the people who are directly responsible for making the

teams Small groups of people who have a common purpose, set their own performance goals and approaches, and hold themselves accountable for success.

employee empowerment An approach to teamwork that moves responsibility for decisions farther down the organizational chart— to the level of the employee actually doing the job.

quality circles Another name for problem-solving teams—small groups of supervisors and employees who meet to identify, analyze, and solve production and quality problems.

MANAGERIAL PRACTICE
Quality and Performance at Steinway & Sons

The first contestant in the Van Cliburn International Piano Competition is about to play Tchaikovsky *Piano Concerto No. 1* before a packed audience. The tension mounts as his fingers approach the keyboard of the Steinway & Sons grand concert piano; both the contestant and piano perform admirably, much to the relief of the contestant and the operations manager of the concert. Why was the Steinway chosen for such a visible event? It is one of the highest-quality grand pianos you can buy. In addition, Steinway has a market share of over 95 percent in concert halls, and it is the piano of choice for professional musicians from Van Cliburn to Billy Joel.

Steinway began operations in the 1880s. Today, the company blends the art of hand crafting, which uses methods essentially the same as when the company started, with twenty-first-century manufacturing technology to produce about 3100 grand pianos a year. Some 12 000 parts are fashioned, mostly in-house, and assembled for each piano; it takes from nine months to a year, as against 20 days for a mass-produced piano. Eight different species of wood go into every grand piano, each selected for its physical properties and aesthetic characteristics. The craft-oriented production process takes pains to ensure quality at every step. For example, every board for a piano is hand-selected for a given part. In a time-consuming process, craftsmen bend 17 laminations of the piano's hard maple rim into place with clamps. The Alaska Sitka spruce soundboard is hand-planed to be arched, thicker at its centre than its tapered edges, to withstand the 1000 pounds of pressure from the more than 200 strings. The piano's "action," containing the keys, whippens, shanks, and hammers, uses 100 parts, manufactured on numerical control machines, to sound each note, and is pieced together at 30 different desks. Quality is checked at every stage to avoid passing defective parts downstream.

There are six characteristics of quality in Steinway pianos:

- *Sound.* Tone and pitch contribute to the fullness and roundness of the sound from the piano. In a process called "voicing," minute adjustments are made to the felt pad of each hammer in the piano's action to either mellow the tone or increase its brilliance. Then a tone regulator listens to the piano's pitch and turns the tuning pins to adjust string tension. Steinways are world-renowned for their sound; however, because of the natural

A worker strings the soundboard of a Concert Grand Model D piano at the Steinway & Sons factory in New York.

characteristics of the wood, every piano will have its own personality.

- *Finish.* Wood veneers are selected for their beauty. Boards not meeting Steinway's standards are discarded, creating a large amount of scrap.

- *Feel.* Each of the 88 keys must require the same amount of pressure to activate. In a process called "action weigh-off," lead is added to each key so that there is a consistent feel. Action parts are held to tolerances within ±13 microns.

- *Durability.* The piano must have a long life and perform to expectations throughout.

- *Image.* There is a certain cult-like mystique associated with the Steinway brand.

- *Service.* Steinway will go out of its way to service a piano that is inoperative, even to the extent of providing a loaner for a major concert.

These six characteristics link up to our definitions of quality: conformance (feel) and high-performance design (sound, finish, durability, service, and image). As for value, Steinway grand pianos cost anywhere from $47 000 to $165 000—unless you want a nine-foot recreation of the famous Alma-Tadema piano built in 1887, which costs $675 000. For the discerning musician, quality comes at a price.[4]

product or providing the service will be best able to consider ways to solve a problem. Also, employees take more pride and interest in their work if they are allowed to help shape it. The teams typically consist of five to twelve volunteers, drawn from different areas of a department or from a group of employees assigned to a particular task, such as automobile assembly or credit application processing. Although problem-solving teams can successfully reduce costs and improve quality, they quickly die if management fails to implement many of the suggestions generated.

special-purpose teams
Groups that address issues of paramount concern to management, labour, or both.

SPECIAL-PURPOSE TEAMS. Special-purpose teams, an outgrowth of the problem-solving teams, address issues of paramount concern to management, labour, or both. For example, management may form a special-purpose team to design and introduce new work policies or new technologies, or to address customer service problems. Essentially, this approach gives workers a voice in high-level decisions.

self-managing team A small group of employees who work together to produce a major portion, or sometimes all, of a product or service.

SELF-MANAGING TEAMS. The **self-managing team** approach takes worker participation to its highest level: a small group of employees work together to produce a major portion, or sometimes all, of a product or service. Members learn all the tasks involved in the operation, rotate from job to job, and take over managerial duties such as work and vacation scheduling, ordering supplies, and hiring. In some cases, team members design the process and have a high degree of latitude as to how it takes shape. Self-managing teams essentially change the way work is organized, because employees have control over their jobs. Only recently have self-managing teams begun to catch on in North America, where they have increased productivity by 30 percent or more in some firms.

CONTINUOUS IMPROVEMENT

continuous improvement
The philosophy of continually seeking ways to improve operations, based on a Japanese concept called *kaizen*.

Continuous improvement, based on a Japanese concept called *kaizen*, is the philosophy of continually seeking ways to improve operations. Continuous improvement involves identifying benchmarks of excellent practice and instilling a sense of employee ownership in the process. The focus can be on reducing the length of time required to process requests for loans at a bank, the amount of scrap generated at a soldering machine, or the number of employee injuries at a construction site. Continuous improvement also can focus on problems with customers or suppliers, such as customers who request frequent changes in shipping quantities and suppliers who fail to maintain high quality. The bases of the continuous improvement philosophy are the beliefs that virtually any aspect of an operation can be improved and that the people most closely associated with an operation are in the best position to identify the changes that should be made. The idea is not to wait until a massive problem occurs before acting.

plan-do-check-act cycle
A cycle, also called the *Deming Wheel*, used by firms actively engaged in continuous improvement to train their work teams in problem solving.

Most firms actively engaged in continuous improvement train their work teams to use the Deming Wheel, which uses a **plan-do-check-act cycle** for problem solving. Figure 6.2 shows this cycle, which lies at the heart of the continuous improvement philosophy. The cycle comprises the following steps:

1. *Plan.* The team selects a process (e.g., activity, method, equipment, or policy) that needs improvement. The team then documents the selected process, usually by analyzing data (using the tools we discuss later in the chapter); sets qualitative goals for improvement; and discusses various ways to achieve the goals. After assessing the benefits and costs of the alternatives, the team develops a plan with quantifiable measures for improvement.

2. *Do.* The team implements the plan and monitors progress. Data are collected continuously to measure the improvements in the process. Any changes in the process are documented, and further revisions are made as needed.

FIGURE 6.2   *Plan-Do-Check-Act Cycle*

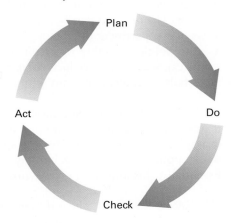

3. *Check.* The team analyzes the data collected during the *do* step to find out how closely the results correspond to the goals set in the *plan* step. If major shortcomings exist, the team may have to re-evaluate the plan or stop the project.

4. *Act.* If the results are successful, the team documents the revised process so that it becomes the standard procedure for all who may use it. The team may then instruct other employees in the use of the revised process.

Problem-solving projects often focus on reducing or eliminating those aspects of operations that do not add value to the product or service. Value is added during operations such as machining a part or serving a customer using a Web page. No value is added in activities such as inspecting parts for quality defects or routing requests for loan approvals to several different departments. In essence, the idea of continuous improvement is to reduce or eliminate activities that do not add value and thus are wasteful.

SYSTEMATICALLY IMPROVING QUALITY

TQM's emphasis on customer satisfaction, employee involvement, and continuous improvement provides a critical foundation for offering better quality services and products. However, this foundation must be translated into systematic approaches for identifying and enhancing quality for a competitive advantage. *Six sigma* is one such model—although it should be combined with other tools, such as quality function deployment, benchmarking, and data analysis, to build quality into process design and new service/product design.

SIX SIGMA

Six sigma, which relies heavily on the principles of TQM, is a comprehensive and flexible system for achieving, sustaining, and maximizing business success by minimizing defects and variability in processes. It has a somewhat different focus than TQM: it is driven by a close understanding of customer needs; the disciplined use of facts, data, and statistical analysis; and diligent attention to managing, improving, and reinventing business processes.

Figure 6.3 shows how six sigma focuses on reducing variation in processes as well as centring processes on their target measures of performance. Either flaw—too much

Six sigma A comprehensive and flexible system for achieving, sustaining, and maximizing business success by minimizing defects and variability in processes.

FIGURE 6.3   *Six-Sigma Approach's Focus on Reducing Spread and Centring the Process*

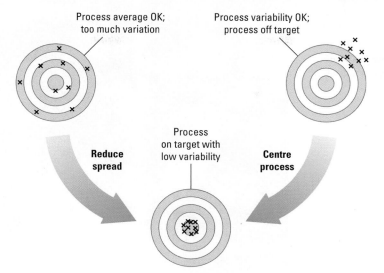

variation or an off-target process—degrades performance of the process. For example, a mortgage loan department of a bank might advertise loan approval decisions in two days. If the actual performance ranges from one day to five days, with an average of two days, those customers who had to wait longer than two days would be upset. Process variability causes customer dissatisfaction. Similarly, if actual performance consistently produced loan decisions in three days, all customers would be dissatisfied. In this case, the process is consistent, but off the target. Six sigma is a rigorous approach to aligning processes with their target performance measures with low variability.

Motorola is credited with developing six sigma more than 20 years ago to improve its manufacturing capability in a world marketplace that was becoming increasingly competitive. Management noticed that some customers were complaining about the quality of Motorola's products and that competitor products were outperforming its products. Motorola began by soliciting new ideas from its employees and benchmarking its competitors. What followed were extensive changes to employee compensation and reward programs, training programs, and critical processes. The procedures were documented and refined. The name "six sigma" relates to the goal of achieving low rates of defective output by developing processes whose mean output for a performance measure is six standard deviations (sigma) from the design specifications for the service or product. We will discuss variability and its implications on the capability of a process to perform at acceptable levels when we present the tools of statistical process control.

Although six sigma was rooted in an effort to improve manufacturing processes, General Electric popularized the application of the approach to nonmanufacturing processes such as sales, human resources, and customer service. The concept of eliminating defects is the same, but the definition of "defect" depends on the process involved. For example, a human resources department's failure to meet a hiring target counts as a defect. Six sigma has been successfully applied to a host of service processes, including financial services, human resources processes, marketing processes, and health-care administrative processes.

SIX SIGMA IMPROVEMENT MODEL. A five-step procedure is used to improve process performance. This *Six Sigma Improvement Model* can be applied to projects involving

Hospital personnel at a trauma centre rush a patient to the emergency room. Six sigma can be used to improve service processes such as those in a trauma centre.

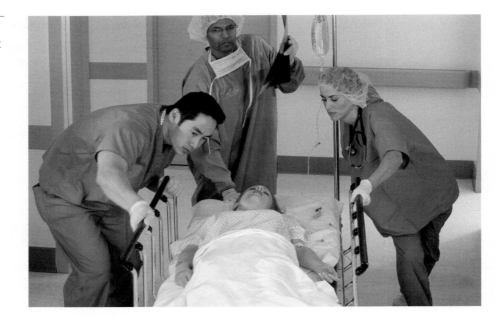

incremental improvements to processes or to projects requiring major changes, including a redesign of an existing process or the development of a new process. The model comprises the following steps:

1. *Define.* Determine the characteristics of the process's output that are critical to customer satisfaction and identify any gaps between these characteristics and the process's capabilities. Get a picture of the current process by documenting it using flowcharts and process charts.

2. *Measure.* Quantify the work the process does that affects the gap. Select what to measure, identify data sources, and prepare a data collection plan.

3. *Analyze.* Use the data on measures to perform process analysis, applying tools such as Pareto charts, scatter diagrams, cause-and-effect diagrams, and the statistical process control (SPC) tools in this chapter, to determine where improvements are necessary. Whether or not major redesign is necessary, establish procedures to make the desired outcome routine.

4. *Improve.* Modify or redesign existing methods to meet the new performance objectives. Implement the changes.

5. *Control.* Monitor the process to make sure that high performance levels are maintained. Once again, data analysis tools such as Pareto charts, bar charts, scatter diagrams, and the statistical process control tools can be used to control the process.

Successful users of six sigma have found that it is essential to rigorously follow these steps, sometimes referred to as the *DMAIC process* (from the first letter of each step). To accomplish the goals of six sigma, employees must be trained in the "whys" and the "how-tos" of quality and what it means to customers, both internal and external.

Successful firms using six sigma develop a cadre of internal teachers who are then responsible for teaching and assisting teams involved in a process improvement project. These teachers might have different titles, depending on their experience and level of achievement. Green Belts devote part of their time to teaching and helping teams with their projects and the rest of their time to their normally assigned duties. Black Belts are full-time teachers and leaders of teams involved in six sigma projects. Finally, Master Black Belts are full-time teachers who review and mentor Black Belts.

NEW SERVICE AND PRODUCT DESIGN

Because design changes often require different methods, materials, or specifications, they can increase defect rates. Change invariably increases the risk of making mistakes, so stable product and service designs can help reduce internal quality problems. However, stable designs may not be possible when a product is sold or service is offered in competitive markets globally. Although these changes have the potential to increase market share, management must be aware of possible quality problems resulting from any changes. If a firm needs to make design changes to remain competitive, it should carefully test new designs and redesign the product or service and the process with a focus on the market and customer expectations. Simulation can improve the quality of new designs. Implementing both strategies involves a trade-off: higher quality and increased competitiveness potentially are exchanged for added time and cost.

reliablity The probability that a product will be functional when used.

Another dimension of quality related to product design is **reliability**, which refers to the probability that the product will be functional when used. Products often consist of a number of components that all must be operative for the product to perform as intended. Sometimes products can be designed with extra components (or subsystems) so that if one component fails, another can be activated.

Suppose that a product has several modules, components, or subsystems, each with its own reliability measure (the probability that it will operate when called upon). The reliability of each module contributes to the quality of the total system; that is, the reliability of the complete product equals the product of all the reliabilities of the modules, or:

$$r_s = (r_1)(r_2)...(r_i)...(r_n)$$

where:

r_s = Reliability of the complete product

n = Number of modules, components, or subsystems

r_i = Reliability of each module, component, or subsystem i

This measure of reliability is based on the assumption that the reliability of each component or subsystem is independent of the others.

Suppose that a small portable radio designed for joggers has three components: a motherboard with a reliability of 0.99, a housing assembly with a reliability of 0.90, and a headphone set with a reliability of 0.85. The reliabilities are the probabilities that each component will still be operating two years from now. The reliability of the portable radio is:

$$r_s = (0.99)(0.90)(0.85) = 0.76$$

The poor headsets and housings hurt the reliability of this product. Suppose that new designs resulted in a reliability of 0.95 for the housing and 0.90 for the headsets. Product reliability would improve to:

$$r_s = (0.99)(0.95)(0.90) = 0.85$$

Managers must be concerned about the quality of every step in the process or component, because the service or product fails when any individual aspect fails.

PROCESS DESIGN

The design of the process used to produce a product or service greatly affects its quality. Managers at the First National Bank noticed that customers' requests for a letter of credit took four days to go through dozens of steps involving nine employees before a letter of credit would be issued. To improve the process and shorten the waiting time for customers, the bank trained letter-of-credit issuers to do all the required tasks so that the customer could deal with just one person. In addition, customers interacted with the same employee each time they requested a letter. The bank now issues letters of credit in less than a day.

The purchase of new machinery can help prevent or overcome potential quality problems. For example, many worker tasks can be very repetitive and prone to error, such as manual data entry. Others may require high skills, such as precision welding, yet those skills may be in short supply locally. Finally, others require intense worker concentration at fast operating speeds, such as bottle inspection after packaging. For each of these situations, automated equipment may dramatically improve quality.

QUALITY FUNCTION DEPLOYMENT

quality function deployment (QFD) A means of translating customer requirements into the appropriate technical requirements for each stage of product or service development and production.

A key to improving quality is linking the design of products or services to the processes that produce them. **Quality function deployment (QFD)**, first described in 1978 by Yoji Akao and Shigeru Mizuno, is a means of translating customer requirements ("voice of the customer") into the appropriate technical requirements ("voice of the engineer") for each aspect of a service or component of a product. Customer requirements and technical specifications are compared to both competitive offerings and the firm's.

These relationships and trade-offs can be presented as a "house of quality" (Hauser and Clausing, 1988). The competitive analysis provides a place to start looking for ways to gain a competitive advantage. Then the relationships between customer needs and technical attributes need to be specified. Finally, the fact that improving one performance measure may detract from another must be recognized.

The QFD approach provides a way to set targets and debate their effects on product quality. Engineering uses the data to focus on significant product design features. Marketing uses this input for determining marketing strategies. Operations uses the information to identify the processes that are crucial to improving product quality as perceived by the customer. As a result, QFD encourages interfunctional communication for the purpose of improving the quality of products and services. Many companies around the world have used the approach, including Toyota, Hewlett-Packard, Samsung, Procter & Gamble, Polaroid, and Deere & Company.

BENCHMARKING

benchmarking A continuous, systematic procedure that measures a firm's products, services, and processes against those of industry leaders.

Benchmarking is a continuous, systematic procedure that measures a firm's products, services, and processes against those of industry leaders, both in the same industry and outside. Companies use benchmarking to understand better how outstanding companies do things so that they can improve their own operations. Typical measures used in benchmarking include cost per unit, service upsets (breakdowns) per customer, processing time per unit, customer retention rates, revenue per unit, return on investment, and customer satisfaction levels. Those involved in continuous improvement efforts rely on benchmarking to formulate goals and targets for performance.

Competitive benchmarking is based on comparisons with a direct industry competitor. *Functional* benchmarking compares areas such as administration, customer service, and sales operations with those of outstanding firms in any industry. For instance, Xerox benchmarked its distribution function against L. L. Bean's because Bean is renowned as a leading retailer in distribution efficiency and customer service.

Finally, *internal* benchmarking involves using an organizational unit with superior performance as the benchmark for other units. This form of benchmarking can be advantageous for firms that have several business units or divisions.

TOOLS FOR DATA ANALYSIS

A key step in improving the quality of an operation is data collection, which can uncover operations requiring improvement and the extent of remedial action needed. There are nine tools for organizing and presenting data to identify areas for quality and performance improvement: flow diagrams, process charts, checklists, histograms and bar charts, Pareto charts, scatter diagrams, cause-and-effect diagrams, graphs, and control charts. We discussed flow diagrams and process charts in Chapter 3, "Process Configuration," and we discuss control charts in depth later when we address statistical process control. In this section we demonstrate the use of the other six methods to emphasize the breadth of applications possible.

checklist A form used to record the frequency of occurrence of certain product or service characteristics related to quality.

histogram A summarization of data measured on a continuous scale, showing the frequency distribution of some quality characteristic (in statistical terms, the central tendency and dispersion of the data).

bar chart A series of bars representing the frequency of occurrence of data characteristics measured on a yes-or-no basis.

Pareto chart A bar chart on which factors are plotted in decreasing order of frequency along the horizontal axis.

scatter diagram A plot of two variables showing whether they are related.

CHECKLISTS. Data collection through the use of a checklist is often the first step in the analysis of quality problems. A **checklist** is a form used to record the frequency of occurrence of certain product or service characteristics related to quality. The characteristics may be measurable on a continuous scale (e.g., weight, diameter, time, or length) or on a yes-or-no basis (e.g., paint discolouration, odours, rude servers, or too much grease).

HISTOGRAMS AND BAR CHARTS. The data from a checklist often can be presented succinctly and clearly with histograms or bar charts. A **histogram** summarizes data measured on a continuous scale, showing the frequency distribution of some quality characteristic (in statistical terms, the central tendency and dispersion of the data). Often the mean of the data is indicated on the histogram. A **bar chart** is a series of bars representing the frequency of occurrence of data characteristics measured on a yes-or-no basis. The bar height indicates the number of times a particular quality characteristic was observed.

PARETO CHARTS. When managers discover several quality problems that need to be addressed, they have to decide which should be attacked first. Vilfredo Pareto, a nineteenth-century Italian scientist whose statistical work focused on inequalities in data, proposed that most of an "activity" is caused by relatively few of its factors. In a restaurant quality problem, the activity could be customer complaints and the factor could be "discourteous waiter." For a manufacturer, the activity could be product defects and a factor could be "missing part." Pareto's concept, called the 80-20 rule, is that 80 percent of the defects are caused by 20 percent of the factors. By concentrating on the 20 percent of the factors (the "vital few"), managers can solve most of the quality problems.

The few vital factors can be visually identified with a **Pareto chart**, a bar chart on which the factors are plotted in decreasing order of frequency along the horizontal axis. The chart has two vertical axes, the one on the left showing frequency (as in a histogram) and the one on the right showing the cumulative percentage of frequency. The cumulative frequency curve identifies the few vital factors that warrant immediate managerial attention.

SCATTER DIAGRAMS. Sometimes managers suspect but are not sure that a certain factor is causing a particular quality problem. A **scatter diagram**, which is a plot of two variables showing whether they are related, can be used to verify or negate the suspicion. Each point on the scatter diagram represents one data observation. For example, the manager of a castings shop may suspect that casting defects are a function of the diameter of the casting. A scatter diagram could be constructed by plotting the number of defective castings found for each diameter of casting produced. After the diagram is completed, any relationship between diameter and number of defects could be observed.

CAUSE-AND-EFFECT DIAGRAMS. An important aspect of TQM is linking each aspect of quality prized by the customer to the inputs, methods, and process steps that build a particular attribute into the product. One way to identify a design problem that needs to be corrected is to develop a **cause-and-effect diagram** that relates a key quality problem to its potential causes. The diagram, first developed by Kaoru Ishikawa, helps management trace customer complaints directly to the operations involved. Operations that have no bearing on a particular defect are not shown on the diagram for that defect.

cause-and-effect diagram
A diagram that relates a key quality problem to its potential causes.

The cause-and-effect diagram sometimes is called a *fishbone diagram*. The main quality problem (effect) is labelled as the fish's "head," the major categories of potential causes as structural "bones," and the likely specific causes as "ribs." When constructing and using a cause-and-effect diagram, an analyst identifies all the major categories of potential causes for the quality problem. For example, these might be People, Equipment, Materials, and Process. For each major category, the analyst lists all the likely causes of the quality problem. For example, under People might be listed "lack of training," "poor communication," and "absenteeism." Each cause can be further explored by asking "Why?" For example, "absenteeism" might be caused by poor morale, or "out of specification" might be caused by adopting a new supplier. Brainstorming helps the analyst identify and properly classify all suspected causes. The analyst then systematically investigates the causes listed on the diagram for each major category, updating the chart as new causes become apparent. The process of constructing a cause-and-effect diagram calls management and worker attention to the primary factors affecting product or service quality.

graphs Representations of data in a variety of pictorial forms, such as line graphs and pie charts.

GRAPHS. **Graphs** represent data in a variety of pictorial formats, such as line graphs and pie charts. *Line graphs* represent data sequentially with data points connected by line segments to highlight trends in the data, for example, in control charts. Pie charts represent quality factors as slices of a pie; the size of each slice is in proportion to the number of occurrences of the factor. Pie charts are useful for showing data from a group of factors that can be represented as percentages totalling 100.

Each of the tools for improving quality that we have just discussed may be used independently, but their power is greatest when they are used together. In solving a quality problem, managers often must act as detectives, sifting data to clarify the issues involved and deducing the causes. Example 6.1 demonstrates four of the tools for improving quality.

EXAMPLE 6.1	*Identifying Causes of Poor Headliner Quality*

The Wellington Fibreboard Company produces headliners, the fibreglass components that form the inner roof of passenger cars. Management wanted to identify which defects were most prevalent and to find the cause.

SOLUTION
Figure 6.4 shows the sequential application of several tools for improving quality:

- *Step 1.* A checklist of different types of defects was constructed from last month's production records.

- *Step 2.* A Pareto chart prepared from the checklist data indicated that broken fibreboard accounted for 72 percent of the quality defects. The manager decided to dig further into the problem of broken fibreboard.

FIGURE 6.4 *Application of the Tools for Improving Quality*

Step 1 Checklist

Headliner defects

Defect type	Tally	Total
A. Tears in fabric	IIII	4
B. Discoloured fabric	III	3
C. Broken fibreboard	HHHHHH HHHHHHI	36
D. Ragged edges	HHII	7
		Total 50

Step 2 Pareto Chart

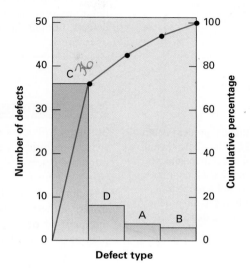

Step 3 Cause-and-Effect Diagram

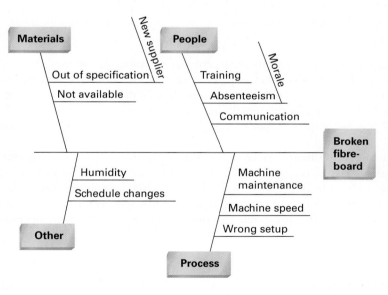

Step 4 Pareto Chart

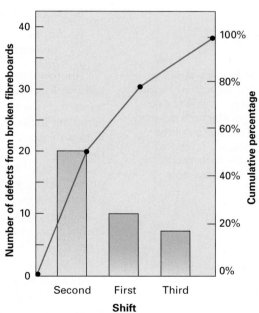

- *Step 3.* A cause-and-effect diagram for broken fibreboard identified several potential causes for the problem. The one strongly suspected by the manager was employee training.
- *Step 4.* The manager reorganized the production reports only for broken fibreboard occurrences into a Pareto chart by shift because the personnel on the three shifts had different levels of experience.

Decision Point The second Pareto chart (step 4) indicated that the second shift, with the least experienced workforce, had the most defects. Further investigation revealed that workers were not using proper procedures for stacking the fibreboards after the press operation, causing cracking and chipping. The manager initiated additional training sessions focused on board handling after the press operation. Although the second shift was not responsible for all the defects, finding the source of many defects enabled the manager to improve the quality of her operations.

STATISTICAL PROCESS CONTROL

statistical process control (SPC) The application of statistical techniques to determine whether the output of a process conforms to the product or service design.

Statistical process control (SPC), another data analysis tool, is the application of statistical techniques to determine whether the output of a process conforms to the product or service design. In SPC, tools called control charts are used primarily to detect production of defective products or services or to indicate that the production process has changed and that products or services will deviate from their design specifications unless something is done to correct the situation. SPC can also be used to inform management of process changes that have changed the output for the better. Some examples of process changes that can be detected by SPC are:

- A decrease in the average number of complaints per day at a hotel
- A sudden increase in the proportion of defective gearboxes
- A consistently low measurement in the diameter of a crankshaft
- A decline in the number of scrapped units at a milling machine
- An increase in the number of claimants receiving late payment from an insurance company

acceptance sampling The application of statistical techniques to determine whether a quantity of material should be accepted or rejected based on the inspection or test of a sample.

Another approach to quality management, **acceptance sampling**, is the application of statistical techniques to determine whether a quantity of material should be accepted or rejected on the basis of the inspection or test of a sample (see Supplement F, "Acceptance Sampling Plans" in MyOMLab). In the remainder of this chapter, we explore the techniques of statistical process control to understand better the role they play in decision making.

We begin with the fundamental reason for SPC techniques: variation in outputs. Earlier, variation was described as one of the three important factors in the process management triangle (see Figure 4.1). Poor quality, which creates higher variability, forces a service or manufacturing firm to add capacity or inventory to compensate. SPC is a powerful approach to controlling the variation in outputs from a process.

VARIATION OF OUTPUTS

No two services or products are exactly alike, because the processes used to produce them contain many sources of variation, even when the processes are working as intended. For example, the diameters of two crankshafts may vary because of differences in tool wear, material hardness, operator skill, or temperature during the period in which they were produced. Similarly, the time required to process a credit card application varies because of the load on the credit department, the financial background of the applicant, and the skills and attitudes of the employees. Nothing can be done to eliminate variation in process output completely, but management should investigate the *causes* of variation to minimize it.

QUALITY MEASUREMENTS. To detect variations in output, employees or their equipment must be able to measure quality characteristics. These characteristics can be evaluated in two ways. One way is to monitor **variables**—that is, product or service characteristics, such as weight, length, volume, or time, that can be *measured*. The advantage of measuring a quality characteristic is that if a product or service misses its quality specifications, the employee knows by how much. The disadvantage is that such measurements typically involve special equipment, employee skills, exacting procedures, and time and effort.

Another way to evaluate quality is to measure **attributes**—that is, product or service characteristics that can be quickly *counted* for acceptable quality. The method allows employees to make a simple yes-or-no decision about whether a product or service meets the specifications. Attributes are often used when quality specifications are complex and measuring by variables is difficult or costly. Some examples of attributes that can be counted are the number of insurance forms containing errors that cause underpayments or overpayments and the proportion of washing machines failing final inspection. The advantage of attribute counts is that less effort and fewer resources are needed than for measuring variables. The disadvantage is that, even though attribute counts can reveal that quality of performance has changed, they may not be of much use in indicating by how much.

SAMPLING. The most thorough approach to inspection is to inspect each product or service at each stage of the process for quality. This method, called *complete inspection*, is used when the costs of passing defects to the next workstation or to external customers outweigh the inspection costs. Firms often use automated inspection equipment that can record, summarize, and display data, particularly in a technology-intensive industry such as electronics. Many companies have found that automated inspection equipment can pay for itself in a reasonably short time.

A well-conceived **sampling plan** can approach the same degree of protection as complete inspection. A sampling plan specifies a **sample size**, which is a quantity of randomly selected observations of process outputs; the time between successive samples; and decision rules that determine when action should be taken. Sampling is appropriate when inspection costs are high because of the special knowledge, skills, procedures, or expensive equipment required to perform the inspections or when testing is destructive.

SAMPLING DISTRIBUTIONS. A process will produce output that can be assessed using particular measures, either variables or attributes. Each of these can be described with a process distribution, which can be characterized by its location, spread, and shape. The mean of the distribution indicates location, while spread is described by the range or standard deviation. Relatively small values for the range or the standard deviation imply that the observations are clustered near the mean. The shape can be simply described as either symmetric or skewed. A symmetric distribution has the same shape above and below the mean (i.e., a mirror image), while a skewed distribution does not.

The mean and variance of the process distribution will be known with 100 percent accuracy only with a complete inspection. The purpose of sampling, however, is to estimate the variable or attribute measure for the output of the process without doing complete inspection. That measure is then used to assess the performance of the process itself.

For example, the time required by a laboratory to analyze patient specimens and report the results to an intensive care unit lab in a hospital (a variable measure) will vary; this is one dimension of service quality (i.e., reliability). If you measured the time to complete an analysis of a large number of patients and plotted the results, the data

variables Product or service characteristics, such as weight, length, volume, or time, that can be measured.

attributes Product or service characteristics that can be quickly counted for acceptable quality.

sampling plan A plan that specifies a sample size, the time between successive samples, and decision rules that determine when action should be taken.

sample size A quantity of randomly selected observations of process outputs.

would form a pattern that is the process distribution. With sampling, we try to estimate the parameters of the process distribution using statistics such as the sample mean and the sample range or standard deviation.

These sample statistics have their own distribution, called a sampling distribution, which is different from the process distribution. For example, in a laboratory, suppose that the process distribution for analyzing and reporting has a mean of 25 minutes. A lab technician who periodically takes a sample of the time required for five analyses and calculates the sample mean could determine how well the process is currently performing. Plotting a large number of these *sample means* would show that they have their own distribution with a mean centred on 25 minutes, as does the process distribution mean, but with *much less* variability. The reason is that the highs and lows of individual times in each sample of five are offset when averaged within each sample.

Some distributions of sample means (e.g., for means with sample sizes of 4 or more and proportions with sample sizes of 20 or more) can be approximated by the *normal* distribution, allowing the use of the normal table if both the mean and standard deviation are known. We can determine the probability that any particular sample mean will fall outside certain limits. The ability to assign probabilities to sample results is important for the construction and use of control charts.

COMMON CAUSES. For SPC, there are two basic categories of variation in output: common causes and assignable causes. These are related to the random and predictable variability described with the process management triangle (recall Figure 4.1 and Table 4.2). However, the terms *common cause* and *assignable cause* are narrower in scope. They focus specifically on service or product quality related to a particular process, rather than other forms of variation, such as demand volume, transit times, or setup times.

common causes of variation The purely random sources of variation inherent in a process and generally considered unavoidable.

Common causes of variation are the purely random, unidentifiable sources of variation that are unavoidable with the current process. So, for the previously mentioned laboratory, the average of 25 minutes per sample includes some random variation from adjusting the equipment, the occasional stuck lid on a vial, and other minor but routine variations. As with many processes, the steps for each sample might be quite repeatable, but not precisely identical. Reducing common-cause variation usually requires a longer-term process redesign, which is primarily management's responsibility. If process variability results solely from common causes of variation, a typical assumption is that the distribution is symmetric, with most observations near the centre.

assignable causes of variation Any variation-causing factors that can be identified and eliminated.

ASSIGNABLE CAUSES. The second category of variation, **assignable causes of variation,** also known as special causes, includes any variation-causing factors that can be identified and eliminated. Assignable causes of variation include an employee needing training or a machine needing repair. Assignable causes can also be related to external changes for process inputs, such as new suppliers, defective shipment of materials, or even weather if the process is sensitive to heat or humidity. The cause may not be known in advance or immediately, but the process doesn't behave in its usual way.

Let us return to the example of the laboratory process. Figure 6.5 shows how assignable causes can change the distribution of output, namely, time for analysis. The green curve is the process distribution when only common causes of variation are present. The red lines depict a change in the distribution because of assignable causes. In Figure 6.5(a), the red line indicates that the process took more time than planned in many of the cases, thereby increasing the average time of analysis. In Figure 6.5(b), an increase in the variability of the time for each case affected the spread of the distribution. Finally, in Figure 6.5(c), the red line indicates that the

FIGURE 6.5   *Effects of Assignable Causes on the Process Distribution for the Lab Analysis Process*

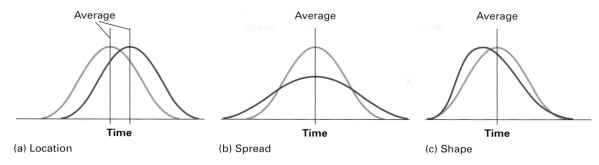

(a) Location   (b) Spread   (c) Shape

process produced a preponderance of the tests in less than average time. Such a distribution is skewed, or no longer symmetric to the average value.

DIAGNOSING VARIATION WITH CONTROL CHARTS

A critical task in managing quality is to separate assignable causes, which need immediate management or worker attention, from common causes, which need longer-term management action, such as process redesign. A process is said to be in statistical control when the location, spread, or shape of its distribution is relatively stable over time. After the process is in statistical control, managers and workers can use control charts to detect the onset of assignable causes so that they can be eliminated. To determine whether observed variations are abnormal, we can measure and plot the quality characteristic taken from the sample on a time-ordered diagram called a **control chart**.

control chart A time-ordered diagram used to determine whether observed variations are abnormal.

    A control chart has a central line, which is the mean of the sample distribution, and two control limits based on the sampling distribution of the quality measure. The control limits are used to judge whether action is required. The larger value represents the *upper control limit* (UCL), and the smaller value represents the *lower control limit* (LCL). Figure 6.6 shows how the control limits relate to the sampling

FIGURE 6.6   *Relationship of Control Limits to Sampling Distribution and Observations from Three Samples*

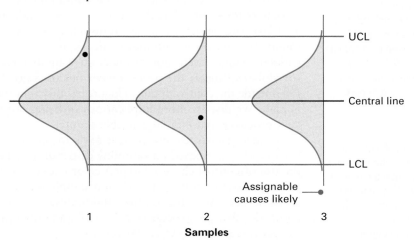

distribution. A sample statistic that falls between the UCL and the LCL indicates that the process is exhibiting common causes of variation; a statistic that falls outside the control limits indicates that the process is exhibiting assignable causes of variation.

Observations falling outside the control limits do not always mean poor quality. For example, in Figure 6.6 the assignable cause may be a new billing process introduced to reduce the number of incorrect bills sent to customers. If the proportion of incorrect bills, the quality statistic from a sample of bills, falls *below* the LCL of the control chart, the new procedure has likely changed the billing process for the better and a new control chart should be constructed.

Managers or employees responsible for monitoring a process can use control charts in the following ways:

1. Take a random sample from the process, measure the quality characteristic, and calculate a variable or attribute measure.

2. If the statistic falls outside the chart's control limits, look for an assignable cause.

3. Eliminate the cause if it degrades quality; incorporate the cause if it improves quality. Reconstruct the control chart with new data.

4. Repeat the procedure periodically.

Sometimes problems with a process can be detected even though the control limits have not been exceeded. There are several rules for detecting the presence of assignable causes (Wheeler, 1995). A lack of control is indicated when:

Rule 1: An observation falls outside a control limit.

Rule 2: Two-of-three successive observations are on the same side of the central line and more than two standard deviations away from the central line.

Rule 3: Four-of-five successive observations are on the same side of the central line and more than one standard deviation away from the central line.

Rule 4: Eight consecutive observations fall on the same side of the central line.

In practice, only Rules 1 and 4 are generally used. Figure 6.7 contains four examples of control charts. Chart (a) shows a process that is in statistical control. No action is needed. However, chart (b) shows a pattern called a *run*, and so violates Rule 4. Here, nine observations are below the central line and show a downward trend. The probability is low that such a result could take place by chance.

Chart (c) shows that the process takes a sudden change from its normal pattern. The last four observations are unusual: three rising toward the UCL and the fourth remaining above the nominal value. A manager should monitor processes with such sudden changes even though the control limits have not been exceeded. Finally, chart (d) violates Rule 1; the process went out of control twice because two sample results fell outside the control limits. The probability that the process distribution has changed is high. We discuss more implications of being out of statistical control when we discuss process capability later in this chapter.

Control charts are not perfect tools for detecting shifts in the process distribution because they are based on sampling distributions. Two types of error are possible with the use of control charts. A **type I error** occurs when the employee concludes that the process is out of control based on a sample result that falls outside the control limits, when in fact it was due to pure randomness. A **type II error** occurs when the employee concludes that the process is in control and only randomness is present, when actually the process is out of statistical control.

type I error An error that occurs when the employee concludes that the process is out of control based on a sample result that falls outside the control limits, when in fact it was due to pure randomness.

type II error An error that occurs when the employee concludes that the process is in control and only randomness is present, when actually the process is out of statistical control.

FIGURE 6.7   *Control Chart Examples*

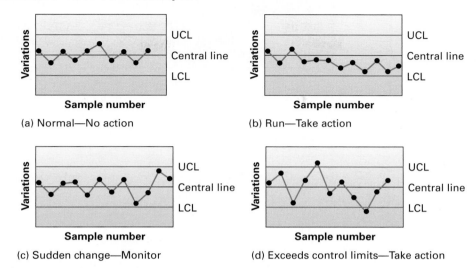

(a) Normal—No action

(b) Run—Take action

(c) Sudden change—Monitor

(d) Exceeds control limits—Take action

These errors can be adjusted by the choice of control limits. The choice would depend on the costs of looking for assignable causes when none exist versus the cost of not detecting a shift in the process. For example, setting control limits at three standard deviations from the mean reduces the type I error because chances are quite small that a sample result will fall outside of the control limits unless the process is out of statistical control. However, the type II error may be significant because more subtle shifts in the nature of the process distribution will go undetected because of the wide spread in the control limits. Alternatively, the spread in the control limits can be reduced to two standard deviations, thereby increasing the likelihood of sample results falling outside of the control limits. Now the type II error is smaller, but the type I error is larger because employees are likely to search for assignable causes when the sample result occurred solely by chance. As a general rule, managers will use wider limits when the cost for searching for assignable causes is large relative to the cost of not detecting a shift in the process distribution.

CONSTRUCTING SPC CHARTS

Statistical process control (SPC) methods are useful for both measuring the current quality of products or services and detecting whether the process itself has changed in a way that will affect quality. In this section, we first discuss mean and range charts for variables and then consider control charts for product or service attributes.

CONTROL CHARTS FOR VARIABLES

The two basic measures of quality, variables and attributes, require different methods to sample and chart, as well as diagnose common versus special causes. Control charts for variables consist of two parts, described next, and are used to monitor the mean and the variability of the process distribution.

R-chart A chart used to monitor changes in process variability.

R-CHARTS. A range chart, or ***R*-chart**, is used to monitor process variability. To calculate the range of a set of sample data, the analyst subtracts the smallest from the largest measurement in each sample. If any of the data fall outside the control limits, the process variability is not in control.

TABLE 6.3	Factors for Calculating Three-Sigma Limits for the x̄-Chart and R-Chart[5]		
SIZE OF SAMPLE (n)	FACTOR FOR UCL AND LCL FOR x̄-CHARTS (A_2)	FACTOR FOR LCL FOR R-CHARTS (D_3)	FACTOR FOR UCL FOR R-CHARTS (D_4)
2	1.880	0	3.267
3	1.023	0	2.575
4	0.729	0	2.282
5	0.577	0	2.115
6	0.483	0	2.004
7	0.419	0.076	1.924
8	0.373	0.136	1.864
9	0.337	0.184	1.816
10	0.308	0.223	1.777

The control limits for the R-chart are:

$$UCL_R = D_4\overline{R} \quad \text{and} \quad LCL_R = D_3\overline{R}$$

where:

$\overline{R}$ = Average of several past R values and the central line of the control chart

D_3, D_4 = Constants that provide three standard deviation (three-sigma) limits for a given sample size

Values for D_3 and D_4 are contained in Table 6.3 and change as a function of the sample size. Note that the spread between the control limits narrows as the sample size increases. This change is a consequence of having more information on which to base an estimate for the process range.

x̄-CHARTS. An x̄-chart (read "x-bar chart") is used to monitor changes in the mean. When the assignable causes of process variability have been identified and the process variability is in statistical control, the analyst can construct an x̄-chart to control the process average. The control limits for the x̄-chart are:

> **x̄-chart** A chart used to monitor changes in the sample mean.

$$UCL_{\overline{x}} = \overline{\overline{x}} + A_2\overline{R} \quad \text{and} \quad LCL_{\overline{x}} = \overline{\overline{x}} - A_2\overline{R}$$

where:

$\overline{\overline{x}}$ = Central line of the chart and either the average of past sample means or a target value set for the process

A_2 = Constant to provide three-sigma limits for the sample mean

The values for A_2 are contained in Table 6.3. Note that the control limits use the value of $\overline{R}$; therefore, the x̄-chart must be constructed *after* the process variability is in control.

Analysts can develop and use x̄- and R-charts in the following way:

Step 1. Collect data on the variable quality measurement (such as weight, diameter, or time) and organize the data by sample number. Preferably, at least 20 samples should be taken for use in constructing a control chart.

Step 2. Compute the range for each sample and the average range, $\overline{R}$, for the set of samples.

Step 3. Use Table 6.3 to determine the upper and lower control limits of the R-chart.

Step 4. Plot the sample ranges. If all are in control, proceed to step 5. Otherwise, find the assignable causes, correct them, and return to step 1.

Step 5. Calculate $\bar{x}$ for each sample and the central line of the chart, $\bar{\bar{x}}$.

Step 6. Use Table 6.3 to determine the parameters for $UCL_{\bar{x}}$ and $LCL_{\bar{x}}$ and construct the $\bar{x}$-chart.

Step 7. Plot the sample means. If all are in control, the process is in statistical control in terms of the process average and process variability. Continue to take samples and monitor the process. If any are out of control, find the assignable causes, correct them, and return to step 1. If no assignable causes are found after a diligent search, assume that the out-of-control points represent common causes of variation and continue to monitor the process.

EXAMPLE 6.2   *Using $\bar{x}$- and R-Charts to Monitor a Process*

The management of West Allis Industries is concerned about the production of a special metal screw used by several of the company's largest customers. The diameter of the screw is critical. Data from five samples are shown in the accompanying table. The sample size is 4. Is the process in control?

SOLUTION

Step 1. For simplicity we have taken only five samples. In practice, more than 20 samples would be desirable. The data are shown in the following table.

Data for the $\bar{x}$- and R-Charts: Observations of Screw Diameter (cm)

SAMPLE NUMBER	OBSERVATION				R	$\bar{x}$
	1	2	3	4		
1	0.5014	0.5022	0.5009	0.5027	0.0018	0.5018
2	0.5021	0.5041	0.5024	0.5020	0.0021	0.5027
3	0.5018	0.5026	0.5035	0.5023	0.0017	0.5026
4	0.5008	0.5034	0.5024	0.5015	0.0026	0.5020
5	0.5041	0.5056	0.5034	0.5047	0.0022	0.5045
				Average	0.0021	0.5027

Step 2. Compute the range for each sample by subtracting the lowest value from the highest value. For example, in sample 1 the range is $0.5027 - 0.5009 = 0.0018$ centimetres. Similarly, the ranges for samples 2, 3, 4, and 5 are 0.0021, 0.0017, 0.0026, and 0.0022 centimetres, respectively. As shown in the table, $\bar{R} = 0.0021$ centimetres.

Step 3. To construct the R-chart, select the appropriate constants from Table 6.3 for a sample size of 4. The control limits are:

$$UCL_R = D_4\bar{R} = 2.282(0.0021) = 0.00479 \text{ cm}$$

$$LCL_R = D_3\bar{R} = 0(0.0021) = 0 \text{ cm}$$

Step 4. Plot the ranges on the R-chart, as shown in Figure 6.8. None of the sample ranges falls outside the control limits. Consequently, the process variability is in statistical control. If any of the sample ranges had fallen outside of the limits, or an unusual pattern had appeared (see Figure 6.7), we would have had to search for the causes of the excessive variability, correct them, and repeat step 1.

FIGURE 6.8   R-*chart Showing That Process Variability Is in Control*

R-chart

Range

0.0050 — UCL$_R$ = 0.00479
0.0045
0.0040
0.0035
0.0030
0.0025 — $\bar{R}$ = 0.0021
0.0020
0.0015
0.0010
0.0005 — LCL$_R$ = 0
0

Sample number
0   1   2   3   4   5   6   7

Step 5. Compute the mean for each sample. For example, the mean for sample 1 is:

$$\frac{0.5014 + 0.5022 + 0.5009 + 0.5027}{4} = 0.5018 \text{ cm}$$

Similarly, the means of samples 2, 3, 4, and 5 are 0.5027, 0.5026, 0.5020, and 0.5045 centimetres, respectively. As shown in the table, $\bar{\bar{x}}$ = 0.5027 centimetres.

Step 6. Now construct the $\bar{x}$-chart for the process average. The average screw diameter is 0.5027 cm, and the average range is 0.0021 cm, so use $\bar{\bar{x}}$ = 0.5027, $\bar{R}$ = 0.0021, and A_2 from Table 6.3 for a sample size of 4 to construct the control limits:

$$\text{UCL}_x = \bar{\bar{x}} + A_2\bar{R} = 0.5027 + 0.729(0.0021) = 0.5042 \text{ cm}$$

$$\text{LCL}_x = \bar{\bar{x}} - A_2\bar{R} = 0.5027 - 0.729(0.0021) = 0.5012 \text{ cm}$$

Step 7. Plot the sample means on the control chart, as shown in Figure 6.9.

The mean of sample 5 falls above the upper control limit, indicating that the process average is out of control and that assignable causes must be explored, perhaps using a cause-and-effect diagram.

Decision Point   A mechanical part in the lathe machine that makes the screw had become damaged on the day the sample was taken. Management initiated maintenance to replace the worn part. Subsequent samples showed that the process was back in statistical control.

FIGURE 6.9 $\bar{x}$-*Chart Showing That Sample 5 Is Out of Control*

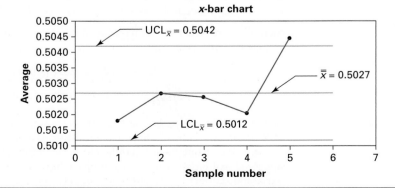

x-bar chart

Average

0.5050
0.5045 — UCL$_{\bar{x}}$ = 0.5042
0.5040
0.5035
0.5030
0.5025 — $\bar{\bar{x}}$ = 0.5027
0.5020
0.5015 — LCL$_{\bar{x}}$ = 0.5012
0.5010

Sample number
0   1   2   3   4   5   6   7

If the standard deviation of the process distribution is known, another form of the $\bar{x}$-chart may be used:

$$\text{UCL}_{\bar{x}} = \bar{\bar{x}} + z\sigma_{\bar{x}} \quad \text{and} \quad \text{LCL}_{\bar{x}} = \bar{\bar{x}} + z\sigma_{\bar{x}}$$

where:

$\sigma_{\bar{x}} = \sigma/\sqrt{n} = $ Standard deviation of sample means

$\sigma = $ Standard deviation of the process distribution

$n = $ Sample size

$\bar{\bar{x}} = $ Average of sample means or a target value set for the process

$z = $ Normal deviate; usually $z = 3$ for control charts

The analyst can use an R-chart to be sure that the process variability is in control before constructing the $\bar{x}$-chart. The advantage of using this form of the $\bar{x}$-chart is that the analyst can adjust the spread of the control limits by changing the value of z.

CONTROL CHARTS FOR ATTRIBUTES

Two charts commonly used for quality measures based on product or service attributes are the p- and c-charts. The p-chart is used for controlling the proportion of defective products or services generated by the process. The c-chart is used for controlling the number of defects when more than one defect can be present in a product or service.

p-chart A chart used for controlling the proportion of defective products or services generated by the process.

***p*-CHARTS.** The **p-chart** is a commonly used control chart for attributes. The quality characteristic is counted rather than measured, and the entire item or service can be declared good or defective. For example, in the banking industry, the attributes counted might be the number of non-endorsed deposits or the number of incorrect financial statements sent. The method involves selecting a random sample, inspecting each item in it, and calculating the sample proportion defective, p, which is the number of defective units divided by the sample size.

Sampling for a p-chart involves a yes-or-no decision: the item or service either is or is not defective. The underlying statistical distribution is based on the binomial distribution. However, for large sample sizes, the normal distribution provides a good approximation to it. The standard deviation of the distribution of proportion defective, σ_p, is:

$$\sigma_p = \sqrt{\bar{p}(1 - \bar{p})/n}$$

where:

$n = $ Sample size

$\bar{p} = $ Historical average population proportion defective or target value and central line on the chart

The central line on the p-chart may be the average of the past sample proportion defective or a target that management has set for the process. We can use σ_p to arrive at the upper and lower control limits for a p-chart:

$$\text{UCL}_p = \bar{p} + z\sigma_p \quad \text{and} \quad \text{LCL}_p = \bar{p} - z\sigma_p$$

where:

$z = $ Normal deviate (number of standard deviations from the average)

The chart is used in the following way. Periodically, a random sample of size n is taken, and the number of defective products or services is counted. The number of defectives is divided by the sample size to get a sample proportion defective, p, which is plotted on the chart. When a sample proportion defective falls outside the control limits, the analyst assumes that the proportion defective generated by the process has changed and searches for the assignable cause. Observations falling below the LCL_p indicate that the process may actually have improved. The analyst may find no assignable cause because there is always a small chance that an "out of control" proportion will have occurred randomly. However, if the analyst discovers assignable causes, those sample data should not be used to calculate the control limits for the chart. See Solved Problem 3 for a detailed solution to a problem requiring the use of the *p*-chart.

c-CHARTS. Sometimes products have more than one defect per unit. For example, a roll of carpeting may have several defects, such as tufted or discoloured fibres, or stains from the production process. Other situations in which more than one defect may occur include defects in a television picture tube face panel, accidents at a particular intersection, and complaints at a hotel. When management is interested in reducing the number of defects per unit, another type of control chart, the **c-chart**, is useful.

c-chart A chart used for controlling the number of defects when more than one defect can be present in a product or service.

The underlying sampling distribution for a *c*-chart is the Poisson distribution. It is based on the assumption that defects occur over a continuous region and that the probability of two or more defects at any one location is negligible. The mean of the distribution is $\bar{c}$ and the standard deviation is $\sqrt{\bar{c}}$. A useful tactic is to use the normal approximation to the Poisson so that the control limits are:

$$UCL_c = \bar{c} + z\sqrt{\bar{c}} \quad \text{and} \quad LCL_c = \bar{c} - z\sqrt{\bar{c}}$$

See Solved Problem 4 for a detailed example of the use of a *c*-chart.

PROCESS CAPABILITY

Statistical process control techniques help managers achieve and maintain a process distribution that does not change in terms of its mean and variance. The control limits on the control charts signal when the mean or variability of the process changes. However, a process that is in statistical control may not be producing products or services according to their design specifications, because the control limits are based on the mean and variability of the process's *sampling distribution*, not the customer's requirements or design specifications. **Process capability** refers to the ability of the process to meet the design specifications for a product or service. Design specifications often are expressed as a **nominal value**, or target, and a **tolerance**, or allowance above or below the nominal value.

process capability The ability of the process to meet the design specifications for a product or service.

nominal value A target for design specifications.

tolerance An allowance above or below the nominal value.

For example, the administrator of an intensive-care-unit lab might have a nominal value for the turnaround time of results to the attending physicians of 25 minutes and a tolerance of ± 5 minutes because of the need for speed under life-threatening conditions. The tolerance gives an *upper specification* of 30 minutes and a *lower specification* of 20 minutes. The lab process must be capable of providing the results of analyses within these specifications; otherwise, it will produce a certain proportion of "defects." The administrator is also interested in detecting occurrences of turnaround times of less than 20 minutes, because something might be learned that can be built into the lab process in the future. For the present, the physicians are pleased with results that arrive within 20 to 30 minutes. A fast food restaurant, such as McDonald's, can monitor service quality using SPC tools to measure variables such as drive-through service time. According to a pilot test in Canada, the design specification for drive-through service is a maximum of 30 seconds from payment to order completion. This provides the upper specification. The capability of the drive-through process at each restaurant can be assessed for its ability to satisfy customer quality expectations before launching a national campaign.

DEFINING PROCESS CAPABILITY

Figure 6.10 shows the relationship between a process distribution and the upper and lower specifications for the lab process turnaround time under two conditions. In Figure 6.10(a), the process is capable because the extremes of the process distribution fall within the upper and lower specifications. In Figure 6.10(b) the process is not capable because the lab process produces too many reports with long turnaround times. The process might not be capable because either the mean has shifted off-centre *or* the distribution has too much spread (i.e., high variance), or both. These situations are analogous to the two upper targets pictured in Figure 6.3.

Figure 6.10 shows clearly why managers are so concerned with reducing process variability. As variability decreases—as seen by a lower standard deviation—poor quality output is produced less frequently. Figure 6.11 shows what reducing variability does for the output of a process with a normal probability distribution. The firm with two-sigma quality (Tolerance limits = Process mean ± 2 standard deviations) produces 4.56 percent defective parts, or 45 600 defective parts per million. The firm with four-sigma quality produces only 0.0063 percent defectives, or 63 defective parts per million. Finally, the firm with six-sigma quality produces only 0.0000002 percent defectives, or 0.002 defective parts per million.

How can a manager determine quantitatively whether a process is capable? Initially, managers must ensure that the process is in control, and all assignable causes are eliminated (see page 220). Process capability, in part, assumes equipment, people, and systems are operating in a stable, consistent manner, that is, in control. If not, it is difficult to know how the process will perform from minute to minute, day to day, or even month to month. Then, two measures are commonly used in practice to assess capability: process capability ratio and process capability index.

PROCESS CAPABILITY RATIO. A process is *capable* for a particular measure of quality if it has a process distribution whose extreme values fall within the upper and lower

FIGURE 6.10 *Relationship Between Process Distribution and Specifications*

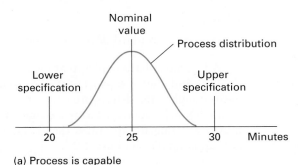

(a) Process is capable

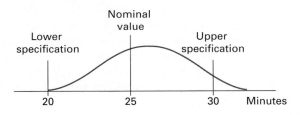

(b) Process is not capable

FIGURE 6.11   *Effects of Reducing Variability on Process Capability*

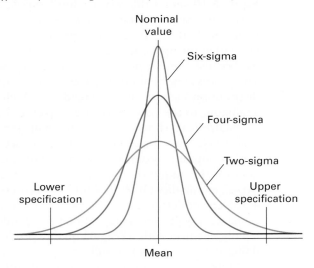

specifications for a product or service. How do we know which extreme values are likely to occur? As a general rule, most values of any process distribution fall within ±3 standard deviations of the mean. For example, if the distribution is normal, 99.74 percent of the values fall within ±3 standard deviations, for a total range of approximately 6 standard deviations. Hence, if a process is capable, the difference between the upper and lower specification, called the *tolerance width*, must be greater than 6 standard deviations. The **process capability ratio**, C_p, is defined as:

process capability ratio, C_p The tolerance width divided by six standard deviations (process variability).

$$C_p = \frac{\text{Upper specification} - \text{Lower specification}}{6\sigma}$$

where:

σ = Standard deviation of the process distribution

A C_p value of 1.0 implies that the firm is producing three-sigma quality (0.26 percent defects) and that the process is consistently producing outputs within specifications even though some defects are generated. C_p values greater than 1.0 imply higher levels of quality achievement. Firms striving to achieve greater than three-sigma quality use a critical value for the ratio that is greater than 1.0. For example, a firm targeting six-sigma quality will use 2.0.

PROCESS CAPABILITY INDEX. The process is capable only when the capability ratio is greater than the critical value and the process distribution is centred on the nominal value of the design specifications. As a general rule, ±3 standard deviations is used as the benchmark. This index also is appropriate to situations with only one specification limit, such as the McDonald's drive-through 30-second limit for good service quality.

The **process capability index**, C_{pk}, is defined as:

process capability index, C_{pk} An index that measures the potential for a process to generate defective outputs relative to either upper or lower specifications.

$$C_{pk} = \text{Minimum of} \left[\frac{\bar{\bar{x}} - \text{Lower specification}}{3\sigma}, \frac{\text{Upper specification} - \bar{\bar{x}}}{3\sigma} \right]$$

We take the minimum of the two ratios because it gives the *worst-case* situation. If C_{pk} is greater than the critical value (say, 1.33 for four-sigma quality) and the process capability ratio is also greater than the critical value, we can finally say the process is capable. If C_{pk} is less than 1.0, the process average is close to one of the tolerance limits and is generating defective output.

The capability index will always be less than or equal to the capability ratio. When C_{pk} equals C_p, the process is centred between the upper and lower specifications and, hence, the mean of the process distribution is centred on the nominal value of the design specifications. See Solved Problem 5 for a detailed example of the process capability ratio and the process capability index.

IMPROVEMENT USING PROCESS CAPABILITY

To determine the capability of a process to produce within the tolerances, use the following steps:

Step 1. Collect data on the process output, and calculate the mean and the standard deviation of the process output distribution.

Step 2. Use the data from the process distribution to compute process control charts, such as an $\bar{x}$- or an R-chart.

Step 3. Take a series of at least 20 random samples from the process and plot the results on the control charts. If sample statistics are within the control limits of the charts, the process is in statistical control. If the process is not in statistical control, look for assignable causes and eliminate them. Recalculate the mean and standard deviation of the process distribution and the control limits for the charts. Continue until the process is in statistical control.

Step 4. Calculate the process capability ratio and the process capability index. If the results are acceptable, document any changes made to the process and continue to monitor the output by using the control charts. If the results are unacceptable, further explore assignable causes for reducing the variance in the output or centring the process distribution on the nominal value. As changes are made, recalculate the mean and standard deviation of the process distribution and the control limits for the charts and repeat step 3.

QUALITY ENGINEERING

quality engineering An approach that involves combining engineering and statistical methods to reduce costs and improve quality by optimizing product design and process characteristics.

quality loss function The rationale that a product or service that barely conforms to the specifications is more like a defective product or service than a perfect one.

Quality engineering, originated by Genichi Taguchi, is an approach that involves combining engineering and statistical methods to reduce costs and improve quality by optimizing product design simultaneously with process characteristics. Statistical methods can be applied to create a product or service design that is insensitive to small variations in the process, increasing the consistency for meeting customer expectations. This design approach is termed *robust design*.

Taguchi also argued that unwelcome costs are associated with any deviation from a quality characteristic's target value. These costs form a **quality loss function**. Taguchi's view is that the value of the quality loss function is zero when the quality characteristic of the product or service is exactly on the target value. As the quality characteristic gets closer to the tolerance limits, the value of the loss function rises exponentially. The rationale is that a product or service that barely conforms to the specifications is more like a defective product or service than a perfect one. By looking at quality in this way, Taguchi emphasizes the need for managers to continually search for ways to reduce *all* variability from the target value in the production process and not be content with merely meeting specification limits.

INTERNATIONAL QUALITY CERTIFICATION

Once a company has gone through the effort of making its processes capable, it must document its level of quality so as to better market its products or services. This is especially important in international trade. However, if each country had its own set of standards, companies selling in international markets would have difficulty complying with quality documentation standards in the countries where they did business. To overcome this problem, the International Organization for Standardization (www.iso.ch) devised a set of standards called ISO 9000 for companies doing business in the European Union and internationally. Subsequently, a new set of documentation standards, ISO 14000, was devised for environmental management systems.

ISO 9000 A family of standards that represents an international consensus for strong quality management systems.

ISO 9000 QUALITY MANAGEMENT STANDARDS

ISO 9000 is really a family of standards that govern how quality is managed and documented within an organization. The primary standard, ISO 9001:2008, now in its fourth revision since 1987, has the broadest scope and ensures a rigorous quality management system is in place. It is the only standard from the family against which an organization can receive externally verified certification. Other standards in the family cover specific topics such as vocabulary, documentation, training, and financial aspects. Over the years, the standards have simplified the necessary documentation, and increasingly focused on customers, the role of top management, and continuous improvement.[6]

ISO 9001:2008 certification, unlike six sigma, does not require a specific quality specification for a service or final product, nor a particular quality level. Instead, it adopts a process approach in which each quality process is clearly mapped, individual responsibilities are clearly defined, and interactions between processes, managers, employees, and customers are delineated. The company must specifically document and ensure that processes are in place to ensure top management commitment and involvement, good design practices, monitoring of quality, and customer satisfaction.

Companies become certified after demonstrating to a qualified external examiner that they consistently follow their documented processes. Becoming certified is not a trivial endeavour, often requiring many months to achieve. Once certified, companies are listed in a directory and can advertise themselves as certified according to a particular standard. Recertification is required every three years.

BENEFITS OF ISO CERTIFICATION

Completing the ISO 9001:2008 certification process can take as long as 18 months and involve many hours of management and employee time. The cost of certification can exceed $1 million for large companies. Despite the expense and commitment involved in ISO certification and other quality awards, they bestow significant external and internal benefits. The external benefits come from the potential sales advantage that companies in compliance have. Companies looking for a supplier will likely select a company that has demonstrated compliance with ISO documentation standards, all other factors being equal. Registered companies report an average of a 48 percent increased profitability and a 76 percent improvement in marketing. Consequently, more and more firms are seeking certification to gain a competitive advantage. Over one million companies worldwide are certified (www.iso.ch).

Internal benefits relate directly to the firm's TQM program. Certification requires a company to analyze and document its procedures, which is necessary for implementing continuous improvement, employee involvement, and similar programs. The internal benefits can be significant. The British Standards Institute, a leading third-party auditor, estimates that most ISO 9001–registered companies experience a 10 percent reduction in the cost of producing a product because of quality improvements made while striving to meet ISO requirements.

QUALITY AND SUSTAINABILITY

Quality is a strategic business issue that must deliver customer value. However, quality rarely stands in isolation. Instead, it is intimately linked to other key areas, including environmental and social aspects of operations. Moreover, in many ways, sustainability performance is analogous to and can borrow from quality management. Senior management must drive environmental and social management systems, employees need ongoing development, and processes must be improved systematically. However, the outcomes are somewhat different, including such environmental aspects as pollutant emissions, raw material consumption, energy intensity, and use of hazardous materials. Social aspects include worker protection, employee well-being, and customer safety. Each of these can be improved by adapting and expanding strong quality management systems.

Three standards are discussed below that are being adopted by many leading firms. The first, ISO 14000, focused on environmental management systems, and closely parallels ISO 9000. The second, SA8000, emphasizes social accountability and worker well-being, both in the firm and in its supply chain. Firms can be certified against both of these two standards using external auditors. The final standard, ISO 26000, which was recently introduced, is a guideline for social responsibility, and captures both environmental and social considerations under an integrated approach.

ISO 14000:2004—ENVIRONMENTAL MANAGEMENT SYSTEMS

ISO 14000:2004 A family of standards governing environmental management of products and processes, including material use, recycling, and disposal of waste.

The **ISO 14000:2004** family of standards addresses a broad range of issues related to the way a firm manages environmental issues. In particular, the focus is on what a firm does to minimize harmful effects on the environment caused by its activities, and to achieve continual improvement of their environmental performance. Like ISO 9001:2008, ISO 14001:2004 does not specify particular outputs or pollutant emission levels. Instead, this standard emphasizes that firms should minimize harmful effects on the environment caused by its activities, and requires companies to prepare a plan for ongoing improvement in their environmental performance. To maintain their certification, companies have to be regularly inspected by outside auditors.

Of the family of standards, several of the most important areas covered include:

- *Environmental management system (14001:2004).* Certifies that a management system is in place to monitor and improve environmental performance, including resource consumption, pollutant emissions, and waste generation.
- *Environmental labelling (14020 series).* Defines terms such as recyclable, energy-efficient, and safe for the ozone layer, as well as the principles and procedures for environmental claims.
- *Life-cycle assessment (14040 series).* Evaluation of the lifetime environmental impact from the manufacture, use, and disposal of a product.
- *Design for the environment (14062).* Incorporating environmental performance in product design and development.

Collectively, this family of standards is structured around the plan-do-check-act cycle of quality improvement discussed earlier (see Figure 6.2).

SA8000—SOCIAL ACCOUNTABILITY

Developed using a collaborative process with multiple parties, SA8000:2008 is currently the most widely recognized global standard for managing human rights in the workplace. It was the first auditable standard based on international workplace norms of International Labour Organization (ILO) conventions, the Universal Declaration of Human Rights, and the UN Convention on the Rights of the Child (www.sa-intl.org). The standard can be used by organizations of all sizes anywhere in the world, and provides a framework to communicate to customers and the community that social issues are being actively managed in a responsible manner. For example, an external examiner might audit a firm's farms or production facilities in developing countries to assess if workers are being treated fairly (www.bsigroup.com).

SA8000:2008 has multiple elements, three of which overlap to some degree with quality management systems:

- *Health and safety.* Provide a safe and healthy work environment; take steps to prevent injuries; regular health and safety worker training; system to detect threats to health and safety; access to bathrooms and potable water.
- *Working hours.* Comply with the applicable law but, in any event, no more than 48 hours per week with at least one day off for every seven-day period; voluntary overtime paid at a premium rate and not to exceed 12 hours per week on a regular basis; overtime may be mandatory if part of a collective bargaining agreement.
- *Management systems.* Facilities seeking to gain and maintain certification must go beyond simple compliance to integrate the standard into their management systems and practices.

In many ways, these elements are minimum conditions needed to foster employee teams and worker involvement in quality improvement processes.

ISO 26000:2010—SOCIAL RESPONSIBILITY

The International Standard ISO 26000:2010, a guidance document for social responsibility, tries to harmonize a firm's approaches to environmental and social issues. Under development for almost a decade, it should be stressed that this is not a management system standard, nor is it intended for certification purposes or regulatory or contractual use (www.iso.ch). Instead, the standard provides managers direction to translate principles into effective actions. ISO 26000 addresses seven core subjects of social responsibility, five of which are directly related to operations: human rights of workers, labour practices, fair operating practices, consumer issues (including service and product safety), and the environment. Given the relative newness of the standard, it is unclear how quickly or enthusiastically managers will move to adopt it, but it is something that can deeply affect many areas of operations.

EQUATION SUMMARY

1. The reliability of a product: $r_s = (r_1)(r_2)\ldots(r_i)\ldots(r_n)$

2. Control limits for variable process control charts:

    a. *R*-chart, range of sample:

    Upper control limit $= \text{UCL}_R = D_4\bar{R}$

    Lower control limit $= \text{LCL}_R = D_3\bar{R}$

    b. $\bar{x}$-chart, sample mean:

    Upper control limit $= \text{UCL}_{\bar{x}} = \bar{\bar{x}} + A_2\bar{R}$

    Lower control limit $= \text{LCL}_{\bar{x}} = \bar{\bar{x}} - A_2\bar{R}$

    c. When the standard deviation of the process distribution, σ, is known:

Upper control limit $= \text{UCL}_{\bar{x}} = \bar{\bar{x}} + z\sigma_{\bar{x}}$

Lower control limit $= \text{LCL}_{\bar{x}} = \bar{\bar{x}} - z\sigma_{\bar{x}}$

where: $\sigma_{\bar{x}} = \dfrac{\sigma}{\sqrt{n}}$

3. Control limits for attribute process control charts:

a. *p*-chart, proportion defective:

Upper control limit $= \text{UCL}_p = \bar{p} + z\sigma_p$

Lower control limit $= \text{LCL}_p = \bar{p} - z\sigma_p$

where: $\sigma_p = \sqrt{\bar{p}(1 - \bar{p})}/n$

b. *c*-chart, number of defects:

Upper control limit $= \text{UCL}_c = \bar{c} + z\sqrt{\bar{c}}$

Lower control limit $= \text{UCL}_c = \bar{c} - z\sqrt{\bar{c}}$

4. Process capability ratio:

$$C_p = \frac{\text{Upper specification} - \text{Lower specification}}{6\sigma}$$

5. Process capability index:

$$C_{pk} = \text{Minimum of} \left[\frac{\bar{\bar{x}} - \text{Lower specification}}{3\sigma}, \frac{\text{Upper specification} - \bar{\bar{x}}}{3\sigma} \right]$$

CHAPTER HIGHLIGHTS

- Total quality management stresses three principles: a customer-driven focus, employee involvement, and continuous improvements in quality.

- The customer may make a quantitative judgment about whether a product or service meets specified design and operating characteristics (conformance). In other situations, assessment of the performance, features, reliability, durability, product or service support, and psychological impressions, such as aesthetics, may take on greater importance. TQM requires firms to listen to customers and report their changing perceptions of quality.

- Responsibility for quality is shared by all employees in the organization. Employee involvement programs include leadership in changing organizational culture, individual development, awards and incentives, and teamwork.

- Continuous improvement involves identifying benchmarks of excellent practice and instilling a sense of ownership in employees so that they will continually identify product, service, and process improvements that should be made.

- Quality management is important because of the costs of poor quality. The four main categories of costs are prevention, appraisal, internal failure, and external failure. If quality is to be improved, prevention costs must increase. Appraisal, internal failure, and external failure costs all decline as quality is improved through preventive measures.

- Six sigma, which relies heavily on the principles of TQM, is a comprehensive and flexible system that focuses on minimizing defects and variability in processes. It is driven by a close understanding of customer needs; the disciplined use of facts, data, and statistical analysis; and diligent attention to managing, improving, and reinventing business processes.

- Benchmarking is a comparative measure. It is used to establish goals for continuous improvement. Forms of benchmarking include competitive, functional, and internal.

- Quality improvement requires close cooperation among functions (design, operations, marketing, purchasing, and others). Quality function deployment (QFD) encourages interfunctional planning and communication.

- Approaches to organizing and presenting quality improvement data include checklists, histograms and bar charts, Pareto charts, scatter diagrams, cause-and-effect diagrams, graphs, and control charts.

- A key to meeting design specifications in a product or service is to reduce output variability. When a process is in a state of statistical control, outputs subject to common causes of variation follow a stable probability distribution. When assignable causes of variation are present, the process is out of statistical control. Statistical process control (SPC) methods are used to detect the presence of assignable causes of variation.

- Statistical process control charts are useful for measuring the current quality generated by the process and for detecting whether the process has changed to the detriment of quality. Thus, *R*-charts are used to monitor process variability, $\bar{x}$- and *p*-charts identify abnormal variations in the process average, and *c*-charts are used for controlling the number of defects when a product or service process could result in multiple defects per unit of output. The presence of abnormal variation triggers a search for assignable causes.

- Process variability should be in control before process control charts are constructed. The reason is that the average range is used in the calculation of control limits for process average control charts. Crucial decisions in the design of control charts are sample size and control limits.

- The central line of a control chart is the average of past averages of the quality measurement. The spread in control limits affects the chances of detecting a shift in the process average or range, as well as the chances of searching for assignable causes when none exist.

- A process can be in statistical control but still not be capable of producing all of its output within design specifications. The process capability ratio and the process capability index are quantitative measures used to assess the capability of a process.

- ISO 9000 is a family of standards governing the development and documentation of quality processes.

Companies can be certified by external examiners for ISO 9001:2008. Similarly, ISO 14001:2004 requires companies seeking certification to develop management systems that track materials use, waste generation, pollutant emissions, and improvement in environmental performance. SA8000 is an international social accountability standard that focuses on labour practices with implications for process management and quality. Like ISO 14001, firms can be certified by external auditors. Finally, ISO 26000 is a guidance document to help firms responsibly integrate their management approaches toward environmental and social issues.

SOLVED PROBLEM 1

Vera Johnson and Merris Williams manufacture vanishing cream. The following are the operations and reliabilities of their packaging operation. The reliabilities are the probabilities that each operation will be performed to the desired specifications.

OPERATION	RELIABILITY
Mix	0.99
Fill	0.98
Cap	0.99
Label	0.97

Johnson and Williams ask their spouses to keep track of and analyze reported defects. They find the following:

DEFECT	FREQUENCY
Lumps of unmixed product	7
Over- or underfilled jars	18
Jar lids did not seal	6
Labels rumpled or missing	29
Total	60

a. What is the reliability of the packaging operation?
b. Draw a Pareto chart to identify the vital defects.

SOLUTION

a. The formula is:

$$r_s = (r_1)(r_2)\ldots(r_n)$$

Substituting $r_1 = 0.99$, $r_2 = 0.98$, ..., gives:

$$r_s = (0.99)(0.98)(0.99)(0.97)$$

$$= 0.9317, \text{ or about 93\% reliability}$$

b. Defective labels account for 48.33% of the total number of defects:

$$\frac{29}{60} \times 100\% = 48.33\%$$

Improperly filled jars account for 30% of the total number of defects:

$$\frac{18}{60} \times 100\% = 30.00\%$$

The cumulative percentage for the two most frequent defects is:

$$48.33\% + 30.00\% = 78.33\%$$

Lumps represent $\frac{7}{60} \times 100\% = 11.67\%$ of defects the cumulative percentage is:

$$78.33\% + 11.67\% = 90.00\%$$

Defective seals represent $\frac{6}{60} \times 100\% = 10\%$ of defects the cumulative percentage is:

$$10\% + 90\% = 100.00\%$$

The Pareto chart is shown in Figure 6.12.

FIGURE 6.12   *Pareto Chart*

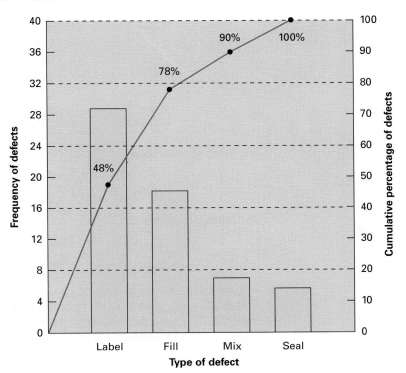

SOLVED PROBLEM 2

The Watson Electric Company produces incandescent light bulbs. The following data on the number of lumens for 40-watt light bulbs were collected when the process was in control.

SAMPLE	OBSERVATION			
	1	2	3	4
1	604	612	588	600
2	597	601	607	603
3	581	570	585	592
4	620	605	595	588
5	590	614	608	604

a. Calculate control limits for an R-chart and an $\bar{x}$-chart.

b. Since these data were collected, some new employees were hired. A new sample obtained the following readings: 570, 603, 623, and 583. Is the process still in control?

SOLUTION

a. To calculate $\bar{x}$, compute the mean for each sample. To calculate R, subtract the lowest value in the sample from the highest value in the sample. For example, for sample 1:

$$\bar{x} = \frac{604 + 612 + 588 + 600}{4} = 601$$

$$R = 612 - 588 = 24$$

SAMPLE	$\bar{x}$	R
1	601	24
2	602	10
3	582	22
4	602	32
5	604	24
Total	2991	112
Average	$\bar{\bar{x}} = 598.2$	$\bar{R} = 22.4$

The R-chart control limits are:

$$UCL_R = D_4\bar{R} = 2.282(22.4) = 51.12$$

$$LCL_R = D_3\bar{R} = 0(22.4) = 0$$

The $\bar{x}$-chart control limits are:

$$UCL_x = \bar{\bar{x}} + A_2\bar{R} = 598.2 + 0.729(22.4) = 614.53$$

$$LCL_x = \bar{\bar{x}} - A_2\bar{R} = 598.2 - 0.729(22.4) = 581.87$$

b. First check to see whether the variability is still in control on the basis of the new data. The range is 53 (or 623 − 570), which is outside the upper control limit for the R-chart. Even though the sample mean, 594.75, is within the control limits for the process average, process variability is not in control. A search for assignable causes must be conducted.

The data processing department of Confederation Bank has five data entry clerks. Each day their supervisor verifies the accuracy of a random sample of 250 records. A record containing one or more errors is considered defective and must be redone. The results of the last 30 samples are shown in the table. All were checked to make sure that none was out of control.

SAMPLE	NUMBER OF DEFECTIVE RECORDS	SAMPLE	NUMBER OF DEFECTIVE RECORDS	SAMPLE	NUMBER OF DEFECTIVE RECORDS
1	7	11	18	21	17
2	5	12	5	22	12
3	19	13	16	23	6
4	10	14	4	24	7
5	11	15	11	25	13
6	8	16	8	26	10
7	12	17	12	27	14
8	9	18	4	28	6
9	6	19	6	29	11
10	13	20	11	30	9
				Total	300

a. Based on these historical data, set up a p-chart using $z = 3$.

b. Samples for the next four days showed the following:

SAMPLE	NUMBER OF DEFECTIVE RECORDS
31	17
32	15
33	22
34	21

What is the supervisor's assessment of the data-entry process likely to be?

SOLUTION

a. From the table, the supervisor knows that the total number of defective records is 300 out of a total sample of 7500 (equal to 30 × 250). Therefore, the central line of the chart is:

$$\bar{p} = \frac{300}{7500} = 0.04$$

The control limits are:

$$UCL_p = \bar{p} + z\sqrt{\frac{\bar{p}(1 - \bar{p})}{n}} = 0.04 + 3\sqrt{\frac{0.04(0.96)}{250}} = 0.077$$

$$LCL_p = \bar{p} - z\sqrt{\frac{\bar{p}(1 - \bar{p})}{n}} = 0.04 - 3\sqrt{\frac{0.04(0.96)}{250}} = 0.003$$

b. Samples for the next four days showed the following:

SAMPLE	NUMBER OF DEFECTIVE RECORDS	PROPORTION
31	17	0.068
32	15	0.060
33	22	0.088
34	21	0.084

Samples 33 and 34 are out of control. The supervisor should look for the problem and, upon identifying it, take corrective action.

SOLVED PROBLEM 4

The Minnow County Highway Safety Department monitors accidents at the intersection of Routes 123 and 14. Accidents at the intersection have averaged three per month.

a. Which type of control chart should be used? Construct a control chart with three-sigma control limits.
b. Last month, seven accidents occurred at the intersection. Is this sufficient evidence to justify a claim that something has changed at the intersection?

SOLUTION

a. The safety department cannot determine the number of accidents that did *not* occur, so it has no way to compute a proportion defective at the intersection. Therefore, the administrators must use a *c*-chart for which:

$$UCL_c = \bar{c} + z\sqrt{\bar{c}} = 3 + 3\sqrt{3} = 8.20$$

$$LCL_c = \bar{c} - z\sqrt{\bar{c}} = 3 - 3\sqrt{3} = -2.196$$

There cannot be a negative number of accidents, so the lower control limit in this case is adjusted to zero.

b. The number of accidents last month falls within the upper and lower control limits of the chart. We conclude that no assignable causes are present and that the increase in accidents was due to chance.

SOLVED PROBLEM 5

Pioneer Chicken advertises "lite" chicken with 30 percent fewer calories. (The pieces are 33 percent smaller.) The process average distribution for "lite" chicken breasts is 420 calories, with a standard deviation of the population of 25 calories. Pioneer randomly takes samples of six chicken breasts to measure calorie content.

a. Design an $\bar{x}$-chart, using the process standard deviation.
b. The product design calls for the average chicken breast to contain 400 ± 100 calories. Calculate the process capability ratio (target = 1.33) and the process capability index. Interpret the results.

SOLUTION

a. For the process standard deviation of 25 calories, the standard deviation of the sample mean is:

$$\sigma_{\bar{x}} = \frac{\sigma}{\sqrt{n}} = \frac{25}{\sqrt{6}} = 10.2 \text{ calories}$$

$$\text{UCL}_{\bar{x}} = \bar{\bar{x}} + z\sigma_{\bar{x}} = 420 + 3(10.2) = 450.6 \text{ calories}$$
$$\text{LCL}_{\bar{x}} = \bar{\bar{x}} - z\sigma_{\bar{x}} = 420 - 3(10.2) = 389.4 \text{ calories}$$

b. The process capability ratio is:

$$C_p = \frac{\text{Upper specification} - \text{Lower specification}}{6\sigma} = \frac{500 \text{ calories} - 300 \text{ calories}}{6(25)} = 1.333$$

The process capability index is:

$$C_{pk} = \text{Minimum of} \left[\frac{\bar{\bar{x}} - \text{Lower specification}}{3\sigma}, \frac{\text{Upper specification} - \bar{\bar{x}}}{3\sigma} \right]$$

$$= \text{Minimum of} \left[\frac{420 - 300}{3(25)} = 1.60, \frac{500 - 420}{3(25)} = 1.07 \right] = 1.07$$

Because the process capability ratio is greater than 1.33, the process should be able to produce the product reliably with four-sigma quality. However, the process capability index is 1.07, so the current process is not centred properly for four-sigma quality. The mean of the process distribution is too close to the upper specification.

PROBLEMS

1. Contented Airlines (CA) is reluctant to begin service at the new Delayed Indefinitely Airport (DIA) until the automated baggage-handling system can transport luggage to the correct location with at least 99 percent reliability for any given flight. Lower reliability will result in damage to CA's reputation for quality service. The baggage system will not deliver to the right location if any of its subsystems fail. The subsystems and their reliability for satisfactory performance during operation for any given flight are shown in the following table.

SUBSYSTEM	RELIABILITY
Power supply	70.0% surge-free
Scanner reading	99.8% accurate
Computer software	98.2% glitch-free
Mechanical systems	97.5% jam-free
Operators	96.0% error-free

a. What is the reliability of the luggage system for any given flight?

b. When the passenger shuttle system operates, power surges trip the motors on the baggage system. Each of the luggage system motors must then be manually reset. Installing surge protectors increases power supply reliability to 99.9 percent. What is the reliability of the luggage system?

c. What could be done to improve the reliability of the luggage system?

2. Smith, Schroeder, and Torn (SST) is a short-haul household furniture moving company. SST's labour force is temporary and part-time. SST is concerned with recent complaints, as tabulated on the following tally sheet.

COMPLAINT	TALLY
Broken glass	### ### ///
Delivered to wrong address	### ////
Furniture rubbed together while on truck	### ### ### ###
Late delivery	###
Late arrival for pickup	### ### ### ///
Missing items	### ### ### ### ### /
Nicks and scratches from rough handling	### ###
Soiled upholstery	### ///

a. Draw a bar chart and a Pareto chart to identify the most serious moving problems.

b. Use a cause-and-effect diagram to identify potential causes of complaints.

3. Regina Fibreboard makes roof liners for the automotive industry. The manufacturing manager is concerned about product quality. She suspects that one particular defect, tears in the fabric, is related to production-run size. An assistant gathers the following data from production records.

RUN	SIZE	DEFECTS (%)	RUN	SIZE	DEFECTS (%)
1	1000	3.5	11	6500	1.5
2	4100	3.8	12	1000	5.5
3	2000	5.5	13	7000	1.0
4	6000	1.9	14	3000	4.5
5	6800	2.0	15	2200	4.2
6	3000	3.2	16	1800	6.0
7	2000	3.8	17	5400	2.0
8	1200	4.2	18	5800	2.0
9	5000	3.8	19	1000	6.2
10	3800	3.0	20	1500	7.0

a. Draw a scatter diagram for these data.

b. Does there appear to be a relationship between run size and percent defects? What implications does this have for Regina Fibreboard's business?

4. Grindwell, Inc., a manufacturer of grinding tools, is concerned about the durability of its products, which depends on the permeability of the sinter mixtures used in production. Suspecting that the carbon content might be the source of the problem, the plant manager collected the following data:

CARBON CONTENT (%)	PERMEABILITY INDEX
5.5	16
3.0	31
4.5	21
4.8	19
4.2	16
4.7	23
5.1	20
4.4	11
3.6	20

a. Draw a scatter diagram for these data.

b. Is there a relationship between permeability and carbon content?

c. If low permeability is desirable, what does the scatter diagram suggest with regard to the carbon content?

5. At Conner Company, a custom manufacturer of printed circuit boards, the finished boards are subjected to a final inspection prior to shipment to its customers. As Conner's quality assurance manager, you are responsible for making a presentation to management on quality problems at the beginning of each month. Your assistant has analyzed the reject memos for all the circuit boards that were rejected during the past month. He has given you a summary statement listing the reference number of the circuit board and the reason for rejection from one of the following categories:

> A = Poor electrolyte coverage
> B = Improper lamination
> C = Low copper plating
> D = Plating separation
> E = Improper etching

For 50 circuit boards that had been rejected last month, the summary statement showed the following:

C B C C D E C C B A D A C C C B C A C D C A C C B A C A C
B C C A C A A C C D A C C C E C C A B A C

a. Prepare a tally sheet (or checklist) of the different reasons for rejection.

b. Develop a Pareto chart to identify the more significant types of rejection.

c. Examine the causes of the most significant type of defect, using a cause-and-effect diagram.

6. The Marlin Company produces plastic bottles to customer order. The quality inspector randomly selects four bottles from the bottle machine and measures the outside diameter of the bottle neck, a critical quality dimension that determines whether the bottle cap will fit properly. The dimensions (in centimetres) from the last six samples are:

	BOTTLE			
SAMPLE	1	2	3	4
1	0.604	0.612	0.588	0.600
2	0.597	0.601	0.607	0.603
3	0.581	0.570	0.585	0.592
4	0.620	0.605	0.595	0.588
5	0.590	0.614	0.608	0.604
6	0.585	0.583	0.617	0.579

a. Assume that only these six samples are sufficient and use the data to determine control limits for an R- and an $\bar{x}$-chart.

b. Suppose that the specification for the bottle neck diameter is 0.600 ± 0.050 centimetres. If the population standard deviation is 0.012 centimetres, and if management has targeted three-sigma quality, is the process capable of producing the bottle?

7. A textile manufacturer wants to set up a control chart for irregularities (e.g., oil stains, shop soil, loose threads, and tears) per 10 square metres of carpet. The following data were collected from a sample of twenty 10-square-metre pieces of carpet.

SAMPLE	IRREGULARITIES	SAMPLE	IRREGULARITIES
1	11	11	11
2	8	12	5
3	9	13	7
4	12	14	12
5	4	15	13
6	16	16	8
7	5	17	19
8	8	18	11
9	17	19	9
10	10	20	10

a. Using these data, set up a c-chart with $z = 3$.

b. Suppose that the next five samples had 15, 18, 12, 22, and 21 irregularities. What do you conclude?

8. The production manager at Sunny Soda, Inc., is interested in tracking the quality of the company's 300 millilitre bottle filling line. The bottles must be filled within the tolerances set for this product, because the dietary information on the label shows 300 millilitres as the serving size. The design standard for the product calls for a fill level of 300.00 ± 2.5 millilitres. The manager collected the following sample data (millilitres per bottle) on the production process:

SAMPLE	OBSERVATION 1	OBSERVATION 2	OBSERVATION 3	OBSERVATION 4
1	300.00	299.25	302.50	302.00
2	297.75	298.50	302.50	299.00
3	297.25	300.50	299.25	299.75
4	302.50	302.25	301.25	298.75
5	302.00	298.00	303.00	301.25
6	298.50	299.50	301.50	302.00
7	302.25	300.00	300.00	300.75
8	300.25	301.00	299.75	298.75
9	300.00	299.00	299.25	300.75
10	298.00	298.50	302.25	300.00
11	297.75	299.75	301.25	302.50
12	300.25	300.00	301.50	299.25
13	299.50	299.75	301.50	300.75
14	300.50	300.00	301.25	298.75
15	300.00	301.25	300.25	299.25

make chart

a. Are the process average and range in statistical control?

b. If management wants three-sigma quality, is the process capable of meeting the design standard? Explain.

9. Management at Webster Chemical Company is concerned about whether caulking tubes are being properly capped. If a significant proportion of the tubes are not being sealed, Webster is placing its customers in a messy situation. Tubes are packaged in large boxes of 144. Several boxes are inspected, and the following numbers of leaking tubes are found:

SAMPLE	TUBES	SAMPLE	TUBES	SAMPLE	TUBES
1	3	8	6	15	5
2	5	9	4	16	0
3	3	10	9	17	2
4	4	11	2	18	6
5	2	12	6	19	2
6	4	13	5	20	1
7	2	14	1	Total	72

Calculate p-chart three-sigma control limits to assess whether the capping process is in statistical control.

10. Janice Sanders, CEO of Pine Crest Medical Clinic, is concerned over the number of times patients have to wait more than 30 minutes beyond their scheduled appointments. She asked her assistant to take random samples of 64 patients to see how many in each sample had to wait more than 30 minutes. Each instance is considered a defect in the clinic process. The table below contains the data for 15 samples of patients.

SAMPLE	NUMBER OF DEFECTS
1	5
2	2
3	1
4	3
5	1
6	5
7	2
8	3
9	6
10	3
11	9
12	9
13	5
14	2
15	3

If LCL is a negative just use 0

a. Assuming Janice Sanders is willing to use three-sigma control limits, construct a p-chart.

b. Based on your p-chart and the data in the table, what can you conclude about the waiting time of the patients?

11. The Farley Manufacturing Company prides itself on the quality of its products. The company is engaged in competition for a very important project. A key element is a part that ultimately goes into precision testing equipment. The specifications are 8.0 ± 3.0 millimetres. Management is

concerned about the capability of the process to produce that part. The following data were randomly
collected during test runs of the process:

	OBSERVATION (MILLIMETRES)							
SAMPLE	1	2	3	4	5	6	7	8
1	9.1	8.9	8.8	9.2	8.1	6.9	9.3	9.1
2	7.6	8.0	9.0	10.1	7.9	9.0	8.0	8.8
3	8.2	9.1	8.2	8.7	9.0	7.0	8.8	10.8
4	8.2	8.3	7.9	7.5	8.9	7.8	10.1	7.7
5	10.0	8.1	8.9	9.0	9.3	9.0	8.7	10.0

Assume that the process is in statistical control. Is the
process capable of producing the part at the three-sigma
level? Explain.

12. A critical dimension of the service quality of a call centre is
the wait time of a caller to reach a sales representative.
Periodically, random samples of three customer calls are
measured for time. The results of the last four samples are
in the following table:

SAMPLE	TIME (SEC)		
1	495	501	498
2	512	508	504
3	505	497	501
4	496	503	492

a. Assuming that management is willing to use three-
sigma control limits, and using only the historical information contained in the four samples, show that the call
centre access time is in statistical control.

b. Suppose that the standard deviation of the process distribution is 5.77. If the specifications for the access time
are 500 ± 18 seconds, is the process capable? Why or
why not? Assume three-sigma quality.

13. An automatic lathe produces rollers for roller bearings, and
the process is monitored by statistical process control
charts. The central line of the chart for the sample means is
set at 8.50 and for the mean range at 0.31 millimetres. The
process is in control, as established by samples of 5 rollers.
The upper and lower specifications for the diameter of the

rollers are $(8.50 + 0.25)$ and $(8.50 - 0.25)$ millimetres,
respectively.

a. Calculate the control limits for the mean and range charts.

b. If the standard deviation of the process distribution is
estimated to be 0.13 mm, is the process capable of
meeting specifications? Assume four-sigma quality.

c. If the process is not capable, what percent of the output
will fall outside the specification limits? (Hint: Use the
normal distribution available in Excel.)

14. The manager of the customer service department of Omega
Credit Card Service Company is concerned about the
number of defects produced by the billing process. Every
day a random sample of 250 statements was inspected for
errors regarding incorrect entries involving account numbers, transactions on the customer's account, interest
charges, and penalty charges. Any statement with one or
more of these errors was considered a defect. The study
lasted 30 days and yielded the data summarized below.
Based on this data, what can you tell the manager about
the performance of the billing process? Do you see any
non-random behaviour in the billing process? If so, what
might cause this behaviour?

SAMPLES	NUMBER OF ERRORS IN SAMPLE OF 250									
1–10	4	9	6	12	8	2	13	10	1	9
11–20	4	6	8	10	12	4	3	10	14	5
21–30	13	11	7	3	2	8	11	6	9	5

15. Red Baron Airlines serves hundreds of cities every day, but
competition is increasing from smaller companies affiliated
with major carriers. One of the key competitive priorities is
on-time arrivals and departures. Red Baron defines *on time*
as any arrival or departure that takes place within 15 minutes
of the scheduled time. To stay on top of the market, management has set the high standard of 98 percent on-time
performance. The operations department was put in charge
of monitoring the performance of the airline. Each week, a
random sample of 300 flight arrivals and departures was
checked for schedule performance. Table 6.4 contains the
numbers of arrivals and departures over the last 30 weeks
that did not meet Red Baron's definition of on-time service.
What can you tell management about the quality of service?
Can you identify any non-random behaviour in the process? If
so, what might cause the behaviour?

TABLE 6.4	*Sample Data for Red Baron Airlines*									
SAMPLES	NUMBER OF LATE PLANES IN SAMPLE OF 300 ARRIVALS AND DEPARTURES									
1–10	3	8	5	11	7	2	12	9	1	8
11–20	3	5	7	9	12	5	4	9	13	4
21–30	12	10	6	2	1	8	4	5	8	2

NOTES FOR CHAPTER

1. L. LaSalle, "Carriers Eye Prime Airwaves; Major Players Are Expecting the Best Frequencies to Be Auctioned Off by Ottawa Next Year," *Kitchener-Waterloo Record,* March 9, 2011; L. LaSalle, "Dropped Calls the Latest Tactic in Wireless Fight Between New and Old Players," *The Canadian Press,* October 2, 2010; Ian Mansfield, "Bell Mobility Wins 4 of 5 Advertising Claims in Court," *cellular-news,* December 17, 2009, www.cellular-news.com/story/41137.php, accessed July 26, 2011; "Judge Rules Bell Can't Yet Claim New Network Is 'Most Reliable' in Canada—Because It's Too New," *ENP Newswire,* December 18, 2009; A. Sharma, "Testing, Testing," *Wall Street Journal,* October 23, 2007; J. Hefler, "Verizon Tester Checks Vineyard Networks," *The Martha's Vineyard Times,* August 30, 2007; Jon Gales, "Ride Along with a Verizon Wireless Test Man," *Mobile Tracker,* April 4, 2005; investor.verizon.com, 2007.

2. Adapted from W. E. Deming, "Transformation of Today's Management," *Executive Excellence,* vol. 4, no. 12 (1987), p. 8.

3. Adapted from J. S. Oakland, *Total Quality Management* (London, UK: Heinemann Professional Publishing Ltd., 1989), pp. 292–293; M. M. Davis, N. J. Aquilano, and R.B. Chase, *Fundamentals of Operations Management,* 4th ed. (Burr Ridge, IL: McGraw-Hill Irwin, 2003), p. 216.

4. A. Serwer, "Happy Birthday, Steinway," *Fortune,* vol. 147, no. 5 (March 17, 2003), pp. 94-97; Leo O'Connor, "Engineering on a Grand Scale," *Mechanical Engineering,* vol. 116, no. 10 (October 1994), pp. 52–58; Steinway Musical Instruments, Inc., annual report (2006), www.steinwaymusical.com; www.steinway.com/factory/tour.shtml, accessed 2007.

5. Source: American Society for Testing Materials, *Manual on Quality Control of Materials.*

6. See: www.iso.ch; West, John E. "Implementing ISO 9001:2000." *Quality Progress,* vol. 34 (2001), no. 5, pp. 65–68.

FURTHER READING

Besterfield, D. *Quality Control,* 6th ed. Upper Saddle River, NJ: Prentice Hall, 2001.

Brady, D. "Will Jeff Immelt's New Push Pay Off for GE?" *Business Week,* October 13, 2003, pp. 94–98.

Brown, E. "The Best Business Hotels." *Fortune,* March 17, 1997, pp. 204–205.

Collier, D. A. *The Service Quality Solution.* New York: Irwin Professional Publishing; Milwaukee: ASQC Quality Press, 1994.

Crosby, P. B. *Quality Is Free: The Art of Making Quality Certain.* New York: McGraw-Hill, 1979.

Deming, W.E. *Out of the Crisis.* Cambridge, MA: Massachusetts Institute of Technology Center for Advanced Engineering Study, 1986.

Denton, D. K. "Lessons on Competitiveness: Motorola's Approach." *Production and Inventory Management Journal,* Third Quarter 1991, pp. 22–25.

Duncan, A. J. *Quality Control and Industrial Statistics,* 5th ed. Homewood, IL: Irwin, 1986.

Feigenbaum, A. V. *Total Quality Control: Engineering and Management,* 3rd ed. New York: McGraw-Hill, 1983.

Garvin, D. A. "Competing on the Eight Dimensions of Quality." *Harvard Business Review,* vol. 65, no. 6 (1987), pp. 101–109.

Hauser, J. R., and D. Clausing. "The House of Quality." *Harvard Business Review,* May/June 1988, pp. 63–73.

Juran, J. M., and A. B. Godfrey. Juran's *Quality Handbook,* 5th ed. New York: McGraw-Hill, 1999.

Kalinosky, I. S. "The Total Quality System—Going Beyond ISO 9000." *Quality Progress,* June 1990, pp. 50–53.

Kerwin, K. "When Flawless Isn't Enough." *Business Week,* December 8, 2003, pp. 80–82.

Lazarus, I. R., and K. Butler. "The Promise of Six Sigma." *Managed Healthcare Executive,* October 2001, pp. 22–26.

Logothetis, N. *Managing for Total Quality: From Deming to Taguchi and SPC.* New York: Prentice Hall, 1992.

Lucier, G. T., and S. Seshadri. "GE Takes Six Sigma Beyond the Bottom Line." *Strategic Finance,* May 2001, pp. 41–46.

Miller, W. "ISO 9000 and the Small Company: Can I Afford It?" *APICS—The Performance Advantage,* September 1994, pp. 45–46.

Mitra, A. *Fundamentals of Quality Control and Improvement,* 2nd ed. Upper Saddle River, NJ: Prentice Hall, 1998.

Pande, P. S., R. P. Neuman, and Roland R. Cavanagh. *The Six Sigma Way.* New York: McGraw-Hill, 2000.

Parasuraman, A., V. A. Zeithaml, and L. L. Berry. *SERVQUAL: A Multiple Item Scale for Measuring Perceptions of Service Quality.* Cambridge, MA: Marketing Science Institute, 1986.

Rust, R. T., T. Keiningham, S. Clemens, and A. Zahorik. "Return on Quality at Chase Manhattan Bank." *Interfaces,* vol. 29, no. 2 (March/April 1999), pp. 62–72.

Schwarz, A. "Listening to the Voice of the Customer Is the Key to QVC's Success." *Journal of Organizational Excellence,* Winter 2004, pp. 3–11.

Sester, D. "Motorola: A Tradition of Quality." *Quality,* October 2001, pp. 30–34.

Sullivan, L. P. "The Power of Taguchi Methods." *Quality Progress,* vol. 20, no. 6 (1987), pp. 76–79.

Wheeler, D. J. *Advanced Topics in Statistical Process Control.* Knoxville, TN: SPC Press, Inc., 1995.

MyOMLab ASSETS

MyOMLab offers the following resources, which allow you to further practise and apply concepts presented in this chapter.

- **Key Equations:** All the equations for this chapter can be found in one convenient location.

- **Discussion Questions.** Six questions will challenge your understanding of the importance of quality for competitive operations.

- **Cases:**

  - *Cranston Nissan.* Analyze the many instances of service quality breakdown that one of the authors of this text experienced.

  - *José's Authentic Mexican Restaurant.* How can quality be improved at this restaurant?

- **Video Case:** *Process Performance and Quality at Starwood Hotels & Resorts.* Implementing TQM and six sigma take considerable time and commitment. Which aspects were critical in the redesign of the Sheraton Service Promise program? How might the new process help to avoid the four costs of poor quality?

- **Virtual Tours:**

  - *Steinway Pianos and Verne Q. Powell Flutes.* Identify the relevant measures of quality in each setting. How is the process designed so that a high-quality product will result?

  - *Beach Beat Surfboards.* Which of the dimensions of quality does Beach Beat emphasize? How does Beach Beat ensure that quality is built into their entire process?

- **Experiential Exercise:** *Statistical Process Control with a Coin Catapult.* Experience the gathering of data and the development of control charts for variable or attribute measures in this entertaining in-class exercise.

- **Internet Exercises:**

  - *International Organization for Standardization.* To learn more background, select "The ISO System" under the heading "About ISO." Then compare ISO standards by selecting "What's different about ISO 9001 and ISO 14001?" from the right-side menu.

  - *SAS Scandinavian Airlines.* The firm's Web site offers a glimpse of its focus on customer service. As a customer, what characteristics of this Web site strike you as being "high-quality"? What might be improved?

  - *Maybach.* As a producer of luxury automobiles, quality is critical. Review the sections on Service, Studios, and Model Range. What key phrases does each page contain that give the consumer an idea of the quality and performance of a Maybach? Which of these attributes does Maybach make the best (and worst) case for? Why?

- **OM Explorer Tutors:** Five tutor programs to enhance your understanding of Pareto charts, $\bar{x}$-charts, p-charts, c-charts, and process capability.

- **Extend LT:** *Service Quality at Best Burger.* Service quality of the drive-through-window operations have to be improved.

- **Supplement F:** *Acceptance Sampling Plans.* Use this supplement to learn how to design single-sampling plans and estimate the average outgoing quality of your plan.

Lean Systems

Learning Goals

After reading this chapter, you will be able to:

1. identify strategic advantages and process characteristics of lean systems.
2. describe how lean systems can facilitate the continuous improvement of processes.
3. understand kanban systems for creating a production schedule in a lean system.
4. use value stream mapping to identify and reduce waste.
5. explain the challenges that arise during the implementation of lean systems.

Across the Organization

Lean systems are important to:

- **marketing**, which relies on lean systems to deliver high-quality products or services on time, at reasonable prices.
- **human resources**, which must recruit, train, and evaluate the employees needed to successfully operate a lean system.
- **engineering**, which must design products that use more common parts so that fewer setups are required and focused factories and group technology can be used.
- **operations**, which is responsible for using the lean system in the production of goods or services.
- **accounting**, which must often adjust its billing and cost accounting practices to take advantage of lean systems.

Sharp Corporation, with revenues of more than $30 billion and approximately 47 000 employees in 2009, is implementing what can be viewed as a ground-breaking step in lean systems. Its newest manufacturing complex in Sakai City, Japan, recently opened with much fanfare and international attention. With capital costs of $11 billion and covering 127 hectares, it is easily Sharp's largest investment in high-tech manufacturing. The largest plant in the complex has a capacity of 72 000 glass panels annually, which are used to produce very large, cutting-edge liquid crystal display (LCD) screens and signage. A second plant employing similar technologies produces thin-film solar energy cells.

Aerial view of Sakai manufacturing complex. The LCD plant is the large facility in the centre.

When consumer spending dropped during the recent recession, many manufacturers, such as Sharp, did not cut costs and curb production quickly enough. Excess inventory quickly piled up and, not surprisingly, contributed to financial losses. For Sharp, this painful lesson reinforced the message that operations must reduce waste, work more closely with suppliers, and improve efficiency—in essence become ever leaner.

Important operational changes combined with the enormous size of this new plant offered three major advantages. First, the new "10th generation" panels are the largest ever produced in a standard process, reducing material waste and improving process efficiency. Measuring 2.88 by 3.13 metres, each panel can be cut to yield up to six 60-inch or eighteen 40-inch (1 inch = 2.54 centimetres) LCD screens, more than double the number at Sharp's next-largest plant. In addition, the plant employs high levels of automation, for example to move the very large sheets of glass, no thicker than a credit card, into finishing ovens.

Larger robots move bundles of 50 sheets, and high-tech equipment precisely monitors process operations to ensure quality.

Second, driven by the need to improve responsiveness, Sharp required key suppliers to have their operations within the manufacturing complex, effectively creating a "hyper-just-in-time" delivery system. In total, 19 suppliers and service providers agreed to pay for and locate their facilities on-site.

For example, glass is made by Corning's plant and transported to Sharp's operations on a conveyer. Across the street, two other suppliers produce colour filters for the LCD panels. In total, roughly half of the expected 5000 workers will be located in suppliers. Sharp has invested significant effort to link its chain and procurement systems with those of suppliers. As a result, kanban signals are delivered in real time as production proceeds around the clock. Sharp expects that its operations and those of suppliers will work as "one virtual company."

Finally, leaner operations can be greener too. The 3 million litres of water used daily to wash the glass is recycled. All indoor and outdoor lighting rely on LEDs (roughly 100 000 in total) to reduce energy consumption. Solar panels on the factory roofs provide nine MW of power, and a central energy control centre collectively manages the energy needs throughout the complex.

Overall, estimated savings from these leaner operations are substantial, as much as 10 percent less than traditional plants. And in this highly competitive market, continuously improving process is the key to maintaining long-term competitiveness. As noted by a senior manager at one supplier, "There's nothing like it anywhere."[1]

lean systems Operations systems that maximize the value added by each of a firm's activities by paring unnecessary activities and delays.

Sharp Corporation is an excellent example of a company that has adopted an approach for designing value chains known as **lean systems**—operations systems that maximize the value added by each of a company's activities by paring unnecessary resources and delays. Lean systems represent a common thread through a company's operations strategy, supply chain, process design, quality management, inventory management, and resource planning to tie together efficient processes.

Lean systems can be leveraged by both service and manufacturing firms. For example, a service business might take an order from a customer, complete a process, and then collect revenue. This firm purchases items or other services, receives and pays for them, and hires and pays employees. Each of these activities often requires many people and other supporting resources, and unfortunately usually includes many inefficiencies. While customer involvement might vary considerably between different processes—from very high in some services such as hospitals to very low in manufacturing commodities—lean systems always emphasize reducing non-value-added time, whether by employees or for customers.

We begin this chapter by considering the overarching philosophy behind and benefits expected from using lean systems. Next, we explore how lean systems are developed within the broader supply chain, followed by a more detailed consideration at the process level. Last, we consider several challenges that companies face when implementing leaner systems.

PHILOSOPHY OF CONTINUOUS IMPROVEMENT

To take advantage of lean systems, managers have to clearly define the value of their products or services, as perceived by their customers. Every product or service category has to be carefully scrutinized for excessive complexity or unnecessary features and options. The goal is to continuously improve the design and delivery of products or services, so that a customer's needs can be precisely met without waste. To do so, a company must identify the sequence of activities and the processes involved that are essential to the creation of the product or service. Activities that are value-added (those tasks that transform the product or service in some measurable way) should be clearly differentiated from those that are non-value-added, in which wasted effort might be eliminated without impact on the customer.

ELIMINATING ALL FORMS OF WASTE

just-in-time (JIT) The concept that customer demand can be met as needed by eliminating all forms of waste and non-value-added activities, and by continuously improving the effectiveness of value-added activities.

Just-in-time (JIT) is one of the most powerful concepts to have reshaped supply chains and process management. JIT aims to precisely meet customer demand, only when needed, as economically as possible. Its core ideas appear deceptively simple, one of which is the elimination of waste by cutting excess capacity or inventory. Table 7.1 shows the eight types of waste that often occur in firms in an interrelated fashion, and which must be eliminated in implementing lean systems. Constant attention must be given to continuously improve the value-added benefits of operations and removing non-value-added activities in processes. This requires a very responsive process, with short order lead times, rapid processing times, and almost no setup times.

By spotlighting areas that need improvement, JIT fosters continuous improvement in quality and productivity. The Japanese term for this approach to process improvement is *kaizen*. The key to *kaizen* is the understanding that excess capacity or inventory hides underlying problems with the processes that produce a service or product. Lean systems provide the mechanism for management to reveal the problems by systematically lowering capacities or inventories until the problems are exposed.

TABLE 7.1	*The Eight Types of Waste (or Muda)*[2]
Waste	**Definition**
1. Overproduction	Manufacturing an item before it is needed, making it difficult to detect defects and creating excessive lead times and inventory.
2. Inappropriate processing	Using expensive, high-precision equipment when simpler machines would suffice. It leads to overutilization of expensive capital assets. Investment in smaller flexible equipment, immaculately maintaining older machines, and combining process steps where appropriate reduce the waste associated with inappropriate processing.
3. Waiting	Wasteful time incurred when product is not being moved or processed. Long production runs, poor material flows, and processes not tightly linked to one another can cause over 90% of a product's lead time to be spent waiting.
4. Transportation	Excessive movement and material handling of product between processes, which can cause damage and deterioration of product quality without adding any significant customer value.
5. Motion	Unnecessary effort related to the ergonomics of bending, stretching, reaching, lifting, and walking. Jobs with excessive motion should be redesigned.
6. Inventory	Excess inventory hides problems on the shop floor, consumes space, increases lead times, and inhibits communication. Work-in-process inventory is a direct result of overproduction, and contributes to waiting.
7. Defects	Quality defects result in rework and scrap, and add wasteful costs to the system in the form of lost capacity, rescheduling effort, increased inspection, and loss of customer goodwill.
8. Underutilization of employees	Failure of the firm to learn from and capitalize on its employees' knowledge and creativity impedes long-term efforts to eliminate waste.

A basic principle underlying continuous improvement with lean systems is illustrated in Figure 7.1. The water surface represents service system capacity, such as staff levels, or queues of customers in services. In manufacturing, the surface may also represent product and component inventory levels. The rocks represent problems encountered in the provision of services or products. When the surface is high enough, the boat passes over the rocks because the high level of capacity or inventory covers up problems. As capacity or inventory shrinks, rocks are exposed. Ultimately, the boat will hit a rock if the surface falls far enough. Through lean systems, workers, managers, engineers, and analysts apply process analysis and quality management tools to demolish the exposed rock. The coordination required for a just-in-time response to customer orders and just-in-time materials flows identifies problems in time for corrective action to be taken.

Periodically stressing the system to identify problems is one approach to identifying weaknesses, a critical first step in continuous improvement. Managers can put stress on the system by setting new short-term performance targets or temporarily reducing the number of employees working until problems become apparent. Alternatively, inventories can be reduced almost to zero. Many firms use this trial-and-error process to develop more efficient manufacturing operations. The problems are exposed, recorded, and later assigned to employees as improvement projects.

Of course, a means for quick recovery is needed, after which problems can be diagnosed and ways for overcoming them explored. After improvements are made,

FIGURE 7.1   *Continuous Improvement with Lean Systems*

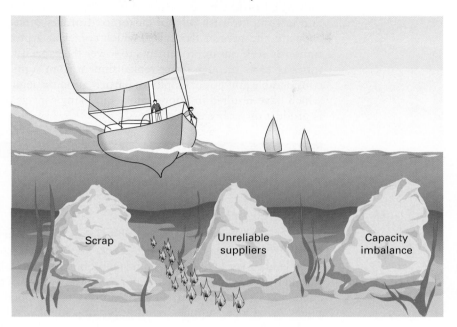

staff levels and inventories are permanently cut to the new level. Other *kaizen* tactics can be used as well. Eliminating the problem of poor quality, scrap materials, and customer complaints might require improving the firm's work processes, providing employees with additional training, or finding higher-quality suppliers. Eliminating capacity imbalances might involve improving the flexibility of the firm's workforce.

STRATEGIC IMPLICATIONS OF LEAN SYSTEMS

When corporate strategy hinges on dramatic improvements in customer service, labour productivity, asset utilization, and inventory turnover, a lean philosophy can be the solution. For example, lean systems form an integral part of an operations strategy that emphasizes time-based competition. Also, low cost and consistent quality are usually emphasized in lean systems.

Lean systems are linked with many operational benefits. A primary benefit is simplicity, as individual operations in the process are coordinated through the use of fewer resources, and straightforward visual signals, such as kanbans, described later. As a company implements and refines leaner systems, processes have:

- Shorter lead times
- Greater productivity of employees, managers, and support staff
- Greater equipment utilization
- Lower inventory investment in purchased parts, raw materials, work-in-process, and finished goods
- Lower space requirements
- Less paperwork, often requiring only simple planning systems
- Clearer priorities for scheduling
- Greater participation by the workforce
- Greater product or service quality

To be fair, firms that provide emergency services, superior features, and customized individual orders have greater difficulty adopting lean systems. The erratic demand and last-minute rush jobs of customized orders forces these processes to have excess capacity and greater flexibility, which comes at a price. But even here, firms can continuously seek out improvements to lower the capacity cushions or "just in case" inventories of parts through faster replenishment from suppliers. Lean systems also involve a considerable amount of employee participation through small-group interaction sessions, which have resulted in improvements in many aspects of operations, not least of which is product or service quality.

SUPPLY CHAIN CONSIDERATIONS

For firms along the supply chain, two aspects of lean systems are particularly important to manage: close supplier ties and small batches.

CLOSE SUPPLIER TIES

Because lean systems operate with low levels of inventory or excess capacity, close relationships with suppliers are necessary. Supplies have to be shipped frequently, have short lead times, arrive on schedule, and be of high quality. A contract might require a supplier to deliver goods to a factory as often as several times per day. Purchasing managers focus on three areas to tighten ties with suppliers: reducing the number of suppliers, using local suppliers, and improving supplier relations.

Typically, one of the first actions undertaken when a lean system is implemented is to pare the number of suppliers. As Xerox implemented lean systems, for example, managers reduced the number of suppliers from 5000 to just 300. This change put a lot of pressure on these suppliers to deliver high-quality components on time. To compensate, contracts with these suppliers are extended to give them fixed advance-order information. In addition, Xerox include their suppliers in the early phases of product design to avoid problems after production has begun. They also work with firms that provide materials to their suppliers to achieve timely inventory flows throughout the entire supply chain.

Manufacturers using lean systems generally utilize local suppliers. For instance, when Toyota located its plant near Cambridge, Ontario, the firm encouraged many suppliers to cluster nearby. Then, supply chain managers worked to coordinate the collection and delivery of parts from multiple suppliers on the same truck. Also, geographic proximity means that the company can reduce the need for safety stock.

Users of lean systems also find that a cooperative orientation with suppliers is essential. Better communication of component requirements, for example, enables more efficient inventory planning and delivery scheduling by suppliers, thereby improving supplier profit margins. And customers can obtain lower prices for components. Suppliers also should be included in the design of new products to develop components that are less expensive to process and ship. To encourage this to happen, suppliers must be viewed as partners, and all parties must have an interest in maintaining a long-term, profitable relationship.

SMALL BATCHES

batch or lot A quantity of identical items processed together.

Rather than build up a cushion of inventory between firms, queue of orders, or waiting line that groups customers together, lean systems use batch sizes or orders that are as small as possible. A **batch** or lot is a quantity of items processed together. Small batch sizes reduce process variability and overall inventory levels by four mechanisms.

First, small batch sizes reduce cycle inventory because products are being ordered more frequently, or customers are being moved with less waiting (see Chapter 5, "Inventory Management"). The average cycle inventory equals one-half the batch size:

as the batch size gets smaller, so does cycle inventory. Reducing cycle inventory reduces the time, space, and costs involved in manufacturing and holding inventory. For example, if an airline uses smaller aircraft on a route, with more frequent departures, a "batch" of passengers will take less time to board, and less luggage is loaded for each trip. As a result, the queue of passengers tends to be shorter and the inventory of luggage is smaller. (Of course, more aircraft might be required to make more frequent trips, but total costs can still be lower, as is demonstrated by WestJet.)

Finally, small batches help achieve uniform operating workloads across the systems. Large batches consume large chunks of processing time on particular workstations and, therefore, complicate scheduling. Small batches can be juggled more effectively, enabling schedulers to utilize capacities more efficiently. In addition, small batches allow workstations to accommodate mixed-model production (more than one item) by reducing waiting-line times for production. We return to this point later when we discuss uniform workstation loads.

Although small batches are beneficial to operations, they have the disadvantage of increased **setup** frequency. In some service and many manufacturing firms, some operations have sizable setup times; increasing the frequency of setups might result in wasting employee and equipment time. For example, the takeoff and landing of aircraft, as well as refuelling, are setup times that must occur with any flight, and take virtually the same time, regardless of the batch size of passengers.

However, managers cannot view setup times as fixed; instead, improvements have to be developed to reduce setup times to achieve the benefits of small-batch operations. Achieving low setup times often requires close cooperation among support services, engineering, management, and labour. For example, changing dies on large presses to form automobile parts from sheet metal can take three or four hours. At one of Honda's plants that produced the Accord, teams worked to identify and implement improvements to reduce the changeover time for these massive dies. As a result, a complete change of dies for a giant 2200-tonne press now takes less than eight minutes. The goal of **single-digit setup** means having setup times shorter than 10 minutes. Some techniques to reduce setup times include using conveyors to move parts (rather than forklifts), having support services standing by, simplifying setup procedures, using computers to automatically feed and position work, and preparing for changeovers while the current job is being processed.

setup The group of activities needed to change or readjust a process between different batches.

single-digit setup The goal of having a setup time shorter than 10 minutes.

PROCESS CHARACTERISTICS OF LEAN SYSTEMS

As noted earlier, leaner processes focus on reducing inefficiency and unproductive time in processes to continuously improve the quality and value of the products or services produced. Managing variability is a critical aspect, as depicted in the process management triangle (recall Figure 4.1). Several characteristics of lean systems reduce process variability: consistent quality at the source, uniform workstation loads, standardized components and work methods, Five S (5S) practices, and preventive maintenance. The reduction of variability makes the process more predictable for managers, reduces investment in equipment and inventories, and offers customers more dependable deliveries and services. In addition, several characteristics help accommodate variability from either external demands or internal operations: the pull method of materials flow, close supplier ties, and a flexible workforce.

PULL METHOD OF WORK FLOW

Lean systems utilize the pull method of work flow. In contrast, another popular method is the push method. To differentiate between these two systems, let's first consider the production system used by McDonald's Restaurants in Canada (and the rest of the world) for many decades. There were four basic operations for producing a hamburger: cooking, preparation, assembly, and packaging. For the cooking operation, a batch of hamburger patties was fried. For the preparation operation, the same-sized batch of buns was toasted on a tray and then dressed with condiments such as mustard, ketchup, pickles, and cheese. The assembly operation placed the cooked patties into prepared buns. Finally, the packaging operation took the tray, wrapped the burgers in paper, and restocked the inventory bins in front of customers. Efforts were made to minimize inventories, because any hamburgers left unsold after ten minutes had to be discarded.

push method A method in which the production of the item begins in advance of customer needs.

The flow of materials was from cooking and preparation to assembly to packaging to the customer. Historically, this flow has been managed using the **push method**, in which the production of the item begins in anticipation of customer needs. With this method, management schedules the receipt of all raw materials (e.g., meat patties, buns, and condiments) and authorizes the start of production, all before customers arrive to purchase hamburgers. The cooking starts production of a batch of hamburgers (often a dozen patties based on the size of the tray) and, when they are completed, pushes them along to assembly and then packaging, where they might have to wait until someone at packaging is ready for them. The packaged hamburgers then wait in a warming bin until a customer purchases one.

pull method A method in which customer demand activates production of the item.

The other way to manage the flow between cooking, preparation, assembly, packaging, and the customer is to use the **pull method**, in which customer demand activates production or assembly of the final product. Since 2000, McDonald's in Canada and the United States has implemented a system that more closely matches the pull method, called "Made for You." Now, as customers purchase hamburgers, the preparation operation is informed of each specific order, and begins toasting and dressing the bun with customer-specific condiments. After completion, the assembly operation removes a cooked patty from a warming oven, places it in the bun, and packages the final product for the customer.

As cooked patties are taken from the warming oven, the assembly operation checks the inventory level of patties. If the level falls below a target range, which varies by time of day, the assembly person calls or signals for the cooking operation to grill more patties. After grilling, the patties are placed in the warming oven. In general, the pull method is better for the production of hamburgers: operations can be visually coordinated to reduce inventories based on customer demand; hot and cold materials are kept

Fast-food workers using the pull system to serve their customers at a McDonald's store in Taipei, Taiwan. Using the older push method, the cooking, assembly, and packaging operations are behind the holding bin, which are available to the workers serving customers at the counter.

separate until just before purchase; and individual customer preferences are quickly accommodated. The production of hamburgers is a highly repetitive process, setup times and process times are low, and the flow of materials is well defined.

The choice between the push and pull methods is often situational. Service and manufacturing firms with highly repetitive processes, well-defined work flows, and standardized outputs (involving either customers or physical goods) often use the pull method because it allows better control. However, there are circumstances where a push system is better. As more of the following conditions are met, the attractiveness of a push system increases:

- Processes that involve long lead times
- Reasonably accurate forecasts of demand
- Variety of products created on common processes with long setup times
- Customers who will not wait long for the product

In many processes, the push and pull methods should be thoughtfully combined, for example, in the form of an assemble-to-order process. The push method is used to produce standardized components in high volumes, and the pull method to fulfill the customer's request for a particular combination of goods or services. So in the case of McDonald's, the push method is used to order food supplies in advance and cook some ingredients in anticipation of orders, such as grilled patties. However, the customer order, including one or more grilled products, is assembled only after it is received, based on a pull method. Thus, pull systems must be applied widely, not universally.

QUALITY AT THE SOURCE

Consistently meeting the customer's expectations is an important characteristic of lean systems. One way to achieve this goal is by adhering to a practice called *quality at the source*, which is an organization-wide effort to improve the quality of a firm's products by having employees act as their own quality inspectors. For workers, the goal is to pass along only high-quality units to the next process. For example, a soldering operation at the Texas Instruments antenna department had a defect rate that varied from zero to 50 percent on a daily basis, averaging about 20 percent. To compensate, production planners increased the batch sizes, which only increased inventory levels and did nothing to reduce the number of defective items. The company's engineers then discovered through experimentation that gas temperature was a critical variable in producing defect-free items. They subsequently devised statistical control charts for the firm's equipment operators to use to monitor the temperature and adjust it themselves. Process yields immediately improved and stabilized at 95 percent, and Texas Instruments was eventually able to implement a lean system.

poka-yoke Mistake-proofing methods aimed at designing fail-safe systems that minimize human and equipment error.

One approach for implementing quality at the source is to use **poka-yoke**, or mistake-proofing. This method aims to design fail-safe systems that attack and minimize human error. Consider, for instance, a company that makes modular products. The company could use the poka-yoke method by making different parts of the modular product in such a way that allows them to be assembled in only one way—the correct way. Similarly, a company's shipping boxes could be designed to be packed only in a particular way that minimizes damage and eliminates chances of missed components and other mistakes.

Another approach for implementing quality at the source is a practice the Japanese call *jidoka*, or making mistakes or problems evident. Workers and machines must have the means to quickly and accurately detect the occurrence of any abnormal condition. In response, employees are then authorized to signal for help and resolve the problem, termed *andon*, which may require stopping the production line. Of course, stopping a production line can cost a company thousands of dollars each minute production is halted. However, this additional attention pushes managers, quality experts, engineers, and workers to jointly identify opportunities to prevent defects, and to recover quickly when they occasionally occur. Management must realize the enormous responsibility this method puts on employees, must prepare them properly with training, and must implement systems that build high quality.

UNIFORM WORKSTATION LOADS

A lean system works best if the daily load on individual workstations is relatively uniform. One option for service processes to create more uniform workstation loads is the use of reservation systems. For example, hospitals schedule surgeries in advance of the actual service so that the facilities and facilitating goods can be ready when the time comes. The load on the surgery rooms and surgeons can be evened out to make the best use of these resources. Another approach is to use differential pricing of the service to manage the demand for it. This is one of the reasons that airlines promote weekend travel or red-eye flights, which begin late in the day and end in the early morning. Efficiencies can be realized when the load on the firm's resources can be managed.

For manufacturing processes, uniform loads can be achieved by assembling the same type and number of units each day, thus creating a uniform daily demand at all workstations. Capacity planning, which recognizes capacity constraints at critical workstations, and line balancing are used to develop the monthly master production schedule. For example, at Toyota, discussed in greater detail later in the chapter, the aggregate production plan may call for 4500 vehicles per week for the next month. That requires two full shifts, five days per week, producing 900 vehicles each day, or 450 per shift. Three models are produced: Camry (C), Avalon (A), and Sienna (S). Suppose that Toyota needs 200 Camrys, 150 Avalons, and 100 Siennas per shift to satisfy market demand. To produce 450 units in one shift of 480 minutes, the line must roll out a vehicle every $480/450 = 1.067$ minutes, or 64 seconds. This time represents the **takt time** of the process, defined as the cycle time needed to match the rate of production to the rate of sales or demand.

While far from ideal, all daily requirements of a model might be produced in one big batch before another model is started. The sequence of 200 C's, 150 A's, and 100 S's would be repeated once per shift. Not only would these big batches increase the average inventory level, but they also would cause "lumpy" (uneven) requirements on all the workstations feeding the assembly line.

But there are two better options for devising a production schedule for the vehicles. These options are based on the Japanese concept of **heijunka**—the levelling of production load by both volume and product mix. It does not build products according to the actual flow of customer orders, but levels out the total volume of orders in a period so that the same amount and mix are being made each day.

Let us explore two possible heijunka options. The first option uses levelled **mixed-model assembly**, producing a mix of models in smaller batches. Note that the production requirements at Toyota are in the ratio of 4 C's to 3 A's to 2 S's, found by dividing the model's production requirements by the greatest common divisor, or 50. Thus, the Toyota planner might develop a production cycle consisting of nine units: 4 C's, 3 A's, and 2 S's. The cycle would repeat in $9(1.067) = 9.60$ minutes, for a total of 50 times per shift (480 min/9.60 min = 50).

The second heijunka option uses a batch size of one, such as the production sequence of C–S–C–A–C–A–C–S–A repeated 50 times per shift. The sequence would achieve the same total output as the other options; however, it is feasible only if the setup times are very short. The sequence generates a steady rate of component requirements for the various models and allows the use of small batch sizes at the feeder workstations. Consequently, the capacity requirements at those stations are greatly smoothed. These requirements can be compared to actual capacities during the planning

---

takt time Cycle time of the process needed to match rate of production to the rate of sales or demand.

heijunka The levelling of production load by both volume and product mix.

mixed-model assembly A type of assembly that produces a mix of models in smaller batches.

phase, and modifications to the production cycle, production requirements, or capacities can be made as necessary.

STANDARDIZED COMPONENTS AND WORK METHODS

In highly repetitive service operations, great efficiencies can be gained by analyzing work methods and documenting the improvements for all employees to use. For example, courier companies, such as UPS, must monitor their work methods and revise them as necessary to improve service. In manufacturing, the standardization of components, called *part commonality* or *modularity*, increases repeatability. For example, a firm producing 10 products from 1000 different components might redesign its products so that they would draw from a common pool of only 100 different components or modules. Because the requirements per component increase, so does repeatability; that is, each worker performs a standardized task or work method more often every day. Productivity tends to increase because, with increased repetition, workers learn to do the task more efficiently. Standardization of components and work methods aids in achieving the high-productivity, low-inventory objectives of lean systems.

FLEXIBLE WORKFORCE

Employees in flexible workforces can be trained to perform more than one job. A benefit of flexibility is the ability to shift workers among workstations to help relieve bottlenecks as they arise without the need for long waiting lines of customers or inventory buffers of parts—an important aspect of the uniform flow of lean systems. Also, workers can step in and do the job for those who are on vacation or who are off sick. Although assigning workers to tasks they do not usually perform can temporarily reduce their efficiency, some job rotation tends to relieve boredom, encourages new ideas, and refreshes workers.

The more customized the service or product is, the greater the firm's need for a multi-skilled workforce. For example, a household appliance repair service requires broadly trained personnel who can identify a wide variety of component problems when the customer brings the defective unit into the shop, or when a service technician must repair an appliance in the field. Alternatively, back-office operations, such as the mail-processing operations at a large post office, have employees with more narrowly

Employees of United Parcel Service work on a small automated package line in the $1 billion air hub in Louisville, Kentucky. The packages (in the centre of the photo) are automatically deposited in the bin dedicated to their destination.

TABLE 7.2	5S Defined
5S Term	**Definition**
Sort	Separate needed from unneeded items (including tools, parts, materials, and paperwork), and discard the unneeded.
Set in order	Neatly arrange what is left, with a place for everything and everything in its place. Organize the work area so that it is easy to find what is needed.
Shine	Clean and wash the work area and make it shine.
Standardize	Establish schedules and methods of performing the cleaning and sorting. Formalize the cleanliness that results from regularly doing the first three S practices so that perpetual cleanliness and a state of readiness is maintained.
Sustain	Create discipline to perform the first four S practices, whereby everyone understands, obeys, and practises the rules when in the plant. Implement mechanisms to sustain the gains by involving people and recognizing them via a performance measurement system.

Note: The Japanese words for these 5S terms are *seiri*, *seiton*, *seiso*, *seiketsu*, and *shitsuke*, respectively.

defined jobs because of the repetitive nature of the tasks they must perform. These employees do not have to acquire as many alternative skills. In situations such as at the Texas Instruments antenna department mentioned earlier, shifting workers to other jobs may require them to undergo extensive, costly training.

FIVE S

five S (5S) A methodology consisting of five workplace practices—sort, set in order, shine, standardize, and sustain—that are conducive to visual controls and lean production.

Five S (5S) practices focus on organizing, cleaning, developing, and sustaining a productive work environment. It represents five related terms, each beginning with an *S*, that describe workplace practices conducive to visual controls and lean production. These five practices are done systematically to achieve lean systems: sort, set in order, shine, standardize, and sustain (see Table 7.2). They are not something that can be done as a stand-alone program. As such, they represent an essential foundation of lean systems.

It is commonly accepted that the 5S practices, when done together, form an important cornerstone of waste reduction and removal of unneeded tasks, activities, and materials. Implementation of 5S practices can lead to lowered costs, improved on-time delivery and productivity, higher product quality, and a safer working environment.

TOTAL PREVENTIVE MAINTENANCE

Because lean systems emphasize finely tuned work flows and little slack capacity or buffer inventory between workstations, unplanned machine downtime—one form of process variability—can be very disruptive. *Total preventive maintenance* (TPM) is designed to reduce the frequency and duration of machine downtime. After performing routine maintenance activities, the technician can test other parts that might need to be replaced. Replacement during regularly scheduled maintenance periods is easier and quicker than dealing with machine failures during production. Maintenance is done on a schedule that balances the cost of the preventive maintenance program against the risks and costs of machine failure. Routine preventive maintenance is particularly important for capital-intensive service or manufacturing processes, such as airlines, telecommunications, and financial services.

A related approach is to make workers responsible for routinely maintaining their own equipment and develop employee pride in keeping their machines in top condition. This practice, however, typically is limited to general housekeeping chores, minor lubrication, and adjustments. Maintenance of high-tech machines needs trained specialists. Doing even simple maintenance tasks goes a long way toward improving machine performance.

DESIGNING LEAN SYSTEM LAYOUTS

Line flows are recommended in designing lean system layouts, because they eliminate waste by reducing the frequency of setups. In a service setting, managers of back-office service processes can similarly organize their employees and equipment to provide uniform work flows through the process, eliminating wasted employee time. Banks use this strategy in their cheque-processing operations, as do couriers such as UPS in its parcel-sorting process. When volumes are not high enough to justify dedicating a single line of multiple workers to a single customer type or product, managers still might be able to derive the benefits of line process—simpler materials handling, lower throughput times, low setups, and reduced labour costs—by creating a similar layout in some portions of the facility, called **cells**—groups of several different workstations located close to each other that process a limited number of parts, products, or customers with similar process requirements. Two techniques for creating such layouts are one-worker, multiple-machines (OWMM) cells and group technology (GT) cells.

cell A group of several different workstations located close to each other that process a limited number of parts, products, or customers with similar process requirements.

CELL FOR ONE WORKER, MULTIPLE MACHINES

If volumes are relatively small for a particular type of customer or product, a manager might set up a one-person cell. Within a OWMM cell, a worker operates several different stations or machines simultaneously to achieve a small-scale line flow. Different cells can be used to serve specific types of customers or manufacture different products.

An OWMM arrangement can reduce customer queues, inventory, and labour requirements. Queues and inventory are cut because, rather than having to wait multiple times ahead of multiple stations, after completing one operation, customers and materials move directly into the next. Labour is cut because more work is automated. The addition of several low-cost automated devices or customer self-service stations can maximize the number of machines included in an OWMM arrangement.

For example, customers renewing their driver's license at a provincial office might be passed from step to step by specialized staff in a line process. One group of workers reviews personal data forms, another performs vision tests, and a third takes up-to-date photographs. Customer queues typically build ahead of each step in the process. In contrast, a OWMM cell arrangement would have each staff member trained to perform all required steps for each customer as needed. Thus, a customer waits only once at the beginning of the process, and interacts with only one staff person for the entire license renewal process. Other cells might focus on applications for new drivers, or complex renewals, such as truck licenses. Of course, the OWMM cell requires additional capital costs to purchase the same equipment for each staff member, such as a computer, vision examination machine and camera. But, the faster service (after the initial waiting line) can pay off in terms of greater customer satisfaction.

CELL FOR GROUP TECHNOLOGY

A second option for achieving product layouts with low-volume processes is GT. This manufacturing technique creates cells not limited to just one worker and has a unique way of selecting work to be done by the cell. The GT method groups parts or products with similar characteristics into families and sets aside groups of machines for their production. Families might be based on size, shape, manufacturing or routing requirements, or demand. The goal is to identify a set of customers or products with similar processing requirements and minimize worker setups or machine changeovers.

A similar logic also applies to services. For example, all patients in a high-volume X-ray clinic who require upper or lower limbs examined (one family) might be sent to one process area, and those who need gastrointestinal X-rays (second family) might be sent to another area. The patients are assigned to the same family because they all require the same basic processing steps regardless of size or age.

Once customers or parts have been grouped into families, the next step is to organize the stations and tools needed to perform the basic processes on these parts into separate cells. The machines in each cell require only minor adjustments to accommodate product changeovers from one customer to the next in the same family. By simplifying customer or product routings, GT cells reduce the time a customer or order is in the facility. Queues waiting to be processed are shortened or eliminated. In manufacturing, materials handling might be further automated so that, after moving materials into a cell, a worker does not handle any parts until the customer order has been completed.

Figure 7.2 compares process flows before and after creation of GT cells. Figure 7.2(a) shows a facility in which machines are grouped according to function: lathing,

FIGURE 7.2 *Process Flows Before and After Use of GT Cells*

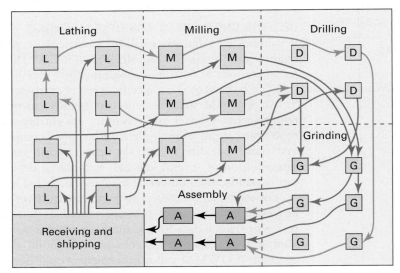

(a) Jumbled flows in a facility without GT cells

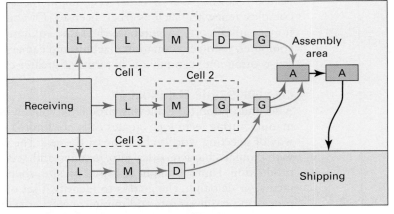

(b) Line flows in a facility with three GT cells

milling, drilling, grinding, and assembly. After lathing, a part is moved to one of the milling machines, where it waits in line until it has a higher priority than any other order competing for the machine's capacity. When the milling operation on the part has been finished, the part is moved to a drilling machine, and so on. The queues can be long, creating significant delays. Flows of materials are jumbled, because the parts being processed in any one area of the shop have so many different routings.

THE KANBAN SYSTEM

kanban A word meaning "card" or "visible record" in Japanese; refers to cards used to control the flow of production through a factory.

One of the most publicized aspects of lean systems, and the Toyota production system in particular, is the kanban system developed by Toyota. **Kanban**, meaning "card" or "visible record" in Japanese, refers to cards used to control the flow of production through a factory. In the most basic kanban system, a card is attached to each container of items that have been produced. The container holds a given percent of the daily requirements for an item. When the user of the parts empties a container, the card is removed from the container and put on a receiving post. The empty container is taken to the storage area. The card signals the need to produce another container of the part. When a container has been refilled, the card is put on the container, which is then returned to a storage area. The cycle begins again when the user of the parts retrieves the container with the card attached.

Figure 7.3 shows how a single-card kanban system works when a fabrication cell feeds two assembly lines. As an assembly line needs more parts, the kanban card for those parts is taken to the receiving post and a full container of parts is removed from the storage area. The receiving post accumulates cards for both assembly lines and sequences the production of replenishment parts. In this example, the fabrication cell will produce product 2 before it produces product 1. The cell consists of three different operations, but operation 2 has two workstations. Once production has been initiated in the cell, the product begins at operation 1 but could be routed to either of the workstations performing operation 2, depending on the workload at the time. Finally, the product is processed in operation 3 before being taken to the storage area.

FIGURE 7.3 *Single-Card Kanban System*

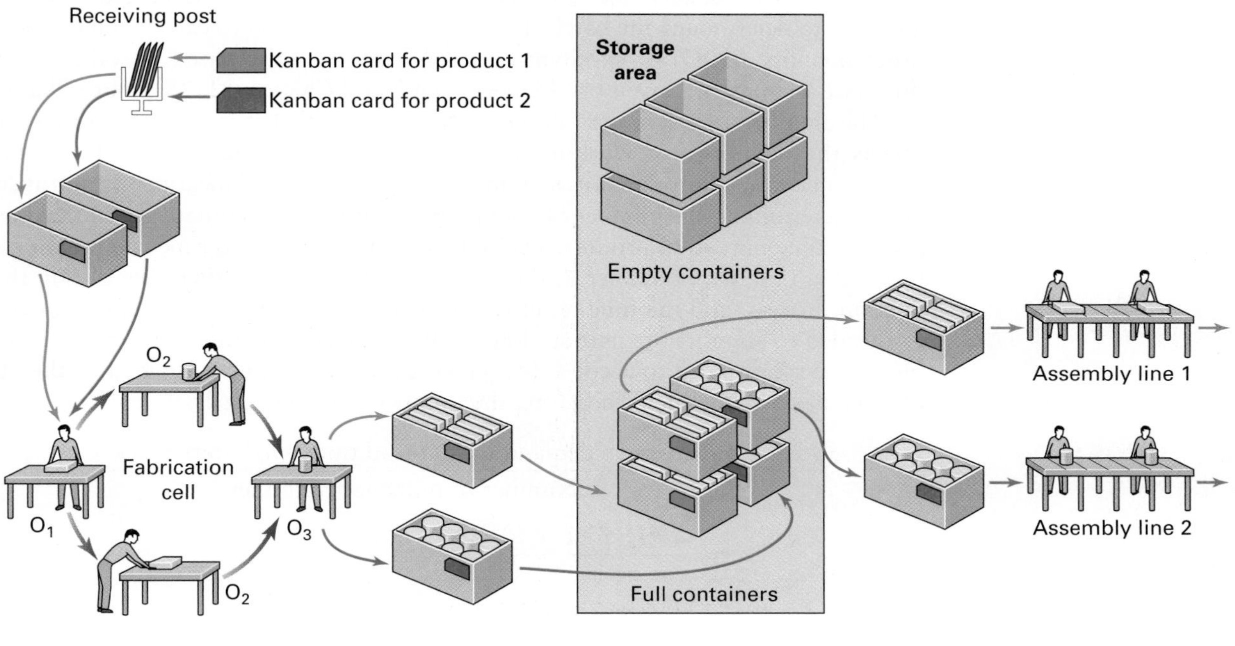

GENERAL OPERATING RULES

The operating rules for the single-card system are simple and are designed to facilitate the flow of materials while maintaining control of inventory levels.

1. Each container must have a card.

2. The assembly line always withdraws materials from the fabrication cell. The fabrication cell never pushes parts to the assembly line because, sooner or later, parts will be supplied that are not yet needed for production.

3. Containers of parts must never be removed from a storage area without a kanban first being posted on the receiving post.

4. The containers should always contain the same number of good parts. The use of nonstandard containers or irregularly filled containers disrupts the production flow of the assembly line.

5. Only nondefective parts should be passed along to the assembly line to make the best use of materials and workers' time.

6. Total production should not exceed the total amount authorized on the kanbans in the system.

Toyota uses a two-card system, based on a withdrawal card and a production-order card, to control withdrawal quantities more closely. The withdrawal card specifies the item and the quantity the user of the item should withdraw from the producer of the item, as well as the stocking locations for both the user and the producer. The production-order card specifies the item and the production quantity to be produced, the materials required and where to find them, and where to store the finished item. Materials cannot be withdrawn without a withdrawal card, and production cannot begin without a production-order card. The cards are attached to containers when production commences.

DETERMINING THE NUMBER OF CONTAINERS

The number of authorized containers in the Toyota production system determines the amount of authorized inventory. Management must make two determinations: (1) the number of units to be held by each container and (2) the number of containers flowing back and forth between the supplier station and the user station. The first decision amounts to determining the batch size and may be compared to calculating the economic order quantity (EOQ) or specifying a fixed order quantity based on other considerations (see Chapter 5, "Inventory Management," and Chapter 12, "Resource Planning").

The number of containers flowing back and forth between two stations directly affects the quantities of work-in-process inventory and safety stock. The containers spend some time in production, in a line waiting, in a storage location, or in transit. The key to determining the number of containers required is to estimate accurately the average lead time needed to produce a container of parts. The lead time is a function of the processing time per container at the supplier station, the waiting time during the production process, and the time required for materials handling. The number of containers needed to support the user station equals the average demand during the lead time plus some safety stock to account for unexpected circumstances, divided by the number of units in one container. Therefore, the number of containers is:

$$k = \frac{\text{Average demand during lead time } plus \text{ safety stock}}{\text{Number of units per container}}$$

$$= \frac{d(\overline{w} + \overline{p})(1 + \alpha)}{c}$$

where:

k = Number of containers for a part

d = Expected daily demand for the part, in units

$\overline{w}$ = Average waiting time during the production process plus materials handling time per container, in fractions of a day

$\overline{p}$ = Average processing time per container, in fractions of a day

c = Quantity in a standard container of the part

α = Policy variable that reflects the efficiency of the workstations producing and using the part (Toyota uses a value of no more than 10 percent)

The number of containers must, of course, be an integer. Rounding k up provides more inventory than desired, whereas rounding k down provides less.

The kanban system allows management to fine-tune the flow of materials in the system in a straightforward way. For example, removing cards from the system reduces the number of authorized containers of the part, thus reducing the inventory of the part.

The container quantity, c, and the efficiency factor, α, are variables that management can use to control inventory. Adjusting c changes the batch sizes, and adjusting α changes the amount of safety stock. The kanban system actually is a special form of the base-stock system (see Chapter 5, "Inventory Management"). In this case, the stocking level is $(\overline{w} + \overline{p})(1 + \alpha)$, and the order quantity is fixed at c units. Each time a container of parts is removed from the base stock, authorization is given to replace it. See the Solved Problem at the end of the chapter for a detailed example of how to apply the equation for the number of containers in a kanban system.

OTHER KANBAN SIGNALS

Cards are not the only way to signal the need for more production of a part. Other, less formal methods are possible, including container and containerless systems.

CONTAINER SYSTEM. Sometimes the container itself can be used as a signal device: an empty container signals the need to fill it. Unisys took this approach for low-value items. The amount of inventory of the part is adjusted by adding or removing containers. This system works well when the container is specially designed for a part and no other parts could accidentally be put in it. Such is the case when the container is actually a pallet or fixture used to position the part during precision processing.

CONTAINERLESS SYSTEM. Systems that require no containers have been devised. In assembly-line operations, operators having their own workbench areas put completed units on painted squares, one unit per square. Each painted square represents a container, and the number of painted squares on each operator's bench is calculated to balance the line flow. When the subsequent user removes a unit from one of the producer's squares, the empty square signals the need to produce another unit. McDonald's uses a containerless system. Information entered by the order taker at the cash register is transmitted to the cooks and assemblers, who produce the sandwiches requested by the customer.

As detailed in the Managerial Practice, the University of Pittsburgh Medical Center Shadyside used principles of kanban systems, 5S methodology, cellular layouts, and continuous flow processes to significantly improve performance in its pathology department.

MANAGERIAL PRACTICE
Lean Systems at the University of Pittsburgh Medical Center Shadyside

The University of Pittsburgh Medical Center (UPMC), comprising 20 hospitals, serves more than four million people every year with 48 000 employees. UPMC at Shadyside, a part of the UPMC system, is a 486-bed advanced-care hospital with a medical staff of more than 600 primary-care physicians and specialists. Always seeking to improve, UPMC first applied principles of the Toyota Production System in 2001 in a 40-bed surgical unit and then systematized the concepts into a lean approach called the Clinical Design Initiative (CDI). This approach focuses on determining the root cause of a problem through direct observation, and then eliminating it by designing solutions that are visual, simple, and unambiguous. These solutions are then tested in a small area and improved until the desired clinical and cost outcomes are achieved, along with enhanced patient and staff satisfaction. Once perfected, the improved process is rolled out to other areas of the hospital.

UPMC used the CDI methodology to speed up turnaround time in the pathology lab. The layout and work flows of the lab were based on a batch-and-queue push system that led to long lead times, complexity in tracking and moving large batches, delays in discovering quality problems, and high storage costs. Before making the transition to the lean system, UPMC ran a workshop on lean concepts for the staff members of the lab and followed it with a 5S exercise to better organize the department. Counter spaces were cleared so that the lab's equipment could be rearranged. Unneeded items were identified with red tags and removed. Visual controls were used to arrange the remaining items in a neat and easy-to-use manner.

The 5S exercise of cleaning house boosted staff morale. Kanban cards with reordering information were then attached to most items. Reordering supplies now takes only a few minutes a day. Stockouts and expensive rush orders have been eliminated and the overall inventory level of supplies has been reduced by 50 to 60 percent.

To move to a system based on line flows, equipment was moved around in the lab to create a cellular layout. The new arrangement allows tissue samples being processed to move through the lab cell from embedding, to cutting, to the oven, and to slide staining. The samples move more quickly, and few or no samples end up waiting between steps. As a result, the overall time needed to prepare and analyze tissue samples fell from one or two days to less than a day. Moreover, the lab

After the pathology lab at the University of Pittsburgh Medical Center adopted a lean operations approach based on a line system as against a batch-and-queue system, the time it took to process samples dropped from days to just hours. Diagnoses were made more quickly as a result, and patients' stays at the hospital were shortened.

does the same amount of work with 28 percent fewer people, and with fewer errors because quality mistakes are discovered immediately. The reduction in turnaround time means doctors get pathology results quicker, which in turn speeds up diagnosis and leads to shorter stays for patients.[3]

VALUE STREAM MAPPING

value stream mapping (VSM) A qualitative lean tool for eliminating waste that involves a current state drawing, a future state drawing, and an implementation plan.

Value stream mapping (VSM) is a widely used qualitative lean tool aimed at eliminating waste (or *muda*). Waste in many processes can be as high as 60 percent. Value stream mapping is helpful because it creates a visual "map" of every process involved in the flow of materials and information in a product's value chain. These maps consist of a current state drawing, a future state drawing, and an implementation plan. Value stream mapping spans the entire value chain, from the firm's receipt of raw materials to the delivery of the finished good to the customer. Thus, it tends to be broader in scope, displaying far more information than a typical process map or a flowchart used with Six Sigma process improvement efforts. Creating such a big picture representation helps managers identify the source of wasteful non-value-added activities.

Value stream mapping follows the steps shown in Figure 7.4. The first step is to focus on one product family for which mapping can be done. It is then followed by drawing a current state map of the existing process: analysts start from the customer and work upstream. The process map is often drawn manually, and actual process times, not "idealized" times, are recorded based on firsthand observation. Information for drawing the material and information flows is gathered from the front lines, including the data related to each process: cycle time (C/T), setup or changeover time (C/O), uptime (on-demand available machine time expressed as a percentage), production batch sizes, number of people required to operate the process, number of product variations, pack size (for moving the product to the next stage), working time (minus breaks), and scrap rate.

Value stream mapping uses a standard set of icons for material flow, information flow, and general information (to denote workers, safety stock buffers, and so on). Even though the complete glossary is extensive, a representative set of these icons is shown in Figure 7.5. These icons provide a common language for describing in detail how a facility should operate to create a better flow.

We use the VSM icons to illustrate in Figure 7.6 what a current state map could look like for a hypothetical bearing manufacturing company, which receives raw material sheets from Kline Steel Company every Monday for a product family of retainers (casings in which ball bearings are held), and then ships its finished product on a daily basis to a second-tier automotive manufacturing customer named GNK Enterprises. The product family of the bearing manufacturing company under consideration

FIGURE 7.4 *Value Stream Mapping Steps*[4]

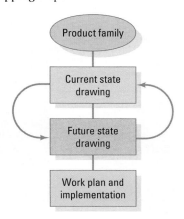

FIGURE 7.5 *Selected Set of Value Stream Mapping Icons*

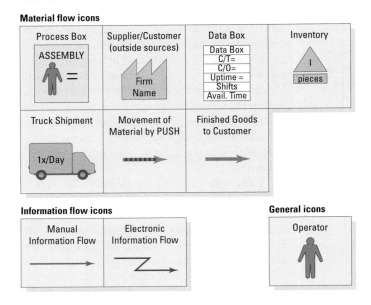

Material flow icons

Process Box	Supplier/Customer (outside sources)	Data Box	Inventory
ASSEMBLY =	Firm Name	Data Box / C/T= / C/O= / Uptime = / Shifts / Avail. Time	I pieces

Truck Shipment	Movement of Material by PUSH	Finished Goods to Customer
1x/Day		

Information flow icons

Manual Information Flow	Electronic Information Flow

General icons

Operator

FIGURE 7.6 *A Representative Current State Map for a Family of Retainers at a Bearings Manufacturing Company*

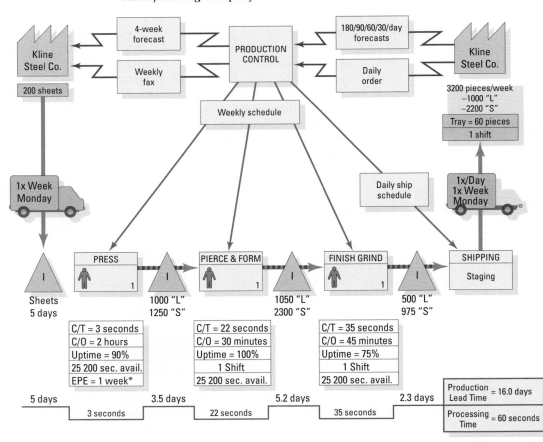

Kline Steel Co.
200 sheets

4-week forecast

Weekly fax

PRODUCTION CONTROL

180/90/60/30/day forecasts

Daily order

Kline Steel Co.

3200 pieces/week
−1000 "L"
−2200 "S"
Tray = 60 pieces
1 shift

Weekly schedule

Daily ship schedule

1x Week Monday

1x/Day 1x Week Monday

I
Sheets
5 days

| PRESS | 1 |

1000 "L"
1250 "S"

| PIERCE & FORM | 1 |

1050 "L"
2300 "S"

| FINISH GRIND | 1 |

500 "L"
975 "S"

SHIPPING
Staging

| C/T = 3 seconds |
| C/O = 2 hours |
| Uptime = 90% |
| 25 200 sec. avail. |
| EPE = 1 week* |

| C/T = 22 seconds |
| C/O = 30 minutes |
| Uptime = 100% |
| 1 Shift |
| 25 200 sec. avail. |

| C/T = 35 seconds |
| C/O = 45 minutes |
| Uptime = 75% |
| 1 Shift |
| 25 200 sec. avail. |

5 days   3.5 days   5.2 days   2.3 days

3 seconds   22 seconds   35 seconds

Production Lead Time = 16.0 days

Processing Time = 60 seconds

consists of two types of retainers—large (L) and small (S)—that are packaged for shipping in returnable trays with 60 retainers in each tray. The manufacturing process consists of a pressing operation, a piercing and forming cell, and a finish grind operation, after which the two types of retainers are staged for shipping. The process characteristics and inventory buffers in front of each process are shown in the current state map of Figure 7.6. One worker occupies each station. Although the total processing time for each retainer is only 1 minute, it takes 16 days for the cumulative production lead time. Clearly, opportunities exist for reconfiguring the existing processes and eliminating inventories.

The process flows shown at the bottom of Figure 7.6 are similar to the flowcharts discussed in Chapter 3, "Process Configuration," except that more detailed information is presented here for each process. However, what really sets the value stream maps apart from flowcharts is the inclusion of information flows at the top of Figure 7.6, which plan and coordinate all the process activities. The value stream maps are more comprehensive than process flowcharts, and meld together planning and control systems with detailed flowcharts to create a comprehensive supply chain view that includes both information and material flows between the firm and its suppliers and customers.

Once the current state map is done, the analysts can then use principles of lean systems such as load levelling, pull scheduling, kanban cards, and such to create a future state map with more streamlined product flows. The future state drawing highlights sources of waste and how to eliminate them. The arrows between the current and future state in Figure 7.4 go both ways, indicating that development of the current and future states are overlapping efforts. Finally, the last step is aimed at preparing and actively using an implementation plan to achieve the future state. It may take only a couple of days from the creation of a future state map to the point where implementation can begin for a single product family. At this stage, the future state map essentially becomes a blueprint for implementing a lean system, and is fine-tuned as implementation progresses. As the future state becomes reality, a new future state map is drawn, thus denoting continuous improvement at the value stream level.

Unlike the theory of constraints (see Chapter 4, "Capacity"), which accepts the existing system bottlenecks and then strives to maximize the throughput given that set of constraint(s), value stream mapping endeavours to understand through current state and future state maps how existing processes can be altered to eliminate bottlenecks and other wasteful activities. The goal is to bring the production rate of the entire process closer to the customer's desired demand rate. The benefits of applying this tool to the waste-removal process include reduced lead times and work-in-process inventories, reduced rework and scrap rates, and lower indirect labour costs.

IMPLEMENTATION CHALLENGES

Even though the benefits of lean systems can be outstanding, implementing a lean system can take a long time. And problems can still arise after significant gains have been made. We address below some of the issues managers should be aware of when implementing a lean system.

ORGANIZATIONAL CONSIDERATIONS

Implementing a lean system requires management to consider issues of worker stress, cooperation and trust among workers and management, and reward systems and labour classifications.

HUMAN COSTS. Lean systems can be coupled with statistical process control (SPC) to reduce variations in outputs. However, this combination requires training and a high degree of regimentation, which can create stress in the workforce. For example, workers must meet specified cycle times and, with SPC, they must follow prescribed problem-solving methods to improve quality. Such systems might make workers feel pushed, causing productivity losses or quality reductions. In addition, workers might feel that they have lost some autonomy because of the close linkages in materials flows between stations with little or no safety stocks. Managers can mitigate some of these effects by emphasizing materials flows instead of worker pace, and judiciously allowing some slack in the system through small safety stock inventories or slack capacity. Managers also can promote the use of work teams and allow them to determine their task assignments or rotations within the team's domain of responsibility.

COOPERATION AND TRUST. Workers and first-line supervisors must take on responsibilities formerly assigned to middle managers and support staff. Activities such as scheduling, expediting, and improving productivity become part of the duties of lower-level personnel. Consequently, organizational relationships must be reoriented to build close cooperation and mutual trust between the workforce and management. Such cooperation and trust may be difficult to achieve, particularly in the light of the typical adversarial positions taken by labour and management in the past.

REWARD SYSTEMS AND LABOUR CLASSIFICATIONS. In some instances, the reward system must be revamped as lean systems are developed and implemented. At General Motors, for example, a plan to reduce stock at one plant ran into trouble because the production superintendent refused to cut back production of unneeded parts. Why? Because his salary was based on his plant's production volume.

The realignment of reward systems is not the only hurdle. Labour contracts traditionally have reduced management's flexibility in reassigning workers as the need arises. A large manufacturer in Canada, such as an automobile plant, might have several unions and dozens of labour classifications. To gain more flexibility, management in some cases has obtained union concessions by granting other types of benefits. In other cases, management has relocated plants to take advantage of nonunion or foreign labour. In contrast, at Toyota, management may deal with only one employee association or union, and there are a much smaller number of labour classifications in a typical plant.

PROCESS CONSIDERATIONS

Firms using lean systems typically have some dominant work flows. During implementation, managers often have to change the layouts of their existing processes. Certain workstations might have to be moved closer together, and cells of machines devoted to particular families of components may have to be established. Moving toward focused cells is often a very effective layout. However, rearranging a plant can be costly. For example, whereas many plants now receive raw materials and purchased parts by rail, to facilitate smaller, more frequent shipments, truck deliveries would be preferable. Loading docks might have to be reconstructed or expanded and certain operations relocated to accommodate the change in transportation mode and quantities of arriving materials.

INVENTORY AND SCHEDULING

Firms need to have stable production schedules, short setups, and frequent, reliable supplies of materials and components to achieve the full potential of the lean systems concept.

PRODUCTION SCHEDULE STABILITY. Daily production schedules in high-volume, make-to-stock environments must be stable for extended periods. At Toyota, the master production schedule is stated in fractions of days over a three-month period and is revised only once a month. The first month of the schedule is frozen to avoid disruptive changes in the daily production schedule for each workstation; that is, the workstations execute the same work schedule each day of the month. At the beginning of each month, kanbans are reissued for the new daily production rate. Stable schedules are needed so that production lines can be balanced and new assignments found for employees who otherwise would be underutilized. Lean systems used in high-volume, make-to-stock environments cannot respond quickly to scheduling changes, because little slack inventory or capacity is available to absorb these changes.

SETUPS. As noted earlier, using small batches can yield big reductions in inventory. However, because small batches require a large number of setups, companies must significantly reduce setup times. Some companies have not been able to achieve short setup times and, therefore, have been compelled to use large-batch production, negating some of the advantages of just-in-time. Also, lean systems are vulnerable when introducing new products because the low levels of finished goods inventory will be insufficient to cover demand while the system is down. If the time to ramp up new products cannot be reduced, large finished goods inventories of the old product must be accumulated to compensate.

PURCHASING AND LOGISTICS. If frequent, small shipments of purchased items cannot be arranged with suppliers, large inventory savings for these items cannot be realized. The shipments of raw materials and components must be reliable because of the low inventory levels in lean systems. A plant can be shut down because of a lack of materials. In Canada, such arrangements can prove to be challenging, because of the geographic dispersion of suppliers. Improvements in the reliability of road and rail transportation have generally contributed to significant inventory reductions (see Chapter 2, "Supply Chain Management").

INTEGRATING SUSTAINABILITY INTO LEAN SYSTEMS

In the past, manufacturing and service firms have often tried to improve the environmental performance of their processes by adding equipment or operations to the end of an existing process. This "end-of-process" pollution control equipment captures and treats pollutants prior to their release into the environment. Pollution controls limit the environmental damage caused by poorly designed equipment, such as when underground tanks leak, or by careless practices. In services, wastes generated by a process often are sent to landfill or incineration. For example, multi-part forms or multi-layered packaging from suppliers creates waste and requires additional handling by workers.

Many firms are starting to shift their emphasis toward identifying environmental shortcomings before they cause serious damage. Starting with an environmental audit, managers can identify problems, measure current levels of wastes, and understand where pollutants are generated in their operations. Reducing waste and pollutants is very consistent with lean systems, and applying a philosophy of continuous improvement can direct efforts toward improving environmental performance. Most importantly, if pollutants are not generated, they need not be captured, treated, or disposed of in landfills.

Investments in lean systems and pollution prevention yield synergistic benefits. In a widely acclaimed program, 3M emphasizes that "pollution prevention pays" (the "3P" program). However, to get such benefits, operations and environmental managers have to work together on continuous improvement efforts, ideally under the leadership of a senior, credible manager with operations. Only then are new areas for cost savings or new competitive opportunities likely to be identified and implemented.

EQUATION SUMMARY

1. Number of containers:

$$k = \frac{\text{Average demand during lead time} + \text{Safety stock}}{\text{Number of units per container}}$$

$$= \frac{d(\overline{w} + \overline{p})(1 + \alpha)}{c}$$

CHAPTER HIGHLIGHTS

- Lean systems are based on a philosophy of continuous improvement, which emphasizes the elimination of waste (in its many forms) and the efficient and timely processing of customers, information, and materials.

- For operations competing on the basis of low cost and consistent quality, lean system advantages include shorter lead times, increased productivity, greater utilization of equipment, reductions in inventory and space requirements, simpler planning and scheduling systems, and improved quality.

- Lean systems require fundamental changes in the way all of the firm's business functions are performed. Several critical changes include increasing cooperation and trust between management and labour, basing rewards on team rather than individual performance, and developing long-term cooperative relationships with suppliers.

- Just-in-time (JIT) systems, a popular type of lean system, are designed to produce or deliver just the right products or services in just the right quantities, at just the right time to serve subsequent processes or customers.

- Some of the key process elements of a lean system are a pull method to manage work flow, quality at the source, small batch sizes, uniform workstation loads, standardized components and work methods, close supplier ties, flexible workforce, 5S practices, and total preventive maintenance.

- Cells (one worker, multiple machines) and group technology (GT) offer a means to implement lean systems if customer demand is relatively small, or of high variety.

- Many methods can be used to signal the movement of customers or materials through a process. In some operations, a kanban is used to control production flow and the replenishment of materials. The authorized inventory of a part is a function of the number of authorized cards for that item. The number of cards depends on average demand, the container size, and a policy variable to adjust for unexpected occurrences.

SOLVED PROBLEM

A company using a kanban system has an inefficient machine group. For example, the daily demand for part L105A is 3000 units. The average waiting time for a container of parts is 0.8 days. The processing time for a container of L105A is 0.2 days, and a container holds 270 units. Currently, there are 20 containers for this item.

   a. What is the value of the policy variable, α?

   b. What is the total planned inventory (work in process and finished goods) for item L105A?

   c. Suppose that the policy variable, α, were 0. How many containers would be needed now? What is the effect of the policy variable in this example?

SOLUTION

   a. We use the equation for the number of containers and then solve for α:

$$k = \frac{d(\overline{w} + \overline{p})(1 + \alpha)}{c}$$

$$= \frac{3000(0.8 + 0.2)(1 + \alpha)}{270} = 20$$

and:

$$1 + \alpha = \frac{20(270)}{3000(0.8 + 0.2)} = 1.8$$

$$\alpha = 1.8 - 1 = 0.8$$

b. With 20 containers in the system and each container holding 270 units, the total planned inventory is 20(270) = 5400 units.

c. If $\alpha = 0$:

$$k = \frac{3000(0.8 + 0.2)(1 + 0)}{270} = 11.11 \quad \text{or} \quad 12 \text{ containers}$$

The policy variable adjusts the number of containers. In this case, the difference is quite dramatic because $\bar{w} + \bar{p}$ is fairly large and the number of units per container is small relative to daily demand.

PROBLEMS

1. Wilson Motorcycle Company produces three models: the Tiger, a sure-footed dirt bike; the LX2000, a nimble racer; and the Golden, a large touring model. This month's production schedule calls for the production of 54 Goldens, 42 LX2000s, and 30 Tigers per seven-hour shift.

    a. What average cycle time is required for the assembly line to achieve the production quota in seven hours?

    b. If mixed-model scheduling is used, how many of each model will be produced before the production cycle is repeated?

    c. Determine a satisfactory production sequence for the ultimate in small-batch production: one unit.

    d. The design of a new model, the Cheetah, includes features from the Tiger, LX2000, and Golden models. The resulting blended design has an ambiguous character and is expected to attract some sales from the other models. Determine a mixed-model schedule resulting in 52 Goldens, 39 LX2000s, 26 Tigers, and 13 Cheetahs per seven-hour shift. Although the total number of motorcycles produced per day will increase only slightly, what problem might be anticipated in implementing this change from the production schedule indicated in part (b)?

2. A fabrication cell at Spradley's Sprockets uses the pull method to supply gears to an assembly line. George Jitson is in charge of the assembly line, which requires 500 gears per day. Containers typically wait 0.20 days in the fabrication cell. Each container holds 20 gears, and one container requires 1.8 days in machine time. Setup times are negligible. If the policy variable for unforeseen contingencies is set at 5 percent, how many containers should Jitson authorize for the gear replenishment system?

3. An assembly line requires two components: gadjits (G) and widjits (W). G is produced by centre 1 and W by centre 2.

Each unit of the end item, called a jit-together (J), requires 3 G's and 2 W's, as shown in Figure 7.7. The daily production quota on the assembly line is 800 J's.

The container for G holds 80 units. The policy variable for centre 1 is set at 0.09. The average waiting time for a container of G is 0.09 days, and 0.06 days are needed to produce a container. The container for W holds 50 units, and the policy variable for centre 2 is 0.08. The average waiting time per container of W is 0.14 days, and the time required to process a container is 0.20 days.

    a. How many containers are needed for gadjits (G)?

    b. How many containers are needed for widjits (W)?

4. A Quick Post supervisor is looking for ways to reduce stress in the mail-sorting department. With the existing arrangement, stamped letters are machine-cancelled and loaded into tubs with 375 letters per tub. The tubs are then pushed to postal clerks, who read and key postal codes into an automated sorting machine at the rate of 1 tub per 375 seconds. To overcome the stress caused when the stamp cancelling machine outpaces the sorting clerks, a pull system is proposed. When the clerks are ready to process another tub of mail, they will pull the tub from the cancelling machine area. How many tubs should circulate between the

FIGURE 7.7 *Component for End Item J*

★ have to convert everything into same units.

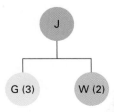

sorting clerks and the cancelling machine if 90 000 letters are to be sorted during an eight-hour shift, the safety stock policy variable, α, is 0.18, and the average waiting time plus materials handling time is 25 minutes per tub?

5. Jitsmart is a retailer of plastic action-figure toys. The action figures are purchased from Tacky Toys, Inc. and arrive in boxes of 48. Full boxes are stored on high shelves out of reach of customers. A small inventory is maintained on child-level shelves. Depletion of the lower-shelf inventory signals the need to take down a box of action figures to replenish the inventory. A reorder card is then removed from the box and sent to Tacky Toys to authorize replenishment of a container of action figures. The average demand rate for a popular action figure, Agent 99, is 36 units per day. The total lead time (waiting plus processing) is 11 days. Jitsmart's safety stock policy variable, α, is 0.25. What is the authorized stock level for Jitsmart?

NOTES FOR CHAPTER

1. Sources for Sharp Corporation information: D. Wakabayashi, "Sharp's New Plant Reinvents Japan Manufacturing Model," *Wall Street Journal*, November 30, 2009, p. B1; "Sharp Electronics Tries Bold New Factory Strategy to Keep Production in Japan," *SupplyChainDigest*, December 16, 2009; sharp-world.com/corporate/news; www.sharp.co.jp/sakai/en.

2. Adapted from David McBride, "The Seven Manufacturing Wastes," August 29, 2003, www.emsstrategies.com.

3. "The Anatomy of Innovation," *Lean Enterprise Institute*, www.lean.org; www.upmc.com, August 2008.

4. Mike Rother and John Shook, *Learning to See* (Brookline, MA: The Lean Enterprise Institute, 2003), p. 9.

FURTHER READING

Ansberry, Clare. "Hurry-Up Inventory Method Hurts Where It Once Helped." *Wall Street Journal Online*, June 25, 2002.

Fuime, Orrest. "Lean Accounting and Finance." *Target*, vol. 18, no. 4 (2002), pp. 6–14.

Greenblatt, Sherwin. "Continuous Improvement in Supply Chain Management." *Chief Executive*, June 1993, pp. 40–43.

Hall, Robert W. "New Balance Athletic Shoe Company." *Target*, vol. 20, no. 5 (2004), pp. 5–10.

Holweg, Matthias. "The Genealogy of Lean Production." *Journal of Operations Management*, vol. 25 (2007), pp. 420–437.

Klassen, R.D., "Just-In-Time Manufacturing and Pollution Prevention Generate Mutual Benefits in the Furniture Industry." *Interfaces*, vol. 30, no. 3 (2000), pp. 95–106.

Klein, J. A. "The Human Costs of Manufacturing Reform." *Harvard Business Review*, March–April 1989, pp. 60–66.

Mascitelli, Ron. "Lean Thinking: It's About Efficient Value Creation." *Target*, vol. 16, no. 2 (2000), pp. 22–26.

Millstein, Mitchell. "How to Make Your MRP System Flow." *APICS—The Performance Advantage*, July 2000, pp. 47–49.

Rother, Mike, and John Shook. *Learning to See*. Brookline, MA: The Lean Enterprise Institute, 2003.

Schaller, Jeff. "A 'Just Do It Now' Philosophy Rapidly Creates a Lean Culture, Produces Dramatic Results at Novametix Medical Systems." *Target*, vol. 18, no. 2 (2002), pp. 48–54.

Schonberger, Richard J. "Japanese Production Management: An Evolution—with Mixed Success." *Journal of Operations Management*, vol. 25 (2007), pp. 403–419.

Shah, Rachna, and Peter T. Ward. "Defining and Developing Measures of Lean Production." *Journal of Operations Management*, vol. 25 (2007), pp. 785–805.

Spear, Steven J. "Learning to Lead at Toyota." *Harvard Business Review* (May 2004), pp. 78–86.

Stewart, Douglas M., and John R. Grout. "The Human Side of Mistake Proofing." *Production and Operations Management*, vol. 10, no. 4 (2001), pp. 440–459.

Tonkin, Lea. "System Sensor's Lean Journey." *Target*, vol. 18, no. 2 (2002), pp. 44–47.

MyOMLab ASSETS

MyOMLab offers the following resources, which allow you to further practise and apply concepts presented in this chapter.

- **Equation Summary:** All the equations for this chapter can be found in one convenient location.

- **Discussion Questions:** Two questions will challenge your understanding of the philosophy of lean systems and the human considerations in implementing these systems.

- **Video Cases:**

  - *Lean Systems at Autoliv.* How were lean concepts developed and integrated into their operations?

  - *Versatile Buildings: Lean Systems.* Which lean concepts transformed the firm's business and improved customer value? Which concepts transfer well to service firms?

- **Case:** *Copper Kettle Catering.* What would you recommend the owners of Copper Kettle Catering do to take advantage of lean concepts in operating their business?

- **OM Explorer Tutor:** OM Explorer contains a tutor program that will help you learn how to apply the equation for determining the number of containers in a kanban system.

- **Extend LT:** *Lean Systems at Heritage Furniture.* Management is exploring reducing the batch size and changing the number of kanbans between operations.

8

Managing Projects

Learning Goals

After reading this chapter, you will be able to:

1. define the major activities associated with organizing, planning, monitoring, and controlling projects.

2. diagram the network of interrelated activities in a project.

3. identify the sequence of critical activities that determines the duration of a project.

4. describe the factors that managers must consider when assessing risks in a project and calculate the probability of completing a project on time.

5. explain how to determine a minimum-cost project schedule.

Across the Organization

Managing project processes is important to:

- **finance**, which uses project processes for financing new business acquisitions.

- **human resources**, which uses project processes for initiating new training and development programs.

- **management information systems**, which uses project processes to design and install information systems to support new business processes.

- **marketing**, which uses project processes to design and execute new product advertising campaigns.

- **operations**, which uses project processes to manage the introduction of new services, products, and processes.

Just a few years ago, Sony dominated the multibillion-dollar market for video games. PlayStation 2, a second-generation console that used a 128-bit processor, had a commanding 67 percent share of the second-generation market. Microsoft's first attempt in the video game market, Xbox, came in a distant second with 17 percent, barely ahead of Nintendo's GameCube at 16 percent. Two of the factors contributing to Sony's success were that it was the first to market, beating Microsoft by 12 months, and that it could build on the prior success of its PlayStation 1. Four years after the introduction of Xbox, Microsoft needed to design, develop, and produce a new product quickly. Developing such a product is a project of massive proportions. The project consisted of four phases: design, analysis, development, and launch (recall Figure 2.6). The result was Xbox 360.

Design

The design of the Xbox 360 was a collaborative effort between Microsoft and many other firms, including Astro Studios in San Francisco, which designed the overall console and controller; IBM, which designed the processor chip; ATI, which designed the graphics chip; and a host of game design firms to develop games for the new product. A key element of the new product was the built-in Internet access that allowed gamers to access online games, buy game add-ons, and access multiplayer games developed exclusively for Xbox 360. Microsoft also included its primary manufacturers, Flextronics and Wistron, in the design process to optimize the production and assembly of the more than 1000 parts contained in an Xbox 360.

Analysis

Getting an estimate of future sales for a new product is always difficult; however, in this case the historic patterns for PlayStation 1, PlayStation 2,

Like the original Xbox 360 hardware, the recently introduced, innovative Kinect game controller requires the management of a complex project with multiple partners.

and Xbox were useful. Analysts found that the peak year for a PlayStation product was four years after its introduction, and that the life cycle for those products is about eleven years. This information provided a basis for estimating the sales potential of Xbox 360, although actual sales may be limited due to supply constraints. Nonetheless, Microsoft realized that the potential was there to open a new generation of game consoles well ahead of the market.

Development

Microsoft worked closely with Flextronics, Wistron, and the various design firms to iron out manufacturing problems in the early phases of Xbox 360 production. Once initial production was under way, Microsoft brought on Celestica to add production capacity. The decision was made to focus manufacturing operations in China. All told, 10 000 workers in China would be involved in Xbox 360 production.

Launch

The promotional campaign for Xbox 360 began seven months before the new gaming system was released. In November 2005, the product was officially available in Canada and the United States, closely followed by Europe and Japan. All told, the product was released in 36 countries in the first year of production, a Herculean effort requiring extensive coordination and a high level of project management skill. Sales of the Xbox 360 exceeded expectations, with more than 10 million units sold in the first year alone. Nonetheless, Microsoft experienced difficulties in getting the supply chain to meet customer demands in a timely fashion. The lesson to be learned is that projects can be planned and executed properly; however, the underlying infrastructure that delivers the product is equally important in the ultimate success of the venture.[1]

project An interrelated set of activities with a definite starting and ending point, which results in a unique outcome for a specific allocation of resources.

Companies such as Microsoft must become experts at managing projects. They need to master the ability to schedule activities and monitor progress within strict time, cost, and performance guidelines. A **project** is an interrelated set of activities with a definite starting and ending point, which results in a unique outcome for a specific allocation of resources.

Project processes can be complex and challenging to manage. Projects often cut across organizational lines, because they need the skills of multiple professions and organizations. Furthermore, each project is unique, even if it has some routine elements, requiring new combinations of skills and resources in the project process. Uncertainties, such as the advent of new technologies or the activities of competitors, can change the character of projects and require responsive countermeasures. Finally, project processes themselves are temporary, because personnel, materials, and facilities are organized to complete a project within a specified time frame and then disbanded.

In this chapter, we discuss three major activities associated with managing project processes: organizing projects, planning projects, and monitoring and controlling projects.

ORGANIZING PROJECTS

Successful projects begin with a clear definition of scope, objectives, and tasks. However, a successful project *process* begins with a clear understanding of its organization and how personnel are going to work together to complete the project. In this section, we will address two important activities in this initial phase of managing projects: defining the objectives and scope, and selecting the project manager and team.

DEFINING THE OBJECTIVES AND SCOPE

Before a project is undertaken, it is important to clearly identify both the purpose and goals that are expected. These might be driven by firm-level strategy, gaps in existing business processes, or opportunities to increase customer value. A thorough statement of the project scope, time frame, and allocated resources is essential to managing the project process. The scope provides a succinct statement of project objectives and captures the essence of the desired project outcomes in the form of major deliverables, which are concrete outcomes of the project process. Changes to the scope of a project inevitably increase costs and delay completion. Collectively, changes to scope are called **scope creep**, and in sufficient quantity are primary causes of failed projects.

scope creep Many small, incremental changes to project objectives, which in total significantly expand the scope.

The time frame for a project should be as specific as possible, even at early stages of the project—for example, the time frame should be "the billing process re-engineering project should be completed by January 1, 2012." Although specifying an allocation of resources to a project can be difficult at the early stages of planning, it is important for managing the project process. The allocation could be expressed as a dollar figure or as full-time equivalents of personnel time. For example, the allocated resources in a project might be $250 000. A specific statement of allocated resources makes it possible to make adjustments to the scope of the project as it proceeds.

SELECTING THE PROJECT MANAGER AND TEAM

Once the project is defined, a project manager must be chosen. Project managers should be good motivators, teachers, and communicators. They should be able to organize a set of disparate activities and work with personnel from a variety of disciplines. These qualities are important because project managers have the responsibility to see that their projects are completed successfully. The project manager is responsible for establishing the project goals and providing the means to achieve them.

The project manager must also specify how the work will be done and ensure that any necessary training is conducted. Finally, the project manager evaluates progress and takes appropriate action when schedules are in jeopardy.

The project team is a group of people led by the project manager. Members of the project team may represent entities internal to the firm, such as marketing, finance, accounting, or operations, or entities external to the firm, such as customers or suppliers. A clear definition of who is on the team is essential, as is a clear understanding of their specific roles and responsibilities, such as helping to create the project plan, performing specific tasks, and reporting progress and problems. Everyone performing work for the project should be a part of the project team. Consequently, the size and makeup of the team may fluctuate during the life of the project.

PLANNING PROJECTS

Once the project has been defined and the project process organized, the team must formulate a plan that identifies the specific tasks to be accomplished and a schedule for their completion. Planning projects involves five steps:

1. Defining the work breakdown structure

2. Diagramming the network

3. Developing the schedule

4. Analyzing cost–time trade-offs

5. Assessing risks

DEFINING THE WORK BREAKDOWN STRUCTURE

work breakdown structure (WBS) A statement of all work that has to be completed.

The **work breakdown structure (WBS)** is a statement of all work that has to be completed. Perhaps the single most important contributor to delay is the omission of work that is germane to the successful completion of the project. The project manager must work closely with the team to identify all work tasks. Typically, in the process of accumulating work tasks, the team generates a hierarchy to the work breakdown. Major work components are broken down to smaller tasks by the project team.

Figure 8.1 shows a WBS for a major project involving the relocation of a hospital. In the interest of better serving the surrounding community, the board of St. John's Hospital has decided to move to a new location. The project involves constructing a new hospital and making it operational. The activities at level 1 in the WBS are major work components that can be broken down into smaller tasks. For example, "Organizing and Site Preparation" can be divided into six tasks at level 2, and "Prepare Final Construction Plans" can be further divided into tasks at level 3 (not shown in the figure). It is easy to conclude that the total WBS for the hospital relocation project may include many more than 100 tasks. Regardless of the project, care must be taken to include all of the important tasks in the WBS to avoid project delays. Often overlooked are the tasks required to plan the project, get management approval at various stages, run pilot tests of new services or products, and prepare final reports.

activity The smallest unit of work effort consuming both time and resources that the project manager can schedule and control.

An **activity** is the smallest unit of work effort consuming both time and resources that the project manager can schedule and control. Each activity in the WBS must have an "owner" who is responsible for doing the work. Task ownership avoids confusion in the execution of activities and assigns responsibility for timely completion. The team should have a defined procedure for assigning tasks to team members, which can be democratic (consensus of the team) or autocratic (assigned by the project manager).

FIGURE 8.1 *Work Breakdown Structure for the St. John's Hospital Project*

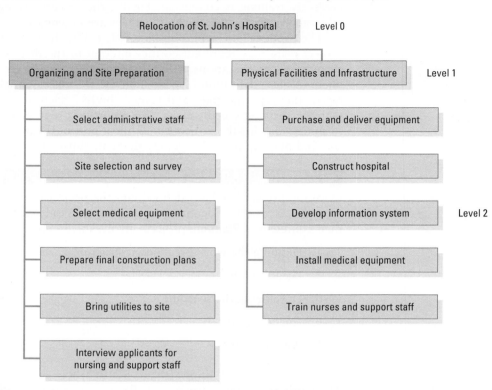

DIAGRAMMING THE NETWORK

Network planning methods can help managers monitor and control projects. These methods treat a project as a set of interrelated activities that can be visually displayed in a **network diagram,** which consists of nodes (circles) and arcs (arrows) that depict the relationships between activities. Two network planning methods were developed in the 1950s. The **program evaluation and review technique (PERT)** was created for the U.S. Navy's Polaris missile project, which involved 3000 separate contractors and suppliers. The **critical path method (CPM)** was developed as a means of scheduling maintenance shutdowns at chemical processing plants. Although early versions of PERT and CPM differed in their treatment of activity-time estimates, today the differences between PERT and CPM are minor. For purposes of our discussion, we refer to them collectively as PERT/CPM. These methods offer several benefits to project managers, including the following:

1. Considering projects as networks forces project teams to identify and organize the data required and to identify the interrelationships of activities. This process also provides a forum for managers of different functional areas to discuss the nature of the various activities and their resource requirements.

2. Networks enable project managers to estimate the completion time of projects, an advantage that can be useful in planning other events and in conducting contractual negotiations with customers and suppliers.

3. Reports highlight the activities that are crucial to completing projects on schedule. They also highlight the activities that may be delayed without

network diagram
A diagram that depicts the relationships between activities, which consists of nodes (circles) and arcs (arrows).

program evaluation and review technique (PERT)
A network planning method created for the U.S. Navy's Polaris missile project.

critical path method (CPM) A network planning method initially developed as a means of scheduling maintenance shutdowns at chemical processing plants.

affecting completion dates, thereby freeing up resources for more critical activities.

4. Network methods enable project managers to analyze the time and cost implications of resource trade-offs.

ESTABLISHING PRECEDENCE RELATIONSHIPS. Diagramming the project as a network requires establishing the precedence relationships among activities. A **precedence relationship** determines a sequence for undertaking activities; it specifies that one activity cannot start until a preceding activity has been completed. For example, brochures announcing a conference for executives must first be designed by the program committee (activity A) before they can be printed (activity B). In other words, activity A must *precede* activity B. For large projects, this task is essential because incorrect or omitted precedence relationships will result in costly delays. The precedence relationships are represented by a network diagram.

ESTIMATING ACTIVITY TIMES. Next, the project team must make time estimates for activities. When the same type of activity has been done many times before, time estimates are apt to have a relatively high degree of certainty. There are several ways to get time estimates in such an environment. First, statistical methods can be used if the project team has access to data on actual activity times experienced in the past. Second, if activity times improve with the number of replications, the times can be estimated using learning curve models (Supplement D, "Learning Curve Analysis"). Finally, the times for first-time activities are often estimated using managerial opinions on the basis of similar prior experiences. However, if there is a high degree of uncertainty in the estimates, probability distributions for activity times can be used. We discuss two approaches for incorporating uncertainty in project networks when we address risk assessment later. For now, we assume that the activity times are known with certainty.

ACTIVITY-ON-NODE (AON) NETWORKS. A networking approach useful for creating a network diagram is the **activity-on-node (AON) network**, in which nodes represent activities and arcs represent the precedence relationships among them. This approach is *activity-oriented*. Here, precedence relationships require that an activity not begin until all preceding activities have been completed. Arrows represent the precedence relationships, and the direction of an arrow represents the sequence of activities. In AON networks, when there are multiple activities with no predecessors, it is usual to show them emanating from a common node called Start. When there are multiple activities with no successors, it is usual to show them connected to a node called Finish. We will use AON networks later to describe assembly lines (see Chapter 9, "Location and Layout").

Modelling a large project as a network forces the project team to identify the necessary activities and recognize the precedence relationships. If this preplanning is skipped, unexpected delays often occur.

precedence relationship
A relationship that determines a sequence for undertaking activities; it specifies that one activity cannot start until a preceding activity has been completed.

activity-on-node (AON) network An approach used to create a network diagram, in which nodes represent activities and arcs represent the precedence relationships among them.

EXAMPLE 8.1   *Diagramming a Hospital Project*

In the interest of better serving the public, St. John's Hospital has decided to relocate to a new, larger facility. The move will involve constructing a new building nearby and making it operational. Judy Kramer, the project manager for the St. John's Hospital project, divided it into two major modules. She assigned John Stewart overall responsibility for the Organizing and Site Preparation module and Sarah Walker for the Physical Facilities and Infrastructure module.

Using the WBS shown in Figure 8.1, the project team developed the precedence relationships, activity time estimates, and activity responsibilities shown in the following table. Draw the network diagram for the hospital project.

ACTIVITY	IMMEDIATE PREDECESSORS	ACTIVITY TIMES (weeks)	RESPONSIBILITY
ST. JOHN'S HOSPITAL PROJECT			Kramer
START		0	
ORGANIZING and SITE PREPARATION			Stewart
A. Select administrative staff	START	12	Johnson
B. Site selection and survey	START	9	Taylor
C. Select medical equipment	A	10	Adams
D. Prepare final construction plans	B	10	Taylor
E. Bring utilities to site	B	24	Burton
F. Interview applicants for nursing and support staff	A	10	Johnson
PHYSICAL FACILITIES and INFRASTRUCTURE			Walker
G. Purchase and deliver equipment	C	35	Sampson
H. Construct hospital	D	40	Casey
I. Develop information system	A	15	Murphy
J. Install medical equipment	E, G, H	4	Pike
K. Train nurses and support staff	F, I, J	6	Ashton
FINISH	K	0	

SOLUTION

The network diagram, activities, and activity times for the hospital project are shown in Figure 8.2. The diagram depicts activities as circles, with arrows indicating the sequence in which they are to be performed. Activities A and B emanate from a start node, because they have no immediate predecessors. The arrows connecting activity A to activities C, F, and I indicate that all three require completion of activity A before they can begin. Similarly, activity B must be completed before activities D and E can begin, and so on. Activity K connects to a finish node, because no activities follow it. The start and finish nodes do not actually represent activities. They merely provide beginning and ending points for the network.

FIGURE 8.2 *Network for the St. John's Hospital Project, Showing Activity Times*

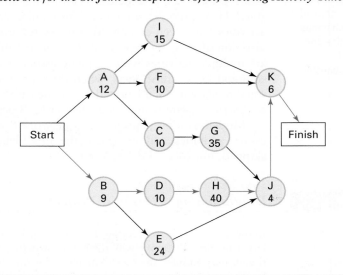

DEVELOPING THE SCHEDULE

CRITICAL PATH. A crucial aspect of project management is estimating the time of completion. If each activity in relocating the hospital were done in sequence, with work proceeding on only one activity at a time, the time of completion would equal the sum of the times for all the activities, or 175 weeks. However, Figure 8.2 indicates that some activities can be carried on simultaneously given adequate resources. We call each sequence of activities between the project's start and finish a **path**. The network describing the hospital relocation project has five paths: A–I–K, A–F–K, A–C–G–J–K, B–D–H–J–K, and B–E–J–K. The **critical path** is the sequence of activities between a project's start and finish that takes the longest time to complete. Thus, the activities along the critical path determine the completion time of the project; that is, if one of the activities on the critical path is delayed, the entire project will be delayed. The estimated times for the paths in the hospital project network are shown in the following table:

path The sequence of activities between a project's start and finish.

critical path The sequence of activities between a project's start and finish that takes the longest time to complete.

PATH	ESTIMATED TIME (weeks)
A–I–K	33
A–F–K	28
A–C–G–J–K	67
B–D–H–J–K	69
B–E–J–K	43

The activity string B–D–H–J–K is estimated to take 69 weeks to complete. As the longest, it constitutes the critical path and is shown in red in Figure 8.2.

Because the critical path defines the completion time of the project, Judy Kramer and the project team should focus on these activities. However, projects can have more than one critical path. If activity A, C, or G were to fall behind by two weeks, the string A–C–G–J–K would become a second critical path. Consequently, the team should be aware that delays in activities not on the critical path could cause delays in the entire project.

PROJECT SCHEDULE. A typical objective is to finish the project as early as possible as determined by the critical path. The project schedule is specified by the start and finish times for each activity. For any activity, managers can use the earliest start and finish times, the latest start and finish times (and still finish the project on time), or times in between these extremes.

The earliest start and earliest finish times are obtained as follows:

earliest start time (ES) The earliest finish time of the preceding activity.

earliest finish time (EF) An activity's earliest start time plus its estimated duration, t, or EF = ES + t.

latest finish time (LF) The latest start time of the activity that immediately follows.

1. The **earliest start time (ES)** for an activity is the earliest finish time of the preceding activity. For activities with more than one preceding activity, ES is the latest of the earliest finish times of the preceding activities.

2. The **earliest finish time (EF)** of an activity equals its earliest start time plus its estimated duration, t, or EF = ES + t.

To calculate the duration of the entire project, we determine the EF for the last activity on the critical path.

To obtain the latest start and latest finish times, we must work backward from the finish node. We start by setting the latest finish time of the project equal to the earliest finish time of the last activity on the critical path.

latest start time (LS)
The latest finish time of an activity minus its estimated duration, t, or $LS = LF - t$.

1. The **latest finish time (LF)** for an activity is the latest start time of the activity following it. For activities with more than one activity immediately following, LF is the earliest of the latest start times of those activities.

2. The **latest start time (LS)** for an activity equals its latest finish time minus its estimated duration, t, or $LS = LF - t$.

EXAMPLE 8.2   *Calculating Start and Finish Times for the Activities*

Using the activity times and precedence relationships noted in Figure 8.2, we can now calculate the start and finish times for all activities, as well as the project as a whole.

To compute the earliest start and earliest finish times, we begin at the start node at time zero. Because activities A and B have no predecessors, the earliest start times for these activities are also zero. The earliest finish times for these activities are:

$$EF_A = 0 + 12 = 12 \qquad \text{and} \qquad EF_B = 0 + 9 = 9$$

Because the earliest start time for activities I, F, and C is the earliest finish time of activity A:

$$ES_I = 12, \quad ES_F = 12, \quad \text{and} \quad ES_C = 12$$

Similarly:

$$ES_D = 9 \qquad \text{and} \qquad ES_E = 9$$

After placing these ES values on the network diagram as shown in Figure 8.3, we determine the EF times for activities I, F, C, D, and E:

$$EF_I = 12 + 15 = 27, \quad EF_F = 12 + 10 = 22, \quad EF_C = 12 + 10 = 22,$$
$$EF_D = 9 + 10 = 19, \quad \text{and} \quad EF_E = 9 + 24 = 33$$

The earliest start time for activity G is the latest EF time of all immediately preceding activities. Thus:

$$
\begin{array}{ll}
ES_G = EF_C & \qquad ES_H = EF_D \\
\quad = 22 & \qquad \quad = 19
\end{array}
$$

$$
\begin{array}{ll}
EF_G = ES_G + t & \qquad EF_H = ES_H + t \\
\quad = 22 + 35 & \qquad \quad = 19 + 40 \\
\quad = 57 & \qquad \quad = 59
\end{array}
$$

Because activity J has several predecessors, the earliest time that activity J can begin is the latest of the EF times of any of its preceding activities: EF_G, EF_H, EF_E. Thus, $ES_J = 59$, and $EF_J = 59 + 4 = 63$. Similarly, $ES_K = 63$ and $EF_K = 63 + 6 = 69$. Because activity K is the last activity on the critical path, the earliest the project can be completed is week 69. The earliest start and finish times for all activities are shown in Figure 8.3.

To compute the latest start and latest finish times, we begin by setting the latest finish activity time of activity K at week 69, its earliest finish time. Thus, the latest start time for activity K is:

$$LS_K = LF_K - t = 69 - 6 = 63$$

If activity K is to start no later than week 63, all its predecessors must finish no later than that time. Consequently:

$$LF_I = 63, \qquad LF_F = 63, \qquad \text{and} \qquad LF_J = 63$$

The latest start times for these activities are shown in Figure 8.3 as:

$$LS_I = 63 - 15 = 48, \qquad LS_F = 63 - 10 = 53, \qquad \text{and} \qquad LS_J = 63 - 4 = 59$$

After obtaining LS_J, we can calculate the latest start times for the immediate predecessors of activity J:

$$LS_G = 59 - 35 = 24, \qquad LS_H = 59 - 40 = 19, \qquad \text{and} \qquad LS_E = 59 - 24 = 35$$

FIGURE 8.3 *Network for the Hospital Project, Showing Activity Start and Finish Times*

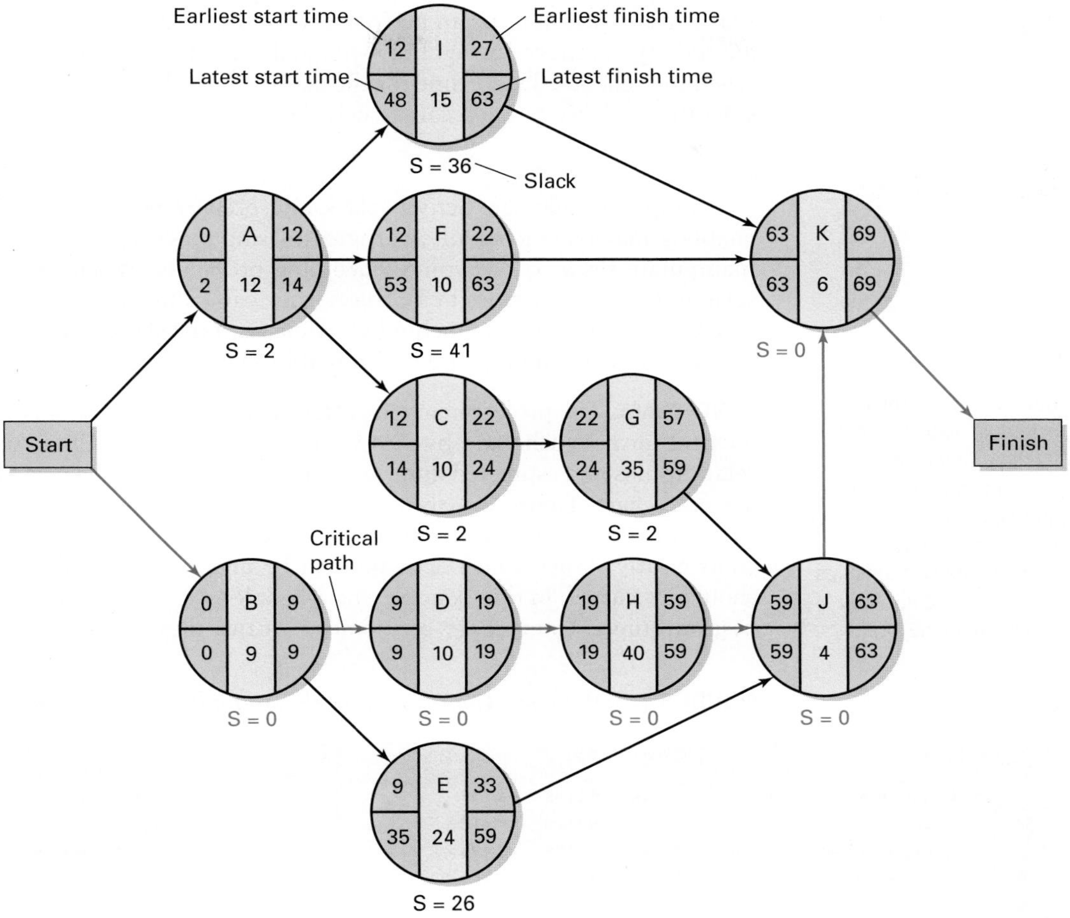

Similarly, we can now calculate latest start times for activities C and D:

$$LS_C = 24 - 10 = 14 \quad \text{and} \quad LS_D = 19 - 10 = 9$$

Activity A has more than one immediately following activity: I, F, and C. The earliest of the latest start times is 14 for activity C. Thus:

$$LS_A = 14 - 12 = 2$$

Similarly, activity B has two immediate followers, D and E. Because the earliest of the latest start times of these activities is 9:

$$LS_B = 9 - 9 = 0$$

Decision Point The earliest or latest start dates can be used for developing a project schedule. For example, Kramer should start activity B immediately, because the latest start date is 0; otherwise, the project will not be completed by week 69. When the LS is greater than the ES for an activity, that activity could be scheduled for any date between ES and LS. Such is the case for activity E, which could be scheduled to start anytime between week 9 and week 35, depending on the availability of resources. The earliest start and earliest finish times and the latest start and latest finish times for all activities are shown in Figure 8.3.

activity slack The maximum length of time that an activity can be delayed without delaying the entire project.

ACTIVITY SLACK. The maximum length of time an activity can be delayed without delaying the entire project is called **activity slack**. Consequently, activities on the critical path have zero slack. Information on slack can be useful, because it highlights activities that need close attention. In this regard, activity slack is the amount of schedule slippage that can be tolerated for an activity before the entire project will be delayed. Slack at an activity is reduced when the estimated time duration of an activity is exceeded or when the scheduled start time for the activity must be delayed because of resource considerations. Activity slack can be calculated in one of two ways for any activity:

$$S = LS - ES \qquad \text{or} \qquad S = LF - EF$$

Computers calculate activity slack and prepare periodic reports for large projects, enabling managers to monitor progress. Using these reports, managers can sometimes manipulate slack to overcome scheduling problems. When resources can be used on several different activities in a project, they can be taken from activities with slack and given to activities that are behind schedule until the slack is used up. The slack for each activity in the hospital project is shown in Figure 8.3.

Gantt chart A project schedule, usually created by the project manager using computer software, that superimposes project activities, with their precedence relationships and estimated duration times, on a time line.

GANTT CHART. The project manager, often with the assistance of computer software, creates the project schedule by superimposing project activities, with their precedence relationships and estimated duration times, on a time line. The resulting diagram is called a **Gantt chart**. Figure 8.4 shows a Gantt chart for the hospital project created with Microsoft Project, a popular software package. The critical path is shown in red. The chart clearly shows which activities can be undertaken simultaneously and when they should be started. In this example, the schedule calls for all activities to begin at their earliest start times. Gantt charts are popular because they are intuitive and easy to construct.

FIGURE 8.4 *MS Project Gantt Chart for the Hospital Project Schedule*

	Task Name	Duration	Start	Finish	Predecessors
1	⊟ St John's Hospital Project	69 wks	9/14/09	1/7/11	
2	Start	0 wks	9/14/09	9/14/09	
3	⊟ Organizing and Site Prep	33 wks	9/14/09	4/30/10	
4	A. Select Staff	12 wks	9/14/09	12/4/09	2
5	B. Select Site	9 wks	9/14/09	11/13/09	2
6	C. Select Equipment	10 wks	12/7/09	2/12/10	4
7	D. Construction Plans	10 wks	11/16/09	1/22/10	5
8	E. Utilities	24 wks	11/16/09	4/30/10	5
9	F. Interviews	10 wks	12/7/09	2/12/10	4
10	⊟ Facilities and Infrastructure	57 wks	12/7/09	1/7/11	
11	G. Purchase Equipment	35 wks	2/15/10	10/15/10	6
12	H. Construct Hospital	40 wks	1/25/10	10/29/10	7
13	I. Information System	15 wks	12/7/09	3/19/10	4
14	J. Install Equipment	4 wks	11/1/10	11/26/10	8,11,12
15	K. Train Staff	6 wks	11/29/10	1/7/11	9,13,14
16	Finish	0 wks	1/7/11	1/7/11	15

ANALYZING COST–TIME TRADE-OFFS

Keeping costs at acceptable levels is almost always as important as meeting schedule dates. The reality of project management is that there are always time and cost trade-offs. For example, a project can often be completed earlier than scheduled by hiring more workers or running extra shifts. Such actions could be advantageous if savings or additional revenues accrue from completing the project early.

Total project costs are the sum of direct costs, indirect costs, and penalty costs. These costs are dependent either on activity times or on project completion time. Direct costs include labour, materials, and any other costs directly related to project activities. Managers can shorten individual activity times by using additional direct resources, such as overtime, personnel, or equipment. Indirect costs include administration, depreciation, financial, and other variable overhead costs that can be avoided by reducing total project time: the shorter the duration of the project, the lower the indirect costs will be. Finally, a project may incur penalty costs if it extends beyond some specific date, whereas a bonus may be provided for early completion. The Managerial Practice feature shows how substantial delays and cost overruns can often be driven by the overall novelty or complexity of the project.

MANAGERIAL PRACTICE
Despite Project Delays, Bridge Retrofit a Modern-Day Miracle

The project went about $25 million over budget and had inflicted more than two years of delays on commuters when it finished 18 months behind schedule. But the buzz surrounding the completed reconstruction of Vancouver's Lions Gate Bridge was that a minor engineering miracle had been performed high above Burrard Inlet. During that time, construction crews had rebuilt this suspension bridge, which connects Vancouver's North Shore to the downtown, piece by piece. The bridge now has wider lanes and sidewalks, features viewing platforms, and can withstand a major earthquake.

The technological marvel in all this was that the retrofit project was done without closing the bridge to weekday traffic. The idea to keep the crossing open during the reconstruction came from the bridge's owner, the Province of British Columbia. Aging bridges that need to be rebuilt are usually closed for two or three months, during which crews work around the clock replacing panels, section by section. That wasn't an option with the Lions Gate, because closing it would have meant gridlock for commuters, as it is one of only two bridges connecting the downtown to the North Shore, with up to 70 000 cars crossing every day.

That meant the work was done on the weekends and at night, during 10-hour periods between 8 p.m. and 6 a.m.—an engineering feat never before attempted on a bridge that size. "You're into major, technical calculations with a project like this," noted one engineering expert. "This has never been done on a major suspension bridge."

But what looked like a doable and daring project on paper ran aground with glitches, delays, and soaring costs. Assistant project manager Carson Carney noted that the task was more difficult than first thought. Delays developed early on, as problems arose with the assembly plan to rebuild the bridge in short time bursts. At night, workers were required to perform a tightly choreographed construction dance, which, on some evenings, called on them to dismantle a 10- or 20-metre section of the bridge, lower it onto a barge, hoist a new panel into place, and then splice it to the existing deck using 800 bolts— all before morning rush hour. However, removing an entire sec-

The retrofit project for the Lions Gate Bridge in Vancouver was done without closing the bridge to weekday traffic.

tion of a suspension bridge changes its shape. To prevent the bridge from buckling when a section was removed, engineers were constantly adjusting the pressure on the bridge's suspended hangers.

"Certainly, it is an engineering first, and in that respect it is a success," Mr. Carney said. "The fact that it was done, that it was able to be done, is really a marvel of modern engineering."[2]

crash cost The additional cost associated with reducing an activity time.

A project manager may consider *crashing*, or expediting, some activities on the critical path (or paths) to reduce overall project completion time. However, reducing the time of an activity comes at an extra cost, termed the **crash cost**, in addition to the normal activity cost. For example, if a particular construction activity was on the critical path, overtime might be used to accelerate its completion. Alternatively, for activities *not* on the critical path, savings might be possible if their times can be extended. For example, materials might be shipped by ground freight rather than air freight if critical activities are not delayed.

minimum-cost schedule A schedule determined by crashing activities along the critical path (or paths) such that the costs of crashing do not exceed the savings from penalty and indirect costs. Non-critical activities also may be extended.

MINIMIZING COSTS. The objective of this cost analysis is to determine the project schedule that minimizes total project costs. In determining the **minimum-cost schedule**, we start with the normal time schedule and crash activities along the critical path—the length of which is the total time of the project. We want to determine by how much we can reduce the time of critical activities, until the crash costs exceed the savings in indirect and penalty costs. The procedure involves the following steps:

- *Step 1.* Determine the project's critical path(s).
- *Step 2.* Find the activity or activities on the critical path(s) with the lowest cost of crashing per week.
- *Step 3.* Reduce the time for this activity until (a) it cannot be further reduced, (b) another path becomes critical, or (c) the increase in direct costs exceeds the savings that result from shortening the project. If more than one path is critical, the time for an activity on each path may have to be reduced simultaneously.
- *Step 4.* Repeat this procedure until the increase in direct costs is larger than the savings generated by shortening the project.

| EXAMPLE 8.3 | *Finding a Minimum-Cost Schedule* |

For the St. John's Hospital project, indirect costs have been estimated at $8000 per week. However, after week 65, if the hospital is not fully operational, provincial government regulators will impose a penalty cost of $20 000 per week. With the current critical path completion time of 69 weeks, the hospital faces large penalty costs unless the schedule is changed. For every week that the project is shortened—to week 65—the hospital saves one week of penalty and indirect costs, or $28 000. For reductions beyond week 65, the savings are only the weekly indirect costs of $8000.

To determine the minimum-cost schedule for the St. John's Hospital project, we need to use the information in Table 8.1 and Figure 8.3.

Without changes, the projected completion time of the project is 69 weeks. The project costs for that schedule are $1 992 000 in direct costs from Table 8.1, 69($8000) = $552 000 in indirect costs based on the total project time, and (69 − 65)($20 000) = $80 000 in penalty costs. In total, the project costs are $2 624 000.

STAGE 1

- *Step 1.* As noted in Figure 8.3, the critical path is B–D–H–J–K.
- *Step 2.* The cheapest activity on the critical path to crash per week is D at $2500, which is much less than the savings in indirect and penalty costs of $28 000 per week.
- *Step 3.* Crash activity D by only 2 weeks, because now a second critical path is present. Now, as depicted in Figure 8.5, the two critical paths are:

A–C–G–J–K: 67 weeks, and B–D–H–J–K: 67 weeks

ACTIVITY	NORMAL ACTIVITY TIME (weeks)	NORMAL COST ($)	MINIMUM ACTIVITY TIME (weeks)	CRASH COST ($ per week)
A	12	$ 12 000	11	$10 000
B	9	50 000	7	7 000
C	10	4 000	5	6 000
D	10	16 000	8	2 500
E	24	120 000	14	8 000
F	10	10 000	6	1 500
G	35	500 000	25	7 000
H	40	1 200 000	35	12 000
I	15	40 000	10	2 500
J	4	10 000	1	3 000
K	6	30 000	5	9 000
Total		$1 992 000		

TABLE 8.1 *Direct Cost and Time Data for the Hospital Project*

The net savings are 2($28 000) − 2($2500) = $51 000. The total project costs are now $2 624 000 − $51 000 = $2 573 000.

FIGURE 8.5 *Project Plan after Stage 1*

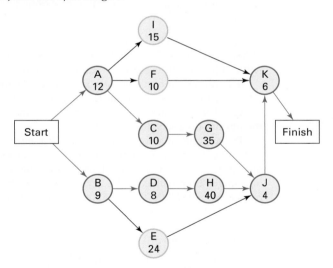

STAGE 2

- *Step 1.* Because we now have two critical paths, both critical paths must now be shortened to realize any savings in indirect project costs. If one is shortened and the other is not, the length of the project remains unchanged.

- *Step 2.* Our alternatives are to crash one of the following combinations of activities—(A, B), (A, D), (A, H), (C, B), (C, D), (C, H), (G, B), (G, D), (G, H)—or to crash either activity J or K, which are on both critical paths.

- *Step 3.* The lowest-cost alternative is to crash J at a cost of $3000 per week for 3 weeks, which is the greatest extent possible for J. As shown in Figure 8.6, updated critical path times are:

   A–C–G–J–K: 64 weeks, and B–D–H–J–K: 64 weeks

FIGURE 8.6   *Project Plan after Stage 2*

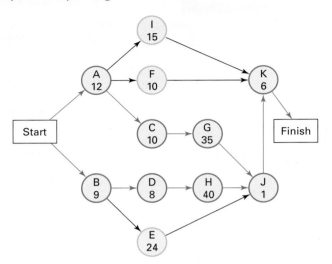

As we are now less than the required 65 weeks, penalty costs are saved for only two weeks, not three. However, indirect costs are saved for all three weeks. As a result, the net savings are 2($28 000) + $8000 − 3($3000) = $55 000. Total project costs are $2 573 000 − $55 000 = $2 518 000.

Decision Point The lowest-cost alternative to crash is now the combination of (C, D) at a cost of $8500 per week. Because this exceeds weekly indirect costs, any other combination of activities will result in a net increase in total project costs.

The minimum-cost schedule is 64 weeks, with a total cost of $2 518 000. To obtain this schedule, the project team must crash activity D to 8 weeks and activity J to its minimum of 1 week. The other activities remain at their normal times. This schedule costs $106 000 less than the normal-time schedule.

If a noncritical activity can be extended without creating a path longer than the existing critical paths, further cost savings are possible. For example, if activity I could be extended from a normal time of 15 weeks to 21 weeks by using part-time instead of full-time staff, further savings might be possible. If the savings were $2000 per week, the total project costs would be reduced to $2 518 000 − (6)($2000) = $2 506 000.

ASSESSING RISKS

Risk is a measure of the probability and consequence of not reaching a defined project goal. Risk involves the notion of uncertainty as it relates to project timing and costs. Often project teams must deal with uncertainty caused by labour shortages, weather, supply delays, or the outcomes of critical tests. A major responsibility of the project manager at the start of a project is to develop a **risk-management plan**. Team members should have an opportunity to describe the key risks to the project's success and prescribe ways to circumvent them, either by redefining key activities or by developing contingency plans in the event problems occur. A good risk-management plan will quantify the risks and predict their impact on the project. For each risk, the outcome is either acceptable or unacceptable, depending on the project manager's tolerance level for risk.

Project risks can be grouped into four categories: strategic alignment, new service or product attributes, team capability, and execution. First, the risk of poor *strategic*

risk-management plan
A plan that identifies the key risks to a project's success and prescribes ways to circumvent them.

alignment can occur when projects work at cross-purposes to each other, or do not fit together to support the broader goals of the firm. Instead, a set of projects, called a program or *portfolio*, should be aligned around a common strategic purpose and collectively enhance customer value. For example, a financial services firm might undertake a set of four related projects: (1) determine what the competition offers in the way of financial reports; (2) design new reporting services; (3) implement changes to the reporting process to reduce customer errors and improve delivery speed; and (4) develop a new Web interface to reach out to new customers. These projects must be integrated in terms of both purpose and timing, and as additional proposals come forward, management must assess and prioritize these based on the fit with the existing portfolio.

Second, many projects involve introducing *new service or product attributes*. Market risk is embedded in project objectives that specify particular market share or sales volumes. Competitive actions, either in parallel to or in response to the project, may weaken the market, or economic conditions may change, resulting in lower demand than expected when the project was initially approved. Technological risk arises from scientific advances made while the project is under way, possibly rendering the project obsolete. For example, a new cell phone under development may be displaced by a new technology developed by a competitor. Also, legal risks, such as liability suits or environmental legislation, may require a change in the design of the service or product after development has begun.

Third, project *team capability* risks are concerns associated with the project team itself. Poor selection of the project manager and team members can compromise the completion of a project. The complexity of the project, relative to what the team or the firm has attempted before, is usually also a good indicator of the likelihood of problems. Complexity might be measured in terms of budget size, number of individuals or groups involved, mix of internal and external resources, and lack of related technological experience.

Finally, project *execution* risk captures potential problems related to implementing the project. The accuracy of information for the work breakdown schedule is critical, as well as all data required for assessing progress, completion times of activities, and costs. Ineffective communication often can contribute to delays. Problems that impede progress must be quickly identified, action items developed, and responsibility clearly assigned.

SIMULATION. PERT/CPM networks can be used to quantify risks associated with project timing. Often the uncertainty associated with an activity can be reflected in the activity's time duration. For example, an activity in a new-product development project might be developing the enabling technology to manufacture it, an activity that may take from eight months to a year. To incorporate uncertainty into the network model, probability distributions of activity times can be used. With simulation, the time for each activity is randomly chosen from its probability distribution. The critical path of the network is determined and the completion date of the project computed. The procedure is repeated many times, which results in a probability distribution for the completion date.

STATISTICAL ANALYSIS. In contrast to simulation, statistical analysis requires that activity times be stated in terms of three reasonable time estimates:

1. The **optimistic time** (*a*) is the shortest time in which the activity can be completed, if all goes exceptionally well.

optimistic time The shortest time in which an activity can be completed, if all goes exceptionally well.

most likely time The probable time required to perform an activity.

pessimistic time The longest estimated time required to perform an activity.

2. The **most likely time (m)** is the probable time required to perform the activity.

3. The **pessimistic time (b)** is the longest estimated time required to perform the activity.

With three time estimates—the optimistic, most likely, and pessimistic—the project manager has enough information to estimate the probability that a project will be completed on schedule. To do so, the project manager must first calculate the mean and variance of a probability distribution for each activity. In PERT/CPM, each activity time is treated as though it were a random variable derived from a beta probability distribution. This distribution can have various shapes, allowing the most likely time estimate, or mode (m), to fall anywhere between the pessimistic (b) and optimistic (a) time estimates.

Two other key assumptions are required. First, we assume that a, m, and b can be estimated accurately, and represent a reasonable time range negotiated between the project manager and the team members responsible for the activities. Second, we assume that the standard deviation, σ, of the activity time is one-sixth the range $b - a$. Thus, the chance that actual activity times will fall between a and b is high.

The mean of the beta distribution can be estimated by using the following weighted average of the three time estimates:

$$t_e = \frac{a + 4m + b}{6}$$

The variance of the beta distribution for each activity is estimated as:

$$\sigma_e^2 = \left(\frac{b - a}{6}\right)^2$$

ANALYZING PROBABILITIES. Because time estimates for activities involve uncertainty, project managers are interested in determining the probability of meeting project completion deadlines. To develop the probability distribution for project completion time, we assume that the duration time of one activity does not depend on that of any other activity. This assumption enables us to estimate the mean and variance of the probability distribution of the time duration of the entire project by summing the duration times and variances of the activities along the critical path. However, if one work crew is assigned two activities that can be done at the same time, the activity times will be interdependent. In addition, if other paths in the network have small amounts of slack, one of them might become the critical path before the project is completed. In such a case, we should calculate a probability distribution for those paths.

Because of the assumption that the activity duration times are independent random variables, we can make use of the central limit theorem, which states that the sum of a group of independent, identically distributed random variables approaches a normal distribution as the number of random variables increases. The mean of the normal distribution is the sum of the expected activity times on the path. In the case of the critical path, it is the earliest expected completion time for the project, T_E:

$$T_E = \Sigma \ (\text{Activity times, } t_e, \text{ on the critical path})$$

Similarly, because of the assumption of activity time independence, we use the sum of the variances of the activities along the path as the variance of the time distribution for that path. That is:

$$\sigma^2 = \Sigma \ (\text{Variances of activities, } \sigma_e, \text{ on the critical path})$$

To analyze probabilities of completing a project by a certain date using the normal distribution, we use the z-transformation formula:

$$z = \frac{T - T_E}{\sqrt{\sigma^2}}$$

where:

T = Due date for the project

The procedure for assessing the probability of completing any activity in a project by a specific date is similar to the one just discussed. However, instead of the critical path, we would use the longest time path of activities from the start node to the activity node in question. See the Solved Problem for an example of calculating the probability of completing a project on time.

MONITORING AND CONTROLLING PROJECTS

Once project planning is over, the challenge becomes keeping the project on schedule within the budget of allocated resources. In this section, we discuss how to monitor project status and resource usage. In addition, we identify the features of project management software useful for monitoring and controlling projects.

PROJECT STATUS

A good tracking system will help the project team accomplish its project goals. Often the very task of monitoring project progress motivates the team as it sees the benefits of its planning efforts come to fruition. It also focuses attention on the decisions that must be made as the project unfolds. Effective tracking systems collect information on three topics: open issues, risks, and schedule status.

OPEN ISSUES AND RISKS. One of the duties of the project manager is to make sure that issues that have been raised during the project actually get resolved in a timely fashion. The tracking system should remind the project manager of due dates for open issues and who was responsible for seeing that they are resolved. Likewise, it should provide the status of each risk to project delays specified in the risk-management plan so that the team can review them at each meeting. To be effective, the tracking system requires team members periodically to update information regarding their respective responsibilities.

SCHEDULE STATUS. Even the best-laid project plans can go awry. Monitoring slack time in the project schedule can help the project manager control activities along the critical path. Periodic updating of the status of ongoing activities in the project allows the tracking system to recalculate activity slacks and indicate those activities that are behind schedule or are in danger of using up all of their slack. Management can then focus on those activities and reallocate resources as needed.

PROJECT RESOURCES

The resources allocated to a project are consumed at an uneven rate that is a function of the timing of the schedules for the project's activities. Projects have a *life cycle* that consists of four major phases: organization, planning, execution, and closeout. Figure 8.7 shows that each of the four phases requires different resource commitments.

We have already discussed the activities associated with the project organization and project planning phases. The phase that takes the most resources is the *execution phase*, during which managers focus on activities pertaining to deliverables. The project schedule becomes very important, because it shows when each resource devoted to a

FIGURE 8.7 *Project Life Cycle*

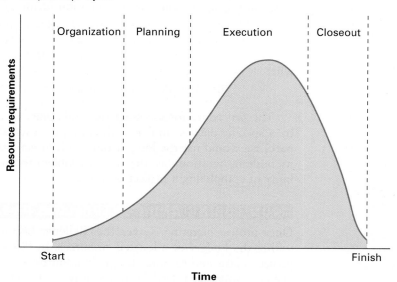

given activity will be required. Monitoring the progress of activities throughout the project is important in order to avoid potential overloading of resources. Problems arise when a specific resource, such as a construction crew or staff specialist, is required on several activities with overlapping schedules. Project managers have several options to alleviate resource problems, including:

- *Resource levelling,* which is an attempt to reduce the peaks and valleys in resource needs by shifting the schedules of conflicting activities within their earliest and latest start dates. If an activity must be delayed beyond its latest start date, the completion date of the total project will be delayed unless activities on the critical path can be reduced to compensate.

- *Resource allocation,* which is an attempt to shift resources from activities with slack to those on the critical path where resources are overloaded. A slack report identifies potential candidates for resource shifting. However, efficiency can be compromised if shifted employees do not have all the skills required for their new assignments.

- *Resource acquisition,* which simply adds more of an overloaded resource to maintain the schedule of an activity.

CONTROLLING PROJECTS

Project managers must account for the effective use of the firm's resources as well as managing the activities to achieve the objectives of the project. Resources include physical assets, human resources, and financial resources. Physical assets are controlled by the timely maintenance of machines and equipment so that their failure does not delay the project. Inventories must be received, stored for future use, and replenished. Project managers are also responsible for human resource deployment and development. Projects provide a rich environment to develop future leaders; project managers can take advantage of the situation by assigning team members important tasks to aid in their managerial development. Last but not least, project managers must control financial expenditures. Project management software assists with accounting reports, budget reports, capital investment controls, and cash flow reports.

Deviations from the project plan, often referred to as *variances*, must be periodically reported and analyzed for their causes. Project managers can exert control over the achievement of the project's time and quality goals by routine monitoring of exception reports, which highlight variances that fall outside specified limits. Unacceptable project progress can trigger levelling, allocation, or acquisition decisions. Industry norms and experience help the project manager know when to take action.

Monitoring and controlling projects are ongoing activities throughout the execution phase of the project life cycle. The project **close out**, however, is an activity that many project managers forget to include in their consideration of resource usage. The purpose of this final phase in the project life cycle is to write final reports and complete remaining deliverables. An important aspect of this phase, however, is compiling the team's recommendations for improving the project process of which they were a part. Many team members will be assigned to other projects where they can apply what they learned.

close out An activity that includes writing final reports, completing remaining deliverables, and compiling the team's recommendations for improving the project process.

SUSTAINABILITY AS A KEY PROJECT OBJECTIVE

Managing projects often requires bringing together many resources in a timely and efficient way. In doing so, environmental and social issues often must enter the project plan in the form of one or more project goals or objectives. For example, when Rio Tinto Group, an international mining company based in the United Kingdom and Australia, considers opening a new mining site, project objectives must include the development of local communities and workforce skills (social objectives), and protection of the neighbouring ecosystems (environmental objectives). Given that mines have a predictable but long lifespan, active planning is required for closing the project decades in advance. The firm's project management track record also affects its future options: a good reputation for earlier mines opens opportunities to develop new mining projects around the world.

Many other industries include environmental objectives in their projects, whether constructing greener buildings, designing new computers, or developing better public transit. For example, the Leadership in Energy and Environmental Design Green Building Rating System (LEED) allows project managers to certify buildings based on the materials used, energy consumed, and sensitivity to lighting and indoor air quality (Lockwood, 2006). And building owners are willing to pay more to achieve Gold or Platinum certification because they can profit from higher rents and lower operating costs (Buhayar, 2009).

Project objectives for new products, such as dishwashers and computers, also can reflect Canada's EnerGuide and Energy Star rating system. Of course, adding more objectives to any project increases complexity, and managers increasingly have to rely on a diverse team of experts to make the right decisions early in the planning process. But there are significant opportunities to enhance customer value by doing so.

EQUATION SUMMARY

1. Start and finish times:

$$ES = max \text{ [EF times of all activities immediately preceding activity]}$$
$$EF = ES + t$$
$$LF = min \text{ [LS times of all activities immediately following activity]}$$
$$LS = LF - t$$

2. Activity total slack:

$$S = LS - ES \quad or \quad S = LF - EF$$

3. Activity time statistics:

$$t_e = \frac{a + 4m + b}{6} \quad \text{(expected activity time)}$$

$$\sigma_e^2 = \left(\frac{b - a}{6}\right)^2 \quad \text{(variance of activity time)}$$

4. z-transformation formula:

$$z = \frac{T - T_E}{\sqrt{\sigma^2}}$$

where:

T = Due date for the project

$T_E = \Sigma$ (expected activity times on the critical path) $= \Sigma t_e$

$\sigma^2 = \Sigma$ (variances of activities on the critical path) $= \Sigma \sigma_e^2$

CHAPTER HIGHLIGHTS

- A project is an interrelated set of activities that often transcends functional boundaries. A project process is the organization and management of the resources dedicated to completing a project. Managing project processes involves organizing, planning, and monitoring and controlling the project.

- Project planning involves defining the work breakdown structure, diagramming the network, developing a schedule, analyzing cost–time trade-offs, and assessing risks.

- Project planning and scheduling focus on the critical path: the sequence of activities requiring the greatest cumulative amount of time for completion. Delay in critical activities will delay the entire project.

- A project manager may consider crashing, or expediting, some activities on the critical path (or paths) to reduce overall project completion time. However, reducing the time of an activity comes at an extra cost, termed the crash cost, in addition to the normal activity cost.

- Risks associated with the completion of activities on schedule can be incorporated in project networks by recognizing three time estimates for each activity and then calculating expected activity times and variances. The probability of completing the schedule by a certain date can be computed with this information.

- Monitoring and controlling the project involves reviewing activity slack time and examining actual resource usage. Overloads on certain resources can be rectified by resource levelling, allocation, or acquisition.

SOLVED PROBLEM

An advertising project manager has gathered the activity information for a new advertising campaign as shown in the table below. The project deadline is 23 weeks. What is the probability of completing the project by that time?

ACTIVITY	TIME ESTIMATES (weeks)			IMMEDIATE PREDECESSOR(S)
	OPTIMISTIC	MOST LIKELY	PESSIMISTIC	
A	1	4	7	—
B	2	6	7	—
C	3	3	6	B
D	6	13	14	A
E	3	6	12	A, C
F	6	8	16	B
G	1	5	6	E, F

SOLUTION

The expected time and variance for each activity are calculated as follows:

$$t_e = \frac{a + 4m + b}{6}, \quad \sigma_e^2 = \left(\frac{b - a}{6}\right)^2$$

ACTIVITY	EXPECTED TIME (weeks)	VARIANCE
A	4.0	1.00
B	5.5	0.69
C	3.5	0.25
D	12.0	1.78
E	6.5	2.25
F	9.0	2.78
G	4.5	0.69

Now we need to calculate the earliest start, latest start, earliest finish, and latest finish times for each activity. Starting with activities A and B, we proceed from the beginning of the network and move to the end, calculating the earliest start and finish times, on the basis of the expected activity times. The earliest finish for the project is week 20, when activity G has been completed. This is shown graphically in Figure 8.8. Using that as a target date, we can work backward through the network, calculating the latest start and finish times (also in Figure 8.8).

FIGURE 8.8   *Network Diagram with Activity Time Estimates*

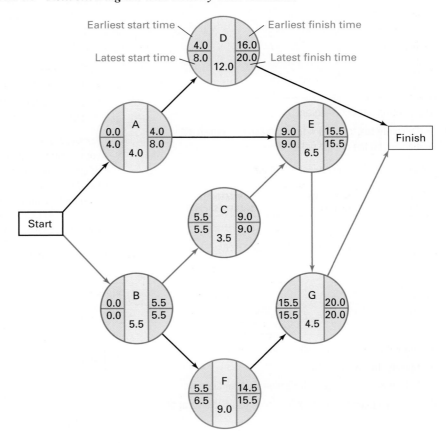

The activities on the critical path can now be identified based on having no slack (i.e., LS − ES = 0). Here the critical path is B–C–E–G, with a total expected time of 20 weeks. The variance of this path is (0.69 + 0.25 + 2.25 + 0.69) = 3.88.

To find the probability of completing the project in 23 weeks or less, we first calculate the z-value:

$$z = \frac{T - T_E}{\sqrt{\sigma^2}} = \frac{23 - 20}{\sqrt{3.88}} = 1.52$$

Using the Normal Distribution in MyOMLab or Excel function NORM.S.DIST(1.52,TRUE), we find that the probability of completing the project in 23 weeks or less is 0.9357. In other words, the probability that the project will exceed 23 weeks is 6 percent. However, the length of path B–F–G, at 19 weeks, is very close to that of the critical path and also has a large variance of 4.16. This path might well become the critical path as the project proceeds. The probability that this path might exceed 23 weeks, for which z = 1.96, is 2.5 percent.

PROBLEMS

1. A project has the following precedence relationships and activity times:

ACTIVITY	ACTIVITY TIME (weeks)	IMMEDIATE PREDECESSOR(S)
A	4	—
B	10	—
C	5	A
D	15	B, C
E	12	B
F	4	D
G	8	E
H	7	F, G

a. Draw the network diagram.

b. Calculate the total slack for each activity. Which activities are on the critical path?

2. Consider the following project information:

ACTIVITY	ACTIVITY TIME (weeks)	IMMEDIATE PREDECESSOR(S)
A	4	—
B	3	—
C	5	—
D	3	A, B
E	6	B
F	4	D, C
G	8	E, C
H	12	F, G

a. Draw the network diagram for this project.

b. Specify the critical path.

c. Calculate the total slack for activities A and D.

d. What happens to the slack for D if A takes five weeks?

3. The following information has been gathered for a project:

ACTIVITY	ACTIVITY TIME (weeks)	IMMEDIATE PREDECESSOR(S)
A	4	—
B	7	A
C	9	B
D	3	B
E	14	D
F	10	C, D
G	11	E, F

a. Draw the network diagram.

b. Calculate the slack for each activity and determine the critical path. How long will the project take?

4. Recently, you were assigned to manage a project for your company. You have constructed a network diagram depicting the various activities in the project (Figure 8.9). In addition, you have asked your team to estimate the amount of time that they would expect each of the activities to take. Their responses are shown in the following table.

FIGURE 8.9 *Project Diagram*

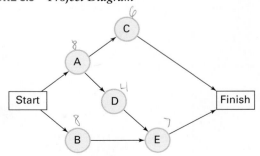

ACTIVITY	TIME ESTIMATES (days)		
	OPTIMISTIC	MOST LIKELY	PESSIMISTIC
A	5	8	11
B	4	8	11
C	5	6	7
D	2	4	6
E	4	7	10

a. What is the expected completion time of the project?

b. What is the probability of completing the project in 21 days or less?

c. What is the probability of completing the project in 17 days or less?

5. Consider the following data for a project never before attempted by your company:

ACTIVITY	EXPECTED TIME t_e (weeks)	IMMEDIATE PREDECESSOR(S)
A	5	—
B	3	—
C	2	A
D	5	B
E	4	C, D
F	7	D

a. Draw the network diagram for this project.

b. Identify the critical path and estimate the project's duration.

c. Calculate the slack for each activity.

6. The director of continuing education at Bluebird University has just approved the planning for a sales training seminar. Her administrative assistant has identified the various activities that must be done and their relationships to each other, as shown in Table 8.2.

TABLE 8.2	*Activities for the Sales Training Seminar*	
ACTIVITY	DESCRIPTION	IMMEDIATE PREDECESSOR(S)
A	Design brochure and course announcement.	—
B	Identify prospective teachers.	—
C	Prepare detailed outline of course.	—
D	Send brochure and student applications.	A
E	Send teacher applications.	B
F	Select teacher for course.	C, E
G	Accept students.	D
H	Select text for course.	F
I	Order and receive texts.	G, H
J	Prepare room for class.	G

Because of the uncertainty in planning the new course, the assistant also has supplied time estimates for each activity.

ACTIVITY	TIME ESTIMATES (days)		
	OPTIMISTIC	MOST LIKELY	PESSIMISTIC
A	5	7	8
B	6	8	12
C	3	4	5
D	11	17	25
E	8	10	12
F	3	4	5
G	4	8	9
H	5	7	9
I	8	11	17
J	4	4	4

The director wants to conduct the seminar 47 working days from now. What is the probability that everything will be ready in time?

7. Paul Silver, owner of Sculptures International, just initiated a new art project. The following data are available for the project:

ACTIVITY	EXPECTED TIME (weeks)	IMMEDIATE PREDECESSOR(S)
A	4	—
B	1	—
C	3	A
D	2	B
E	3	C, D

a. Draw the network diagram for the project.

b. Determine the project's critical path and duration.

c. What is the slack for each activity?

8. You are the manager of a project to improve a billing process at your firm. Table 8.3 contains the data you will need to conduct a cost analysis of the project. Indirect costs are $1600 per week, and penalty costs are $1200 per week after week 12.

TABLE 8.3		*Data for the Billing Process Project*			
ACTIVITY	IMMEDIATE PREDECESSOR(S)	NORMAL TIME (weeks)	CRASH TIME (weeks)	NORMAL COST ($)	CRASH COST ($)
A	—	4	1	5 000	8 000
B	—	5	3	8 000	10 000
C	A	1	1	4 000	4 000
D	B	6	3	6 000	12 000
E	B, C	7	6	4 000	7 000
F	D	7	6	4 000	7 000

a. What is the minimum-cost schedule for this project?

b. What is the difference in total project costs between the earliest completion time of the project using "normal" times and the minimum-cost schedule you derived in part (a)?

9. Consider the office renovation project data in Table 8.4. A "zero" time estimate means that the activity could take a very small amount of time and should be treated as a numeric zero in the analysis.

a. Based on the critical path, find the probability of completing the office renovation project by 39 days.

b. Find the date by which you would be 90 percent sure of completing the project.

TABLE 8.4		Data for the Office Renovation Project		
ACTIVITY	OPTIMISTIC	MOST LIKELY	PESSIMISTIC	IMMEDIATE PREDECESSOR(S)
START	0	0	0	—
A	6	10	14	START
B	0	1	2	A
C	16	20	30	A
D	3	5	7	B
E	2	3	4	D
F	7	10	13	C
G	1	2	3	D
H	0	2	4	G
I	2	2	2	C, G
J	2	3	4	I
K	0	1	2	H
L	1	2	3	J, K
FINISH	0	0	0	E, F, L

10. The project manager of Good Public Relations has gathered the data shown in Table 8.5 for a new advertising campaign.

a. How long is the project likely to take?

b. What is the probability that the project will take more than 38 weeks?

c. Consider the path A–E–G–H–J. What is the probability that this path will exceed the expected project duration?

TABLE 8.5	Activity Data for Advertising Project			
	TIME ESTIMATES (days)			IMMEDIATE PREDECESSOR(S)
ACTIVITY	OPTIMISTIC	MOST LIKELY	PESSIMISTIC	
A	8	10	12	—
B	5	8	17	—
C	7	8	9	—
D	1	2	3	B
E	8	10	12	A, C
F	5	6	7	D, E
G	1	3	5	D, E
H	2	5	8	F, G
I	2	4	6	G
J	4	5	8	H
K	2	2	2	H

NOTES FOR CHAPTER

1. David Holt, Charles Holloway, and Hau Lee, "Evolution of the Xbox Supply Chain," Stanford Graduate School of Business, Case GS-49, April 14, 2006; "Xbox 360," *Wikipedia, The Free Encyclopedia*, en.wikipedia.org/wiki/Xbox_360.

2. Jane Armstrong, "Bridge Retrofit a Modern Miracle," *The Globe and Mail*, January 7, 2002, p. A8. Reprinted with permission from *The Globe and Mail*. All rights reserved.

FURTHER READING

Buhayar, N. "Old Wine, New Bottles: Retrofits of Existing Buildings Can Cut Energy Use, Save Money—and Attract Tenants." *Wall Street Journal*, September 21, 2009.

Caland, D. I. *Project Management: Strategic Design and Implementation.* New York: McGraw-Hill, 1994.

Goldratt, E. M. *Critical Chain.* Great Barrington, MA: North River Press, 1997.

Kerzner, Harold. *Advanced Project Management: Best Practices on Implementation,* 2nd ed. New York: John Wiley & Sons, 2004.

Kerzner, Harold. *Project Management: A Systems Approach to Planning, Scheduling, and Controlling,* 6th ed. New York: John Wiley & Sons, 1998.

Leach, Larry P. "Critical Chain Project Management Improves Project Performance." *Project Management Journal* (June 1999), pp. 39–51.

Lewis, J. P. *Mastering Project Management.* New York: McGraw-Hill, 1998.

Lockwood, C. "Building the Green Way." *Harvard Business Review,* vol. 84, no. 6 (2006), pp. 129–137.

Mantel, Jr., Samuel J., Jack R. Meredith, Scott M. Shafer, and Margaret M. Sutton. *Project Management in Practice,* 2nd ed. New York: John Wiley & Sons, 2005.

Pellegrinelli, Sergio, and Cliff Bowman. "Implementing Strategy Through Projects." *Long Range Planning,* vol. 27, no. 4 (1994), pp. 125–132.

"Project Management Body of Knowledge." Available from the Project Management Institute, www.pmi.org.

MyOMLab ASSETS

MyOMLab offers the following resources, which allow you to further practise and apply concepts presented in this chapter.

- **Key Equations:** All the equations for this chapter can be found in one convenient location.

- **Discussion Questions:** Three questions will challenge your understanding of the role of project management by asking you to reflect on your experiences.

- **Microsoft Project:** A student version is included to develop project plans.

- **Case:** *The Pert Studebaker*. Will Vikky Roberts complete the project on time and within budget?

- **Video Cases:**

  - *Project Management at Starwood's Phoenician*. Explore intangible factors and the timing for the spa selection process.

  - *Nantucket Nectars: ERP*. The firm defined a set of objectives, developed a specific project format, and reviewed the results after implementation.

- **Internet Exercise:**

  - *Olympic Movement: London 2012*. Planning begins years in advance. How does the multi-cultural focus of the Games affect planning?

  - *Ch2M Hill*. The firm offers many project-related capabilities in engineering, construction, and operations. How might scope and risk be managed?

- **Virtual Tours:**

  - *Rieger Orgelbau Pipe Organ Factory:* Follow a customer's visit to the factory while his congregation's pipe organ was being restored.

  - *Alaskan Way Viaduct:* This site details the Alaskan Way Viaduct Project that will completely overhaul a major artery in Seattle's transportation system.

- **Extend LT:** Connect Telecom must improve its process for new product introductions.

- **Supplement C:** *Work Measurement*. This supplement presents several tools for estimating the time to perform predictable or repetitive project tasks after learning effects have worn off.

- **Supplement D:** *Learning Curve Analysis*. This supplement provides the background to estimate the time or resources required to perform an activity consisting of the production of a given number of identical units.

9

Location and Layout

Learning Goals

After reading this chapter, you will be able to:

1. discuss the managerial challenges in global operations.
2. describe the factors affecting location choices, in both manufacturing and services.
3. apply the load-distance method and break-even analysis to single-site location problems.
4. describe the four basic layout types and when each is best used.
5. identify the types of performance criteria that are important in evaluating layouts.
6. recommend how to design flexible-flow and line-flow layouts.

Across the Organization

Location and layout are important to:

- **accounting,** which prepares cost estimates for changing layouts and operating at new locations.
- **distribution,** which seeks warehouse layouts that make materials handling easier and make customer response times shorter.
- **engineering,** which considers the impact of product design choices on layout.
- **finance,** which performs the financial analysis for investments in new layouts or in facilities at new locations.
- **human resources,** which hires and trains employees to support new or relocated operations.
- **management information systems,** which provide information technologies that link operations at different locations.
- **marketing,** which assesses how new locations and revised layouts will appeal to customers.
- **operations,** which seeks facility locations and layouts that best balance multiple performance criteria.

Bavarian Motor Works (BMW), founded in 1917 and headquartered in Munich, Germany, is a manufacturer of select premium-segment brands such as BMW, MINI, and Rolls-Royce Motor Cars in the international automobile market. When faced with fluctuating exchange rates and increasing production costs in the late 1980s, BMW decided that it was time to consider operating a new production facility outside the European borders. A "blank page" approach was used to compile a list of 250 potential worldwide plant sites. Further analysis pared the list down to ten viable options; a plant location in the United States was preferred due to its proximity to a large market segment for BMW's automobiles.

Fluctuating exchange rates and other economic factors led Bavarian Motor Works (BMW) to consider manufacturing outside of Europe. The question was, where? After an extensive study and numerous government concessions, the South Carolina location was chosen. The plant is now an exclusive manufacturer of the X-series vehicles.

The selection of the plant site involved many factors that had to be analyzed prior to its construction. BMW considered the labour climate in each country, geographical requirements and constraints, and its relations with the governments of the countries in which the prospective sites were located. In terms of the labour climate, a technologically capable workforce was needed due to the complex nature of the automotive manufacturing process. Because the cost to train a single worker in the automotive industry is between $10 000 and $20 000, this factor was especially critical. Additionally, BMW decided that if the plant were located in the United States, it should be in a "right-to-work" state in which workers could decide for themselves whether they want to join or financially support a union.

Geographical factors had to be examined because thousands of automobile parts needed to be delivered from both domestic and foreign suppliers. In order to keep the supply chain costs down, it was decided that the new location should have ample highway/interstate access and be reasonably close to a port from which both supplies and finished automobiles could be easily transported. Another consideration was easy access to an airport for BMW's executives travelling back and forth to its headquarters in Germany.

The final set of location factors was government related. BMW wanted to move to a location that was "business friendly" in terms of making concessions on issues such as infrastructural improvements, tax abatements, and employee screening and education programs. The overall goal was to make the relationship between BMW and the local community as mutually beneficial as possible through a coordinated improvement effort.

After a search process that stretched over three years and stringently evaluated the ten options, BMW finally decided to build a new 185 800 square metre production facility in Spartanburg, South Carolina. The final decision was made on the basis of a good match between the selection criteria and this location. State lawmakers proved flexible and open as to how the state would address the needs set forth by BMW. For instance, they agreed to acquire the more than 200 hectares necessary to build the plant, improve the highway system around the facility for $10 million, and lengthen the runway and modernize the terminal at the Spartanburg airport for an additional $40 million. The legislature also agreed to provide tax incentives and property tax relief, and establish an employee screening and training program to ensure the right mix of workers was available. (Processing the applications alone proved to be a daunting task, because more than 50 000 applications were received.) While this location may not have scored the highest on each decision criterion, taken as a whole, this site was best for BMW.

This location has proven to be a good choice. The plant, which opened in 1994, subsequently underwent a $550 million expansion over the next six years. Recently, a further $750 million dollar expansion was completed in October 2010, adding 111 500 square metres of manufacturing space. As a key plant in BMW Group's global manufacturing network, it will soon become the exclusive producer for all its X-series vehicles. As BMW also brought about 40 suppliers, the local community also reaped rewards in the form of business growth, infrastructural improvement, and high-skill employment—a success story all around.[1]

Every year in Canada, manufacturing firms and service providers build and remodel innumerable plants, stores, office buildings, warehouses, and other facilities. Choosing where to locate new manufacturing facilities, service outlets, or branch offices, and how to lay them out, have both strategic and tactical dimensions. The location and layout of a business's facilities have significant impacts on the company's operating costs, the prices it charges for goods and services, and its ability to compete in the marketplace.

Analyzing location patterns to discover a firm's underlying strategy is fascinating. For example, White Castle, a U.S. hamburger chain started in 1921, locates restaurants near manufacturing plants. This is consistent with the firm's strategy to cater to blue-collar workers. As a result, restaurants tend to be located near the target population and away from competitors such as Wendy's and McDonald's, and are open around the clock. In contrast, why do competing new-car sales showrooms deliberately cluster near one another? In this case, customers prefer to do their comparison shopping in one area. For either industry, management's location decision reflects a particular strategy.

Recognizing the strategic impact that location decisions have on implementing a firm's strategy and supply chain design, we first consider the qualitative factors that influence location choices. Subsequently, we examine an important trend in location patterns—the use of geographical information systems (GIS) to identify market segments—and how serving each segment can profitably affect the firm's location decisions. Next we present some analytic techniques for making single- or multiple-facility location decisions. Finally, we turn to facility layout, beginning with strategic issues and then describing ways to design effective layouts.

FACTORS AFFECTING LOCATION DECISIONS

Managers of both service and manufacturing organizations have to weigh many factors when assessing the desirability of particular locations, such as their proximity to customers and suppliers, labour costs, and transportation costs. In essence, critical factors have a high impact on the company's ability to generate customer value. For example, although different facilities will be located at different distances from suppliers, if the shipments from them can take place overnight and the communication with them is done via fax or e-mail, the distance is not likely to have a large impact on the firm's ability to deliver customer value.

Location factors can be divided into dominant and secondary factors. Dominant factors are derived from competitive priorities (cost, quality, time, flexibility, customer experience, and innovation) and have a particularly strong impact on sales or costs. For example, Roots has emphasized natural living and the environmental sustainability of its products when entering the Chinese market in 2007. To create visibility and build its brand image, Roots chose to locate its new retail stores near well-known high-end

The location of Roots stores in China focused on access to customers and building its brand image.

international rivals, such as Gucci and Versace.[2] Secondary factors also are important, but management may downplay or even ignore some of these factors if others are more important. Thus, the cost of the retail site was a secondary factor for Roots in China. We discuss ten basic sets of factors here.

PROXIMITY TO CUSTOMERS AND MARKETS. Location is a key factor in determining how conveniently customers can carry on business with a firm. For example, few people will patronize a remotely located dry cleaner or supermarket if another is more convenient. Thus, the influence of location on revenues tends to be the dominant factor. The key is proximity to customers who will patronize the facility and seek its services. For manufacturers, locating near markets is particularly important when the final goods are bulky or heavy, breakage in shipment is high, and quick customer delivery is critical.

PROXIMITY TO SUPPLIERS AND RESOURCES. Firms dependent on inputs of bulky, perishable, or heavy raw materials emphasize proximity to suppliers and resources. In such cases, inbound transportation costs become a dominant factor, encouraging such firms to locate facilities near suppliers. For example, locating paper mills near forests and grain processing facilities near farms is practical, because smaller quantities of value-added materials can be shipped more efficiently. Another advantage of locating near suppliers is the ability to maintain lower inventories.

LABOUR CLIMATE. A favourable labour climate may be the most important factor for labour-intensive firms in industries such as textiles, furniture, and consumer electronics. Labour climate is a function of wage rates, training requirements, attitude toward work, worker productivity, and union strength. Having a favourable climate applies not just to the workforce already on site, but, in the case of relocation decisions, also to the employees that a firm hopes will transfer or will be attracted there.

PROXIMITY TO THE FIRM'S OTHER FACILITIES. In many companies, plants supply parts to other facilities or rely on other facilities for management and staff support. These ties require frequent coordination and communication, which can become more difficult as distance increases. Also, close proximity can help a new facility start up more quickly through sharing personnel and other resources. For example, Toyota's new plant in Woodstock, Ontario, is less than 50 kilometres from a large, well-established facility in Cambridge.

LOCATION OF OTHER FIRMS. One complication in estimating the sales potential at different locations is the impact of competitors. Management must not only consider the current location of competitors but also try to anticipate their reaction to the firm's new location. Avoiding areas where competitors are already well established can pay.

critical mass The clustering of several competing firms in one location to attract more customers than the total number that would be attracted if the same stores were scattered.

However, in some industries, such as new-car sales showrooms, locating near competitors is actually advantageous. The strategy is to create a **critical mass**, whereby several competing firms clustered in one location attract more customers than the total number who would shop at the same stores at scattered locations. Firms that offer complementary products and services also can co-locate. For example, several home decorating stores might locate close together so that customer can buy furniture, bedding, rugs, and other products from neighbouring stores. Finally, firms that focus on innovation in related technologies can build facilities near each other to spur the development of knowledge, such as the biotechnology cluster that has developed in the Ottawa area, and Silicon Valley in the United States. Recognizing this effect, some firms use a follow-the-leader strategy when selecting new sites.

TRANSPORTATION COSTS. For warehousing and distribution operations, transportation costs and proximity to markets are extremely important. With a warehouse nearby, many firms can hold inventory closer to the customer, reducing delivery time and promoting sales. In addition, the costs of transportation vary by country on the basis of many factors, such as fuel prices or weather. Thus, rail might make sense to move goods in Canada, while truck transport might be favoured to move the same distance in the United States.

SITE-SPECIFIC FACTORS. Retailers also must consider the level of retail activity, residential density, traffic flow, and site visibility. Retail activity in the area is important, as shoppers often decide on impulse to go shopping or to eat in a restaurant. Traffic flows and visibility are important, because businesses' customers often arrive in cars. Management considers possible traffic tie-ups, traffic volume and direction by time of day, traffic signals, intersections, and the position of traffic medians. Visibility involves distance from the street and size of nearby buildings and signs. High residential density ensures evening and weekend business when the population in the area fits the firm's competitive priorities and target market segment.

UTILITIES, TAXES, AND REAL ESTATE COSTS. Other important factors that may emerge include utility costs (telephone, energy, and water), local and provincial taxes, financing incentives offered by local or provincial governments, relocation costs, and land costs. Currently, there is increasing pressure on provincial and local governments in Canada to provide major tax and financial incentives to international manufacturers, in order to compete with aggressive offers from states in the southern United States.

QUALITY OF LIFE. Good schools, recreational facilities, cultural events, and an attractive lifestyle contribute to quality of life for employees. This factor is relatively unimportant on its own, but it can make the difference in location decisions within a region or country. In North America, Japan, and Europe, many new manufacturing jobs are shifting outside of urban centres. Reasons for this movement include high costs of living, high crime rates, and general decline in the quality of life in many large cities.

OTHER FACTORS. Still other factors may need to be considered, including room for expansion, construction costs, accessibility to multiple modes of transportation, the cost of shuffling people and materials between plants, insurance costs, competition from other firms for the workforce, local ordinances (such as pollution or noise control regulations), community attitudes, and many others. For global operations, firms are emphasizing local employee skills and education and the local infrastructure. Many firms are concluding that large, centralized manufacturing facilities in low-cost countries with poorly trained workers are not sustainable. Smaller, flexible facilities serving multiple markets allow the firm to deal with nontariff barriers such as sales volume limitations, regional trading blocs, political risks, and exchange rates.

GEOGRAPHICAL INFORMATION SYSTEMS

geographical information system (GIS) A computer-based system of databases that enable the manipulation, analysis, and presentation of location-related information.

Managers can use a **geographical information system** (GIS), comprising multiple databases, to manipulate, analyze, and present information relevant to a location decision. A GIS can also create a visual representation of a firm's location choices. Among other things, it can be used to (1) store databases of location-related characteristics, such as population demographics, transportation infrastructure, and competitor locations; (2) display maps; and (3) create models that can take information from existing datasets, apply analytic functions, and write results into new, derived datasets.

A GIS can be a really useful decision-making tool because many of the decisions made by businesses today have a geographical aspect. Information is stored in databases and can be naturally linked to places; for example, customer sales can be mapped to locations, or to demographic information about that location, such as the percentage of residents in a neighbourhood with a particular income level. More generally, demographics include the number of people in the metropolitan statistical area, city, or postal code; average income; number of families with children; and so forth. These demographics may all be important variables in the decision of how best to reach the target market. Similarly, the road system, including bridges and highways, location of nearby airports and seaports, and the terrain (mountains, forests, lakes, and so forth) play an important role in facility location decisions. As such, a GIS can have a diverse set of location-related applications that can be used in different industries, such as retail, real estate, government, transportation, and logistics.

Governmental data can provide a wealth of statistical information used to make better GIS-based location decisions. For example, the federal government is working to develop the Canadian Geospatial Data Infrastructure (www.cgdi.ca), which provides access to a wide variety of location-based information through a network of data, service, and technology suppliers. When combined with a database, such as the results of a Canadian census or a company's own customer files, managers have the ability to ask various "what if" questions about location alternatives.

Many different types of GIS packages are available, and some have been tailored to a specific application such as locating retail stores, analyzing logistics and marketing data, environmental management, and so forth. Here, we illustrate the use of one GIS program, Microsoft's MapPoint. Its ability to display information on maps can be a powerful decision-making tool.

USING GIS TO IDENTIFY LOCATIONS AND DEMOGRAPHIC CUSTOMER SEGMENTS

GIS can be useful for identifying locations that relate well to a firm's target market based on customer demographics. When coupled with other location models, sales forecasting models, and geodemographic systems, GIS can give a firm a formidable array of decision-making tools for its location decisions. The Managerial Practice feature illustrates how Starbucks makes one of its most important strategic decisions: the location of its stores. A GIS also can be used to estimate drive times from a central site

MANAGERIAL PRACTICE
Location Challenges at Starbucks

With 17 000 stores in 50 countries, Starbucks knows that an important part of its service strategy is location. The pace of new store openings slowed somewhat in 2010, to just over 200, down somewhat from the 1600 added in 2008. This continuing growth is aided by new site-selection technology. Starbucks relies on location analysis to evaluate where to place new stores.

In Starbucks' early days, a relatively small number of people participated in new store decisions, which was more of an experiential than a systematic process. As Starbucks grew, however, more planners became involved in the process and used a more standard, formal analysis. If a site's potential is not within a certain set of parameters, its planners do not waste their time giving it additional consideration.

Starbucks' original strategy was to expand in major urban areas, clustering in prime locations and placing outlets across from one another, sometimes even in the same block. This approach maximized the company's market share in areas with the highest volume potential—usually urban, affluent areas. Then rural areas began demanding Starbucks be located there too. Over the past few years, Starbucks' domestic expansion strategy definitely evolved. Smaller city markets and new store types, like those located in retail and airport locations, are being utilized.

Another change to the original strategy is the implementation of a geodemographic GIS as a productivity and process tool. It provides a description of different characteristics about people based upon the location where they live. The system determines the impact over the course of a year of opening an additional store one day sooner or one day later. Starbucks' site-acquisition process includes a number of elements that use spatial models, geodemographics, and sales-forecasting models. To identify potential locations, maps (such as those shown in Figures 9.1 and 9.2) are used by the company to show walk-time trade areas that pinpoint hotspots for gourmet coffee consumption.

TRADE AREA MAP - HAMILTON, ON

In addition to those in North America, Starbucks also opened stores in Asia, the Middle East, Europe, and South America. When seeking potentially viable sites abroad, Starbucks encounters additional challenges, such as the lack of available and accurate data. In many regions of the world, important statistics are not available and the systems that use any available data vary. There is no central place to get information about data availability in certain countries, which translates into comparability issues and increases the risks of erring in expansion analyses.

Although Starbucks continues to grow rapidly, it has already taken the premium locations in many markets. The company is now forced to look for lower-volume locations that will still provide a good return. More than ever before, the use of location analysis limits Starbucks' risk, and has become paramount to the firm.[3]

to surrounding locations, which is critical when locating emergency services, such as fire stations and ambulance dispatch facilities.

To get more practical insights into the application of GIS and demographics for understanding location choices made by Starbucks, let us examine further the Hamilton, Ontario, area showcased in the trade area map in Figure 9.1. The Starbucks store addresses within about 30 kilometres of Hamilton were obtained from the Starbucks Web site and imported into MapPoint. These store locations are denoted by yellow dots around a coffee cup pushpin. Then, demographics that come with MapPoint were overlaid on the map. The first map shows the population density per square kilometre for each census subdivision. Hamilton (the darkest area) has a population density of 2730 per square kilometre, while Oakville has a population density of 1024 per square kilometre. Yet Oakville has more stores than Hamilton. It suggests that store location is not being driven by population density alone. The most densely populated area around Hamilton has only one Starbucks store; further investigation reveals that it is on a road leading to the airport. In contrast, Ancaster, in the bottom left corner of the map, has a Starbucks, even though its population density is only 141 per square kilometre.

FIGURE 9.1   *Trade Area and Population Map for Hamilton, Ontario*

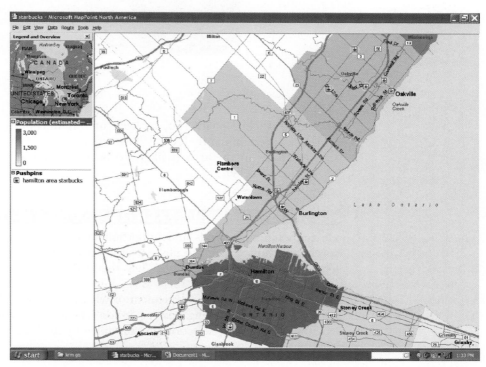

We then look to see whether per capita income could explain the locations of the Starbucks store. Figure 9.2 shows the demographics by average per capita household income. Applying these data to the map, we see that Oakville and Ancaster (the darkest cities in Figure 9.2) have a per capita income of $96 545 and $98 422, respectively. Burlington has a moderate population density and moderate per capita income. Oakville has five stores while Burlington has three stores, all of them located

FIGURE 9.2 *Per Capita Household Income Map of Hamilton*

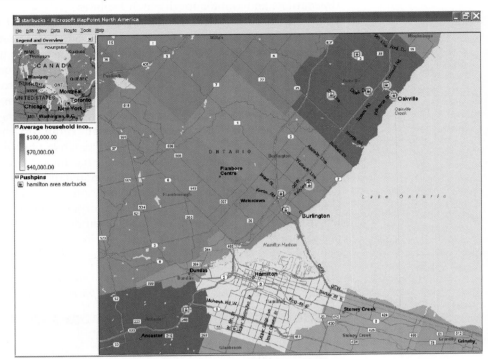

on well-trafficked roads. So, at least in this one particular case, it appears that Starbucks predominantly locates its stores in more affluent areas, and future expansion of stores in the area is likely to occur in and around Ancaster if population grows there further.

LOCATING A SINGLE FACILITY

Having examined trends and important factors in location, we now consider more specifically how a firm can make location decisions. To begin, we consider the case of locating only one new facility. When the facility is part of a firm's larger network of facilities, we assume that there is no interdependence; that is, a decision to open a restaurant in Calgary is independent of whether the chain has a restaurant in Halifax. Let's begin by considering how to decide whether a new location is needed and then examine a systematic selection process aided by the load-distance method to deal with proximity.

SELECTING ON-SITE EXPANSION, NEW LOCATION, OR RELOCATION

Management must first decide whether to expand on-site, build another facility, or relocate. A survey of Fortune 500 firms showed that 45 percent of expansions were on-site, 43 percent were in new plants at new locations, and only 12 percent were relocations of all facilities. On-site expansion has the advantage of keeping management together, reducing construction time and costs, and avoiding splitting up operations.

However, a firm may expand a facility too much, at which point diseconomies of scale set in (see Chapter 4, "Capacity"). Poor materials handling, increasingly complex production control, and simple lack of space all are reasons for building a new plant or relocating the existing one.

The advantages of building a new plant or moving to a new retail or office space are that the firm does not have to rely on production from a single plant, it can hire new and possibly more productive labour, it can modernize with new technology, and it can reduce transportation costs. Most firms that choose to relocate are small (fewer than ten employees). They tend to be single-location companies cramped for space and needing to redesign their production processes and layouts. More than 80 percent of all relocations are within 35 kilometres of the first location, which enables the firm to retain its current workforce.

COMPARING SEVERAL SITES

A systematic selection process begins after there is a perception or evidence that opening a retail outlet, warehouse, office, or plant in a new location will increase profits. A team may be responsible for the selection decision in a large corporation, or an individual may make the decision in a small company. The process of selecting a new facility location involves a series of steps.

1. Identify the important location factors and categorize them as dominant or secondary.

2. Consider alternative regions; then narrow the choices to alternative communities and finally to specific sites.

3. Collect data on the alternatives from location consultants, provincial development agencies, city and county planning departments, chambers of commerce, land developers, electric power companies, banks, and on-site visits. Some of these data and information may also be contained inside the GIS.

4. Analyze the data collected, beginning with the *quantitative* factors—factors that can be measured in dollars, such as annual transportation costs or taxes. These dollar values may be broken into separate cost categories (e.g., inbound and outbound transportation, labour, construction, and utilities) and separate revenue sources (e.g., sales, stock or bond issues, and interest income). These financial factors can then be converted to a single measure of financial merit and used to compare two or more sites.

5. Bring the qualitative factors pertaining to each site into the evaluation. A *qualitative* factor is one that cannot be evaluated in dollar terms, such as community attitudes or quality of life. To merge quantitative and qualitative factors, some managers review the expected performance of each factor, while others assign each factor a weight of relative importance and calculate a weighted score for each site, using a preference matrix. What is important in one situation may be unimportant or less important in another. The site with the highest weighted score is best.

After thoroughly evaluating between 5 and 15 sites, those making the study prepare a final report containing site recommendations, along with a summary of the data and analyses on which they are based. A presentation of the key findings usually is delivered to top management in large firms.

EXAMPLE 9.1   *Calculating Weighted Scores in a Preference Matrix*

A new medical facility, Health-Watch, is to be located in Edmonton. The following table shows the location factors, weights, and scores (1 = poor, 5 = excellent) for one potential site. The weights in this case add up to 100 percent. A weighted score will be calculated for each site. What is the weighted score for this site?

LOCATION FACTOR	WEIGHT	SCORE
Total patient kilometres per month	25	4
Facility utilization	20	3
Average time per emergency trip	20	3
Expressway accessibility	15	4
Land and construction costs	10	1
Employee preferences	10	5

SOLUTION

The weighted score (WS) for this particular site is calculated by multiplying each factor's weight by its score and adding the results:

$$WS = (25 \times 4) + (20 \times 3) + (20 \times 3) + (15 \times 4) + (10 \times 1) + (10 \times 5)$$
$$= 100 + 60 + 60 + 60 + 10 + 50$$
$$= 340$$

The total weighted score of 340 can be compared with the total weighted scores for other sites being evaluated.

APPLYING THE LOAD-DISTANCE METHOD

In the systematic selection process, the analyst must identify attractive candidate locations and compare them on the basis of quantitative factors. The load-distance method can facilitate this step. Several location factors relate directly to distance: proximity to markets, average distance to target customers, proximity to suppliers and resources, and proximity to other company facilities. The **load-distance method** is a mathematical model used to evaluate locations on the basis of proximity factors. The objective is to select a location that minimizes the total weighted loads moving into and out of the facility. An alternative approach is to use time rather than distance.

load-distance method
A mathematical model used to evaluate locations on the basis of proximity factors.

DISTANCE MEASURES. To calculate distance, we can use the driving distance between any two points estimated by a GIS system. Alternatively, a Euclidean or a rectilinear distance measure may be used. Euclidean distance is the straight-line distance, or shortest possible path, between two points. To calculate the **Euclidean distance**, we create a graph with grid coordinates. The distance between two points, say points A and B, is:

Euclidean distance The straight-line distance, or shortest possible path, between two points.

$$d_{AB} = \sqrt{(x_A - x_B)^2 + (y_A - y_B)^2}$$

where:

d_{AB} = Distance between points A and B

x_A = x-coordinate of point A

y_A = y-coordinate of point A

x_B = x-coordinate of point B

y_B = y-coordinate of point B

rectilinear distance The distance between two points with a series of 90° turns, as along city blocks.

Rectilinear distance measures distance between two points with a series of 90° turns, as along city blocks. The distance travelled in the x-direction is the absolute value of the difference in x-coordinates. Adding this result to the absolute value of the difference in the y-coordinates gives:

$$d_{AB} = |x_A - x_B| + |y_A - y_B|$$

CALCULATING A LOAD-DISTANCE SCORE. Suppose that a firm planning a new location wants to select a site that minimizes the distances that larger *loads* must travel to and from the site. Depending on the industry, loads may be expressed as the number of customers or workers that must travel to a facility. Loads may also be shipments from suppliers.

To calculate a load distance for any potential location, we multiply the loads flowing to and from the facility by their distances. The *ld score* is simply the sum of the load-distance products. By selecting a new location based on a low *ld score*, customer service is improved or transportation costs reduced.

$$ld = \sum_i l_i d_i$$

The goal is to find one acceptable facility location that minimizes the score, where the location is defined by its x-coordinate and y-coordinate. Practical considerations rarely allow managers to select the exact location with the lowest possible score. For example, land may not be available there at a reasonable price, or other location factors may make the site undesirable.

centre of gravity A good starting point in evaluating locations is with the load-distance model; the centre of gravity's x-coordinate is found by multiplying each point's x-coordinate by its load (l), summing these products, and then dividing by the sum of the loads.

CENTRE OF GRAVITY. Testing different locations with the load-distance model is relatively simple if some systematic search process is followed. A good starting point is the **centre of gravity** of the target area. The centre of gravity's x-coordinate, denoted x^*, is found by multiplying each point's x-coordinate (x_i) by its load (l_i), summing these products ($\Sigma l_i x_i$), and then dividing by the sum of the loads (Σl_i). The y-coordinate, denoted y^*, is found the same way, with the y-coordinates used in the numerator. The formulas are:

$$x^* = \frac{\sum_i l_i x_i}{\sum_i l_i} \quad \text{and} \quad y^* = \frac{\sum_i l_i y_i}{\sum_i l_i}$$

This location usually is not the optimal one for the Euclidean or rectilinear distance measures, but it is still an excellent starting point. Calculate the load-distance scores for locations in its vicinity until you're satisfied that your solution is near-optimal.

| EXAMPLE 9.2 | *Finding the Centre of Gravity* |

The new Health-Watch facility is targeted to serve seven areas, with customers travelling from these areas when they need health care. What is the centre of gravity for these target areas for the Health-Watch medical facility?

SOLUTION

To calculate the centre of gravity, we begin with the information in the following table, in which population is given in thousands:

TARGET AREA	GEOGRAPHIC LOCATION (x,y)	POPULATION (thousands) (l)	LOAD-DISTANCE	
			lx	ly
A	(2.5, 4.5)	2	5	9
B	(2.5, 2.5)	5	12.5	12.5
C	(5.5, 4.5)	10	55	45
D	(5, 2)	7	35	14
E	(8, 5)	10	80	50
F	(7, 2)	20	140	40
G	(9, 2.5)	14	126	35
	Totals	68	453.5	205.5

Next we solve for x^* and y^*:

$$x^* = \frac{453.5}{68} = 6.67$$

$$y^* = \frac{205.5}{68} = 3.02$$

Decision Point   The centre of gravity is (6.67, 3.02), which is not necessarily optimal. Using the centre of gravity as a starting point, managers can now search in its vicinity for the optimal location.

USING BREAK-EVEN ANALYSIS

Break-even analysis can help a manager compare location alternatives on the basis of quantitative factors that can be expressed in terms of total cost (see Chapter 3, "Process Configuration," for a similar analysis with process equipment). It is particularly useful when the manager wants to define the ranges over which each alternative is best. The basic steps for graphic and algebraic solutions are as follows:

1. Determine the variable costs and fixed costs for each site. Recall that *variable* costs are the portion of the total cost that varies directly with the volume of output. Recall that fixed costs are the portion of the total cost that remains constant regardless of output levels.

2. Plot the total cost lines—the sum of variable and fixed costs—for all the sites on a single graph.

3. Identify the approximate ranges for which each location has the lowest cost.

4. Solve algebraically for the break-even points over the relevant ranges.

EXAMPLE 9.3   *Break-Even Analysis for Location*

An operations manager has narrowed the search for a new facility location to four communities. The annual fixed costs (land, property taxes, insurance, equipment, and buildings) and the variable costs (labour, materials, transportation, and variable overhead) are:

COMMUNITY	FIXED COSTS PER YEAR	VARIABLE COSTS PER UNIT
A	$150 000	$62
B	$300 000	$38
C	$500 000	$24
D	$600 000	$30

a. Plot the total cost curves for all the communities on a single graph. Identify on the graph the approximate range over which each community provides the lowest cost.

b. Using break-even analysis, calculate the break-even quantities over the relevant ranges.

c. If the expected demand is 15 000 units per year, what is the best location?

SOLUTION

a. To plot a community's total cost line, let us first compute the total cost for two output levels: $Q = 0$ and $Q = 20\,000$ units per year. For the $Q = 0$ level, the total cost is simply the fixed costs. For the $Q = 20\,000$ level, the total cost (fixed plus variable costs) is:

COMMUNITY	FIXED COSTS	VARIABLE COSTS (COST PER UNIT)(NO. OF UNITS)	TOTAL COST (FIXED + VARIABLE)
A	$150 000	$62(20 000) = $1 240 000	$1 390 000
B	$300 000	$38(20 000) = $ 760 000	$1 060 000
C	$500 000	$24(20 000) = $ 480 000	$ 980 000
D	$600 000	$30(20 000) = $ 600 000	$1 200 000

Figure 9.3 shows the graph of the total cost lines. The line for community A goes from $(0, 150)$ to $(20, 1390)$. The graph indicates that community A is best for low volumes, B for intermediate volumes, and C for high volumes. We should no longer consider community D, as both its fixed *and* its variable costs are higher than community C's.

FIGURE 9.3   *Break-Even Analysis of Four Candidate Locations*

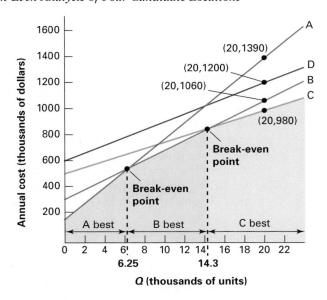

b. The break-even quantity between A and B lies at the end of the first range, where A is best, and the beginning of the second range, where B is best. We find it by setting their total cost equations equal to each other and solving:

$$\begin{array}{cc} \text{(A)} & \text{(B)} \end{array}$$

$$\$150\,000 + \$62Q = \$300\,000 + \$38Q$$
$$Q = 6250 \text{ units}$$

The break-even quantity between B and C is at the end of the range over which B is best and the beginning of the final range, where C is best. It is:

$$(B) \qquad\qquad (C)$$

$$\$300\ 000 + \$38Q = \$500\ 000 + \$24Q$$

$$Q = 14\ 286 \text{ units}$$

No other break-even quantities are needed. The break-even point between A and C does not mark either the start or the end of one of the three relevant ranges.

Decision Point   Management located the new facility at community C, because the 15 000-units-per-year demand forecast lies in the high-volume range.

LOCATING A FACILITY WITHIN A NETWORK OF FACILITIES

When a firm with a network of existing facilities plans a new facility, one of two conditions exists: either the facilities operate independently (e.g., a chain of restaurants, health clinics, banks, or retail establishments) or the facilities interact (e.g., component manufacturing plants, assembly plants, and warehouses). Independently operating units can be located by treating each as a separate single facility, as described in the preceding section. Locating interacting facilities introduces new issues, such as how to allocate work between the facilities and how to determine the best capacity for each. Changing work allocations in turn affects the size (or capacity utilization) of the facilities. Thus, the multiple-facility location problem has three dimensions—location, allocation, and capacity—that must be solved simultaneously. In many cases, the analyst can identify a workable solution merely by looking for patterns in the cost, demand, and capacity data and using trial-and-error calculations. In other cases, more formal approaches are needed.

Many location analysis problems are very complex. Consider the situation that a medium-sized manufacturer faces when distributing products through warehouse, or distribution centres, to various communities. The problem is to determine the number, size, allocation pattern, and location of the warehouses. The situation may involve thousands of individual retail outlets, hundreds of potential warehouse locations, several plants, and multiple product lines. Transportation rates depend on the direction of shipment, product, quantity, rate breaks, and geographic area. Such complexity requires the use of a computer for a comprehensive evaluation. Four basic approaches are briefly described here for locating multiple facilities: (1) GIS methods, (2) heuristics, (3) simulation, and (4) optimization.

GIS METHODS

As discussed earlier in this chapter, the use of GIS tools often simplifies the search for solutions. Visualizing customer locations and data, as well as the transportation structure of roads and highways, allows the analyst to quickly arrive at a reasonable solution to the multiple facility location problems. Load-distance score and centre of gravity data can be merged with customer databases in Excel to arrive at trial locations for facilities, which can then be evaluated for annual driving time or distance using a GIS such as MapPoint. Such an approach can have many applications, including the design of supply chain distribution networks. A five-step framework that captures the use of GIS for locating multiple facilities is outlined here.

1. Map the data for existing customers and facilities in the GIS.

2. Visually split the entire operating area into the number of parts or subregions that equal the number of facilities to be located.

3. Assign a facility location for each region based on the visual density of customer concentration or other factors. Alternately, determine the centre of gravity for each part or subregion identified in step 2 as the starting location point for the facility in that subregion.

4. Search for alternate sites around the centre of gravity to pick a feasible location that meets the firm's managerial criteria, such as proximity to major metropolitan areas or highways.

5. Compute total load-distance scores and perform capacity checks before finalizing the locations for each region.

HEURISTICS

heuristics Solution guidelines, or rules of thumb, that find feasible—but not necessarily the best—solutions to problems.

Solution guidelines, or rules of thumb, that find feasible—but not necessarily the best—solutions to problems are called **heuristics**. Their advantages include efficiency and an ability to handle general views of a problem. The systematic search procedure utilizing a target area's centre of gravity, described earlier for single-facility location problems, is a typical heuristic procedure. One of the first heuristics to be computerized for location problems was proposed more than five decades ago to handle several hundred potential warehouse sites and several thousand demand centres (Kuehn and Hamburger, 1963). Many other heuristic models are available today for analyzing a variety of situations.

SIMULATION

simulation A modelling technique that reproduces the behaviour of a system.

A modelling technique that reproduces the behaviour of a system is called **simulation**. Simulation allows certain variables to be manipulated and shows what effect they have on select operating measures. Simulation models allow the analyst to evaluate different location alternatives by trial-and-error. It is up to the analyst to propose the most reasonable alternatives. A simulation model can handle more realistic views of a problem and involves the analyst in the solution process itself. For each run, the analyst inputs the facilities to be opened, and the simulator typically makes the allocation decisions based on some reasonable assumptions that have been written into the computer program. The Ralston-Purina Company used simulation to assist the company in locating warehouses to serve 137 demand centres, five warehouses, and four plants. Random demand at each demand centre by product type was simulated over a period of time. Demand was met by the closest warehouse that had available inventory. Based on the results of the simulation, the firm consolidated five warehouses down to three to reduce supply chain costs.

OPTIMIZATION

optimization A procedure used to determine the "best" solution; generally utilizes simplified and less realistic views of a problem.

In contrast to heuristics and simulation, **optimization** involves procedures to determine the *best* solution. The transportation method is one such optimization approach that can help solve multiple facility location problems, and it is based on linear programming (see Supplement I, "Linear Programming," in MyOMLab). This method only finds the best shipping pattern between plants and warehouses for a particular set of plant locations, each with a given capacity. The analyst must try a variety of location–capacity combinations and find the optimal distribution for each. In the end, the payoffs can be substantial.

WHAT IS LAYOUT PLANNING?

After the location of a facility is determined, management attention can shift to develop the layout within that facility. In essence, layouts put other decisions on processes in tangible, physical form by converting process structures, flowcharts, technology choices, and capacity plans into bricks and mortar. Revising layouts also is a way to improve processes.

layout planning Planning that involves decisions about the physical arrangement of economic activity centres within a facility.

Layout planning involves decisions about the physical arrangement of "economic activity centres" within a facility. An economic activity centre can be anything that consumes space: a person or group of people, a teller window, a machine, a workstation, a department, an aisle, a storage room, and so on. Layout planning translates the broader decisions about a firm's competitive priorities, process, and capacity into actual physical arrangements of people, equipment, and space. The goal is to allow workers and equipment to operate most effectively. Before a manager can make decisions regarding physical arrangement, four questions must be addressed:

1. *What centres should the layout include?* Centres should reflect process decisions and maximize productivity. For example, a central storage area for tools is most efficient for certain processes, but keeping tools at individual workstations makes more sense for other processes.

2. *How much space and capacity does each centre need?* Inadequate space can reduce productivity, deprive employees of privacy, and even create health and safety hazards. However, excessive space is wasteful, can reduce productivity, and can isolate employees unnecessarily.

3. *How should each centre's space be configured?* The amount of space, its shape, and the elements in a centre are interrelated. For example, the placement of a desk and chair relative to the other furniture is determined by the size and shape of the office, as well as the activities performed there. Providing a pleasing atmosphere also should be considered as part of the layout configuration decisions, especially in retail outlets and offices.

4. *Where should each centre be located?* Location can significantly affect productivity. For example, employees who must frequently interact with one another face to face should be placed in a central location rather than in separate, remote locations to reduce time lost travelling back and forth.

The location of a centre has two dimensions: (1) *relative location*, or the placement of a centre relative to other centres, and (2) *absolute location*, or the particular space that the centre occupies within the facility. Both affect a centre's performance. Look at the grocery store layout in Figure 9.4(a). It shows the location of five departments, with the dry groceries department allocated twice the space of each of the

FIGURE 9.4   *Identical Relative Locations and Different Absolute Locations*

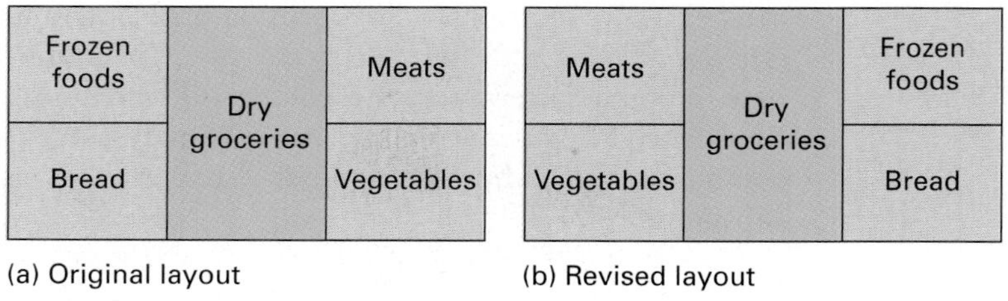

(a) Original layout   (b) Revised layout

others. The location of frozen foods relative to bread is the same as the location of meats relative to vegetables, so the distance between the first pair of departments equals the distance between the second pair of departments. Relative location is normally the crucial issue when travel time, materials handling cost, and communication effectiveness are important.

Now look at the plan in Figure 9.4(b). Although the relative locations are the same, the absolute locations have changed. This modified layout might prove unworkable. For example, the cost of moving the meats to the northwest corner could be excessive. Or customers might react negatively to the placement of vegetables in the southwest corner, preferring them to be near the entrance.

STRATEGIC ISSUES

Layout choices can help immensely in communicating an organization's product plans and competitive priorities. If a retailer plans to upgrade the quality of its merchandise, the store layout should convey more exclusiveness and luxury. Or alternatively, layout can simplify and improve customer experience. Since 2008, Canadian Tire has introduced changes to its store layout with the newly designed "Smart" stores. This layout offers stand-alone specialty areas that showcase key departments, such as tools, hardware, or hockey apparel, with better signage and logically grouped products. For example, work boots and work wear were moved into the tools area.

Layout has many practical and strategic implications. Altering a layout can affect how well an organization meets its competitive priorities by:

- Facilitating the flow of materials and information
- Increasing the efficient utilization of labour and equipment
- Increasing customer convenience and sales at a retail store
- Reducing hazards to workers
- Improving employee morale
- Improving communication

Since 2008, Canadian Tire has introduced changes to its store layout to simplify the customer's shopping experience.

The type of operation also determines the layout requirements. For example, in warehouses, materials flows and stock picking costs are dominant considerations. In retail stores, customer convenience and sales may dominate, whereas communication effectiveness and team building may be crucial in an office.

Among the several fundamental layout choices available to managers are whether to plan for current or future (and less predictable) needs, whether to select a single-storey or multi-storey design, whether to open the planning process to employee suggestions, what type of layout to choose, and what performance criteria to emphasize. Thus, designing a new layout or changing an existing one often requires making trade-offs between multiple factors. For example, the capital investment and flexibility of the process varies based on the layout, and the customer experience also is likely to vary. Each of the performance outcomes must be assessed before large-scale implementation, possibly by using a pilot store or test facility.

LAYOUT TYPES

The choice of layout type depends largely on process configuration (Chapter 3). Three basic types of layout are covered: flexible-flow, line process, and fixed-position. By combining two or more of these, hybrid layouts are possible. For example, process "cells," described in Chapter 7 "Lean Systems," offer a means to use line-flow principles for low volumes of customers and parts.

flexible-flow layout
A layout that groups workstations or departments according to function.

FLEXIBLE-FLOW LAYOUT. With a batch process, the demand levels are often too low or have high variability for management to set aside human and capital resources exclusively for a particular product line or type of customer. A **flexible-flow layout**, which groups workstations or departments according to function, accomplishes this purpose. For example, in the metalworking shop shown in Figure 9.5(a), all drills are located in one area of the machine shop and all milling machines are located in another. The flexible-flow layout is most common when the same operation must intermittently produce many different products or serve many different customers.

The flexible-flow layout has a number of advantages over the line-flow layout shown in Figure 9.5(b), described next. In general, equipment tends to be more general-purpose and less capital-intensive. The process is also very responsive to changes in product mix or new marketing strategies. When volumes are low, multiple products or services can be routed through similar equipment. Finally, employee supervision can

FIGURE 9.5 *Two Layout Types*

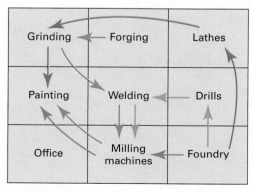

(a) Flexible-flow layout

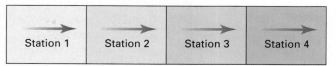

(b) Line-flow layout

be more specialized, an important factor when job content requires a good deal of technical knowledge. However, processing rates can be lower, and productive time is lost in changing from one product or service to another. In addition, long queues can build as customers or products move between processing steps.

LINE PROCESS LAYOUT. Back offices, assembly lines, and continuous-flow processes typically have linear workflows and repetitive tasks. For such processes, the manager should dedicate resources to individual services, products, or tasks. This strategy is achieved by a **line process layout**, illustrated by Figure 9.5(b), in which workstations or departments are arranged in a linear path. As in an automated car wash, the product or customer moves along in a smooth, continuous path. Resources are arranged around the product's route rather than shared across many products. Although this layout often follows a straight line, an L, O, S, or U shape is also possible.

Line process layouts often rely heavily on specialized, capital-intensive resources. When volumes are high, this layout allows for faster processing rates, lower inventories, and less unproductive time lost to changeovers and materials handling. As a result, throughput time can be can dramatically reduced. However, it is important that each operation be very reliable (i.e., have low variability), or buffer inventory must be added between adjacent operations. Line process layouts also tend to be less able to accommodate changes in product mix (without significant investment).

FIXED-POSITION LAYOUT. The third basic type of layout is the **fixed-position layout**. In this arrangement, the product is fixed in place; workers, along with their tools and equipment, come to the product to work on it. Many project processes have this arrangement. This type of layout makes sense when the product is particularly massive or difficult to move, as in shipbuilding, assembling locomotives, making huge pressure vessels, building dams, or repairing home furnaces. A fixed-position layout minimizes the number of times that the product must be moved and is often the only feasible solution. Resources, including workers and equipment, must be mobile to move between products or service sites.

DESIGNING FLEXIBLE-FLOW LAYOUTS

The approach to designing a layout depends on whether a flexible-flow layout or a line-flow layout has been chosen. A fixed-position format basically eliminates the layout problem, whereas the design of the hybrid layout partially uses flexible-flow layout principles and partially uses line-flow layout principles.

Process layout involves three basic steps, whether the design is for a new layout or for revising an existing one: (1) gather information, (2) develop a block plan, and (3) design a detailed layout.

STEP 1: GATHER INFORMATION

The Office of Budget Management (OBM), which is a major division in a large provincial government, consists of 70 employees assigned to six different departments. It is one of several divisions occupying a relatively new office tower. Workloads have expanded to the extent that 30 new employees must be hired and somehow housed in the space allocated to OBM. While changing the layout, it also makes sense to review the layout to make sure that it is arranged as effectively as possible. The goal is to improve communication among people who must interact and to create a good work environment. Three types of information are needed to begin designing the revised layout for OBM: (1) space requirements by centre, (2) available space, and (3) closeness factors.

---

line process layout
A layout in which workstations or departments are arranged in a linear path.

fixed-position layout An arrangement in which the product is fixed in place; workers, along with their tools and equipment, come to the product to work on it.

SPACE REQUIREMENTS BY CENTRE. OBM has grouped its processes into six different departments: administration, social services, institutions, accounting, education, and internal audit. The exact space requirements of each department, in square metres, are as follows:

DEPARTMENT	AREA NEEDED (m²)
1. Administration	110
2. Social services	105
3. Institutions	85
4. Accounting	130
5. Education	90
6. Internal audit	80
Total	600

The layout designer must tie space requirements to capacity and staffing plans; calculate the specific equipment and space needs for each centre; and allow circulation space, such as aisles and the like. At OBM, a way must be found to include all 150 employees in its assigned area. Consulting with the managers and employees involved can help avoid excessive resistance to change and make the transition smooth.

block plan A plan that allocates space and indicates placement of each department.

AVAILABLE SPACE. A **block plan** allocates space and indicates placement of each department. To describe a new facility layout, the plan need only provide the facility's dimensions and space allocations. When an existing facility layout is being modified, the current block plan also is needed. OBM's available space is 30 metres by 20 metres, or 600 square metres. The designer could begin the design by dividing the total amount of space into six equal blocks (100 square metres each), even though Internal Audit needs only 80 square metres and Accounting needs 130 square metres. The equal-space approximation shown in Figure 9.6 is sufficient until the detailed layout stage, when larger departments (such as Accounting) are assigned more space than smaller departments.

FIGURE 9.6   *Current Block Plan for Office of Budget Management*

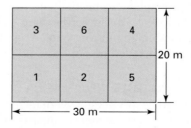

closeness matrix
A matrix that gives the number of trips (or some other measure capturing the movement of people or materials) between each pair of departments per day.

CLOSENESS FACTORS. The layout designer must also know which centres need to be located close to one another. The following table shows OBM's **closeness matrix**, which gives a measure of the relative importance of each pair of centres being located close together. The specific metric used to quantify "closeness" depends on the type of processes involved and the organizational setting. It can be a qualitative judgment on a scale from 0 to 10 that the manager uses to account for multiple performance criteria, as in the OBM's case. Only the upper right-hand portion of the matrix is used.

Closeness Matrix

DEPARTMENT	NEED FOR INTERACTION					
	1	2	3	4	5	6
1. Administration	—	3	6	5	6	10
2. Social services		—	8	1	1	
3. Institutions			—	3	9	—
4. Accounting				—	2	
5. Education					—	1
6. Internal audit						—

The closeness factors are indicators of the need for proximity based on an analysis of information flows and the need for face-to-face meetings. They give clues as to which departments should be located close together. For example, the most important interaction is between the administration and internal audit departments for OBM, with a score of 10 (first row and last column). Thus, the designer should locate departments 1 and 6 close together, which is not the arrangement in the current layout. Entries in both the columns and rows result in five factor scores for each department.

At a manufacturing plant, the closeness factor could be the number of trips (or some other measure of materials movement) between each pair of centres per day. This information can be gleaned by conducting a statistical sampling, polling supervisors and materials handlers, or using the routings and ordering frequencies for typical items made at the plant.

OTHER CONSIDERATIONS. Finally, the information gathered for OBM includes performance criteria that depend on the absolute location of a department. OBM has two criteria based on absolute location:

1. Education (department 5) should remain where it is because it is next to the office library.
2. Administration (department 1) should remain where it is because that location has the largest conference room, which administration uses often. Relocating the conference room would be costly.

Noise levels and management preference are other potential sources of performance criteria that depend on absolute location. The closeness matrix cannot reflect these criteria because it reflects only relative location considerations. The layout designer must list these criteria separately.

STEP 2: DEVELOP A BLOCK PLAN
The second step in layout design is to develop a block plan that best satisfies performance criteria and area requirements. The most elementary way to do so is by trial and error. Because success depends on the designer's ability to spot patterns in the data, this approach does not guarantee the selection of the best or even a nearly best solution. When supplemented by the use of a computer to evaluate solutions, however, such an approach often compares quite favourably with more sophisticated computerized techniques.

EXAMPLE 9.4   *Developing a Block Plan*

Develop an acceptable block plan for the Office of Budget Management, using trial and error. The goal is to locate the departments that have the greatest interaction between them (largest closeness factor) as close to each other as possible.

SOLUTION

A good place to start is with the largest closeness ratings (say, 8 and above). Beginning with the largest factor scores and working down the list, you might plan to locate departments as follows:

    a. Departments 1 and 6 close together

    b. Departments 3 and 5 close together

    c. Departments 2 and 3 close together

Departments 1 and 5 should remain at their current locations because of the "other considerations."

If after several attempts you cannot meet all three requirements, drop one or more and try again. If you can meet all three easily, add more (such as for interactions below 8). The block plan in Figure 9.7 shows a trial-and-error solution that satisfies all three requirements. We started by keeping departments 1 and 5 in their original locations. As the first requirement is to locate departments 1 and 6 close to each other, we put 6 in the upper-left corner of the layout. The second requirement is to have departments 3 and 5 close to each other, so we placed 3 in the space just above the 5, and so on.

FIGURE 9.7   *Proposed Block Plan*

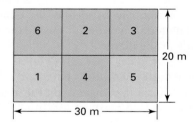

Decision Point   This solution fell into place easily for this particular problem, but it might not be the best layout. Management wants to consider several alternative layouts before making a final choice and needs some measure of effectiveness with which to compare them.

When *relative* locations are a primary concern, such as for effective materials handling, stock picking, and communication, the load-distance method can be used to compare alternative block plans. Just as with facility location decisions, we can use the total load-distance (*ld*) score by multiplying each load by the distance travelled and then summing over all of the loads. Here the loads are just the closeness factors (i.e., need for interaction) between each department in the closeness matrix. Each load goes between two centres (each represented by a row and a column in the matrix). The distance (actual, Euclidean, or rectilinear) between them is calculated from the block plan being evaluated.

EXAMPLE 9.5   *Calculating the Total Load-Distance Score*

How much better, in terms of the load-distance (ld) score, is the proposed block plan in Figure 9.7 than the current plan that was shown in Figure 9.6? Use the rectilinear distance measure.

SOLUTION

The accompanying table lists each pair of departments that has a nonzero closeness factor in the closeness matrix. For the third column, calculate the rectilinear distances between the departments in the current layout. For example, departments 3 and 5 in the current plan are in the upper-left corner and bottom-right corner of the building, respectively. The distance between the centres of these blocks is three units (two horizontally and one vertically). For the fourth column, we multiply the weights (closeness factors) by the distances, and then add the results for a total ld score of 112 for the current plan. Similar calculations for the proposed plan produce an ld score of only 82. For example, between departments 3 and 5 is just one unit of distance (one vertically and zero horizontally).

		CURRENT PLAN		PROPOSED PLAN	
DEPARTMENT PAIR	CLOSENESS FACTOR, *l*	DISTANCE *d*	LOAD-DISTANCE SCORE, *ld*	DISTANCE *d*	LOAD-DISTANCE SCORE, *ld*
1, 2	3	1	3	2	6
1, 3	6	1	6	3	18
1, 4	5	3	15	1	5
1. 5	6	2	12	2	12
1, 6	10	2	20	1	10
2, 3	8	2	16	1	8
2, 4	1	2	2	1	1
2, 5	1	1	1	2	2
3, 4	3	2	6	2	6
3, 5	9	3	27	1	9
4, 5	2	1	2	1	2
5, 6	1	2	2	3	3
			Total = 112		Total = 82

Current Plan

3	6	4
1	2	5

Proposed Plan

6	2	3
1	4	5

To be more precise, we could multiply the two ld total scores by 10 because each unit of distance represents 10 metres. However, the relative difference between the two totals remains unchanged.

Decision Point Although the ld score in Example 9.5 for the proposed layout represents an almost 27 percent improvement, the designer may be able to do better. However, the designer must first determine whether the revised layout is worth the cost of relocating four of the six departments (all but 1 and 5). If relocation costs are too high, a less expensive proposal must be found.

STEP 3: DESIGN A DETAILED LAYOUT

After finding a satisfactory block plan, the layout designer translates it into a detailed representation, showing the exact size and shape of each centre, the arrangement of elements (e.g., desks, machines, and storage areas), and the location of aisles, stairways, and other service space. These visual representations can be two-dimensional drawings, three-dimensional models, or computer-aided graphics. This step helps decision makers discuss the proposal and problems that might otherwise be overlooked. Such visual representations can be particularly important when evaluating high-customer-contact processes.

DESIGNING LINE PROCESS LAYOUTS

As noted in Chapter 3, "Process Configuration," products created by a line process include the assembly of computers, automobiles, appliances, and toys. Such assembly lines can exist in providing services as well. For instance, putting together a standard hamburger with a fixed sequence of steps is akin to operating an assembly line. While the product mix or demand volumes do not change as rapidly for line processes as for job or batch processes, the load can shift between work centres in a line as the final product being assembled is changed or the total output rate of the line is altered. Constraints arising out of such actions can be managed by balancing the workload between different stations in a line, which we explain next in greater detail.

LINE BALANCING

line balancing The assignment of work to stations in a line so as to achieve the desired output rate with the smallest number of workstations.

Line balancing is the assignment of work to stations in a line process so as to achieve the desired output rate with the smallest number of workstations. Normally, one worker is assigned to a station. Thus, the line that produces at the desired pace with the fewest workers is the most efficient one. Achieving this goal is much like the theory of constraints (Chapter 4) because both approaches are concerned about bottlenecks. However, line balancing differs in how it addresses bottlenecks. Rather than (1) taking on new customer orders to best use bottleneck capacity or (2) scheduling so that bottleneck resources are conserved, line balancing takes a third approach.

Line balancing creates workstations with workloads as evenly balanced as possible. It seeks to create workstations so that the capacity utilization for the bottleneck is not much higher than for the other workstations in the line. Another difference is that line balancing applies only to line processes that do assembly work, or to work that can be bundled in many ways to create the jobs for each workstation in the line. The latter situation can be found both in manufacturing and service settings.

Line balancing must be performed when a line is set up initially, when a line must change its hourly output rate, or when a product or process is modified significantly. The goal is to obtain workstations with well-balanced workloads (e.g., every station takes roughly three minutes per customer in a cafeteria line with different food stations).

work elements The smallest units of work that can be performed independently.

The analyst begins by separating the work into **work elements**, the smallest units of work that can be performed independently. The analyst then obtains the labour standard (see Supplement C, "Work Measurement," in MyOMLab) for each element and identifies the work elements, called **immediate predecessors**, that must be done before the next can begin.

immediate predecessors Work elements that must be done before the next element can begin.

precedence diagram A diagram that allows you to visualize immediate predecessors better; work elements are denoted by circles, with the time required to perform the work shown below each circle.

PRECEDENCE DIAGRAM. Most lines must satisfy some technological precedence requirements—that is, certain work elements must be done before the next can begin. However, most lines also allow for some latitude and more than one sequence of operations. To help you visualize immediate predecessors better, let us run through the construction of a **precedence diagram**. (Precedence diagrams are also very important in Chapter 8, "Managing Projects.") We denote the work elements by circles, with the time required to perform the work shown below each circle. Arrows lead from immediate predecessors to the next work element.

EXAMPLE 9.6	*Constructing a Precedence Diagram*

Green Grass, Inc., a manufacturer of lawn and garden equipment, is designing an assembly line to produce a new fertilizer spreader, the Big Broadcaster. Using the following information on the production process, construct a precedence diagram for the Big Broadcaster.

WORK ELEMENT	DESCRIPTION	TIME (sec)	IMMEDIATE PREDECESSOR(S)
A	Bolt leg frame to hopper	40	None
B	Insert impeller shaft	30	A
C	Attach axle	50	A
D	Attach agitator	40	B
E	Attach drive wheel	6	B
F	Attach free wheel	25	C
G	Mount lower post	15	C
H	Attach controls	20	D, E
I	Mount nameplate	18	F, G
		Total 244	

SOLUTION

Figure 9.8 shows the complete diagram. We begin with work element A, which has no immediate predecessors. Next, we add elements B and C, for which element A is the only immediate predecessor. After entering labour standards and arrows showing precedence, we add elements D and E, and so on. The diagram simplifies interpretation. Work element F, for example, can be done anywhere on the line after element C is completed. However, element I must await completion of elements F and G.

FIGURE 9.8 *Precedence Diagram for Assembling the Big Broadcaster*

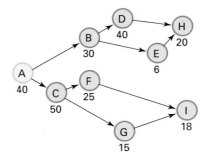

Decision Point Management now has enough information to develop a layout that clusters work elements to form workstations, with a goal being to balance the workloads and in the process minimize the number of workstations required.

DESIRED OUTPUT RATE. The goal of line balancing is to match the output rate to the production plan. For example, if the production plan calls for 4000 units per week and the line operates 80 hours per week, the desired output rate ideally would be 50 units (4000/80) per hour. Matching output to demand ensures on-time delivery and prevents buildup of unwanted inventory. However, managers should avoid rebalancing a line too frequently: every time a line is rebalanced many workers' jobs on the line have to be redesigned, temporarily hurting productivity and sometimes even requiring a new detailed layout for some stations.

Some automobile plants avoid frequent changes by eliminating a shift entirely when demand falls and inventory becomes excessive, rather than gradually scaling back the output rate. Managers can also add shifts to increase equipment utilization, which is crucial for capital-intensive facilities. However, higher pay rates or low demand may make multiple shifts undesirable or unnecessary.

cycle time The maximum time allowed for work on a unit at each station.

CYCLE TIME. After determining the desired output rate for a line, the analyst can calculate the line's cycle time. A line's **cycle time** is the maximum time allowed for work on a unit at each station.[†] If the time required for work elements at a station exceeds the line's cycle time, the station will be a bottleneck, preventing the line from reaching its desired output rate. The target cycle time is the reciprocal of the desired hourly output rate:

$$c = \frac{1}{r}$$

where:

c = Cycle time (e.g., minutes per unit)

r = Desired output rate (e.g., units per minute)

For example, if the line's desired output rate is 60 units per hour, the cycle time is $c = 1/60$ hour per unit, or 1 minute per unit.

THEORETICAL MINIMUM. To achieve the desired output rate, managers use line balancing to assign every work element to a station, making sure to satisfy all precedence requirements and to minimize the number of stations, n, formed. If each station is operated by a different worker, minimizing n also maximizes worker productivity. Perfect balance is achieved when the sum of the work-element times at each station equals the cycle time, c, and no station has any idle time. For example, if the sum of each station's work-element times is 1 minute, which is also the cycle time, there is perfect balance. Although perfect balance usually is unachievable in practice, owing to the unevenness of work-element times and the inflexibility of precedence requirements, it sets a benchmark for the smallest number of stations possible. The **theoretical minimum (TM)** for the number of stations is:

theoretical minimum (TM) A benchmark or goal for the smallest number of stations possible, where the total time required to assemble each unit (the sum of all work-element standard times) is divided by the cycle time.

$$TM = \frac{\Sigma t}{c}$$

where:

Σt = Total time required to assemble each unit (the sum of all work-element standard times) (e.g., minutes)

c = Cycle time (e.g., minutes per unit)

For example, if the sum of the work-element times is 15 minutes and the cycle time is 1 minute, TM = 15/1, or 15 stations. Any fractional values obtained for TM are rounded up because fractional stations are impossible.

IDLE TIME, EFFICIENCY, AND BALANCE DELAY. Minimizing n automatically ensures (1) minimal idle time, (2) maximal efficiency, and (3) minimal balance delay. Idle time is the total unproductive time for all stations in the assembly of each unit:

$$\text{Idle time} = nc - \Sigma t$$

where:

n = Number of stations

c = Cycle time

Σt = Total standard time required to assemble each unit

[†]The term *cycle time* can have multiple meanings. In addition to this definition for line balancing, cycle time can also mean the elapsed time between starting and finishing a component or product, or the time between successive units being completed for a process. You must be careful to clarify the use of the term in different settings with different people.

Efficiency is the ratio of productive time to total time, expressed as a percent:

$$\text{Efficiency (percent)} = \frac{\Sigma t}{nc}(100)$$

balance delay The amount by which efficiency falls short of 100 percent.

Balance delay is the amount by which efficiency falls short of 100 percent:

$$\text{Balance delay (percent)} = 100 - \text{Efficiency}$$

As long as c is fixed, we can optimize all three goals by minimizing n.

| EXAMPLE 9.7 | *Calculating the Cycle Time, Theoretical Minimum, and Efficiency* |

Green Grass's plant manager has just received marketing's latest forecasts of Big Broadcaster sales for the next year. She wants its production line to be designed to make 2400 spreaders per week for at least the next three months. The plant will operate 40 hours per week.

    a.   What should be the line's cycle time?

    b.   What is the smallest number of workstations that she could hope for in designing the line for this cycle time?

    c.   Suppose that she finds a solution that requires only five stations. What would be the line's efficiency?

SOLUTION

    a.   First, convert the desired output rate (2400 units per week) to an hourly rate by dividing the weekly output rate by 40 hours per week to get $r = 60$ units per hour. Then the cycle time is:

$$c = \frac{1}{r} = \frac{1}{60} \text{ hour/unit} = 1 \text{ minute/unit} = 60 \text{ seconds/unit}$$

    b.   Now calculate the theoretical minimum for the number of stations by dividing the total time, Σt, by the cycle time, $c = 60$ seconds. Assuming perfect balance, we have:

$$\text{TM} = \frac{\Sigma t}{c} = \frac{244 \text{ seconds}}{60 \text{ seconds}} = 4.067, \quad \text{or} \quad 5 \text{ stations}$$

    c.   Now calculate the efficiency of a five-station solution, assuming for now that one can be found:

$$\text{Efficiency (percent)} = \frac{\Sigma t}{nc}(100) = \frac{244}{5(60)}(100) = 81.3\%$$

Decision Point Thus, if the manager finds a solution with five stations, that is the minimum number of stations possible. However, the efficiency (sometimes called the *theoretical maximum efficiency*) will be only 81.3 percent. Perhaps the line should be operated fewer than 40 hours per week and the employees transferred to other kinds of work when the line does not operate.

FINDING A SOLUTION. Often, many assembly-line solutions are possible, even for such simple problems as those of Green Grass. The goal is to cluster the work elements into workstations so that (1) the number of workstations required is minimized and (2) the

FIGURE 9.9   *Big Broadcaster Precedence Diagram Solution*

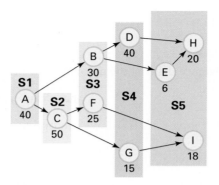

precedence and cycle-time requirements are not violated. Here we use the trial-and-error method to find a solution, although commercial software packages are also available. Figure 9.9 shows a good solution that creates just five workstations, which we already calculated as the theoretical minimum. All of the precedence and cycle-time requirements are also satisfied. For example, workstation S5 consists of work elements E, H, and I, which one worker will perform on each unit that comes along the assembly line. The total processing time per unit is 44 seconds (or 6 + 20 + 18), which does not exceed the cycle time of 60 seconds (see Example 9.7). Furthermore, the immediate predecessors of these three work elements are assigned to this workstation or upstream workstations, so their precedence requirements are satisfied. For example, the worker at workstation S5 can do element I at any time but will not start element H until element E is finished.

MANAGERIAL CONSIDERATIONS

In addition to balancing a line for a given cycle time, managers must also consider four other options: pacing, behavioural factors, number of models produced, and cycle times.

pacing The movement of product from one station to the next after the cycle time has elapsed.

PACING. The movement of product from one station to the next as soon as the cycle time has elapsed is called **pacing**. Pacing allows materials handling to be automated and requires less inventory storage area. However, it is less flexible in handling unexpected delays that require either slowing down the entire line or pulling unfinished work off-line to be completed later.

BEHAVIOURAL FACTORS. The most controversial aspect of line process layouts is behavioural response. Studies have shown that installing production lines increases absenteeism, turnover, and grievances. Paced production and high specialization (e.g., cycle times of less than two minutes) lower job satisfaction. Workers generally favour inventory buffers as a means of avoiding mechanical pacing. One study even showed that productivity increased on unpaced lines.

mixed-model line A product line that produces several items belonging to the same family.

NUMBER OF MODELS PRODUCED. A **mixed-model line** produces several items belonging to the same family. In contrast, a single-model line produces one model with no variations. Mixed-model production enables a plant to achieve both high-volume production *and* product variety. However, it complicates scheduling and increases the need for good communication about the specific parts to be produced at each station.

CYCLE TIMES. A line's cycle time depends on the desired output rate (or sometimes on the maximum number of workstations allowed). In turn, the maximum line efficiency varies considerably with the cycle time selected. Thus, exploring a range of cycle times makes sense. A manager might go with a particularly efficient solution even if it does not match the output rate. The manager can compensate for the mismatch by varying the number of hours the line operates through overtime, extending shifts, or adding shifts. Multiple lines might even be the answer.

LOCATION OFFERS A MEANS TO IMPROVE SUSTAINABILITY

Location, or, more precisely, co-location, is becoming a very important factor as firms work to make their operations more sustainable. Two aspects are emerging as key: where suppliers and customers are located (and how materials and products are transported between each); and whether a facility can become a member of a bigger local system that becomes more sustainable. We will look briefly at each of these.

Many international firms located facilities in North America to serve growing markets, such as Toyota and BMW (described in the opening vignette). When they did so, they often brought critical suppliers from their home countries, and also developed new local suppliers. This approach for locating suppliers nearby brought two benefits. First, experienced suppliers could help the new facility ramp up production quickly. Second, responsive delivery schedules could be used, without the delays of shipping long distances (see Chapter 7, "Lean Systems"). However, an interesting parallel benefit was reduced carbon dioxide emissions from small, frequent shipments, relative to long-distance international transport. Thus, locating a Corolla manufacturing plant in Cambridge, Ontario, to serve the North American market also can help Toyota reduce its carbon footprint, relative to importing vehicles or parts from Japan.

Co-location is not limited anymore to just the suppliers and customers. Increasingly, one facility is able to productively use *byproducts and waste products* of another facility (Ehrenfeld and Gertler, 1997). For example, an oil refinery might transfer waste energy (in the form of heat) to a greenhouse, waste sulphur to an acid production plant, and wastewater to a power plant. And each of these facilities is owned by a different firm. This clustering of non-competing firms can create an **industrial ecosystem**, whereby facilities exchange or transfer wastes, recycle materials, and use each other's byproducts. One important example is an industrial district in Kalundborg, Denmark, where approximately 11 physical linkages transfer wastes, byproducts, and energy between firms. Others are now developing in Canada, the United Kingdom, and elsewhere (Bansal and McKnight, 2009). Firms linked in an industrial ecosystem become highly dependent on each other, and operational decisions must take into account the processes of other facilities.

industrial ecosystem The exchange or transfer of wastes, recyclable materials, and byproducts between closely located, non-competing facilities.

EQUATION SUMMARY

1. Euclidean distance: $d_{AB} = \sqrt{(x_A - x_B)^2 + (y_A - y_B)^2}$

2. Rectilinear distance: $d_{AB} = |x_A - x_B| + |y_A - y_B|$

3. Load-distance score: $ld = \sum_i l_i d_i$

4. Centre of gravity: $x^* = \dfrac{\sum_i l_i x_i}{\sum_i l_i}$ and $y^* = \dfrac{\sum_i l_i y_i}{\sum_i l_i}$

5. Cycle time: $c = \dfrac{1}{r}$

6. Theoretical minimum number of workstations: $TM = \dfrac{\Sigma t}{c}$

7. Idle time (in seconds): $nc - \Sigma t$

8. Efficiency (percent): $\dfrac{\Sigma t}{nc}(100)$

9. Balance delay (percent): $100 - $ Efficiency

CHAPTER HIGHLIGHTS

- Location decisions depend on many factors. For any situation some factors may be disregarded entirely; the remainder may be divided into dominant and secondary factors.

- Factors that might be considered include: proximity to customers and markets; proximity to suppliers and resources; labour climate; proximity to the firm's other facilities; location of other firms; transportation costs; quality of life; site-specific factors; and utilities, taxes, and real estate costs. Competition is a complicating factor in estimating the sales potential of a location. Having competitors' facilities nearby may be an asset or a liability, depending on the type of business.

- One way of evaluating qualitative factors is to calculate a weighted score for each alternative location by using the preference matrix approach. The load-distance (*ld*) method brings together concerns of proximity (to markets, suppliers, resources, and other company facilities) during the early stages of location analysis. By making a full grid or patterned search of an area, an analyst identifies locations resulting in lower *ld* scores. The centre of gravity of an area is a good starting point for making a patterned search. Break-even analysis can help compare location alternatives when location factors can be expressed in terms of variable and fixed costs.

- Locating multiple facilities can be very complex. A variety of computerized heuristic, simulation, and optimization models have been developed over the last two decades to help analysts deal with this complexity.

- Layout decisions identify the placement of departments, individual operations or activities within a service or manufacturing facility. This analysis must also identify which centres to include, how much space they need, and how to configure their space.

- Three basic types of layout were discussed: flexible-flow, line process, and fixed-position. Management's choice should reflect process structure. Low volume, customized products or services favour a flexible-flow layout. Standardized, high-volume flows call for a line process layout.

- Capital investment, materials handling cost, and flexibility are important criteria in judging most layouts. Entirely different criteria, such as encouraging sales or communication, might be emphasized for stores or offices.

- Designing a flexible-flow layout involves gathering the necessary information, developing an acceptable block plan, and translating the block plan into a detailed layout. Information needed includes space requirements by centre, available space, the block plan for existing layouts, closeness ratings, and performance criteria relating to absolute location concerns. A manual approach to finding a block plan begins with listing key requirements, which may be based on high closeness ratings or on other considerations. Trial-and-error is then used to find a block plan that satisfies most of the requirements. A load-distance score is helpful in evaluating the plan for relative location concerns.

- In line process layouts, workstations are arranged in a somewhat naturally occurring, common-sense sequence as required for high-volume production of only one product or a narrow family of products. Because the physical arrangement is determined by the product's design, management concerns become line balance, pacing, behaviour, number of models, and cycle times.

- In line balancing, tasks are assigned to stations so as to satisfy all precedence and cycle-time constraints while minimizing the number of stations required. Balancing minimizes idle time, maximizes efficiency, and minimizes delay. The desired output rate from a line depends not only on demand forecasts but also on frequency of rebalancing, capacity utilization, and job specialization.

SOLVED PROBLEM 1

An electronics manufacturer must expand by building a second facility. The search has been narrowed to four locations, all acceptable to management in terms of dominant factors. Assessment of these sites in terms of seven location factors is shown in Table 9.1. For example, location A has a factor score of 5 (excellent) for labour climate; the weight for this factor (20) is the highest of any.

TABLE 9.1	*Factor Information for Electronics Manufacturer*				
		FACTOR SCORE FOR EACH LOCATION			
LOCATION FACTOR	**FACTOR WEIGHT**	**A**	**B**	**C**	**D**
1. Labour climate	20	5	4	4	5
2. Quality of life	16	2	3	4	1
3. Transportation system	16	3	4	3	2
4. Proximity to markets	14	5	3	4	4
5. Proximity to materials	12	2	3	3	4
6. Taxes	12	2	5	5	4
7. Utilities	10	5	4	3	3

Calculate the weighted score for each location. Which location should be recommended?

SOLUTION

On the basis of the weighted scores in Table 9.2, location C is the preferred site, although location B is a close second.

TABLE 9.2	*Calculating Weighted Scores for Electronics Manufacturer*				
		WEIGHTED SCORE FOR EACH LOCATION			
LOCATION FACTOR	**FACTOR WEIGHT**	**A**	**B**	**C**	**D**
1. Labour climate	20	100	80	80	100
2. Quality of life	16	32	48	64	16
3. Transportation system	16	48	64	48	32
4. Proximity to markets	14	70	42	56	56
5. Proximity to materials	12	24	36	36	48
6. Taxes	12	24	60	60	48
7. Utilities	10	50	40	30	30
Totals	100	348	370	374	330

SOLVED PROBLEM 2

The operations manager for Fizzy Beverage Company has narrowed the search for a new facility location to seven communities. Annual fixed costs (land, property taxes, insurance, equipment, and buildings) and variable costs (labour, materials, transportation, and variable overhead) are shown in Table 9.3.

  a. Which of the communities can be eliminated from further consideration because they are dominated (both variable and fixed costs are higher) by another community?

TABLE 9.3	Fixed and Variable Costs for Fizzy Beverage Company	
COMMUNITY	FIXED COSTS PER YEAR	VARIABLE COSTS PER CASE
Aurora	$1 600 000	$17
Boulder	$2 000 000	$12
Cranbrook	$1 500 000	$16
Deerfield	$3 000 000	$10
Essex	$1 800 000	$15
Farber	$1 200 000	$15
Grafton	$1 700 000	$14

b. Plot the total cost curves for all remaining communities on a single graph. Identify on the graph the approximate range over which each community provides the lowest cost.

c. Using break-even analysis, calculate the break-even quantities to determine the range over which each community provides the lowest cost.

SOLUTION

a. Aurora and Cranbrook are dominated by Farber, as both fixed and variable costs are higher for those communities than for Farber. Essex is dominated by Grafton.

b. Figure 9.10 shows that Farber is best for low volumes, Boulder for intermediate volumes, and Deerfield for high volumes. Although Grafton is not dominated by any community, it is the second or third choice over the entire range. Grafton does not become the lowest-cost choice at any volume.

FIGURE 9.10

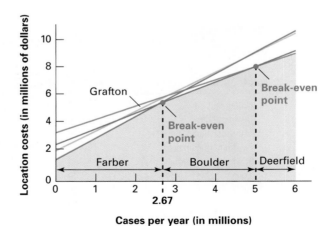

c. The break-even point between Farber and Boulder is:

$$\$1\ 200\ 000 + \$1.50Q = \$2\ 000\ 000 + \$1.20Q$$
$$Q = 2.67 \text{ million cases per year}$$

The break-even point between Deerfield and Boulder is:

$$\$3\ 000\ 000 + \$1Q = \$2\ 000\ 000 + \$1.20Q$$
$$Q = 5.0 \text{ million cases per year}$$

SOLVED PROBLEM 3

A supplier to the electric utility industry in the U.S. has a heavy product, and transportation costs are high. One market area includes the lower part of the Great Lakes region and the upper portion of the southeastern region. More than 600 000 tonnes are to be shipped to eight major customer locations, as shown in Table 9.4.

TABLE 9.4	*Markets for Electric Utilities Supplier*	
CUSTOMER LOCATION	**TONNES SHIPPED**	**XY-COORDINATES**
Three Rivers, MI	5 000	(7,13)
Fort Wayne, IN	92 000	(8,12)
Columbus, OH	70 000	(11,10)
Ashland, KY	35 000	(11,7)
Kingsport, TN	9 000	(12,4)
Akron, OH	227 000	(13,11)
Wheeling, WV	16 000	(14,10)
Roanoke, VA	153 000	(15,5)

a. Calculate the centre of gravity, rounding distance to the nearest tenth.

b. Calculate the load-distance score for this location, using rectilinear distance.

SOLUTION

a. The centre of gravity is (12.4, 9.2).

$$\sum_i l_i = 5 + 92 + 70 + 35 + 9 + 227 + 16 + 153 = 607$$

$$\sum_i l_i x_i = 5(7) + 92(8) + 70(11) + 35(11) + 9(12) + 227(13) + 16(14) + 153(15)$$

$$= 7504$$

$$x^* = \frac{\sum_i l_i y_i}{\sum_i l_i} = \frac{7504}{607} = 12.4$$

$$\sum_i l_i y_i = 5(13) + 92(12) + 70(10) + 35(7) + 9(4) + 227(11) + 16(10) + 153(5) = 5572$$

$$y^* = \frac{\sum_i l_i y_i}{\sum_i l_i} = \frac{5572}{607} = 9.2$$

b. The load-distance score is:

$$ld = \sum_i l_i d_i = 5(5.4 + 3.8) + 92(4.4 + 2.8) + 70(1.4 + 0.8) + 35(1.4 + 2.2)$$

$$+ 9(0.4 + 5.2) + 227(0.6 + 1.8) + 16(1.6 + 0.8) + 153(2.6 + 4.2)$$

$$= 2662.4$$

where:

$$d_i = |x_i - x^*| + |y_i - y^*|$$

A defence contractor is evaluating its machine shop's current process layout. Figure 9.11 shows the current layout, and the table shows the trip matrix for the facility. Safety and health regulations require departments E and F to remain at their current locations.

FIGURE 9.11   *Current Layout*

E	B	F
A	C	D

DEPARTMENT	A	B	C	D	E	F
					TRIPS BETWEEN DEPARTMENTS	
A	—	8	3		9	5
B		—		3		
C			—		8	9
D				—		3
E					—	3
F						—

a. Use trial and error to find a better layout.

b. How much better is your layout than the current one in terms of the *ld* score? Use rectilinear distance.

a. In addition to keeping departments E and F at their current locations, a good plan would locate the following department pairs close to each other: A and E, C and F, A and B, and C and E. Figure 9.12 was worked out by trial and error and satisfies all these requirements. Start by placing E and F at their current locations. Then, because C must be as close as possible to both E and F, put C between them. Place A directly south of E, and B next to A. All of the heavy traffic concerns have now been accommodated. Department D is located in the remaining space.

FIGURE 9.12   *Proposed Layout*

E	C	F
A	B	D

DEPARTMENT PAIR	NUMBER OF TRIPS (1)	CURRENT PLAN		PROPOSED PLAN	
		DISTANCE (2)	LOAD × DISTANCE (1) × (2)	DISTANCE (3)	LOAD × DISTANCE (1) × (3)
A, B	8	2	16	1	8
A, C	3	1	3	2	6
A, E	9	1	9	1	9
A, F	5	3	15	3	15
B, D	3	2	6	1	3
C, E	8	2	16	1	8
C, F	9	2	18	1	9
D, F	3	1	3	1	3
E, F	3	2	6	2	6
			$ld = 92$		$ld = 67$

b. The table reveals that the ld score drops from 92 for the current plan to 67 for the revised plan, a 27 percent reduction.

SOLVED PROBLEM 5

A company is setting up an assembly line to produce 192 units per eight-hour shift. The following table identifies the work elements, times, and immediate predecessors.

WORK ELEMENT	TIME (SEC)	IMMEDIATE PREDECESSOR(S)
A	40	None
B	80	A
C	30	D, E, F
D	25	B
E	20	B
F	15	B
G	120	A
H	145	G
I	130	H
J	115	C, I
Total	720	

a. What is the desired cycle time?

b. What is the theoretical minimum number of stations?

c. Use trial and error to work out a solution, and show your solution on a precedence diagram.

d. What are the efficiency and balance delay of the solution found?

SOLUTION

a. Substituting in the cycle-time formula, we get:

$$c = \frac{1}{r} = \frac{8 \text{ hours}}{192 \text{ units}} (3600 \text{ seconds/hour}) = 150 \text{ seconds/unit}$$

b. The sum of the work-element times is 720 seconds, so:

$$TM = \frac{\Sigma t}{c}$$

$$= \frac{720 \text{ seconds/unit}}{150 \text{ seconds/unit-station}} = 4.8, \quad \text{or} \quad 5 \text{ stations,}$$

which may not be achievable.

c. The precedence diagram is shown in Figure 9.13. Each row in the following table shows work elements assigned to each of the five workstations in the proposed solution.

FIGURE 9.13

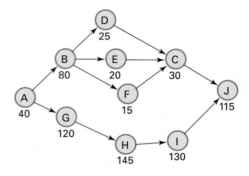

STATION	WORK ELEMENT	WORK-ELEMENT TIME (sec)	CUMULATIVE TIME TIME (sec)	IDLE TIME ($c = 150$ sec)
S1	A	40	40	110
	B	80	120	30
	D	25	145	5
S2	G	120	120	30
	E	20	140	10
S3	H	145	145	5
S4	I	130	130	20
	F	15	145	5
S5	C	30	30	120
	J	115	145	5

d. Calculating the efficiency, we get:

$$\text{Efficiency} = \frac{\Sigma t}{nc}(100)$$

$$= \frac{720 \text{ seconds/unit}}{5(150 \text{ seconds/unit})}(100)$$

$$= 96\%$$

Thus, the balance delay is only 4 percent (100 − 96).

PROBLEMS

1. Calculate the weighted score for each location (A, B, C, and D) shown in Table 9.5. Which location would you recommend?

TABLE 9.5 Factors for Locations A–D

	FACTOR WEIGHT	FACTOR SCORE FOR EACH LOCATION			
LOCATION FACTOR		A	B	C	D
1. Labour climate	5	5	4	3	5
2. Quality of life	30	2	3	5	1
3. Transportation system	5	3	4	3	5
4. Proximity to markets	25	5	3	4	4
5. Proximity to materials	5	3	2	3	5
6. Taxes	15	2	5	5	4
7. Utilities	15	5	4	2	1
Total	100				

2. John and Jane Darling are newlyweds trying to decide among several available rentals. Alternatives were scored on a scale of 1 to 5 (5 = best) against weighted performance criteria, as shown in Table 9.6. The criteria included rent, proximity to work and recreational opportunities, security, and other neighbourhood characteristics associated with the couple's values and lifestyle. Alternative A is an apartment, B is a bungalow, C is a condo, and D is a downstairs apartment in Jane's parents' home.

TABLE 9.6 Factors for Newlyweds

	FACTOR WEIGHT	FACTOR SCORE FOR EACH LOCATION			
LOCATION FACTOR		A	B	C	D
1. Rent	25	3	1	2	5
2. Quality of life	20	2	5	5	4
3. Schools	5	3	5	3	1
4. Proximity to work	10	5	3	4	3
5. Proximity to recreation	15	4	4	5	2
6. Neighbourhood security	15	2	4	4	4
7. Utilities	10	4	2	3	5
Total	100				

Which location is indicated by the preference matrix? What qualitative factors might cause this preference to change?

3. Two alternative locations are under consideration for a new plant: Winnipeg and Montreal. The Winnipeg location is superior in terms of costs. However, management believes that sales volume would decline if this location were chosen because it is farther from the market and the firm's customers prefer local suppliers. The selling price of the product is $250 per unit in either case. Use the following information to determine which location yields the higher total profit contribution per year.

LOCATION	ANNUAL FIXED COST	VARIABLE COST PER UNIT	FORECAST DEMAND PER YEAR
Winnipeg	$1 500 000	$50	30 000 units
Montreal	$2 800 000	$85	40 000 units

4. Fall-Line, Inc., is a Great Falls, Montana, manufacturer of a variety of downhill skis. Fall-Line is considering four locations for a new plant: Aspen, Colorado; Medicine Lodge, Kansas; Broken Bow, Nebraska; and Wounded Knee, South Dakota. Annual fixed costs and variable costs per pair of skis are shown in the following table:

LOCATION	ANNUAL FIXED COSTS	VARIABLE COSTS PER PAIR
Aspen	$8 000 000	$250
Medicine Lodge	$2 400 000	$130
Broken Bow	$3 400 000	$90
Wounded Knee	$4 500 000	$65

a. Plot the total cost curves for all the communities on a single graph (see Solved Problem 2). Identify on the graph the range in volume over which each location would be best.

b. What break-even quantity defines each range?

Although Aspen's fixed and variable costs are dominated by those of the other communities, Fall-Line believes that both the demand and the price would be higher for skis made in Aspen than for skis made in the other locations. The following table shows those projections:

LOCATION	PRICE PER PAIR	FORECAST DEMAND PER YEAR
Aspen	$500	60 000 pairs
Medicine Lodge	$350	45 000 pairs
Broken Bow	$350	43 000 pairs
Wounded Knee	$350	40 000 pairs

c. Determine which location yields the highest total profit contribution per year.

d. Is this location decision sensitive to forecast accuracy? At what minimum sales volume does Aspen become the location of choice?

5. The following three points are the locations of important facilities in a transportation network: (20, 20), (30, 50), and (60, 0). The coordinates are in kilometres.

a. Calculate the Euclidean distances (in kilometres) between each of the three pairs of facilities.

b. Calculate these distances using rectilinear distances.

6. Sam Hutchins is planning to operate a specialty bagel sandwich kiosk but is undecided about whether to locate in the downtown shopping plaza or in a suburban shopping mall. Based on the following data, which location would you recommend?

LOCATION	DOWNTOWN	SUBURBAN
Annual rent, including offices	$12 000	$8 000
Expected annual demand (sandwiches)	30 000	25 000
Average variable costs per sandwich	$1.50	$1.00
Average selling price per sandwich	$3.25	$2.85

7. Centura High School is to be located at the population centre of gravity of three communities: Boelus, population 228; Cairo, population 737; and Dannebrog, population 356. The Boelus community is located at 106.72°E, 46.31°N; Cairo at 106.68°E, 46.37°N; and Dannebrog at 106.77°E, 46.34°N. Where should Centura be located?

8. A larger and more modern main post office is to be constructed at a new location. Growing suburbs have shifted the population density from where it was 40 years ago, when the current facility was built. Annette Werk, the postmaster, asked her assistants to draw a grid map of the seven points where mail is picked up and delivered in bulk. The coordinates and trips per day to and from the seven mail source points and the current main post office, M, are shown in the following table. M will continue to act as a mail source point after relocation.

MAIL SOURCE POINT	ROUND TRIPS PER DAY	XY-COORDINATES (km)
1	6	(2,8)
2	3	(6,1)
3	3	(8,5)
4	3	(13,3)
5	2	(15,10)
6	7	(6,14)
7	5	(18,1)
M	3	(10,3)

a. Calculate the centre of gravity as a possible location for the new facility (round to the nearest whole number).

b. Compare the load-distance scores for the location in part (a) and the current location, using rectilinear distance.

9. *Note:* This question requires Microsoft MapPoint software. Snappy Pizza decided to locate a pizza and takeout delivery restaurant in Fargo, North Dakota. It wants to locate near the densely populated areas of the town. Snappy management created a map of the population density of the various census tracts in Fargo. The map can be found in the file "Snappy.ptm" in MyOMLab. Choose a site that has as many people as possible within a five-minute drive time zone. Print the map with your five-minute drive time zone. You might wish to watch the Tyler EMS video on MyOMLab before starting this problem.

10. Baker Machine Company specializes in manufacturing precision parts for firms in the aerospace industry. Figure 9.14 shows the current block plan for the key manufacturing centres of the 7500-square-metre facility. Referring to the trip matrix below the figure, use rectilinear distance (the current distance from inspection to shipping and receiving is 3 units) to calculate the change in the load-distance, ld, score if Baker exchanges the locations of the tool crib and inspection.

FIGURE 9.14   *Current Layout*

Trip Matrix

DEPARTMENT	TRIPS BETWEEN DEPARTMENTS					
	1	2	3	4	5	6
1. Burr and grind	—	8	3		9	5
2. NC equipment		—	3			
3. Shipping and receiving			—		8	9
4. Lathes and drills				—		3
5. Tool crib					—	3
6. Inspection						—

11. The head of the information systems group at Conway Consulting must assign six new analysts to offices. The following closeness matrix shows the expected frequency of contact between analysts. The block plan in Figure 9.15 shows the available office locations (1–6) for the six analysts (A–F). Assume equal-sized offices and rectilinear distance. Owing to their tasks, Analyst A must be assigned to location 4 and Analyst D to location 3. What are the best locations for the other four analysts? What is the load-distance score for your layout?

FIGURE 9.15 *Conway Consulting's Block Plan*

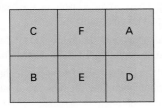

Closeness Matrix

ANALYST	CONTACTS BETWEEN ANALYSTS					
	A	B	C	D	E	F
Analyst A	—		6			
Analyst B		—		12		
Analyst C			—	2	7	
Analyst D				—		4
Analyst E					—	
Analyst F						—

12. Richard Garber is the head designer for Matthews and Novak Design Company. Garber has been called in to design the layout for a newly constructed office building. From statistical samplings over the past three months, Garber developed the trip matrix shown here for daily trips between the department's offices.

Trip Matrix

DEPARTMENT	TRIPS BETWEEN DEPARTMENTS					
	A	B	C	D	E	F
A	—	25	90			165
B		—			105	
C			—		125	125
D				—	25	
E					—	105
F						—

a. If other factors are equal, which two offices should be located closest together?

b. Figure 9.16 shows an alternative layout for the department. What is the total load-distance score for this plan, using rectilinear distance and assuming that offices A and B are 3 units of distance apart?

c. Switching which two departments will most improve the total load-distance score?

FIGURE 9.16 *Alternative Block Plan*

C	F	A
B	E	D

13. The department of engineering at a university in Alberta must assign six faculty members to their new offices. The following closeness matrix indicates the expected number of contacts per day between professors. The available office spaces (1–6) for the six faculty members are shown in Figure 9.17. Assume equal-sized offices. The distance between offices 1 and 2 (and between offices 1 and 3) is 1 unit, whereas the distance between offices 1 and 4 is 2 units.

Closeness Matrix

PROFESSOR	CONTACTS BETWEEN PROFESSORS					
	A	B	C	D	E	F
A	—		4			
B		—		12		10
C			—	2	7	
D				—		4
E					—	
F						—

a. Because of their academic positions, Professor A has to be assigned to office 1, Professor C to office 2, and Professor D to office 6. Which faculty members should be assigned to offices 3, 4, and 5, respectively, to minimize the total weighted distance score (assuming rectilinear distance)?

b. What is the load-distance score of your solution?

FIGURE 9.17 *Available Space*

1	2
3	4
5	6

14. In order to meet holiday demand, Penny's Pie Shop requires a production line that is capable of producing 50 pecan pies per week, while operating only 40 hours per week. Only 4 steps are required to produce a single pecan pie with respective processing times of 5, 5, 45, and 15 minutes.

a. What should the line's cycle time be?

b. What is the smallest number of workstations Penny could hope for in designing the line considering this cycle time?

c. Suppose that Penny finds a solution that requires only four stations. What would be the efficiency of this line?

15. Johnson Cogs wants to set up a line to produce 60 units per hour. The work elements and their precedence relationships are shown in the following table.

WORK ELEMENT	TIME (sec)	IMMEDIATE PREDECESSOR(S)
A	40	None
B	30	A
C	50	A
D	40	B
E	6	B
F	25	C
G	15	C
H	20	D, E
I	18	F, G
J	30	H, I
	Total 274	

a. What is the theoretical minimum number of stations?

b. How many stations are required, using trial and error to find a solution?

c. Suppose that a solution requiring five stations is obtained. What is its efficiency?

16. Jane produces custom greeting cards using six distinct work elements. She would like to produce 10 cards in each 8-hour card-making session. Figure 9.18 details each work element and its associated durations in minutes as well as their precedence relationships.

a. What cycle time is required to satisfy the required output rate?

b. What is the theoretical minimum number of workstations required?

c. If Jane identifies a five-station solution, what is the associated efficiency and balance delay?

d. If the cycle time increased by 100 percent, would the theoretical minimum number of workstations also increase by 100 percent?

FIGURE 9.18   *Precedence Diagram for Custom Greeting Cards*

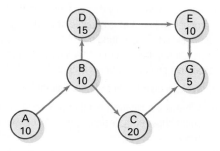

17. A paced assembly line has been devised to manufacture calculators, as the following data show:

STATION	WORK ELEMENT ASSIGNED	WORK ELEMENT TIME (min)
S1	A	2.7
S2	D, E	0.6, 0.9
S3	C	3.0
S4	B, F, G	0.7, 0.7, 0.9
S5	H, I, J	0.7, 0.3, 1.2
S6	K	2.4

a. What is the maximum hourly output rate from this line?
   Hint: The line can go only as fast as its slowest workstation.

b. What cycle time corresponds to this maximum output rate?

c. If a worker is at each station and the line operates at this maximum output rate, how much idle time is lost during each 10-hour shift?

d. What is the line's efficiency?

18. The associate administrator at Getwell Hospital wants to evaluate the layout of the outpatient clinic. Table 9.7 shows the interdepartmental flows (patients/day) between departments; Figure 9.19 shows the current layout.

TABLE 9.7   *Trip Matrix*

	TRIPS BETWEEN DEPARTMENTS							
DEPARTMENT	1	2	3	4	5	6	7	8
1. Reception	—	25	35	5	10	15		20
2. Business office		—	5	10	15			15
3. Examining room			—	20	30	20		10
4. X-ray				—	25	15		25
5. Laboratory					—	20		25
6. Surgery						—	40	
7. Postsurgery							—	15
8. Doctor's office								—

FIGURE 9.19   *Current Layout*

4	6	5	7
2	8	3	1

a. Determine the effectiveness of the current layout, as measured by the total load-distance score, using rectilinear distances.

b. Try to find the best possible layout on the basis of the same effectiveness measure.

c. What is the impact on your new solution if it must be revised to keep department 1 at its present location?

d. How should the layout developed in part (c) be revised if the interdepartmental flow between the examining room and the X-ray department is increased by 50 percent? decreased by 50 percent?

NOTES FOR CHAPTER

1. "Manager's Journal: Why BMW Cruised into Spartanburg," *Wall Street Journal*, July 6, 1992, p. A10; "BMW Announces Its Plans for a Plant in South Carolina," *Wall Street Journal*, June 24, 1992, p. B2; P. Galuszka, "The South Shall Rise Again," *Chief Executive*, November 2004, pp. 50–54; Southern Business & Development, www.sb-d.com, June 2005; www.bmwusfactory.com, July 2008.

2. G. York, "Roots Plants the Flag in China," *The Globe and Mail*, September 21, 2007.

3. "Location Analysis Tools Help Starbucks Brew Up New Ideas," *Business Geographics*, www.geoplace.com; V. Vishwanath and D. Hardling, "The Starbucks Effect," *Harvard Business Review*, March/April 2000, pp. 17–18; www.starbucks.com, June 2011.

FURTHER READING

Andel, T. "Site Selection Tools Dig Data." *Transportation & Distribution*, vol. 37, no. 6 (1996), pp. 77–81.

Bansal, P., and B. McKnight. "Looking Forward, Pushing Back and Peering Sideways: Analyzing the Sustainability of Industrial Symbiosis." *Journal of Supply Chain Management*, vol. 45, no. 4 (2009): 26–37.

Bartness, A. D. "The Plant Location Puzzle." *Harvard Business Review*, March/April 1994, pp. 20–30.

Chittum, Ryan. "Location, Location, and Technology: Where to Put That New Store? Site-Selection Software May Be Able to Help." *Wall Street Journal*, July 18, 2005, p. R7.

Cook, David P., Chon-Huat Goh, and Chen H. Chung. "Service Typologies: A State of the Art Survey." *Production and Operations Management*, vol. 8, no. 3 (1999), pp. 318–338.

Drezner, Z. *Facility Location: A Survey of Applications and Methods*. Secaucus, NJ: Springer-Verlag, 1995.

Ehrenfeld, J., and N. Gertler, N., "Industrial Ecology in Practice: The Evolution of Interdependence at Kalundborg," *Journal of Industrial Ecology*, vol. 1, no. 1 (1997): 67–79.

Ferdows, Kasra. "Making the Most of Foreign Factories." *Harvard Business Review*, March/April 1997, pp. 73–88.

Heragu, Sunderesh. *Facilities Design*. Boston, MA: PWS Publishing Company, 1997.

Kuehn, Alfred A., and Michael J. Hamburger. "A Heuristic Program for Locating Warehouses." *Management Science*, vol. 9, no. 4 (1963): pp. 643–666.

"Location Analysis Tools Help Starbucks Brew Up New Ideas." *Business Geographics*, www.geoplace.com.

MacCormack, A. D., L. J. Newman, III, and D. B. Rosenfield. "The New Dynamics of Global Manufacturing Site Location." *Sloan Management Review*, Summer 1994, pp. 69–77.

"Making Malls (Gasp!) Convenient." *Wall Street Journal*, February 8, 2000.

"MapInfo Delivers Location Intelligence for Marco's Pizza." *Directions Magazine*, December 14, 2004, www.directionsmag.com/press.releases/?duty=Show&id=10790.

Sule, D. R. *Manufacturing Facilities: Location, Planning, and Design*. Boston, MA: PWS Publishing Company, 1994.

"Tools of the Remote Trade." *BusinessWeek*, March 27, 2000, p. F20.

"Will This Open Space Work?" *Harvard Business Review*, May/June 1999, p. 28.

MyOMLab ASSETS

MyOMLab offers the following resources, which allow you to further practise and apply concepts presented in this chapter.

- **Equation Summary:** All the equations for this chapter can be found in one convenient location.
- **Discussion Questions:** Six questions will challenge your understanding of location factors, ethical obligations in location, layout criteria, office layout, and layout differences between a health system and a steel factory.
- **Cases:**
  - *Tyler Emergency Medical Services.* A growing community requires the addition of a new facility to shorten response times.
  - *Locating Multiple Facilities at Witherspoon Automotive.* An aging distribution centre is being closed and two new sites need to be chosen to better service customers based on multiple criteria.
  - *Imaginative Toys.* What are the dominant and secondary factors in this location decision?
  - *Industrial Repair.* Assess options to locate one or more new facilities.
  - *Hightec, Inc.* What block plan do you propose, and why is it effective?
  - *The Pizza Connection.* Prepare a revised layout and explain why it addresses the issues that Dave Collier identified.
  - *R.U. Reddie for Location.* To maximize the net present value of the investment in a new plant, should Rhonda Reddie build the plant in Denver or St. Louis?
- **Videos of MapPoint:** Three videos demonstrate the use of Microsoft MapPoint software.
  - *Starbucks.* Explore how customer demographics determine service location, as described earlier in the Managerial Practice feature.
  - *Tyler Emergency Medical Services.* (A description of the case is provided separately.)
  - *Witherspoon Automotive.* (A description of the case is provided separately.)
- **Virtual Tours:** *McCadam Cheese Company and Jack Daniels Distillery Tour.* Why are these firms located where they are?
- **Internet Exercises:**
  - *Dunkin Donuts* use a variety of arrangements to expand their "outlets."
  - *An increasing number of mapping and analysis options are available.* Mapquest, Expedia, Yahoo, and GeoConnections.org.
- **OM Explorer Tutors:** Five tutor programs will help you learn how to use the reference matrix, distance measures, centre of gravity, break-even analysis, and line balancing.
- **Supplement A:** *Decision Making.* See how to do break-even analysis that can be applied to location analysis.
- **Supplement C:** *Work Measurement.* See how to obtain the labour standards needed for the task times in line balancing.
- **Supplement I:** *Linear Programming.* Learn about linear programming, an important tool in solving multiple-facility location problems.

10

Managing Demand and Forecasting

Learning Goals

After reading this chapter, you will be able to:

1. Identify the different demand patterns and options for managing demand.
2. describe the various judgmental forecasting approaches.
3. explain collaborative planning, forecasting, and replenishment (CPFR).
4. explain the use of regression to make forecasts.
5. compute forecasts using the most common approaches for time-series analysis.
6. describe the various measures of forecast and explain how they are used to monitor and control forecast performance.

Across the Organization

Forecasting is important to:

- **human resources,** which uses forecasts to estimate the need for workers.
- **management information systems,** which designs and implements forecasting systems.
- **marketing,** which develops sales forecasts that are used for medium- and long-range plans.
- **operations,** which develops and uses forecasts for decisions such as scheduling workers, short-term inventory replenishment, and long-term planning for capacity.

One of the critical drivers in managing value chains is effective customer demand planning (CDP), which begins with accurate forecasts. CDP is a business-planning process that enables sales teams (and customers) to develop demand forecasts as input to service-planning processes, production and inventory planning, and revenue planning.

Unilever—the purveyor of fast-moving consumer products such as Dove, Lipton, Hellmann's, and hundreds of other brands—has a state-of-the-art CDP system. Using computer software, historical shipment data is blended with promotional data, allowing information sharing and collaboration with important customers.

The system begins with shipment history and current order information; reliable data is a critical requirement for constructing an initial baseline forecast. However, because data frequently are collected from disparate legacy systems, they may contain errors and may not necessarily lead to the best forecast. Moreover, historical statistical information is of limited use for forecasting the outcomes of special events, promotions, rollouts, and special packages, which are common in the industry.

To overcome these problems, planners must adjust initial forecasts with additional input from others. For each promotion, special sales teams predict the "lift," or projected increase in sales. These data are routed to the demand-planning system, where changes are applied weekly to specific stock-keeping units (SKUs) and distribution centres. In turn, these forecasts are reviewed and further adjusted if needed. Unilever also conducts external market research, which is analyzed and combined with the retail customer promotions, and fed into the demand-planning system.

To further improve the accuracy of its forecasts and reduce inventory lead times, Unilever compares point-of-sale (POS) data with its own forecasts. Unfortunately, not all customers provide POS data, and integrating the data from those that do is challenging given the many different formats. Because of this complexity, Unilever only collects POS data from its largest customers. Ultimately, planners must negotiate the final numbers each week and feed these forecasts into the demand-planning system.

Overall, the current CDP system has been a success. Unilever has reduced its inventory and improved its customer service. However, if collaboration and the usage of POS data were to increase, Unilever would likely reap even larger benefits.[1]

Lipton Tea is one of the many Unilever products, and its demand must be forecast for many markets around the world.

forecast A prediction of future events used for planning purposes.

Balancing supply and demand begins with making accurate forecasts. A **forecast** is a prediction of future events used for planning purposes. Planning, on the other hand, is the process of making management decisions on how to deploy resources to best respond to the demand forecasts. Forecasting methods might be based on mathematical models that use available historical data or on qualitative methods that draw on managerial experience and judgments, or they might be based on a combination of both. Unilever's CDP system illustrates the value of merging forecasts from multiple sources.

In this chapter, our focus is on demand forecasts. We begin with different types of demand patterns and designing the forecasting system. We examine forecasting methods in three basic categories: judgment, causal, and time-series methods. Forecast errors are defined, providing important clues for making better forecasts. We conclude with multiple techniques, which bring together insights from several sources, and an overall process for making forecasts.

Forecasts are useful for both managing processes and managing supply chains. At the supply chain level, a firm needs forecasts to coordinate with its customers and suppliers. At the process level, output forecasts are needed to design the various processes throughout the organization, including identifying and dealing with in-house bottlenecks. For example, Hewlett-Packard produces network cards that turn dedicated HP printers into network-shared printers. Changing its forecasting process reduced its inventory levels by 20 to 30 percent while maintaining high levels of product availability. Recognizing the important role of the forecasting process resulted in better overall performance of the supply chain.

DEMAND PATTERNS

At the root of most business decisions is the challenge of forecasting customer demand. It is a difficult task, because the demand for goods and services can vary greatly. For example, demand for lawn fertilizer predictably increases in the spring and summer months; however, the particular weekends when demand is heaviest may depend on uncontrollable factors such as the weather. Sometimes patterns are more predictable. Thus, weekly demand for haircuts at a local barbershop may be quite stable from week to week, with daily demand being heaviest on Saturday mornings and lightest on Mondays and Tuesdays. Forecasting demand in such situations requires uncovering the underlying patterns from available information. In this section, we first discuss the basic patterns of demand.

time series The repeated observations of demand for a product or service in their order of occurrence.

The repeated observations of demand for a product or service in their order of occurrence form a pattern known as a **time series**. The five basic patterns of most demand time series are:

1. *Horizontal*, or the fluctuation of data around a constant mean

2. *Trend*, or systematic increase or decrease in the mean of the series over time

3. *Seasonal*, or a repeatable pattern of increases or decreases in demand, depending on the time of day, week, month, or season

4. *Cyclical*, or less predictable gradual increases or decreases in demand over longer periods of time (years or decades)

5. *Random*, or unforecastable, variation in demand

Cyclical patterns arise from two influences. The first is the business cycle, which includes factors that cause the economy to go from recession to expansion over a number of years. The other influence is the product or service life cycle, which reflects the stages of demand from development through decline. Business cycle movement is difficult to predict because it is affected by national or international events, such as parliamentary elections or political turmoil in other countries. Predicting the rate of demand increase or decline in the life cycle also is difficult. Sometimes firms estimate demand for a new product by starting with the demand history for the product it is replacing.

Four of the patterns of demand—horizontal, trend, seasonal, and cyclical—combine in varying degrees to define the underlying time pattern of demand for a product or service. The fifth pattern, random variation, results from chance causes and, thus, cannot be predicted. Random variation is an aspect of demand that makes every forecast wrong. Figure 10.1 shows the first four patterns of a demand time series, all of which contain random variation. A time series may comprise any combination of these patterns.

FIGURE 10.1 *Patterns of Demand*

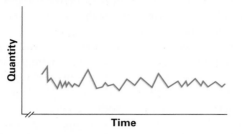

(a) Horizontal: Data cluster about a horizontal line.

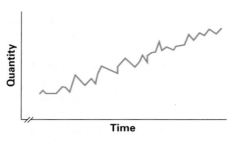

(b) Trend: Data consistently increase or decrease.

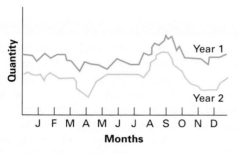

(c) Seasonal: Data consistently show peaks and valleys.

(d) Cyclical: Data reveal gradual increases and decreases over extended periods of time.

MANAGING DEMAND

Matching supply to demand becomes a challenge when forecasts call for high variability in demand patterns (see Chapter 4). Demand swings can be from one month to the next, one week to the next, or even one hour to the next. Peaks and valleys in demand also can cause poor customer service. For example, Canadian National Railways can lose sales because its railcar capacity is exceeded on a particular route and date, yet at other times, little demand might materialize. If nothing is done to even out demand, sales are lost or greater capacity cushions must be added. Fortunately, marketing and operations managers can jointly influence demand through one or more options.

COMPLEMENTARY SERVICES AND PRODUCTS

One demand option for a company to even out the load on resources is to produce complementary products or services that have similar resource requirements but different demand cycles. For example, a city parks and recreation department can counterbalance seasonal staffing requirements for summer activities by offering ice skating, tobogganing, or indoor activities during the winter months. The key is to find services and products that can be produced with the existing resources and can level off the need for resources over the year.

PROMOTIONAL PRICING

Promotional campaigns are designed to increase sales with creative pricing. Examples include automobile rebate programs, price reductions for winter clothing in the late summer months, reduced prices for hotel rooms during off-peak periods, and "two for the price of one" automobile tire sales. Lower prices can increase demand for the product or service from new and existing customers, take sales from competitors, or encourage customers to move up future buying. The first two outcomes increase overall demand, while the third shifts demand to the current period.

PRESCHEDULED APPOINTMENTS AND RESERVATIONS

Service providers often can schedule customers for specific times. In doing so, demand is levelled to not exceed supply capacity. The advantages of this method are timely customer service and the high utilization of service personnel. Doctors, dentists, lawyers, and automobile repair shops are examples of service providers that use appointment systems. Doctors can use the system to schedule parts of their day to visit hospital patients, and lawyers can set aside time to prepare cases. If timely service is to be provided, however, care must be taken to tailor the length of appointments to individual customer needs rather than merely scheduling customers at equal time intervals.

Alternatively, based on their needs for a service, customers can make advance reservations for such services as hotel rooms, new automobiles, airline tickets, and concert seats. The major advantage of reservation systems is the lead time they give service managers and the ability to level demand. Managers can deal with no-shows with a blend of overbooking, deposits, and cancellation penalties. Sometimes overbooking means that a customer with reservations cannot be served as promised. In such cases, bonuses can be offered for compensation. For example, an airline passenger might not only get on the next available flight, but also may be given a free ticket for a second flight sometime in the future.

REVENUE MANAGEMENT

A specialized combination of the pricing and reservation options for service providers is revenue management. Revenue management (sometimes called yield management) is the process of adjusting price at the right time for different customer segments to maximize revenues generated from existing capacity. It works best if customers can be segmented, prices can be varied by segment in real time, fixed costs are high, variable costs are low, service duration is predictable, and capacity is lost if not used (sometimes called perishable capacity).

Airlines, hotels, cruise lines, and rental cars are good examples. Computerized reservation systems can make hour-by-hour updates, using decision rules for opening or closing price categories depending on the difference between capacity and updated demand forecasts. In the airlines industry, prices are lowered if a particular airline flight is not selling as fast as expected, until more seats are booked. In contrast, if larger than expected demand is developing, prices for the remaining seats might be increased. Last-minute business travellers pay the higher prices, whereas leisure travellers making reservations well in advance and staying over the weekend get the bargain prices.

BACKLOGS, BACKORDERS, AND STOCKOUTS

backlog An accumulation of customer orders that a manufacturer has promised for delivery at some future date.

Much like the appointments or reservations of service providers, a **backlog** is an accumulation of customer orders that a manufacturer has promised for delivery at some future date. Manufacturers in the supply chain that maintain a backlog of orders as a normal business practice can allow the backlog to grow during periods of high demand and then reduce it during periods of low demand. Airplane manufacturers do not promise instantaneous delivery, as do wholesalers or retailers further forward in the supply chain. Instead, they impose a lead time between when the order is placed and when it is delivered.

Firms that are most likely to use backlogs—and increase the size of them during periods of heavy demand—make customized products and tend to have a make-to-order strategy. Backlogs reduce the uncertainty of future production requirements and also can be used to level demand. However, they become a competitive disadvantage if they get too big.

backorder A customer order that cannot be filled when promised or demanded but is filled later.

A last resort in demand management is to use lower levels of customer service during peak periods, in the form of either backorders or stockouts (see Chapter 5). A **backorder**—not to be confused with a backlog—is a customer order that cannot be filled immediately but is filled as soon as possible; although the customer might not be pleased with the delay, the order is not lost and is filled. In contrast, a backlog refers to the total accumulation of backorders currently waiting to be filled. In practical terms, backlogs for service firms are waiting lines of customers or orders; examples include TV repair shops, restaurants, banks, grocery stores, and barbershops.

stockout An order that is lost and causes the customer to go elsewhere.

In contrast, a **stockout** occurs when the customer goes elsewhere and the order is lost. Unlike a backorder, which adds to the next period's demand requirement, a stockout does not. Backorders and stockouts can lead dissatisfied customers to do their future business with another firm. Generally, stockouts are to be avoided.

These options for managing demand can be combined and used to varying degrees throughout the year as part of a sales and operations plan. For example, a manufacturer of lighting equipment had several products characterized as "slow movers with spikes." Several weeks would go by with sales of only two or three units, and then suddenly an huge order would arrive for 10 000 units the following week from a contractor or commercial property manager. The result was a forecasting nightmare, and the firm had to resort to high-cost supply options to meet these demand spikes. The breakthrough to solve this problem was found in combining the pricing and backlog options. Contractors were offered a 3 percent discount (the pricing option) on any order in excess of 10 000 units that was placed five or more weeks before it was needed (the backlog option). The advanced warning allowed the firm to smooth out its production processes, saving millions of dollars annually.

DESIGNING THE FORECASTING SYSTEM

Before using forecasting techniques to analyze operations management problems, a manager must make three decisions: (1) what organizational inputs to use, (2) what to forecast, and (3) what type of forecasting technique to use. We discuss each of these decisions before examining specific forecasting techniques.

ORGANIZATIONAL INPUTS

Many inputs to the forecasting process are informational, beginning with the history of past demand. A history file is kept up to date with the actual demand data. Clarifying notes and adjustments are made to the database to explain unusual demand behaviour, such as the impact of special promotions and closeouts. Final forecasts just made at the end of the prior cycle are entered in the history file, so as to track forecast errors. Other information sources include sales-force estimates, outstanding bids on new orders, booked orders, market research studies, competitor behaviour, economic outlook, new product introductions, pricing, and promotions.

collaborative planning, forecasting, and replenishment (CPFR) An approach to forecasting that allows a manufacturer and its customers to work together to make and refine a forecast over the Internet.

An important development in forecasting is a general approach whereby a firm uses software to share information and work together with its customers to make and refine forecasts over the Internet. The **collaborative planning, forecasting, and replenishment** (CPFR) model calls for the comparison of two forecasts, one from each partner in a supply chain (e.g., manufacturer and retailer). If the forecasts differ by more than a predetermined percentage, the partners share comments and supporting data until an acceptable forecast is achieved.

Benefits of CPFR can be significant for both firms. Experience reported by companies such as Walmart, Unilever, and Warner-Lambert show that the retailer has products in stock with greater reliability, thus increasing sales. The manufacturer benefits from smoother production plans and lower overall costs. However, factors such as legacy systems, mutual trust, and geography have limited adoption of CPFR to date.

DECIDING WHAT TO FORECAST

Although some sort of demand estimate is needed for the individual goods or services produced by a company, forecasting total demand for groups or clusters and then deriving individual product or service forecasts may be easiest. Also, selecting the correct unit of measurement (e.g., product or service units or machine-hours) for forecasting may be as important as choosing the best method.

aggregation The act of clustering several similar products or services so that companies can obtain more accurate forecasts.

LEVEL OF AGGREGATION. Few companies err by more than 5 percent when forecasting total demand for all their products. However, errors in forecasts for individual items may be much higher. By clustering several similar products or services in a process called **aggregation**, companies can obtain more accurate forecasts. Many companies utilize a two-tier forecasting system, first making forecasts for families of goods or services that have similar demand requirements and common processing, labour, and materials requirements and then deriving forecasts for individual items. This approach maintains consistency between planning for the final stages of manufacturing (which requires the unit forecasts) and longer-term planning for sales, profit, and capacity (which requires the product family forecasts).

UNITS OF MEASUREMENT. The most useful forecasts for planning and analyzing operations problems are those based on product or service units, such as customers needing maintenance service or repairs for their cars, rather than dollars. Forecasts of sales revenue are not very helpful, because prices often fluctuate. Forecasting the number of units of demand—and then translating these estimates to sales revenue estimates by multiplying them by the price—is often the better method. If accurately forecasting the number of units of demand for a product or service is not possible, forecasting the standard labour- or machine-*hours* required of each of the critical resources, based on historical patterns, is often better.

judgment method A fore-casting method that trans-lates the opinions of managers, expert opinions, consumer surveys, and sales-force estimates into quantitative estimates.

causal method A fore-casting method that uses historical data on related variables, such as promotional campaigns, economic conditions, and competitors' actions, to predict demand.

time-series analysis A statistical approach that relies heavily on historical demand data to project the future size of demand and recognizes trends and seasonal patterns.

CHOOSING THE TYPE OF FORECASTING TECHNIQUE

The forecaster's objective is to develop a useful forecast from the information at hand with the technique appropriate for the different characteristics of demand. This choice sometimes involves a trade-off between forecast accuracy and costs, such as software purchases, the time required to develop a forecast, and personnel training. Three general types of forecasting techniques are used for demand forecasting: judgment methods, causal methods, and time-series analysis. **Judgment methods** translate the opinions of managers, expert opinions, consumer surveys, and sales-force estimates into quantitative estimates. **Causal methods** use historical data on related variables, such as promotional campaigns, economic conditions, and competitors' actions, to predict demand. **Time-series analysis** is a statistical approach that relies heavily on historical demand data to project the future size of demand and recognizes trends and seasonal patterns.

JUDGMENT METHODS

When adequate historical data are lacking, as when a new product is introduced or technology is expected to change, firms rely on managerial judgment and experience to generate forecasts. Judgment methods can also be used to modify forecasts generated by quantitative methods. In this section, we discuss four of the more successful methods currently in use: sales-force estimates, executive opinion, market research, and the Delphi method.

sales-force estimates The forecasts that are compiled from estimates of future demands made periodically by members of a company's sales force.

SALES-FORCE ESTIMATES

Sometimes the best information about future demand comes from the people closest to the customer. **Sales-force estimates** are forecasts compiled from estimates of future demands made periodically by members of a company's sales force. Forecasts of individual sales-force members can be combined easily to get regional or national sales estimates. However, individual biases of the salespeople may taint the forecast.

For example, some people are naturally optimistic, whereas others are more cautious. Adjustments in forecasts may need to be made.

EXECUTIVE OPINION

executive opinion
A forecasting method in which the opinions, experience, and technical knowledge of one or more managers are summarized to arrive at a single forecast.

When a new product or service is contemplated, the sales force may not be able to make accurate demand estimates. **Executive opinion** is a forecasting method in which the opinions, experience, and technical knowledge of one or more managers are summarized to arrive at a single forecast. As we discuss later, executive opinion can be used to modify an existing sales forecast to account for unusual circumstances, such as a new sales promotion or unexpected international events. Executive opinion can also be used for **technological forecasting**, as the quick pace of technological change makes keeping abreast of the latest advances difficult. The key to effective use of executive opinion is to ensure that the forecast reflects not a series of independent modifications but consensus among executives.

technological forecasting
An application of executive opinion to account for the difficulties of keeping abreast of the latest advances in technology.

MARKET RESEARCH

market research
A systematic approach to gathering market information to determine customer interest in a product or service, including surveys of potential customers.

Market research is a systematic approach to gathering market information to determine customer interest in purchasing a product or service. A variety of techniques are possible, including assessing the demand for a related product, using focus groups, and administering data-gathering surveys. Although market research yields important information, one shortcoming is the numerous qualifications and hedges typically included in the findings.

DELPHI METHOD

Delphi method A process of gaining consensus from a group of experts while maintaining their anonymity.

The **Delphi method** is a process of gaining consensus from a group of experts while maintaining their anonymity. This form of forecasting is useful when there are no historical data from which to develop statistical models and when managers inside the firm have limited experience on which to base informed projections. A coordinator sends questions to each member of the group of outside experts, who may not even know who else is participating. Anonymity is important when some members of the group tend to dominate discussion or command a high degree of respect in their fields. The coordinator prepares a statistical summary of the responses along with a summary of arguments for particular responses. The report is sent to the same group for another round, and the participants may choose to modify their previous responses. These rounds continue until consensus is obtained.

CAUSAL METHODS: LINEAR REGRESSION

linear regression A causal method in which one variable (the dependent variable) is related to one or more independent variables by a linear equation.

Causal methods are used when historical data are available and the relationship between the factor to be forecasted and other external or internal factors (e.g., government actions or advertising promotions) can be identified. These relationships are expressed in mathematical terms and can be very complex. Causal methods provide the most sophisticated forecasting tools and are very good for predicting turning points in demand and preparing long-range forecasts. Although many causal methods are available, we focus here on linear regression, one of the best-known and most commonly used causal methods.

dependent variable The measure or quantity that is being forecast.

independent variables Variables assumed to be related to the dependent variable and therefore predict or "cause" the results observed in the past.

In **linear regression**, one variable, called a **dependent variable**, is related to one or more **independent variables** by a linear equation. The dependent variable, such as demand for doorknobs, is the one the manager wants to forecast. The independent variables, such as advertising expenditures and new housing starts, are assumed to affect the dependent variable and thereby "cause" the results observed in the past. Figure 10.2 shows how a linear regression line relates to the data. In technical terms, the regression line minimizes the squared deviations from the actual data.

FIGURE 10.2 *Linear Regression Line Relative to Actual Data*

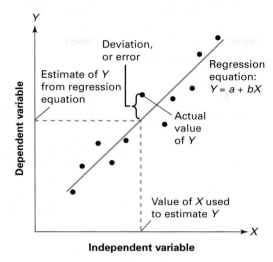

In the simplest linear regression models, the dependent variable is a function of only one independent variable, and therefore the theoretical relationship is a straight line:

$$Y = a + bX$$

where:

   Y = Dependent variable
   X = Independent variable
   a = Y-intercept of the line
   b = Slope of the line

The objective of linear regression analysis is to find values of a and b that minimize the sum of the squared deviations of the actual data points from the graphed line. Computer programs are used for this purpose. For any set of matched observations for Y and X, the program computes the values of a and b and provides measures of forecast accuracy. Three measures commonly reported are the sample correlation coefficient, the sample coefficient of determination, and the standard error of the estimate.

The *sample correlation coefficient*, r, measures the direction and strength of the relationship between the independent variable and the dependent variable. The value of r can range from -1 to $+1$. A correlation coefficient of 1 implies that period-by-period changes in direction (increases or decreases) of the independent variable are always accompanied by changes in the same direction by the dependent variable. An r of -1 means that decreases in the independent variable are always accompanied by increases in the dependent variable, and vice versa. A zero value of r means that there is no relationship between the variables. The closer the value of r is to ± 1, the better the regression line fits the points.

The *sample coefficient of determination* measures the amount of variation in the dependent variable about its mean that is explained by the regression line. The coefficient of determination is the square of the correlation coefficient, or r^2, and its value ranges from 0 to 1. Higher values of r^2 indicate that more variance is explained, which indicates that the forecasts generated by the regression equation are closely related to the dependent variable.

The *standard error of the estimate*, s_{yx}, measures how closely the data on the dependent variable cluster around the regression line. Although it is similar to the sample standard deviation, it measures the error from the dependent variable, Y, to the regression line, rather than to the mean. More specifically, it is the standard deviation of the difference between the actual demand and the estimate provided by the regression equation. When determining which independent variable to include in the regression equation, you should choose the one with the smallest standard error of the estimate.

| EXAMPLE 10.1 | *Using Linear Regression to Forecast Product Demand* |

The supply chain manager seeks a better way to forecast the demand for door hinges, and believes that the demand is related to advertising expenditures. The following are sales and advertising data for the past five months:

MONTH	SALES (thousands of units)	ADVERTISING (thousands of $)
1	264	2.5
2	116	1.3
3	165	1.4
4	101	1.0
5	209	2.0

The marketing manager says that next month the company will spend $1750 on advertising for the product. Use linear regression to develop an equation and a forecast for this product.

SOLUTION

We assume that sales are linearly related to advertising expenditures. In other words, sales are the dependent variable, Y, and advertising expenditures are the independent variable, X. Using the paired monthly observations of sales and advertising expenditures supplied by the marketing manager, we use software, such as Excel, to determine the best values of a, b, the correlation coefficient, the coefficient of determination, and the standard error of the estimate.

$$a = -8.137$$
$$b = 109.230$$
$$r = 0.980$$
$$r^2 = 0.960$$
$$s_{yx} = 15.603$$

The regression equation is:

$$Y = -8.137 + 109.230X$$

and the regression line is shown in Figure 10.3.

Are advertising expenditures a good choice to use in forecasting sales? Note that the sample correlation coefficient, r, is 0.98. Because the value of r is very close to 1, we conclude that there is a strong positive relationship between sales and advertising expenditures and that the choice was a good one.

Next, we examine the sample coefficient of determination, r^2, or 0.96. This value of r^2 implies that 96 percent of the variation in sales is explained by advertising expenditures. Most relationships between advertising and sales in practice are not this strong, because other variables, such as general economic conditions and the strategies of competitors, often combine to affect sales.

As the advertising expenditure will be $1750, the forecast for month 6 is:

$$Y = -8.137 + 109.230(1.75)$$
$$= 183.016 \quad \text{or} \quad 183\ 016 \text{ units}$$

FIGURE 10.3 *Linear Regression Line for Sales Data*

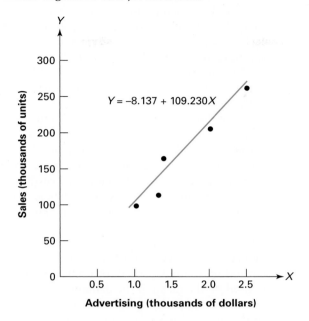

Decision Point The production scheduler can use this forecast to determine the quantity of brass door hinges needed for month 6. Suppose that she has 62 500 units in stock. The requirement to be filled from production is 183 015 − 62 500 = 120 015 units, assuming that she does not want to lose any sales.

Often several independent variables may affect the dependent variable. For example, advertising expenditures, new corporation startups, and residential building contracts may be important for estimating the demand for door hinges. In such cases, *multiple regression analysis* is helpful in determining a forecasting equation for the dependent variable as a function of several independent variables. Such models can be analyzed with Excel or OM Explorer, and they can be quite useful for predicting turning points and solving many planning problems.

TIME-SERIES METHODS

Rather than using independent variables for the forecast as regression models do, time-series methods use historical information regarding only the dependent variable. These methods are based on the assumption that the dependent variable's past pattern will continue in the future. Time-series analysis identifies the underlying patterns of demand that combine to produce an observed historical pattern of the dependent variable and then develops a model to replicate it. In this section, we focus on time-series methods that address the horizontal, trend, and seasonal patterns of demand. Before we discuss statistical methods, let us take a look at the simplest time-series method for addressing all patterns of demand—the naive forecast.

NAIVE FORECAST

naive forecast A time-series method whereby the forecast for the next period equals the demand for the current period.

A method often used in practice is the **naive forecast,** whereby the forecast for the next period equals the demand for the current period. So, if the actual demand for Wednesday is 35 customers, the forecasted demand for Thursday is 35 customers. If the actual demand on Thursday is 42 customers, the forecasted demand for Friday is 42 customers.

The naive-forecast method may take into account a demand trend. The increase (or decrease) in demand observed between the last two periods is used to adjust the current demand to arrive at a forecast. Suppose that last week the demand was 120 units and the week before it was 108 units. Demand increased 12 units in one week, so the forecast for next week would be 120 + 12 = 132 units. If the actual demand next week turned out to be 127 units, the next forecast would be 127 + 7 = 134 units. The naive-forecast method also may be used to account for seasonal patterns. If the demand last July was 50 000 units, the forecast for this July is 50 000 units. Similarly, forecasts of demand for each month of the coming year may simply reflect actual demand in the same month last year.

The advantages of the naive-forecast method are its simplicity and low cost. The method works best when the horizontal, trend, or seasonal patterns are stable and random variation is small. If random variation is large, using last period's demand to estimate next period's demand can result in highly variable forecasts that are not useful for planning purposes. Nonetheless, if its level of accuracy is acceptable, the naive forecast is an attractive approach for time-series forecasting.

ESTIMATING THE AVERAGE

We begin our discussion of statistical methods of time-series forecasting with demand that has no trend, seasonal, or cyclical patterns. The horizontal pattern in a time series is based on the mean of the demands, so we focus on forecasting methods that estimate the average of a time series of data. Consequently, for all the methods of forecasting we discuss in this section, the forecast of demand for *any* period in the future is the average of the time series computed in the current period. For example, if the average of past demand calculated on Tuesday is 65 customers, the forecasts for Wednesday, Thursday, and Friday are 65 customers each day.

Consider Figure 10.4, which shows patient arrivals at a medical clinic over the past 28 weeks. Assume that the demand pattern for patient arrivals has only a horizontal and random pattern. Three statistical techniques useful for forecasting such a time series are (1) simple moving averages, (2) weighted moving averages, and (3) exponential smoothing.

FIGURE 10.4   *Weekly Patient Arrivals at a Medical Clinic*

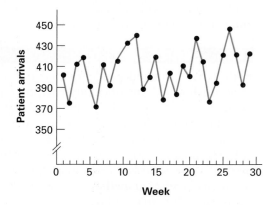

simple moving average method A time-series method used to estimate the average of a demand time series by averaging the demand for the *n* most recent time periods.

SIMPLE MOVING AVERAGES. The **simple moving average method** is used to estimate the average of a demand time series and thereby remove the effects of random fluctuation. Applying a moving average model simply involves calculating the average demand for the *n* most recent time periods and using it as the forecast for the next time period. For the next period, after the demand is known, the oldest demand from the previous average is replaced with the most recent demand and the average is recalculated. In this way, the n most recent demands are used, and the average "moves" from period to period.

Specifically, the forecast for period $t + 1$ can be calculated as:

$$F_{t+1} = \frac{\text{Sum of last } n \text{ demands}}{n} = \frac{D_t + D_{t-1} + D_{t-2} + \cdots + D_{t-n+1}}{n}$$

where:

$$D_t = \text{Actual demand in period } t$$
$$n = \text{Number of most recent periods in the average}$$
$$F_{t+1} = \text{Forecast for period } t + 1$$

With the moving average method, the forecast of next period's demand equals the average calculated at the end of this period.

EXAMPLE 10.2   *Using the Moving Average Method to Estimate Average Demand*

a. Compute a *three-week* moving average forecast for the arrival of medical clinic patients in week 4. The numbers of arrivals for the past three weeks were:

WEEK	PATIENT ARRIVALS
1	400
2	380
3	411

b. If the actual number of patient arrivals in week 4 is 415, what is the forecast for week 5?

SOLUTION

a. The moving average forecast at the end of week 3 is:

$$F_4 = \frac{411 + 380 + 400}{3} = 397.0$$

b. The forecast for week 5 requires the actual arrivals from weeks 2–4, the three most recent weeks of data.

$$F_5 = \frac{415 + 411 + 380}{3} = 402.0$$

Decision Point Thus, the forecast at the end of week 3 would have been 397 patients for week 4. The forecast for week 5, made at the end of week 4, would have been 402 patients. In addition, at the end of week 4 the forecast for week 6 and beyond is also 402 patients.

The moving average method may involve the use of as many periods of past demand as desired. Large values of n should be used for demand series that are stable and small values of n for those that are susceptible to changes in the underlying average.

weighted moving average method A time-series method in which each historical demand in the average can have its own weight; the sum of the weights is equal to 1.

WEIGHTED MOVING AVERAGES. In the simple moving average method, each demand has the same weight in the average—namely, $1/n$. In the **weighted moving average method**, each historical demand in the average can have its own weight, with the sum of the weights equalling 1. For example, in a *three-period* weighted moving average model, the most recent period might be assigned a weight of 0.50, the second most recent might be weighted 0.30, and the third most recent might be weighted 0.20. The average is obtained by multiplying the weight of each period by the value for that period and adding the products together (see Solved Problem 2 for a numerical example). The advantage of a weighted moving average method is that it allows you to emphasize recent demand over earlier demand.

exponential smoothing method A weighted moving average method that calculates the average of a time series by giving recent demands more weight than earlier demands.

EXPONENTIAL SMOOTHING. The **exponential smoothing method** is a sophisticated weighted moving average method that calculates the average of a time series by giving recent demands more weight than earlier demands. It is the most frequently used formal forecasting method because of its simplicity and the small amount of data needed to support it. Unlike the weighted moving average method, which requires n periods of past demand and n weights, exponential smoothing requires only three items of data: the last period's forecast; the demand for this period; and a smoothing parameter, alpha (α), which has a value between 0 and 1. To obtain an exponentially smoothed forecast, calculate a weighted average of the most recent demand and the forecast calculated last period. The equation for the forecast is:

$$F_{t+1} = \alpha(\text{Demand this period}) + (1 - \alpha)(\text{Forecast calculated last period})$$
$$= \alpha D_t + (1 - \alpha)F_t$$

An equivalent equation is:

$$F_{t+1} = F_t + \alpha(D_t - F_t)$$

This form of the equation shows that the forecast for the next period equals the forecast for the current period plus a proportion of the forecast error for the current period.

The emphasis given to the most recent demand levels can be adjusted by changing the smoothing parameter. Larger α values emphasize recent levels of demand and result in forecasts more responsive to changes in the underlying average. Smaller α values treat past demand more uniformly and result in more stable forecasts. This approach is analogous to adjusting the value of n in the moving average methods, except smaller values of n emphasize recent demand and larger values give greater weight to past demand. In practice, various values of α are tried and the one producing the best forecasts is chosen.

Exponential smoothing requires an initial forecast to get started. There are two ways to get this initial forecast: either use last period's demand or, if some historical data are available, calculate the average of several recent periods of demand. The effect of the initial estimate of the average on successive estimates of the average diminishes over time.

| EXAMPLE 10.3 | *Using Exponential Smoothing to Estimate Average Demand* |

Again consider the patient arrival data in Example 10.2. It is now the end of week 3. Using $\alpha = 0.10$, calculate the exponential smoothing forecast for week 4.

SOLUTION

The exponential smoothing method requires an initial forecast. Suppose that we take the demand data for the past two weeks and average them, obtaining $(400 + 380)/2 = 390$ as an initial forecast. To obtain the forecast for week 4, using exponential smoothing with $\alpha = 0.10$, we calculate the average at the end of week 3 as:

$$F_4 = 0.10(411) + 0.90(390) = 392.1$$

Thus, the forecast for week 4 would be 392 patients. If the actual demand for week 4 proved to be 415, the new forecast for week 5 would be:

$$F_5 = 0.10(415) + 0.90(392.1) = 394.4$$

or 394 patients. Note that we used F_4, not the integer-value forecast for week 4, in the computation for F_5. In general, we round off (when it is appropriate) only the final result to maintain as much accuracy as possible in the calculations.

Decision Point Using this exponential smoothing model, the analyst's forecasts would have been 392 patients for week 4 and all future weeks. Then, when actual demand turned out to be 415 patients, the revised estimate would be 394 patients for week 5 and beyond. As soon as the actual demand for week 5 is known, then the forecast for week 6 will be updated.

Exponential smoothing has the advantages of simplicity and minimal data requirements. It is inexpensive to use and, therefore, very attractive to firms that make thousands of forecasts for each time period. However, its simplicity is also a disadvantage when the underlying average is changing, as in the case of a demand series with a trend. Like any method geared solely to the assumption of a stable average, exponential smoothing results will lag behind changes in the underlying average of demand. Typically, if large α values (e.g., greater than 0.5) are required for an exponential smoothing application, chances are good that a more sophisticated model is needed because of a significant trend or seasonal influence in the demand series.

INCLUDING A TREND

Let's now consider a demand time series that has a trend. A trend in a time series is a systematic increase or decrease in the average of the series over time. Where a trend is present, exponential smoothing approaches must be modified; otherwise, the forecasts always will be below or above the actual demand.

To improve the forecast we need to calculate an estimate of the trend. We start by calculating the *current* estimate of the trend, which is the difference between the average of the series computed in the current period and the average computed last period. To obtain an estimate of the long-term trend, you can average the current estimates. The method for estimating a trend is similar to that used for estimating the demand average with exponential smoothing.

The method for incorporating a trend in an exponentially smoothed forecast is called the **trend-adjusted exponential smoothing method**. With this approach the estimates for both the average and the trend are smoothed, requiring two smoothing constants. For each period, we calculate the average and the trend:

trend-adjusted exponential smoothing method The method for incorporating a trend in an exponentially smoothed forecast.

$$A_t = \alpha(\text{Demand this period}) + (1 - \alpha)(\text{Average} + \text{Trend estimate last period})$$

$$= \alpha D_t + (1 - \alpha)(A_{t-1} + T_{t-1})$$

$$T_t = \beta(\text{Average this period} - \text{Average last period}) + (1 - \beta)(\text{Trend estimate last period})$$

$$= \beta(A_t - A_{t-1}) + (1 - \beta)T_{t-1}$$

$$F_{t+1} = A_t + T_t$$

where:

A_t = Exponentially smoothed average of the *series* in period t

T_t = Exponentially smoothed average of the *trend* in period t

α = Smoothing parameter for the average, with a value between 0 and 1

β = Smoothing parameter for the trend, with a value between 0 and 1

F_{t+1} = Forecast for period $t + 1$

To make forecasts for periods beyond the next period, we multiply the trend estimate (T_t) by the number of additional periods that we want in the forecast and add the results to the current average (A_t). For a numerical example of the trend-adjusted exponential smoothing method, see Solved Problem 4.

Estimates for last period's average and trend needed for the first forecast can be derived from past data or based on an educated guess if no historical data exist. To find values for α and β, often an analyst systematically adjusts α and β until the forecast errors are lowest. This process can be carried out in an experimental setting with the model used to forecast historical demands.

SEASONAL PATTERNS

Many organizations experience seasonal demand for their goods or services. Seasonal patterns are regularly repeating upward or downward movements in demand measured in periods of less than one year (hours, days, weeks, months, or quarters). In this context, the time periods are called *seasons*. For example, customer arrivals at a fast-food shop on any day may peak between 11 a.m. and 1 p.m. and again from 5 to 7 p.m. Here the seasonal pattern lasts a day, and each hour of the day is a season. Seasonal patterns can be any length of time, such as a day, a month, a semester, or a year. Examples include the monthly volumes of mail processed and the monthly demand for automobile tires.

An easy way to account for seasonal effects is to use one of the techniques already described but to limit the data in the time series to those time periods in the same season. For example, if there is day-of-the-week seasonal effect, then one time series would be for Mondays, one for Tuesdays, and so on. If the naive forecast is used, then the forecast for this Tuesday is the actual demand seven days ago (last Tuesday), rather than the actual demand one day ago (Monday). This method accounts for seasonal effects but has the disadvantage of discarding considerable information on past demand.

multiplicative seasonal method A method whereby seasonal factors are multiplied by an estimate of average demand to arrive at a seasonal forecast.

Other methods are available that analyze all past data, using one model to forecast demand for all of the seasons. We describe only the **multiplicative seasonal method**, whereby seasonal factors are multiplied by an estimate of average demand to arrive at a seasonal forecast. The four-step procedure presented here involves the use of simple averages of past demand, although more sophisticated methods for calculating averages, such as a moving average or exponential smoothing approach, could

Greeting cards have a strong seasonal demand pattern, requiring careful forecasting and management of inventory.

be used. The following description is based on a seasonal pattern lasting one year and seasons of one month, although the procedure can be used for any seasonal pattern and seasons of any length.

1. For each seasonal pattern, for example a year, calculate the average demand per season by dividing total demand by the number of seasons per year. For example, if the total demand for a year is 6000 units and each month is a season, the average demand per season is 6000/12 = 500 units.

2. For each year, divide the actual demand for a season by the average demand per season. The result is a *seasonal index* for each season, which indicates the level of demand relative to the average demand. For example, suppose that the demand for March was 400 units. The seasonal index for March then is 400/500 = 0.80, which indicates that March's demand is 20 percent below the average demand per month. Similarly, a seasonal index of 1.14 for April implies that April's demand is 14 percent greater than the average demand per month.

3. Calculate the average seasonal index for each season, using the results from step 2. Add the seasonal indices for a season and divide by the number of years of data. For example, suppose that we have calculated seasonal indices for April based on the last three years: 1.14, 1.18, and 1.04. The three-year average seasonal index for April is (1.14 + 1.18 + 1.04)/3 = 1.12. This is the index we will use for forecasting April's demand.

4. Calculate each season's forecast for next year. Begin by estimating the average demand per season for next year. Use the naive method, moving averages, exponential smoothing, trend-adjusted exponential smoothing, or linear regression to forecast annual demand. Divide annual demand by the number of seasons per year. Then obtain the seasonal forecast by multiplying the seasonal index by the average demand per season.

For a detailed numerical example of the multiplicative seasonal method, see Solved Problem 5.

CHOOSING A TIME-SERIES METHOD

We now turn to factors that managers must consider in selecting a method for time-series forecasting. One important consideration is forecast performance, as determined by forecast errors. Managers need to know how to measure forecast errors and how to detect when something is going wrong with the forecasting system. After examining forecast errors and their detection, we discuss criteria that managers can use to choose an appropriate time-series forecasting method.

FORECAST ERROR

Forecasts almost always contain errors. Forecast errors can be classified as either *bias errors* or *random errors*. Bias errors are the result of consistent mistakes—the forecast is always too high or too low. These errors often are the result of neglecting or not accurately estimating patterns of demand, such as a trend, seasonal, or cyclical pattern.

The other type of forecast error, random error, results from unpredictable factors that cause the forecast to deviate from the actual demand. Forecasting analysts try to minimize the effects of bias and random errors by selecting appropriate forecasting models, but eliminating all forms of errors is impossible.

forecast error The difference found by subtracting the forecast from actual demand for a given period.

MEASURES OF FORECAST ERROR. Before they can think about minimizing forecast error, managers must have some way to measure it. **Forecast error** is simply the difference between the forecast and actual demand for a given period, or:

$$E_t = D_t - F_t$$

where:

E_t = Forecast error for period t

D_t = Actual demand for period t

F_t = Forecast for period t

However, managers are usually more interested in measuring forecast error over a relatively long period of time.

The **cumulative sum of forecast errors** (CFE) measures the total forecast error:

$$\text{CFE} = \Sigma E_t$$

cumulative sum of forecast errors (CFE) A measurement of the total forecast error that assesses the bias in a forecast.

Large positive errors tend to be offset by large negative errors in the CFE measure. Nonetheless, CFE is useful in assessing bias in a forecast. For example, if a forecast is always lower than actual demand, the value of CFE will gradually get larger and larger. This increasingly large error indicates some systematic deficiency in the forecasting approach. Perhaps the analyst omitted a trend element or a cyclical pattern, or perhaps seasonal influences changed from their historical pattern. Note that the average forecast error is simply:

$$\overline{E} = \frac{\text{CFE}}{n}$$

mean squared error (MSE) A measurement of the dispersion of forecast errors.

standard deviation (σ) A measurement of the dispersion of forecast errors.

mean absolute deviation (MAD) A measurement of the dispersion of forecast errors.

The **mean squared error** (MSE), **standard deviation** (σ), and **mean absolute deviation** (MAD) measure the dispersion of forecast errors:

$$\text{MSE} = \frac{\Sigma E_t^2}{n}$$

$$\sigma = \sqrt{\frac{\Sigma(E_t - \overline{E})^2}{n - 1}}$$

$$\text{MAD} = \frac{\Sigma |E_t|}{n}$$

The mathematical symbol $|\,|$ is used to indicate the absolute value—that is, it tells you to disregard positive or negative signs. If MSE, σ, or MAD is small, the forecast is typically close to actual demand; a large value indicates the possibility of large forecast errors. The measures differ in the way they emphasize errors. Large errors get far more weight in MSE and σ, because the errors are squared. MAD is a widely used measure of forecast error because managers can easily understand it; it is merely the mean of the forecast errors over a series of time periods, without regard to whether the error was an overestimate or an underestimate. MAD also is used in tracking signals and inventory control. Earlier, we discussed how MAD or σ can be used to determine safety stocks for inventory items (see Chapter 5, "Inventory Management").

mean absolute percent error (MAPE) A measurement that relates the forecast error to the level of demand.

The **mean absolute percent error** (MAPE) relates the forecast error to the level of demand and is useful for putting forecast performance in the proper perspective:

$$\text{MAPE} = \frac{\Sigma \dfrac{|E_t|}{D_t}}{n} (100) \text{ (expressed as a percent)}$$

For example, an absolute forecast error of 100 results in a larger percentage error when the demand is 200 units than when the demand is 10 000 units.

EXAMPLE 10.4   *Calculating Forecast Error Measures*

The following table shows the actual sales of upholstered chairs for a furniture manufacturer and the forecasts made for each of the last eight months. Calculate CFE, MSE, σ, MAD, and MAPE for this product.

MONTH, t	DEMAND, D_t	FORECAST, F_t	ERROR, E_t	ERROR SQUARED, E_t^2	ABSOLUTE ERROR, $|E_t|$	ABSOLUTE PERCENT ERROR, $(|E_t|/D_t)(100)$
1	200	225	−25	625	25	12.5%
2	240	220	20	400	20	8.3
3	300	285	15	225	15	5.0
4	270	290	−20	400	20	7.4
5	230	250	−20	400	20	8.7
6	260	240	20	400	20	7.7
7	210	250	−40	1600	40	19.0
8	275	240	35	1225	35	12.7
		Total	−15	5275	195	81.3%

SOLUTION

Using the formulas for the measures, we get:

Cumulative forecast error: $\text{CFE} = -15$

Average forecast error: $\bar{E} = \dfrac{\text{CFE}}{8} = -1.875$

Mean squared error: $\text{MSE} = \dfrac{\Sigma E_t^2}{n} = \dfrac{5275}{8} = 659.4$

Standard deviation: $\sigma = \sqrt{\dfrac{\Sigma [E_t - (-1.875)]^2}{7}} = 27.4$

Mean absolute deviation: $\text{MAD} = \dfrac{\Sigma |E_t|}{n} = \dfrac{195}{8} = 24.4$

Mean absolute percent error: $\text{MAPE} = \dfrac{[\Sigma |E_t|/D_t]\,100}{n} = \dfrac{81.3\%}{8} = 10.2\%$

A CFE of −15 indicates that the forecast has a tendency to overestimate demand. The MSE, σ, and MAD statistics provide measures of forecast error variability. A MAD of 24.4 means that the average forecast error was 24.4 units in absolute value. The value of σ, 27.4, indicates that the sample distribution of forecast errors has a standard deviation of 27.4 units. A MAPE of 10.2 percent implies that, on average, the forecast error was about 10 percent of actual demand. These measures become more reliable as the number of periods of data increases.

Decision Point   Although reasonably satisfied with these forecast performance results, the analyst decided to test out a few more forecasting methods before reaching a final forecasting method to use for the future.

tracking signal A measure that indicates whether a method of forecasting is accurately predicting actual changes in demand.

TRACKING SIGNALS. A **tracking signal** is a measure that indicates whether a method of forecasting is accurately predicting actual changes in demand. The tracking signal measures the number of MADs represented by the cumulative sum of forecast errors, the CFE. The CFE tends to be zero when a correct forecasting system is being used.

At any time, however, random errors can cause the CFE to be a nonzero number. The tracking signal formula is:

$$\text{Tracking signal} = \frac{\text{CFE}}{\text{MAD}}$$

Each period, the CFE and MAD are updated to reflect current error, and the tracking signal is compared to some predetermined limits. The MAD can be calculated in one of two ways: (1) as the simple average of all absolute errors (as demonstrated in Example 10.4) or (2) as a weighted average determined by the exponential smoothing method:

$$\text{MAD}_t = \alpha |E_t| + (1 - \alpha)\text{MAD}_{t-1}$$

If forecast errors are normally distributed with a mean of 0, there is a simple relationship between σ and MAD:

$$\sigma = (\sqrt{\pi/2})\,(\text{MAD}) \cong 1.25(\text{MAD})$$

$$\text{MAD} = 0.7978\sigma \cong 0.8\sigma$$

(Recall that: $\pi \cong 3.1416$.)

This relationship allows use of the normal probability tables to specify limits for the tracking signal. If the tracking signal falls outside those limits, the forecasting model no longer is tracking demand adequately. A tracking system is useful when forecasting systems are computerized because it alerts analysts when forecasts are getting far from desirable limits.

Figure 10.5 shows tracking signal results for 23 periods plotted on a *control chart*. (recall Chapter 6, "Quality and Process Improvement"). The control chart is useful for determining whether any action needs to be taken to improve the forecasting model. In the example, the first 20 points cluster around zero, as we would expect if the forecasts are not biased. The CFE will tend toward zero. When the underlying characteristics of demand change but the forecasting model does not, the tracking signal eventually goes out of control. The steady increase after the 20th point in Figure 10.5 indicates that the process is going out of control. The 21st and 22nd points are acceptable, but the 23rd point is not.

FIGURE 10.5   *Tracking Signal*

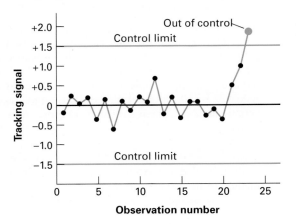

CRITERIA FOR SELECTING TIME-SERIES METHODS

Forecast error measures provide important information for choosing the best forecasting method for a product or service. They also guide managers in selecting the best values for the parameters needed for a particular time-series method. For example, measures of error can assist in selecting n for the moving average method. Two guidelines based on statistical criteria that help when searching for the best time-series models are:

1. For projections of more stable demand patterns, use lower α and β values for the exponential smoothing method or larger n values for the moving average method to emphasize historical experience.

2. For projections of more dynamic demand patterns, try higher α and β values or smaller n values. When historical demand patterns are changing, recent history should be emphasized.

Often the forecaster must make trade-offs between bias (CFE) and the measures of forecast error dispersion (MAD, MSE, and MAPE). Managers also must recognize that the best technique in explaining the past data is not necessarily the best to predict the future. For this reason, some analysts prefer to use a **holdout set** as a final test. To do so, they set aside some of the more recent periods from the time series and use only the earlier time periods to develop and test different models. Once the final models have been selected in the first phase, then they are tested again with the holdout set. Whether or not this idea is used, managers should monitor future forecast errors, perhaps with tracking signals, and modify their forecasting approaches as needed. Maintaining data on forecast performance is the ultimate test of forecasting power—rather than how well a model fits past data or holdout samples.

holdout set Actual demands from the more recent time periods in the time series, which are set aside to test different models developed from the earlier time periods.

USING MULTIPLE TECHNIQUES

We have described several individual forecasting methods and shown how to assess their forecast performance. As with all business processes, forecasting is a process and should be continually reviewed for improvements. A better process will foster better relationships between departments such as marketing, sales, and operations. It will also produce better forecasts. This principle is the first one in Table 10.1 to guide process improvements.

There is no need to rely on only a single forecasting method. For example, Unilever and Fiskars combine several different forecasts to arrive at the final forecast. Initial statistical forecasts using several time-series methods and regression can be distributed to knowledgeable individuals, such as marketing directors and sales teams, for their adjustments. They can account for current market and customer conditions that are not necessarily reflected in past data. Multiple forecasts may come from different sales teams, and some teams may have a better record on forecast errors than others. Finally, the collaborative process of CPFR introduces forecasts from suppliers and even customers. There are two approaches to using several forecasting techniques in unison—combination forecasts and focus forecasting.

TABLE 10.1	*Some Principles for the Forecasting Process*[2]

1. Better processes yield better forecasts.
2. Demand forecasting is being done in virtually every company, either formally or informally. The challenge is to do it well—better than the competition.
3. Better forecasts result in better customer service and lower costs, as well as better relationships with suppliers and customers.
4. The forecast can and must make sense based on the big picture, economic outlook, market share, and so on.
5. The best way to improve forecast accuracy is to focus on reducing forecast error.
6. Bias is the worst kind of forecast error; strive for zero bias.
7. Whenever possible, forecast at more aggregate levels. Forecast in detail only where necessary.
8. Far more can be gained by people collaborating and communicating well than by using the most advanced forecasting technique or model.

COMBINATION FORECASTS

combination forecasts
Forecasts produced by
averaging independent
forecasts based on
different methods or
different data, or both.

Research during the last two decades suggests that combining forecasts from multiple sources often produces more accurate forecasts. **Combination forecasts** are forecasts that are produced by averaging independent forecasts based on different methods or different data, or both. It is intriguing that combination forecasts often perform better over time than does even the *best* single forecasting method.

For example, suppose that the forecast for next period is 100 units from method #1 and 120 units from method #2, and that method #1 has been the single best method to date. The combination forecast for next period, giving equal weight to each technique, is 110 units (or $0.5 \times 100 + 0.5 \times 120$). When this averaging technique is used consistently into the future, its combination forecasts often will be much more accurate than either method on its own. Combining methods is most effective when the individual forecasts bring different kinds of information into the forecasting process. Forecasters have achieved excellent results by weighting forecasts equally, and this is a good starting point. However, unequal weights may provide better results under some conditions.

FOCUS FORECASTING

focus forecasting
A method of forecasting
that selects the best
forecast from a set of
forecasts generated by
simple techniques.

Another way to take advantage of multiple techniques is **focus forecasting**, which selects the best forecast from a set of several, often simpler, forecast methods. Using historical data as a starting point, a set of forecasts is prepared using each method for each item and then compared to actual demand for each item. On the basis of this exhaustive analysis, the method that produces the forecast with the least error is used to make the forecast for the next period, again on an item-by-item basis. Thus, many different methods might be used in the same period (for different items) and the method used for a particular item may change from period to period. This analysis must be conducted on a computer, because forecasts for tens of thousands of different items are made using half a dozen or more different methods.

DEMAND MANAGEMENT AND FORECASTING UNDERPIN SUSTAINABILITY

In contrast to some of the earlier chapters, managing demand and developing forecasts have linkages to sustainability because they represent important inputs to process decisions. In this light, two key principles emerge. First, actively managing demand is one means to reduce waste and inefficiencies, which invariably hurt the natural environment or social outcomes. For example, setting appointments for a health-care clinic helps doctors' time to be highly utilized, while at the same time reducing the chance that patients arrive, but must be turned away and come back later. A related benefit is customer satisfaction.

Second, a more accurate forecast also reduces waste and inefficiencies, as there is less need for safety stock and smaller capacity cushions. Less safety stock can translate into less obsolete or damaged product. Also, smaller capacity cushions mean less energy, less maintenance, and less materials for equipment. For example, if a pharmaceutical firm is able to better forecast customer demand for its eye care products, less requires disposal after the "best before" dates (in addition to the energy required to transport it for disposal). Also, the firm doesn't need to keep extra capacity "just in case" customer demand is much higher than forecast.

A growing area that is challenging managers' abilities to forecast is returned products (called the *reverse supply chain* in Chapter 2). Return policies for new products have become very generous over the past decade, and with increasing returns come increasing waste. Often customers can return products within 30 days, with no questions asked. Also, more products are being returning at the end of their useful life,

MANAGERIAL PRACTICE
Combination Forecasts and the Forecasting Process

Fiskars Brands, Inc., has totally overhauled its forecasting process. It serves 2000 customers, ranging from large discounters to local craft stores providing about 2300 finished SKUs. Its parent company, Fiskars Corporation, is the second-oldest incorporated entity in the world and produces a variety of high-quality products, such as garden shears, pruners, hand tools, scissors for preschoolers, ratchet tools, screwdrivers, and the like. Business is highly seasonal and prices quite variable. About 10 to 15 percent of the annual revenue comes from one-time promotions, and 25 to 35 percent of its products are new every year.

Fiskars introduced a statistical-based analysis along with a Web-based business intelligence tool for reporting. It put much more emphasis on combination forecasts. Instead of asking members of the sales staff to provide their own forecasts, forecasts were sent to them, and they were asked for their validation and refinement. Their inputs are most useful relative to additions, deletions, and promotions. Converting multiple forecasts into one number (forecasts from time-series techniques, sales input, and customer input) creates more accurate forecasts by SKU. Fiskars's software has the ability to weigh each input. It gives more weight to a statistical forecast for in-line items, and inputs from the sales staff get much more weight for promoted products and new items.

It also segments SKUs by value, variability, and historical forecast error levels so as to focus forecasting efforts on SKUs that have the biggest impact on the business. High-value items ("A" items identified with ABC analysis in Chapter 5, "Inventory Management") that also have *high* forecastability (i.e., low variability in demand with low forecast errors to date) tend to do well with the time-series techniques, and judgmental adjustments are made with caution. High-value items with *low* forecastability get additional attention to improve forecasting using such techniques as CPFR. Much less consideration is given to improving forecasts for "C" items, for which there is some history and fairly steady demand.

Finally, Fiskars has instituted a Web-based program that gives the entire company visibility to forecast information in

This power-point bypass pruner is one of 2300 SKUs for which Fiskars Brands needs demand forecasts. Sales are quite seasonal, and one-time promotions can be a factor. This garden tool is especially designed for people with limited hand strength. Combination forecasts that modify statistical forecasts with judgmental inputs from the sales staff improved their forecasting process.

whatever form it needs. For example, Finance wants monthly, quarterly, and yearly projections in dollars, whereas Operations wants projections in units as well as accuracy measures. Everybody can track updated forecast information by customer, brand, and SKU.[3]

either because managers are seeing opportunities to recycle materials and components, or because governments are mandating their return.

Managers must forecast product returns to design collection and processing systems that can accommodate the volume. Many factors also affect how long customers want to keep their mobile phones, computers, carpets, and other goods, which in turn can adversely affect initial forecasts. And given the small residual economic value of many end-of-life products, a firm has few options to manage demand. For example, a manufacturer of computer printers reported that the average length of time that a printer is used is roughly three years. But these printers are not discarded immediately; instead, they are typically stored in an office closet, basement, or garage for another five years before finally being discarded. So, managing and forecasting returns are very difficult, yet essential for more sustainable outcomes.

EQUATION SUMMARY

1. Naive forecasting: $\text{Forecast} = D_t$

2. Simple moving average: $F_{t+1} = \dfrac{D_t + D_{t-1} + D_{t-2} + \cdots + D_{t-n+1}}{n}$

3. Weighted moving average:

$$F_{t+1} = \text{Weight}_1(D_t) + \text{Weight}_2(D_{t-1}) + \text{Weight}_3(D_{t-2}) + \cdots + \text{Weight}_n(D_{t-n+1})$$

4. Exponential smoothing: $F_{t+1} = \alpha D_t + (1 - \alpha)F_t$

5. Trend-adjusted exponential smoothing:

$$A_t = \alpha D_t + (1 - \alpha)(A_{t-1} + T_{t-1})$$
$$T_t = \beta(A_t - A_{t-1}) + (1 - \beta)T_{t-1}$$
$$F_{t+1} = A_t + T_t$$

6. Forecast error: $E_t = D_t - F_t$

$$\text{CFE} = \Sigma E_t$$

$$\bar{E} = \text{CFE}/n$$

$$\text{MSE} = \dfrac{\Sigma E_t^2}{n}$$

$$\sigma = \sqrt{\dfrac{\Sigma(E_t - \bar{E})^2}{n - 1}}$$

$$\text{MAD} = \dfrac{\Sigma |E_t|}{n}$$

$$\text{MAPE} = \dfrac{\Sigma \dfrac{|E_t|}{D_t}}{n}(100)$$

7. Exponentially smoothed error: $\text{MAD}_t = \alpha|E_t| + (1 - \alpha)\text{MAD}_{t-1}$

8. Tracking signal: $\dfrac{\text{CFE}}{\text{MAD}}$

CHAPTER HIGHLIGHTS

- The five basic patterns of demand are horizontal, trend, seasonal, cyclical, and random variation.

- Managing demand involves options to shift the timing or quantity of customer demand. In doing so, forecasting can be simplified, production or service rates can be smoothed, or inventory can be reduced. Options include complementary services or products, promotional pricing, customer appointments and reservations, revenue management, backlogs, backorders, and stockouts.

- Designing a forecasting system involves determining what to forecast, which forecasting technique to use, and how computerized forecasting systems can assist managerial decision making.

- Level of data aggregation and units of measure are important considerations in managerial decisions about what to forecast. Three general types of demand forecasting are used: judgment methods, causal methods, and time-series analysis.

- Collaborative planning, forecasting, and replenishment (CPFR) uses software to enable a supplier and customer to work together over the Internet to develop a better forecast. If the forecasts from each firm differ by more than a predetermined percentage, they share comments and supporting data until an acceptable forecast is achieved.

- Judgment methods of forecasting are useful in situations where relevant historical data are lacking. Sales-force estimates, executive opinion, market research, and the Delphi method are judgment methods. Judgment methods require the most human interaction and so can be very costly.

- Causal forecasting methods, such as linear regression, hypothesize a functional relationship between the factor to be forecasted and other internal or external factors. Causal methods identify turning points in demand patterns but require more extensive analysis to determine the appropriate relationships between the item to be forecast and the external and internal factors.

- Time-series analysis is often used with computer systems to generate quickly the large number of short-term forecasts required for scheduling products or services. Simple moving averages, weighted moving averages, and exponential smoothing are used to estimate the average of a time series. The exponential smoothing technique has the advantage of requiring that only a minimal amount of data be kept for use in updating the forecast. Trend-adjusted exponential smoothing is a method for including a trend estimate in exponentially smoothed forecasts.

- Although many techniques allow for seasonal influences, a simple approach is the multiplicative seasonal method, which is based on the assumption that the seasonal influence is proportional to the level of average demand.

- The cumulative sum of forecast errors (CFE), mean squared error (MSE), standard deviation of forecast errors (σ), mean absolute deviation (MAD), and mean absolute percent error (MAPE) are all measures of forecast error used in practice. The CFE and MAD are used to develop a tracking signal that determines when a forecasting method no longer is yielding acceptable forecasts. Forecast error measures also are used to select the best forecast methods from available alternatives.

- Combination forecasts produced by averaging two or more independent forecasts often provide more accurate forecasts.

SOLVED PROBLEM 1

Chicken Palace periodically offers take-out five-piece chicken dinners at special prices. Let Y be the number of dinners sold and X be the price. On the basis of the historical observations and calculations in the following table, determine the regression equation, correlation coefficient, and coefficient of determination. How many dinners can Chicken Palace expect to sell at $3 each?

OBSERVATION	PRICE, X	DINNERS SOLD, Y
1	$ 2.70	760
2	$ 3.50	510
3	$ 2.00	980
4	$ 4.20	250
5	$ 3.10	320
6	$ 4.05	480
Total	$19.55	3300
Average	$ 3.26	550

SOLUTION

We use the computer to calculate the best values of a, b, the correlation coefficient, and the coefficient of determination.

$$a = 1450.12$$
$$b = -276.28$$
$$r = -0.84$$
$$r^2 = 0.71$$

The regression line is:

$$Y = a + bX = 1450.12 - 276.28X$$

The correlation coefficient ($r = -0.84$) shows a negative correlation between the variables. The coefficient of determination ($r^2 = 0.71$) indicates that other variables (in addition to price) appreciably affect sales.

If the regression equation is satisfactory to the manager, estimated sales at a price of $3 per dinner may be calculated as follows:

$$Y = a + bX = 1450.12 - 276.28(3)$$
$$= 621.27, \text{ or } 621 \text{ dinners}$$

SOLVED PROBLEM 2

The Polish General's Pizza Parlour is a small restaurant catering to patrons with a taste for European pizza. One of its specialties is Polish Prize pizza. The manager must forecast weekly demand for these special pizzas so that he can order pizza shells weekly. Recently demand has been as follows:

WEEK OF:	PIZZAS	WEEK OF:	PIZZAS
June 2	50	June 23	56
June 9	65	June 30	55
June 16	52	July 7	60

a. Forecast the demand for pizza for June 23 to July 14 by using the simple moving average method with $n = 3$. Then repeat the forecast by using the weighted moving average method with $n = 3$ and weights of 0.50, 0.30, and 0.20, with 0.50 applying to the most recent demand.

b. Calculate the MAD for each method.

SOLUTION

a. The simple moving average method and the weighted moving average method give the following results.

CURRENT WEEK	SIMPLE MOVING AVERAGE FORECAST FOR NEXT WEEK	WEIGHTED MOVING AVERAGE FORECAST FOR NEXT WEEK
June 16	$\dfrac{52 + 65 + 50}{3} = 55.7$, or 56	$[(0.5 \times 52) + (0.3 \times 65) + (0.2 \times 50)] = 55.5$, or 56
June 23	$\dfrac{56 + 52 + 65}{3} = 57.7$, or 58	$[(0.5 \times 56) + (0.3 \times 52) + (0.2 \times 65)] = 56.6$, or 57
June 30	$\dfrac{55 + 56 + 52}{3} = 54.3$, or 54	$[(0.5 \times 55) + (0.3 \times 56) + (0.2 \times 52)] = 54.7$, or 55
July 7	$\dfrac{60 + 55 + 56}{3} = 57$	$[(0.5 \times 60) + (0.3 \times 55) + (0.2 \times 56)] = 57.7$, or 58

b. The mean absolute deviation is calculated as follows:

		SIMPLE MOVING AVERAGE		WEIGHTED MOVING AVERAGE	
WEEK	**ACTUAL DEMAND**	**Forecast**	**Absolute Errors, $|E_t|$**	**Forecast**	**Absolute Errors, $|E_t|$**
June 23	56	56	$|56 - 56| = 0$	56	$|56 - 56| = 0$
June 30	55	58	$|55 - 58| = 3$	56	$|55 - 57| = 2$
July 7	60	54	$|60 - 54| = 6$	56	$|60 - 55| = 5$
			MAD $= \dfrac{0 + 3 + 6}{3} = 3$		MAD $= \dfrac{0 + 2 + 5}{3} = 2.3$

For this limited set of data, the weighted moving average method resulted in a slightly lower mean absolute deviation. However, final conclusions can be made only after analyzing much more data.

SOLVED PROBLEM 3

The monthly demand for units manufactured by the Acme Rocket Company has been as follows:

MONTH	UNITS	MONTH	UNITS
May	100	September	105
June	80	October	110
July	110	November	125
August	115	December	120

a. Use the exponential smoothing method to forecast the number of units for June to January. The initial forecast for May was 105 units; $\alpha = 0.2$.

b. Calculate the absolute percentage error for each month from June through December and the MAD and MAPE of forecast error as of the end of December.

c. Calculate the tracking signal as of the end of December. What can you say about the performance of your forecasting method?

SOLUTION

a.

CURRENT MONTH, t	$F_{t+1} = \alpha D_t + (1 - \alpha)F_t$	FORECAST FOR MONTH $t + 1$
May	$0.2(100) + 0.8(105)\ \ = 104.0$, or 104	June
June	$0.2(80)\ \ + 0.8(104.0) = \ \ 99.2$, or 99	July
July	$0.2(110) + 0.8(99.2)\ \ = 101.4$, or 101	August
August	$0.2(115) + 0.8(101.4) = 104.1$, or 104	September
September	$0.2(105) + 0.8(104.1) = 104.3$, or 104	October
October	$0.2(110) + 0.8(104.3) = 105.4$, or 105	November
November	$0.2(125) + 0.8(105.4) = 109.3$, or 109	December
December	$0.2(120) + 0.8(109.3) = 111.4$, or 111	January

b.

MONTH, t	ACTUAL DEMAND, D_t	FORECAST, F_t	ERRORS, $E_t = D_t - F_t$	ABSOLUTE ERRORS, $\lvert E_t \rvert$	ABSOLUTE PERCENTAGE ERROR, $(\lvert E_t \rvert / D_t)(100\%)$
June	80	104	−24	24	30.0%
July	110	99	11	11	10.0
August	115	101	14	14	12.2
September	105	104	1	1	0.9
October	110	104	6	6	5.4
November	125	105	20	20	16.0
December	120	109	11	11	9.2
Total	765		39	87	83.7%

$$\text{MAD} = \frac{\Sigma \lvert E_t \rvert}{n} = \frac{87}{7} = 12.4 \quad \text{and} \quad \text{MAPE} = \frac{\Sigma [\lvert E_t \rvert (100)]/D_t}{n} = \frac{83.7\%}{7} = 11.9$$

c. As of the end of December, the cumulative sum of forecast errors (CFE) is 39. Using the mean absolute deviation calculated in part (b), we calculate the tracking signal:

$$\text{Tracking signal} = \frac{\text{CFE}}{\text{MAD}} = \frac{39}{12.4} = 3.14$$

The probability that a tracking signal value of 3.14 could be generated completely by chance is very small. Consequently, we should revise our approach. The long string of forecasts lower than actual demand suggests use of a trend method.

SOLVED PROBLEM 4

The demand for Krispee Crunchies, a favourite breakfast cereal of people born in the 1940s, is experiencing a decline. The company wants to monitor demand for this product closely as it nears the end of its life cycle. The trend-adjusted exponential smoothing method is used with $\alpha = 0.1$ and $\beta = 0.2$. At the end of December, the January estimate for the average number of cases sold per month, A_t, was 900 000 and the trend, T_t, was −50 000 per month. The following table shows the actual sales history for January, February, and March. Generate forecasts for February, March, and April.

MONTH	SALES
January	890 000
February	800 000
March	825 000

SOLUTION

We know the initial condition at the end of December and actual demand for January, February, and March. We must now update the forecast method and prepare a forecast for April. All data are expressed in thousands of cases. Our equations for use with trend-adjusted exponential smoothing are:

$$A_t = \alpha D_t + (1 - \alpha)(A_{t-1} + T_{t-1})$$
$$T_t = \beta(A_t - A_{t-1}) + (1 - \beta)T_{t-1}$$
$$F_{t+1} = A_t + T_t$$

For January, we have:

$$A_{Jan} = 0.1(890\,000) + 0.9(900\,000 - 50\,000)$$

$$= 854\,000 \text{ cases}$$

$$T_{Jan} = 0.2(854\,000 - 900\,000) + 0.8(-50\,000)$$

$$= -49\,200 \text{ cases}$$

$$F_{Feb} = A_{Jan} + T_{Jan} = 854\,000 - 49\,200 = 804\,800 \text{ cases}$$

For February, we have:

$$A_{Feb} = 0.1(800\,000) + 0.9(854\,000 - 49\,200)$$

$$= 804\,320 \text{ cases}$$

$$T_{Feb} = 0.2(804\,320 - 854\,000) + 0.8(-49\,200)$$

$$= -49\,296 \text{ cases}$$

$$F_{Mar} = A_{Feb} + T_{Feb} = 804\,320 - 49\,296 = 755\,024 \text{ cases}$$

For March, we have:

$$A_{Mar} = 0.1(825\,000) + 0.9(804\,320 - 49\,296)$$

$$= 762\,022 \text{ cases}$$

$$T_{Mar} = 0.2(762\,022 - 804\,320) + 0.8(-49\,296)$$

$$= -47\,897 \text{ cases}$$

$$F_{Apr} = A_{Mar} + T_{Mar} = 762\,022 - 47\,897 = 714\,125 \text{ cases}$$

SOLVED PROBLEM 5

The Northville Post Office experiences a seasonal pattern of daily mail volume every week. The following data for two representative weeks are expressed in thousands of pieces of mail:

DAY	WEEK 1	WEEK 2
Sunday	5	8
Monday	20	15
Tuesday	30	32
Wednesday	35	30
Thursday	49	45
Friday	70	70
Saturday	15	10
Total	224	210

a. Calculate a seasonal factor for each day of the week.
b. If the postmaster estimates that there will be 230 000 pieces of mail to sort next week, forecast the volume for each day of the week.

SOLUTION

a. Calculate the average daily mail volume for each week. Then for each day divide the mail volume by the week's average to get the seasonal factor. Finally, for each day, add the two seasonal factors and divide by 2 to obtain the average seasonal factor to use in the forecast (see part (b)).

| | WEEK 1 | | WEEK 2 | | AVERAGE SEASONAL FACTOR [(1) + (2)]/2 |
DAY	Mail Volume	Seasonal Factor (1)	Mail Volume	Seasonal Factor (2)	
Sunday	5	5/32 = 0.15625	8	8/30 = 0.26667	0.21146
Monday	20	20/32 = 0.62500	15	15/30 = 0.50000	0.56250
Tuesday	30	30/32 = 0.93750	32	32/30 = 1.06667	1.00209
Wednesday	35	35/32 = 1.09375	30	30/30 = 1.00000	1.04688
Thursday	49	49/32 = 1.53125	45	45/30 = 1.50000	1.51563
Friday	70	70/32 = 2.18750	70	70/30 = 2.33333	2.26042
Saturday	15	15/32 = 0.46875	10	10/30 = 0.33333	0.40104
Total	224		210		
Average	224/7 = 32		210/7 = 30		

b. The average daily mail volume is expected to be 230 000/7 = 32 857 pieces of mail. Using the average seasonal factors calculated in part (a), we obtain the following forecasts:

DAY	CALCULATION	FORECAST
Sunday	0.21146(32 857) =	6 948
Monday	0.56250(32 857) =	18 482
Tuesday	1.00209(32 857) =	32 926
Wednesday	1.04688(32 857) =	34 397
Thursday	1.51563(32 857) =	49 799
Friday	2.26042(32 857) =	74 271
Saturday	0.40104(32 857) =	13 177
	Total	230 000

PROBLEMS

1. Sales for the past 12 months at Dalworth Company are given here.

MONTH	SALES ($ MILLIONS)	MONTH	SALES ($ MILLIONS)
January	20	July	53
February	24	August	62
March	27	September	54
April	31	October	36
May	37	November	32
June	47	December	29

a. Use a three-month moving average to forecast the sales for the months April through December.

b. Use a four-month moving average to forecast the sales for the months May through December.

c. Compare the performance of the two methods by using the mean absolute deviation as the performance criterion. Which method would you recommend?

d. Compare the performance of the two methods by using the mean absolute percent error as the performance criterion. Which method would you recommend?

e. Compare the performance of the two methods by using the mean squared error as the performance criterion. Which method would you recommend?

2. Karl's Copiers sells and repairs photocopy machines. The manager needs weekly forecasts of service calls so that he can schedule service personnel. The forecast for the week of July 3 was 24 calls. The manager uses exponential smoothing with $\alpha = 0.20$. Forecast the number of calls for the week of August 7, which is next week.

WEEK OF:	ACTUAL SERVICE CALLS
July 3	24
July 10	32
July 17	36
July 24	23
July 31	25

3. Community Bank in Saskatoon recently installed a new automatic teller machine to perform the standard banking

services and handle loan applications and investment transactions. The new machine is a bit complicated to use, so management is interested in tracking its past use and projecting its future use. Additional machines may be needed if projected use is high enough.

At the end of April, the average monthly use was 600 customers and the trend was +60 customers per month. The actual use figures for May, June, and July are 680, 710, and 790, respectively. Use trend-adjusted exponential smoothing with $\alpha = 0.3$ and $\beta = 0.2$ to forecast usage for June, July, and August.

4. A convenience store recently started to carry a new brand of soft drink in its territory. Management is interested in estimating future sales volume to determine whether it should continue to carry the new brand or replace it with another brand. At the end of April, the average monthly sales volume of the new soft drink was 700 cans and the trend was +50 cans per month. The actual sales volume figures for May, June, and July are 760, 800, and 820, respectively. Use trend-adjusted exponential smoothing with $\alpha = 0.2$ and $\beta = 0.1$ to forecast usage for June, July, and August.

5. The number of heart surgeries performed at Heartville General Hospital has increased steadily over the past several years. The hospital's administration is seeking the best method to forecast the demand for such surgeries in year 6. The data for the past five years are shown.

YEAR	DEMAND
1	45
2	50
3	52
4	56
5	58

The hospital's administration is considering the following forecasting methods. Begin error measurement in year 3, so all methods are compared for the same years.

   i. Exponential smoothing, with $\alpha = 0.6$. Let the initial forecast for year 1 be 45, the same as the actual demand.

   ii. Exponential smoothing, with $\alpha = 0.9$. Let the initial forecast for year 1 be 45, the same as the actual demand.

   iii. Trend-adjusted exponential smoothing, with $\alpha = 0.6$ and $\beta = 0.1$. Use the actual demand for year 1 for the initial average for the first year and 0 for the initial trend.

   iv. Two-year moving average.

   v. Two-year weighted moving average, using weights 0.6 and 0.4, with more recent data given more weight.

   vi. Regression model, $Y = 42.6 + 3.2X$, where Y is the number of surgeries and X is the index for the year (e.g., $X = 1$ for year 1, $X = 2$ for year 2, and so forth).

a. If MAD is the performance criterion chosen by the administration, which forecasting method should it choose?

b. If MSE is the performance criterion chosen by the administration, which forecasting method should it choose?

c. If MAPE is the performance criterion chosen by the administration, which forecasting method should it choose?

6. The following data are for calculator sales in units at an electronics store over the past five weeks:

WEEK	SALES
1	46
2	49
3	43
4	50
5	53

Use trend-adjusted exponential smoothing with $\alpha = 0.2$ and $\beta = 0.2$ to forecast sales for weeks 3–6. Assume that the average of the time series was 45 units and that the average trend was +2 units per week just before week 1.

7. The manager of Snyder's Garden Centre must make her annual purchasing plans for rakes, gloves, and other gardening items. One of the items she stocks is Fast-Grow, a liquid fertilizer. The sales of this item are seasonal, with peaks in the spring, summer, and fall months. Quarterly demand (in cases) for the past two years follows:

QUARTER	YEAR 1	YEAR 2
1	40	60
2	350	440
3	290	320
4	210	280
Total	890	1100

If the expected sales for Fast-Grow are 1150 cases for year 3, use the multiplicative seasonal method to prepare a forecast for each quarter of the year.

8. The manager of a utility company wants to develop quarterly forecasts of power loads for the next year. The power loads are seasonal, and the data on the quarterly loads in megawatts (MW) for the last four years are as follows:

YEAR	QUARTER 1	QUARTER 2	QUARTER 3	QUARTER 4
1	103.5	94.7	118.6	109.3
2	126.1	116.0	141.2	131.6
3	144.5	137.1	159.0	149.5
4	166.1	152.5	178.2	169.0

The manager has estimated the total demand for the next year at 780 MW. Use the multiplicative seasonal method to develop the forecast for each quarter.

9. Demand for oil changes at Garcia's Garage has been as follows:

MONTH	NUMBER OF OIL CHANGES
January	41
February	46
March	57
April	52
May	59
June	51
July	60
August	62

a. Use simple linear regression analysis to develop a forecasting model for monthly demand. In this application, the dependent variable, Y, is monthly demand and the independent variable, X, is the month. For January, let $X = 1$; for February, let $X = 2$; and so on.

b. Use the model to forecast demand for September, October, and November. Here, $X = 9$, 10, and 11, respectively.

10. Forrest and Dan make boxes of chocolates for which the demand is uncertain. Forrest says, "That's life." On the other hand, Dan believes that some demand patterns exist that could be useful for planning the purchase of sugar, chocolate, and shrimp. Forrest insists on placing a surprise chocolate-covered shrimp in some boxes so that "You never know what you'll get." Quarterly demand (in boxes of chocolates) for the last three years follows:

QUARTER	YEAR 1	YEAR 2	YEAR 3
1	3000	3300	3502
2	1700	2100	2448
3	900	1500	1768
4	4400	5100	5882
Total	10 000	12 000	13 600

a. Use intuition and judgment to estimate quarterly demand for the fourth year.

b. If the expected sales for chocolates are 14 800 cases for year 4, use the multiplicative seasonal method to prepare a forecast for each quarter of the year. Are any

of the quarterly forecasts different from what you thought you would get in part (a)?

11. The past demands at a medical clinic follow:

WEEK	DEMAND	WEEK	DEMAND
1	400	15	383
2	380	16	402
3	411	17	387
4	415	18	410
5	393	19	398
6	375	20	433
7	410	21	415
8	395	22	380
9	406	23	394
10	424	24	412
11	433	25	439
12	391	26	416
13	396	27	395
14	417	28	419

The clinic's administration is considering the following forecasting methods. Start error measurement in the fourth week, so all methods are evaluated over the same periods.

i. Naive (1-period moving average).

ii. 3-period weighted moving average, using weights of 0.70, 0.20, and 0.10, with more recent data given more weight

iii. Exponential smoothing, with $\alpha = 0.10$. Use 400 as the initial forecast.

iv. Trend-adjusted exponential smoothing, with $\alpha = 0.10$ and $\beta = 0.10$. Use 400 for the initial average and an initial trend of 0.

a. If CFE (or mean bias) is the performance criterion chosen by the administration, which forecasting method should it choose?

b. If MAD is the performance criterion chosen by the administration, which forecasting method should it choose?

c. If MSE is the performance criterion chosen by the administration, which forecasting method should it choose?

d. If MAPE is the performance criterion chosen by the administration, which forecasting method should it choose?

12. The materials handling manager of a manufacturing company is trying to forecast the cost of maintenance for the company's fleet of over-the-road tractors. The manager believes that the cost of maintaining the tractors increases with their age. The following data was collected:

AGE (YEARS)	YEARLY MAINTENANCE COST ($)	AGE (YEARS)	YEARLY MAINTENANCE COST ($)
4.5	619	5.0	1194
4.5	1049	0.5	163
4.5	1033	0.5	182
4.0	495	6.0	764
4.0	723	6.0	1373
4.0	681	1.0	978
5.0	890	1.0	466
5.0	1522	1.0	549
5.5	987		

a. Use linear regression software to assess the relationship between age and maintenance costs, and then to forecast the yearly maintenance cost based on the age of a tractor.

b. If a section has 20 three-year-old tractors, what is the forecast for the annual maintenance cost?

NOTES FOR CHAPTER

1. Robert L. Mitchell, "Case Study: Unilever Crosses the Data Streams," *Computerworld,* December 17, 2001; Robert L. Mitchell, "Tech Check: Getting Demand Planning Right," *Computerworld,* December 17, 2001; Chana R. Schoenberger, "The Weakest Link," *Forbes,* October 1, 2001, p. 114.

2. Adapted from Thomas F. Wallace and Robert A. Stahl, *Sales Forecasting: A New Approach* (Cincinnati, OH: T. E. Wallace & Company, 2002), p. 112.

3. David Montgomery, "Flashpoints for Changing Your Forecasting Process," *The Journal of Business Forecasting,* Winter 2006–2007, pp. 35–37; www.fiskars.com, July 6, 2008.

FURTHER READING

Armstrong, J. S. *Long-Range Forecasting: From Crystal Ball to Computer.* New York: John Wiley & Sons, 1995.

Armstrong, J. S. (ed.). *Principles of Forecasting: A Handbook for Researchers and Practitioners.* Norwell, MA: Kluwer Academic Publishers, 2001. (Also visit http://www.forecastingprinciples.com for valuable information on forecasting, including frequently asked questions, a forecasting methodology tree, and a dictionary.)

Bowerman, B. L., and R. T. O'Connell. *Forecasting and Time Series: An Applied Approach,* 3rd ed. Belmont, CA: Duxbury Press, 1993.

Clemen, R. T. "Combining Forecasts: A Review and Annotated Bibliography." *International Journal of Forecasting,* vol. 5 (1989), pp. 559–583.

Hudson, W. J. *Executive Economics: Forecasting and Planning for the Real World of Business.* New York: John Wiley & Sons, 1993.

Klassen, R. D., and B. E. Flores. "Forecasting Practices of Canadian Firms: Survey Results and Comparisons." *International Journal of Production Economics,* vol. 70, no. 2 (2001), pp. 163–174.

Li, X. "An Intelligent Business Forecaster for Strategic Business Planning." *Journal of Forecasting,* vol. 18, no. 3 (1999), pp. 181–205.

Lim, J. S., and M. O'Connor. "Judgmental Forecasting with Time Series and Causal Information." *International Journal of Forecasting,* vol. 12 (1996), pp. 139–153.

Mentzer, John T., and Mark A. Moon. "Understanding Demand." *Supply Chain Management,* May/June 2004, pp. 38–45.

Mitchell, R. L. "Case Study: Unilever Crosses the Data Streams." *Computerworld,* December 17, 2001.

Moon, M. A., J. T. Mentzer, and D. E. Thomas, Jr. "Customer Demand Planning at Lucent Technologies: A Case Study in Continuous Improvement Through Sales Forecast Auditing." *Industrial Marketing Management,* vol. 29, no. 1 (2000).

Sanders, N. R., and L. P. Ritzman. "Bringing Judgment into Combination Forecasts." *Journal of Operations Management,* vol. 13 (1995), pp. 311–321.

Sanders, N. R., and L. P. Ritzman. "The Need for Contextual and Technical Knowledge in Judgmental Forecasting." *Journal of Behavioral Decision Making*, vol. 5, no. 1 (1992), pp. 39–52.

Schachtman, Noah. "Trading Partners Collaborate to Increase Sales." *InformationWeek.com,* October 9, 2000. www.informationweek.com/807/cpfr.htm.

Seifert, D. *Collaborative Planning, Forecasting, and Replenishment: How to Create a Supply-Chain Advantage.* Bonn, Germany: Galileo Press, 2002.

Smith, L. "West Marine: A CPFR Success Story." *Supply Chain Management Review,* March 2006, pp. 29–36.

Steerman, H. "A Practical Look at CPFR: The Sears-Michelin Experience." *Supply Chain Management Review,* July/August 2003, pp. 46–53.

Wallace, T. F., and R. A. Stahl. *Sales Forecasting: A New Approach.* Cincinnati, OH: T. E. Wallace & Company, 2002.

MyOMLab ASSETS

MyOMLab offers the following resources, which allow you to further practise and apply concepts presented in this chapter.

- **Key Equations:** All the equations for this chapter can be found in one convenient location.

- **Discussion Questions:** Two questions will challenge your understanding of forecasting.

- **Case:** *Yankee Fork and Hoe Company.* What are your forecasts for bow rakes in year 5?

- **Video Case:** *Forecasting and Supply Chain Management at Deckers Outdoor Corporation.* Assess and explore improvements for this footwear manufacturer.

- **Virtual Tours:**

  - *Ferrara Pan* produces candy using a high-volume batch process. The forecasting challenges are quite different from those of a low-volume specialty producer.

  - *Cape Cod Chips* turns raw potatoes into crispy potato chips. What might the demand pattern look like? How would managers forecast sales for new flavours?

  - *Stihl Chain Saws.* Which products have relatively stable demand? Which products might be complementary, and which components of a chain saw might be used in other products?

- **Experiential Exercises:**

  - Use the *Yankee Fork and Hoe Company* case as an in-class team experience.

  - *Forecasting with the Holdout Sample.* Put your forecasting tools and insights into practice.

- **OM Explorer Tutors:** Four Tutor programs will help you to learn how to use the moving average, weighted moving average, exponential smoothing, and trend-adjusting exponential smoothing techniques.

11

Operations Planning and Scheduling

Learning Goals

After reading this chapter, you will be able to:

1. describe the operations planning and scheduling process.
2. explain why the process of matching supply with demand begins with aggregation.
3. identify options to manage demand and supply.
4. explain how operations plans and schedules relate to other plans.
5. use spreadsheets to create sales and operations plans.
6. develop employee schedules.

Across the Organization

Operations planning is important to:

- **accounting,** which prepares cost accounting information needed to evaluate operations plans.
- **distribution,** which coordinates the outbound flow of materials in the supply chain with plans and schedules.
- **finance,** which develops plans to finance the cash flows created by plans and schedules.
- **human resources,** which is aware of how labour market conditions and training capacities constrain plans and schedules.
- **marketing,** which provides demand forecasts and information on competition and customer preferences.
- **operations,** which develops plans and schedules that are the best compromise among cost, customer service, inventory investment, stable workforce levels, and facility utilization.
- **purchasing,** which provides information on supplier capabilities and coordinates the inbound flow of materials and services in the supply chain with plans and schedules.

The MacMillan Yard, a 400-hectare marshalling yard just north of Toronto, is critical to transferring much of Canadian National Railways' freight that crosses the continent. This freight-classification yard breaks trains apart and reassembles them for local deliveries or onward carriage. Everything is running well here, and trains are on time. The reason things are going so smoothly is a rigorous new approach called "Precision Railroading" by CN. Using this model, CN runs regularly scheduled trains that leave at predetermined times. And each railcar has an individual "trip plan," a unique and sacrosanct timetable that the railway must honour for its customers. Scheduling is making one of the most dramatic changes in railways since the introduction of diesel power.

It may come as a surprise that freight railways haven't run on schedules like those that discipline airlines, bus lines, and couriers. But within the capital-intensive and traditional world of freight railways, the notion of scheduling is a splendid and fearsome revolution. Until recently, most rail companies could not be specific about how many days it might take for their customer's products to get to market—a real problem in the era of just-in-time deliveries.

Before CN began developing its concept of a schedule railway about a dozen years ago, service from Edmonton to Chicago would be quoted as taking six to eight days—give or take another day. So how did the customer respond? Plan for the worst: increase safety stock inventory, as well as order extra railcars in case the train didn't arrive. Costs for both the customer and CN were higher. The result: the market share for railways declined for more than 40 years as trucking snatched high-value, time-sensitive goods and left the railways with high-volume, low-margin commodities.

The chief architect of scheduling trains was CN's executive vice-president and chief operating officer. Scheduled service sounds simple, but its execution is symphonic in its complexity. And like a symphony, it comprises three principal parts. First, service is enshrined at the front line, not just in upper management; second, costs must be controlled; and third, asset utilization must be maximized.

CN's commitment to deliver freight in hours—not days—and its ability to deliver on the promise have transformed it into the best railroad in North America. Over a four-year period, the volume of railcars that MacMillan Yard could handle jumped 50 percent. And similar gains occurred in labour productivity. By 2009, about 35 cars per labour hour were being handled in the terminals, a 23 percent improvement over the previous two years.

But the gains aren't limited to just lower costs. In 2009, CN reported that on-time arrival, a key customer metric, averaged 89 percent across its vast and complex network. Scheduling improvements are now being leveraged in key competitive markets. For example, CN offers scheduled potash service to improve the shipment of potash (a common fertilizer) from mines in Saskatchewan to key distribution centres. Total cycle time for the customer-owned railcars from mine to distribution centre, and then back to the mine, has fallen by 25 percent. Customers also can track their shipments over the Internet. Benefits come from better fleet productivity, smaller inventories, and improved responsiveness.

All this better scheduling and improved efficiency translates into smoother flows and less congestion in terminals. By 2009, the total time railcars spent in terminals being transferred or waiting for departure had fallen by 11 percent across the system since 2007. Most importantly, "Precision Railroading" has earned kudos from customers, for example, with Walmart Canada naming CN Innovator of the Year for its "truck-like" service and cutting-edge supply chain solutions.[1]

Canadian National Railways' commitment to delivering freight on time across a vast North American network has dramatically transformed the railroad.

Planning for operations at companies such as CN must cover both the long-term planning horizon for resources and short-term schedules for facilities, equipment, and personnel. While long-term plans can stretch out five years or more, much management attention is often focused on some form of annual plan. The annual plan is then further broken down into detailed, short-term schedules for specific jobs, customers, and employees. In this chapter, we examine planning and scheduling that falls within this annual planning time frame.

The starting point is usually a financial assessment of the organization's near future—that is, for one or two years ahead. Service firms, such as a retail store or firm of lawyers, and manufacturing firms prepare business plans that are usually accompanied by budgets, a projected (pro forma) balance sheet, and a projected cash flow statement. The business plan unifies the plans and expectations of a firm's marketing, sales, operations, and finance managers, aggregating plans for such areas as market penetration, new product introduction, and capital investment. Not-for-profit or government organizations, such as the United Way or a regional hospital, prepare a similar type of plan, often termed an *annual plan*.

At the next level below, operations planning and scheduling is the process of making sure that demand and supply plans are in balance, from the aggregate level down to the specific detailed scheduling level. Operations planning and scheduling lies at the core of supply chain integration (see Chapter 2), around which plans are made up and down the supply chain, from supplier deliveries to customer due dates and services. Table 11.1 defines several types of plans related to operations planning and scheduling.

TABLE 11.1	*Types of Plans*
KEY TERM	**DEFINITION**
Business plan	A projected plan of revenue, costs, and profits.
Sales and operations plan (S&OP)	A plan of future aggregate resource levels that tries to balance supply with demand. It states a company's or department's production rates, workforce levels, and inventory holdings that are consistent with demand forecasts and capacity constraints. The S&OP is time-phased, meaning that it is projected for several time periods (such as months or quarters) into the future.
Aggregate plan	Another term for the sales and operations plan.
Production plan	A manufacturing firm's sales and operations plan that centres on production rates and inventory holdings.
Staffing plan	A sales and operations plan for a service firm, which centres on staffing and on other human resources–related factors.
Resource plan	An intermediate step in the planning process that lies between S&OP and scheduling. It determines requirements for materials and other resources on a more detailed level than the S&OP. This topic is covered in Chapter 12, "Resource Planning."
Schedule	A detailed plan that allocates resources over shorter time horizons to accomplish specific tasks.

An analogy for the different planning levels is a student's calendar. Basing the choice of a school on career goals—a plan covering four or five years—corresponds to the highest planning level. Basing the choice of classes on that school's requirements—a plan for the next school year—corresponds to the middle planning level (or aggregate plan).

Finally, scheduling group meetings and study times around work requirements in current classes—a plan for the next few weeks—corresponds to the most detailed planning level.

THE PURPOSE OF A SALES AND OPERATIONS PLAN

In this section, we explain why companies begin with a macro, or big-picture, view of their business. The sales and operations plan is useful because it focuses on a general course of action, consistent with the company's strategic goals and objectives, without getting bogged down in details. For this reason, production and staffing plans are prepared by grouping, or aggregating, similar products, services, units of labour, or units of time. For instance, a manufacturer of bicycles that produces 12 different models of bikes might divide them into two groups, mountain bikes and road bikes, for the purpose of preparing the aggregate plan. It might also consider its workforce needs in terms of units of labour needed per month. In general, companies aggregate products or services, workforce, and time.

PRODUCT FAMILIES

Recall that a group of products or services that have similar demand requirements and common processing, labour, and materials requirements is called a *product family*. Sometimes product families relate to market groupings or, in the case of production plans, to specific manufacturing processes. A firm can aggregate its products or services into a set of relatively broad families, avoiding too much detail at this stage of the planning process.

WORKFORCE

A company can aggregate its workforce in various ways, depending on workforce flexibility. For example, if workers at the bicycle manufacturer are trained to work on either mountain bikes or road bikes, for planning purposes, management can consider its workforce to be a single aggregate group, even though the skills of individual workers may differ. Alternatively, in service operations, such as a city government, workers are aggregated by the type of service they provide: firefighters, police officers, sanitation workers, and administrators.

TIME

planning horizon The length of time covered by an aggregate plan.

A **planning horizon** is the length of time covered by an aggregate plan. Typically, the planning horizon is one year, although it can differ in various situations. To avoid the expense and disruptive effect of frequent changes in output rates and the workforce, adjustments usually are made monthly or quarterly. In other words, the company looks at time in the aggregate—months, quarters, or seasons, rather than days or hours. In practice, planning periods reflect a balance between the needs for (1) a limited number of decision points to reduce planning complexity and (2) flexibility to adjust output rates and workforce levels when demand forecasts exhibit seasonal variations.

SALES AND OPERATIONS PLANS

Developing sales and operations plans means making decisions. In this section, we concentrate on the information inputs, the supply options themselves, and strategies that go into the sales and operations planning (S&OP) decisions.

INFORMATION INPUTS

Just as it is needed to manage the demand side, consensus is needed among the firm's departments when decisions for the supply side are made. Information inputs are sought to create a plan that works for all. Figure 11.1 lists inputs from each functional

FIGURE 11.1   *Managerial Inputs from Functional Areas to Sales and Operations Plans*

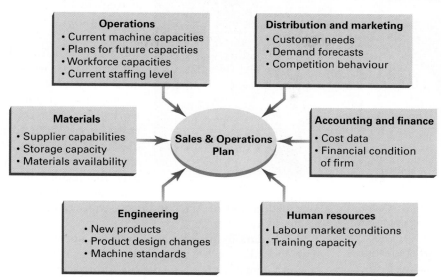

area. They must be accounted for to make sure that the plan is a good one and also doable. Such coordination helps synchronize the flow of services, materials, and information through the supply chain to best balance supply with customer demand.

SUPPLY OPTIONS

Given demand forecasts, as modified by demand management choices (see Chapter 10, "Managing Demand and Forecasting"), operations managers must develop a plan to meet that demand, drawing from a number of supply options. An operations manager can modify inventory levels, workforce levels, worker utilization, and vacation schedules, or employ subcontracting.

ANTICIPATION INVENTORY. A plant facing seasonal demand can stock *anticipation inventory* (see Chapter 5, "Inventory Management") during light demand periods and use it during heavy demand periods. For example, Whirlpool uses this option to meet demand for air conditioners. Although this approach stabilizes output rates and workforce levels, it can be costly because the value of the product is greatest in its finished state. Stocking components and subassemblies that can be assembled quickly when customer orders come in might be preferable to stocking finished goods.

Service providers generally cannot use anticipation inventory because services can't be stocked. In some instances, however, services can be performed prior to actual need. For example, telephone company workers usually lay cables for service to a new subdivision before housing construction begins. They can do this work during a period when the workload for scheduled services is low.

WORKFORCE ADJUSTMENT. Management can adjust workforce levels through the hiring or layoff of employees. The use of this alternative can be attractive if the workforce is largely unskilled or semiskilled and the labour pool is large. However, for a particular company, the size of the qualified labour pool may limit the number of new employees that can be hired at any one time. Also, new employees must be trained, and the capacity of the training facilities themselves might limit the number of new hires at any one time. In some industries, the layoff of employees is difficult or unusual for

A retail employee stocks a Whirlpool air conditioner at a Lowe's store. The demand for window-unit air conditioners fluctuates not only by season but also by year—some summers are hotter than others. Instead of ramping production up or down on the basis of a particular year, Whirlpool bases its sales and operations plans on the average year.

contractual reasons (unions); in other industries, such as tourism and agriculture, seasonal hiring and layoffs are the norm.

WORKFORCE UTILIZATION. An alternative to workforce adjustment is workforce utilization, which might involve overtime and undertime. **Overtime** means that employees work longer than the regular workday or workweek and receive additional pay for the extra hours. It can be used to satisfy output requirements that cannot be completed on regular time. However, overtime is expensive (typically 50 percent premium over the regular-time pay rate). Moreover, workers often do not want to work a lot of overtime for an extended period of time, and excessive overtime may result in declining quality and productivity.

Undertime means that employees do not work *productively* for the entire regular-time workday or workweek. Undertime occurs when labour capacity exceeds a period's demand requirements (net of anticipation inventory) and this excess capacity cannot or should not be used to build up inventory or to satisfy customer orders earlier than the delivery dates already promised. Depending on their contract, employees can either be paid for undertime, which avoids layoffs, or be sent home earlier without pay.

A related option is to hire part-time workers, who are paid only for the hours and days worked. Perhaps they only work during the peak times of the day or peak days of the week. Sometimes, part-time arrangements provide predictable work schedules, but in other cases workers are not called in if the workload is light. Such arrangements are more common in low-skill positions or when the supply of workers seeking such an arrangement is sufficient.

overtime The time that employees work that is longer than the regular workday or workweek, for which they receive premium pay for the extra hours.

undertime The situation that occurs when employees do not work *productively* for the regular-time workday or workweek.

VACATION SCHEDULES. A firm can shut down during an annual lull in sales, leaving a skeleton crew to cover operations and perform maintenance. Employees might be required to take all or part of their allowed vacation time during this period. Use of this alternative depends on whether the employer can mandate the vacation schedules of its employees. In any case, employees may be strongly discouraged from taking vacations during peak periods or encouraged to take vacations during slack periods.

SUBCONTRACTORS. Subcontractors can be used to overcome short-term capacity shortages, such as during peaks of the season or business cycle (see Chapter 2, "Supply Chain Management"). Subcontractors can supply services, make components and subassemblies, or even assemble an entire product. If the subcontractor can supply components or subassemblies of equal or better quality less expensively than the company can produce them itself, these arrangements may become permanent.

PLANNING STRATEGIES

Managers often combine supply options with demand management (see Chapter 10) to develop an acceptable sales and operations plan. For the remainder of this chapter, let us assume that the expected results of managing demand have already been incorporated into the forecasts of product families or services. This assumption allows us to focus on the supply options that define output rates and workforce levels. Countless plans are possible even when just a few supply options are considered. Here we focus on two basic strategies that are useful starting points in searching for the best plan.

chase strategy A strategy that involves hiring and laying off employees to match the demand forecast.

1. *Chase strategy.* The **chase strategy** involves hiring and laying off employees to match the demand forecast over the planning horizon. Varying the workforce's regular-time capacity to equate supply to demand requires no inventory investment, overtime, or undertime. The drawbacks are the expense of continually adjusting workforce levels, the potential alienation of the workforce, and the loss of productivity and quality because of constant changes in the workforce.

level strategy A strategy that keeps the workforce constant, but varies its utilization via overtime, undertime, and vacation planning to match the demand forecast.

2. *Level strategy.* The **level strategy** involves keeping the workforce constant (except possibly at the beginning of the planning horizon). It can vary its utilization to match the demand forecast via overtime, undertime (paid or unpaid), and vacation planning (i.e., paid vacations when demand is low). A constant workforce can be sized at many levels: managers can choose to maintain a large workforce so as to minimize the planned use of overtime during peak periods (which, unfortunately, also maximizes the need for undertime during slack periods). Alternatively, they can choose to maintain a smaller workforce and rely heavily on overtime during the peak periods (which puts a strain on the workforce and endangers quality).

mixed strategy A strategy that considers and implements a full range of supply options.

These two "pure" strategies used alone usually do not produce the best sales and operations plan. It might not be best to keep the workforce exactly level, or to vary it to exactly match forecasted demand on a period-by-period basis. The best strategy, therefore, is usually a **mixed strategy** that considers the full range of supply options. While the chase strategy is limited to just hiring and laying off employees and the level strategy is limited to overtime, undertime, and vacation schedules, the mixed strategy opens things up to all options, including anticipation inventory, part-time workers, and subcontractors (in addition to backorders and stockouts to manage demand).

THE PLANNING PROCESS

Figure 11.2 shows the process for preparing a sales and operations plan. It is dynamic and continuing, as aspects of the plan are updated periodically when new information becomes available and new opportunities emerge.

FIGURE 11.2   *The Process for Preparing a Sales and Operations Plan*

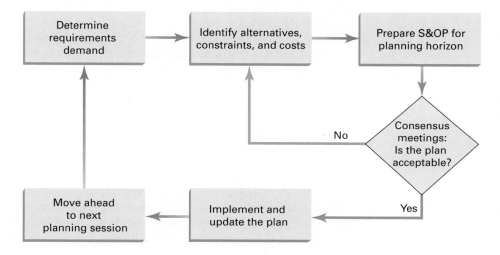

DETERMINING DEMAND REQUIREMENTS

The first step in the planning process is to determine the demand requirements for each period of the planning horizon using one of the many methods that we have already discussed (see Chapter 10). For staffing plans, the planner bases forecasts of staff requirements for each workforce group on historical levels of demand, managerial judgment, and existing backlogs for services. For example, a director of nursing in a hospital can develop a direct-care index for a nursing staff and translate a projection of the month-to-month patient census into an equivalent total amount of nursing care time—and, thus, the number of nurses—required for each month of the year.

For production plans, however, the requirements represent the demand for finished goods and the external demand for replacement parts. The planner can derive future requirements for finished goods from backlogs (for make-to-order operations) or from forecasts for product families made to stock (for make-to-stock operations). Sometimes distributors or dealers indicate their requirements for finished goods in advance of actual orders, providing a reliable forecast of requirements from those sources.

IDENTIFYING ALTERNATIVES, CONSTRAINTS, AND COSTS

The second step is to identify the alternatives, constraints, and costs for the plan. We presented the capacity alternatives used in aggregate plans earlier, so we now focus on constraints and costs.

Constraints represent physical limitations or managerial policies associated with the aggregate plan. Examples of physical constraints might include training facilities capable of handling only so many new hires at a time, machine capacities that limit maximum output, or inadequate inventory storage space. Policy constraints might include limitations on the amount of backordering or the use of subcontracting or overtime, as well as the minimum inventory levels needed to achieve desired safety stocks.

PREPARING AN ACCEPTABLE PLAN

The third step is to prepare the sales and operations plan. Developing an acceptable plan is an iterative process; that is, plans may need to go through several revisions and adjustments (see Figure 11.2). A prospective, or tentative, plan is developed to start. A production plan with monthly periods, for example, must specify monthly production rates, inventory and backorder accumulations, subcontracted production, and monthly workforce levels (including hires, layoffs, and overtime). The plan must then be checked against constraints and evaluated in terms of strategic objectives. If the prospective plan is not acceptable for either of those reasons, a new prospective plan must be developed.

One or more meetings should be held to gain some degree of consensus among the stakeholders about how to best balance supply with demand. Participants might include the supply chain manager, plant manager, controller, purchasing manager, production control manager, or logistics manager. The goal is to prepare one set of recommendations for the the firm's senior management, but, where agreement cannot be reached, to prepare scenarios of alternative plans.

IMPLEMENTING AND UPDATING THE PLAN

The final step is implementing and updating the sales and operations plan. Implementation requires the commitment of managers in all functional areas. The planning committee may recommend changes in the plan during implementation or updating to balance conflicting objectives better. Acceptance of the plan does not necessarily mean that everyone is in total agreement, but it does imply that everyone will work to achieve it. Once implementation is underway, management can begin the planning process again.

USING SOFTWARE TO ASSIST WITH PLANNING

Large firms can employ "enterprise software" to help develop sales and operations plans. This software, offered by companies such as SAP, integrates information across functional areas, business units, geographic regions, and product lines. The software can also coordinate information and planning among customers, internal operations, and suppliers. For simplicity here, we use a *spreadsheet* approach that involves adopting a planning strategy, identifying alternatives, developing a plan, comparing the developed plan to other plans, and finally modifying the plan or strategy as necessary, until we are satisfied with the results. We demonstrate this approach by developing three aggregate plans: the first using a chase strategy, the second using a level strategy, and the third using a mixed strategy. For service or manufacturing companies where inventory is not possible, the level strategy is usually adjusted using overtime or undertime to reduce the number of employees.

After a planning strategy has been stated and a plan developed, it is evaluated using a spreadsheet. One part of the spreadsheet shows the *input values* that give the demand requirements and the capacity alternative choices period by period. Another part shows the *derived values* that must follow from the input values. The final part of the spreadsheet shows the *calculated costs* of the plan. Along with qualitative considerations, the calculated cost of each plan determines whether the plan is satisfactory or whether a revised plan should be considered. When seeking clues about how to improve a plan already evaluated, we identify its highest-cost elements. Revisions that would reduce these specific costs might produce a new plan with lower overall costs.

| EXAMPLE 11.1 | *Using the Chase and Level Strategies as Starting Points* |

The manager of a large distribution centre must determine how many part-time stock pickers to keep on the payroll. She wants to develop a staffing plan that minimizes total costs, and wants to begin with the chase strategy and level strategy. For the level strategy, she wants to first try the workforce level that meets demand with the minimum use of undertime and not consider vacation scheduling.

First, the manager divides the next year into six time periods, each two months long. Each part-time employee can work a maximum of 20 hours per week on regular time, but the actual number can be less. Instead of paying undertime, each worker's day is shortened during slack periods. Once on the payroll, each worker is used each day, but they may work only a few hours. Overtime can be used during peak periods.

The distribution centre's forecasted demand is shown as the number of part-time employees required for each time period at the maximum regular time of 20 hours per week. For example, in period 3, an estimated 18 part-time employees working 20 hours per week on regular time will be needed.

	1	2	3	4	5	6	TOTAL
Forecasted demand (number of part-time employees)	6	12	18	15	13	14	78

Currently, 10 part-time clerks are employed. They have not been subtracted from the forecasted demand shown. Constraints and cost information are as follows:

a. The size of training facilities limits the number of new hires in any period to no more than 10.

b. No backorders are permitted; demand must be met each period.

c. Overtime cannot exceed 20 percent of the regular-time capacity (that is, 4 hours) in any period. Therefore, the most that any part-time employee can work is 1.20(20) = 24 hours per week.

d. The following costs can be assigned:

Regular-time wage rate	$2000 per time period at 20 hours per week
Overtime wages	150 percent of the regular-time rate
Hires	$1000 per person
Layoffs	$500 per person

SOLUTION

Chase Strategy

This strategy simply involves adjusting the workforce as needed to meet demand, as is shown in Figure 11.3. Rows in the spreadsheet that do not apply (such as inventory and vacations) are hidden. The workforce level row is identical to the forecasted demand row. A large number of hirings and layoffs begin with laying off 4 part-time employees immediately because the current staff is 10 and the staff level required in period 1 is only 6. However, many employees, such as college students, prefer part-time work. The total cost is $173 500, and most of the cost increase comes from frequent hiring and layoffs, which add $17 500 to the cost of utilized regular-time costs.

FIGURE 11.3 *Spreadsheet for Chase Strategy*

	1	2	3	4	5	6	Total
Inputs							
Forecasted demand	6	12	18	15	13	14	78
Workforce level	6	12	18	15	13	14	78
Undertime	0	0	0	0	0	0	0
Overtime	0	0	0	0	0	0	0
Derived							
Utilized time	6	12	18	15	13	14	78
Hires	0	6	6	0	0	1	13
Layoffs	4	0	0	3	2	0	9
Calculated							
Utilized time cost	$12 000	$24 000	$36 000	$30 000	$26 000	$28 000	$156 000
Undertime cost	$ 0	$ 0	$ 0	$ 0	$ 0	$ 0	$ 0
Hiring cost	$ 0	$ 6 000	$ 6 000	$ 0	$ 0	$ 1 000	$ 13 000
Layoff cost	$ 2 000	$ 0	$ 0	$ 1 500	$ 1 000	$ 0	$ 4 500
Total cost	$14 000	30 000	42 000	31 500	27 000	29 000	$173 500

Level Strategy

To minimize undertime, the maximum use of overtime possible has to occur in the peak period. For this particular level strategy (other workforce options are possible), the most overtime the manager can use is 20 percent of the regular-time capacity, w, so:

$$1.2w = 18 \text{ employees required in peak period (period 3)}$$

$$w = \frac{18}{1.2} = 15 \text{ employees}$$

A 15-employee staff size minimizes the amount of undertime for this level strategy. Because the staff already includes 10 part-time employees, the manager should immediately hire 5 more. The complete plan is shown in Figure 11.4. The total cost is $164 000, which seems reasonable because the minimum conceivable cost is only $156 000 (78 periods × $2000/period). This cost could be achieved only if the manager found a way to cover the forecasted demand for all 78 periods with regular time. The plan seems reasonable, primarily because it involves the use of large amounts of undertime (15 periods), which in this example are unpaid.

Decision Point The manager, now having a point of reference with which to compare other plans, decided to evaluate some other plans before making a final choice, beginning with the chase strategy. The only way to reduce costs is to somehow reduce the premium for 3 overtime employee periods (3 periods × $3000/period) or to reduce the hiring cost of 5 employees

FIGURE 11.4 *Spreadsheet for Level Strategy*

	1	2	3	4	5	6	Total
Inputs							
Forecasted demand	6	12	18	15	13	14	78
Workforce level	15	15	15	15	15	15	90
Undertime	9	3	0	0	2	1	15
Overtime	0	0	3	0	0	0	3
Derived							
Utilized time	6	12	15	15	13	14	75
Hires	5	0	0	0	0	0	5
Layoffs	0	0	0	0	0	0	0
Calculated							
Utilized time cost	$12 000	$24 000	$30 000	$30 000	$26 000	$28 000	$150 000
Undertime cost	$ 0	$ 0	$ 0	$ 0	$ 0	$ 0	$ 0
Overtime cost	$ 0	$ 0	$ 9 000	$ 0	$ 0	$ 0	$ 9 000
Hiring cost	$ 5 000	$ 0	$ 0	$ 0	$ 0	$ 0	$ 5 000
Layoff cost	$ 0	$ 0	$ 0	$ 0	$ 0	$ 0	$ 0
Total cost	$17 000	24 000	39 000	30 000	26 000	28 000	$164 000

(5 hires × $1000/person). Nonetheless, better solutions may be possible. For example, undertime can be reduced by delaying the hiring until period 2, because the current workforce is sufficient until then. This delay would decrease the amount of unpaid undertime, which is a qualitative improvement.

As noted previously, a key difference between the service and manufacturing firms is the potential options of building inventory or allowing backorders between periods with a mixed strategy. To capture these options, additional rows can be added into the spreadsheet; for planning purposes, these options allow the firm to potentially avoid overtime.

MANAGERIAL CONSIDERATIONS

Although a series of operations plans can be tried and compared to find the best plan, managers also can use a variety of mathematical techniques and software packages to assist with meeting particular management objectives. For example, Supplement I, "Linear Programming," in MyOMLab shows how to formulate different operations plans and scheduling problems as linear programming models—and how to solve them once modelled. In their simplest form, the models allow management to minimize cost, subject to meeting demand, given the costs of supply options. Spreadsheets also routinely include extra software modules that assist with optimizing against particular criteria determined by management, such as minimum cost (e.g., Excel has an add-in module called "Solver").

Although such techniques can be useful in developing sound operations plans, they are only aids to the planning process. The planning process is dynamic and often complicated by conflicting objectives. Analytic techniques can help managers evaluate plans and resolve conflicting objectives, but managers—not techniques—make the decisions. As a result, a minimum-cost plan might only serve as a guide or benchmark against which to compare alternatives that more effectively balance other customer- and operations-related objectives, such as flexibility and risk.

IMPLEMENTING THE OPERATIONS PLAN: SCHEDULING

Scheduling operations is a key part of implementing the plan in Figure 11.2, and is where "the rubber meets the road." This important aspect of supply chain management is itself a process. It requires gathering data from sources such as demand forecasts or specific customer orders, resource availability from the sales and operations plan, and specific constraints to be reckoned with from employees and customers. It then involves generating a work schedule for employees or sequences of jobs or customers at workstations. The schedule has to be coordinated with the employees and suppliers to make sure that all constraints are satisfied. Here we cover Gantt charts, employee schedules, and job sequencing at workstations.

GANTT CHARTS

Schedules can be displayed in various ways. For different jobs or activities they can simply list their due dates, show in a table their start and finish times, or show in a graph their start and finish times. The Gantt chart uses the third approach. Recall that Figure 8.4 demonstrates how a "picture can be worth a thousand words" in managing projects. A similar visual tool can be used with scheduling; staff not familiar with scheduling techniques can still grasp the essence of the plan. This tool can be used to monitor the progress of work and to view the load on workstations.

The chart takes two basic forms: (1) the job or activity progress chart and (2) the workstation chart. The Gantt progress chart graphically displays the current status of each job or activity relative to its scheduled completion date. For example, suppose that an automobile parts manufacturer has three jobs under way, one each for Ford, Honda, and BMW. The actual status of these orders is shown by the coloured bars in

MANAGERIAL PRACTICE

Scheduling of Resources at Air New Zealand

How important is scheduling to an airline company? Certainly, customer satisfaction regarding on-time schedule performance is critical in a highly competitive industry such as air transportation. In addition, airlines lose a lot of money when expensive equipment, such as an aircraft, is idle. Flight and crew scheduling, however, is a complex process. For example, Air New Zealand is a group of five airlines with a combined fleet of over 100 aircraft. It directly serves 50 ports—26 domestic and 24 international within 15 countries. It carries 1.7 million passengers annually, and its network incorporates flight times ranging from 15 minutes to 13 hours. Operations planning and scheduling at the aggregate level begins with a market plan that identifies the new and existing flight segments that are needed to remain competitive. This general plan is further refined to a three-year plan, and then is put into an annual budget in which flight segments have specific departure and arrival times.

Next, crew availability must be matched to the flight schedules. The two types of crews—pilots and attendants—each comes with its own set of constraints. Pilots, for example, cannot be scheduled for more than 35 hours in a seven-day week and no more than 100 hours in a 28-day cycle. They also must have a 36-hour break every seven days and 30 days off in an 84-day cycle. Each pilot's tour of duty begins and ends at a crew base and consists of an alternating sequence of duty periods and rest periods, with duty periods including one or more flights. The schedule must ensure that each flight has a qualified crew and that each crew member has a feasible tour of

Operations planning and scheduling at an airline such as Air New Zealand goes through several stages to match supply with demand, from aggregate plans to short-term schedules.

duty over the roster period. From the crew's point of view, it is also important to satisfy as many crew requests and preferences as possible.

Scheduling does not end with matching flights to crew rosters. Daily disruptions such as severe weather conditions or mechanical failures can cause schedule changes to crews, pilots, and even aircraft. Customers expect a fast resolution of the problem, and the company needs to find the least-cost solution. In the airline industry, the aggregate planning and scheduling process for a firm can become a long-term competitive strength.[2]

FIGURE 11.5 *Gantt Progress Chart for an Auto Parts Company*

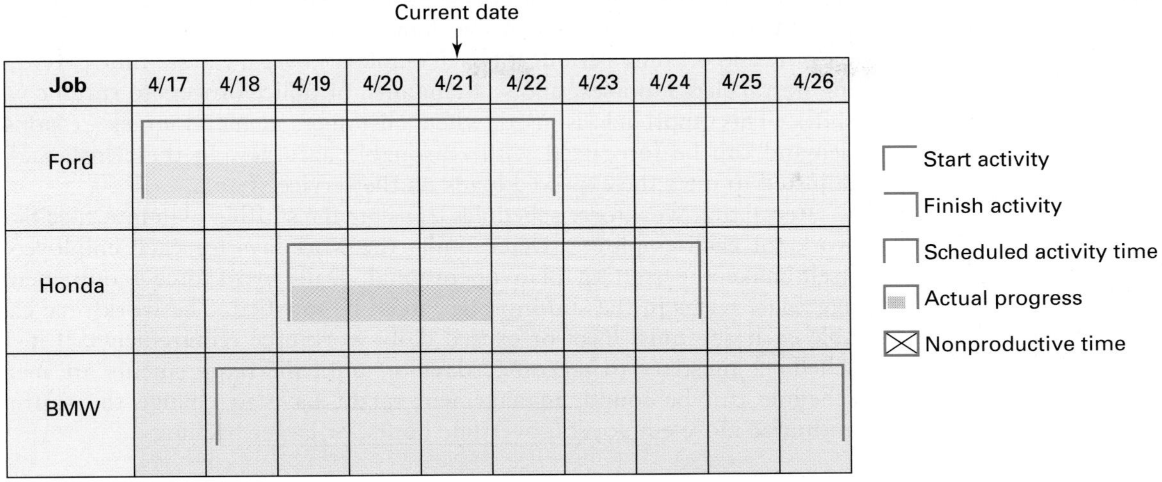

Figure 11.5; the red lines indicate the desired schedule for the start and finish of each job. For the current date, April 21, this Gantt chart shows that the Ford order is behind schedule because operations has completed only the work scheduled through April 18. The Honda order is exactly on schedule, and the BMW order is ahead of schedule.

Figure 11.6 shows a Gantt workstation chart of the operating rooms at a hospital for a particular day. Here, the focus is on the equipment, physical space, or staff, rather than the customer order. Using the same notation as in Figure 11.5, the chart shows the load on the operating rooms and the non-productive time. The time slots assigned to each doctor include the time needed to clean the room prior to the next surgery. The chart can be used to identify time slots for unscheduled emergency surgeries. It can also be used to accommodate requests to change the time of surgeries. For example, Dr. Flowers may be able to change the start of her surgery to 2 p.m. by swapping time slots with Dr. Gillespie in operating room C or by asking Dr. Brothers to start her surgery one hour earlier in operating room A and asking Dr. Bright to schedule her surgery for the morning in operating room C. In any event, the hospital administrator would have to get involved in rescheduling the surgeries.

FIGURE 11.6 *Gantt Workstation Chart for Operating Rooms at a Hospital*

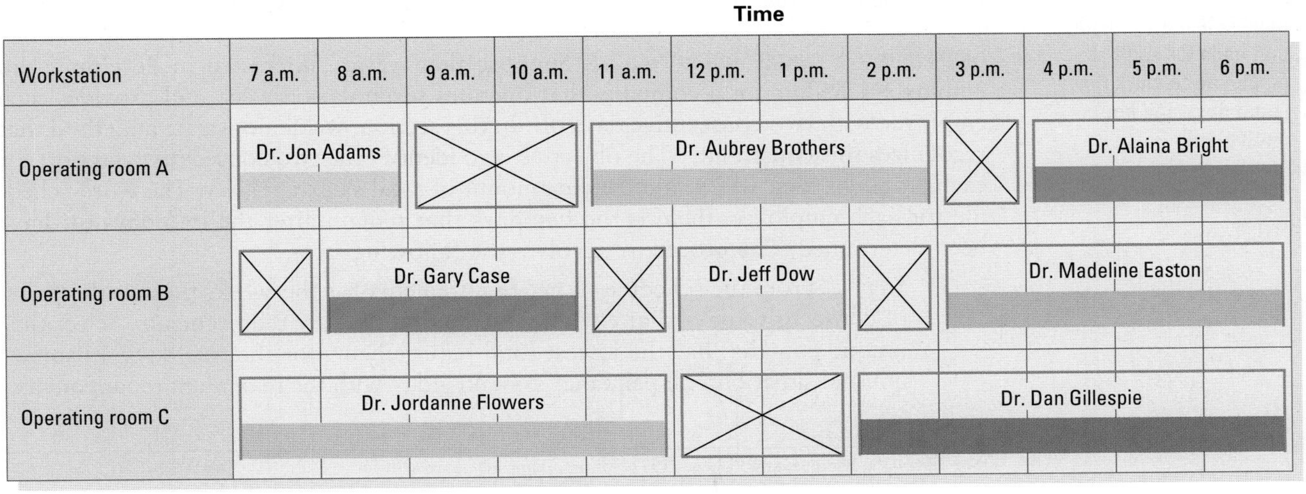

SCHEDULING EMPLOYEES

workforce scheduling
Developing a timetable that determines when employees work.

Another way to manage capacity is **workforce scheduling**, a type of scheduling that determines when employees work. A scheduling system for workers is necessary to specify the on-duty and off-duty periods for each employee over a certain time period, as in assigning postal clerks, nurses, pilots, attendants, or police officers to specific workdays and shifts. This approach is used when customers demand quick response and total demand can be forecasted with reasonable accuracy. In these instances, capacity is adjusted to meet the expected loads on the service system.

Recall that workforce schedules translate the staffing plan into specific schedules of work for each employee. Determining the workdays for each employee does not in itself make the staffing plan operational. Daily workforce requirements, stated in aggregate terms in the staffing plan, must be satisfied. The workforce capacity available each day must meet or exceed daily workforce requirements. If it does not, the scheduler must try to rearrange days off until the requirements are met. If no such schedule can be found, management might have to change the staffing plan and authorize more employees, overtime hours, or larger backlogs.

CONSTRAINTS. The technical constraints imposed on the workforce schedule are the resources provided by the staffing plan and the requirements placed on the operating system. However, other constraints, including legal and behavioural considerations, also can be imposed. For example, Air New Zealand, described in the Managerial Practice feature, is required to have at least a minimum number of flight attendants on duty at all times. Similarly, a minimum number of fire and safety personnel must be on duty at a fire station at all times. Such constraints limit management's flexibility in developing workforce schedules.

The constraints imposed by the psychological needs of workers complicate scheduling even more. Some of these constraints are written into labour agreements. For example, an employer may agree to give employees a certain number of consecutive days off per week or to limit employees' consecutive workdays to a certain maximum. Other provisions might govern the allocation of vacation, days off for holidays, or rotating shift assignments. In addition, preferences of the employees themselves need to be considered.

rotating schedule
A schedule that rotates employees through a series of workdays or hours.

One way that managers deal with certain undesirable aspects of scheduling is to use a **rotating schedule**, which rotates employees through a series of workdays or hours. Thus, over a period of time, each person has the same opportunity to have weekends and holidays off and to work days, as well as evenings and nights. A rotating schedule gives each employee the next employee's schedule the following week. In contrast, a **fixed schedule** calls for each employee to work the same days and hours each week.

fixed schedule A schedule that calls for each employee to work the same days and hours each week.

DEVELOPING A WORKFORCE SCHEDULE. Suppose that we are interested in developing an employee schedule for a company that operates seven days a week and provides each employee with two consecutive days off. In this section, we demonstrate a method that recognizes this constraint.† The objective is to identify the two consecutive days off for each employee that will minimize the amount of total slack capacity. The work schedule for each employee, then, is the five days that remain after the two days off have been determined. The procedure involves the following steps:

● *Step 1.* From the schedule of net requirements for the week, find all the pairs of consecutive days that exclude the maximum daily requirements. Select the unique pair that has the lowest total requirements for the two days. In some unusual situations, all pairs may contain a day with the maximum requirements.

---

†See Tibrewala, Philippe, and Browne (1972) for an optimizing approach.

If so, select the pair with the lowest total requirements. Suppose that the numbers of employees required are:

Monday	8	Friday	7
Tuesday	9	Saturday	4
Wednesday	2	Sunday	2
Thursday	12		

The maximum capacity requirement is 12 employees on Thursday. The pair having the lowest total requirements is Saturday–Sunday, with $4 + 2 = 6$.

- *Step 2.* If a tie occurs, choose one of the tied pairs, consistent with provisions written into the labour agreement, if any. Alternatively, the tie could be broken by asking the employee being scheduled to make the choice. As a last resort, the tie could be broken arbitrarily. For example, preference could be given to Saturday–Sunday pairs.

- *Step 3.* Assign the employee the selected pair of days off. Subtract the requirements satisfied by the employee from the net requirements for each day the employee is to work. In this case, the employee is assigned Saturday and Sunday off. After requirements are subtracted, Monday's requirement is 7, Tuesday's is 8, Wednesday's is 1, Thursday's is 11, and Friday's is 6. Saturday's and Sunday's requirements do not change because no employee is yet scheduled to work those days.

- *Step 4.* Repeat steps 1–3 until all requirements have been satisfied or a certain number of employees have been scheduled.

This method reduces the amount of slack capacity assigned to days having low requirements and forces the days having high requirements to be scheduled first. It also recognizes some of the behavioural and contractual aspects of workforce scheduling in the tie-breaking rules. However, the schedules produced might *not* minimize total slack capacity. Different rules for finding the days-off pair and breaking ties are needed to ensure minimal total slack capacity.

EXAMPLE 11.2

Developing a Workforce Schedule

Amalgamated Parcel Service is open seven days a week. The schedule of requirements is:

Day	M	T	W	Th	F	S	Su
Number of employees	6	4	8	9	10*	3	2

The manager needs a workforce schedule that provides two consecutive days off and minimizes the amount of total slack capacity. To break ties in the selection of off days, the scheduler gives preference to Saturday–Sunday if it is one of the tied pairs. If not, she selects one of the tied pairs arbitrarily.

SOLUTION

Friday contains the maximum requirements (designated by *), and the pair S–Su has the lowest total requirements. Therefore, employee 1 is scheduled to work Monday–Friday. The revised set of requirements, after scheduling employee 1, is:

Day	M	T	W	Th	F	S	Su
Number of employees	5	3	7	8	9*	3	2

Note that Friday still has the maximum requirements and that the requirements for S–Su are carried forward because these are employee 1's days off. These updated requirements are the ones the scheduler uses for the next employee.

The unique minimum again is on S–Su, so the scheduler assigns employee 2 to a M–F schedule. She then reduces the requirements for M–F to reflect the assignment of employee 2.

The day-off assignments for the remaining employees are shown in Table 11.2. In this example, Friday always has the maximum requirements and should be avoided as a day off. The schedule for the employees is shown in Table 11.3.

TABLE 11.2							*Scheduling Days Off*	
M	**T**	**W**	**Th**	**F**	**S**	**Su**	**EMPLOYEE**	**COMMENTS**
4	2	6	7	8*	3	2	3	S–Su has the lowest total requirements. Reduce the requirements to reflect a M–F schedule for employee 3.
3	1	5	6	7*	3	2	4	M–T has the lowest total requirements. Assign employee 4 to a W–Su schedule and update the requirements.
3	1	4	5	6*	2	1	5	S–Su has the lowest total requirements. Assign employee 5 to a M–F schedule and update the requirements.
2	0	3	4	5*	2	1	6	M–T has the lowest total requirements. Assign employee 6 to a W–Su schedule and update the requirements.
2	0	2	3	4*	1	0	7	S–Su has the lowest total requirements. Assign employee 7 to a M–F schedule and update the requirements.
1	0	1	2	3*	1	0	8	Three pairs have the minimum requirement and the lowest total: S–Su, M–T, and T–W. Choose S–Su according to the tie-breaking rule. Assign employee 8 a M–F schedule and update the requirements.
0	0	0	1	2*	1	0	9	Arbitrarily choose Su–M to break ties because S–Su does not have the lowest total requirements. Assign employee 9 to a T–S schedule.
0	0	0	0	1*	0	0	10	Choose S–Su according to the tie-breaking rule. Assign employee 10 a M–F schedule.

TABLE 11.3	*Final Schedule*							
EMPLOYEE	**M**	**T**	**W**	**Th**	**F**	**S**	**Su**	**TOTAL**
1	X	X	X	X	X	Off	Off	
2	X	X	X	X	X	Off	Off	
3	X	X	X	X	X	Off	Off	
4	Off	Off	X	X	X	X	X	
5	X	X	X	X	X	Off	Off	
6	Off	Off	X	X	X	X	X	
7	X	X	X	X	X	Off	Off	
8	X	X	X	X	X	Off	Off	
9	Off	X	X	X	X	X	Off	
10	X	X	X	X	X	Off	Off	
Capacity, C	7	8	10	10	10	3	2	50
Requirements, R	6	4	8	9	10	3	2	42
Slack, $C - R$	1	4	2	1	0	0	0	8

Decision Point With its substantial amount of slack capacity, the schedule is not unique. Employee 9, for example, could have Su–M, M–T, or T–W off without causing a capacity short-age. Indeed, the company might be able to get by with one fewer employee because of the total of eight slack days of capacity. However, all ten employees are needed on Fridays. If the manager were willing to get by with only nine employees on Fridays or if someone could work one day of overtime on a rotating basis, he would not need employee 10. As indicated in the table, the net requirement left for employee 10 to satisfy amounts to only one day, Friday. Thus, employee 10 can be used to fill in for vacationing or sick employees.

Managers try to staff their call centres to meet certain performance measures, one of which is the percentage of calls answered within a specified time interval. Typically in a call centre, the objective might be to answer 80 to 90 percent of calls within 15 to 30 seconds. The problem is that the requirements for agents change over time, depending on the time of day and day of the year. Also, the callers are likely to speak different languages. Fortunately, employee scheduling software is available to estimate call volumes, project skill requirements, and identify employee start and end times or preferred days off.

Workforce scheduling often entails myriad constraints and concerns, and computerized scheduling systems are used to cope with the complexity. For example, in some types of firms, such as telephone companies, web retailers, or emergency hotline agencies, employees must be on duty 24 hours a day, seven days a week. Sometimes a portion of the staff is part-time, allowing management a great deal of flexibility in developing schedules but adding considerable complexity to the requirements. The flexibility comes from the opportunity to match anticipated loads closely by using overlapping shifts or odd shift lengths; the complexity comes from having to evaluate the numerous possible alternatives. Management also must consider the timing of lunch breaks and rest periods, the number and starting times of shift schedules, and the days off for each employee. An additional typical concern is that the number of employees on duty at any particular time be sufficient to answer calls within a reasonable amount of time.

SEQUENCING JOBS AT A WORKSTATION

sequencing Determining the order in which jobs or customers are processed in the waiting line at a workstation.

Another aspect of scheduling is sequencing of specific jobs at workstations. **Sequencing** determines the order in which specific customers are processed from a waiting line at a workstation, or if finished goods are put in inventory, which product to process next. When combined with the expected processing time, the sequence allows you to estimate the start and finish times of each job.

PRIORITY SEQUENCING RULES. One way to determine what job or customer to process next is with the help of a priority sequencing rule. The following three priority sequencing rules are commonly used in practice.

1. *First-Come, First-Served.* The job or customer arriving at the workstation first has the highest priority under a First-Come, First-Served (FCFS) rule. This rule is the most "democratic" in that each job is treated equally, with no one stepping ahead of others already in line. It is commonly used at service facilities, and is the rule that was assumed in Supplement 4S, "Waiting Lines."

Earliest Due Date (EDD)
A priority sequencing rule that specifies that the job or customer with the earliest due date is the next job to be processed.

2. *Earliest Due Date.* The job or customer with the **Earliest Due Date (EDD)** is the next one to be processed. The due date specifies when work on a job or customer should be finished. Due dates are commonly used by manufacturers and suppliers in the supply chain. For example, a product cannot be assembled until all of its purchased and produced components are available. If these components were not already in inventory, they must be ordered prior to when the product assembly can begin. Their due date is the start date for assembling the product to be assembled. This simple relationship is fundamental to coordinating with suppliers and with the manufacturer's own shops in

expediting The process of completing a job or finishing with a customer sooner than would otherwise be done.

Shortest Processing Time A priority sequencing rule that specifies that the job or customer with the lowest processing time is the next job to be processed.

the supply chain. It is also the key to **expediting**, which is the process of completing a job sooner than would otherwise be done. Expediting can be done by revising the due date, moving the job to the front of the waiting line, making a special appeal by phone or e-mail to the supplier, adding extra capacity, or even putting a red tag on the job that says it is urgent.

3. *Shortest Processing Time.* With the **Shortest Processing Time** rule, the job or customer that requires the least amount of service or operations processing time is pulled out of the waiting line to be served first. At first glance, this might sound unfair. But many grocery stores use a variation of this rule with "express" and "regular" cashier lanes. The rationale is that customers who require little work should be served quickly. Of course, limits may need to be in place, and similar jobs or customers continue to be served on a FCFS basis.

None of these rules guarantees finding an optimal solution, partly because it depends on the performance measure being used, discussed next. A schedule that does well on one measure may do poorly on another.

PERFORMANCE MEASURES. The quality of a schedule can be judged in various ways. Two commonly used performance measures are throughput time and past due.

1. *Throughput time (or flow time).* Recall that the amount of time a customer or product spends in the service or manufacturing system is called *throughput time* (Chapter 4), also termed *flow time*. It is the sum of the waiting time for servers or machines; the process time, including setups; the time spent moving between operations; and delays resulting from machine breakdowns, unavailability of facilitating goods or components, and the like.

Throughput time at a workstation = Finish time − Arrival time

When using this equation, we assume for convenience that the first job scheduled starts at time zero (0). At time 0, all the jobs were available for processing at the workstation.

past due The amount of time by which a job missed its due date.

2. *Past due.* The **past due** measure can be expressed as the amount of time by which a job missed its due date (also referred to as tardiness) or as the percentage of total jobs processed over some period of time that missed their due dates. Minimizing the past due measure supports the competitive priorities of cost (penalties for missing due dates), quality, customer experience, and time.

EXAMPLE 11.3 *Using the First-Come, First-Served Rule*

Currently a consulting company has five jobs in its backlog. The time since the order was placed, processing time, and promised due dates are given in the following table. Determine the schedule by using the First-Come, First-Served rule, and calculate the average days past due and throughput time. How can the schedule be improved, if average throughput time is the most critical?

CUSTOMER	DAYS SINCE ORDER ARRIVED	PROCESSING TIME (days)	DUE DATE (days from now)
A	15	25	29
B	12	16	27
C	5	14	68
D	10	10	48
E	0	12	80

SOLUTION

a. The FCFS rule states that customer A should be the first one in the sequence, because that order arrived earliest—15 days ago. Customer E's order arrived today, so it is processed last. The sequence is shown in the following table, along with the days past due and throughput times.

CUSTOMER SEQUENCE	START TIME (days)	PROCESSING TIME (days)	FINISH TIME (days)	DUE DATE	PAST DUE (days)	DAYS SINCE ORDER ARRIVED	THROUGHPUT TIME (days)
A	0	+ 25	= 25	29	0	15	40
B	25	+ 16	= 41	27	14	12	53
D	41	+ 10	= 51	48	3	10	61
C	51	+ 14	= 65	68	0	5	70
E	65	+ 12	= 77	80	0	0	77

The *finish time* for a job is its start time plus the processing time. Its finish time becomes the start time for the next job in the sequence, assuming that the next job is available for immediate processing. The days past due for a job are zero (0) if its due date is equal to or exceeds the finish time. Otherwise it equals the shortfall. The throughput time for each job equals its finish time plus the number of days ago since the order first arrived at the workstation. For example, customer C's throughput time must account for the order's scheduled finish time of 65 days, combined with fact that the order arrived 5 days ago. Thus, the total throughput time is $65 - (-5) = 70$ days. The days past due and average throughput time performance measures for the FCFS schedule are:

$$\text{Average days past due} = \frac{0 + 14 + 3 + 0 + 0}{5} = 3.4 \text{ days}$$

$$\text{Average throughput time} = \frac{40 + 53 + 61 + 70 + 77}{5} = 60.2 \text{ days}$$

b. The average throughput time can be reduced. One possibility is the sequence shown in the following table, which uses the Shortest Processing Time. (Yet another possibility is the Earliest Due Date rule, illustrated in Solved Problem 3.)

CUSTOMER SEQUENCE	START TIME (days)	PROCESSING TIME (days)	FINISH TIME (days)	DUE DATE	PAST DUE (days)	DAYS SINCE ORDER ARRIVED	THROUGHPUT TIME (days)
D	0	+ 10	= 10	48	0	10	20
E	10	+ 12	= 22	80	0	0	22
C	22	+ 14	= 36	68	0	5	41
B	36	+ 16	= 52	27	25	12	64
A	52	+ 25	= 77	29	48	15	92

$$\text{Average days past due} = \frac{0 + 0 + 0 + 25 + 48}{5} = 14.6 \text{ days}$$

$$\text{Average throughput time} = \frac{20 + 22 + 41 + 64 + 92}{5} = 47.8 \text{ days}$$

This schedule reduces the average throughput time from 60.2 to 47.8 days—a 21 percent improvement. However, the past due times for jobs A and B have increased significantly.

Decision Point Management decided to use a modified version of the second schedule, adding overtime when customer B is processed. Further, customer A agreed to extend its due date to 77 days, because in this case the advanced warning allowed it to reschedule its own operations with little problem.

CHAPTER HIGHLIGHTS

- Operations plans (aggregate production plans or staffing plans) are statements of strategy that specify time-phased production or service rates, workforce levels, and (in manufacturing) inventory investment. These plans show how the organization will work toward longer-term objectives while considering the demand and capacity that are likely to exist during a planning horizon of only a year or two.

- To reduce the level of detail required in the planning process, products or services are aggregated into families, and labour is aggregated along product family lines or according to the general skills or services provided. Time is aggregated into periods of months or quarters.

- Information inputs are required from the various functional areas in the organization. This approach typically raises conflicting objectives, such as high customer service, a stable workforce, and low inventory investment. Creativity and cross-functional compromise are required to reconcile these conflicts.

- Supply options generally take customer demand as a given. Two pure, but generally high-cost, planning strategies are the level strategy, which maintains a constant workforce size, and the chase strategy, which varies workforce level to match fluctuations in demand.

- Developing operations plans is an iterative process of determining demand requirements; identifying relevant constraints, alternatives, and costs; preparing and approving a plan; and implementing and updating the plan.

- Although spreadsheets, linear programming, and other software tools can help analyze complicated alternatives, operations planning is primarily an exercise in consensus building, conflict resolution, and compromise. Ultimately, decisions are made by managers, not by quantitative methods.

- Scheduling is the allocation of resources over a period of time to accomplish a specific set of tasks. Gantt charts are useful for depicting the sequence of work at a particular workstation and for monitoring the progress of customer orders in the system.

- Capacity considerations are important for scheduling services. A workforce schedule translates a staffing plan into a specific work schedule for each employee. Typical workforce scheduling considerations include capacity limits, service targets, consecutive days off, maximum number of workdays in a row, type of schedule (fixed or rotating), and vacation and holiday time

- No approach to scheduling is best for all situations. Performance measures that can be used to evaluate schedules include throughput time and percent of jobs past due. The choice of priority rule can affect the schedule performance measures.

SOLVED PROBLEM 1

The Cranston Telephone Company employs workers who lay telephone cables and perform various other construction tasks. The company prides itself on good service and strives to complete all service orders within the planning period in which they are received.

Each worker puts in 600 hours of regular time per planning period and can work as many as 100 hours overtime. The operations department has estimated the following workforce requirements for such services over the next four planning periods:

Planning period	1	2	3	4
Demand (hours)	21 000	18 000	30 000	12 000

Cranston pays regular-time wages of $6000 per employee per period for any time worked up to 600 hours (including undertime). The overtime pay rate is $15 per hour after 600 hours. Hiring, training, and outfitting a new employee cost $8000. Layoff costs are $2000 per employee. Currently, 40 employees work for Cranston in this capacity. No delays in service or backorders are allowed. Use the spreadsheet approach to answer the following questions:

a. Develop a level workforce plan that uses only the overtime and undertime alternatives. Maximize the use of overtime during the peak period so as to minimize the workforce level and amount of undertime.

b. Prepare a chase strategy using only the workforce adjustment alternative of hiring and layoffs. What are the total numbers of employees hired and laid off?

c. Propose an effective mixed-strategy plan.

d. Compare the total costs of the three plans.

SOLUTION

a. The peak demand is 30 000 hours in period 3. As each employee can work 700 hours per period (600 on regular time and 100 on overtime), the workforce level that minimizes undertime is 30 000/700 = 42.86, or 43, employees. The level strategy calls for three employees to be hired in the first quarter and for none to be laid off. To convert the demand requirements into employee-period equivalents, divide the demand in hours by 600. For example, the demand of 21 000 hours in period 1 translates into 35 employee-period equivalents (21 000/600) and demand in the third period translates into 50 employee-period equivalents (30 000/600). Figure 11.7 shows one solution using the level strategy option.

FIGURE 11.7   *Spreadsheet for Level Strategy*

	1	2	3	4	Total
Inputs					
Forecasted demand	35	30	50	20	135
Workforce level	43	43	43	43	172
Undertime	8	13	0	23	44
Overtime	0	0	7	0	7
Derived					
Utilized time	35	30	43	20	128
Hires	3	0	0	0	3
Layoffs	0	0	0	0	0
Calculated					
Utilized time cost	$210 000	$180 000	$258 000	$120 000	$ 768 000
Undertime cost	$ 48 000	$ 78 000	$ 0	$138 000	$ 264 000
Overtime cost	$ 0	$ 0	$ 63 000	$ 0	$ 63 000
Hiring cost	$ 24 000	$ 0	$ 0	$ 0	$ 24 000
Layoff cost	$ 0	$ 0	$ 0	$ 0	$ 0
Total cost	$282 000	258 000	321 000	258 000	$1 119 000

b. The chase strategy workforce is calculated by dividing the demand for each period by 600 hours, or the amount of regular-time work for one employee during one period. This strategy calls for a total of 20 workers to be hired and 40 to be laid off during the four-period plan. Figure 11.8 shows the "chase strategy" solution.

FIGURE 11.8   *Spreadsheet for Chase Strategy*

	1	2	3	4	Total
Inputs					
Forecasted demand	35	30	50	20	135
Workforce level	35	30	50	20	135
Undertime	0	0	0	0	0
Overtime	0	0	0	0	0
Derived					
Utilized time	35	30	50	20	135
Hires	0	0	20	0	20
Layoffs	5	5	0	30	40
Calculated					
Utilized time cost	$210 000	$180 000	$300 000	$120 000	$ 810 000
Undertime cost	$ 0	$ 0	$ 0	$ 0	$ 0
Overtime cost	$ 0	$ 0	$ 0	$ 0	$ 0
Hiring cost	$ 0	$ 0	$160 000	$ 0	$ 160 000
Layoff cost	$ 10 000	$ 10 000	$ 0	$ 60 000	$ 80 000
Total cost	$220 000	190 000	460 000	180 000	$1 050 000

FIGURE 11.9 *Spreadsheet for Mixed Strategy*

	1	2	3	4	Total
Inputs					
Forecasted demand	35	30	50	20	135
Workforce level	35	35	43	30	143
Undertime	0	5	0	10	15
Overtime	0	0	7	0	7
Derived					
Utilized time	35	30	43	20	128
Hires	0	0	8	0	8
Layoffs	5	0	0	13	18
Calculated					
Utilized time cost	$210 000	$180 000	$258 000	$120 000	$ 768 000
Undertime cost	$ 0	$ 30 000	$ 0	$ 60 000	$ 90 000
Overtime cost	$ 0	$ 0	$ 63 000	$ 0	$ 63 000
Hiring cost	$ 0	$ 0	$ 64 000	$ 0	$ 64 000
Layoff cost	$ 10 000	$ 0	$ 0	$ 26 000	$ 36 000
Total cost	$220 000	210 000	385 000	206 000	$1 021 000

c. The mixed strategy plan that we propose uses a combination of hires, layoffs, and overtime to reduce total costs. The workforce is reduced by 5 at the beginning of the first period, increased by 8 in the third period, and reduced by 13 in the fourth period. Figure 11.9 shows the results.

d. The total cost of the level strategy is $1 119 000. The chase strategy results in a total cost of $1 050 000. The mixed-strategy plan was developed by trial-and-error and results in a total cost of $1 021 000. Further improvements to the mixed strategy are possible.

SOLVED PROBLEM 2

The Food Bin grocery store operates 24 hours per day, seven days per week. Fred Bulger, the store manager, has been analyzing the efficiency and productivity of store operations recently. Bulger decided to observe the need for checkout clerks on the first shift for a one-month period. At the end of the month, he calculated the average number of checkout registers that should be open during the first shift each day. His results showed peak needs on Saturdays and Sundays.

Day	M	T	W	Th	F	S	Su
Number of employees	3	4	5	5	4	7	8

Bulger now has to come up with a workforce schedule that guarantees each checkout clerk two consecutive days off but still covers all requirements.

a. Develop a workforce schedule that covers all requirements while giving two consecutive days off to each clerk. How many clerks are needed? Assume that the clerks have no preference regarding which days they have off.

b. Plans can be made to use the clerks for other duties if slack or idle time resulting from this schedule can be determined. How much idle time will result from this schedule and on what days?

SOLUTION

a. We use the method demonstrated in Example 11.2 to determine the number of clerks needed. The minimum number of clerks is eight.

	M	T	W	Th	F	S	Su
				DAY			
Requirements	3	4	5	5	4	7	8*
Clerk 1	Off	Off	X	X	X	X	X
Requirements	3	4	4	4	3	6	7*
Clerk 2	Off	Off	X	X	X	X	X
Requirements	3	4	3	3	2	5	6*
Clerk 3	X	X	X	Off	Off	X	X
Requirements	2	3	2	3	2	4	5*
Clerk 4	X	X	X	Off	Off	X	X
Requirements	1	2	1	3	2	3	4*
Clerk 5	X	Off	Off	X	X	X	X
Requirements	0	2	1	2	1	2	3*
Clerk 6	Off	Off	X	X	X	X	X
Requirements	0	2*	0	1	0	1	2*
Clerk 7	X	X	Off	Off	X	X	X
Requirements	0	1*	0	1*	0	0	1*
Clerk 8	X	X	X	X	Off	Off	X
Requirements	0	0	0	0	0	0	0

*Maximum requirements.

b. On the basis of the results in part (a), the number of clerks on duty minus the requirements is the number of idle clerks available for other duties:

	M	T	W	Th	F	S	Su
				DAY			
Number on duty	5	4	6	5	5	7	8
Requirements	3	4	5	5	4	7	8
Idle clerks	2	0	1	0	1	0	0

The slack in this schedule would indicate to Bulger the number of employees he might ask to work part-time (fewer than five days per week). For example, clerk 7 might work Tuesday, Saturday, and Sunday, and clerk 8 might work Tuesday, Thursday, and Sunday to eliminate slack from the schedule.

SOLVED PROBLEM 3

Revisit Example 11.3, in which the consulting company has five jobs in its backlog. Create a schedule using the Earliest Due Date priority rule, calculating the average days past due and throughput time. In this case, does this rule outperform the First-Come, First-Served rule?

SOLUTION

CUSTOMER SEQUENCE	START TIME (days)	PROCESSING TIME (days)	FINISH TIME (days)	DUE DATE	PAST DUE (days)	DAYS SINCE ORDER ARRIVED	THROUGHPUT TIME (days)
B	0	+ 16	= 16	27	0	12	28
A	16	+ 25	= 41	29	12	15	56
D	41	+ 10	= 51	48	3	10	61
C	51	+ 14	= 65	68	0	5	70
E	65	+ 12	= 77	80	0	0	77

The days past due and average throughput time performance measures for the EDD schedule are:

$$\text{Average days past due} = \frac{0 + 12 + 3 + 0 + 0}{5} = 3.0 \text{ days}$$

$$\text{Average throughput time} = \frac{28 + 56 + 61 + 70 + 77}{5} = 58.4 \text{ days}$$

By both measures, EDD outperforms the FCFS (3.0 versus 3.4 past due and 58.4 versus 60.2 throughput time). However, the solution found using the Shortest Processing Time (b) of Example 11.3 still has the best average throughput time of only 47.8 days.

PROBLEMS

1. The Barberton Municipal Division of Road Maintenance is charged with road repair in the city of Barberton and surrounding area. Cindy Sarker, road maintenance director, must submit a staffing plan for the next year based on a set schedule for repairs and on the city budget. Sarkar estimates that the labour hours required for the next four quarters are 6000, 12 000, 19 000, and 9000, respectively. Each of the 11 workers on the workforce can contribute 500 hours per quarter. Payroll costs are $6000 in wages per worker for regular time worked up to 500 hours, with an overtime pay rate of $18 for each overtime hour. Overtime is limited to 20 percent of the regular-time capacity in any quarter. Although unused overtime capacity has no cost, unused regular time is paid at $12 per hour. The cost to hire a worker is $3000, and the cost to lay off a worker is $2000. Subcontracting is not permitted.

   a. Find a level workforce plan that allows no delay in road repair and minimizes undertime. Overtime can be used to its limits in any quarter. What is the total cost of the plan and how many undertime hours does it call for?

   b. Use a chase strategy that varies the workforce level without using overtime or undertime. What is the total cost of this plan?

   c. Propose a plan of your own. Compare your plan with those in parts (a) and (b) and discuss its comparative merits.

2. Bob Carlton's golf camp estimates the following workforce requirements for its services over the next two years:

Quarter	1	2	3	4
Demand (hours)	4200	6400	3000	4800

Quarter	5	6	7	8
Demand (hours)	4400	6240	3600	4800

Each certified instructor puts in 480 hours per quarter regular time and can work up to 120 hours overtime. Regular-time wages and benefits cost Carlton $7200 per employee per quarter for regular time worked up to 480 hours, with an overtime cost of $20 per hour. Unused regular time for certified instructors is paid at $15 per hour. There is no cost for unused overtime capacity. The cost of hiring, training, and certifying a new employee is $10 000. Layoff costs are $4000 per employee. Currently, eight employees work in this capacity.

   a. Find a workforce plan using a level strategy that allows for no delay in service and minimizes undertime. What is the total cost of this plan?

   b. Use a chase strategy that varies the workforce level with minimal undertime and without using overtime. What is the total cost of this plan?

   c. Propose a better plan and calculate its total cost.

3. Continuing Problem 2, now assume that Carlton is permitted to employ some uncertified, part-time instructors, provided they represent no more than 15 percent of the total work-force hours in any quarter. Each part-time instructor can work up to 240 hours per quarter, with no overtime or undertime cost. Labour costs for part-time instructors are $12 per hour. Hiring and training costs are $2000 per uncertified instructor, and there are no layoff costs.

   a. Propose a low-cost, mixed-strategy plan and calculate its total cost.

   b. What are the primary advantages and disadvantages of having a workforce consisting of both regular and temporary employees?

4. The Donald Fertilizer Company produces industrial chemical fertilizers. The projected manufacturing requirements (in thousands of litres) for the next four quarters are 80, 50, 80, and 130, respectively. A workforce plan using a level strategy is desired, relying only on anticipation inventory as a supply option. Stockouts and backorders are to be avoided, as are overtime and undertime.

   a. Determine the quarterly production rate required to meet total demand for the year, and minimize the anticipation inventory that would be left over at the end of the year. Beginning inventory is zero.

   b. Specify the anticipation inventory that will be produced.

   c. Suppose that the requirements for the next four quarters are revised to 80, 130, 50, and 80, respectively. If total demand is the same, what level of production rate is needed now, using the same strategy as part (a)?

5. The Twilight Clothing Company makes jeans for children. Management has just prepared a forecast of sales (in pairs of jeans) for next year and now must prepare a production plan. The company has traditionally maintained a level workforce strategy. Currently, there are eight workers who have been with the company for a number of years. Each employee can produce 2000 pairs of jeans during a two-month planning period. Every year management authorizes overtime in periods 1, 5, and 6, up to a maximum of 20 percent of regular-time capacity. Management wants to avoid stockouts and backorders and will not accept any plan that calls for such shortages. At present, there are 12 000 pairs of jeans in finished goods inventory. The demand forecast is as follows:

Period	1	2	3
Sales	25 000	6 500	15 000

Period	4	5	6
Sales	19 000	32 000	29 000

   a. Is the level workforce strategy feasible with the current workforce, assuming that overtime is used only in periods 1, 5, and 6? Explain.

   b. Find two alternative plans that would satisfy management's concern over stockouts and backorders, disregarding costs. What trade-offs between these two plans must be considered?

6. Gretchen's Kitchen is a fast-food restaurant located in an ideal spot near the local high school. Gretchen Lowe has to prepare an annual staffing plan. The only menu items are hamburgers, chili, soft drinks, shakes, and french fries. A sample of 1000 customers taken at random revealed that they purchased 2100 hamburgers, 200 litres of chili, 1000 soft drinks and shakes, and 1000 bags of french fries. Thus, for purposes of estimating staffing requirements, Lowe assumes that each customer purchases 2.1 hamburgers, 0.2 litres of chili, 1 soft drink or shake, and 1 bag of french fries. Each hamburger requires 4 minutes of labour, a litre of chili requires 3 minutes, and a soft drink or shake and a bag of fries each take 2 minutes of labour.

   The restaurant currently has 10 part-time employees who work 80 hours a month on staggered shifts. Wages are $800 per month for regular time and $15 per hour for overtime. Hiring and training costs are $500 per new employee, and layoff costs are $100 per employee.

   Lowe realizes that building up seasonal inventories of hamburgers (or any of the products) would not be wise because of shelf-life considerations. Also, any demand not satisfied is a lost sale and must be avoided. Three strategies come to mind.

   ● Use a level strategy relying on overtime and under-time, with up to 20 percent of regular-time capacity on overtime.

   ● Maintain a base of 10 employees, hiring and laying off as needed to avoid any overtime.

   ● Utilize a chase strategy, hiring and laying off employees as demand changes to avoid overtime.

   When performing her calculations, Lowe always rounds to the next-highest integer for the number of employees. She also follows a policy of not using an employee more than 80 hours per month, except when overtime is needed. The projected demand by month (number of customers) for next year is as follows:

January	3200	July	4800
February	2600	August	4200
March	3300	September	3800
April	3900	October	3600
May	3600	November	3500
June	4200	December	3000

a. Develop the schedule of service requirements for the next year.

b. Which strategy is most effective?

c. Suppose that an arrangement with the high school enables the manager to identify good prospective employees without having to advertise in the local newspaper. This source reduces the hiring cost to $100, which is mainly the cost of charred hamburgers during training. If cost is her only concern, will this method of hiring change Gretchen Lowe's strategy? Considering other objectives that may be appropriate, do you think she should change strategies?

7. Cara Ryder manages a ski school in a large resort and is trying to develop a schedule for instructors. The instructors receive little salary and work just enough to earn room and board. They do receive free skiing, spending most of their free time tackling the resort's notorious double black diamond slopes. Hence, the instructors work only four days a week. One of the lesson packages offered at the resort is a four-day beginner package. Ryder likes to keep the same instructor with a group over the four-day period, so she schedules the instructors for four consecutive days and then three days off. Ryder uses years of experience with demand forecasts provided by management to formulate her instructor requirements for the upcoming month:

Day	M	T	W	Th	F	S	Su
Requirements	7	5	4	5	6	9	8

a. Determine how many instructors Ryder needs to employ. Give preference to Saturday and Sunday off. *Hint:* Look for the group of three days with lowest requirements.

b. Specify the work schedule for each employee. How much slack does your schedule generate for each day?

8. The mayor of Black Creek, wanting to be environmentally progressive, has decided to implement a recycling plan. All residents of the city will receive a special three-part bin to separate their glass, plastic, and aluminum, and the city will be responsible for picking up the materials. A young city and regional planning graduate, Janet Sanchez, has been hired to manage the recycling program. After carefully studying the city's population density, Sanchez decides that the following numbers of recycling collectors will be needed:

Day	M	T	W	Th	F	S	Su
Requirements	12	7	9	9	5	3	6

The requirements are based on the populations of the various housing developments and subdivisions in the city and surrounding communities. To motivate residents of some areas to have their pickups scheduled on weekends, a special tax break will be given.

a. Find the minimum number of recycling collectors required if each employee works five days a week and has two consecutive days off. Give preference to S-Su when that pair is involved in a tie.

b. Specify the work schedule for each employee. How much slack does your schedule generate for each day?

c. Suppose that Sanchez can smooth the requirements further through greater tax incentives. The requirements then will be 8 on Monday and 7 on the other days of the week. How many employees will be needed now? Find the optimal solution in terms of minimal total slack capacity. Does smoothing of requirements have capital investment implications? If so, what are they?

9. A manager faces peak (weekly) demand for one of her operations, but is not sure how long the peak will last. She can either use overtime from the current workforce, or hire/lay off and just pay regular-time wages. Regular-time pay is $500 per week, overtime is $750 per week, the hiring cost is $2000, and the layoff cost is $3000. Assuming that people are available seeking such a short-term arrangement, how many weeks must the surge in demand last to justify a temporary hire? *Hint:* Use break-even analysis (see Chapter 3, "Process Configuration"). Let w be the number of weeks of the high demand (rather than using Q for the break-even quantity). What is the fixed cost for the regular-time option? Overtime option?

10. Little 6, Inc., an accounting firm, forecasts the following weekly workload during the tax season:

	DAY						
	M	T	W	Th	F	S	Su
Personal tax returns	24	14	18	18	10	28	16
Corporate tax returns	18	10	12	15	24	12	4

Corporate tax returns each require four hours of an accountant's time, and personal returns each require 90 minutes. During tax season, each accountant can work up to ten hours per day. However, error rates increase to unacceptable levels when accountants work more than five consecutive days per week.

a. Create an effective and efficient work schedule.

b. Assume that Little 6 has three part-time employees available to work three days per week. How might these employees be effectively utilized?

11. The Hickory Company manufactures wooden desks. Management schedules overtime every weekend to reduce the backlog on the most popular models. The automatic

routing machine is used to cut certain types of edges on the desktops. The following orders need to be scheduled for the routing machine:

ORDER	TIME SINCE ORDER ARRIVED (hours ago)	ESTIMATED MACHINE TIME (hours)	DUE DATE (hours from now)
1	6	10	12
2	5	3	8
3	3	15	18
4	1	9	20
5	0	7	21

The due dates reflect the need for the order to be at its next operation.

a. Develop separate schedules by using the First-Come, First-Served and Earliest Due Date rules. Compare the schedules on the basis of average throughput time and average past due hours.

b. Comment on the performance of the two rules relative to these measures.

12. Currently a company that designs Web sites has five customers in its backlog. The day when the order arrived, processing time, and promised due dates are given in the following table. The customers are listed in the order of when they arrived. They are ready to be scheduled today, which is the start of day 190.

CUSTOMER	DAY ORDER ARRIVED	PROCESSING TIME (days)	DUE DATE
A	180	20	216
B	182	12	240
C	184	28	256
D	187	24	248
E	188	32	290

a. Develop separate schedules by using the First-Come, First-Served, Earliest Due Date, and Shortest Processing Time rules. Compare the schedules on the basis of average throughput time and average days past due.

b. Comment on the performance of the three rules relative to these measures. Which gives the best schedule? Why?

13. The Mowry Machine Shop still has five jobs to be processed as of 8 a.m. today (day 23) at its bottleneck operation. The day when the order arrived, processing time, and promised due dates are given in the following table. The jobs are listed in the order of arrival.

JOB	DAY ORDER ARRIVED	PROCESSING TIME (days)	DUE DATE
A	12	10	45
B	13	8	36
C	15	4	42
D	17	4	39
E	22	3	53

a. Develop separate schedules by using the First-Come, First-Served, Earliest Due Date, and Shortest Processing Time rules. Compare the schedules on the basis of average throughput time and average days past due.

b. Which rule gives the best schedule, in your judgment? Why?

NOTES FOR CHAPTER

1. Sources: J. Mitchell, "This Train Runs on Time," originally published in *National Post Business,* April 2002, pp. 50–58; *CN Annual Report* (2009), pp. 10–12; "CN's Scheduled Potash Service Drives New Supply Chain Efficiencies for Key Customers," media release, CN site, May 3, 2011, www.cn.ca/en/media-news-scheduled- potash-service-20110503.htm, accessed July 29, 2011.

2. "Service Scheduling at Air New Zealand," Video Library, *Operations Management,* 9th ed. (Upper Saddle River, NJ: Prentice Hall, 2010); "Our History," Air New Zealand site, www.pacificislands.airnewzealand.com/aboutus/consulting/history.htm, accessed July 29, 2011; www.airnz.com, June 1, 2011.

FURTHER READING

Baker, K. R. *Elements of Sequencing and Scheduling.* Hanover, NH: Baker Press, 2002.

Browne, J. J. "Simplified Scheduling of Routine Work Hours and Days Off." *Industrial Engineering,* December 1979, pp. 27–29.

Chiang, Wen-Chyuan, Jason C. H. Chen, and Xiaojing Xu. "An Overview of Research on Revenue Management: Current Issues and Future Research." *International Journal of Revenue Management,* vol. 1, no. 1 (2007), pp. 97–128.

Dougherty, John R., and Christopher Gray. *Sales & Operations Planning— Best Practices.* Victoria, B.C. Trafford Publishing, 2006.

Fisher, M. L., J. H. Hammond, W. R. Obermeyer, and A. Raman. "Making Supply Meet Demand in an Uncertain World." *Harvard Business Review,* vol. 72, no. 3 (1994), pp. 83–93.

Heskett, J., W. E. Sasser, and C. Hart. *Service Breakthroughs: Changing the Rules of the Game.* New York: The Free Press, 1990.

Kimes, Sheryl E., and Richard B. Chase. "The Strategic Levers of Yield Management." *Journal of Service Research,* vol. 1, no. 2 (1998), pp. 298–308.

Lesaint, David, Christos Voudouris, and Nader Azarmi. "Dynamic Workforce Scheduling for British Telecommunications plc." *Interfaces,* January/ February 2000, pp. 45–56.

Muzumdar, Maha, and John Fontanella. "The Secrets to S&OP Success." *Supply Chain Management,* April 2006, pp. 34–41.

Ramani, K. V. "Scheduling Doctors' Activities at a Large Teaching Hospital." *Production and Inventory Management Journal,* First/Second Quarter 2002, pp. 56–62.

Rennie, Elizabeth. "All Fired Up: Why Food and Beverage Professionals Must Put S&OP on the Menu." *APICS Magazine,* July/August 2006, pp. 32–35.

Silver, E. A., F. F. Pyke, and R. Peterson. *Inventory Management and Production Planning and Scheduling.* New York: Wiley, 1998.

Tibrewala, R. K., D. Philippe, and J. J. Browne. "Optimal Scheduling of Two Consecutive Idle Periods." *Management Science,* vol. 19, no. 1 (1972), pp. 71–75.

Trottman, Melanie. "Choices in Stormy Weather: How Airline Employees Make Hundreds of Decisions to Cancel or Reroute Flights." *Wall Street Journal,* February 14, 2006, pp. B1–B3.

Vollmann, Thomas E., William Berry, D. Clay Whybark, and Robert Jacobs. *Manufacturing Planning and Control Systems for Supply Chain Management,* 5th ed. New York: McGraw-Hill/Irwin, 2005.

Wallace, Thomas F. *Sales & Operations Planning: The How-To Handbook,* 3rd ed. Cincinnati, OH: T. E. Wallace & Company, 2008.

MyOMLab ASSETS

MyOMLab offers the following resources, which allow you to further practise and apply concepts presented in this chapter.

- **Key Equations:** All the equations for this chapter can be found in one convenient location.
- **Discussion Questions:** Four questions raise important considerations in layoff costs, workforce variability, and a company's responsibilities to a community.
- **Cases:**
  - *Memorial Hospital.* What nurse staffing plan do you propose?
  - *Food King.* What schedule do you propose for stockers and baggers?

- **Video Case:**
  - *Air New Zealand.* Service scheduling.
  - *Starwood.* Sales and operations planning.

- **Virtual Tours:** *Statton Furniture Company.* As the demand varies throughout the year, what operations planning strategies might Statton employ?
- **Experiential Exercise:** Use the Memorial Hospital case as an in-class team experience.
- **Internet Exercise:**
  - *United Parcel Service.* How much volume variability do you imagine each of the business units face? What resources do you imagine are required to provide capacity in each of the business units?
  - *Canada Revenue Agency: H&R Block.* What operations scheduling complications does seasonality create? What actions are taken to address these issues?

- **OM Explorer Tutors:** OM Explorer contains four tutor programs that will help you learn how to implement basic level and chase strategies (five periods), various staffing strategies, and workforce scheduling.
- **Extend LT:** *Scheduling Vehicle Repair at Precision Autobody.* While the shop had an excellent reputation for quality, significant improvements were needed to better schedule customer delivery of repairs.
- **Supplement I:** *Linear Programming.* See how linear programming problems can be solved and how both operations planning and scheduling problems can be modelled.
- **Supplement J:** *Operations Scheduling.* Read about various scheduling approaches in job shop and small batch settings.

12

Resource Planning

Learning Goals

After reading this chapter, you will be able to:

1. explain how enterprise resource planning (ERP) systems can foster better resource planning.

2. distinguish between independent and dependent demand and their differences when planning for the replenishment of materials.

3. explain the logic of material requirements planning, how it can be used to plan distribution inventories, and how to schedule the receipt of materials to meet promised delivery dates.

4. identify the key outputs from the resource planning process and how they are used.

5. provide examples of the effective use of manufacturing resource planning and its benefits to various functional areas of the firm.

6. discuss resource planning for service firms.

Across the Organization

Resource planning is important to:

- **finance**, which plans for adequate working capital to support the schedules generated in the resource plan.

- **human resources**, which determines the implications of the resource plan on personnel requirements.

- **management information systems**, which must identify the information requirements of managers and the information that can be generated from the resource plan.

- **marketing**, which makes reliable delivery commitments to customers.

- **operations**, which is responsible for inventories and the utilization of the resources required by the firm's processes to meet customer demand.

Dow Corning, created as a joint venture between Corning Incorporated and the Dow Chemical Company in 1943, is a global leader that offers over 7000 innovative products and services using silicon-based technology in such diverse industries as electronics, aviation and aerospace, textile, automotive, and health care. As an example, Dow Corning's Electrical Insulating Compounds are used for creating moisture-proof seals for aircraft, automotive, and marine ignition systems. With 10 000 employees, over 20 000 customers, and 45 manufacturing and warehouse locations worldwide, its annual revenues of $6 billion generated an income of almost $900 million in 2010. In order to integrate different business functions and enhance resource planning across the entire firm and its supply chain, Dow Corning turned to a leading provider of enterprise resource planning (ERP) software solutions. It installed the SAP R/3 and mySAP Supply Chain Management solution.

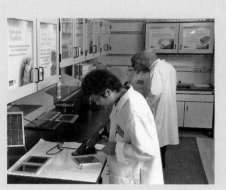

Dow Corning scientists research next-generation solar technologies at the company's Solar Application Center.

Prior to the ERP implementation, limited transparency and redundancy within the existing legacy systems made it difficult to access and analyze data needed for effective resource planning, and also hampered decision making and responsiveness. A sequenced implementation of the SAP modules facilitated the linking of key processes from order generation to production planning to warehousing to delivery and final billing (see Chapter 2, "Supply Chain Management"). This system allowed the linkage of shop floor processes and manufacturing operations with the rest of the business. With a clear view of orders, materials, equipment, product quality, and cost information, Dow Corning could now coordinate plants and processes with greater ease, and also better match production to market requirements around the world. Employee productivity and satisfaction also increased, due mostly to faster response times and accurate, on-time deliveries.[1]

resource planning A process that takes sales and operations plans; processes information in the way of time standards, routings, and other information on how the firm produces its services or products; and then plans the input requirements.

Dow Corning demonstrates that companies can gain a competitive edge by using an effective information system to help with their **resource planning**. Companies must ensure that all of the resources they need to produce finished services or products are available at the right time. If they are not, they risk losing business. For a manufacturer, this task can mean keeping track of thousands of subassemblies, components, raw materials, and key equipment capacities. For a service provider, this task can mean keeping track of numerous supplies and carefully scheduling the time and capacity requirements of different employees and types of equipment.

We begin this chapter by describing enterprise resource planning (ERP) systems, which have become a valuable tool for, among other things, resource planning. We then examine a specific approach to resource planning, called *material requirements planning (MRP)*. The concluding section of the chapter illustrates how service providers manage their supplies, human resources, equipment, and financial resources.

ENTERPRISE RESOURCE PLANNING

enterprise process A companywide process that cuts across functional areas, business units, geographic regions, and product lines.

enterprise resource planning (ERP) systems Large, integrated information systems that support many enterprise processes and data storage needs.

An **enterprise process** is a company-wide process that cuts across functional areas, business units, geographic regions, and product lines. **Enterprise resource planning (ERP) systems** are large, integrated information systems that support many enterprise processes and data storage needs. By integrating the firm's functional areas, ERP systems allow an organization to view its operations as a whole rather than having to try to put together the different information pieces produced by its various functions and divisions. Today, ERP systems are being used by traditional brick-and-mortar organizations such as manufacturers, restaurants, hospitals, and hotels, as well as by Internet companies that rely extensively on Web connectivity to link their customers and suppliers.

HOW ERP SYSTEMS ARE DESIGNED

ERP revolves around a single comprehensive database that can be made available across the entire organization (or enterprise). Passwords are generally issued to allow certain personnel to access certain areas of the system. Having a single database for all of the firm's information makes it much easier for managers to monitor all of the company's products at all locations and at all times. The database collects data and feeds them into the various modular applications (or suites) of the software system. As new information is entered as a transaction in one application, related information is automatically updated in the other applications, including the firm's financial and accounting databases, human resource and payroll databases, sales and customer databases, and so forth.

In many ways, an ERP system streamlines the data flows throughout the organization and provides employees with direct access to a wealth of real-time operating information. This process eliminates many of the cross-functional coordination problems older, non-integrated systems suffered from. Figure 12.1 shows some of the typical

FIGURE 12.1 *ERP Application Modules*[3]

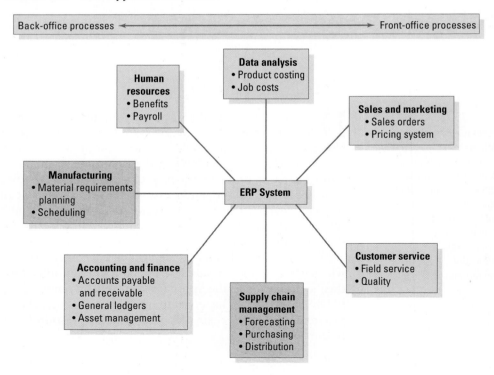

VF Corporation is the world's largest apparel producer, with more than 50 000 workers and $7 billion in sales. Data on quality and demand for products such as backpacks and outdoor equipment are important inputs for VF's ERP system.

applications with a few subprocesses nested in each. Some of the applications are for back-office operations such as manufacturing and payroll, while others are for front-office operations such as customer service.

Chapters.Indigo is one company that uses an ERP system. The supply chain application was to increase sales by adjusting the mix of inventory, centralizing forecasting and replenishment, and reducing maintenance of "legacy" information systems. The $13 million project, with a full-time project team of more than 50 external consultants and full-time employees, took over 18 months to design and implement.[2]

Other applications are more important in other businesses. For example, universities put particular emphasis on the human resources and accounting and finance applications, and manufacturers have an interest in almost every application suite. Not all applications in Figure 12.1 need to be integrated into an ERP system, but those left out will not share their information with the ERP system.

Designing an ERP system requires that a company carefully analyze its major processes so that appropriate decisions about the coordination of legacy systems and new software can be made. Sometimes, a company's processes must be completely reengineered before the firm can enjoy the benefits of an integrated information system. However, a recent study showed that companies reap the greatest rewards when they keep their ERP implementations simple, work with a small number of vendors, and use standardized systems rather than customizing them extensively. Firms can otherwise end up spending excessive amounts of money on ERP systems that are complex to use and costly to manage.

Most ERP systems today use a graphical user interface, although the older, keyboard-driven, text-based systems are still popular because of their dependability and technical simplicity. Users navigate through various screens and menus. Training, such as during ERP implementation, focuses on these screens and how users can utilize them to get their jobs done. One of the biggest suppliers of these off-the-shelf commercial ERP packages is SAP AG, a German company that was used by such companies as Dow Corning and Chapters.Indigo.

ERP systems have undergone significant changes over the past several years. One direction relates to their **interoperability**—the ability of one piece of software to interact with others. Electronic data interchange, a system that allows data to be transferred between companies on a batch basis, and XML (Extensible Markup Language) let companies structure and exchange information without rewriting their existing software or having to purchase new software or hardware. The goal of these and other such methods is to automate, in almost real time, the sharing of information across enterprise boundaries.

interoperability The ability of one piece of software to interact with others.

material requirements planning (MRP) A computerized information system developed specifically to aid in managing dependent demand inventory and scheduling replenishment orders.

MATERIAL REQUIREMENTS PLANNING

Material requirements planning (MRP)—a computerized information system—was developed specifically to help companies manage dependent demand inventory and schedule replenishment orders. MRP systems have proven to be beneficial to many companies. In this section, we discuss the nature of dependent demands and identify some of the benefits that firms have experienced with these systems.

DEPENDENT DEMAND

To illustrate the concept of dependent demand, let us consider a bicycle produced by Rocky Mountain Bicycle, a fast-growing manufacturer of high-performance bikes, with its operations in Vancouver. Demand for a final product such as a bicycle is called *independent demand*, because it is influenced only by market conditions and not by demand for any other type of bicycle produced or held in inventory (see Chapter 5, "Inventory Management"). Management must *forecast* that demand on the basis of a variety of market factors. For bicycle models in higher demand, management might decide to hold some inventory at the manufacturing plant to speed delivery. However, another alternative is to keep many of the items used to make completed bicycles in inventory, including frames, wheels and wheel rims, handlebars, and pedals. Each of these items has a **dependent demand**, because the quantity required is directly related to the demand for completed bicycles. Operations can *calculate* the demand for dependent demand items once the production levels for bicycles are established. If a bicycle of a particular style needs two wheels, then 20 completed bicycles need 20(2) = 40 wheels. Statistical forecasting techniques aren't needed for these wheels.

The bicycle, or any other good manufactured from one or more components, is called a **parent**. The wheel is an example of a **component**—an item that may go through one or more operations to be transformed into or become part of one or more parents. In turn, each wheel is assembled from subcomponents, including a tire and a rim. For complex products, the list of components can be very lengthy, with many components made from other subcomponents. In addition, the wheel might have several different parents, because it might be used for more than one style of bicycle.

The parent–component relationship can cause erratic dependent demand patterns for components. Suppose that every time inventory falls to 10 units (a reorder point), an order for 20 more bicycles is placed, as shown in Figure 12.2(a). The assembly supervisor then authorizes the production of 40 wheels, along with other components for the finished product; demand for the wheel is shown in Figure 12.2(b). So, even though customer demand for the finished bicycle is continuous and uniform, the production demand for wheels is "lumpy"; that is, it occurs sporadically, usually in relatively large quantities.

dependent demand The quantity required is a function of the demand for other items produced or held in inventory.

parent Any item manufactured from one or more components.

component An item that may go through one or more operations to be transformed into or become part of one or more parents.

FIGURE 12.2 *Lumpy Dependent Demand Resulting from Continuous Independent Demand*

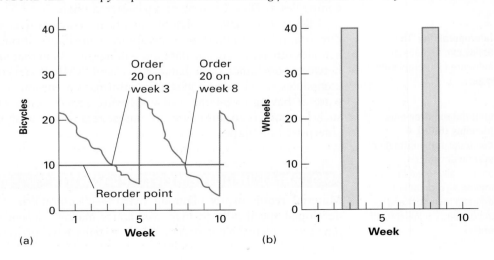

Managing dependent demand inventories is complicated, because some components may be subject to both dependent and independent demand. For example, operations might need 40 wheels for new bicycles, but Rocky Mountain Bicycle can also sell replacement wheels for old bicycles to retail dealers. This practice places an independent demand on the inventory of wheels. Material requirements planning can be used in complex situations involving components that may have independent demand as well as dependent demand inventories.

The use of MRP enables businesses to reduce inventory levels, utilize labour and facilities better, and improve customer service. These successes are due to three advantages of material requirements planning.

1. MRP calculates the dependent demand of components from the production schedules of their parents, thereby providing a better forecast of component requirements.

2. MRP systems translate production schedules and materials purchases into capacity requirements and dollar amounts projected into future time periods. Planners can also identify times when needed components may be unavailable because of capacity shortages, supplier delivery delays, and the like.

3. MRP systems automatically update the dependent demand and inventory replenishment schedules of components when the production schedules of parent items change. Planners are alerted whenever action is needed on any component.

BILL OF MATERIALS

The replenishment schedule for a component is determined from the production schedules of its parents. Hence, the system needs accurate information on parent–component relationships. A **bill of materials** (BOM) is a record of all the components of an item, the parent–component relationships, and usage quantities derived from engineering and process designs. In Figure 12.3, the BOM of a simple ladder-back chair shows that the chair is made from a ladder-back subassembly, a seat subassembly, legs, and leg supports. In turn, the ladder-back subassembly is made from legs and back slats, and the seat subassembly is made from a seat frame and a cushion. Finally, the seat frame is made from seat-frame boards. For convenience, we refer to these items by the letters shown in the figure.

All items except A are components because they are needed to make a parent. Items A, B, C, and H are parents, because they all have at least one component. The BOM also specifies the **usage quantity**, or the number of units of a component needed to make one unit of its immediate parent. Figure 12.3 shows usage quantities for each parent–component relationship in parentheses. Note that one chair (item A) is made from one ladder-back subassembly (item B), one seat subassembly (item C), two front legs (item D), and four leg supports (item E). In addition, item B is made from two back legs (item F) and four back slats (item G). Item C needs one seat frame (item H) and one seat cushion (item I). Finally, item H needs four seat-frame boards (item J).

Four terms frequently used to describe inventory items are end items, intermediate items, subassemblies, and purchased items. An **end item** typically is the final product sold to the customer; it is a parent but not a component. Item A in Figure 12.3, the completed ladder-back chair, is an end item. Accounting statements classify inventory of end items as either work-in-process (WIP), if work remains to be done, or finished goods. An **intermediate item** is one such as B, C, or H that has at least one parent and at least one component. Some products have several levels of intermediate items; the parent of one intermediate item also is an intermediate item. Inventory of intermediate

bill of materials (BOM)
A record of all the components of an item, the parent–component relationships, and usage quantities derived from engineering and process designs.

usage quantity The number of units of a component needed to make one unit of its immediate parent.

end item The final product sold to a customer.

intermediate item An item that has at least one parent and at least one component.

FIGURE 12.3   *Bill of Materials for a Ladder-Back Chair*

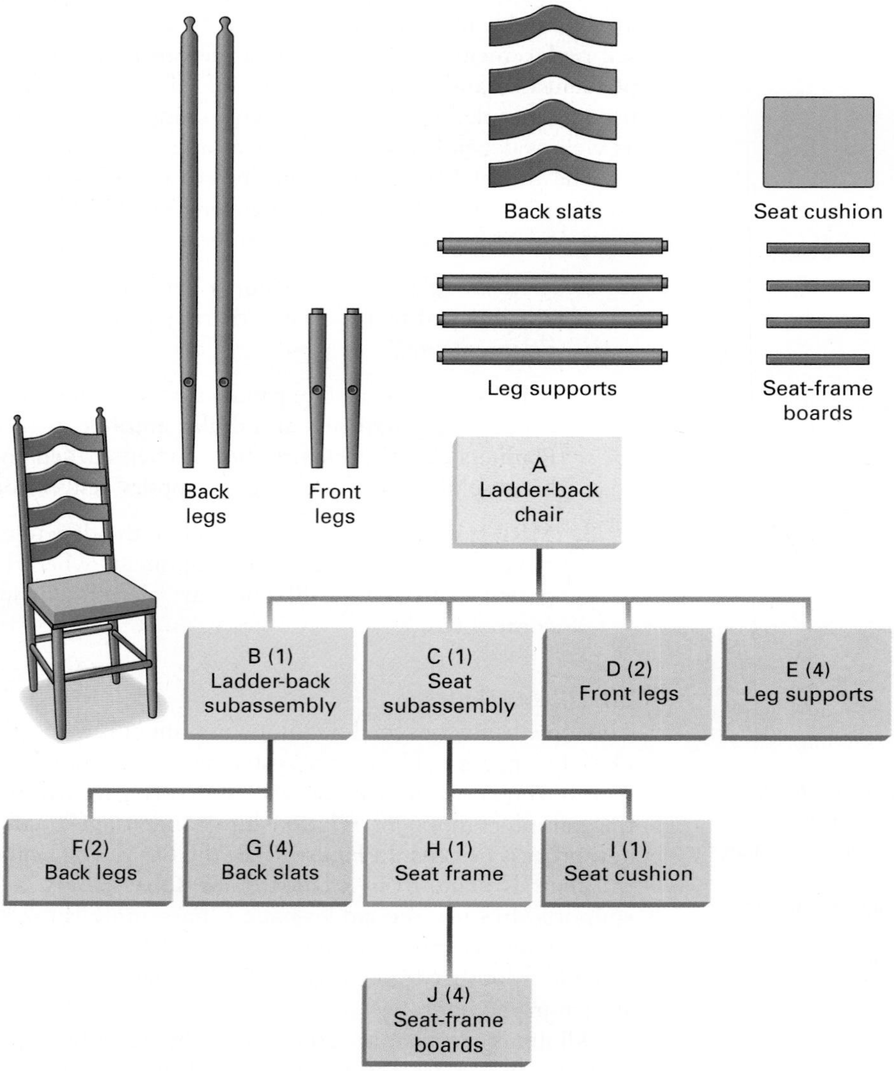

subassembly An intermediate item that is *assembled* (as opposed to being transformed by other means) from *more* than one component.

purchased item An item that has one or more parents but no components because it comes from a supplier.

part commonality The degree to which a component has more than one immediate parent.

items—whether completed or still on the shop floor—is classified as WIP. A **subassembly** is an intermediate item that is *assembled* (as opposed to being transformed by other means) from *more* than one component. Items B and C are subassemblies. A **purchased item** has no components, because it comes from a supplier, but it has one or more parents. Examples are items D, E, F, G, I, and J in Figure 12.3. Inventory of purchased items is treated as raw materials in accounting statements.

A component may have more than one parent. **Part commonality**, sometimes called *standardization of parts* or *modularity*, is the degree to which a component has more than one immediate parent. As a result of commonality, the same item may appear in several places in the bill of materials for a product, or it may appear in the bills of materials for several different products. For example, the seat assembly in Figure 12.3 is a component of the ladder-back chair and of a kitchen chair that is part of the same family of products. The usage quantity specified in the bill of materials relates to a specific parent–component relationship. The usage quantity for any component can change, depending on the parent item. Part commonality increases volume and

FIGURE 12.4   *Master Production Schedule for a Family of Chairs*

	April				May			
	1	2	3	4	5	6	7	8
Ladder-back chair	150					150		
Kitchen chair				120			120	
Desk chair		200	200		200			200
Operations production plan for chair family	670				670			

repeatability for some items—which has advantages for new product introduction, process design, and quality—and helps minimize inventory costs. Today, with the need for greater efficiency in all firms, part commonality is used extensively.

MASTER PRODUCTION SCHEDULE

master production schedule (MPS) A part of the material requirements plan that details how many end items will be produced within specified periods of time.

The second input into a material requirements plan is the **master production schedule** (**MPS**), which details how many end items will be produced within specified periods of time. It breaks down the operations plan (see Chapter 11, "Operations Planning and Scheduling") into specific product schedules. Figure 12.4 shows how an operations plan for a family of chairs breaks down into the weekly master production schedule for each specific chair type (the time period can be hours, days, weeks, or months). Here the scheduled quantities are shown in the week they must be released to the plant to start final assembly so as to meet customer delivery promises, based on the MPS. The chair example demonstrates the following aspects of master scheduling:

1. Total quantities of all end items, that is, ladder-back, kitchen, and desk chairs, in the MPS must equal those in the operations plan. This consistency between the plans is needed because of the capacity and economic analysis done earlier to develop the best operations plan.

2. Production quantities must be allocated efficiently over time. The specific mix of chair types—the amount of each type as a percentage of the total aggregate quantity—is based on historical demand and marketing and promotional considerations. The planner must select lot sizes for each chair type, taking into consideration economic factors such as production setup costs and inventory carrying costs.

3. Capacity limitations, such as machine or labour capacity, and other resources, such as storage space and working capital, differ between chair styles. These factors must be taken into account when setting the timing and size of the production quantities.

The MPS is then used by the MRP system to determine the timing and quantities of components needed. Further details of how to develop the MPS are contained in Supplement K, "Master Production Scheduling," in MyOMLab.

INVENTORY RECORDS

Inventory records are the final input to MRP, and the basic building blocks of up-to-date records are inventory transactions. Transactions include releasing new orders, receiving scheduled receipts, adjusting due dates for scheduled receipts, withdrawing inventory, cancelling orders, correcting inventory errors, rejecting shipments, and verifying scrap losses and stock returns. Recording such transactions is essential for maintaining the accurate records of on-hand inventory balances and scheduled receipts necessary for an effective MRP system.

inventory record A record that shows an item's lot-size policy, lead time, and various time-phased data.

The **inventory record** divides the future into time periods called *time buckets*. In our discussion, we use weekly time buckets for consistency with our MPS example, although other time periods could as easily be used. The inventory record shows an item's lot-size policy, lead time, and various time-phased data. The purpose of the inventory record is to keep track of inventory levels and component replenishment needs. The time-phased information contained in the inventory record consists of (1) gross requirements, (2) schedule receipts, (3) projected on-hand inventory, (4) planned receipts, and (5) planned order releases. We illustrate the discussion of inventory records with the seat subassembly, item C, shown in Figure 12.3. It is used in two products: a ladder-back chair and a kitchen chair.

gross requirements The total demand derived from *all* parent production plans.

GROSS REQUIREMENTS. The **gross requirements** are the total demand derived from *all* parent production plans. They also include demand not otherwise accounted for, such as demand for replacement parts for units already sold. Figure 12.5 shows an inventory record for item C, the seat subassembly. Item C is produced in lots of 230 units and has a lead time of two weeks. The inventory record also shows item C's gross requirements for the next eight weeks, which come from the master production schedules for the ladder-back and kitchen chairs (see Figure 12.4). If both types of chairs were

FIGURE 12.5   *Material Requirements Planning Record for the Seat Subassembly*

Item: C Description: Seat subassembly		Lot Size: 230 units Lead Time: 2 weeks							
		Week							
		1	2	3	4	5	6	7	8
Gross requirements		150	0	0	120	0	150	120	0
Scheduled receipts		230	0	0	0	0	0	0	0
Projected on-hand inventory	37	117	117	117	−3	−3	−153	−273	−273
Planned receipts									
Planned order releases									

Explanation:
Gross requirements are the total demand for the two chairs. Projected on-hand inventory in week 1 is 37 + 230 − 150 = 117 units.

produced in the same week, these quantities would be added together. The seat sub-assembly's gross requirements exhibit lumpy demand: operations will withdraw seat subassemblies from inventory in only four of the eight weeks.

The MRP system works with release dates to schedule production and delivery for components and subassemblies. Its program logic anticipates the removal of all materials required by a parent's production order from inventory at the *beginning* of the parent item's lead time—when the scheduler first releases the order to the shop.

SCHEDULED RECEIPTS. Recall that *scheduled receipts* (sometimes called *open orders*) are orders that have been placed but not yet completed. For a purchased item, the scheduled receipt could be in one of several stages: being processed by a supplier, being transported to the purchaser, or being inspected by the purchaser's receiving department. If production is making the item in-house, the order could be on the shop floor being processed, waiting for components, waiting in queue, or waiting to be moved to its next operation. According to Figure 12.5, one 230-unit order of item C is due in week 1. Given the two-week lead time, the inventory planner released the order two weeks ago.

projected on-hand inventory An estimate of the amount of inventory available each week after gross requirements have been satisfied.

PROJECTED ON-HAND INVENTORY. The **projected on-hand inventory** is an estimate of the amount of inventory available each week after gross requirements have been satisfied. The beginning inventory, shown as the first entry (37) in Figure 12.5, indicates on-hand inventory available at the time the record was computed. As with scheduled receipts, entries are made for each actual withdrawal and receipt to update the MRP database. Then, when the MRP system produces the revised record, the correct inventory will appear.

Other entries in the row show inventory expected in future weeks. Projected on-hand inventory is calculated as:

$$\begin{pmatrix} \text{Projected on-hand} \\ \text{inventory balance} \\ \text{at end of week } t \end{pmatrix} = \begin{pmatrix} \text{Inventory on} \\ \text{hand at end of} \\ \text{week } t-1 \end{pmatrix} + \begin{pmatrix} \text{Scheduled} \\ \text{or planned} \\ \text{receipts in} \\ \text{week } t \end{pmatrix} - \begin{pmatrix} \text{Gross} \\ \text{requirements} \\ \text{in week } t \end{pmatrix}$$

planned receipts Orders that are not yet released to the shop or the supplier.

The projected on-hand calculation includes the consideration of **planned receipts**, which are orders not yet released to the shop or the supplier. In any week, there will never be both a scheduled receipt and a planned receipt. In Figure 12.5, the planned receipts are all zero. The on-hand inventory calculations for each week are:

Week 1:	37 +	230 −	150 =	117
Weeks 2 and 3:	117 +	0 −	0 =	117
Week 4:	117 +	0 −	120 =	−3
Week 5:	−3 +	0 −	0 =	−3
Week 6:	−3 +	0 −	150 =	−153
Week 7:	−153 +	0 −	120 =	−273
Week 8:	−273 +	0 −	0 =	−273

In week 4, the balance drops to −3 units; this indicates that a shortage of 3 units will occur unless more seat subassemblies are built. This condition signals the need for a planned receipt to arrive in week 4. In addition, unless more stock is received, the shortage will grow to 273 units in weeks 7 and 8.

FIGURE 12.6   *Completed Inventory Record for the Seat Subassembly*

Item: C								Lot Size: 230 units	
Description: Seat subassembly								**Lead Time:** 2 weeks	

		Week							
		1	2	3	4	5	6	7	8
Gross requirements		150	0	0	120	0	150	120	0
Scheduled receipts		230	0	0	0	0	0	0	0
Projected on-hand inventory	37	117	117	117	227	227	77	187	187
Planned receipts					230			230	
Planned order releases			230			230			

Explanation:
Without a new order in week 4, there will be a shortage of 3 units: 117 + 0 + 0 − 120 = −3 units. Adding the planned receipt brings the balance to 117 + 0 + 230 − 120 = 227 units. Offsetting for a two-week lead time puts the corresponding planned order release back to week 2.

Explanation:
The first planned order lasts until week 7, when projected inventory would drop to 77 + 0 + 0 − 120 = −43 units. Adding the second planned receipt brings the balance to 77 + 0 + 230 − 120 = 187 units. The corresponding planned order release is for week 5 (or week 7 minus 2 weeks).

PLANNED RECEIPTS. Planning for receipt of new orders will keep the projected on-hand balance from dropping below zero. The planned receipt row is developed as follows:

1. Weekly on-hand inventory is projected until a shortage appears. Completion of the initial planned receipt is scheduled for the week when the shortage is projected. The addition of the newly planned receipt should raise the projected on-hand balance so that it equals or exceeds zero. It will exceed zero when the lot size exceeds requirements in the week it is planned to arrive.

2. Projection of on-hand inventory continues until the next shortage occurs. This shortage signals the need for the second planned receipt.

This process is repeated until the end of the planning horizon by proceeding column by column through the MRP record—filling in planned receipts as needed and completing the projected on-hand inventory row. Figure 12.6 shows the planned receipts for the seat subassembly. In week 4, the projected on-hand inventory will drop below zero, so a planned receipt of 230 units is scheduled for week 4. The updated inventory on-hand balance is 117 (inventory at end of week 3) + 230 (planned receipts) − 120 (gross requirements) = 227 units. The projected on-hand inventory remains at 227 for week 5, because there are no scheduled receipts or gross requirements. In week 6, the projected on-hand inventory is 227 (inventory at end of week 5) − 150 (gross requirements) = 77 units. This quantity is greater than zero, so no new planned receipt is needed. In week 7, however, a shortage will occur unless more seat subassemblies are received. With a planned receipt in week 7, the updated inventory balance is 77 (inventory at end of week 6) + 230 (planned receipts) − 120 (gross requirements) = 187 units.

planned order release
An indication of when an order for a specified quantity of an item is to be issued.

PLANNED ORDER RELEASES. A **planned order release** indicates when an order for a specified quantity of an item is to be issued. We must place the planned order release quantity in the proper time bucket. To do so, we must assume that all inventory flows—scheduled receipts, planned receipts, and gross requirements—occur at the same point of time in a time period. Some firms assume that all flows occur at the beginning of a time period; others assume that they occur at the end of a time period or at the middle of the time period. Regardless of when the flows are assumed to occur, we find the release date by subtracting the lead time from the receipt date. For example, the release date for the first planned order release in Figure 12.6 is 4 (planned receipt date) − 2 (lead time) = 2 (planned order release date). Figure 12.6 shows the planned order releases for the seat subassembly.

PLANNING FACTORS

The planning factors in an MRP inventory record play an important role in the overall performance of the MRP system. By manipulating these factors, managers can fine-tune inventory operations. In this section, we discuss the planning lead time, the lot-sizing rule, and safety stock.

PLANNING LEAD TIME
Planning lead time is an estimate of the time between placing an order for an item and receiving it in inventory. Accuracy is important in planning lead time. If an item arrives in inventory sooner than needed, inventory holding costs increase. If an item arrives too late, stockouts or excessive expediting costs (or both) may occur.

For purchased items, the planning lead time is the time allowed for receiving a shipment from the supplier after the order has been sent, including the normal time to place the order. Often, the purchasing contract stipulates the delivery date. For items manufactured in-house, the planning lead time consists of estimates for:

- Setup time
- Process time
- Materials handling time between operations
- Waiting time

Each of these times must be estimated for every operation along the item's route.

LOT-SIZING RULES
A lot-sizing rule determines the timing and size of order quantities. A lot-sizing rule must be assigned to each item before planned receipts and planned order releases can be computed. The choice of lot-sizing rules is important, because they determine the number of setups required and the inventory holding costs for each item. We present three lot-sizing rules: fixed order quantity, periodic order quantity, and lot-for-lot.

fixed order quantity (FOQ)
A rule that maintains the same order quantity each time an order is issued.

FIXED ORDER QUANTITY. The **fixed order quantity (FOQ)** rule maintains the same order quantity each time an order is issued. For example, the lot size might be the size dictated by equipment capacity limits, as when a full lot must be loaded into a furnace at one time.

For purchased items, the FOQ could be determined by the quantity discount level, truck-load capacity, or minimum purchase quantity. Alternatively, the lot size could be determined by the economic order quantity (EOQ) formula (see Chapter 5, "Inventory Management"). Figure 12.6 illustrates the FOQ rule. However, if an item's gross requirement within a week is particularly large, the FOQ might be insufficient to avoid a shortage. In such unusual cases, the inventory planner must increase the lot size beyond the FOQ, typically to a size large enough to avoid a shortage. Another option is to make the order quantity an integer multiple of the FOQ. This option is appropriate when capacity constraints limit production to FOQ sizes (at most) and setup costs are high.

periodic order quantity (POQ) A rule that allows a different order quantity for each order issued but tends to issue the order at predetermined time intervals.

PERIODIC ORDER QUANTITY. The **periodic order quantity (POQ)** rule allows a different order quantity for each order issued but tends to issue the order at predetermined time intervals, such as every two weeks. The order quantity equals the amount of the item needed during the predetermined time between orders and must be large enough to prevent shortages. Specifically, the POQ is:

$$\begin{pmatrix} \text{POQ lot size} \\ \text{to arrive in} \\ \text{week } t \end{pmatrix} = \begin{pmatrix} \text{Total gross requirements} \\ \text{for } P \text{ weeks, including} \\ \text{week } t \end{pmatrix} - \begin{pmatrix} \text{Projected on-hand} \\ \text{inventory balance at} \\ \text{end of week } t-1 \end{pmatrix}$$

This amount exactly covers P weeks' worth of gross requirements. That is, the projected on-hand inventory should equal zero at the end of the Pth week. The POQ rule does *not* mean that operations must issue a new order every P weeks. Rather, when an order *is* planned, its lot size must be enough to cover P successive weeks. One way to select a P value is to divide the average lot size desired, such as the EOQ (see Chapter 5, "Inventory Management"), or some other applicable lot size, by the average weekly demand. That is, express the target lot size as desired weeks of supply (P) and round to the nearest integer. See Solved Problem 2 for a detailed example of the POQ rule.

lot-for-lot (L4L) A rule under which the lot size ordered covers the gross requirements of a single week.

LOT-FOR-LOT. A special case of the POQ rule is the **lot-for-lot (L4L)** rule, under which the lot size ordered covers the gross requirements of a single week. Thus, $P = 1$, and the goal is to minimize inventory levels. This rule ensures that the planned order is just large enough to prevent a shortage in the single week it covers. The L4L lot size is:

$$\begin{pmatrix} \text{L4L lot size} \\ \text{to arrive in} \\ \text{week } t \end{pmatrix} = \begin{pmatrix} \text{Gross requirements} \\ \text{for week } t \end{pmatrix} - \begin{pmatrix} \text{Projected on-hand} \\ \text{inventory balance at} \\ \text{the end of week } t-1 \end{pmatrix}$$

The projected on-hand inventory combined with the new order will equal zero at the end of week t. Following the first planned order, an additional planned order will be used to match each subsequent gross requirement. See Solved Problem 2 for a detailed example of the L4L rule.

COMPARISON OF LOT-SIZING RULES. Choosing a lot-sizing rule can have important implications for inventory management. Lot-sizing rules affect inventory costs and setup or ordering costs. The FOQ, POQ, and L4L rules differ from one another in one or both respects. We can make the following three generalizations:

1. The FOQ rule generates a high level of average inventory because it creates inventory *remnants*. A remnant is inventory carried into a week that is too small to prevent a shortage. Remnants occur because the FOQ does not match requirements exactly. For example, according to Figure 12.6, the stockroom

must receive a planned order in week 7, even though 77 units are on hand at the beginning of that week. The remnant is the 77 units that the stockroom will carry for three weeks, beginning with receipt of the first planned order in week 4. Although they increase average inventory levels, inventory remnants introduce stability into the production process by buffering unexpected scrap losses, capacity bottlenecks, inaccurate inventory records, or unstable gross requirements.

2. The POQ rule reduces the amount of average on-hand inventory because it does a better job of matching order quantity to requirements. It adjusts lot sizes as requirements increase or decrease.

3. The L4L rule minimizes inventory investment, but it also maximizes the number of orders placed. This rule is most applicable to expensive items or items with small ordering or setup costs. It is the only rule that can be used for a low-volume item made to order.

By avoiding remnants, both the POQ and the L4L rule may actually *introduce* instability by tying the lot-sizing decision so closely to requirements. If any requirement changes, so must the lot size, which can disrupt component schedules. Last-minute increases in parent orders may be hindered by missing components.

SAFETY STOCK

An important managerial issue is the quantity of safety stock needed. It is more complex for dependent demand items than for independent demand items. Safety stock for dependent demand items with lumpy demand (gross requirements) is valuable only when future gross requirements, the timing or size of scheduled receipts, and the amount of scrap are uncertain. Safety stock should be reduced and ultimately removed as the causes of the uncertainty are eliminated. The usual policy is to use safety stock for end items and purchased items to protect against fluctuating customer orders and unreliable suppliers of components, and to avoid using safety stock as much as possible for intermediate items. Safety stocks can be incorporated in the MRP logic by scheduling a planned receipt whenever the projected on-hand inventory balance drops below the desired safety stock level (rather than to zero, as before). The objective is to keep a minimum level of planned inventories equal to the safety stock quantity. Figure 12.7 shows what happens when there is a requirement for 80 units of safety stock for the seat assembly using a FOQ of 230 units. Compare these results with Figure 12.6. The net effect is to move the second planned order release from week 5 to week 4 to avoid going below 80 units in week 6.

FIGURE 12.7   *Inventory Record for the Seat Subassembly Showing the Application of a Safety Stock*

Tutor: FOQ, POQ, and L4L Rules									
FOQ Rule						Lot Size			230
						Lead Time			2
						Safety Stock			80
		1	2	3	4	5	6	7	8
Gross Requirements		150	0	0	120	0	150	120	0
Scheduled Receipts		230	0	0	0	0	0	0	0
Projected On-Hand Inventory	37	117	117	117	227	227	307	187	187
Planned Receipts		0	0	0	230	0	230	0	0
Planned Order Releases		0	230	0	230	0	0	0	0

OUTPUTS FROM MRP

Material requirements planning systems provide many reports, schedules, and notices to help managers control dependent demand inventories, as indicated in Figure 12.8. In this section, we discuss the MRP explosion process, action notices that alert managers to items needing attention, and capacity reports that project the capacity requirements implied by the material requirements plan.

FIGURE 12.8   *Material Requirements Planning Outputs*

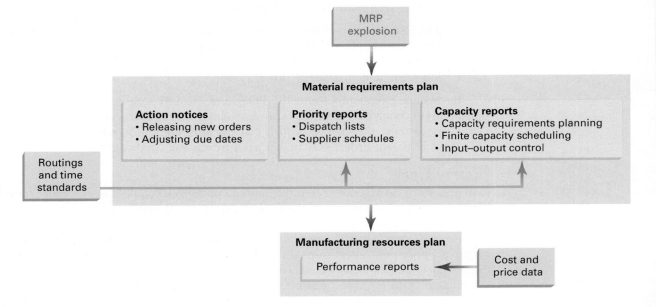

MRP EXPLOSION

MRP translates, or *explodes*, the master production schedule and other sources of demand into the requirements for all subassemblies, components, and raw materials needed to produce parent items. This process generates the material requirements plan for each component item.

An item's gross requirements are derived from three sources:

1. MPS for immediate parents that are end items

2. Planned order releases for parents below the MPS level

3. Other requirements not originating in the MPS, such as the demand for replacement parts

Consider the seat subassembly (item C) for which we have developed the inventory record shown in Figure 12.6. The seat subassembly requires a seat cushion and a seat frame, which in turn needs four seat-frame boards. Its BOM is shown in Figure 12.3. How many seat cushions should we order from the supplier? How many seat frames should we produce to support the seat subassembly schedule? How many seat-frame boards do we need to make? The answers to these questions depend on the inventories we already have of these items and the replenishment orders already in progress. MRP can help answer these questions through the explosion process.

Figure 12.9 shows the MRP records for the seat subassembly and its components. We have already shown how to develop the MRP record for the seat subassembly. We

FIGURE 12.9 *MRP Explosion of Seat Assembly Components*

Item: Seat subassembly
Lot size: 230 units
Lead time: 2 weeks

	Week							
	1	2	3	4	5	6	7	8
Gross requirements	150	0	0	120	0	150	120	0
Scheduled receipts	230	0	0	0	0	0	0	0
Projected inventory 37	117	117	117	227	227	77	187	187
Planned receipts				230			230	
Planned order releases		230			230			

Usage quantity: 1   Usage quantity: 1

Item: Seat frames
Lot size: 300 units
Lead time: 1 week

	Week							
	1	2	3	4	5	6	7	8
Gross requirements	0	230	0	0	230	0	0	0
Scheduled receipts	0	300	0	0	0	0	0	0
Projected inventory 40	40	110	110	110	180	180	180	180
Planned receipts					300			
Planned order releases				300				

Item: Seat cushion
Lot size: L4L
Lead time: 1 week

	Week							
	1	2	3	4	5	6	7	8
Gross requirements	0	230	0	0	230	0	0	0
Scheduled receipts	0	0	0	0	0	0	0	0
Projected inventory 0	0	0	0	0	0	0	0	0
Planned receipts		230			230			
Planned order releases	230			230				

Usage quantity: 4

Item: Seat-frame boards
Lot size: 1500 units
Lead time: 1 week

	Week							
	1	2	3	4	5	6	7	8
Gross requirements	0	0	0	1200	0	0	0	0
Scheduled receipts	0	0	0	0	0	0	0	0
Projected inventory 200	200	200	200	500	500	500	500	500
Planned receipts				1500				
Planned order releases			1500					

now concentrate on the MRP records of its components. The lot-size rules are an FOQ of 300 units for the seat frame, L4L for the seat cushion, and an FOQ of 1500 for the seat-frame boards. All three components have a one-week lead time. The key to the explosion process is to determine the proper timing and size of the gross requirements for each component. When we have done that, we can derive the planned order release schedule for each component by using the logic we have already demonstrated.

In our example, the components have no independent demand for replacement parts. Consequently, in Figure 12.9, the gross requirements of a component come from the planned order releases of its parents. The seat frame and the seat cushion get their gross requirements from the planned order release schedule of the seat subassembly. Both components have gross requirements of 230 units in weeks 2 and 5, the same weeks in which we will be releasing orders to make more seat subassemblies. In week 2, for example, the materials handler for the assembly department will withdraw 230 seat frames and 230 seat cushions from inventory so that the assembly department can produce the seat subassemblies in time to avoid a stockout in week 4. The materials plans for the seat frame and the seat cushion must allow for that.

Using the gross requirements in weeks 2 and 5, we can develop the MRP records for the seat frame and the seat cushion, as shown in Figure 12.9. For a scheduled receipt of 300 in week 2, an on-hand quantity of 40 units, and a lead time of one week, we need to release an order of 300 seat frames in week 4 to cover the assembly schedule for the seat subassembly. The seat cushion has no scheduled receipts and no inventory on hand; consequently, we must place orders for 230 units in weeks 1 and 4, using the L4L logic with a lead time of one week.

Once we have determined the replenishment schedule for the seat frame, we can calculate the gross requirements for the seat-frame boards. We plan to begin producing 300 seat frames in week 4. Each frame requires 4 boards, so we need to have $300(4) = 1200$ boards available in week 4. Consequently, the gross requirement for seat-frame boards is 1200 in week 4. Given no scheduled receipts, 200 boards in stock, a lead time of one week, and an FOQ of 1500 units, we need a planned order release of 1500 in week 3.

The questions we posed earlier can now be answered. The following orders must be released: 300 seat frames in week 4, 230 seat cushions in each of weeks 1 and 4, and 1500 seat-frame boards in week 3.

ACTION NOTICES

action notice A computer-generated memo alerting planners about releasing new orders and adjusting the due dates of scheduled receipts.

Once computed, inventory records for any item appearing in the bills of materials can be printed in hard copy or displayed on a computer screen. Inventory planners use a computer-generated memo called an **action notice** to make decisions about releasing new orders and adjusting the due dates of scheduled receipts. These notices are generated every time the system is updated. The action notice alerts planners to only the items that need their attention such as those items that have a planned order release in the current period or those that need their due dates adjusted because of changes to parent item schedules or the availability of raw materials and components. They can then view the full records for those items and take the necessary actions. An action notice can simply be a list of part numbers for items needing attention. Or it can be the full record for such items, with a note at the bottom identifying the action needed.

CAPACITY REPORTS

By itself, the MRP system does not recognize capacity limitations when computing planned orders. That is, it may call for a planned order release that exceeds the amount that can be physically produced. An essential role of managers is to monitor the capacity requirements of material requirements plans, adjusting a plan when it cannot be met. Particular attention is paid to bottlenecks. The planner can apply theory of constraints (TOC) principles (see Chapter 4, "Capacity") to keep bottleneck operations fed by adjusting some lot sizing rules or occasionally overriding planned order releases. To facilitate this process, various types of capacity reports can be provided. For example, **capacity requirements planning (CRP)** projects time-phased capacity requirements for workstations. They calculate workload according to the work required to complete the scheduled receipts already in the shop and to complete the planned order releases not yet released. Bottlenecks are those workstations at which the projected loads exceed station capacities.

Other types of outputs are also possible, such as priority reports on orders already placed to the shop or with suppliers. Priority reports begin with the due dates assigned to scheduled receipts, which planners keep up to date so that they continue to reflect when receipt is really needed. The Managerial Practice illustrates how Winnebago created and adapted its own homegrown software for the MRP system to achieve business self-sufficiency.

capacity requirements planning (CRP) A technique used for projecting time-phased capacity requirements for workstations; its purpose is to match the material requirements plan with the plant's key processes.

MANAGERIAL PRACTICE
Material Requirements Planning at Winnebago Industries

Established in 1959, Winnebago Industries continues to be a leading manufacturer of motor homes and related products and services for North America, with sales of $449 million in 2010. In a tough business environment, the firm improved the quality of its products and lowered production costs by emphasizing employee teamwork and involvement. So it is no surprise that Winnebago has for decades kept away from software packages, preferring instead to create and adapt its own applications. Managers can thereby achieve a closer fit to the company's business needs, an objective that is at times not met by the ERP vendors described at the beginning of this chapter. These applications also can be more responsive to users at lower cost because code can be reused as needed.

An example of Winnebago's home-grown approach is its MRP system, which is used to plan material needs and schedule production orders. When the company added a new model to its fleet of motor homes, it took only a few hundred hours of development, including a new bill of materials, to make the required changes to the MRP system in order to support production of the new vehicle. Given that more than 55 percent of the 2010 model year product was new or redesigned, such agility in adapting the MRP system to manufacturing and supplier needs can be especially rewarding. Winnebago offered

Winnebago Industries keeps innovating with new models that require detailed planning for thousands of parts and components, typically customized with optional equipment.

24 different models, each of which can be outfitted with a variety of options including colours, wood stains, and drawer pulls. When you are in the business of building customized homes-on-wheels ranging in price from $70 000 to over $300 000, combining cost-consciousness with employee involvement in developing your own MRP, sales order management, and purchasing systems can prove valuable.[4]

MRP AND SUSTAINABILITY

Consumer and governmental concerns about deterioration of the natural environment have driven manufacturers to re-engineer their processes to become more environmentally friendly. Disassembly and recycling of base materials is becoming more commonplace, and products are being designed for a fate other than disposal at the end of their useful lives. Despite these improvements, manufacturing processes often produce a number of wastes that need to be properly disposed of. Wastes come in many forms, including the following:

- Effluents such as carbon monoxide, sulphur dioxide, and hazardous chemicals associated with the processes used to manufacture the product
- Materials such as metal shavings, oils, and chemicals associated with specific operations
- Packaging materials such as unusable cardboard and plastics associated with products or purchased items
- Scrap associated with unusable product or component defects generated by the manufacturing process

Companies can modify their MRP systems to assist them in tracking these wastes and planning for their disposition. The type and amount of waste associated with each item can be entered into its bill of materials by treating the waste much like you would a component of the item. When the master production schedule is developed for a product, reports can be generated that project the amount of waste that is expected and when it will occur. Although this approach requires substantial modification of a firm's bills of materials, the benefits are also substantial. Firms can identify their waste problems in advance and consequently plan for the recycle or proper disposal of them. The firms also have a means to generate any formal documentation required by the government to verify compliance with environmental laws and policies.

RESOURCE PLANNING FOR SERVICE FIRMS

We have seen how manufacturing companies can disaggregate a master production schedule of finished products into the plans for assemblies, components, and purchased materials, which in turn can be translated into the needs for resources such as staff, equipment, supporting materials, and financial assets. Service providers must plan for the same resources; however, the focus is on maintaining capacity to serve as opposed to producing a product to stock. Utilization of resources is important because materials are only a fraction of a typical service provider's investment in capital and people. In this section, we will discuss the concept of dependent demands for service providers and the use of a bill of resources in managing capacity.

DEPENDENT DEMAND

When we discussed planning and control systems earlier in this chapter, we introduced the concept of *dependent demand*, which is demand for an item that is a function of the demand for some other item the company produces. For service resource planning, it is useful to define the concept of dependent demand to include demands for resources that are driven by forecasts of customer requests for services or by plans for various activities in support of the services the company provides. Here are some other examples of dependent demands for service providers.

RESTAURANTS. Every time you order from the menu at a restaurant, you initiate the need for supporting materials (uncooked food items, plates, and napkins), staff (chef, servers, and dishwashers), and equipment (stoves, ovens, and cooking utensils). Using a forecast of the demand for each type of meal, the manager of the restaurant can estimate the need for resources. Many restaurants have "specials" on certain days, such as fish on Fridays or prime rib on Saturdays. Specials improve the accuracy of the forecast for meal types and typically signal the need for above-average levels of staff help.

AIRLINES. Whenever an airline schedules a flight, there are requirements for supporting materials (meals, beverages, and fuel), staff (pilots, flight attendants, and airport services), and equipment (plane and airport gate). Forecasts of customer patronage of each flight help determine the amount of supporting materials and the type of plane needed. A master schedule of flights based on the forecasts can be exploded to determine the resources needed to support the schedule.

HOSPITALS. With the exception of the emergency room, appointments—a form of master schedule for specific services—generally drive the short-term need for health-care resources in hospitals. Forecasts of requests for various services provided by the hospital drive the long-term needs. When you schedule a surgical procedure, you generate a need for supporting materials (medicines, surgical gowns, and linens), staff (surgeon, nurses, and anesthesiologist), and equipment (operating room, surgical tools, and recovery bed). Hospitals must take care so that certain equipment or personnel do not become overcommitted. That is why an appointment for a hernia operation is put off until the surgeon is available, even though the appropriate operating room, nurses, and other resources are available.

HOTELS. The major fixed assets at a hotel are the rooms where guests stay. Given the high capital costs involved, hotels try to maintain as high a utilization rate as possible by offering group rates or special promotions at certain times of the year. Reservations, supplemented by forecasts of "walk-in" customers, provide a master schedule of needs for the hotel's services. When a traveller makes a reservation at a hotel, a need is generated for supporting materials (soap and towels), staff (front desk, housekeeping, and concierge), and facilities (parking).

BILL OF RESOURCES

The service analogy to the BOM in a manufacturing company is the **bill of resources (BOR)**, which is a record of all the required materials, equipment time, staff, and other resources needed to provide a service, the parent–component relationships, and the usage quantities. Given a master schedule of services, we can use the bills of resources to derive the time-phased requirements for the firm's critical resources, as we did for the inventory records in MRP.

A BOR for a service provider can be as complex as a BOM for a manufacturer. Consider a hospital that has just scheduled treatment of a patient with an aneurysm. As shown in Figure 12.10, the BOR for treatment of an aneurysm has seven levels, starting at the top (end item): (1) discharge; (2) intermediate care; (3) postoperative care—step down; (4) postoperative care—intensive; (5) surgery; (6) preoperative care—angiogram; and (7) preoperative care—testing. Each level of the BOR has a set of material and resource requirements and a lead time. For example, at level 6 shown in Figure 12.10(b), the patient needs 6 hours of nurses' time, 1 hour of the primary MD's time, 1 hour of the respiratory therapist's time, 24 hours of bed time, 3 different lab tests, 1 dietary

bill of resources (BOR)
A record of all the required materials, equipment time, staff, and other resources needed to provide a service, the parent–component relationships, and the usage quantities.

A concierge for the Hotel Gritti Palace greets customers: a rowing team. This hotel is one of many properties of Starwood Hotels & Resorts Worldwide that faces complex resource planning issues.

FIGURE 12.10a   *Bill of Resources for Treating an Aneurysm*

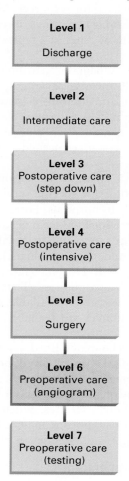

meal, and 10 different medicines from the pharmacy. The lead time for this level is 1 day. The lead time for the entire stay for treatment of the aneurysm is 12.2 days. A master schedule of patient admissions and the BORs for each illness enable the hospital to manage their critical resources. Capacity reports and action notices can be generated for the managers of the major processes in the hospital.

FIGURE 12.10B   *Detailed Bill of Resources for Preoperative Care*

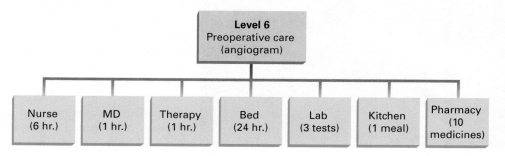

CHAPTER HIGHLIGHTS

- Enterprise resource planning (ERP) is a large, integrated information system. Its applications cut across many processes, functional areas, business units, regions, and products.

- Dependent demand for component items can be calculated from production schedules of parent items in a manufacturing company. Dependent demands can be calculated from forecasts and other resource plans in a service company.

- Material requirements planning (MRP) is a computerized scheduling and information system that offers benefits in managing dependent demand inventories because it (1) recognizes the relationship between production schedules and the demand for component items, (2) provides forward visibility for planning and problem solving, and (3) provides a way to change materials plans in concert with production schedule changes. MRP has three basic inputs: bills of materials, the master production schedule, and inventory records.

- A bill of materials is a diagram or structured list of all components of an item, the parent–component relationships, and usage quantities.

- A master production schedule (MPS) states the number of *end items* to be produced during specific time periods within an intermediate planning horizon. The MPS is developed on the basis of the operations plan.

- The MRP is prepared from the most recent inventory records for all items. The basic elements in each record are gross requirements, scheduled receipts, projected on-hand inventory, planned receipts, and planned order releases. Several quantities must be determined for each inventory record, including lot size, lead time, and safety stock.

- The MRP explosion procedure determines the production schedules of the components that are needed to support the master production schedule. The planned order releases of a parent, modified by usage quantities shown in the bill of materials, become the gross requirements of its components.

- MRP systems provide outputs such as the material requirements plan, action notices, capacity reports, and performance reports. Action notices bring to a planner's attention new orders that need to be released or items that have open orders with misaligned due dates.

- Capacity requirements planning (CRP) is a technique for estimating the workload required by a master schedule. CRP uses routing information to identify the workstations involved and MRP information about existing inventory, lead-time offset, and replacement part requirements to calculate accurate workload projections.

- Enterprise resource planning (ERP) ties the basic MRP system to the financial and accounting systems. Advanced systems integrate management decision support for all business functions.

- Service providers can take advantage of MRP principles by developing bills of resources that include requirements for materials, labour, and equipment.

SOLVED PROBLEM 1

Refer to the bill of materials for item A shown in Figure 12.11.

FIGURE 12.11 *Bill of Materials for Product A*

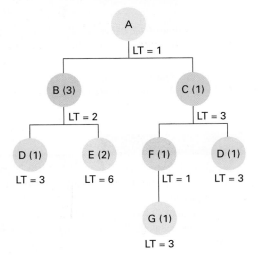

If there is no existing inventory, how many units of G, E, and D must be purchased to produce five units of end item A?

SOLUTION

Five units of G, 30 units of E, and 20 units of D must be purchased to make 5 units of A. The usage quantities shown in Figure 12.11 indicate that 2 units of E are needed to make 1 unit of B and that 3 units of B are needed to make 1 unit of A; therefore, 5 units of A require 30 units of E ($2 \times 3 \times 5 = 30$). One unit of D is consumed to make 1 unit of B, and 3 units of B per unit of A result in 15 units of D ($1 \times 3 \times 5 = 15$); plus 1 unit of D in each unit of C and 1 unit of C per unit of A result in another 5 units of D ($1 \times 1 \times 5 = 5$). The total requirements to make 5 units of A are 20 units of D ($15 + 5$). The calculation of requirements for G is simply $1 \times 1 \times 1 \times 5 = 5$ units.

SOLVED PROBLEM 2

The MPS for product A calls for the assembly department to begin final assembly according to the following schedule: 100 units in week 2; 200 units in week 4; 120 units in week 6; 180 units in week 7; and 60 units in week 8. Develop a material requirements plan for the next eight weeks for items B, C, and D. The BOM for A is shown in Figure 12.12, and data from the inventory records are shown in Table 12.1.

FIGURE 12.12 *Bill of Materials for Product A*

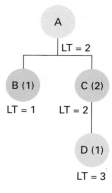

TABLE 12.1 *Inventory Record Data*

DATA CATEGORY	ITEM		
	B	C	D
Lot-sizing rule	POQ ($P = 3$)	L4L	FOQ = 500 units
Lead time	1 week	2 weeks	3 weeks
Scheduled receipts	None	200 (week 1)	None
Beginning (on-hand) inventory	20	0	425

SOLUTION

We begin with items B and C and develop their inventory records, as shown in Figure 12.13. The MPS for item A must be multiplied by 2 to derive the gross requirements for item C, because of the usage quantity. Once the planned order releases for item C are found, the gross requirements for item D can be calculated.

Notice that an action notice would call for delaying the scheduled receipt for item C from week 1 to week 2. Other action notices would notify planners that items B and D have a planned order release in the current week.

FIGURE 12.13   *Inventory Records for Items B, C, and D*

Item: B Description:								Lot Size: POQ ($P = 3$) Lead Time: 1 week		
	Week									
	1	2	3	4	5	6	7	8	9	10
Gross requirements		100		200		120	180	60		
Scheduled receipts										
Projected on-hand inventory 20	20	200	200	0	0	240	60	0	0	0
Planned receipts		280				360				
Planned order releases	280				360					

Item: C Description:								Lot Size: L4L Lead Time: 2 weeks		
	Week									
	1	2	3	4	5	6	7	8	9	10
Gross requirements		200		400		240	360	120		
Scheduled receipts	200 →									
Projected on-hand inventory 0	200	0	0	0	0	0	0	0	0	0
Planned receipts				400		240	360	120		
Planned order releases		400		240	360	120				

(continued on next page)

FIGURE 12.13   (cont'd)

Item: D								Lot Size: FOQ = 500 units	
Description:								**Lead Time:** 3 weeks	

		Week								
		1	2	3	4	5	6	7	8	9	10
Gross requirements			400		240	360	120				
Scheduled receipts											
Projected on-hand inventory	425	425	25	25	285	425	305	305	305	305	305
Planned receipts					500	500					
Planned order releases		500	500								

PROBLEMS

1. Consider the bill of materials in Figure 12.14.

   a. How many immediate parents (one level above) does item I have? How many immediate parents does item E have?

   b. How many unique components does item A have at all levels?

   c. Which of the components are purchased items?

   d. How many intermediate items does item A have at all levels?

   e. Given the lead times noted on Figure 12.14, how far in advance of shipment is the earliest purchase commitment required?

2. Item A is made from components B, C, and D. Item B is a subassembly that requires 2 units of C and 1 unit of E. Item D also is an intermediate item, made from F. All other usage quantities are 2. Draw the bill of materials for item A.

FIGURE 12.14   *Bill of Materials for Product A*

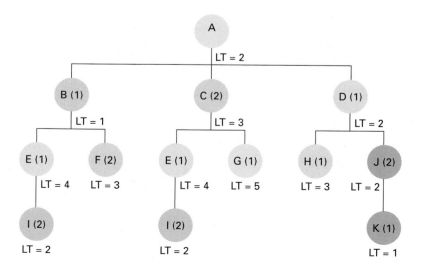

3. What is the lead time (in weeks) to respond to a customer order for product A, on the basis of the BOM shown in Figure 12.15, assuming no existing inventories or scheduled receipts?

FIGURE 12.15   *BOM for Product A*

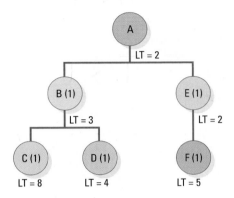

4. Product A is made from components B and C. Item B, in turn, is made from D and E. Item C also is an intermediate item, made from F and H. Finally, intermediate item E is made from H and G. Note that item H has two parents. The following are item lead times:

Item	A	B	C	D	E	F	G	H
Lead time (weeks)	1	2	2	6	5	6	4	3

a. What lead time (in weeks) is needed to respond to a customer order for product A, assuming no existing inventories or scheduled receipts?

b. What is the customer response time if all purchased items (i.e., D, F, G, and H) are in inventory?

c. If you were allowed to keep just one purchased item in stock, which one would you choose?

5. The partially completed inventory record in Figure 12.16 shows gross requirements, scheduled receipts, lead time, and current on-hand inventory.

a. Complete the last three rows of the record for an FOQ of 110 units.

b. Complete the last three rows of the record by using the L4L lot-sizing rule.

c. Complete the last three rows of the record by using the POQ lot-sizing rule, with $P = 2$.

FIGURE 12.16   *Inventory Records for Tabletop Assembly*

Item: M405-X
Description: Tabletop assembly

Lot Size:
Lead Time: 2 weeks

		Week									
		1	2	3	4	5	6	7	8	9	10
Gross requirements		90		85		80		45	90		
Scheduled receipts		110									
Projected on-hand inventory	40										
Planned receipts											
Planned order releases											

6. The partially completed inventory record for the rotor sub-assembly in Figure 12.17 shows gross requirements, scheduled receipts, lead time, and current on-hand inventory.

   a. Complete the last three rows of the record for an FOQ of 150 units.

   b. Complete the last three rows of the record by using the L4L lot-sizing rule.

   c. Complete the last three rows of the record by using the POQ lot-sizing rule, with $P = 2$.

FIGURE 12.17   *Inventory Record for the Rotor Subassembly*

Item: Rotor subassembly							Lot Size:		
					Week				
		1	2	3	4	5	6	7	8
Gross requirements		65	15	45	40	80	80	80	80
Scheduled receipts		150							
Projected on-hand inventory	20								
Planned receipts									
Planned order releases									

(Lead Time: 2 weeks)

7. The BOM for product A is shown in Figure 12.18, and data from the inventory records are shown in Table 12.2. In the master production schedule for product A, 500 units are needed in week 8. The lead time for production of A is two weeks. Develop the material requirements plan for the next six weeks for items B, C, and D. *Hint:* You cannot derive an item's gross requirements unless you know the planned order releases of all its parents.

FIGURE 12.18   *BOM for Product A*

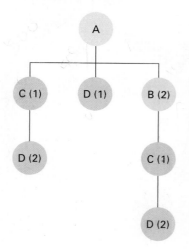

TABLE 12.2   *Inventory Record Data*

	ITEM		
DATA CATEGORY	B	C	D
Lot-sizing rule	L4L	L4L	FOQ = 2000
Lead time	3 weeks	1 week	1 week
Scheduled receipts	None	None	2000 (week 1)
Beginning inventory	0	0	200

8. The BOMs for products A and B are shown in Figure 12.19. Data from inventory records are shown in Table 12.3. The master production schedule calls for 85 units of product A to be started in week 3 and 100 units in week 6. The master production schedule for product B calls for 180 units to be started in week 5. Develop the material requirements plan for the next six weeks for items C, D, E, and F. Identify any action notices.

TABLE 12.3	*Inventory Record Data*			
	ITEM			
DATA CATEGORY	**C**	**D**	**E**	**F**
Lot-sizing rule	FOQ = 220	L4L	FOQ = 300	POQ (P = 2)
Lead time	3 weeks	2 weeks	3 weeks	2 weeks
Scheduled receipts	280 (week 1)	None	300 (week 3)	None
Beginning inventory	25	0	150	600

FIGURE 12.19   *Bill of Materials for Product A and Product B*

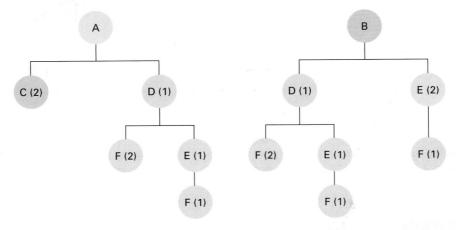

9. A partially completed inventory record for the motor sub-assembly is shown in Figure 12.20.

   a. Complete the last three rows of the record for an FOQ of 60 units.

   b. Revise the planned order release row by using the L4L rule.

   c. Revise the planned order release row by using the POQ rule. Find the value of P that should (in the long run) yield an average lot size of 60 units. Assume that the average weekly demand for the foreseeable future is 15 units.

FIGURE 12.20   *Inventory Record for the Motor Subassembly*

Item: GF-4 Description: Motor subassembly										Lot Size: Lead Time: 3 weeks		
	Week											
	1	2	3	4	5	6	7	8	9	10	11	12
Gross requirements		50		35		55		30		10		25
Scheduled receipts		60										
Projected on-hand inventory 40												
Planned receipts												
Planned order releases												

FIGURE 12.21   *Bill of Materials for Product A*

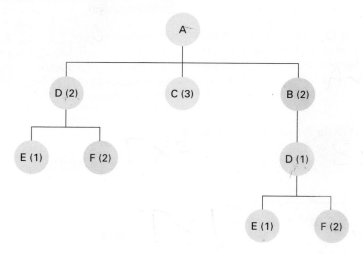

10. The BOM for product A is shown in Figure 12.21. The master production schedule for product A calls for 120 units to be started in weeks 2, 4, 5, and 8. Table 12.4 shows data from the inventory records. Develop the material requirements plan for the next eight weeks for each item. *Warning:* Note that item E has a safety stock requirement.

TABLE 12.4	*Inventory Record Data*				
			ITEM		
DATA CATEGORY	**B**	**C**	**D**	**E**	**F**
Lot-sizing rule	L4L	FOQ = 700	FOQ = 700	L4L	L4L
Lead time	3 weeks	3 weeks	4 weeks	2 weeks	1 week
Safety stock	0	0	0	50	0
Scheduled receipts	150 (week 2)	450 (week 2)	700 (week 1)	None	1400 (week 1)
Beginning inventory	125	0	235	750	0

11. Develop the material requirements plan for all components and intermediate items associated with end item A for the next ten weeks. Refer to Solved Problem 1 for the bill of materials (Figure 12.11) and Table 12.5 for component inventory record information. The master production schedule for product A calls for 50 units to be started in weeks 2, 6, 8, and 9. *Warning:* Note that items B and C have safety stock requirements.

TABLE 12.5	*Inventory Record Data*					
			ITEM			
DATA CATEGORY	**B**	**C**	**D**	**E**	**F**	**G**
Lot-sizing rule	L4L	L4L	POQ (P = 2)	L4L	L4L	FOQ = 100
Lead time	2 weeks	3 weeks	3 weeks	6 weeks	1 week	3 weeks
Safety stock	30	10	0	0	0	0
Scheduled receipts	150 (week 2)	50 (week 2)	None	400 (week 6)	40 (week 3)	None
Beginning inventory	30	20	60	400	0	0

NOTES FOR CHAPTER

1. "End to End Supply Chain Management at Dow Corning," www.sap.com/usa/solutions/business-suite/erp/operations/pdf/CS_Dow_Corning.pdf; Dow Corning, "Optimizing Operational Performance to Sharpen Competitive Advantage," www.sap.com; "Dow Corning Fast Facts," Dow Corning Web site, www.dowcorning.com/content/about/aboutmedia/fastfacts.asp, accessed August 2, 2011.

2. "Change Management at Chapters.Indigo: A Case Study," HR Transformations site, www.hrtransformations.com/pdfs/change_management_case_study.pdf, accessed July 30, 2011.

3. Reprinted by permission of Harvard Business School Press. From *Enterprise Resource Planning (ERP)* by Scalle and Cotteleer. Boston, MA, 1999, No. 9-699-020. © 1999 by the Harvard Business School Publishing Corporation; all rights reserved.

4. "Road Rules: Creating and Adapting Homegrown Software Is the Key to Winnebago's Drive for Business Self Sufficiency," October 15, 2006; www.winnebagoind.com, accessed July 2008; and *Winnebago Industries Annual Report,* 2010.

FURTHER READING

Conway, Richard W. "Linking MRP II and FCS." *APICS—The Performance Advantage,* June 1996, pp. 40–44.

Davenport, Thomas H. "Putting the Enterprise into the Enterprise System." *Harvard Business Review,* July–August 1998, pp. 121–131.

Hendricks, Kevin B., Vinod R. Singhal, and Jeff K. Stratman. "The Impact of Enterprise Systems on Corporate Performance: A Study of ERP, SCM and CRM System Implementations." *Journal of Operations Management,* vol. 25, no. 1 (2007), pp. 65–82.

Jacobs, F. Robert, and Weston, F.C. (Ted), Jr. "Enterprise Resource Planning (ERP)—A Brief History." *Journal of Operations Management,* vol. 25, no. 2 (2007), pp. 357–363.

Jacobs, F. Robert, and D. Clay Whybark. *Why ERP?* New York: Irwin McGraw-Hill, 2000.

Mabert, Vincent A. "The Early Road to Materials Requirements Planning." *Journal of Operations Management,* vol. 25, no. 2 (2007), pp. 346–356.

Melnyk, Steven A., Robert Stroufe, Frank Montabon, Roger Calantone, R. Lal Tummala, and Timothy J. Hinds. "Integrating Environmental Issues into Material Planning: 'Green' MRP." *Production and Inventory Management Journal,* Third Quarter 1999, pp. 36–45.

Ormsby, Joseph G., Susan Y. Ormsby, and Carl R. Ruthstrom. "MRP II Implementation: A Case Study." *Production and Inventory Management,* vol. 31, no. 4 (1990), pp. 77–82.

Ptak, Carol. *MRP and Beyond.* Homewood, IL: Irwin Professional Publications, 1996.

Roth, Aleda V., and Roland Van Dierdonck. "Hospital Resource Planning: Concepts, Feasibility, and Framework." *Production and Operations Management,* vol. 4, no. 1 (1995), pp. 2–29.

Scalle, Cedric X., and Mark J. Cotteleer. *Enterprise Resource Planning (ERP),* No. 9-699-020. Boston: Harvard Business School Publishing, 1999.

Vollmann, T. E., W. L. Berry, and D. C. Whybark. *Manufacturing Planning and Control Systems,* 4th ed. Homewood, IL: Irwin Professional Publications, 1997.

Wallace, Thomas F. *Sales & Operations Planning: The How-To Handbook,* 3rd ed. Cincinnati, OH: T. E. Wallace & Company, 2008.

Wallace, Thomas F., and Robert A. Stahl. *Master Scheduling in the 21st Century.* Cincinnati, OH: T. E. Wallace & Company, 2003.

My OMLab ASSETS

MyOMLab offers the following resources, which allow you to further practise and apply concepts presented in this chapter.

- **Discussion Questions:** Three questions will challenge your understanding of the usefulness of MRP to all functional areas of a business and of how the principles of resource planning can be applied to service firms.

- **Case:** *Flashy Flashers, Inc.* Determine the requirements for materials and components in a practical setting and assess the implications for MRP implementation at an automotive electric component manufacturer.

- **Video Cases:**

  - *Inventory and Textbooks.* Following one product, a typical textbook, from printing through distribution to the final retail sale.

  - *Nantucket Nectars: ERP.* The firm defined a set of objectives, developed a specific project format, and reviewed the results after implementation.

- **OM Explorer Tutor:** OM Explorer contains a tutor program that will help you learn how to use the FOQ, POQ, and L4L decision rules for inventory lot-sizing decisions.

- **Internet Exercise:**

  - *Schwinn Bicycle and Hewlett-Packard.* Explore how each firm uses part commonality across its enormous variety of products.

  - *FedEx Services.* How do services such as those offered by FedEx help a company with its resource management?

- **Virtual Tours:**

  - *Vaughn Hockey Equipment* specializes in equipment for hockey goalies. After seeing this tour, can you draw a bill of materials for a goalie mask?

  - *Winslow Life Rafts.* Pick any process step and indicate all materials and resources that an MRP would track.

- **Supplement J:** *Operations Scheduling.* Use this supplement to see how resource planning systems link up with advanced planning systems in practice.

- **Supplement K:** *Master Production Scheduling.* Learn how to develop master production schedules and how customer due-date promises are linked to production schedules.

Name Index

Page references that contain letters (F.1, G.3, and the like) indicate materials that are in the MyOMLab Supplements.

Note: f denotes a figure and *t* denotes a table.

Subject Index

Page references that contain letters (F.1, G.3, and the like) indicate materials that are in the MyOMLab Supplements.

Note: *f* denotes a figure and *t* denotes a table.